# THE GREEK AND LATIN LITERARY
# TEXTS FROM GRECO-ROMAN EGYPT

# THE GREEK AND LATIN LITERARY TEXTS FROM GRECO-ROMAN EGYPT

*Second Revised and Enlarged Edition*

ROGER A. PACK

Ann Arbor    The University of Michigan Press

Library of Congress Catalog Card No. 65-10786


Published in the United States of America by
The University of Michigan Press and simultaneously
in Toronto, Canada, by Ambassador Books Limited
Manufactured in the United States of America

*To*
*Marion and Philip Pack*

# PREFACE

Since 1952, when the first edition of this repertory appeared, many new papyri have been published, including a few of exceptional importance. Several of the old fragments have been definitely identified, some have been persuasively attributed to different authors or genres than before, and still others have been joined when found to belong to the same papyrus. Again, many of the old texts have been reedited, emended, or variously analyzed in books, monographs, or articles. I have now attempted to bring my list into line with these developments, as far as this can be done for such a constantly proliferating branch of study. It has proved necessary to renumber the old items, but the new numbers can be easily learned from the Concordance, and writers who have used "Pack 330," for example, as a form of brief citation, may now refer, if they wish, to "Pack 2. 455" or "Pack$^2$ 455."

Professor Alphonse Dain has placed me in his debt by proposing various improvements (BAGB, Sér. 4. 3, 1959, 395-400). As I have infinite respect for his judgment, I should have liked to comply with all of his demands, but unfortunately his prophecy that "arrivera un moment où ce labeur dépassera la mesure des forces d' un seul travailleur" is very near fulfillment. He will especially regret that the papyri from Herculaneum have not been added, even now, to those chiefly from Egypt. It would have been easy enough to insert the references to these that were gathered as a by-product to revision, but I decided to withhold material of this class, at least for the present, because the work entailed in handling it on the same scale as the rest, that is, with verification and attention to the secondary bibliography and the quotations within the texts, would have delayed the appearance of this edition longer than seemed desirable. On the other hand, there are certain new features which will possibly earn M. Dain's good opinion.

Another friendly critic, Professor M. F. Galiano, has renewed and extended Dain's desiderata (Studia Papyrologica 1, 1962, 9-37). He envisions an agency which would issue to subscribers, at frequent intervals, sets of file-cards supplying some twenty-seven items of information about a given text as well as a small facsimile of it. All Greek and Latin literary texts would be covered, not barring those of Biblical or magical contents, inscribed on papyrus or any other material except stone and discovered, at any site whatsoever, by either excavation or casual finds. It is obvious that this would be a service of immense value, but that only an international group of workers could render it. Galiano's enthusiasm and the careful thought which he has devoted to his plan suggest that he is best fitted to make it a reality. Meanwhile, it is hoped that the present list may enjoy a season of usefulness.

Professor Paul Mertens, of the University of Liège, has kindly transmitted information about several European collections. All who concern themselves with papyri will augur success for his "Centre de Documentation Photographique des Papyrus Littéraires." Beside Professors Dain, Galiano, Mertens, and the reviewers of the first edition, I am indebted to Professor Herbert C. Youtie, who showed, as before, a friendly and helpful interest in my endeavors. Professor Alexander Turyn and Dr. Edith Jones smoothed the way for me to revisit the excellent Classics Library of the University of Illinois. Many others obliged me with advice, corrections, offprints, or words of encouragement—A. Bataille, J. Bingen, W. E. Blake, J. A. Davison, S. Dow, B. Einarson, G. F. Else, C. Gallavotti, H. G. Gundel, E. Heitsch, Harriet C. Jameson, P. Maas, V. Martin, O. Masson, R. Merkelbach, H. Musurillo, M. Naoumides, O. Neugebauer, R. P. Oliver, K. Preisendanz, C. H. Roberts, B. Snell, E. G. Turner, Mrs. M. L. West, W. H. Willis, and G. Zuntz. W. R. Clayton, of the University Press, patiently instructed me in the preparation of the typescript. To all of these I am sincerely grateful.

R. A. P.

# CONTENTS

# INTRODUCTION

1. <u>Scope of the Inventory</u>.  Pragmatic considerations have led me to use the term "literary" in the sense prevalent among the papyrologists, who generally apply it to most or all of the texts that were intended to reach the eyes of a reading public or at least possessed a more than ephemeral interest or usefulness.  In practice, this means that virtually nothing is excluded save documents and private letters, so that many of the fragments listed here are really "quasi-literary," that is, they can lay only a dubious claim to literary merit.  I have also included texts which, like most of the papyri, come from Egypt, but are inscribed on materials other than papyrus, such as parchment, potsherds (ostraca), and wooden tablets.  The many verse epitaphs from Egyptian stelae have been omitted, though I have registered a few graffiti of historical importance.  An exception to the geographical limitation has been made in the case of certain papyrus fragments from other areas of the Greco-Roman world, such as Palestine and Mesopotamia, but the Herculanean papyri, which belong to a rather specialized field of study, have been excluded, or perhaps reserved for later treatment (see the Preface).  Treatises on divination have been listed, but not magical texts, because the most important of these are covered by Preisendanz in his bibliography and the two volumes of his collection, but the verse passages contained in them have been entered under the appropriate captions.  Similarly, horoscopes have been barred from the listing of the astrological texts.  (These have been published by O. Neugebauer and H. B. Van Hoesen, Greek Horoscopes, Memoirs of the American Philosophical Society 48, 1959, 16-75, 205; see, further, Neugebauer and Van Hoesen, Astrol. Pap. Ostr., Appendix I: "New Horoscopes.").

The cataloguing of the Biblical and other Jewish and Christian (or Gnostic) texts has been left to specialists, except that the major patristic fragments have been entered in an Appendix.  (It is reported in Gnomon 33, 1961, 735, that J. van Haelst is preparing a catalogue of the Christian papyri.  For those of the New Testament, see now K. Aland, Kurzgefasste Liste der griechischen Handschriften des Neuen Testaments 1, Berlin 1963, 29-33).

2. <u>Method of Reference and Description</u>.  For ease in locating the texts, reference to those published in the standard papyrological collections is made in terms of volumes and serial numbers, though the inventory numbers employed by libraries and museums are supplied wherever possible.

Each entry is arranged as follows: (1) the list number, the author's name, if identified, and the title or caption, (2) the reference to the major publication, (3) the present location and inventory number, if ascertained, (4) the date and the provenience, when stated by the editor, with a note on the material and the book form, when requisite (see below), (5) the citations of other authors, if any, or the contents, if these are varied, (6) the secondary references, when such are given.  Only materials other than papyrus are noted specifically: when the material is not mentioned, it is to be inferred that it is papyrus.  Similarly, whenever a text is said by its editor to have formed a part of a codex, the fact is recorded: in other instances it is to be assumed that the original is either a roll (volumen) or a separate sheet of papyrus.  Cases have likewise been noted in which pieces of inscribed papyrus were used as mummy wrappings (cartonnage).

3. <u>Classification</u>.  The basic principle of the classification here adopted is that the fragments identified by author are separated from the adespota and are of course arranged in an alphabetical sequence, without regard to the literary form which they represent.  Apart from its mechanical convenience, this procedure, it is believed, has the advantage of emphasizing the most immediate problem in the study of literary papyri, that is, their identification; for the ideal goal is clearly to transfer as many items as possible from the provisional subdivisions of the adespota to the final alphabetical listing.  Pursuing a rigorous method, then, one would include in the alphabetical category only those fragments whose authorship is placed beyond any reasonable doubt, generally through the presence of a title or a subscription, or else by a whole or partial coincidence with a text otherwise attested.  Yet many a fragment for which such conclusive proof of authorship is lacking contains internal evidence which, in the opinion of some ackowledged expert, or, better, in the consensus of several, weighs so heavily in favor of some one attribution that it would be presumptuous to relegate it to the adespota.  In other cases even the experts disagree, or propose attributions with considerable caution or hesitancy; these fragments appear still to find a more proper place among the adespota, but the results of such study are not lost to view, because the various authors suggested are cross-catalogued, without serial numbers of their own, in the alphabetical listing.

In the classification of the adespota, verse and prose fragments have been separated as far as possible, with further subdivisions for the various literary genera represented in verse and prose; and the most exiguous and desperate fragments, which have not been assigned with confidence to any genus of adespota, far less to definite authors, are gathered under the final rubrics, respectively, of "Verse, Unidentified" and "Prose, Unidentified."

Any single text of varied contents, such as a florilegium or a papyrus inscribed on recto and verso with compositions of a different nature, is, when practicable, entered but once, wnile its elements are spread over the record in the form of unnumbered cross references; but in many cases it has appeared expedient or necessary to depart from this principle and to give separate descriptions with cross references.

4. Citations within the Texts. Many of the fragments, both the adespota and those fully identified, contain citations which clearly possess an independent value. These have been noted as a part of the descriptions of the texts in which they occur, and have been cross-indexed, but of course without numbers, in the alphabetical sequence.

5. Secondary References. I have ventured to supply also a number of references to the vast body of critical literature which has gathered around the editiones principes themselves. The inclusion of those special collections which deal solely or substantially with papyri offers no serious difficulty, but it is a formidable task to handle the scores of articles scattered among numerous journals. If the reader desires an exhaustive bibliography for a given fragment, he is urged to make an independent search of L' Année philologique, which will guide him to occasional articles which have appeared in journals of limited circulation and which, without being examined, cannot be precisely related to the papyri in question. Further, it is evident that a complete bibliography of such a text as Aristotle's Constitution of Athens would entail a protracted search and would form a substantial publication in itself. But a fairly extended treatment of Menander's Dyscolus seems justified by the strong current interest in that recent discovery.

--------

*Perhaps it will be of service to note here the magical texts which have been published since the date of Preisendanz' second volume: O. Bodl. 2.2161-62 (inv. 1900-1; liturgical or magical?); ibid. 2180 (inv. 1129); O. Edfu 3.329; P. Antin. 2.65-66; P.S.A. Athen. 70; P. Bad. 4.61-64; P. Erl. 15 (inv. 37); P. Harris 55 (see S. Eitrem, SO 17, 1937, 103-4; for P. Harris 56, see now No. 1602 below); P. Iand. 5.87 (inv. 266; Gundel 48); P. Merton 2.58; P. Mich. 3.154-56; P. Michael. 27; P. Oslo 3.75 (from the same text as A. S. Hunt, Proc. Brit. Acad. 15, 1929, 4-10 = Preisendanz, PGM 2, No. 57, pp. 184-86); P. Princ. 2.76, 159; P. Rain. 1.28-30; P. Rein. 2.88 (see P. Collart, Rev. Phil. 4, 1930, 248-56), ibid. 89; PSI 13.1362; P. Varsov. 4 (or a medical prescription?); H. I. Bell, A. D. Nock, and H. Thompson, Proc. Brit. Acad. 17 (1931) 235-87; O. Guéraud, Mél. Maspero 201-12 (see Ann. Serv. 38, 1938, 247-49); T. Hopfner, Archiv Orientalni 10 (1938) 128-48; A. S. Hunt, Studies Presented to F. LL. Griffith (London 1932) 233-40 (republished as P. Warren 21, in Papyrologica Lugduno-Batava 1: The Warren Papyri, London 1941); E. J. Knudtzon, Bakchiastexte u. andere Papyri der Lunder Papyrussammlung 4 (Lund 1946), No. 12 (inv. 32); K. Preisendanz, DLZ 61 (1940) 739, ibid. 80 (1959) 310 (a magical Christian prayer in Latin: P. Heid.; Cavenaile, CPL 316; Lowe, CLA 8.1222; A. Traversa, Aeg. 33 (1953) 57-62 (P. Med. inv. 23); D. Wortmann, Philol. 107 (1963) 157-61 (Univ.-Bibl., Köln, inv. 851; a Christian amulet against fever).

Note. In case an abbreviation is not entered separately (e.g., TGFP.), it will be found under the name of the individual in question (e.g., Hunt, TGFP).

Abh. Berl. Akad. = Abhandlungen der (Königlich-) Preussischen Akademie der Wissenschaften zu Berlin. Berlin 1815-.

Abh. Leipzig = Abhandlungen der (Königlich-) Sächsischen Gesellschaft der Wissenschaften zu Leipzig: Philologisch-historische Klasse. Leipzig 1850-.

Acme = Acme: Annali della Facoltà di Filosofia e Lettere dell' Università Statale di Milano. Milano 1948-.

Act. Ant. Hung. = Acta Antiqua Academiae Scientiarum Hungaricae. Budapest 1951-.

Act. Class. = Acta Classica: Proceedings of the Classical Association of South Africa. Cape Town 1958-.

Actas PCEEC. = Actas del Primer Congreso Español de Estudios Clásicos ... 1956. Madrid 1958.

Actes Pap. V = Actes du V^e Congrès International de Papyrologie, Oxford 1937. Bruxelles 1938.

Adrados, F. R., "La poesía de Arquíloco e Hiponacte a la luz de los últimos descubrimientos papirológicos y epigráficos," Actas PCEEC. 184-90.

Aeg. = Aegyptus: Rivista italiana di egittologia e di papirologia. Milano 1920-.

Aevum = Aevum: Rassegna di scienze filologiche, linguistiche, e storiche. Milano 1927-.

AJA = American Journal of Archaeology. Second Series, Norwood, Mass., 1897- (latterly, Princeton, N.J.).

AJP = American Journal of Philology. Baltimore 1880-.

Akten Pap. VIII = Akten des VIII. Internationalen Kongresses für Papyrologie, Wien 1955. Mitteilungen aus der Papyrussammlung der Oesterreichischen Nationalbibliothek, NS 5. Wien 1956.

Allen = T. W. Allen., Homeri Ilias, Tomus 1. Oxonii 1931.

An. fil. clás. = Anales de filología clásica (Anales del Instituto de Literaturas Clásicas). Buenos Aires 1939-.

Ann. Inst. Ph. H. O. = Annuaires de l' Institut de Philologie et d' Histoire Orientales et Slaves. Bruxelles 1932-.

Ann. Sc. Pisa = Annali della Scuola Normale Superiore di Pisa. Pisa 1873-.

Ann. Serv. = Annales du Service des Antiquités de l' Égypte. Le Caire 1899-.

Ann. Univ. Sarav. = Annales Universitatis Saraviensis, Philosophische Fakultät. Saarbrücken 1952-.

Ant. Class. = L' Antiquité classique. Louvain 1932-33; Wetteren, 1933-.

Anz. AW = Anzeiger für die Altertumswissenschaft. Wien 1948-.

AR = Atene e Roma: Bulletino della Società Italiana per la Diffusione degli Studi Classici. Firenze 1898-.

Arch. Bibliogr. = Archiv für Bibliographie, Buch- und Bibliothekswesen. Linz-Donau 1926-.

Arch. Gesch. N. T. = Archiv für Geschichte der Naturwissenschaft und der Technik. Leipzig 1909-31.

Archeol. Class. = Archeologia Classica: Rivista dell' Istituto di Archeologia della Università di Roma. Roma 1949-.

Archiv = Archiv für Papyrusforschung und verwandte Gebiete. Leipzig 1901-.

Arnim, SE = H. von Arnim, Supplementum Euripideum. Lietzmann's Kleine Texte, Nr. 112. Bonn 1913. (Cited by page.)

Årsb., Lund = Humanistiska Vetenskapssamfundet i Lund: Års berättelse (Bulletin de la Société des Lettres de Lund). Lund 1918-.

ARW = Archiv fur Religionswissenschaft. Freiburg im Breisgau (last published at Leipzig and Berlin) 1898-.

Athen. = Athenaeum: Studi periodici di letteratura e storia. Pavia 1913-.

Athena = Athêna: Syngramma Periodikon tês en Athênais Epistêmonikês Hetaireiâs. Athênai 1889-.

Atti Acc. Napoli = Atti della Reale Accademia di Archeologia, Lettere e Belle-Arti di Napoli. Napoli, Nuova Serie 1910-.

Atti Pap. IV = Atti del IV Congresso Internazionale di Papirologia. Aegyptus, Serie scientifica, Vol. 5. Milano 1936.

Baar, J., Index zu den Ilias-Scholien: Die wichtigeren Ausdrücke. Baden-Baden 1961. (Cites papyri: Nos. 1173, 1175, 1184, 1186, 1194, 1205.)

BAGB = Bulletin de l' Association G. Budé. Paris 1923-.

Bassi, MIG = S. Bassi, Monumenta Italiae Graphica, I-II. Cremona 1956-57. (Cited by number.)

Bates, W. N., Euripides: A Student of Human Nature. Philadelphia 1930.

Bates, W. N., Sophocles: Poet and Dramatist. Philadelphia 1940.

Bates, W. N., "The Euripides Papyri," American Journal of Philology 62 (1941) 469-75.

Baviera = J. Baviera, Fontes Iuris Romani Antejustiniani, Pars Altera: Auctores. Florentiae 1940.

BCH = Bulletin de correspondance hellénique. Paris 1877-.

Berard, V., Introduction à l'Odyssée, Tome 1. Paris 1924.

Ber. Berl. Mus. = Berliner Museen: (Amtliche) Berichte aus den Königlichen (Preussischen) Kunstsammlungen. Berlin 1907-.

Ber. Leipzig = Berichte der (Königlich-) Sächsischen Gesellschaft der Wissenschaften zu Leipzig: Philologisch-historische Klasse. Leipzig 1849-.

Bergk = T. Bergk, Poetae Lyrici Graeci, Editio Quarta, Vols. 1-3. Lipsiae 1878-82.

Berl. Phil. Woch. = Berliner philologische Wochenschrift. Leipzig 1881-1920. Cf. Phil. Woch., Woch. Phil.

BFC = Bolletino di filologia classica. Torino 1894-1929; Nuova Serie, 1930-42.

BFLS = Bulletin de la Faculté des Lettres de Strasbourg. Strasbourg 1921-.

BGU = Ägyptische Urkunden aus den Königlichen (Staatlichen) Museen zu Berlin: Griechische Urkunden, Vols. 1-9. Berlin 1895-1937.

BICSL = Bulletin of the Institute of Classical Studies of the University of London. London 1954-.

BIDR = Bulletino dell' Istituto di Diritto Romano. Milano 1888-.

BIFAO = Bulletin de l' Institut Français d'Archéologie Orientale. Le Caire 1901-.

Bilabel = F. Bilabel, Die kleineren Historikerfragmente auf Papyrus. Lietzmann's Kleine Texte, Nr. 149. Bonn 1922.

BKT = Berliner Klassikertexte herausgegeben von der Generalverwaltung der Königlichen Museen in Berlin, Hefte 1-7. Berlin 1904-23.

Blake, Char. = W. E. Blake, Charitonis Aphrodisiensis de Chaerea et Callirhoe ... Libri Octo. Oxonii 1938.

Bodl. Rec. = The Bodleian Quarterly Record. Oxford 1914-38. The Bodléian Library Record. Oxford 1938-.

Bowra, Pindar' = C. M. Bowra, Pindari Carmina cum Fragmentis. Oxonii 1935.

Breccia, Alexandrea = E. Breccia, Alexandrea ad Aegyptum. Bergamo 1922².

BSAA = Bulletin de la Sociète Archéologique d'Alexandrie. Nouvelle Série, Alexandrie 1904-.

Bull. Acad. Belg. = Académie Royale ... de Belgique: Bulletin de la classe des lettres. Bruxelles 1899-.

Bull. Ryl. Libr. = Bulletin of the John Rylands Library. Manchester 1903-.

Byz. = Byzantion: Revue internationale des études byzantines. Paris 1924-.

Byz. neugr. Jahrb. = Byzantinisch-neugriechische Jahrbücher. Berlin-Wilmersdorf 1920-.

Byz. Zeitschr. = Byzantinische Zeitschrift. Leipzig 1892-.

C. P. Jud. = V. A. Tcherikover and A. Fuks, Corpus Papyrorum Judaicarum, Vols. 1-2. Cambridge, Mass., 1957, 1960. (Only vol. 2 is cited, by serial numbers.)

Calderini, A., Manuale di papirologia antica greca e romana. Milano 1938.

Calderini, PL = A. Calderini, Papiri latini. Milano 1945.

Calderini, A. et R., "De papyris ad historiarum scriptores pertinentibus nuper repertis ...," Proc. IX Int. Congr. Pap. 139-51.

Cantarella = R. Cantarella, I nuovi frammenti Eschilei di Ossirinco. Napoli 1947.

Cavenaile, CPL = R. Cavenaile, Corpus Papyrorum Latinarum, Lieferungen 1-4. Wiesbaden 1956-58. (Cited by serial number.)

Charist. Przychocki = Charisteria Gustavo Przychocki a discipulis oblata. Varsoviae 1934.

ChLA 1 = A. Bruckner et R. Marichal, Chartae Latinae Antiquiores 1. Olten-Lausanne 1954.

Chr. Ég. = Chronique d'Égypte: Bulletin périodique de la Fondation Égyptologique Reine Élisabeth. Bruxelles 1925-. (Cited by "Année," not "Nombre.")

Class. Med. = Classica et Mediaevalia: Revue danoise d'histoire et de philologie publiée par la Société Danoise pour les Études Anciennes et Médiévales. Kφbenhavn 1938-.

Collart = P. Collart, "Les Papyrus de l'Iliade," Revue de philologie, Sér. 3.6 (1932) 315-49, ibid. 7 (1933) 33-61; "Les Papyrus de l'Iliade et de l'Odyssée," ibid. 13 (1939) 289-307.

Collart, PLL = P. Collart, "Les Papyrus littéraires latins," Revue de philologie, Sér. 3.15 (1941) 112-28.

Collart, P., "Les Papyrus scolaires," Mélanges offerts à A.-M. Desrousseaux ... (Paris 1937) 69-80.

Collart, P., "Les Fragments des tragiques grecs sur papyrus," Revue de philologie, Sér. 3.17 (1943) 5-36.

Coppola = G. Coppola, Introduzione a Pindaro. Roma 1931.

Coptic Bibl. = W. Kammerer, E. M. Husselman, and L. A. Shier, A Coptic Bibliography. University of Michigan General Library Publications, No. 7. Ann Arbor 1950.

Couvreur, P., "Inventaire sommaire des textes grecs classiques retrouvés sur papyrus," Revue de philologie 20 (1896) 165-74.

CP = Classical Philology. Chicago 1906-.

CQ = Classical Quarterly. Oxford 1907-.

CR = Classical Review. Oxford 1887-.

CRAI = Comptes rendus de l'Académie des Inscriptions et Belles-Lettres. Paris 1857-.

Dain, A., "Les Fragments lyriques des tragiques à la lueur des découvertes papyrologiques," Actas PCEEC 180-84.

David, Gaius = M. David, Gai Institutiones ... Editio Minor. Leiden 1948. (Studia Gaiana 1).

Davison, J. A., "The Study of Homer in Graeco-Roman Egypt," Akten Pap. VIII, 51-58.

Dawson = C. M. Dawson, "The Iambi of Callimachus," Yale Classical Studies 11 (1950) 1-157.

Del Corno, Il. = D. del Corno, "I papiri dell'Iliade anteriori al 150 A. CR., "Rendiconti del Istituto Lombardo 94 (1960) 73-146. (Cited by page.)

Del Corno, Od. = D. del Corno, "I papiri dell'Odissea anteriori al 150 A. C., "Rendiconti del Istituto Lombardo 95 (1961) 3-54. (Cited by page.)

Demiańczuk = J. Demiańczuk, Supplementum Comicum. Cracoviae 1912. (Cited by page.)

Denkschr. Wien. Akad. = Denkschriften der (Kaiserlichen) Akademie der Wissenschaften in Wien: Philosophisch-historische Klasse. Berlin 1850-.

Didask. = Didaskaleion: Studi filologici di letteratura cristiana antica. Torino 1912-.

Diehl, Anth. Lyr. 2¹ = E. Diehl, Anthologia Lyrica Graeca, Editio Prima, Vol. 2. Lipsiae 1925. (Cited by page.)

Diehl, Anth. Lyr. 1² = E. Diehl, Anthologia Lyrica Graeca, Editio Altera, Vol. 1, fasc. 1-4. Lipsiae 1936. (Cited by volume, fascicle, and page.)

Diehl, Anth. Lyr. 1³, 2³, 3³ = E. Diehl et R. Beutler, Anthologia Lyrica Graeca, Editio Tertia, fasc. 1, 2, 3. Lipsiae 1949, 1950, 1952. (Cited by fascicle and page.)

Diehl, Hypomn. = E. Diehl, Hypomnema: De Callimachi librorum fatis capita selecta. Acta Universitatis Latviensis, Ser. Fac. Philol. et Philos. 4.2. Riga 1937.

Diehl, SL = E. Diehl, Supplementum Lyricum. Lietzmann's Kleine Texte, Nr. 33-34. Bonn 1917.

Diehl, SS = E. Diehl, Supplementum Sophocleum. Lietzmann's Kleine Texte, Nr. 113. Bonn 1913.

Dion. = Dioniso: Bolletino dell'Istituto del Dramma Antico. Siracusa 1931-.

DLZ = Deutsche Literaturzeitung. Berlin 1880-.

Drerup = E. Drerup, Isocratis Opera Omnia, Vol. 1. Lipsiae 1906.

Edmonds, LG = J. M. Edmonds, Lyra Graeca, Vols. 1-3. The Loeb Classical Library; London and New York 1922-27. (Cited by page.)

Eos = Eos: Commentarii Societatis Philologae Polonorum. Lwow 1894-.

Eranos = Eranos: Acta Philologica Suecana. Goteborg 1906-.

Est. Clás. = Estudios clásicos. Madrid 1950-.

Ét. Cl. = Les Études classiques. Namur 1932-.

Ét. Pap. = Société (Royale) Égyptienne de Papyrologie: Études de papyrologie. Le Caire 1932-.

Euphros. = Euphrosyne: Philologarum Rerum Commentarii. Olisipone 1957-.

Festschr. Gomperz = Festschrift Theodor Gomperz dargebracht ... Wien 1902.

Festschr. Kapp = Thesaurismata: Festschrift für Ida Kapp. München 1954.

Festschr. Sommer = Corolla Linguistica: Festschrift F. Sommer ... dargebracht ... Wiesbaden 1955.

FF = Forschungen und Fortschritte. Berlin 1925-.

Fifty Years Cl. Schol. = M. Platnauer and others, Fifty Years of Classical Scholarship. Oxford 1954.

Fin. Vet. Soc. = Finska Vetenskaps-Societeten (Societas Scientiarum Fennica): Commentationes Humanarum Litterarum. Helsingfors 1922-.

Fischer = F. Fischer, Thucydidis Reliquiae in Papyris et Membranis Aegyptiacis Servatae. Lipsiae 1913.

Fritsch = C. E. Fritsch, Neue Fragmente des Aischylos und Sophokles. Hamburg 1936.

Galiano, Aesch. = M. F. Galiano, "Les Papyrus d' Eschyle," Proc. IX Int. Congr. Pap. 81-133.

Galiano, LG = M. F. Galiano, "La lírica griega a la luz de los descubrimientos papirológicos, "Actas PCEEC 59-180. (Cited by page. )

Galiano, Pind. = M. F. Galiano, "Los papiros pindáricos," Emérita 16 (1948) 165-200. (Cited by serial numbers. )

Galiano, M. F., "Los papiros de comedias griegas descubiertos en los últimos años," Arbor 6 (1946) 131-50.

Galiano, M. F., "Los papiros de tragedias griegas, en los últimos años," Investigación y Progreso 16 (1945) 139-53.

Gallavotti, Callim. = C. Gallavotti, Callimaco: Il libro dei Giambi. Napoli 1946. (Cited by page. )

Gallavotti, C., Saffo e Alceo. Napoli 1947-48. (Collana di studi greci diretta da Vittorio de Falco 10, 15).

Gallavotti, C., Theocritus Quique Feruntur Bucolici Graeci. Romae 1946. ("Papyrorum Index, " p. VIII).

Gazza = V. Gazza, "Prescrizioni mediche nei papiri dell' Egitto greco-romano, " Aegyptus 35 (1955) 86-110, ibid. 36 (1956) 73-114. (The first installment only is cited, by page. )

Gentili, Anacr. = B. Gentili, Anacreon. Romae 1958. (Cited by page. )

Gerhard, Phoinix = G. A. Gerhard, Phoinix von Kolophon. Leipzig und Berlin 1909.

Gesch. der Textüberlief. = H. Hunger, E. Erbse, und Andere, Geschichte der Textüberlieferung, Band 1. Zürich 1961.

Giabbani, L., Testi letterari greci di provenienza egiziana (1920-45). Pubblicazioni dell' Istituto di Papirologia "G. Vitelli" della Università di Firenze. Firenze 1947.

GIF = Giornale italiano di filologia: Rivista trimestrale di cultura. Napoli 1948-.

Girard = P. F. Girard, Textes de droit romain, Sizième édition. Paris 1937.

Glotta = Glotta: Zeitschrift für griechische und lateinische Sprache. Göttingen 1907-.

Gnomon = Gnomon: Kritische Zeitschrift für die gesamte klassische Altertumswissenschaft. Berlin 1925-.

Göt. Högsk. Årsskr. = Göteborgs Högskolas Årsskrift. Göteborg 1894-.

Gött. Abh. = Abhandlungen der (Königlichen) Gesellschaft (Akademie) der Wissenschaften zu (in) Göttingen: Philologisch-historische Klasse. Göttingen, Neue Folge 1896-.

Gött. Anz. = Göttingische gelehrte Anzeigen. Göttingen 1739-.

Gött. Nachr. = Nachrichten von der (Königlichen) Gesellschaft (Akademie) der Wissenschaften zu (in) Göttingen: Philologisch-historische Klasse. Göttingen 1845-.

Gow = A. S. F. Gow, Theocritus, Edited with a Translation and Commentary, Vol. 1. Cambridge 1950.

Gow, A. S. F., Bucolici Graeci. Oxonii 1952.

GR = Greece & Rome. Oxford 1931-.

GRBS = Greek, Roman, and Byzantine Studies. Cambridge, Mass., 1958-. (Vol. 1: Greek and Byzantine Studies).

Guéraud-Jouguet = O. Guéraud et P. Jouguet, Un livre d' écolier du IIIe siècle avant J. -C. Publications de la Société Royale Égyptienne de Papyrologie: Textes et documents, Vol. 2. Le Caire 1938.

Gundel = H. G. Gundel, "Die literarischen Papyri in der Giessener Universitätsbibliothek, " Kurzberichte aus den Giessener Papyrus-Sammlungen 12 (1962). (Cited by serial number. )

Gymnas. = Gymnasium: Zeitschrift für Kultur der Antike und humanistische Bildung. Heidelberg 1890-.

Häberlin, C., "Griechische Papyri, "Centralblatt für Bibliothekswesen 14 (1897) 1-13, 201-25, 263-83, 337-61, 389-412, 473-99.

Hall, CGT = H. R. Hall, Coptic and Greek Texts of the Christian Period from Ostraka, Stelae, Etc., in the British Museum. London 1905.

Harv. Theol. Rev. = Harvard Theological Review. Cambridge, Mass., 1908-.

Heitsch, GDRK = E. Heitsch, "Die griechischen Dichterfragmente der römischen Kaiserzeit, " Abhandlungen der Akademie der Wissenschaften in Göttingen, Philol. -hist. Klasse, Dritte Folge 49 (1961; Zweite verbesserte Auflage, 1963). (Cited by number of fragment. )

Hellen. = Hellênika: Historikon Periodikon Dêmosievma. Athênai 1928-.

Hemmerdinger, Thucyd. = B. Hemmerdinger, Essai sur l' histoire du texte de Thucydide. Paris 1955.

Hermathena = Hermathena: A Series of Papers on Literature, Science, and Philosophy. Dublin and London 1874-.

Hermes = Hermes: Zeitschrift für klassische Philologie. Berlin 1866-.

Hesperia = Hesperia: Journal of the American School of Classical Studies at Athens. Cambridge, Mass., 1932-.

Historia = Historia: Zeitschrift für Alte Geschichte. Baden-Baden (Heft 2 usw.: Wiesbaden) 1950-.

Hlk. = Helikon: Rivista di tradizione e cultura classica. Napoli 1961-.

HSCP = Harvard Studies in Classical Philology. Cambridge, Mass., 1890-.

Human. = Humanitas. Faculdade de Letras da Universidade de Coimbra, Instituto de Estudos Clássicos. Coimbra 1947-.

Hunt, TGFP = A. S. Hunt, Tragicorum Graecorum Fragmenta Papyracea Nuper-Reperta. Oxonii 1912.

IFC Trieste = Università degli Studi di Trieste, Facoltà di Lettere (Lettere e Filosofia): Istituto di Filologia Classica. Trieste 1955-.

Ihm, M., "Lateinische Papyri, " Centralblatt für Bibliothekswesen 16 (1899) 341-57.

Irigoin, J., "Les Papyrus de Pindare, " Histoire du texte de Pindare (Paris 1952) 77-90.

Isis = Isis: International Review Devoted to the History of Science and Civilization. Cambridge, Mass., 1913-.

Iura = Iura: Rivista internazionale di diritto romano e antico. Napoli 1950-.

Jacoby, FGH = F. Jacoby, Die Fragmenta der griechischen Historiker. Berlin und Leiden 1923-. (Cited generally by volume and page. )

Jander = K. Jander, Oratorum et Rhetorum Graecorum Fragmenta Nuper Reperta. Lietzmann's Kleine Texte, Nr. 118. Bonn 1913. (Cited by page. )

JAW = Bursian's Jahresbericht über die Fortschritte der Altertumswissenschaft. Leipzig 1873-1955. Cf. Lustrum.

JEA = Journal of Egyptian Archaeology. London 1914-.

Jebb-Pearson = R. C. Jebb and A. C. Pearson, The Fragments of Sophocles, Vols. 1-3. Cambridge 1917.

Jensen = C. Jensen, Menandri Reliquiae in Papyris et Membranis Servatae. Berlin 1929.

JHS = Journal of Hellenic Studies. London 1880-.

JJP = Journal of Juristic Papyrology. New York 1946; Warsaw 1947-.

Jones, H. S., et J. E. Powell, Thucydidis Historiae. Oxonii 1942. (The "Conspectus Siglorum" lists the papyri cited in the critical apparatus. )

Jouguet, P., "Les Papyrus latins d'Égypte, " Revue des études latines 3 (1925) 35-50.

Journ. Philol. = Journal of Philology. London 1868-1920.

Journ. Sav. = Journal des savants. Paris, Nouvelle Série, 1903-.

JRS = Journal of Roman Studies. London 1911-.

JWCI = Journal of the Warburg and Courtauld Institutes. London 1937-.

Kenyon, Class. Texts = F. G. Kenyon, Classical Texts from Papyri in the British Museum. London 1891.

Kenyon, Pal. GP = F. G. Kenyon, The Palaeography of Greek Papyri. Oxford 1899.

Kirchner, Scr. LL = J. Kirchner, Scriptura Latina Libraria. Monachii 1955.

Klio = Klio: Beitrage zur Alten Geschichte. Leipzig 1901-.

Knox, Herodes = A. D. Knox, Herodes, Cercidas and the Greek Choliambic Poets. The Loeb Classical Library; London and New York 1929. (Follows Theophrastus, Characters, edited by J. M. Edmonds.)

Kock = T. Kock, Comicorum Atticorum Fragmenta, Vols. 1-3. Lipsiae 1880-88.

Koerte, Men. = A. Koerte, Menandri Quae Supersunt, Pars Prior; Reliquiae in Papyris et Membranis Vetustissimis Servatae. Lipsiae 1938.

Lameere = W. Lameere, Aperçus de paléographie Homérique à propos des papyrus de l'Iliade et de l'Odyssée des collections de Gand, de Bruxelles et de Louvain. Paris-Bruxelles 1960. (Les Publications de "Scriptorium," Vol. 4). (The "Supplément au catalogue de Pack," pp. 255-58, is cited by serial number; other citations are by page.)

Lasserre = F. Lasserre et A. Bonnard, Archiloque: Fragments. Paris 1958. (Cited by number of fragment.)

Lavagnini, Aglaia = B. Lavagnini, Aglaia: Nuova antologia della lirica greca. Torino 1937. (Cited by page.)

Lavagnini, EGFP = B. Lavagnini, Eroticorum Graecorum Fragmenta Papyracea. Lipsiae 1922.

Lavagnini, Mimn. Call. = B. Lavagnini, Da Mimnermo a Callimaco. Torino 1949.

Lavagnini, Studi RG = B. Lavagnini, Studi sul romanzo greco. Messina-Firenze 1950.

Lesky, GGL = A. Lesky, Geschichte der griechischen Literatur. Bern 1957-58.

Listy Fil. = Listy Filologické. NS, Praha 1953-.

Lit. Zentralbl. = Literarisches Zentralblatt für Deutschland. Leipzig 1850-.

Lloyd-Jones, Aesch. = H. Lloyd-Jones, in an appendix to H. W. Smyth, Aeschylus, Vol. 2. The Loeb Classical Library; London and Cambridge, Mass., 1957. (Cited by number of fragment, unless page is specified.)

Lobel, Alcaeus = E. Lobel, Alkaiou Melê: The Fragments of the Lyrical Poems of Alcaeus. Oxford 1927. (Cited by page, unless the number is specified.)

Lobel, Sappho = E. Lobel, Sapphous Melê: The Fragments of the Lyrical Poems of Sappho. Oxford 1925. (Cited by page, unless the number is specified.)

Lobel-Page, PLF = E. Lobel et D. Page, Poetarum Lesbiorum Fragmenta. Oxford 1955. (Cited by page.)

Lowe, CLA = E. A. Lowe, Codices Latini Antiquiores: A Palaeographical Guide to Latin Manuscripts prior to the Ninth Century. Parts 1-10. Oxford 1934-63. (Cited by part and number.)

Ludwich, PC = A. Ludwich, "Über die Papyrus-Commentare zu den Homerischen Gedichten," Verzeichniss ... der Vorlesungen, Königsberg, Sommer 1902.

Lustrum = Lustrum: Internationale Forschungsberichte aus dem Bereich des klassischen Altertums. Göttingen 1956-. A continuation of JAW: see above.

Madan, F., and H. H. E. Craster, A Summary Catalogue of Western Manuscripts in the Bodleian Library at Oxford, Vol. 6. Oxford 1924.

MAI = Mémoires de l'Institut National de France: Académie des Inscriptions et Belles-Lettres. Paris 1815-.

Maia = Maia: Rivista di letterature classiche. Messina-Firenze (Firenze) 1948-.

Mallon, EL = J. Mallon, R. Marichal, et C. Perrat, L'Écriture latine de la capitale romaine à la minuscule. Paris 1939.

Mallon, PR = J. Mallon, Paléographie romaine. Madrid 1952. (Scripturae Monumenta et Studia 3).

Manteuffel, Opusc. = G. Manteuffel, De Opusculis Graecis Aegypti e Papyris, Ostracis Lapidibusque Collectis. Travaux de le Société des Sciences et des Lettres de Varsovie, No. 12. Warszawa 1930.

Marichal = R. Marichal, "Paléographie précaroline et papyrologie," Scriptorium 4 (1950) 116-42, ibid. 9 (1955) 127-33.

Marouzeau, J., et J. Ernst, L'Année philologique: Bibliographie critique et analytique de l'antiquité gréco-latine. Paris 1914-.

Martin, Texte d'Aratos = J. Martin, Histoire du texte des Phénomènes d'Aratos. Paris 1956.

Martin, V., "La Poésie lyrique et la poésie dramatique dans les découvertes papyrologiques des trente dernières années," Museum Helveticum 4 (1947) 74-100.

Meander = Meander: Revue de civilisation du monde antique. Warszawa 1946-.

Medeiros = W. de Sousa Medeiros, "Hipponactis Fragmenta," Humanitas 13-14 (Coimbra 1961-62), pp. VIII-LXXXI, 1-282. (Cited by number of fragment, unless page is specified.)

Meineke = A. Meineke, Fragmenta Comicorum Graecorum, Vols. 1-5. Berolini 1839-57.

Mél. Bidez = Mélanges Bidez. Annuaires de l'Institut de Philologie et d'Histoire Orientales et Slaves, Vol. 2. Bruxelles 1934.

Mél. Boisacq = Mélanges Boisacq. Annuaires de l'Institut de Philologie et d'Histoire Orientales et Slaves, Vol. 5. Bruxelles 1937.

Mél. Chatelain = Mélanges offerts à M. Émile Chatelain ... Paris 1910.

Mél. Ernout = Mélanges de philologie, de litterature et d'histoire anciennes offerts à Alfred Ernout. Paris 1940.

Mél. Glotz = Mélanges Gustave Glotz, Tomes 1-2. Paris 1932.

Mél. Graux = Mélanges Graux. Paris 1884.

Mél. Maspero = Mélanges Maspero. Mémoires publiées par les membres de l'Institut Français d'Archéologie Orientale du Caire, Vol. 67, fasc. 1-2. Le Caire 1934-37.

Mél. Nicole = Mélanges Nicole. Genève 1905.

Mél. Perrot = Mélanges Perrot. Paris 1903.

Mél. Weil = Mélanges Henri Weil. Paris 1898.

Menandrea = Menandrea: Miscellanea Philologica. Facoltà di Lettere, Istituto di Filologia Classica, Università di Genova, 1960.

Merkelbach, Hes. = R. Merkelbach, "Die Hesiodfragmente auf Papyrus," Archiv für Papyrusforschung 16 (1956) 26-81. (Cited by the serial letters.)

Merkelbach, Quellen = R. Merkelbach, Die Quellen des griechischen Alexanderromans. München 1954. (Zetemata, Heft 9).

Mertens, P., "Archives photographiques de papyrologie littéraire," Chronique d'Égypte 36 (1961) 428-30.

Mette, FTA = H. J. Mette, Die Fragmente der Tragödien des Aischylos. Deutsche Akademie der Wissenschaften zu Berlin: Schriften der Sektion für Altertumswissenschaft 15. Berlin 1959. (Cited by number of fragment.)

Mette, Il., Od. = H. J. Mette, "Neue Homer-Papyri," Revue de Philologie, Sér. 3.29 (1955) 193-205; idem, Lustrum 1 (1956) 9, Anm. 1 (addenda). (Continues the lists by P. Collart; see above.)

Mette, Nachtrag = H. J. Mette, Nachtrag zum Supplementum Aeschyleum. Lietzmann's Kleine Texte, Nr. 169a. Berlin 1949. (Cited by page.)

Mette, SA = H. J. Mette, Supplementum Aeschyleum. Lietzmann's Kleine Texte, Nr. 169. Berlin 1939.

MIFAO = Mémoires publiés par les membres de la Mission Archéologique Française au Caire (l' Institut Francais d' Archéologie Orientale du Caire). Le Caire 1884-.

Milne, Gr. Shorthand. Man. = H. J. M. Milne, Greek Shorthand Manuals: Syllabary and Commentary, Edited from Papyri and Waxed Tablets in the British Museum and from the Antinoë Papyri in the Possession of the Egypt Exploration Society. London 1934.

Mizraim = Mizraim: Journal of Papyrology, Egyptology, etc. New York 1933-38.

Mnemos. = Mnemosyne: Bibliotheca Classica Batava. Leiden 1852-.

Mon. Epiphan. = H. G. Evelyn-White, The Monastery of Epiphanius at Thebes, Part 2: Greek Ostraca and Papyri. New York 1926.

Murray, Aesch. = G. Murray, Aeschyli Septem Quae Supersunt Tragoediae, Editio Altera. Oxonii 1955. (Cited by page.)

Mus. Belge = Musée Belge: Revue de philologie classique. Louvain 1897-1920; Liege 1921-32.

Mus. Helv. = Museum Helveticum: Revue suisse pour l' étude de l' antiquité classique. Basel 1944-.

Musurillo = H. A. Musurillo, S. J., The Acts of the Pagan Martyrs: Acta Alexandrinorum, Edited with Commentary. Oxford 1954. (Cited by serial number and page.) Musurillo's later edition, Acta Alexandrinorum: De Mortibus Alexandriae Nobilium Fragmenta Papyracea Graeca (Lipsiae 1961), is not cited separately, as the serial numbers, though not the pages, correspond to those of his Oxford edition, except that his No. XXII is added as a new text (see No. 2242 below.)

Nauck = A. Nauck, Tragicorum Graecorum Fragmenta. Lipsiae 1856.

Nauck[2] = the second edition of the preceding, 1889.

Neue Heidelb. Jahrb. = Neue Heidelberger Jahrbücher. Heidelberg 1891-.

Neue Jahrb. = (Neue) Jahrbücher für Philologie und Pädagogik. Leipzig 1826-97. Neue Jahrbücher für das classische Altertum. Leipzig 1898-1925. Neue Jahrbücher für Wissenschaft und Jugendbildung. Leipzig 1925-36.

Neugebauer, Astron. Pap. Ostr. = O. Neugebauer, "Astronomical Papyri and Ostraca: Bibliographical Notes," Proceedings of the American Philosophical Society 106 (1962) 383-91. (Cited by serial number, unless page is specified.)

Neugebauer, Exact Sc. = O. Neugebauer, The Exact Sciences in Antiquity. Providence 1957[2].

Neugebauer-Van Hoesen, Astrol. Pap. Ostr. = O. Neugebauer and H. B. Van Hoesen, "Astrological Papyri and Ostraca: Bibliographical Notes," to appear in Proceedings of the American Philosophical Society.

New Chapters = J. U. Powell, E. A. Barber, and others, New Chapters in the History of Greek Literature, Series 1-3. Oxford 1921-33.

New Pal. Soc. = The New Palaeographical Society: Facsimiles of Ancient Manuscripts, Etc., Edited by E. M. Thompson, G. F. Warner, F. G. Kenyon, and J. P. Gilson. Series 1, London 1903-12; Series 2, London 1913-30. See also: Pal. Soc.

Norsa, SLG = M. Norsa, La scrittura letteraria greca dal secolo IV a. C. all' VIII d. C. Firenze 1939.

O. Bodl. 1 = J. G. Tait, Greek Ostraca in the Bodleian Library at Oxford and Various Other Collections, Vol. 1. London 1930. (Cited by page.)

O. Bodl. 2 = J. G. Tait and C. Préaux, Greek Ostraca in the Bodleian Library at Oxford, Vol. 2: Ostraca of the Roman and Byzantine Periods. London 1955. (Cited by number.)

O. Edfu = B. Bruyère, J. Manteuffel, K. Michalowski, et autres, Fouilles Franco-Polonaises: Rapports, Parts 1-3. Institut Français d' Archéologie Orientale du Caire. Le Caire 1937-50.

O. Mich. 1 = L. Amundsen, Greek Ostraca in the University of Michigan Collection, Part 1. University of Michigan Studies, Humanistic Series, Vol. 34. Ann Arbor 1935.

O. Strassb. = P. Viereck, Griechische und griechisch-demotische Ostraka der Universitäts- und Landesbibliothek zu Strassburg im Elsass, Band 1. Berlin 1923.

Oldfather, C. H., The Greek Literary Texts from Greco-Roman Egypt. University of Wisconsin Studies in the Social Sciences and History, No. 9. Madison 1923.

Olivieri = A. Olivieri, Frammenti della commedia greca e del mimo nella Sicilia e nella Magna Grecia. Napoli 1930.

Orph. = Orpheus: Rivista di umanità classica e cristiana. Catania 1954-.

Osiris = Osiris: Studies in the History and Philosophy of Science, and in the History of Culture. Bruges 1936-. (Later subtitled: Commentationes de Scientiarum et Eruditionis Historia Rationeque. Brugis etc.)

P. Aberdeen = E. G. Turner, Catalogue of Greek and Latin Papyri and Ostraca in the Possession of the University of Aberdeen. Aberdeen University Studies, No. 116. Aberdeen 1939.

P. Achmîm = P. Collart, "Les Papyrus grecs d' Achmîm à la Bibliothèque Nationale de Paris," Bulletin de l' Institut Français d' Archéologie Orientale 31 (1931) 33-111.

P. Amh. = B. P. Grenfell and A. S. Hunt, The Amherst Papyri, Being an Account of the Greek Papyri in the Collection of the Right Hon. Lord Amherst of Hackney, Parts 1-2. London 1900-01.

P. Antin. = C. H. Roberts, J. W. B. Barns, and H. Zilliacus, The Antinoöpolis Papyri, Parts 1-2. The Egypt Exploration Society. London 1950, 1960.

P. S. A. Athen. = G. A. Petropulos, Papyri Societatis Archaeologicae Atheniensis, Vol. 1. Athenae 1939.

P. Bad. = F. Bilabel und G. A. Gerhard, Veröffentlichungen aus den Badischen Papyrus-Sammlungen, Hefte 4, 6. Heidelberg 1924, 1938. Cf. P. Heid. Siegmann.

P. Bodmer I = V. Martin, Papyrus Bodmer I: Iliade, chants 5 e 6. Cologny-Genève 1954. (Bibliotheca Bodmeriana 3).

P. Bodmer IV: see No. 1298, below.

P. Bon. 1 = O. Montevecchi, Papyri Bononienses 1. Pubblicazioni dell' Università Cattolica del Sacro Cuore, NS 42. Milano 1953. (First provisional publication: O. Montevecchi e G. B. Pighi, Aegyptus 27, 1947, 159 -84).

P. Bouriant = P. Collart, Les Papyrus Bouriant. Paris 1926.

P. Cairo Crawford = D. S. Crawford, Fuad I University Papyri. Publications de la Société Fouad I de Papyrologie, Vol. 8. Alexandrie 1949.

P. Cairo Goodspeed = E. J. Goodspeed, Greek Papyri from the Cairo Museum. Decennial Publications of the University of Chicago, Vol. 5. Chicago 1904.

P. Cairo G. H. = B. P. Grenfell and A. S. Hunt. Greek Papyri. Catalogue général des antiquités égyptiennes du Musée du Caire. Oxford 1903.

P. Cairo Zen. = C. C. Edgar, Zenon Papyri, Vols. 1-4. Catalogue général des antiquités égyptiennes du Musée du Caire, Nos. 79, 82, 85, 90. Le Caire 1925-31.

P. Colt = L. Casson and E. L. Hettich, Excavations at Nessana, Vol. 2: Literary Papyri. Princeton 1950.

P. Cornell = W. L. Westermann and C. J. Kraemer, Jr.,
Greek Papyri in the Library of Cornell University. New
York 1926.

P. Didot = H. Weil, Monuments grecs publiés par l' Association pour l' encouragement des études grecques en
France, Vol. 1, No. 8 (Paris 1879), pp. 1-34. (Cited by
page.)

P. Dura = C. B. Welles, R. O. Fink, and J. F. Gilliam,
The Excavations at Dura-Europos, Final Report 5, Part
1: The Parchments and Papyri. New Haven 1959.

P. Erl. = W. Schubart, Die Papyri der Universitätsbibliothek Erlangen. Katalog der Handschriften der Universitätsbibliothek Erlangen, Neubearbeitung, Band 3, Teil 1.
Leipzig 1942.

P. Fay. = B. P. Grenfell, A. S. Hunt, and D. G. Hogarth,
Fayum Towns and Their Papyri. London 1900.

P. Flor. = D. Comparetti e G. Vitelli, Papiri greco-egizii:
Papiri Fiorentini, Vols. 2-3. Milano 1911-15.

P. Freib. = W. Aly und M. Gelzer, Mittheilungen aus der
Freiburger Papyrussammlung. Sitzungsberichte der
Heidelberger Akademie der Wissenschaften, Philoso-
phisch-historische Klasse, 1914, Abhandlung 2.

P. Fuad = P. Jouguet, O. Guéraud, et autres, Les Papyrus Fouad I. Publications de la Société Fouad I de
Papyrologie: Textes et Documents, Vol. 3. Le Caire
1939.

P. Genève = J. Nicole, Textes grecs inédits de la collection papyrologique de Genève. Genève 1909.

P. Giss. = E. Kornemann, P. M. Meyer, und O. Eger,
Griechische Papyri im Museum des Oberhessischen
Geschichtsvereins zu Giessen, Band 1, Heft 1. Leipzig
1910. Cf. P. Iand.

P. Goth. = H. Frisk, Papyrus grecs de la Bibliothèque
Municipale de Gothembourg. Göteborgs Högskolas Årsskrift, Vol. 35, No. 1. Göteborg 1929.

P. Grenf. 1 = B. P. Grenfell, An Alexandrian Erotic Fragment and Other Greek Papyri, Chiefly Ptolemaic. Oxford 1896.

P. Grenf. 2 = B. P. Grenfell and A. S. Hunt, New Classical
Fragments and Other Greek and Latin Papyri. Oxford
1897.

P. Groning. = A. G. Roos, Papyri Groninganae: Griechische Papyri der Universitätsbibliothek zu Groningen,
nebst zwei Papyri der Universitätsbibliothek zu Amsterdam. Verhandelingen der Koninklijke Akademie
van Wetenschappen te Amsterdam, Afdeeling Letterkunde, Nieuwe Reeks, Deel 32, No. 4. Amsterdam 1933.

P. Gurob = J. G. Smyly, Greek Papyri from Gurob. Royal
Irish Academy: Cunningham Memoirs, No. 12. Dublin
1921.

P. Hal. = Dikaiomata, Auszüge aus Alexandrinischen
Gesetzen und Verordnungen in einem Papyrus des Philo-
logischen Seminars der Universität Halle mit einem Anhang
weiterer Papyri derselben Sammlung, herausgegeben von
der Graeca Halensis. Berlin 1913.

P. Hamb. = Griechische Papyri der Hamburger Staats- und
Universitäts-Bibliothek mit einigen Stücken aus der
Sammlung Hugo Ibscher, herausgegeben vom Seminar
für Klassische Philologie der Universität Hamburg, ein-
geleitet von B. Snell. (Veröffentlichungen aus der Hamburger Staats- und Universitätsbibliothek, Band 4). Hamburg 1954.

P. Harris = J. E. Powell, The Rendel Harris Papyri of
Woodbrooke College, Birmingham. Cambridge 1936.

P. Haun. = T. Larsen, Papyri Graecae Haunienses, Fasc.
1. Hauniae 1942.

P. Hawara = W. M. Flinders Petrie, Hawara, Biahmu, and
Arsinoe. London 1889. (Cited by page.)

P. Heid. Lit. = G. A. Gerhard, Griechische literarische
Papyri, 1: Ptolemäische Homerfragmente. Veröffentlichungen aus der Heidelberger Papyrussammlung, Band
4, Heft 1. Heidelberg 1911.

P. Heid. Siegmann = E. Siegmann, Literarische griechische
Texte der Heidelberger Papyrussammlung. Veröffentlichungen aus der Heidelberger Papyrussammlung, Neue
Folge. Herausgegeben von der Heidelberger Akademie
der Wissenschaften, Philos.-hist. Klasse, Nr. 2. Heidelberg 1956. (Continues P. Bad. 6.)

P. Hibeh = B. P. Grenfell and A. S. Hunt, E. G. Turner
and M.-T. Lenger, The Hibeh Papyri, Parts 1-2. London
1906, 1955.

P. Holm. = O. Lagercrantz, Papyrus Graecus Holmiensis.
Uppsala 1913.

P. Iand. = K. Kalbfleisch, E. Schaefer, und J. Sprey, Papyri Iandanae, fasc. 1, 5. Leipzig 1912, 1931.

P. Ibscher = P. Hamb., pp. 127-32 (see above).

P. Lit. Goodspeed = E. J. Goodspeed, Chicago Literary
Papyri. Chicago 1908.

P. Lit. Lond. = H. J. M. Milne, Catalogue of the Literary
Papyri in the British Museum. London 1927.

P. Lond. = F. G. Kenyon and H. I. Bell, Greek Papyri in
the British Museum: Catalogue with Texts, Vols. 1-5.
London 1893-1917.

P. Maspero = J. Maspero, Papyrus grecs d' époque byzantine, Vols. 1-3. Catalogue général des antiquités
égyptiennes du Musée du Caire, Nos. 51, 54, 73. Le
Caire 1911-16.

P. Med. = A. Calderini, Papiri Milanesi. Aegyptus, Serie
Scientifica, Vol. 1, fasc. 1. Milano 1928.

P. Merton = H. I. Bell, C. H. Roberts, B. R. Rees, and
J. W. B. Barns. A Descriptive Catalogue of the Greek
Papyri in the Collection of Wilfred Merton, F. S. A.,
Vols. 1-2. London 1948; Dublin 1959.

P. Mich. 3 = J. G. Winter and others, Papyri in the University of Michigan Collection; Miscellaneous Papyri.
University of Michigan Studies, Humanistic Series, Vol.
40. Ann Arbor 1936.

P. Mich. 7 = H. A. Sanders and J. E. Dunlap, Latin Papyri
in the University of Michigan Collection. University of
Michigan Studies, Humanistic Series, Vol. 48. Ann
Arbor 1947.

P. Mich. 8 = H. C. Youtie and J. G. Winter, Papyri and
Ostraca from Karanis, Second Series. University of
Michigan Studies, Humanistic Series, Vol. 50. Ann
Arbor 1951.

P. Michael. = D. S. Crawford and E. G. Turner, Papyri
Michaelidae: Being a Catalogue of the Greek and Latin
Papyri, Tablets and Ostraca in the Library of Mr. G.
A. Michailidis of Cairo. Aberdeen 1955.

P. Mil. Vogl. 2 = I. Cazzaniga, A. Colonna, C. Gallavotti, A. Gianformaggio, G. Pugliese-Carratelli, M.
Vandoni, ed altri. Papiri della Università degli Studi
di Milano, Vol. 2. Milano 1961. (The first volume was
called PRIMI; see below.)

P. Mur. = P. Benoît, J. T. Milik, et R. de Vaux, Les
Grottes de Murabba'at. Oxford 1961. (Discoveries in the
Judaean Desert 2). The "Texte" and the "Planches" are
bound in separate volumes. (See No. 1983 below; the
others appear in the Supplement.)

P. Oslo = S. Eitrem og L. Amundsen, Papyri Osloenses,
fasc. 1-3. Oslo 1925-36.

P. Oxy. = B. P. Grenfell, A.S. Hunt, H. I. Bell, E. Lobel,
C. H. Roberts, E. G. Turner, J. W. B. Barns, J. Rea,
and others, The Oxyrhynchus Papyri, Parts 1-27. The
Egypt Exploration Society. London 1898-1962.

P. Par. = W. Brunet de Presle et E. Egger, Les Papyrus grecs du Musée du Louvre et de la Bibliothèque Imperiale. Notices et extraits des manuscrits de la Bibliothèque Nationale, Vol. 18. Paris 1865.

P. Petrie = J. P. Mahaffy and J. G. Smyly, The Flinders Petrie Papyri, Parts 1-3. Royal Irish Academy: Cunningham Memoirs, Nos. 8, 9, 11. Dublin 1891-1905.

P. Princ. = E. H. Kase, Jr., A. C. Johnson, and S. P. Goodrich, Papyri in the Princeton University Collections, Vols. 2-3. Princeton 1936, 1942.

P. Rain = H. Gerstinger, H. Oellacher, und K. Vogel, Mitteilungen aus der Papyrussammlung der National-bibliothek in Wien: Papyrus Erzherzog Rainer, Neue Serie, Erste Folge und Dritte Folge. Baden bei Wien 1932, 1939. (Cf. Raineri F., Raineri M., Akten Pap. VIII).

P. Rein. 1 = T. Reinach, Papyrus grecs et démotiques. Paris 1905.

P. Rein. 2 = P. Collart, Les Papyrus Theodore Reinach, Tome 2. Bulletin de l' Institut Français d' Archéologie Orientale, Vol. 39. Le Caire 1940.

PRIMI = A. Vogliano, Papiri della Regia Università di Milano, Vol. 1. Milano 1937. (The second volume is called P. Mil. Vogl.; see above.)

P. Ross. Georg. = G. Zereteli, O. Krueger, und P. Jernstedt, Papyri russischer und georgischer Sammlungen, Vols. 1, 5. Tiflis 1925, 1935.

P. Ryl. = J. de M. Johnson, V. Martin, A. S. Hunt, C. H. Roberts, and E. G. Turner, Catalogue of the Greek (and Latin) Papyri in the John Rylands Library, Manchester, Vols. 1-4. Manchester 1911, 1915, 1938, 1952.

P. Schubart = W. Schubart, "Griechische literarische Papyri," Berichte über die Verhandlungen der Sächsischen Akademie der Wissenschaften zu Leipzig (Philologisch-historische Klasse) 97.5 (1950).

PSI = G. Vitelli, M. Norsa, V. Bartoletti, ed altri, Pubblicazioni della Società Italiana per la Ricerca dei Papiri Greci e Latini in Egitto: Papiri greci e latini, Vols. 1-14. Firenze 1912-57.

P. Tebt. = B. P. Grenfell, A. S. Hunt, J. G. Smyly, and E. J. Goodspeed, The Tebtunis Papyri, Parts 1-3. London 1902-38.

P. Théad. = P. Jouguet, Papyrus de Théadelphie. Paris 1911.

P. Univ. Giss. = E. Eberhart und A. von Premerstein, Mitteilungen aus der Papyrussammlung der Giessener Universitätsbibliothek, Teile 4-5. Giessen 1935-39.

P. Varsov. = G. Manteuffel et alii, Papyri Varsovienses. Universitas Varsoviensis: Acta Facultatis Litterarum, Vol. 1. Varsoviae 1935.

P. Vat. Gr. 11 = M. Norsa e G. Vitelli, Il Papiro Vaticano Greco 11. Città del Vaticano 1931.

P. Würzb. = U. Wilcken, Mitteilungen aus der Würzburger Papyrussammlung. Abhandlungen der Preussischen Akademie der Wissenschaften: Philosophisch-historische Klasse, Nr. 6. Berlin 1934.

Paap = A. H. R. E. Paap, De Herodoti Reliquiis in Papyris et Membranis Aegyptiis Servatis. Papyrologica Lugduno-Batava, Vol. 4. Lugduni-Batavorum 1948.

Pack = R. A. Pack, The Greek and Latin Literary Texts from Greco-Roman Egypt. Ann Arbor 1952. (University of Michigan General Library Publications, No. 8).

Pack 2 = this repertory, a revision of Pack.

Page, Corinna = D. L. Page, "Corinna," The Society for the Promotion of Hellenic Studies, Supplementary Paper No. 6. London 1953.

Page, GLP = D. L. Page, Greek Literary Papyri, Vol. 1. The Loeb Classical Library; London and New York 1942: London and Cambridge, Mass., 1950[2].

Page, PMG = D. L. Page, Poetae Melici Graeci. Oxford 1962. (Cited by number of fragment, unless page is specified.)

Page, SA = D. L. Page, Sappho and Alcaeus: An Introduction to the Study of Ancient Lesbian Poetry. Oxford 1955. (Cited by page.)

Paid. = Paideia: Rivista letteraria di informazione bibliografica. Genova 1946-.

Pal. Soc. = The Palaeographical Society: Facsimiles of Manuscripts and Inscriptions, Edited by E. A. Bond, E. M. Thompson, and G. F. Warner. Series 1, London 1873-83; Series 2, London 1884-94. See also: New Pal. Soc.

Pasquali, Stor. Testo = G. Pasquali, Storia della tradizione e critica del testo. Firenze, Seconda edizione, 1952.

Pauli Sent. Fr. Leid. = G. G. Archi, M. David, E. Levy, R. Marichal, and H. L. W. Nelson, Pauli Sententiarum Fragmentum Leidense (Cod. Leid. B. P. L. 2589). Leiden 1956. (Studia Gaiana, Vol. 4). (See especially No. 2956 below.)

Peremans, W., "Heuristique des papyrus grecs," Les Études classiques 12 (1944) 257-72.

Perry, Aesopica = B. E. Perry, Aesopica, Vol. 1. Urbana 1952.

Perry, Studies = B. E. Perry, Studies in the Text History of the Life and Fables of Aesop. Monographs of the American Philological Association, No. 7. Haverford 1936.

Persson = A. W. Persson, "Zur Textgeschichte Xenophons," Lunds Universitets Årsskrift 10, Nr. 2 (1914).

Pfeiffer, Callim. = R. Pfeiffer, Callimachus, Vols. 1-2. Oxonii 1949, 1953. (Cited by number of fragment, unless page is specified.)

Pfeiffer, CFNR = R. Pfeiffer, Callimachi Fragmenta Nuper Reperta. Lietzmann's Kleine Texte, Nr. 145. Bonn 1921.

Philol. = Philologus: Zeitschrift für das Klassische Altertum. Leipzig 1841-.

Philol., Suppl. = Philologus, Supplementbände. Leipzig 1860-.

Phil. Woch. = Philologische Wochenschrift. Leipzig 1921-1944. Cf. Berl. Phil. Woch., Woch. Phil.

Phoenix = The Phoenix: Journal of the Classical Association of Canada. Toronto 1952-.

Platon = Platôn: Deltion tês Hetaireias Hellênôn Philologôn. Athênai 1949-. (Cited by "Tomos.")

Pöhlmann, GMF = E. Pöhlmann, Griechische Musikfragmente: Ein Weg zur altgriechischen Musik. Nürnberg 1960. (Erlanger Beiträge zur Sprach- und Kunstwissenschaft, Band 8).

Powell, J. E.: see under Jones, H. S.

Powell, CA = J. U. Powell, Collectanea Alexandrina. Oxonii 1925. (Cited by page.)

PP = La parola del passato: Rivista di studi classici. Napoli 1946-.

Preisendanz, PFF = K. Preisendanz, Papyrusfunde und Papyrusforschung. Leipzig 1933. (Pp. 260-300: "Papyrologische Sammlungen").

Preisendanz, PGM = K. Preisendanz, Papyri Graecae Magicae: Die griechischen Zauberpapyri, Vols. 1-2. Leipzig und Berlin 1928-31.

Preisendanz, K., "Die griechischen Zauberpapyri," Archiv fur Papyrusforschung 8 (1927) 104-67.

Proc. Brit. Acad. = Proceedings of the British Academy. London 1904-.

Proc. IX Int. Congr. Pap. = Proceedings of the IX International Congress of Papyrology, Oslo ... 1958. Oslo 1961.

Proc. Soc. Bibl. Arch. = Proceedings of the Society of Biblical Archaeology. London 1879-.

Prolegom. = Prolegomena: Documenti e studi storici e filologici. Roma 1952-.

Publ. Obs. U. M. = Publications of the Astronomical Observatory of the University of Michigan. Ann Arbor 1912-.

Racc. Lumbroso = Raccolta di scritti in onore di Giacomo Lumbroso. Milano 1925.

Radt = S. L. Radt, Pindars zweiter und sechster Paian. Amsterdam 1958.

Raineri F. = Papyrus Erzherzog Rainer: Führer durch die Ausstellung. Wien 1894. Cf. P. Rain., Raineri M.

Raineri M. = Mittheilungen aus der Sammlung der Papyrus Erzherzog Rainer, Vols. 1-6. Wien 1887-97.

RE = A. Pauly, G. Wissowa, und W. Kroll, Realencyklopädie der klassischen Altertumswissenschaft. Stuttgart 1894-.

Rec. Champollion = Recueil d' études égyptologiques dédiées à la mémoire de Jean-François Champollion. Paris 1922.

Recherches Pap. = Recherches de papyrologie. Publications de la Faculté des Lettres et Sciences humaines de Paris, Série "Recherches." Paris 1961-.

Reggers, Zuster E., Catalogus van de grieksche letterkundige Papyrusteksten uitgegeven in de Jaren 1922-38. Katholieke Universiteit te Leuven: Philologische Studien, Teksten en Verhandelingen, Reeks 2, Deel 2. Leuven 1942.

Rend. Acc. Linc. = Rendiconti della Reale Accademia dei Lincei. Roma, Serie 6, 1892-1924; Serie 7, 1925-45; Serie 8, 1946-.

Rend. Ist. Lomb. = Rendiconti del Reale Istituto Lombardo di Scienze e Lettere. Milano 1864-.

Rev. Arch. = Revue archéologique. Paris 1844-.

Rev. Dr. Fr. = (Nouvelle) Revue historique de droit français et étranger. Paris 1855-.

Rev. Ég. = Revue égyptologique. Paris, Nouvelle Série, 1919-24.

Rev. Ég. Anc. = Revue de l' Égypte ancienne. Paris 1925-.

Rev. Ét. Anc. = Revue des études anciennes. Paris 1899-.

Rev. Ét. Gr. = Revue des études grecques. Paris 1888-.

Rev. Phil. = Revue de philologie. Paris, Nouvelle Série, 1877-1926; Troisième Série 1927-.

Rh. Mus. = Rheinisches Museum für Philologie. Frankfurt, Neue Folge, 1842-.

Riv. CCM = Rivista di cultura classica e medioevale. Roma 1959-.

Riv. Fil. = Rivista di filologia e d' istruzione classica. Torino 1873-.

Riv. Ind Gr. Ital. = Rivista indo-greco-italica di filologia, lingua, antichità. Napoli 1917-37.

Roberts, GLH = C. H. Roberts, Greek Literary Hands 350 B. C. - A. D. 400. Oxford 1955.

Roberts, C. H., "Literature and Society in the Papyri," Museum Helveticum 10 (1953) 264-79.

Robinson, Hist. Alex. = C. A. Robinson, Jr., The History of Alexander the Great, Vol. 1. Providence 1953. (Brown University Studies 16).

Sav. Zeitschr. = Zeitschrift der Savigny-Stiftung für Rechtsgeschichte: Romanistische Abteilung. Weimar 1880-.

Schroeder = O. Schroeder, Pindari Carmina. Lipsiae 1900.

Schroeder[5] = the fifth edition of the preceding. Lipsiae 1923.

Schroeder, NCF = O. Schroeder, Novae Comoediae Fragmenta in Papyris Reperta Exceptis Menandreis. Lietzmann's Kleine Texte, Nr. 135. Bonn 1915. (Cited by page. )

Schubart, Einführung = W. Schubart, Einführung in die Papyruskunde. Berlin 1918.

Schubart, Gr. Pal. = W. Schubart, Griechische Palaeographie. München 1925. (I. von Müller, Handbuch der Altertumswissenschaft, Band 1, Abteilung 4).

Schubart, PGB = W. Schubart, Papyri Graecae Berolinenses. Bonnae 1911.

Schwartz, Ps.-Hes. = J. Schwartz, Pseudo-Hesiodeia: Recherches sur la composition, la diffusion et la disparition ancienne d' oeuvres attribuées à Hésiode. Leiden 1960.

Script. = Scriptorium: Revue internationale des études relatives aux manuscrits. Bruxelles 1946-.

Scritti Nogara = Scritti in onore di Bartolomeo Nogara. Città del Vaticano 1937.

Scritti Rosellini = Scritti dedicati alla memoria di Ippolito Rosellini nel primo centenario della morte. Firenze 1945.

Sic. Gymn. = Siculorum Gymnasium: Rassegna Semestrale della Facoltà di Lettere e Filosofia dell' Università di Catania. Catania 1948-.

Sierl, L. E., Supplementum ad Ottonis Lenel Palingenesiam Iuris Civilis ad Fidem Papyrorum ... Graz 1960. (An addendum to Vol. 2 of Lenel's work).

SIFC = Studi italiani di filologia classica. Firenze 1893-1919; Nuova Serie, 1920-.

Sitzb. Berl. Akad. = Sitzungsberichte der (Königlich-) Deutschen (Preussischen) Akademie der Wissenschaften zu Berlin: Philosophisch- historische Klasse (Klasse fur Sprachen, Literatur und Kunst). Berlin 1882-.

Sitzb. Heid. Akad. = Sitzungsberichte der Heidelberger Akademie der Wissenschaften: Philosophisch-historische Klasse. Heidelberg 1910-.

Sitzb. Münch. Akad. = Sitzungsberichte der (Königlich-) Bayerischen Akademie der Wissenschaften zu München: Philosophisch-historische Klasse. Munchen 1871-.

Sitzb. Wien. Akad. = Sitzungsberichte der (Kaiserlichen) (Österreichischen) Akademie der Wissenschaften in Wien: Philosophisch-historische Klasse. Wien 1849-.

Snell, Bacchyl. = B. Snell, Bacchylidis Carmina cum Fragmentis, Editio sexta. Lipsiae 1949. (Cited by page. )

Snell, Pindarus = B. Snell, Pindari Carmina cum Fragmentis. Lipsiae 1953. (Cited by number of fragment. )

SO = Symbolae Osloenses. Oslo 1922-.

Srebrny, Stud. Scaen. = S. Srebrny, Studia Scaenica. Polska Akademia Nauk, Archiwum Filologiczne 5. Wroclaw 1960.

Stark, R., "Textgeschichtliche und literarkritische Folgerungen aus neueren Papyri," Annales Universitatis Saraviensis, Philosophische Fakultät, 8 (1959) 31-49.

Steffen, Sat. Gr. Fr. = V. Steffen, Satyrographorum Graecorum Fragmenta. Poznan 1952. (Cited by page. )

Steffen, Stud. Aesch. = W. (V. ) Steffen, Studia Aeschylea Praecipue ad Deperditarum Fabularum Fragmenta Pertinentia. Polska Akademia Nauk, Archiwum Filologiczne 1. Wroclaw 1958.

Stud. Cl. Or. = Studi classici e orientali. Pisa 1951-.

Stud. Jachmann = H. Dahlmann und R. Merkelbach, Studien zur Textgeschichte und Textkritik Günther Jachmann ... gewidmet. Köln und Opladen 1959.

Stud. Pal. = Studien zur Paläographie und Papyruskunde, herausgegeben von C. Wessely, Vols. 1-23. Leipzig 1901-24.

Studi Bonfante = Studi in onore di Pietro Bonfante. Milano 1929-30.

Studi Calderini-Paribeni 2 = Studi in onore di Aristide Calderini e Roberto Paribeni, Vol. 2: Studi di papirologia e antichità orientali. Milano 1957.

Studi Castiglioni = Studi in onore di Luigi Castiglioni, 1-2.
Firenze 1960.

Studi Paoli = Studi in onore di Ugo Enrico Paoli. Firenze
1955.

Sudhaus = S. Sudhaus, Menandri Reliquiae Nuper Repertae.
Lietzmann's Kleine Texte, Nr. 44-46. Bonn 1914.

TAPA = Transactions of the American Philological Association. Hartford, Conn. (last published at Ithaca, N. Y. )
1869-.

Theol. Lit. Zeit. = Theologische Literaturzeitung. Leipzig
1876-.

Thompson, GLP = Sir E. M. Thompson, An Introduction to
Greek and Latin Palaeography. Oxford 1912.

Tijdschr. v. Rechtsg. = Tijdschrift voor Rechtsgeschied-
enis: Revue d' histoire du droit. Haarlem 1918-.

Trans. Amer. Philos. Soc. = Transactions of the American
Philosophical Society. Philadelphia, New Series, 1818-.

Traversa, Hes. Cat. = A. Traversa, Hesiodi Catalogi sive
Eoearum Fragmenta. Napoli, n. d. (1949?). (Cited by
page.)

Traversa, A., "I papiri epici nell' ultimo trentennio, "
Proc. IX Intr. Congr. Pap. 49-80.

Treu, Alkaios = M. Treu, Alkaios. München 1952. (Cited
by page.)

Treu, Archil. = M. Treu, Archilochus. München 1959.
(Cited by page.)

Treu, Sappho = M. Treu, Sappho. München 1954. (Cited
by page.)

Trieste: see IFC Trieste.

Turner, E. G., "Scribes and Scholars of Oxyrhynchus, "
Akten Pap. VIII, 141-46.

Turyn = A. Turyn, Pindari Carmina cum Fragmentis.
Academia Polona Litterarum et Scientiarum. Cracoviae 1948.

Van Hoesen = H. B. Van Hoesen, Roman Cursive Writing.
Princeton 1915.

Van Looy, H., "Les Fragments d' Euripide, " L' Antiquité
classique 32 (1963) 162-99.

Vid. Forh., Christiania = Vidensskabsselskabets Forhand-
linger, Christiania 1858-.

Vilborg, Ach. Tat. = E. Vilborg, Achilles Tatius: Leucippe and Clitophon. Stockholm 1955.

Viljoen = H. G. Viljoen, Herodoti Fragmenta in Papyris
Servata. Groningae 1915.

Waddell, W. G., "Papyrology, Latin, " Oxford Classical
Dictionary (Oxford 1949) 646-47.

Wattenbach, SGS = G. (W.) Wattenbach, Scripturae Graecae
Specimina. Berolini 1897.[3]

Weitzmann, Anc. Bk. Ill. = K. Weitzmann, Ancient Book
Illumination. Cambridge, Mass., 1959. (Martin Classical Lectures 16).

Weitzmann, Ill. RC = K. Weitzmann, Illustrations in Roll
and Codex. Princeton 1947. (Studies in Manuscript
Illumination 2).

Werre-De Haas = M. Werre-De Haas, Aeschylus' Dictyulci:
An Attempt at Reconstruction of a Satyric Drama. Lug-
duni Batavorum 1961. (Papyrologica Lugduno-Batava 10).

Wessely, SALP = C. Wessely, Schrifttafeln zur älteren
lateinischen Palaeographie. Leipzig und Wien 1898.

Wieacker, Textstufen = F. Wieacker, Textstufen klass-
ischer Juristen. Göttingen 1960. Abhandlungen der
Akad. der Wiss. in Göttingen, Philol. -hist. Klasse,
Dritte Folge, Nr. 45.

Wifstrand, Kallim. Nonn. = A. Wifstrand, Von Kallimachos
zu Nonnos. Lund 1933. Skrifter utgivna av Vetenskaps-
Societeten i Lund, 16.

Wilamowitz, Gr. Versk. = U. von Wilamowitz-Mollendorff,
Griechische Verskunst. Berlin 1921.

Wilamowitz, Pindaros = U. von Wilamowitz-Möllendorff,
Pindaros. Berlin 1922.

Wilcken, Chrest. u. Grundzüge = L. Mitteis und U.
Wilcken, Grundzüge und Chrestomathie der Papyrus-
kunde, Vol. 1, Part 1 (Grundzüge), Vol. 1, Part 2
Chrestomathie). Leipzig und Berlin 1912.

Wilcken, Gr. Ostr. = U. Wilcken, Griechische Ostraka
aus Ägypten und Nubien, Vols. 1-2. Leipzig und Berlin
1899.

Wilcken, TAGP = U. Wilcken, Tafeln zur aelteren griechischen Palaeographie. Leipzig und Berlin 1891.

Wilcken, UPZ = U. Wilcken, Urkunden der Ptolemäerzeit,
Parts 1-2. Berlin und Leipzig 1922-35.

Willis, W. H., "Greek Literary Papyri from Egypt and the
Classical Canon, " Harvard Library Bulletin 12 (1958)
5-34.

Winter, LLP = J. G. Winter, Life and Letters in the Papyri. University of Michigan: The Jerome Lectures.
Ann Arbor 1933.

WJA = Würzburger Jahrbücher für die Altertumswissenschaft. Würzburg 1946-50.

Woch. Phil. = Wochenschrift für klassische Philologie,
Berlin 1884-1920. Cf. Berl. Phil. Woch., Phil. Woch.

WS = Wiener Studien: Zeitschrift für klassische Philologie. Wien 1879-.

Wyss = B. Wyss, Antimachi Colophonii Reliquiae. Berlin
1936.

Yale Class. Stud. = Yale Classical Studies. New Haven
1928-.

Young, Theognis = D. Young, Theognis, Ps. -Pythagoras,
Ps. -Phocylides, Chares, Anonymi Aulodia, Fragmentum
Teliambicum. Lipsiae 1961.

Zalateo, G., "Papiri scolastici, " Aegyptus 41 (1961) 160-
235.

Zawadzka, I., "Papirusowe fragmenty Sofoklesa, " Meander 17 (1962) 302-6; "Papirusowe fragmenty Eurypidesa, "
ibid. 343-50.

Zeitschr. Aeg. Spr. = Zeitschrift für Aegyptische Sprache
und Altertumskunde. Leipzig 1863-.

Zeitsch. Deutsch. Ver. Buchw. = Zeitschrift des Deutsch-
en Vereins für Buchwesen und Schrifttum. Leipzig 1918-.

Zeitschr. Math. Phys. = Zeitschrift für Mathematik und
Physik. Leipzig 1856-1917.

Zeitschr. Vergl. Spr. = Zeitschrift für Vergleichende
Sprachforschung. Berlin 1852-.

Zeitz = H. Zeitz, Die Fragmente des Äsopromans in Pa-
pyrushandschriften. Giessen 1935.

Ziebarth = E. Ziebarth, Aus der antiken Schule. Lietzmann's Kleine Texte, Nr. 65. Bonn 1910.

Ziebarth 2 = the second edition of the preceding. Bonn 1913.

Ziebarth, Gr. Schulwesen = E. Ziebarth, Aus dem griechischen Schulwesen. Leipzig und Berlin 1914.[2]

Zimmermann, GRP = F. Zimmermann, Griechische
Roman-Papyri und verwandte Texte. Heidelberg 1936.

## OTHER ABBREVIATIONS

Abb. = Abbildung

Abh. = Abhandlung

Abt. = Abteilung

Avh. = Avhandling

Beih. = Beiheft

bibl. = bibliography

Bibl. = Biblioteca, Bibliotek,
        Bibliothek, Bibliothèque

cart. = cartonnage

cod. = codex

col. = column

Coll. = College

ed. pr. = editio princeps

Einzelschr. = Einzelschrift

fasc. = fascicle, fascicolo,
        fascicule, fasciculus

fig. = figure

fr., frr. = fragment, fragments

Inst. = Institut, Institute

inv. = inventory number

Ist. = Istituto

Libr. = Library

Mus. = Musée, Museo, Museum

NS = New Series, Nova Series,
        Nouvelle Série, Nuova Serie

ostr. = ostracon

Oxy. = Oxyrhynchus

pap. = papyrus

parch. = parchment

pl. = planche, plate

Sch. = School

sch. ex. = school exercise

Ser., Sér. = Serie, Series, Série

Soc. = Society

tab. = tabula

Taf. = Tafel

tav. = tavola

Univ. = Università, Université, Universitet,
        Universiteit, University

Univ.-Bibl. = Universitätsbibliothek

Vol. = Volume

# KEY TO THE LOCATIONS OF THE PAPYRI

Note. The reader is forewarned that the information of this class supplied, chiefly from publications, both here and in the list of texts below, is unavoidably incomplete and at some points probably obsolete or otherwise faulty. Anyone who is acquainted with the fortunes of papyri will understand why this is so. To eliminate this defect one would have to engage in a prolonged correspondence with the directors of many libraries and museums, not to mention private owners. Yet those readers who wish to communicate with the present holders of the papyri will find clues to most of the institutions or individuals to whom their first inquiries might reasonably be addressed.

The "Lists of Papyri Distributed" which have appeared in P. Oxy., Parts 4, 5, 11, and 16, record the various institutions to which papyri of the collections P. Oxy., P. Fay.,and P. Hibeh have been donated so far. It is assumed that those not listed are still in the possession of the Egypt Exploration Society, London.

Precise addresses of many of these institutions, and the names of their current directors, can be obtained from The World of Learning, published periodically in London.

The abbreviations marked with asterisks refer to the collections published in the special series listed in the Bibliography; the others refer to collections from which papyri have been published in various series or periodicals, as noted ad loc. in the list of texts.

Académie des Inscriptions et Belles-Lettres, Paris.
Archaeological Institute of America, New York, N. Y., U.S.A.
*Årsb., Lund: Lunds Universitet, Lund.
Ashmolean Museum, Oxford.
Belfast Museum and Art Gallery, Belfast.
Berliner Stadtbibliothek, Berlin.
*BGU: see BKT.
Biblioteca Ambrosiana, Milano.
Bibliotheek der Universiteit Gent.
Bibliothèque Nationale, Paris.
Bibliothèque de l' Université Catholique de Louvain.
*BKT: Staatliche Museen zu Berlin (see Chr. Ég. 23, 1948, 181-82). W. Schubart, Archiv 5 (1913) 196, mentions five literary papyri loaned at that time to the Cairo Museum; these are noted below ad loc.
Bodleian Library, Oxford.
Bristol Museum and Art Gallery, Bristol.
British Museum, London.
Brooklyn Museum, Brooklyn, N. Y., U.S.A.
Brotherton Library, The University of Leeds, Leeds 2.
Cambridge University Library, Cambridge.
Chadwick Museum, Bolton, Lancashire.
Chicago Natural History Museum (formerly Field Museum), Chicago, Illinois, U.S.A.
Christie Library, The Victoria University of Manchester, Manchester 13.
Christ's Hospital, West Horsham, Sussex.
Collection of E. von Scherling, Leiden.
Columbia University Library, New York, N. Y., U.S.A.
Cornell University Library, Ithaca, N. Y., U.S.A.
Crozer Theological Seminary, Chester, Pennsylvania, U.S.A.
Dominion Museum, Wellington, New Zealand.
Dulwich College, London.
Edinburgh University Library, Edinburgh.

Fitzwilliam Museum, Cambridge.
Fondation Égyptologique Reine Élisabeth: see Musées Royaux, Bruxelles.
Glasgow University Library, Glasgow.
Hibbard Library, Chicago, Illinois, U.S.A.
Houghton Library, Harvard University, Cambridge, Massachusetts, U.S.A. (The Oxyrhynchus papyri formerly in Harvard's Semitic Library are now housed here.)
Institut de Papyrologie de la Sorbonne: see P. Sorbonne.
Institut für Österreichische Geschichtsforschung, Wien.
Istituto Papirologico "Girolamo Vitelli": see PSI.
Johns Hopkins University Library, Baltimore, Maryland, U.S.A.
Kongelige Biblioteket, København.
Kungliga Humanistiska Vetenskapssamfundet i Lund, Lund.
Library of the Princeton Theological Seminary, Princeton, New Jersey, U.S.A.
Library of the University of Melbourne, Melbourne, Australia.
Library of Victoria College, Toronto, Ontario, Canada.
Liverpool University Library, Liverpool.
Manchester Museum, Oxford Road, Manchester 13.
Marlborough College, Marlborough, Wiltshire.
Merchant Taylors' School, London.
*Mon. Epiphan.: Metropolitan Museum of Art, New York, N. Y., U.S.A.
Morgan Library: Pierpont Morgan Library, New York, N. Y., U.S.A.
Mt. Holyoke College, South Hadley, Massachusetts, U.S.A.
Muhlenberg College, Allentown, Pennsylvania, U.S.A.
Musée Archéologique du Chateau Borelly, Marseille.
Musées Royaux d' Art et d' Histoire (Fondation Égyptologique Reine Élisabeth), Bruxelles.
Musei del Castello Sforzesco, Milano.
Museo Archeologico, Firenze.
Museo Egiziano Vaticano, Città del Vaticano.
Museum of the New York Historical Society, New York, N. Y., U.S.A.
Newton Theological Institute, Newton Centre, Massachusetts, U.S.A.
Oriental Institute, University of Chicago, Chicago, Illinois, U.S.A.
*O. Bodl.: Bodleian Library, Oxford.
*O. Edfu: Institut Français d' Archéologie Orientale du Caire, Cairo.
*O. Mich.: see P. Mich.
O. Petrie: Bodleian Library, Oxford.
*O. Strassb.: see P. Strassb.
*P. Aberdeen: University of Aberdeen Library, Aberdeen.
*P. Achmîm: Bibliothèque Nationale, Paris.
*P. Amh.: Pierpont Morgan Library, New York, N. Y., U.S.A.
*P. Antin.: Egypt Exploration Society, London.
P. Argent.: see P. Strassb.
*P. S. A. Athen.: Archaiologikî Hetairia, Athînai (Societas Archaeologica Atheniensis).
*P. Bad.: Universitätsbibliothek, Heidelberg.
P. Berol.: see BKT.
*P. Bodmer: Bibliothèque Bodmer, Cologny-Genève.
*P. Bon.: Biblioteca Universitaria, Università degli Studi, Bologna.
*P. Bouriant: Université de Paris, Institut de Papyrologie de la Sorbonne.

P. Cairo: Musée des Antiquités Égyptiennes du Caire, Cairo.

*P. Cairo Crawford: Cairo University (Fuad I University), Cairo.

*P. Cairo G.H., *P. Cairo Goodspeed, *P. Cairo Zen.: see P. Cairo.

*P. Colt (P. Nessana): Pierpont Morgan Library, New York, N. Y., U.S.A. (Papyri on permanent loan to the Morgan Library by the Colt Archaeological Institute.)

*P. Cornell: Cornell University Library, Ithaca, N. Y., U. S.A.

*P. Didot: Musée du Louvre, Paris.

*P. Dura: Yale University Library, New Haven, Connecticut, U.S.A.

*P. Erl.: Universitätsbibliothek, Erlangen.

*P. Fay.: as for P. Cairo, but some papyri are now distributed among several institutions, as noted ad loc.

*P. Flor.: see PSI.

*P. Freib.: Universitätsbibliothek, Freiburg-im-Breisgau.

*P. Fuad: Société Fouad I de Papyrologie, Cairo.

*P. Genève: Bibliothèque Publique et Universitaire de Genève, Genève.

*P. Giss.: Museum des Oberhessischen Geschichtsvereins zu Giessen.

P. Golenischeff: State Museum of Fine Arts, Moscow.

*P. Goth.: Göteborgs Stadsbibliotek (Bibliothèque Municipale de Gothembourg), Göteborg.

*P. Grenf.: British Museum, London, and Bodleian Library, Oxford, as noted ad loc.

*P. Groning.: Bibliotheek der Rijksuniversiteit te Groningen, and Bibliotheek der Universiteit van Amsterdam, as noted ad loc.

*P. Gurob: (Royal) Irish Academy, Dublin.

*P. Hal.: Philologisches Seminar der Universität Halle, Halle.

*P. Hamb.: Staats- und Universitäts-Bibliothek, Hamburg.

*P. Harris: Woodbrooke College, Birmingham, but some papyri have been distributed as noted ad loc.

*P. Haun.: Institutum Papyrologiae Graecae Universitatis Hauniensis, Universitetsbiblioteket, København.

*P. Hawara: University College, London, and Bodleian Library, Oxford, as noted (where possible) ad loc.

P. Heid.: Universitätsbibliothek, Heidelberg.

*P. Heid. Lit.: see P. Heid.

*P. Heid. Siegmann: see P. Heid.

*P. Hibeh: Egypt Exploration Society, London, but papyri have been distributed among many institutions, as noted ad loc.

*P. Holm.: Kungliga Vitterhets- Historie- och Antikvitets-Akademien, Stockholm.

*P. Iand.: Klassisches Seminar der Universität Giessen (cf. P. Univ. Giss.)

*P. Ibscher: see P. Hamb.

PIFAO: Institut Français d' Archéologie Orientale du Caire, Cairo.

P. Leid.: Bibliotheek der Rijksuniversiteit, Leiden.

*P. Lit. Goodspeed: said to be in the Library of the University of Chicago, but direct inquiries have proved unavailing.

*P. Lit. Lond.: British Museum, London.

*P. Lond.: British Museum, London.

P. Louvre: Musée du Louvre, Paris.

*P. Maspero: see P. Cairo.

*P. Med.: Università Cattolica del Sacro Cuore, Milano.

*P. Merton: Chester Beatty Library, Dublin.

*P. Mich.: Rare Book Room (Dr. H. Jameson, Librarian), General Library, University of Michigan, Ann Arbor, Michigan, U.S.A.

*P. Michael.: Library of G. A. Michailides, Cairo (papyri published for the Egypt Exploration Society, London, by the Aberdeen University Press).

*P. Mil. Vogl(iano) 2: Università Statale (Università degli Studi), Milano (cf. PRIMI, P. Univ. Statale di Milano).

P. Monac.: Bayerische Staatsbibliothek, München.

P. Mus. Alex.: Greco-Roman Museum, Alexandria.

P. Nessana: see P. Colt.

*P. Oslo: Det Norske Videnskaps-Akademi i Oslo, Universitetsbiblioteket, Oslo.

*P. Oxy.: Egypt Exploration Society, London, but many papyri have been distributed among various institutions, as noted ad loc.

*P. Par.: Bibliothèque Nationale and Musée du Louvre, Paris, as noted ad loc.

*P. Petrie: (Royal) Irish Academy, Dublin, and British Museum and University College, London, as noted ad loc.

*P. Princ.: Princeton University Library, Princeton, New Jersey, U.S.A.

*P. Rain.: Österreichische Nationalbibliothek, Wien. Cf. P. Vindob.

*P. Rein.: Université de Paris, Institut de Papyrologie de la Sorbonne.

*PRIMI: Università Statale (Università degli Studi), Milano (cf. P. Mil. Vogl. 2, P. Univ. Statale di Milano).

P. Robinson: University of Mississippi Library, Oxford, Mississippi, U.S.A.

*P. Ross. Georg.: Library of the State Hermitage Museum, Leningrad, State Museum of Fine Arts, Moscow, and Collections of M. Maximova and G. Zereteli, as noted ad loc.

*P. Ryl.: John Rylands Library, Manchester.

*P. Schubart: as for BKT, above.

P. Soc. Pap. Alex.: Société Papyrologique d' Alexandrie, Alexandria.

P. Sorbonne: Université de Paris, Institut de Papyrologie de la Sorbonne.

P. Strasb., P. Strassb.: Bibliothèque Nationale et Universitaire, Strasbourg (Universitäts- und Landesbibliothek, Strassburg).

*PSI: Istituto Papirologico "Girolamo Vitelli, " Università degli Studi, Firenze. (Some papyri of this collection are evidently in the Biblioteca Laurenziana, Firenze.)

*P. Tebt.: Egypt Exploration Society, London.

*P. Thead.: Musée des Antiquités Égyptiennes du Caire, Cairo.

*P. Univ. Giss.: Klassisches Seminar der Universität Giessen, Giessen (cf. P. Iand.).

P. Univ. Statale di Milano: cf. PRIMI and P. Mil. Vogl. 2.

*P. Varsov.: Uniwersytet Warszawski (Universitas Varsoviensis), Warszawa.

P. Vat.: Museo Egiziano Vaticano, Città del Vaticano.

*P. Vat. Gr.: see P. Vat.

P. Vindob.: see P. Rain.

*P. Würzb.: Universitätsbibliothek, Würzburg.

P. Zereteli: Professor George Zereteli, Oriental Faculty of the University Tbilisi, U.S.S.R.

Peabody Mudseum of Natural History, Yale University, New Haven, Connecticut, U.S.A.

Philologisches Seminar der Universität Jena, Jena.

*Raineri F., *Raineri M.: see P. Rain.

Rijksmuseum van Oudheden, Leiden.

Rossall School, Fleetwood, Lancashire.

Royal Ontario Museum, University of Toronto, Toronto, Ontario, Canada.

Shrewsbury School, Shrewsbury, Shropshire.

Smithsonian Institution, Washington, D. C., U.S.A.

Southern Methodist University Library, Dallas, Texas, U.S.A.

St. Andrews University Library, Fife.
St. Paul's School, London.
Stanford University Library, Palo Alto, California, U.S.A.
Toledo Museum of Art, Toledo, Ohio, U.S.A.
Tonbridge School, Tonbridge, Kent.
Trinity College Library, Dublin.
Università degli Studi di Genova, Genova.
Universitätsbibliothek, Basel.
Universitätsbibliothek, Giessen.
Universitätsbibliothek, Graz.
Universitätsbibliothek, Leipzig.
University College, London.
University of Illinois Library, Urbana, Illinois, U.S.A.

University of Pennsylvania Museum, Philadelphia, Pennsylvania, U.S.A.
University of Sydney Library, Sydney, New South Wales, Australia.
Uppsala Universitets Bibliotek, Uppsala.
Walters Art Gallery, Baltimore, Maryland, U.S.A.
Washington University Library, St. Louis, Missouri, U.S.A.
Wellesley College, Wellesley, Massachusetts, U.S.A.
Western Reserve University Library, Cleveland, Ohio, U.S.A.
Westminster School, London.
Williams College, Williamstown, Massachusetts, U.S.A.
Winchester College, Winchester, Hampshire.
Yale University Library, New Haven, Connecticut, U.S.A.

# LIST OF TEXTS: GREEK

## A. TEXTS IDENTIFIED BY AUTHORS

Abas: see No. 2339.
Achaeus: see Nos. 1739, 2290.

1 ACHILLES TATIUS: Clitophon and Leucippe ii. 2. 3-5, 14. 5-7. P. Schubart 30 (III, Hermupolis Magna; pap. cod.). Vilborg, Ach. Tat. XVI, XLII-XLIII.

2 --- ii. 7. 7, 8. 1-3, 2, 3. 1-2, 9. 1-2 (sic). P. Oxy. 10. 1250 (Bodleian Libr., Gr. class. d. 97 (P)) (III-IV, Oxy.). JAW 170. 226; Vilborg, Ach. Tat. XV, XXXV-XLII. F. Garin, Riv. Fil. 47 (1919) 351-57, on the relation to the text tradition; C. F. Russo, Rend. Acc. Linc., Ser. 8. 10 (1955) 397-403. W. Schubart, under P. Schubart 30, assigns this papyrus to the third century.

3 --- vi. 14-15, 16-17. A. Vogliano, SIFC 15 (1938) 121-30 (P. Univ. Statale di Milano) (II?, Oxy. ?; pap. cod.). Vilborg, Ach. Tat. XVI-XVII, XLIII-XLIV.

Acusilaus of Argos: see Nos. 2290, 2810.
Aegimius of Elis: see No. 2339.

4 AESCHINES: Contra Timarchum 53-54. M.-T. Lenger, Phoibos 5 (= Mél. Joseph Hombert, 1950-51) 88-93 (P. Fuad inv. 222) (II). Identified by W. G. Waddell. M. Hombert, Chr. Ég. 28 (1953) 388-89.

--- 165: see No. 2289.

5 --- 171-81. P. Genève 1 (inv. 256) (II-III; on the verso of a document).

6 --- 177-78, 191-92, 194-95. P. Hal. 6 (inv. 13) (II; on the verso of a document).

--- See also No. 307.

--- De Falsa Legatione 10: see No. 2289.

7 --- 21, 26-27, 29-30. P. Oxy. 3. 458 (Houghton Libr., Harvard Univ.) (II-III, Oxy.). Archiv 3. 293.

8 --- 42, 74-75. P. Oxy. 3. 440 (a) (Manchester Mus.) (III, Oxy.). Identified by F. Blass, Archiv 3. 293. J. Bingen, Chr. Ég. 34 (1959) 93-94, reedits the text.

9 --- 149-53. P. Erl. 11 (inv. 103) (III). Identified by A. Oguse, Chr. Ég. 27 (1952) 393-95; J. Bingen, ibid. 34 (1959) 91-94, identifies another fragment of the text and reedits it.

--- 158: see No. 2128.

10 --- In Ctesiphontem 14-27. P. Oxy. 13. 1625 (P. Cairo) (II, Oxy.).

11 --- 24, 26-27. W. H. Willis, TAPA 86 (1955) 129-34 (P. Robinson inv. 1) (II-III).

12 --- 47. P. Groning. 1, pp. 57-58 (Amsterdam) (II-III).

13 --- 51-53. P. Oxy. 24. 2404 (II, Oxy.). R. Merkelbach, Stud. Jachmann 162-64.

14 --- 86-87. P. Mil. Vogl. 2. 41 (inv. 221) (I-II, Oxy.). I. Cazzaniga, Rend. Ist. Lomb. 70 (1937) 129-32 (ed. pr.).

15 --- 94, 96. P. Oxy. 4. 703 (Bodleian Libr., Gr. class. g. 51 (P)) (III, Oxy.). Archiv 3. 494.

16 --- 166-67. P. Oxy. 3. 457 (Royal Ontario Mus., Univ. of Toronto) (II, Oxy.). Archiv 3. 293.

17 --- 178-86. W. von Hartel, Feierliche Sitzung der Kaiserlichen Akad. der Wiss. (Wien 1886) 57-60; Vortrag über die griechischen Papyri Erzherzog Rainer (Wien 1886) 44-49 (V, Fayum; parch. cod.). Gesch. der Textüberlief. 268.

18 --- 194-200. P. Hamb. 165 (inv. 406) (II).

Aeschines: see also No. 2070.

19 AESCHINES SOCRATICUS: Alcibiades. P. Oxy. 13. 1608; P. Lit. Lond. 148 (Brit. Mus. inv. 2469) (II, Oxy.). Archiv 7. 155; New Chapters 2. 103-4. P. Collart, Rev. Phil. 43 (1919) 55-57; E. G. Berry, TAPA 81 (1950) 1-8.

Aeschines Socraticus: see also Nos. 2103, 2120.

20 AESCHYLUS: Agamemnon 7-17, 20-30. P. Oxy. 18. 2178 (II, Oxy.). In the same hand as Nos. 21, 26-28, 33, 36, 42, 44. Galiano, Aesch. 91.

--- Choëphoroe 49: see No. 455.

21 --- Septem contra Thebas 155-59. P. Oxy. 18. 2179 (and ibid. 20, p. 167) (II, Oxy.). In the same hand as Nos. 20, 26-28, 33, 36, 42, 44.

22 --- 498, 501-3, 529-52. P. Oxy. 22. 2334 (II. Oxy.).

23 --- 621-31, 634-38, 644-56. P. Oxy. 22. 2333 (II, Oxy.).

--- Septem: see also No. 46.
--- Supplices: see No. 46.

24 --- A choral fragment (Aigyptioi? Ixion?). P. Oxy. 20. 2251 (II, Oxy.). Galiano, Aesch. 101-2; Lloyd-Jones, Aesch., fr. 280 (bibl.), lists as an "unknown play"; Mette, FTA, fr. 496. Archiv 16. 100; M. L. Cunningham, Rh. Mus. 96 (1953) 223-31, suggests the Aigyptioi; B. Snell, Gnomon 25 (1953) 436-37; J. T. Kakridis, Acme 8, fasc. 2-3 (1955) 91; D. Bindzus, Dion., NS 19 (1956) 227-28; E. A. Wolff, Eranos 56 (1958) 125-27; F. C. Görschen, Archiv 17 (1960) 26, 57, attributes fragments to the Aigyptioi and the Ixion.

25   --- Aitnaiai or Philoktetes (?).   P. Oxy. 20.2246
     (II, Oxy.).  Galiano, Aesch. 118 (bibl.);  Mette,
     FTA, fr. 494.  F. C. Görschen, Gymnas. 62 (1955)
     200, suggests the Philoktetes;  H. J. Mette, ibid.
     406, favors the Aitnaiai;  R. Merkelbach, Archiv
     16 (1956) 101;  F. C. Görschen, Archiv 17 (1960) 25,
     57;  idem, Archiv 17 (1962) 163-85, reedits the text.

     --- Aitnaiai:  see Nos. 46-47.
     --- Alexandros:  see No. 49.
     --- Amymone:  see No. 46.
     --- Danaïdes:  see Nos. 45-46, 1699.
     --- "Dike fragment":  see No. 46.

26   --- Diktyoulkoi.   PSI 11.1209;  P. Oxy. 18.2161 (II,
     Oxy.).  In the same hand as Nos. 20-21, 27-28, 33,
     36, 42, 44.  M. Norsa and G. Vitelli, BSAA, NS 8,
     No. 28 (1933) 115-21 (partial ed. pr. of PSI 1209),
     Mel. Bidez 965-68 (ditto).  Cantarella 36-59;  Fritsch,
     No. 1;  Galiano, Aesch. 102-4;  Lesky, GGL 248-49;
     Lloyd-Jones, Aesch., frr. 274-75 (bibl.);  Mette,
     SA, No. 178, Nachtrag 24-26, FTA, frr. 464, 467,
     474;  G. Murray, Aeschylus the Creator of Tragedy
     (Oxford 1940), Preface ix-x;  Page, GLP 1, No. 2;
     Steffen, Sat. Gr. Fr. 11-16, Stud. Aesch. 23-39;
     Werre-De Haas 11-78 et passim.  Archiv 11.249-50,
     16.99.  A. Koerte, Hermes 68 (1933) 267-75;  G.
     Vitelli, BSAA, NS 8, No. 29 (1934) 229-48;  R.
     Goossens, Chr. Ég. 10 (1935) 120-28, 376-77;  idem,
     ibid. 16 (1941) 107-8, 17 (1942) 113;  R. Pfeiffer,
     Sitzb. Münch. Akad., 1938, Heft 2, 1-22;  M. Unter-
     steiner, BFC 45 (1939) 199-205;  E. Fraenkel, Proc.
     Brit. Acad., 1942, 240-44;  W. Steffen, Eos 42 (1947)
     153-56;  A. Setti, Ann. Sc. Pisa, Ser. 2.17 (1948)
     2-36;  E. Siegmann, Philol. 97 (1948) 71-124;  V.
     Steffen, JJP 3 (1949) 119-35;  J. C. Kamerbeek,
     Mnemos., Ser. 4.7 (1954) 90-110;  R. Pfeiffer, Fest-
     schr. Sommer 177-80;  H. J. Mette, Gnomon 30
     (1958) 567;  T. P. Howe, GR, Ser. 2.6 (1959) 152-65;
     R. Stark, Rh. Mus. 102 (1959) 2-4;  G. Vita, Dion.,
     NS 22 (1959) 214-19.

     --- Diktyoulkoi:  see also Nos. 45-46.
     --- Dionysou Trophoi:  see No. 45.
     --- Eleusinioi:  see Nos. 32, 339.

27   --- Glaukos Pontios.   P. Oxy. 18.2159 (II, Oxy.).
     In the same hand as Nos. 20-21, 26, 28, 33, 36,
     42, 44.  Cantarella 9-15;  Galiano, Aesch. 115-16;
     Lloyd-Jones, Aesch., fr. 273 (bibl.);  Mette, Nach-
     trag 5-6, FTA, fr. 55;  Steffen, Sat. Gr. Fr. 8-9.
     Archiv 16.99;  W. Steffen, Eos 42 (1947) 152-53;  E.
     Siegmann, Philol. 97 (1948) 59-62;  F. C. Görschen,
     Dion., NS 13 (1950) 42-43;  B. Snell, Gnomon 25
     (1953) 438;  Z. K. Vysoky, Listy Fil., NS 4 (1956)
     14-23, 161-70;  H. J. Mette, Gnomon 30 (1958) 566-
     67;  R. P. Winnington-Ingram, BICSL 6 (1959) 58-60;
     Z. K. Vysoky, Listy Fil., NS 8 (1960) 162-64.

     --- Glaukos Pontios:  see also No. 45.

28   --- Glaukos Potnieus.   PSI 11.1210;  P. Oxy. 18.2160
     (cf. ibid., p. 182) (II, Oxy.).  In the same hand as
     Nos. 20-21, 26-27, 33, 36, 42, 44.  Cantarella
     21-30;  Fritsch, No. 2;  Galiano, Aesch. 110-11;
     Mette, SA, No. 171, Nachtrag 20-23, FTA, frr.

                                    441-44, 447-49;  Murray, Aesch. 97.  Archiv 13.97,
                                    16.99;  JAW 259.28.  R. Goossens, Chr. Ég. 11
                                    (1936) 508-11;  E. Siegmann, Philol. 97 (1948) 62-71;
                                    F. C. Görschen, Dion., NS 13 (1950) 43-47.

                               29   --- Herakleidai.   G. Lefebvre, BSAA 14 (1912) 192
                                    (II-III, Fayum).  Fritsch, No. 3;  Galiano, Aesch.,
                                    113-14 (bibl.);  Lloyd-Jones, Aesch., fr. 285 (bibl.);
                                    Mette, SA, No. 57, FTA, fr. 110;  Page, GLP 1, No.
                                    35;  Steffen, Stud. Aesch. 53-65.  Archiv 7.141-42.

                                    --- Herakleidai:  see also Nos. 38, 45.
                                    --- Hiereiai:  see No. 45.
                                    --- Hoplon Krisis:  see Nos. 30, 46-47.

                               30   --- Iphigeneia (?):  Verses from the beginning of a
                                    prologue (?).  P. Oxy. 20.2253 (II, Oxy.).  Gali-
                                    ano, Aesch. 87-88;  Lloyd-Jones, Aesch., fr. 283
                                    (bibl.);  Mette, FTA, fr. 223a (Myrmidones?).
                                    Archiv 16.101.  B. Snell, Gnomon 25 (1953) 437, sug-
                                    gests a Trojan play;  R. Stark, Hermes 82 (1954)
                                    372-75, suggests the Iphigeneia;  J. T. Kakridis,
                                    Acme 8, fasc. 2-3 (1955) 91;  H. J. Mette, Gnomon
                                    30 (1958) 569-70;  F. C. Görschen, Archiv 17 (1960)
                                    34, 57 (Phryges vel Hektoros Lytra, Hoplon Krisis,
                                    Iphigeneia?).

                                    --- Iphigeneia:  see also No. 46.
                                    --- Ixion:  see No. 24.

                               31   --- Kares vel Europa (?).   P. Didot, pp. 18-22
                                    (P. Louvre inv. 7171 + 7172) (II B.C., Serapaeum,
                                    Memphis;  sch. ex.;  from a composite roll con-
                                    taining also Nos. 401, 1319-20, 1435).  Galiano,
                                    Aesch. 92-93 (bibl.);  Lloyd-Jones, Aesch., pp.
                                    599-603 (bibl.);  Mette, FTA, fr. 145;  Steffen,
                                    Stud. Aesch. 81-87.  JAW 17.44-46;  F. Blass,
                                    Rh. Mus. 35 (1880) 83-88;  F. Buecheler, ibid.
                                    93-97;  E. Fraenkel, Proc. Brit. Acad., 1942,
                                    237.

                                    --- Laios:  see No. 46.
                                    --- Leon:  see No. 46.

                               32   --- Lykourgeia (?) or Eleusinioi (?).  W. Buchwald,
                                    Studien zur Chronologie der attischen Tragödie
                                    (Konigsberg 1939) 57 (P. Med.) (I).  Galiano, Aesch.
                                    107-8;  Lloyd-Jones, Aesch., p. 527, queries the
                                    ascription to Aeschylus;  Mette, Nachtrag 32, FTA,
                                    fr. 596;  K. Deichgräber, Gött. Nachr. 1.3 (1938-
                                    39) 276, note 3, queries the editor's attribution to
                                    the Lykourgeia;  E. Eichgrün, Prolegom. 2 (1953)
                                    9-20, holds that the text consists of three distinct
                                    citations, of which one belongs to the Eleusinioi.

                               33   --- Myrmidones.   P. Oxy. 18.2163 (cf. ibid. 20,
                                    p. 167) (II, Oxy.).  In the same hand as Nos. 20-21,
                                    26-28, 36, 42, 44.  Cantarella 99-104;  Galiano,
                                    Aesch. 87;  Mette, Nachtrag 10-12, FTA, frr. 213-
                                    218, 220-23.  F. C. Görschen, Dion., NS 13 (1950)
                                    179-83;  Z. K. Vysoky, Listy Fil., NS 6 (1958) 148-
                                    56, ibid. 7 (1959) 8-31.

                               34   --- Myrmidones (?).   PSI 11.1211 (I-II, Oxy.).
                                    M. Norsa and G. Vitelli, Mél. Bidez 2.968-78 (ed.
                                    pr.).  Fritsch, No. 4;  Galiano, Aesch. 86-87;

Lesky, GGL 248; Lloyd-Jones, Aesch., fr. 286
(bibl.); Mette, SA, No. 73, FTA, fr. 225a; Page,
CLP 1, No. 20; Steffen, Stud. Aesch. 89-98. Archiv 11. 250-52. R. Sulzberger, Ant. Class. 3 (1934)
447-50; R. Goossens, Chr. Ég. 10 (1935) 376, regards the attribution as probable; T. Kalén, Eranos
33 (1935) 39-62; W. Schadewaldt, Hermes 71 (1936)
25-69; L. A. Stella, Rend. Ist. Lomb. 69 (1936)
553-62, queries Aeschylean authorship; C. Fries,
Phil. Woch. 57 (1937) 478-80; E. Fraenkel, Proc.
Brit. Acad., 1942, 239-40; Z. K. Vysoky, Listy
Fil., NS 6 (1958) 156-71.

35   --- Myrmidones (?). P. Cairo Zen. 4.59651 (III
B.C., Philadelphia). Cited in a "Memorandum to
Zenon from Nikarchos." Galiano, Aesch. 86;
Mette, FTA, fr. 412e, as from the Mysoi.

--- Myrmidones: see also Nos. 30, 45-46.
--- Mysoi: see No. 35.

36   --- Niobe. PSI 11.1208 (II, Oxy.). In the same hand
as Nos. 20-21, 26-28, 33, 42, 44. Ed. pr.: M.
Norsa and G. Vitelli, BSAA 28 (1933) 108-14, ibid.
29 (1934) 229-48. Fritsch, No. 5; Galiano, Aesch.,
84-85; Lesky, GGL 248; Lloyd-Jones, Aesch.,
fr. 277 (bibl.); Mette, SA, No. 116, FTA, fr. 273;
Page, GLP 1, No. 1; Steffen, Stud. Aesch. 99-117.
Archiv 11. 248-49; JAW 259. 30-73. I. Cazzaniga,
Rend. Ist. Lomb. 66 (1933) 843-52; A. Koerte,
Hermes 68 (1933) 250-66; K. Latte, Gött. Nachr.,
1933, 22-29; P. Maas, Gnomon 9 (1933) 289-92;
W. Schadewaldt, Sitzb. Heid. Akad., 1933-34, Abh.
3; A. Lesky, WS 52 (1934) 1-18; R. Pfeiffer, Philol.
89 (1934)1-18; H. Kloesel, Hermes 72 (1937) 466-
69; I. Cazzaniga, Athen., NS 17 (1939) 49; Q. Ca-
taudella, Riv. Fil. 69 (1941) 34-36; E. Fraenkel,
Proc. Brit. Acad., 1942, 238-39; A. D. Fitton
Brown, CQ, NS 4 (1954) 175-80, reprints the text
and discusses the plot; R. E. Wycherley, CP 49
(1954) 38; H. Lloyd-Jones, JHS 76 (1956) 63; H.
J. Mette, Gnomon 30 (1958) 568; J. C. Kamerbeek,
Mnemos., Ser. 4.13 (1960) 327-28; Z. K. Vysoky,
Listy Fil., NS 8 (1960) 165-66.

--- Niobe: see also No. 1700.
--- Oidipous: see No. 46.
--- Philoktetes: see Nos. 25, 46.
--- Phineus: see Nos. 46, 1186.
--- Phorkides: see No. 1700.
--- Phryges vel Hektoros Lytra: see Nos. 30, 46, 49.

37   --- Prometheus Pyrkaeus (or Pyrphoros?). P. Oxy.
20.2245 (II, Oxy.). E. Fraenkel, Proc. Brit. Acad.,
1942, 245-47 (first description). Galiano, Aesch.
111-13; Lloyd-Jones, Aesch., fr. 278 (bibl.); Mette,
FTA, frr. 343-50; Murray, Aesch. 99-100. Archiv
16. 100. B. Snell, Gnomon 25 (1953) 435; N. Terzaghi, Riv. Fil. 82-(1954) 337-52, Rend. Acc. Linc.,
Ser. 8.10 (1955) 532-34, Athen., NS 39 (1961) 6, prefers the P. Pyrphoros; R. Stark, Maia 8 (1956) 89-
91; F. C. Görschen, Archiv 17 (1960) 25, 32-34, 57;
Z. K. Vysoky, Listy Fil., NS 8 (1960) 166.

38   --- Prometheus Pyrkaeus (?). P. Oxy. 20.2252 (II,
Oxy.). Galiano, Aesch. 113; Mette, FTA, fr. 342.
B. Snell, Gnomon 25 (1953) 436, suggests the Pro-
metheus Pyrkaeus; F. C. Görschen, Archiv 17

(1960) 57 (Herakleidai, Prometheus Pyrkaeus?).

--- Prometheus Pyrkaeus (or P. Lyomenos): see
No. 2172.

39   --- Prometheus Pyrphoros (or P. Lyomenos?). P.
Heid. Siegmann 185 (inv. 1131) (ca. 200 B.C.). Gali-
ano, Aesch. 108-9; Mette, FTA, fr. 323a. H.
Lloyd-Jones, Gnomon 29 (1957) 426; K. Reinhardt,
Hermes 85 (1957) 12-17, 125-26, argues for the P.
Pyrphoros; M. Gigante, PP 13 (1958) 278, suggests
the P. Lyomenos; N. Terzaghi, Athen., NS 39 (1961)
3-10, further develops Reinhardt's identification.

--- Salaminiai: see No. 46.

40   --- Semele vel Hydrophoroi (?). P. Oxy. 20.2248
(II, Oxy.). Galiano, Aesch. 107; Mette, FTA, fr.
357. F. C. Görschen, Archiv 17 (1960) 25, 57.

41   --- Semele vel Hydrophoroi (?). P. Oxy. 20.2249
(II, Oxy.). Galiano, Aesch. 107; Mette, FTA, fr.
356. B. Snell, Gnomon 25 (1953) 436; F. C. Görschen, Archiv 17 (1960) 25, 57.

--- Semele vel Hydrophoroi: see also Nos. 44-45.
--- Sphinx: see Nos. 45-46.
--- Tenes: see No. 46.

42   --- Theoroi vel Isthmiastai (?). P. Oxy. 18.2162
(and ibid. 20, p. 167: an additional fr.) (II, Oxy.).
In the same hand as Nos. 20-21, 26-28, 33, 36, 44.
Cantarella 71-90; Galiano, Aesch. 120-22; Lesky,
GGL 249; Lloyd-Jones, Aesch., fr. 276 (bibl.);
Mette, Nachtrag 27-31, FTA, frr. 17-18; Steffen,
Sat. Gr. Fr. 17-20, Stud. Aesch. 67-80. Archiv
16. 100. E. Fraenkel, Proc. Brit. Acad., 1942,
244-45; A. Tovar, Emérita 11 (1943) 438-40; W.
Steffen, Eos 42 (1947) 156-57; M. Untersteiner,
Dion., NS 14 (1951) 19-45; A. Setti, Ann. Sc. Pisa,
Ser. 2.21 (1953) 205-44; B. Snell, Gnomon 25 (1953)
436; A. Barigazzi, Ann. Sc. Pisa., Ser. 2.23 (1954)
338-43; F. C. Görschen, Dion., NS 17 (1954) 3-21;
J. C. Kamerbeek, Mnemos., Ser. 4.8 (1955) 1-13;
N. Terzaghi, Studi Paoli 685-93; B. Snell, Hermes
84 (1956) 1-11, rearranges the fragments, discusses
the plot, and assigns No. 43 to the same play; D.
L. Page, CR, NS 7 (1957) 191; K. Reinhardt, Her-
mes 85 (1957) 1-12, 123-25; H. Schaefer, Charites:
Studien zur Altertumswiss. (E. Langlotz gewidmet)
(Bonn 1957) 231-32; H. J. Mette, Gnomon 30 (1958)
567-68; idem, Hermes 86 (1958) 255, 384; R.
Stark, Rh. Mus. 102 (1959) 6-9; Z. K. Vysoky,
Listy Fil., NS 8 (1960) 164-65.

43   --- Theoroi vel Isthmiastai (?). P. Oxy. 20.2250
(II, Oxy.). Galiano, Aesch. 122; Mette, FTA, fr.
16. B. Snell, Gnomon 25 (1953) 436, idem, Hermes
84 (1956) 10, conjectures that this belongs to the
same papyrus and play as No. 42; J. T. Kakridis,
Acme 8, fasc. 2-3 (1955) 91; F. C. Görschen, Archiv 17 (1960) 57.

--- Theoroi vel Isthmiastai: see also Nos. 45-46.

44 --- Xantriai or Semele (?). P. Oxy. 18.2164 (cf. ibid. 20, p. 10) (II, Oxy.). In the same hand as Nos. 20-21, 26-28, 33, 36, 42. Cantarella 108-24; Galiano, Aesch. 105-7, favors the Semele, as do Lloyd-Jones, Aesch., fr. 279 (bibl.), and Mette, FTA, fr. 355, Nachtrag 14-16. Archiv 16.100. E. R. Dodds, Euripides: Bacchae (Oxford 1944), p. xxvii, 2nd ed. (1960), p. xxx, prefers the Xantriai; K. Latte, Philol. 97 (1948) 47-56, the Semele; F. Lasserre, Mus. Helv. 6 (1949) 140-56, the Xantriai; M. Nilsson, Ant. Class. 24 (1955) 336-40; H. J. Mette, Gnomon 30 (1958) 568; Z. K. Vysoky, Listy Fil., NS 8 (1960) 166-67.

45 --- Fragments attributed to various plays. P. Oxy. 20.2255 (II, Oxy.). Galiano, Aesch. 88, 94, 102, 104-5; Mette, FTA, frr. 19 (Theoroi vel Isthmiastai), 56 (Glaukos Pontios), 125 (Danaïdes), 183b (Sphinx), 219 (Myrmidones), 468-73 (Diktyoulkoi), 498-504, 505-27 ("unbekannten Ortes"). Archiv 16.100. B. Snell, Gnomon 25 (1953) 437-38; J. T. Kakridis, Acme 8, fasc. 2-3 (1955) 92; F. M. Heichelheim, SO 34 (1958) 15-18, on fr. 5; F. C. Görschen, Archiv 17 (1960) 26-27, 34-38, 57, attributes fragments to the Danaïdes, Herakleidai, Hiereiai, Myrmidones, Semele (trilogy), Diktyoulkoi, Dionysou Trophoi, Glaukos Pontios, Theoroi vel Isthmiastai, and Sphinx.

46 --- Hypotheses to the Laios, the Danaïd tetralogy, and the Philoktetes; and fragments attributed to various plays. P. Oxy. 20.2256 (II-III?, Oxy.). Frr. 2+4+1 = a hypothesis to the Laios, referring to Aeschylus' Laios, Oidipous, Septem, and Sphinx; Aristias, a tragedian; and Polyphradmon, a tragedian, and his Lycurgean tetralogy. Fr. 3 = a hypothesis to the Danaïd tetralogy, bearing upon the disputed chronology of the Pentekontaëtia, perhaps challenging the traditional dating of the Supplices (Hiketides), and referring to Aeschylus' Amymone, Danaides, and Supplices; Sophocles, Kophoi and Poimenes; and one "Mesatos" (a tragic poet?). Fr. 5 = a hypothesis to the Philoktetes. Frr. 8-9: a satyr play (Aitnaiai?). (Fr. 9a = the "Dike fragment.") Fr. 71: choral (Hoplon Krisis?). Fr. 72: Diktyoulkoi (?).

Fr. 3: reprinted by Murray, Aesch. 2; Galiano, Aesch. 95-101, 123. D. Pieraccioni, Maia 5 (1952) 289-91; J. A. Davison, CR, NS 3 (1953) 144, defends the identity of Mesatos; F. R. Earp, GR 22 (1953) 118-23, defends the traditional early dating of the Supplices; J. T. Kakridis, Hellen. 13 (1954) 165-70; A. Lesky, Hermes 82 (1954) 1-13; T. B. L. Webster, Fifty Years Cl. Schol. 74-75, on the date of the Supplices; E. C. Yorke, CQ, NS 4 (1954) 183-84, defends the identity of Mesatos; E. C. Yorke, CR, NS 4 (1954) 10-11, and E. G. Turner, ibid. 21-23, discuss the date of the Supplices; F. Lasserre, Hermes 83 (1955) 128, reads "Naiades" for the tragedy of Sophocles; P. Orgels, Bull. Acad. Belg., Ser. 5.41 (1955) 528-36, on the Supplices; D. del Corno, Dion., NS 19 (1956) 277-91; Lesky, GGL 227-28; D. L. Page, CR, NS 7 (1957) 192; E. A. Wolfe, Eranos 56 (1958) 119-39, on the date of the Danaïd tetralogy. Lloyd-Jones, Aesch., fr. 288.

Frr. 8-9: Lloyd-Jones, Aesch., fr. 282; W. J. Verdenius, Mnemos., Ser. 4.6 (1953) 207; E. Fraenkel, Eranos 52 (1954) 64-75; F. C. Görschen,

Dion., NS 18 (1955) 139-61, attributes frr. 9 a-b, 12, to the Theoroi vel Isthmiastai; H. Lloyd-Jones, JHS 76 (1956) 59-60; R. Stark, Maia 8 (1956) 83-89, on fr. 8; Z. K. Vysoky, Listy Fil., NS 5 (1957) 164-73, ibid. 6 (1958) 7-26, ibid. 8 (1960) 41-44; H. J. Mette, Gnomon 30 (1958) 568-69; F. C. Görschen, Dion., NS 22 (1959) 147-88, on the concept of peace here and in other authors; Ph. J. Kakridis, Eranos 60 (1962) 111-21, on fr. 9 a.

Fr. 72: Werre-De Haas 33-34; Z. K. Vysoky, Listy Fil., NS 8 (1960) 164.

Further: Galiano, Aesch. 88-91, 93-101, 105, 113, 118-20; Archiv 16.101-2; B. Snell, Gnomon 25 (1953) 435-36, 438-40; F. C. Görschen, Gymnas. 62 (1955) 200-6, attributes frr. 85, 87-88, and P. Oxy. 2246 (see No. 25) to the Philoktetes; J. T. Kakridis, Hellen. 13 (1954) 171, on fr. 2; idem, Acme 8, fasc. 2-3 (1955) 92, on frr. 2, 9 a, 71; idem, Acta Congressus Madvigiani: Proceedings of the Second International Congress of Class. Studies (Copenhagen 1958) 142-45 (ob fr. 71), 145-47 (frr. 8-9), 147-52 (fr. 3); F. C. Görschen, Archiv 17 (1960) 28-31, 38-56, 58-60, attributes fragments to a number of plays; S. G. Kossyphopoulos, Hellen. 14 (1955-56) 449-51, on fr. 5 a; G. Andresen, Dion., NS 19 (1956) 229-31, attributes fr. 10 (a) to the Phineus; F. M. Heichelheim, SO 34 (1958) 15-18, would combine fr. 71 (Hoplon Krisis?) with P. Oxy. 2255, fr. 5 (see No. 45) and P. Berol. inv. 6870, fr. C (see No. 2439). Mette, FTA, frr. 122 (Danaïdes), 137-40 (Iphigeneia), 169, 174 (Laios), 186-90 (Leon), 229b (Myrmidones), 246a, 250b, 251-53 (Phryges vel Hektoros Lytra), 283a (Hoplon Krisis), 296 (Salaminiai), 388-90 (Tenes?), 392 (Philoktetes), 465 (Diktyoulkoi), 528-89 ("unbekannten Ortes").

47 --- Hypothesis to the Aitnaiai, and other fragments. P. Oxy. 20.2257 (II?, Oxy.). Fr. 1 = hypothesis to the Aitnaiai, referring to Sophocles, Achilleos Erastai: Archiv 16.102; Lloyd-Jones, Aesch., fr. 287; Lesky, GGL 226; Srebrny, Stud. Scaen. 59 (note 41), 91 (note 89); F. C. Görschen, Dion., NS 19 (1956) 217-26; E. Grassi, PP 11 (1956) 208-9, ibid. 12 (1957) 374. Galiano, Aesch. 116-18; Mette, FTA, frr. 26 (Aitnaiai), 284b (Hoplon Krisis), 590-95 ("unbekannten Ortes"); B. Snell, Gnomon 25 (1953) 440; E. Fraenkel, Eranos 52 (1954) 63, 75, notes that fr. 4 matches Aeschylus, fr. 350, Nauck[2] (lines 1-2).

48 --- Aeschylus (?). P. Oxy. 20.2247 (II, Oxy.). Mette, FTA, fr. 495 ("unbekannten Ortes").

49 --- Aeschylus (?). P. Oxy. 20.2254 (II, Oxy.). Mette, FTA, fr. 497 ("unbekannten Ortes"); F. C. Görschen, Archiv 17 (1960) 57 (Hektoros Lytra, Alexandros?); Galiano, Aesch. 92, notes the attributions.

Aeschylus: see also Nos. 1205, 1699, 1701, 1950, 2160, 2172.

50 AESOP (?): Fables. P. Ryl. 3.493 (I). Traces of 14 fables; those recognizable correspond to Nos. 269, 208, 110 (or 174?), 111, 437, 93 (?), in Perry, Aesopica (cf. ibid., No. 75). Perhaps the version of Demetrius of Phalerum. Archiv 14.138; B. Snell, Gnomon 15 (1939) 542; Lesky, GGL 147-48; E. L. B. Meurig Davies, CP 45 (1950) 112; F. R. Adrados,

Emérita 20 (1952) 337-88 (a detailed study).

51   --- Fable of the homicide (No. 48, ed. C. Halm,
     Lipsiae 1872).   P. Grenf. 2.84 (Bodleian Libr.,
     Gr. class. e. 72 (P)) (IV-V, Fayum; sch. ex.),
     W. A. Oldfather, Aeg. 10 (1929) 255-56; Chr. Ég.
     22 (1936) 503; Ziebarth, No. 25; Ziebarth 2, No.
     38.

52   --- Fable with a Latin translation.   PSI 7.848 (III-
     IV, Medinet-el-Fayum).   The same fable as in the
     Hermeneumata Pseudo-Dositheana (G. Goetz,
     Corpus Glossariorum Latinorum, 3.45-46); Greek
     text on the recto, Latin on the verso.   The Latin:
     Cavenaile, CPL 39; Lowe, CLA 3.291.

     Aesop: see also Nos. 211, 215, 219, 2070, 2072-76,
     2294, 2917, 3010.

53   JULIUS AFRICANUS: Kestoi, Bk. xviii.   P. Oxy.
     3.412; P. Lit. Lond. 174 (Brit. Mus. inv. 2040)
     (III, Oxy.).   J. R. Viellefond, Jules Africain:
     Fragments des Cestes (Paris 1932), Introduction,
     xxii-xxiii.  New Pal. Soc., Ser. 1, vol. 1, pl.
     104; Norsa, SLG, tav. 14a; Roberts, GLH, pl.
     23a.  Archiv 3.297-98; JAW 220.240; Winter,
     LLP 42-43, 264-65.  Africanus quotes 27 hexa-
     meters and holds that they belong to Odyssey xi;
     on these lines, see Archiv 8.126; A. Ludwich,
     Berl. Phil. Woch. 23 (1903) 1467-70, 1502-4; E.
     Hefermehl, ibid. 26 (1906) 413-15; Preisendanz,
     PGM, No. 23; L. Robert, Hellenica: Recueil
     d' épigraphie ... 1 (1940) 144-48, on the library at
     Nysa, in Caria, one of those where Africanus
     claims that editions containing these plus-verses
     were to be found.

     Julius Africanus: see also No. 1998.
     Agathinus of Lacedaemon: see No. 2380.

54   ALCAEUS: Fragment of Bk. i or iv (?).   P. Oxy.
     23.2358 (II, Oxy.).   Recto: parts of 4 lines; verso:
     title, Alkaiou melon.

55   --- Fragments.   P. Oxy. 15.1789 (cf. ibid. 21, pp.
     146-47), 18.2166 (e) (I, Oxy.).  Diehl, Anth. Lyr.
     $1^2.4.149$-54; Galiano, LG 101-2; Lobel, Alcaeus
     1-9; Lobel-Page, PLF 112-23; Page, SA 182-85,
     291-94; Treu, Alkaios 42, 46, 76.  Archiv 7.132-
     33; G. Coppola, Aeg. 4 (1923) 285-87; E. Lobel,
     Bodl. Rec. 3 (1923) 289-90; K. F. W. Schmidt,
     Gött. Anz., 1924, 4-5; E. Diehl, Rh. Mus. 92
     (1943) 1-26; C. Theander, Eranos 41 (1943) 158-60,
     idem, Aeg. 32 (1952) 182-85; B. Snell, Philol. 96
     (1944) 288-90; A. Y. Campbell, CR, NS 7 (1957)
     4-5.

56   --- Fragments.   P. Oxy. 10.1233 (Bodleian Libr.,
     Gr. class. b. 18 (P)), 17.2081 (d), 18.2166 (b) (cf.
     ibid. 21, pp. 127-30) (II, Oxy.).   P. Oxy. 1233, fr.
     29, belongs to P. Oxy. 2176 (No. 551: Hipponax);
     see P. Oxy. 18, p. 184, and Galiano, LG 87, note
     144.  Diehl, Anth. Lyr. $1^2.4.122$-33; Edmonds, LG
     1.326, 328-31, 336-39, 396-97, 400, 404, 420-23;
     Galiano, LG 102; Lavagnini, Aglaia 152-54, 157-60;
     Lobel, Alcaeus 9-21; Lobel-Page, PLF 124-36;
     Page, SA 265-67, 278-83, 286-88, 300-3; Treu,
     Alkaios 24, 32, 34, 56, 58, 64, 66.  J. M. Ed-

monds, CR 28 (1914) 75-77, ibid. 30 (1916) 103-4,
ibid. 33 (1919) 127-28; A. S. Hunt, CR 28 (1914)
127; H. Jurenka, WS 36 (1914) 220-32; Wilamowitz,
Neue Jahr. 33 (1914) 231-34; G. Coppola, Aeg. 4
(1923) 291-95; E. Lobel, Bodl. Rec. 4 (1923) 20-21;
Q. Cataudella, AR, NS 9 (1928) 81-85; C. M. Bowra, Hermes 70 (1935) 238-39; W. Schubart, Philol.
97 (1948) 319; C. Theander, Human. 2 (1948-49)
37-39; M. Treu, WJA 4 (1949-50) 219-25, compares
Alcaeus in P. Oxy. 1233 with Horace, Carm. i. 26;
A. W. Gomme, JHS 77 (1957) 257-58.

57   --- Fragment.   P. Bad. 6.174 (II-III).   From the
     same poem, but not the same papyrus, as in No.
     56.  Archiv 14.111.  Lobel-Page, PLF 129; Treu,
     Alkaios 64.

58   --- Fragments.   BKT 5.2.6-8 (inv. 9810) (II).
     Schubart, PGB, tab. 29b.  Diehl, Anth. Lyr. $1^2$.
     4.120-21, 227; idem, SL, No. 4; Edmonds, LG
     1.414-15; Lobel, Alcaeus, No. 36; Lobel-Page,
     PLF 137; Treu, Alkaios 60.  Archiv 5.549.  J. M.
     Edmonds, CR 31 (1917) 9-11; S. Luria, PP 2, fasc.
     4 (1947) 80-81; W. Schubart, Philol. 97 (1948) 318-
     19.

59   --- Fragments, with marginalia.   P. Oxy. 10.1234
     (Bodleian Libr., Gr. Class. a. 16 (P)), 11.1360
     (ditto), 18.2166 (c) (cf. ibid. 18, pp. 182-83, ibid.
     21, pp. 130-34) (II, Oxy.).  Nicanor (?) and Sap-
     pho are mentioned in the marginalia of P. Oxy. 18.
     2166 (c).  Schubart, Gr. Pal., Abb. 84.  Diehl,
     Anth. Lyr. $1^2.4.96$-98, 104-12; idem, SL, Nos.
     21-32; Edmonds, LG 1.362-71; Galiano, LG 102-
     103, 104-5; Lobel, Alcaeus 22-31; Lobel-Page,
     PLF 138-58; Page, SA 171-74, 189-90, 226-27,
     235-37; Treu, Alkaios 36, 40, 42, 44, 46, 48, 50,
     52, 58, 76.  Archiv 7.130-31.  J. M. Edmonds, CR
     28 (1914) 77-78, ibid. 30 (1916) 104-7, ibid. 33 (1919)
     128-30; H. Jurenka, WS 36 (1914) 232-42; Wilamo-
     witz, Neue Jahrb. 33 (1914) 234-38; K. F. W. Schmidt,
     Gött. Anz., 1918, 89-91; G. Coppola, Aeg. 4 (1923)
     287-91; C. M. Bowra, Hermes 70 (1935) 239; B.
     Snell, Philol. 96 (1944) 286; W. Schubart, Philol.
     97 (1948) 316; C. Theander, Aeg. 32 (1952) 179-81,
     186-88; J. C. Kamerbeek, Mnemos., Ser. 4.6
     (1953) 89; M. Treu, Festschr. Sommer 226-28;
     R. Merkelbach, Archiv 16 (1956) 92-96, on the al-
     legory in P. Oxy. 1234, fr. 3; S. Luria, Act. Ant.
     Hung. 8 (1960) 265-66.

60   --- Fragments with scholia.   BKT 5.2.1-6 (inv. 9569);
     P. Aberdeen 7 (I-II, Fayum; on the verso of a
     cursive text).  Diehl, Anth. Lyr. $1^2.4.100$-3, SL,
     No. 1 A-B; Edmonds, LG 1.346-49; Galiano, LG
     101; Lobel, Alcaeus 31-33; Lobel-Page, PLF 158-
     61; Treu, Alkaios 38.  Archiv 2.353.  E. O. Win-
     stedt, CQ 1 (1907) 262 (ed. pr. of P. Aberdeen); T.
     Reinach, Rev. Ét. Gr. 18 (1905) 295-99, 413-14; J.
     M. Edmonds, CR 31 (1917) 33-36; W. Schubart,
     Philol. 97 (1948) 316-17.

61   --- Fragments.   P. Oxy. 15.1788 (cf. ibid. 21, pp.
     139-45, 23, pp. 105-6); Lobel, Alcaeus, Nos. 58-
     59, 64, 67, 69 (additional frr. of the same roll)
     (II, Oxy.).  Marginalia mention Didymus.  Diehl,
     Anth. Lyr. $1^2.4.141$-49; Galiano, LG 105-6; Lo-

bel, Alcaeus 33-42; Lobel-Page, PLF 162-75; Page, PMG 918 (a), SA 288; Treu, Alkaios 32, 68, 70, 72. Archiv 7.131-32. K. F. W. Schmidt, Gött. Anz., 1924, 3-4; C. M. Bowra, Hermes 70 (1935) 239-40; C. Theander, Aeg. 32 (1952) 188-90.

62 --- Fragments. P. Oxy. 18.2165 (II, Oxy.). Galiano, LG 106-7 (extended bibl.); Lobel-Page, PLF 176-81; Page, SA 161-69 (bibl.), 198-209; Treu, Alkaios 18, 20, 54. Archiv 16.91. C. Gallavotti, Aeg. 22 (1942) 109-13, PP 1 (1946) 123-25; L. Deubner, Abh. Berl. Akad., 1943, Abh. 7; E. Diehl, Rh. Mus. 92 (1943) 1-26; M. F. Galiano, Emérita 11 (1943) 441-47; C. Préaux, Bull. Acad. Belg., Sér. 5.29 (1943) 147-58, Chr. Ég. 18 (1943) 279-90; A. Vogliano, Athen. 31 (1943) 125-26; L. Alfonsi, Aeg. 24 (1944) 113-18; P. Collart, CRAI, 1944, 344-60; R. Goossens, Chr. Ég. 19 (1944) 265-68; A. Ardizzoni, Riv. Fil., NS 22-23 (1944-45) 16-20; A. Colonna, SIFC, NS 21 (1946) 30-40; C. Picard, BCH 70 (1946) 455-73; B. Gentili, SIFC, NS 22 (1947) 105-8; J. C. Kamerbeek, Mnemos., Ser. 3.13 (1947) 94-120, 161-82; K. Latte, Mus. Helv. 4 (1947) 141-46; S. Luria, PP 2, fasc. 4 (1947) 81-87; A. Ardizzoni, SIFC, NS 23 (1948) 223-27; B. Gentili, ibid. 229-33; B. Gentili, Maia 1 (1948) 62-63, ibid. 3 (1950) 255-57; V. Pisani, Acme 1 (1948) 292; C. Theander, Human. 2 (1948-49) 34-37; V. Pisani, Paid. 4 (1949) 401; A. Luppino, PP 5 (1950) 206-14; CR, NS 1 (1951) 14-15; W. J. W. Koster, Mnemos., Ser. 4.4 (1951) 9-29, 112; E. Will, Rev. Arch. 39 (1952) 156-59; J. C. Kamerbeek, Mnemos., Ser. 4.6 (1953) 91-92; J. G. Griffith, Fifty Years Cl. Schol. 45-47; A. J. Beattie, CR, NS 6 (1956) 189-91; R. Merkelbach, Archiv 16 (1956) 92, joins fr. 6 with P. Oxy. 2303, fr. 1 (a) (see No. 71): Lobel-Page, PLF, pp. 181, 233; L. A. Stella, PP 11 (1956) 321-34; A. M. Dale, Lustrum 2 (1957) 6-7; V. Pisani, Paid. 15 (1960) 246-47; G. M. Bolling, AJP 82 (1961) 161-63.

63 --- Sixty-three exiguous fragments, with scholia. P. Oxy. 21.2295 (I, Oxy.). Lobel-Page, PLF 182-200; Page, SA 234; Treu, Alkaios 16, 36, 50.

64 --- Four small fragments. P. Oxy. 21.2296 (II-III, Oxy.). Fr. 1 overlaps frr. 45, 50, and 46 of No. 63. Lobel-Page, PLF 201-2, 274; Treu, Alkaios 36.

65 --- Forty-eight small fragments. P. Oxy. 21.2297 (II, Oxy.). Lobel-Page, PLF 203-13; Treu, Alkaios 8, 10. D. Pieraccioni, Maia 5 (1952) 133-34; J. C. Kamerbeek, Mnemos., Ser. 4.6 (1953) 89-91; C. Gallavotti, Studi Castiglioni 1. 321-29, joins fr. 3 with Alcaeus, fr. 20 Bergk.

66 --- Fragment. P. Oxy. 21.2298 (I?, Oxy.). Includes a strophe quoted by Athenaeus xv. 695a as a scolion. Lobel-Page, PLF 214-15; Page, SA 196-97; Treu, Alkaios 10.

67 --- Thirty-one small fragments, with a few marginalia. P. Oxy. 21.2299 (I?, Oxy.). Lobel-Page, PLF 215-24 (as by Alcaeus); Page, SA 296-97; Treu, Sappho 19-21 (as by Sappho). D. Pieraccioni, Maia 5 (1952) 134; C. Gallavotti, Aeg. 33 (1953) 171.

68 --- Fragment. P. Oxy. 21.2300 (II-III, Oxy.). Lobel-Page, PLF 225-26; Page, SA 275-78; Treu, Alkaios 6. D. Pieraccioni, Maia 5 (1952) 134-35; C. Gallavotti, Aeg. 33 (1953) 166-67; L. Alfonsi, ibid. 34 (1954) 215-19, studies the influence on Horace; A. Colonna, Paid. 10 (1955) 310-11; A. Setti, SIFC 27-28 (1956) 519-35.

69 --- Ten small fragments, with a few marginalia. P. Oxy. 21.2301 (II?, Oxy.). Lobel-Page, PLF 227-29; Page, SA 289-90; Treu, Alkaios 10. D. Pieraccioni, Maia 5 (1952) 135.

70 --- Fragments. P. Oxy. 21.2302 (II-III, Oxy.). Lobel-Page, PLF 230-33; Page, SA 297-99; Treu, Alkaios 12, 16. P. Maas, CR, NS 6 (1956) 200, restores an allusion to the tyranny of Antileon of Chalcis.

71 --- Fragment. P. Oxy. 21.2303 (I?, Oxy.). Lobel-Page, PLF 233-34, Page, SA 283-85; Treu, Alkaios 8. C. Gallavotti, Aeg. 33 (1953) 167; A. Colonna, Paid. 10 (1955) 311-12.

72 --- Fragment. P. Oxy. 21.2304 (II?, Oxy.). Lobel-Page, PLF 235.

73 --- Alcaeus (?). P. Oxy. 21.2305 (II-III, Oxy.). Lobel-Page, PLF 236; Treu, Alkaios 62.

74 --- Commentary on Alcaeus. P. Oxy. 21.2306 (II, Oxy.). Lobel-Page, PLF 238-39; Page, SA 180-81, 241-42; Treu, Alkaios 12. C. Gallavotti, Aeg. 33 (1953) 167-68.

75 --- Commentary on Alcaeus. P. Oxy. 21.2307 (II, Oxy.). Mentions Anacreon. Lobel-Page, PLF 240-59; Page, SA 191-96, 240-41; Treu, Alkaios 12, 14, 40, 48, 52. C. Gallavotti, Aeg. 33 (1953) 168-71; M. Treu, Festschr. Sommer 223-28.

Alcaeus: see also Nos. 83, 455, 1173, 1186, 1205, 1452, 1898-1903, 2143.

Alcaeus of Messene: see No. 1601.
Alcamenes of Abydos: see No. 2339.

76 ALCIDAMAS: Life of Homer (extracts from the Mouseion, etc.?). J. G. Winter, TAPA 56 (1925) 120-29 (P. Mich. inv. 2754) (II-III, Karanis; on the verso of accounts). Archiv 8.261-64; New Chapters 2.37-38, 118-19; Winter, LLP 196-97. C. Gallavotti, Riv. Fil. 57 (1929) 31-59; F. Solmsen, Hermes 67 (1932) 141-44; S. Abramowicz, Eos 39 (1938) 483-85; G. S. Kirk, CQ 44 (1950) 149-67, suggests that lines 1-14 are an interpolation not by Alcidamas; E. R. Dodds, ibid., NS 2 (1952) 187-88, suggests that the text is a collection of extracts on Homer, including Alcidamas; E. Vogt, Rh. Mus. 102 (1959) 208-11.

77 --- Mouseion (Fragment on the Contest of Homer and Hesiod). P. Petrie 1.25; P. Lit. Lond. 191 (Brit. Mus. inv. 500) (III B.C., Gurob; cart.). The text corresponds to Homeri et Hesiodi Agon, lines 67-95, ed. A. Rzach. Quotes Homer, Od. ix. 5-11; Theognis 425-27. New Chapters 2.37; Lesky, GGL 88; Wilamowitz, Vitae Homeri et

Hesiodi (Lietzmann's Kleine Texte, Nr. 137) 45-
47. A. Rzach, WS 14 (1892) 139-45; E. Vogt, Rh.
Mus. 102 (1959) 206-8.

Alcimus: see No. 2145.

78   ALCMAN: Partheneion, with marginalia.   P. Par.
71 (P. Louvre inv. 3320, Nouv. No. 71) (I, Memphis).   The marginalia refer to Aristarchus, Aristophanes (of Byzantium?), Pamphilus (a glosso-
grapher), Pherecydes (the historian), Sosiphanes
(the Alexandrian dramatist), and one Stasicles;
quote Hesiod, Theogonia 116, and Homer, Od. xxiv.
11-12. Diehl, Anth. Lyr. 2$^1$.7-14; Edmonds, LG
1.50-59; A. Farina, Studi sul Partenio di Alcmane
(Napoli 1950); Galiano, LG 129-30 (bibl.); A. Garzya, Alcmane: I frammenti (Napoli 1954), fr. 1, pp.
9-76, 177-78; Lavagnini, Aglaia 184-93; Lesky,
GGL 142-43; D. L. Page, Alcman: The Partheneion (Oxford 1951; detailed study, with bibl.);
Page, PMG 1. F. Blass, Rh. Mus. 25 (1870) 177-
201, ibid. 40 (1885) 1-24; idem, Hermes 13 (1878)
15-32, ibid. 14 (1879) 466-68; G. Bruschi, Riv.
Fil. 23 (1895) 504-63; H. Diels, Hermes 31 (1896)
339-74; H. Jurenka, Sitzb. Wien. Akad., 1896,
1-35; R. C. Kukula, Philol. 66 (1907) 202-30; W.
W. Wilson, AJP 33 (1912) 57-67; F. Wiedemann,
Berl. Phil. Woch. 33 (1913) 1405-6; C. M. Bowra,
CQ 28 (1934) 35-44; B. A. van Groningen, Mnemos.,
Ser. 3.3 (1935-36) 241-61; D. L. Page, CQ 31
(1937) 94-101; F. Schwenn, Rh. Mus. 86 (1937)
289-315; J. A. Davison, Hermes 73 (1938) 440-
58; F. Stoessl, Eumusia: Festgabe für Ernst
Howald ... (Erlenbach-Zürich 1947) 93-106; F.
Scheidweiler, Rh. Mus. 93 (1950) 242-49; A. Gar-
zya, GIF 5 (1952) 263-66; J. Taillardat, Rev. Phil.,
Sér. 3.27 (1953) 131-34; J. G. Griffith, Fifty Years
Cl. Schol. 40-41, 65-66; E. Risch, Mus. Helv.
11 (1954) 20-37; M. Treu, Gnomon 26 (1954) 168-74;
P. von der Mühll, Mus. Helv. 15 (1958) 83; J. A.
Davison, Proc. IX Int. Congr. Pap. 30-42, discusses various problems in their relation to the
newer papyri of Alcman; P. Janni, Riv. Fil., NS
40 (1962) 180-85.

79   --- Partheneia, with marginalia.   P. Oxy. 24.2387
(I B.C. - I, Oxy.).   The marginalia refer to an
Aristonicus (?) and a Ptolemaeus as critics of the
text. Page, PMG 3. A. Giannini, Rend. Ist. Lomb.
93 (1959) 183-202; W. Peek, Philol. 104 (1960) 163-
180; W. S. Barrett, Gnomon 33 (1961) 683-85; A.
Garzya, Maia 14 (1962) 209, note 2.

80   --- Alcman (?).   P. Oxy. 24.2388 (II, Oxy.). Page,
PMG 4.

81   --- Commentary on Alcman.   P. Oxy. 24.2389 (I,
Oxy.).   Refers to Aristarchus, Aristotle (Res
Publica Lacedaemoniorum?), and Sosibius (or
Sosiphanes?). Page, PMG, pp. 7-9, 11, 27-28,
32-33. W. S. Barrett, Gnomon 33 (1961) 685-88;
J. A. Davison, Proc. IX Int. Congr. Pap. 42-48;
A. Garzya, Maia 14 (1962) 209-11.

82   --- Commentary on Alcman.   P. Oxy. 24.2390 (II,
Oxy.).   Refers to Mimnermus and the grammari-
ans Theon and Tyrannion. Page, PMG 5; W. S.
Barrett, Gnomon 33 (1961) 688-89.

83   --- Commentary on Alcman (?).   P. Oxy. 24.2391
(I, Oxy.).   Mentions Alcaeus (?).   Page, PMG 6.

84   --- Dionysius: Commentary on Alcman, Melê, Bk.
iv (colophon only).   P. Oxy. 24.2392 (II, Oxy.).
Page, PMG 18.   D. Sidêtos, Sidonius, or Thrax?

85   --- Lexicon to Alcman (?).   P. Oxy. 24.2393 (II,
Oxy.).   Page, PMG, p. 10 and No. 12.

Alcman: see also Nos. 166, 186, 197, 246, 1839,
1889-90, 1950, 2172.

Alexander Philalethes: see No. 2339.
Alexis: see Nos. 1639, 1641, 2121.
Ammonius: see Nos. 1039, 1205.
Amymon of Sicyon: see No. 2071.
Amyntas: see No. 1595.

86   ANACREON: Fragments.   P. Oxy. 22.2321 (II, Oxy.).
Galiano, LG 112-17; Gentili, Anacr. 44-51, 179-
206; Page, PMG 346. L. Alfonsi, Aeg. 35 (1955)
201-5; K. Latte, Gnomon 27 (1955) 496-97; P.
Maas, Acme 8, fasc. 2-3 (1955) 113-14; C. Gallavotti, PP 10 (1955) 47-50; A. Barigazzi, Athen.
44 (1956) 139-51; B. Gentili, Maia 8 (1956) 181-96;
R. Merkelbach, Archiv 16 (1956) 96-98, reprints
and interprets fr. 1; A. M. Dale, Lustrum 2 (1957)
7.

87   --- Anacreon (?).   P. Oxy. 22.2322 (II-III, Oxy.).
Galiano, LG 117-19; Gentili, Anacr. 52-54, 206-18;
Page, PMG 347. Archiv 16.96. C. Gallavotti, PP
10 (1955) 41-47, thinks of an imitator of Anacreon;
K. Latte, Gnomon 27 (1955) 495-96; B. Marzullo,
Rh. Mus. 100 (1957) 81; J. A. Davison, CR, NS
11 (1961) 202-3, on line 17, supporting a lection in
Aristophanes, Aves 996.

Anacreon: see also Nos. 75, 246, 1205, 2151, 2172,
2595.

Ananius: see No. 1186.
Anaxandrides: see No. 1573.
Anaxilaus: see No. 1998.

88   ANAXIMENES: Rhetorica ad Alexandrum 15.3 — 31.20
(with lacunae).   P. Hibeh 1.26 (Bodleian Libr., Gr.
class. d.80 (P)) (III B.C., Hibeh; cart.).   New
Chapters 2.114-16.

Anaximenes: see also Nos. 317, 339, 1574.

Andocides: De Mysteriis 110-16: see No. 157.
Andron: see No. 2127.
Androtion: see No. 339.
Antenor: see No. 2127.
Anthestius: see No. 2089.
Anticlides: see No. 2127.
Antigonus: see No. 103.

89   ANTIMACHUS OF COLOPHON: Commentary on the
Artemis and the Thebaïs (?).   PRIMI 1.17 (II,
Hermupolis).   Quotes or refers to Antimachus
(Wyss, Nos. 173-89; No. 173 is from Thebaïs, Bk.
iii); Callimachus, Aetia (?) (Pfeiffer, Callim. 1,
fr. 65); Dercylus and Hagias, Argolica; Hecataeus (G. Tibiletti, Athen. 43, 1955, 345-50, compares

this quotation with the paraphrase in Pausanias iii. 25. 5); Hesiod, Catalogus and op. incert. (cf. fr. 11, Rzach, from Catalogus, Bk. v; Merkelbach, Hes., fr. Z 3; Traversa, Hes. Cat. 104, 123-24); Homer, Il. vi. 268, x. 394, Od. xiii. 106, xvi. 317 (Collart, Il., No. 325, Od., No. 90); Mimnermus, Smyrneïs (Page, GLP 1, No. 101; Diehl, Anth. Lyr. 1³. 54; Galiano, LG 61: bibl.); Panyasis; and Theophrastus, De aquis. Wyss 76-90. Archiv 13. 81-84. B. Snell, Gnomon 15 (1939) 533-34.

Antimachus: see also Nos. 1186, 1577, 1776-79, 2131, 2144.

Antimachus of Heliopolis: see No. 1849.
Antipater: see No. 2093.
Antipater of Sidon: see No. 1595.
Antipater of Tarsus: see No. 2088.

90 ANTIPHANES: Anthropogonia. P. Oxy. 3. 427; P. Lit. Lond. 87 (Brit. Mus. inv. 1525) (III, Oxy.; on the verso of a document). Parts of the last 3 verses, and subscription. Demiańczuk 8. Archiv 3. 277; JAW 174. 184.

Antiphanes: see also Nos. 1568, 1573, 1579, 2121.

91 ANTIPHON: Apologia. J. Nicole, L'Apologie d'Antiphon (Genève-Bâle 1907) (P. Genève inv. 264 bis + 267) (II-III). Jander 3-5. Archiv 6. 235-236 (bibl.).

92 ANTIPHON SOPHISTA: Peri aletheias, Bk. i. P. Oxy. 11. 1364 (Cambridge Univ. Libr., add. 6355) (III, Oxy.). L. Gernet, Antiphon: Discours, suivis des fragments d'Antiphon le Sophiste (Paris 1923) 176-78. Archiv 7. 153-54; JEA 6. 126-27, 7. 90, 11. 87; New Chapters 2. 95-96. B. Brugi, Rend. Acc. Linc., Ser. 5. 25 (1916) 243-52, studies the ideas; H. Diels, Sitzb. Berl. Akad., 1916, 931-36, reedits the text; A. Croiset, Rev. Ét. Gr. 30 (1917) 1-19, doubts that the sophist Antiphon was distinct from the orator; K. F. W. Schmidt, Gött. Anz., 1918, 95-98; E. Bignone, Rend. Ist. Lomb. 52 (1919) 564-78, distinguishes the sophist from the orator; S. Luria, Aeg. 5 (1924) 326-30, studies the relation to Euripides, Alexandros; P. Merlan, CP 45 (1950) 163-64.

93 --- Bk. i (?). P. Oxy. 15. 1797 (III, Oxy.). Archiv 7. 154-55; JEA 10. 152, 14. 133; New Chapters 2. 96-97. E. Bignone, Riv. Fil. 51 (1923) 145-66, 309-32; S. Luria, ibid. 55 (1927) 80-83. Perhaps from the same papyrus as No. 92.

94 --- Fragments. P. Oxy. 3. 414 (Columbia Univ. Libr.) (II-III, Oxy.). Archiv 3. 295. Assigned to Antiphon by S. Luria, CQ 22 (1928) 176-78.

Antiphon tragicus: Andromacha: see No. 1710.
Antisthenes: see Nos. 2573, 2584.

95 ANTONIUS DIOGENES (?): Ta hyper Thoulên apista (?). PSI 10. 1177 (II-III, Fayum; on the verso of a document). C. Gallavotti, SIFC, NS 8 (1931) 247-57 (ed. pr.). Zimmermann, GRP, No. 10. Archiv 10.

233-34; F. Zimmermann, Phil. Woch. 55 (1935) 474-80, idem, Hermes 71 (1936) 312-19.

96 ANUBION: An astrological poem in 60 distichs. P. Schubart 15 (P. Berol. inv. 9587) (III). S. Weinstock, Chr. Ég. 27 (1952) 210-17, identifies the text as by Anubion, noting that Firmicus Maternus vi. 31. 78-85 is an almost literal translation of it. Archiv 16. 86-87 (reprints lines 29-40). Neugebauer - Van Hoesen, Astrol. Pap. Ostr., No. 106.

Anyte: see No. 1593.
Pseudo-Apicius: see No. 2097.
Apion: see Nos. 1039, 1216, 2089.
Apollodorus of Athens: see Nos. 1197, 2127, 2471.
Apollodorus of Carystus: see Nos. 1568, 1659.
Apollonius: see No. 2146.
Apollonius of Acharnae: see No. 2130.

97 APOLLONIUS MYS: Peri euporistôn pharmakôn. P. Oxy. 2. 234 (St. Andrews Univ. Libr.) (II-III, Oxy.; on the verso of a lease). Archiv 1. 538-39; JAW 158. 157-58, 192. A. Olivieri, BFC 8 (1902) 229-31; identified by M. Wellmann, Hermes 45 (1910) 469.

Apollonius Mys: see also No. 2386.

98 APOLLONIUS OF RHODES: Argonautica i. 699-719. PRIMI 1. 6 (I, Oxy.; on the verso of a document).

99 --- i. 775-94. P. Amh. 2. 16, verso (II-III; on the verso of No. 1793). Archiv 2. 349. Wilamowitz, Hermes 58 (1923) 73; A. Dain, Rev. Phil. 69 (1943) 56-61.

100 --- i. 1195-1219, 1221. PSI 10. 1172 (I).

101 --- ii. 101-10. P. Oxy. 9. 1179 (Newton Theological Institute) (II-III, Oxy.).

102 --- ii. 729-34, 754-61. P. Rain. 3. 16 (inv. 29785) (VI; parch. cod.).

103 --- ii. 917-53, iv. 317-22, 416-61, 468-512, with scholia. P. Kingston, BICSL 7 (1960) 45-56 (P. Oxy. inedita) (II, Oxy.). The scholia mention Antigonus (of Carystus?) and Artemidorus of Ephesus (the geographer).

104 --- Scholia on Argonautica ii. 1075, 1099, 1103, 1127. A. Wifstrand, Eranos 30 (1932) 2-6 (P. Berol. inv. 13413) (I-II).

105 --- iii. 145-61, 173-91. R. Reitzenstein, Hermes 35 (1900) 605-7 (P. Strassb. inv. 173 ?) (VIII-IX; parch. cod.). Archiv 1. 515. D. N. Levin, CP 58 (1963) 107.

106 --- iii. 263-73. P. Oxy. 6. 874 (P. Ryl. inv. 449) (II-III, Oxy.; on the verso of a list of persons).

107 --- iii. 727-45. P. Oxy. 4. 690 (Musées Royaux, Bruxelles, inv. E. 5934) (III, Oxy.). Archiv 3. 478.

108 --- iii. 908-13. P. Oxy. 4. 691 (Wellesley Coll.) (II, Oxy.). Archiv 3. 478.

109 --- iii. 1055-63. P. Oxy. 10. 1243 (Muhlenberg Coll.) (II, Oxy.; on the verso of a survey list).

110    --- iii.1358-64, 1398-1406.   A. Wifstrand, Eranos
       30 (1932) 1-6 (P. Berol. inv. 13248) (V, Hermupolis
       Magna; pap. cod.).

111    --- iv.77-90.   P. Oxy. 4.692 (Wellesley Coll.) (II,
       Oxy.).   Archiv 3.479.

       --- iv.317-512: see No. 103.

112    --- iv.675-96, 724-44.   C. W. Keyes, AJP 50 (1929)
       263-65 (Columbia Univ. Libr., inv. 437) (III; on
       the verso of a register).

          Apollonius of Rhodes: see also Nos. 2069, 2144.
             Apollonius of Rhodes (or son of Chaeris?): see
             No. 1175.

       Apollonius Sophista: Homeric Lexicon: see No. 1217.
       Apollonius Syrus: see No. 2573.

113    APPIAN: Bellum Mithridaticum 101.         P. Dura 2
       (inv. 84 + 91) (III, Dura; pap. cod.).   C. B. Welles,
       TAPA 70 (1939) 203-12 (ed. pr.).   Roberts, GLH,
       pl. 16b.

       ARATUS:  Phaenomena 148: see No. 186.

       --- 480-94: see No. 1621.

114    --- 642-55, 684-802, 855-83, 922-34.   BKT 5.1.47-
       54 (inv. 7503 + 7804) (I-II).   Martin, Texte d' Ara-
       tos 210-12.   A. Ludwich, Berl. Phil. Woch. 27
       (1907) 489-90.

115    --- 741-53, 804-12, 814-16.   H. I. Bell, CQ 1 (1907)
       1-3; P. Lit. Lond. 34 (Brit. Mus. inv. 273 B)
       (IV; bound in the same pap. cod. as No. 343).
       Martin, Texte d' Aratos 214-15.

116    --- 746-56, 810-13, 815-20, with scholia.   P. Rain.
       3.17 (inv. 29776) (IV; pap. cod.).   Martin, Texte
       d' Aratos 215-16.

117    --- 914-33, with other fragments.   P. Oxy. 15.1807
       (Edinburgh Univ. Libr., Ox. P. 14) (II, Oxy.).
       Martin, Texte d' Aratos 213-14.

118    --- 944-57.   P. Lond. 2.484 e; P. Lit. Lond. 35
       (Brit. Mus. inv. 484 E) (I-II).   Martin, Texte
       d' Aratos 212-13.

119    --- Scholia on Phaenomena 146-47, 167, 173, 184, 191,
       194, 294, 329, 337.   BKT 5.1.54 (inv. 5865) (Late;
       pap. cod.).   F. Blass, Zeitschr. Aeg. Spr. 18 (1880)
       35 (first mention).   E. Maass, Commentariorum in
       Aratum Reliquiae (Berolini 1898), pp. LXIX-LXX,
       556-58 (ed. pr.).   Martin, Texte d' Aratos 216-18.

120    --- Phaenomena ... (?).   Mentioned by Neugebauer,
       Astron. Pap. Ostr. 383, note 1 (P. Hamb. inv. 121,
       inedita) (?).

       Archagathus: see No. 2407.
       Archelaus: see No. 2184.
       Archibius: see No. 2354.

121    ARCHILOCHUS: Elegeia (Nauagion).   P. Oxy. 23.
       2356 (II, Oxy.).   Galiano, LG 77;  Lasserre, fr. 3;
       Treu, Archil. 26.

122    --- Elegeia.   P. Oxy. 6.854 (Toledo Mus. of Art)
       (II, Oxy.; on the verso of a document).   Diehl, SL,
       No. 1, Anth. Lyr. $1^2$.3.5-6, ibid. $3^3$.3-4;  Las-
       sere, fr. 12;  Treu, Archil. 22.   Archiv 5.542;
       JAW 174.22.   A. Garzya, Maia 10 (1958) 66-71,
       notes an echo of the text in Synesius, Ep. 32.

123    --- Trimetra.   P. Oxy. 22.2312 (II-III, Oxy.).
       Galiano, LG 73;  Lasserre, frr. 20, 27, 41-44,
       55-58, 63, 71-75;  Treu, Archil. 16-17, 36.   Archiv
       16.87-88.   W. Peek, Philol. 99 (1955) 208-17;  F. R.
       Adrados, PP 11 (1956) 43-47;  A. Giannini, Acme 11
       (1958) 43-45, 51-57;  G. Morelli, Maia 12 (1960)
       132-33;  S. Luria, Philol. 105 (1961) 179-81.

124    --- Trimetra (Archilochus?).   P. Oxy. 22.2319 (II,
       Oxy.).   Listed by the editor as "Ionic verses."
       Galiano, LG 76;  Lasserre, frr. 20, 67-69;  Treu,
       Archil. 18.   Archiv 16.87-88.   W. Peek, Philol.
       99 (1955) 216-17, 219;  G. Morelli, Maia 12 (1960)
       131-32.

125    --- Trimetra (Archilochus?).   P. Oxy. 22.2310 (II,
       Oxy.).   Galiano, LG 69-72;  Lasserre, frr. 35-37,
       60-62;  Treu, Archil. 8, 10, 20-21, 32, 36.   Archiv
       16.87-88.   K. Latte, Gnomon 27 (1955) 493;  W.
       Peek, Philol. 99 (1955) 193-206;  F. R. Adrados,
       PP 11 (1956) 38-42;  F. Lasserre, Mus. Helv. 13
       (1956) 226-35, idem, Rev. Phil., Sér. 3.31 (1957)
       52-62;  D. Giordano, Aeg. 37 (1957) 209-18, sees
       four distinct poems, rejects Archilochus, and sug-
       gests Phoenix of Colophon;  G. W. Bond, Gnomon
       32 (1960) 597-98;  H. J. Mette, Hermes 88 (1960)
       493-94;  J. C. Kamerbeek, Mnemos., Ser. 4.14
       (1961) 9-15;  W. Steffen, Proc. IX Int. Congr. Pap.
       18-29.

126    --- Trimetra.   P. Oxy. 22.2311 (II, Oxy.).   Galiano,
       LG 73;  Lasserre, frr. 38-39, 70;  Treu, Archil.
       21, 34.   Archiv 16.87-88.   W. Peek, Philol. 99
       (1955) 206-7;  F. R. Adrados, PP 11 (1956) 42-43;
       A. Giannini, Acme 11 (1958) 45-50.

127    --- Trimetra (Archilochus?).   P. Oxy. 22.2318 (II,
       Oxy.).   Listed by the editor as "Iambic trimeters
       (?) in Ionic."   Galiano, LG 76;  Lasserre, frr. 59,
       64-66, 76-79;  Treu, Archil. 14, 19, 187.   Archiv
       16.87-88.   W. Peek, Philol. 99 (1955) 217-19.

128    --- Tetrametra.   P. Oxy. 22.2313 (I-II, Oxy.;  in
       the same hand as No. 474).   Galiano, LG 74;  Las-
       serre, frr. 82, 101, 110, 113-14, 124, 126, 128-52;
       Treu, Archil. 6, 8, 14, 18-19, 56, 60, 64, 74.   Ar-
       chiv 16.87-88.   K. Latte, Gnomon 27 (1955) 495;  M.
       G. Dervisopoulos, Hellén. 14 (1955-56) 451-52;  F.
       R. Adrados, PP 11 (1956) 47-48;  W. Peek, Philol.
       100 (1956) 1-16;  A. Giannini, Acme 11 (1958) 70-78.

129    --- Tetrametra, with marginalia.   P. Oxy. 22.2314
       (III, Oxy.).   Galiano, LG 75;  Lasserre, p. XC,
       rejects as not Archilochian;  Treu, Archil. 6, 8.
       Archiv 16.87-88.   K. Latte, Gnomon 27 (1955) 495;
       M. G. Dervisopoulos, Hellén. 14 (1955-56) 451-52,
       notes that P. Oxy. 2313, fr. 27 (see No. 128), joins

P. Oxy. 2314, col. I. 9-12 (cf. Treu, Archil. 176).

130       --- Tetrametra. P. Lit. Lond. 54 (Brit. Mus. inv.
2652 A) (III B.C., Philadelphia; on the verso of an
account). Text identified by W. Croenert, reprinted by A. Koerte, Archiv 10.43. Roberts, GLH, pl.
4b. Diehl, Anth. Lyr. $3^3$. 25-26; Lasserre, fr.
104; Page, GLP 1, No. 80; Treu, Archil. 66, 68.
P. Maas, Zeitschr. Vergl. Spr. 60 (1933) 286; J.
Wackernagel, Mus. Helv. 1 (1944) 229-30; F. R.
Adrados, Aeg. 35 (1955) 206-10.

131       --- Tetrametra. P. Petrie 1.4 (2); P. Lit. Lond.
55 (Brit. Mus. inv. 487 B) (III B.C., Gurob; cart.).
Identified by F. Blass, Hermes 33 (1898) 656; idem,
Rh. Mus. 55 (1900) 102-3. Diehl, Anth. Lyr. $3^3$.
71-72; Galiano, LG 64 (bibl.); Lasserre, frr. 126-
27; Treu, Archil. 64, 66. Archiv 16.88.

132       --- Epodoi. P. Oxy. 22.2316 (III, Oxy.). Galiano,
LG 75; Lasserre, fr. 170; Treu, Archil. 86.
Archiv 16.87-88. F. R. Adrados, Emérita 23
(1955) 16-17; W. Peek, Philol. 100 (1956) 27-28;
J. C. Kamerbeek, Mnemos., Ser. 4.14 (1961) 7-8;
H. J. Mette, Mus. Helv. 18 (1961) 35-36.

133       --- Epodoi. P. Oxy. 22.2315 (II, Oxy.). Galiano,
LG 75; Lasserre, frr. 173, 199; Treu, Archil.
86, 88. Archiv 16.87-88. F. R. Adrados, Emérita 23 (1955) 18-19; W. Peek, Philol. 100 (1956)
25-26; A. Giannini, Acme 11 (1958) 85-96.

134       --- Fragments (Archilochus?). P. Oxy. 22.2317
(II, Oxy.). Listed by the editor as "Trochaic
tetrameters in Ionic." Galiano, LG 75-76; Lasserre, p. XC, rejects as not Archilochian; Treu,
Archil. 10, 12, 185, favors the attribution. Archiv
16.87-88. K. Latte, Gnomon 27 (1955) 495, queries
the attribution; W. Peek, Philol. 100 (1956) 19-21;
S. Luria, ibid. 105 (1961) 188.

135       --- Fragment (Archilochus?). P. Oxy. 22.2320
(III, Oxy.). Listed by the editor as "Iambic or
trochaic verses in Ionic." Galiano, LG 76; Lasserre, p. XC, rejects Archilochus. Archiv 16.
87-88. W. Peek, Philol. 100 (1956) 21-24.

136       --- Homeric parallels to verses of Archilochus (by
Heraclides Ponticus?). P. Hibeh 2.173 (Brit. Mus.
inv. 2946) (ca. 270-240 B.C., Hibeh; cart.). In-
cludes Homer, Il. iv.182, v.130, xiv.66. Galiano,
LG 77; Treu, Archil. 6. J. A. Davison, Akten
Pap. VIII, 51, favors the attribution to Heraclides;
D. L. Page, CR, NS 7 (1957) 192.

Archilochus: see also Nos. 222, 234, 1186, 1205,
1752, 1895-97.

Archimedes: see No. 2089.
Archimedes or Archonides: see No. 456.
Arctinus: see No. 2290.
Argyrippus: see No. 196.
Aristarchus: see Nos. 78, 81, 183, 483, 616, 1173,
1205, 1361, 1479, 1594, 2290.
Aristias: see No. 46.
Aristides, Aelius: see Nos. 1535, 2089.
Aristippus: see No. 2289.

137       ARISTODEMUS: Historical fragment, in a revised
version). P. Oxy. 27.2469 (II, Oxy.). The text,
on the preliminaries to the Battle of Plataea, corresponds to Jacoby, FGH II A, No. 104, II C, pp.
319 ff.

Aristodemus: see No. 190.
Ariston: see No. 1320.
Ariston of Chios: see No. 2597.
Aristonicus: see Nos. 79, 1205.

138       ARISTOPHANES: Scholia on Acharnenses 108-671.
P. Oxy. 6.856 (Musées Royaux, Bruxelles, inv.
E. 5972) (III, Oxy.). Mention Aristophanes, Baby-
lonii; Euripides, Telephus; Hieronymus comicus;
and Theognis tragicus. Archiv 6.255; JAW 152.
268-69.

--- Acharnenses 345: see No. 2121.

139       --- Acharnenses 598-600, 631-33, 747-975 (with
lacunae); Ranae 234-300, 404-10, 607-11; Aves
819-29, 860-64. BKT 5.2.99-108 (inv. 13231)
(V-VI, Hermupolis Magna; pap. cod.). JAW
152.268. Pasquali, Stor. Testo 196-97.

--- Aves 28: see No. 339.

--- Aves 382, 460-61: see No. 1578.

--- Aves 819-29, 860-64: see No. 139.

--- Aves 884: see No. 157.

140       --- Aves 1057-85, 1101-27. H. Weil, Rev. Phil.
6 (1882) 179-85 (P. Louvre) (VI, Arsinoë; parch.
cod.). G. Zuntz, Byz. 13 (1938) 686.

--- Equites 6-15, 1013-17, etc.: see No. 151.

141       --- Equites 37-46, 86-95, with scholia. B. P.
Grenfell and A. S. Hunt, Mél. Nicole 212-17
(Bodleian Libr., Gr. class. f.72 (P)) (IV-V,
Hermupolis Magna; pap. cod.). JAW 152.267;
G. Zuntz, Byz. 13 (1938) 659-77.

142       --- Scholia on Equites 546-51, 574-80. G. Zuntz,
Byz. 13 (1938) 635-57 (P. Berol. inv. 13929)
(IV; parch. cod.).

--- Equites 655-56: see No. 2126.

143       --- Lysistrata 307-13, 342-46. P. Antin. 2.75
(V-VI, Antinoöpolis; pap. cod.).

--- Lysistrata 354: see No. 2121.

144       --- Lysistrata 433-47, 469-84. B. P. Grenfell and
A. S. Hunt, Mél. Nicole 217-20 (Bodleian Libr.,
Gr. class. e.87 (P)) (IV-V, Hermupolis Magna;
pap. cod.).

145       --- Nubes 1-11, 38-48, with marginal scholia. P.
Oxy. 11.1371 (P. Princ. AM. 9054) (V, Oxy.; pap.
cod.). K. F. W. Schmidt, Gött. Anz., 1918, 101-2;
G. Zuntz, Byz. 13 (1938) 677-85.

146     --- Nubes 177-80, 207-9, 234-35, 268-70, 936-44,
        959-72.   BKT 5.2.108-10  (inv. 13225 + 13226)
        (V; parch. cod.).

147     --- Nubes 577-635.   PSI 10.1171 (III; parch. cod.).
        Galiano, Pind., No. 36, on Aristophanes' citation
        of Pindar.

148     --- Nubes 945-1015.   BKT 5.2.110-12 (inv. 13219;
        loaned to the Cairo Mus.) (V-VI; parch. cod.).
        Pasquali, Stor. Testo 197-98.

149     --- Nubes 1371-85, 1391, 1407-28.   R. Reitzenstein,
        Hermes 35 (1900) 602-4 (P. Strassb. inv. 621)
        (V-VII; parch. cod.).   Archiv 1.511; G. Zuntz,
        Byz. 13 (1938) 685-86; W. J. W. Koster and D.
        Holwerda, Mnemos., Ser. 4.15 (1962) 267-68.

150     --- Pax 721-827, with lacunae.   PSI 6.720 (III, Oxy.;
        pap. cod.?).

        --- Pax 922 ff.: see No. 157.

151     --- Pax 1326-35; Equites 6-15, 1013-17, 1057-62.
        P. Oxy. 11.1373 (P. Princ., AM.9056) (V, Oxy.;
        pap. cod.).   K. F. W. Schmidt, Gött. Anz., 1918,
        102.

152     --- Plutus 1-56.   P. Oxy. 13.1617(Bibl. de l' Univ.
        de Louvain, D.371.2) (V, Oxy.; pap. cod.).

        --- Plutus: see No. 2092.

153     --- Ranae 44-50, 85-91, 840-61, 879-902.   P. Oxy.
        11.1372 (P. Princ., AM.9055) (V, Oxy.; pap. cod.).
        K. F. W. Schmidt, Gött. Anz., 1918, 102.

        --- Ranae 234-300, etc.: see No. 139

        --- Ranae 237: see No. 339.

        --- Ranae 1217: see No. 246.

154     --- Thesmophoriazusae 139-56, 237-45, 273-88,
        594-96, 804-9.   PSI 11.1194 (II, Oxy.).   R.  Goos-
        sens, Chr. Ég. 16 (1941) 105-6; E. Grassi, SIFC,
        NS 27-28 (1956) 48, publishes the fr. containing
        lines 139-44 (cf. PSI 14, p. XV); W. J. W. Koster,
        Acme 8, fasc. 2-3 (1955) 93-103.

        --- Thesmophoriazusae 335-37, 374-75: see No. 1456.

155     --- Vespae 443-67, 486-513, 558-77, 607-26, 746-60,
        790-808, 814-30, 863-78.   P. Oxy. 11.1374 (P.
        Princ., AM.9052) (V, Oxy.; pap. cod.).   K. F.
        W. Schmidt, Gött. Anz., 1918, 102-3.  Pasquali,
        Stor Testo 198.

        --- Vespae 1435-40; see No. 2298.

        --- Vespae 1530: see No. 2121.

        --- Anagyrus: see No. 157.

        --- Babylonii: see No. 138.

        --- Danaïdes: see No. 157.

        --- Geras: see No. 2126.

        --- Gerytades: see Nos. 157, 1456, 1625.

        --- Polyïdus: see No. 2121.

156     --- Thesmophoriazusae Secundae (?).   P. Oxy. 2.212;
        P. Lit. Lond. 85 (Brit. Mus. inv. 1180) (I-II, Oxy.).
        Demiańczuk 91-92;  Page, GLP 1, No. 44.  Archiv 1.
        512; JAW 116.304; G. Fraccaroli, Riv. Fil. 28 (1900)
        87-89, favors the attribution;  H. van Herwerden,
        Mnemos. 28 (1900) 122-25.

        --- Thesmophoriazusae Secundae: see No. 1625.

        --- Triphales: see No. 157.

157     --- Scholia on a lost comedy (Anagyrus, Gerytades,
        or Triphales?).   P. Flor. 2.112 (II-III).  Demiań-
        czuk 17-19.  Archiv 6.254; JAW 152.269-71; Berl.
        Phil. Woch. 28 (1908) 1390-91; J. van Leeuwen,
        Mnemos. 37 (1909) 67-70, prefers the Anagyrus. The
        scholia refer to Andocides, De Mysteriis 110-16; Aris-
        tophanes, Aves 884, Pax 922 ff., Danaïdes (?); Cal-
        listratus of Alexandria; Didymus (added by a second
        hand); Homer, Il. v.253; Iophon (?); and Philocles
        (?; restored by van Leeuwen, loc. cit.).  J. Tail-
        lardat, Rev. Phil., Sér. 3.33 (1959) 64.

        Aristophanes: see also Nos. 551, 1456, 1625-30, 1664,
        1952, 2087, 2121, 2289-90.

        Aristophanes of Byzantium: see Nos. 78, 1205, 1298,
        1361, 1471, 1473, 1479.
        Aristophanes of Thebes: see No. 2861.

158     ARISTOTLE: Analytica Posteriora i.71B.19—72A.38.
        H. Landwehr, Philol. 44 (1885) 21-29 (P. Berol. inv.
        166) (VI-VII; pap. cod.).

        --- Aporemata Homerica: see No. 1205.

159     --- Categoriae 11A.24-B.1, 13B.21-27, 14A.13-15.   P.
        Oxy. 24.2403 (III, Oxy.).   R. Stark, Ann. Univ.
        Sarav. 8 (1959) 36.

160     --- Ethica Nicomachea vi.1142B.11-17, 1144A.6-11.   P.
        Oxy. 24.2402 (II, Oxy.).

        --- Eudemus: see No. 2087.

161     --- Historia Animalium x.3.10, 4.2.   P. Rein. 2.80
        (P. Sorbonne inv. 2144) (II; text on recto, No. 684
        on verso).

        --- Historia Animalium: see also Nos. 197, 1205, 2120,
        2127, 2144.

        --- Nomima Barbarika, Epigram, Paean for Hermias:
        see No. 339.

162     --- Protrepticus.   P. Oxy. 4.666 (Bodleian Libr., Gr.
        class. d.76 (P)) (II, Oxy.).   New Chapters 2.101-3;
        R. Walzer, Aristotelis Dialogorum Fragmenta (Flo-
        rentiae 1934) 24-26.  Archiv 3.496; JEA 8.87.

163 --- Res Publica Atheniensium. P. Lit. Lond. 108
(Brit. Mus. inv. 131, verso) (I, Meir; from the
same papyrus as Nos. 197 and 307). Aristotle on
the Constitution of Athens: Facsimile of Papyrus
CXXXI in the British Museum (London 1891); Thompson, GLP, No. 11 (p. 128), No. 30 (p. 167); Wattenbach, SGS, tab. V. Editions and critical articles
are too numerous to list here. Ed. pr.: Kenyon,
1891. Later editions (listed by Milne, P. Lit. Lond.
108) include: H. van Herwerden and J. van Leeuwen
(Leiden 1891); F. G. Kenyon (Supplementum Aristotelicum, Vol. 3, Pars 2, Berolini 1903); J. E.
Sandys (London 1912); G. Mathieu and B. Haussoullier (Paris 1922); H. Oppermann (Lipsiae 1928;
bibl., pp. VIII-XV); idem (Stutgardiae 1961; extended bibl.). G. T. Griffith, Fifty Years Cl.
Schol. 162-64, 183-84 (bibl.); New Chapters 1.133-
42; Preisendanz, PFF 152-53; Winter, LLP 242-43.
JAW 75.1-54, 83.181-264, 88.4-8. For the quotations from Solon, see Diehl, Anth. Lyr. $1^2$.1.33-35,
45-48, $1^3$.30-31, 43-46; A. Ludwich, Berl. Phil.
Woch. 23 (1903) 700-2, 732-35, 765.

164 --- Res Publica Atheniensium. H. Diels, Abh.
Berl. Akad., 1885, Abh. 2 (P. Berol.) (IV, Fayum;
sch. ex.; pap. cod. or loose sheets?).

--- 53.2-6: see No. 308.

--- 54.2: see No. 2120.

--- See also No. 2089.

--- Res Publica Lacedaemoniorum: see Nos. 81, 317.
--- Res Publica Neapolitanorum: see No. 2089.
--- Res Publica Parianorum: see No. 196.
--- Res Publica Soleorum, R. P. Thessalorum: see
No. 2127.

165 --- Commentary or paraphrase of Topica ii.2.
P. Fay. 3; P. Lit. Lond. 180 (Brit. Mus. inv.
815) (I-II, Theadelphia). Archiv 2.367; R. Stark,
Ann. Univ. Sarav. 8 (1959) 37-38.

Aristotle: see also Nos. 187, 1501-2, 1990, 2069,
2089, 2181, 2183, 2204, 2339, 2564-65.

166 ARISTOXENUS (?): Rhythmica (?). P. Oxy. 1.9
(Trinity Coll. Libr., Dublin, Pap. B.1) (III, Oxy.).
Quotations (Powell, CA 192-93; Page, PMG 926,
for the lyric adespota): dithyrambs (4 frr.); Ps.-
Alcman, Partheneion (New Chapters 1.54; Page,
GLP 1, No. 88). J. F. Mountford, New Chapters
2.178-80, queries the attribution; Manteuffel,
Opusc., No. 35.1, p. 189; Wilamowitz, Gr. Versk.
67, doubts the attribution. Archiv 1.117; JAW 104.
22-25, 125.2-8; T. Reinach, Rev. Ét. Gr. 11 (1898)
389-415; Wilamowitz, Gött. Anz., 1898, 698-703;
K. von Jahn, Berl. Phil. Woch. 19 (1899) 475-79,
508-11.

167 --- Aristoxenus (?): Discussion of music. P. Oxy.
4.667 (Trinity Coll. Libr., Dublin, Pap. F.10)
(III, Oxy.). J. F. Mountford, New Chapters 2.
180-81, favors the attribution. Archiv 3.497; JAW
144.1-2. C. E. Ruelle, Rev. Phil. 29 (1905) 201-4.

Aristoxenus: see also Nos. 361-62.

168 ARRIAN (?): Life of Tilliborus (?). P. Oxy. 3.416
(Musées Royaux, Bruxelles, inv. E.5927) (III-IV,
Oxy.; on the verso of an alphabetical vocabulary).
Lavagnini, EGFP 35-36; R. M. Rattenbury, New
Chapters 3.249-50. Archiv 3.296. Identified by
F. Zimmermann, Archiv 11 (1935) 165-75.

Arrian: see also No. 2202.

Artemidorus of Ephesus: see No. 103.
Asclepiades: see Nos. 196, 1209, 1598, 1601, 2127.
Asclepiades (medicus): see No. 2339.

169 ASTYDAMAS (?): Hector (?). P. Amh. 2.10 (II
B.C., Soknopaiou Nesos; a leaf of pap. written
in cursive). Page, GLP 1, No. 29, and A. W.
Pickard-Cambridge, New Chapters 3.152-53,
query the attribution. Archiv 2.355; JAW 125.
183-84. Attribution suggested by H. Weil, Journ.
Sav., 1901, 737-41, and L. Radermacher, Rh. Mus.
57 (1902) 138.

170 --- Astydamas (?): Hector (?). B. Snell, Hermes,
Einzelschr. 5 (1937) 84-89 (P. Strassb. WG 304, 2)
(III-II B.C.?; cart.; from the same composite
roll as Nos. 426, 1349, 1592, 1698, 1735). A.
Koerte, Archiv 13.100, favors the attribution, Page,
GLP 1, No. 29, queries it.

171 --- Hector (?). P. Hibeh 2.174 (Brit. Mus. inv.
2947) (II B.C., Hibeh; cart.; on the verso are
traces of tragic trimeters, perhaps from an anthology). T. B. L. Webster, Hermes 82 (1954) 305-
307, on this and other papyri of Astydamas.

Astydamas: see also No. 1594.

Athenocles: see Nos. 1205, 2299.
Autoclides: see No. 2127.
Axiopistus: see Nos. 363-64.

BABRIUS: Fables, Prologue 1-11: see No. 2643.

172 --- Fables 11, 16-17, with a Latin translation.
P. Amh. 2.26 (III-IV). Van Hoesen, No. 65 (pp.
124-26). Calderini, PL, No. 1; Cavenaile, CPL
40; Collart, PLL, No. 4; Marichal, No. 136.
Archiv 2.356; JAW 133.163. M. Ihm, Hermes
37 (1902) 147-51; L. Radermacher, Rh. Mus. 57
(1902) 142-45.

173 --- Fables 43, 110, 118, 25 (sic). P. Oxy. 10.1249
(II, Oxy.).

174 --- Fables 142, 156, 78, 97, 163, 117, 91, 103, 107,
147, 160, 215, 218, 43, 123, 121 (sic). D. C.
Hesseling, JHS 13 (1893) 293-314 ("Tabulae Ceratae Assendelftianae," Bibliotheek der Rijksuniversiteit, Leiden) (III, Palmyra?; sch. ex.;
seven waxed tablets, forming a codex including
also No. 491). JAW 92.111-13.

Babrius: see also Nos. 1877, 3010.

175  BACCHYLIDES: Epinician Odes and Dithyrambs.
P. Lond. 733; P. Lit. Lond. 46 (Brit. Mus. inv.
733); PSI 12.1278 (four small frr. from the same
roll) (I-II, Meir). Ed. pr. of the London papyrus:
F. G. Kenyon, 1897; ed. pr. of the Florence frr.:
M. Norsa, Ann. Sc. Pisa 10 (1941) 155-63. The
Poems of Bacchylides: Facsimile of Papyrus
DCCXXXIII in the British Museum (London 1897);
Bassi, MIG, No. 112, tav. XL; Kenyon, Pal. GP,
pl. XIII; Norsa, SLG, tav. 10a; Schubart, Gr.
Pal., Abb. 85; Thompson, GLP, No. 6 (p. 118).
F. Blass, G. Suess, and B. Snell, Bacchylidis
Carmina cum Fragmentis (Lipsiae 1934⁵) 50-55
(earlier bibl.); Edmonds, LG 3.92-116, 126-99;
Galiano, LG 136-37 (bibl.); Preisendanz, PFF 154;
Snell, Bacchyl. 6-12, and passim. JAW 104.132-
140; Archiv 14.112-13; L. Radermacher, WS 52
(1934) 139-40, ibid. 56 (1938) 1-2; F. N. Pryce,
JHS 56 (1936) 77-78, on a vase-painting as an
illustration to the text; B. Snell, Hermes 71
(1936) 124-26, ibid. 76 (1941) 208-19; B. Lavagnini, Riv. Fil. 65 (1937) 372-73; H. Oellacher,
SIFC, NS 18 (1941) 109-12; G. B. Pighi, Aeg. 24
(1944) 176-83; C. Gallavotti, Riv. Fil. 72-73
(1944-45) 1-15; E. François, An. fil. clás. 4
(1947-49) 91-113; Q. Cataudella, Aeg. 31 (1951)
231-34; L. Alfonsi, Riv. Fil. 80 (1952) 26-37, on
B. and Varro; B. Gentili, PP 8 (1953) 199-208,
idem, Archeol. Class. 6 (1954) 121-25, on Dithyramb 17 in relation to a vase-painting from Ruvo;
J. G. Griffith, Fifty Years Cl. Schol. 60-61; W.
S. Barrett, Hermes 84 (1956) 248-53, examines
B's. dactylo-epitrites; C. del Grande, Filologia
minore (Milano-Napoli 1956) 125-72, 345-47; W.
Steffen, Eos 51 (1961) 11-20, on Ode 5; J. Irigoin,
Rev. Ét. Gr. 75 (1962) 45-63, writes prolegomena
to a new edition of Bacchylides.

176  --- Ode 14 A-B.  P. Oxy. 23.2363 (II-III, Oxy.).
Snell, Bacchyl. 12-13, 50-51 (ed. pr.). Archiv
16.98; Galiano, LG 137-38.

177  --- Dithyramb 17.47-78, 91-92.  P. Oxy. 8.1091;
P. Lit. Lond. 47 (Brit. Mus. inv. 2056) (II, Oxy.).
Snell, Bacchyl. 12, 61-63. J. M. Edmonds, CR
36 (1922) 160.

178  --- Paean.  P. Oxy. 3.426 (Libr. of Victoria Coll.,
Toronto) (III, Oxy.; sch. ex.; on the verso of a
document). Edmonds, LG 3.212-15; Galiano, Pind.,
No. 61, idem, LG 139; Snell, Bacchyl. 13, 76-77.
Archiv 3.267; P. Maas, Philol. 63 (1904) 308;
identified by Snell, Hermes 67 (1932) 1-13; P.
Maas, ibid. 469-71; F. M. Heichelheim, SO 30
(1953) 77-81; W. S. Barrett, Hermes 82 (1954)
421-44.

179  --- Scolia (or Encomia?).  P. Oxy. 11.1361 (Brit.
Mus. inv. 2443), P. Oxy. 17.2081 (e); P. Lit.
Lond. 48 (I, Oxy.). Pindar is perhaps mentioned
in a scholium (Galiano, Pind., No. 57). Diehl,
SL, Nos. 1-5; Edmonds, LG 3.216-21; Galiano,
LG 139-40; Snell, Bacchyl. 13, 83-92. Archiv
7.139; JEA 6.123; K. F. W. Schmidt, Gött. Anz.,
1918, 91-93; C. M. Bowra, New Chapters 3.56-58;
B. Snell, Hermes 80 (1952) 156-63; P. Maas, Neue
Beiträge zur klass. Altertumswiss.: Festschrift
Bernhard Schweitzer (Stuttgart 1954) 139.

180  --- Scolia or Encomia (?).  P. Oxy. 23.2362 (II-
III, Oxy.). Galiano, LG 143.

181  --- Erotikon (?).  P. Oxy. 23.2361 (II-III, Oxy.).
Galiano, LG 142-43. C. Gallavotti, Gnomon 29
(1957) 420-21.

182  --- Commentary on Odes 3-5.  P. Oxy. 23.2367
(II?, Oxy.; on the verso of a document). Galiano,
LG 146.

183  --- Commentary on Bacchylides (?), Dithyrambs or
Paeans (a fragment on the poem "Cassandra").
P. Oxy. 23.2368 (II, Oxy.; in the same hand as
No. 74 above, a commentary on Alcaeus). Relates that Aristarchus says that the "Cassandra"
is dithyrambic, while Callimachus and Dionysius
"ho Phaselites" wrongly classify it as a paean.
Galiano, LG 146. C. Gallavotti, Gnomon 29 (1957)
420.

184  --- A choral lyric (Bacchylides or Simonides?).
P. Oxy. 23.2364 (II?, Oxy.). By the same copyist as No. 185; partially coincides with P. Berol.
inv. 16139 (see No. 1906). Galiano, LG 143-45,
prefers Bacchylides; C. Gallavotti, Gnomon 29
(1957) 421-22.

185  --- Lyric.  Snell, Pindarus, fr. 343 (Ashmolean
Mus., P. Oxoniensis inv. 20) (?). By the same
copyist as No. 184. For the attribution to Bacchylides, see E. Lobel on P. Oxy. 23.2364. Archiv
16.98. Galiano, LG 142, 144, 148.

Bacchylides: see also Nos. 204, 455, 1365, 1906-8,
1912-14, 1949.

Baton of Sinope: see No. 998.
Bion: see No. 1858.
Boëthus: see No. 2093.
Bryon: see No. 339.
Caecilius Calactinus: see No. 2289.

186  CALLIMACHUS: Hymni i.53-60, 76-83, ii.1-18,
24-40, iii.2-4, 12-14, 28-29, 36-39, iv.130-34,
158-62, 169-74, 196-99, 232-35, 240-45, 260-63,
268-73, 282-83, 308-9, vi.125-34; Aetia iii, iv (?)
and Libri Incerti; argumentum Hecalae; Coma
Berenices 44-64, 67-78; Sosibi Victoria; two
unidentified fragments; and numerous marginalia.
P. Oxy. 20.2258 (VI-VII, Oxy.; pap. cod.). The
marginalia quote or refer to Alcman; Aratus,
Phaen. 148; a poem on astronomy by one Diophil(..);
Hesiod, Theog. 378 and 984, and Astronomia (?;
Merkelbach, Hes., fr. Z 4); Philetas, Demeter
(?); and Theopompus (Jacoby, FGH, Dritter Teil
b 398). Ed. pr.: Pfeiffer, Callim. 1, pp. ix, 114-
122, 226, 311-16, 501, 503, 506; see also ibid. 2,
pp. xxiv-xxv, liii, 46-47, 55-56, 76-77, 123-24.
Archiv 16.115; D. Pieraccioni, Maia 5 (1952) 291-
294; B. Snell, Gnomon 25 (1953) 433-34; T. Cire-
sola, Rend. Ist. Lomb. 91 (1957) 123-36, 483-504,
makes two studies of the Coma, with special reference to this papyrus, and ibid. 92 (1958) 269-85,
examines especially the identity of Diophil(..) and
that of the author of the scholia (Theon, Epaphroditus, or Salustius?). On the relation to Catullus
66.75-78, see C. Bailey, Fifty Years Cl. Schol.

299; H. J. Mette, Hermes 83 (1955) 500; G. B.
Pighi, Euphros. 2 (1959) 203-8; N. I. Herescu,
Eranos 55 (1957) 153-70, idem, Orph. 7 (1960)
189-90; B. Axelson, Studi Castiglioni 1. 15-21; A.
Luppino, Riv. Fil. 86 (1958) 339-45, ibid. 89
(1961) 309-13.

--- Hymnus i. 50: see No. 1201.

187  --- Scholia on Hymni ii. 38-76, iii. 37-94.   P. Antin.
1. 20 (IV-V, Antinoöpolis; pap. cod. ).  The scholia
refer to Aristotle.  Pfeiffer, Callim. 2, pp. lii,
48-49, 53-55.

188  --- Hymnus iii.1-6, 16, 22-54.   P. Mil. Vogl. 2. 42
(inv. 174) (I B.C., Tebtunis).  Pfeiffer, Callim.
2, p. li.  A. Vogliano, Atti Pap. IV, 489-91 (first
mention); A. Mariotti, Acme 1 (1948) 121-30 (ed.
pr. ).

189  --- Hymnus iii. 46-54, 78-84, with scholia.   C. C.
Edgar, Ann. Serv. 26 (1926) 203 (P. Cairo inv.
47993 b) (I, Oxy. ).  Pfeiffer, Callim. 2, pp. li,
55.  W. G. Waddell, Ét. Pap. 1 (1932) 13 (No. 5);
A. Mariotti, Acme 1 (1948) 128-29, reprints the
text.

190  --- Hymnus iii. 107-63, 172-78.   P. Amh. 2. 20
(Morgan Libr. ) (IV; pap. cod. ).  Refers to one
Aristodemus (?), and to Clitodemus.  Pfeiffer,
CFNR, pp. 90-92, Callim. 2, pp. lii, 56-58. Ar-
chiv 2. 348.  L. Radermacher, Rh. Mus. 57 (1902)
141-42.

191  --- Hymnus iv. 11-25, 38-40, 68-75, 81-92, 102-10,
141-46, 156-81, 186-205, 209-18, 230-43.   P. Oxy.
19. 2225 (II, Oxy. ).  Pfeiffer, Callim. 2, p. lii.

192  --- Hymnus iv. 53-69, 80-98, with marginalia.
Mentioned by E. Lobel, P. Oxy. 19, p. 68, note 1
(Bodleian Libr., Gr. Class. f. 109 (P)) (V-VI; pap.
cod. ).  Pfeiffer, Callim. 2, pp. lii-liii.

193  --- Hymnus iv. 84-94.   Breccia, Alexandrea 140
(P. Mus. Alex. inv. 5) (II?).  Pfeiffer, Callim.
2, p. li (bibl. ).

194  --- Hymnus vi. 32-37, 41-43, 54-63, 79-117, 138, with
part of a new line.  P. Oxy. 19. 2226 (II, Oxy. ).
Pfeiffer, Callim. 2, p. lii.

195  --- Aetia i, with Prologue, ibid. i (?), iii (?).
P. Oxy. 17. 2079, 18. 2167 (cf. ibid. 19, pp. 147-
149); PSI 11. 1217 A-B (II, Oxy. ).  Mimnermus is
mentioned in P. Oxy. 2079, fr. 1, line 11 (for bibl.
on this, see Galiano, LG 60, note 12).  Pfeiffer,
Callim. 1, frr. 1, 7, 11 (lines 1-7), 17 (14-17), 18
(1-12), 115 (1-21), 116-17, ibid. 2, pp. xiv-xv (bibl. ).
Ed. pr. of PSI 1217: G. Vitelli, Ann. Sc. Pisa,
Ser. 2. 3 (1934) 1-12.  Archiv 10. 32-35, 11. 225-27;
JAW 255. 96 and passim.  Q. Cataudella, Riv. Fil.
56 (1928) 509-10, on imitations by Gregory of Nazianzus; A. S. Hunt, CR 42 (1928) 6; J. T. Kakridis,
Phil. Woch. 48 (1928) 1214-15; R. Pfeiffer, Hermes
63 (1928) 302-41; J. U. Powell, CQ 22 (1928) 113;
A. Rostagni, Riv. Fil. 56 (1928) 1-35; A. Vogliano,
BFC 34 (1928) 201-11; H. J. M. Milne, CR 43 (1929)
214; M. Pohlenz, Gött. Nachr., 1929, 150-55; A.

Wifstrand, Eranos 27 (1929) 116-18; W. M. Edwards, CQ 24 (1930) 109-12; A. Rostagni, Riv. Fil.
58 (1930) 115-16; C. Gallavotti, SIFC, NS 10 (1933)
231-39, ibid. 11 (1934) 91-96; G. Coppola, ibid. 10
(1933) 333-38; A. Rostagni, Riv. Fil. 61 (1933)
189-210; P. Maas, Gnomon 10 (1934) 162-65; A.
Rostagni, Riv. Fil. 62 (1934) 67-70; E. Lobel,
Hermes 70 (1935) 31-41, restores the beginning of
the Aetia from these and other papyri; E. Diehl,
Hermes 71 (1936) 472-73; C. Gallavotti, Aeg. 22
(1942) 114-16; Q. Cataudella, AR 45 (1943) 41-44;
Lavagnini, Mimn. Call. 3-4, holds that the megalê
gynê to which Callimachus refers is the Nanno of
Mimnermus; E. A. Barber and P. Maas, CQ 44
(1950) 168, restore Pfeiffer, Callim. 1, fr. 7, lines
31-33; A. Colonna, Athen. 40 (1952) 191-95, suggests that the megalê gynê is Mimnermus' poem,
the Smyrneïs; G. de Vico, GIF 6 (1953) 252-58, on
Callimachus' literary rivals; A. Garzya, Emérita
21 (1953) 113-15, argues that the megalê gynê is
Nanno, not the Smyrneïs; M. Puelma, Mus. Helv.
11 (1954) 101-16, and Philol. 101 (1957) 90-100, on
Callimachus' relations with Philetas, Mimnermus,
and Antimachus; E. A. Barber, CR, NS 5 (1955)
241; C. Corbato, IFC Trieste 3 (1955) 20; A. Barigazzi, Hermes 84 (1956) 162-82, on Callimachus'
relations with Mimnermus, Philetas, Antimachus,
and Choerilus (the megalê gynê refers to the Lyde
of Antimachus); A. Luppino, Riv. Fil. 86 (1958)
345-49; W. Wimmel, Hermes 86 (1958) 346-54,
on Callimachus and Philetas; Q. Cataudella, Riv.
Fil. 87 (1959) 148-50, on Aetia, fr. 1 Pfeiffer; W.
Wimmel, Kallimachos in Rom, Hermes, Einzel-
schriften 16 (1960) 71-123, on the prologue to the
Aetia; D. del Corno, Acme 15 (1962) 57-58, on the
megalê gynê; H. Diller, Hermes 90 (1962) 119-20.

196  --- Scholia on Aetia, Bk. i.   PSI 11. 1219 (II-III, Oxy. ).
The so-called "Scholia Florentina. "  Ed. pr.: M.
Norsa and G. Vitelli, BSAA 28 (1933) 123-32.  Pfeif-
fer, Callim. 1, pp. 3, 11, 13, 17, 31, ibid. 2, p.
xviii (bibl. ).  Mentions or cites Aristotle, Res
Publica Parianorum; Callimachus, Aetia (Tel-
chines); critics of Callimachus: Argyrippus (?),
Asclepiades (?), Posidippus, and Praxiphanes of
Mitylene (?); Dercylus and Hagias; Mimnermus;
Philetas.  Archiv 11. 229-31; JAW 255. 97 and pas-
sim.  M. Pohlenz, Hermes 68 (1933) 313-27; Q.
Cataudella, Riv. Fil. 62 (1934) 55-66; P. Maas,
Gnomon 10 (1934) 162-65; A. Rostagni, Riv. Fil.
62 (1934) 289-312; Diehl, Hypomn. 418-21; R.
Goossens, Chr. Ég. 18 (1943) 134-37, and many
of the articles cited under No. 195, above.

197  --- Scholia on Aetia, Bk. i.   P. Lit. Lond. 181
(Brit. Mus. inv. 131) (I, Meir; from the same
papyrus as Nos. 163, 307).  Quotes Alcman, fr. 1,
Bergk; Aristotle, Hist. Animal. vi. 35. 580. A. 17;
Homer, Il. xiii. 64 (?), Od. xxiv. 62.  Pfeiffer,
Callim. 1, pp. 3, 7-8, ibid. 2, pp. x-xi (bibl).
Archiv 10. 35-36; W. M. Edwards, CQ 24 (1930)
109-12.

198  --- Aetia, Bk. i, i(?), iii(?).   P. Oxy. 19. 2208
(III, Oxy. ).  Pfeiffer, Callim. 1, frr 2, 113, 114
(lines 1-15), ibid. 2, p. xix.  R. Pfeiffer, JWCI
25 (1952) 20-32, discusses Callimachus' evidence
for the statue of the Delian Apollo; R. Kassel,
Rh. Mus. 101 (1958) 235.

199       --- Callimachus(?): Aetia i (?).   P. Oxy. 20.2261
          (II, Oxy.).  Pfeiffer, Callim. 2, pp. xiv, 107, 109-
          110.

200       --- Aetia, Bk. i, with scholia.  Wilamowitz, Sitzb.
          Berl. Akad., 1912, 544-47 ("Commentarius Bero-
          linensis": P. Berol. inv. 11521) (II).  Cites Cli-
          demus, Atthis; Homer, Il. xiii.685; Pindar, fr.
          76, Schroeder (Galiano, Pind., No. 18).  Pfeiffer,
          CFNR, No. 4; idem, Callim. 1, fr. 7 (lines 23-29)
          and p. 19, ibid. 2, pp. xv-xvi (bibl.).  Archiv 5.546.
          C. Corbato, IFC Trieste 3 (1955) 13-20, on the re-
          lation to Apollonius Rhodius.

201       --- Aetia, Bks. i, iii; Lyrica; Hecala.   P. Oxy.
          18.2168; Wilamowitz, Sitzb. Berl. Akad., 1914,
          222-44 (P. Berol. inv. 11629 A-B); idem, ibid.,
          1912, 524-44 (P. Berol. inv. 13417 A-B); PSI 2.
          133 (III, Oxy.; pap. cod.).  Pfeiffer, CFNR, Nos.
          1-2, 6-7, 33; idem, Callim. 1, frr. 12, 18 (lines
          9-15), 23-24, 57, 59 (18-22), 227-28, 253, ibid.
          2, pp. xx-xxi (bibl.); I. Kapp, Callimachi Heca-
          lae Fragmenta (Berolini 1915), Nos. 37, 41.  Ar-
          chiv 5.545, 7.117, 120-21.  P. Maas, Berl. Phil.
          Woch. 32 (1912) 959; idem, Hermes 60 (1925) 259;
          A. Ardizzoni, Riv. Fil. 63 (1935) 452-67; Galla-
          votti, Callim. 67-71; C. Corbato, IFC Trieste 3
          (1955) 7-12, on the relation to Apollonius Rhodius;
          P. Maas, Maia 9 (1957) 157; V. Bartoletti, SIFC,
          NS 31 (1959) 179-81; H. Diller, Hermes 90 (1962)
          120-21.

202       --- Aetia, Bk. i, and Liber Incertus.  P. Oxy. 19.
          2209, A-B (II, Oxy.).  Pfeiffer, Callim. 1, frr.
          21, 118, ibid. 2, p. xiii.

203       --- Aetia, Bk. i.   P. Ryl. 1.13 (I-II, Oxy.; on the
          verso of accounts).  Pfeiffer, CFNR, No. 3; idem,
          Callim. 1, fr. 26, ibid. 2, p. xiv.  Archiv 5.544;
          identified by Wilamowitz, Hermes 46 (1911) 471-73.

204       --- Commentary on Aetia, Bk. i.   P. Oxy. 20.2262
          (II, Oxy.).  Includes a new citation from Bacchy-
          lides; quotes Homer, Il. xi.21.  Pfeiffer, Callim.
          1, p. 499 (on fr. 2), ibid. 2, pp. xvii, 100-106.  C.
          Gallavotti, Aeg. 33 (1953) 160-61; B. Snell, Gno-
          mon 25 (1953) 434; L. Alfonsi, Hermes 83 (1955)
          379-83, on the relation to Propertius.

205       --- Diegeseis to Aetia i (frr. 26-31, Pfeiffer), and
          another Aetion.  P. Oxy. 20.2263 (II-III, Oxy.;
          on the verso of a blank piece of pap.).  Refers to
          Dercylus and Hagias(Jacoby, FGH, III B, p. 757,
          III b, p. 399).  Pfeiffer, Callim 1, p. 499 (on frr.
          26-21), ibid. 2, pp. xviii-xix, 107-8, 110-12.

206       --- Aetia, Bk. ii, with marginalia.  P. Oxy. 17.
          2080 (cf. ibid. 19, p. 147) (II, Oxy.).  Pfeiffer,
          Callim. 1, fr. 43, ibid. 2, p. xvi (bibl.).  Archiv
          10.36-41; E. A. Barber, New Chapters 2.6-8;
          E. Lobel, CQ 22 (1928) 115-16; J. U. Powell, ibid.
          113; W. Ehlers, Die Gründung von Zankle in den
          Aitia des Kallimachos (Diss. Berlin 1933); R.
          Pfeiffer, Philol. 93 (1938) 61-66; L. Deubner,
          ibid. 95 (1942) 26-28; E. A. Barber, CR, NS 5
          (1955) 241; C. Corbato, IFC Trieste 3 (1955) 5-7,
          on the relation to Apollonius Rhodius.

207       --- Aetia, Bk. ii, and Libri Incerti.   P. oxy.  19.
          2210 (II, Oxy.).  Pfeiffer, Callim. 1, frr. 43
          (lines 8-19), 119 (2-7), 120-37, ibid. 2, p. xiii.

208       --- Aetia, Bk. iii (and i, iii?).   P. Oxy. 19.2212
          (cf. ibid. 19, p. 144, ibid. 20, p. 167) (II, Oxy.).
          Pfeiffer, Callim. 1, frr. 59 (lines 1-11), 80, 82
          (1-3), 83-84, 114 (15-17), 138-57, ibid. 2, pp. xiii,
          113.

209       --- Aetia, Bk. iii.   P. Oxy. 18.2169 (II, Oxy.).
          Pfeiffer, Callim. 1, fr. 59 (lines 8-25), ibid. 2,
          p. xvii.

210       --- Aetia, Bk. iii (and i, iii?).   P. Oxy. 19.2211
          III, Oxy.; pap. cod.).  Pfeiffer, Callim. 1, frr.
          63-64, 66-67, 114 (lines 14-25), 115 (lines 11-21),
          and pp. 502-3 (on. fr. 114), ibid. 2, pp. xix-xx.
          R. Merkelbach, Archiv 16 (1956) 89, on fr. 67
          (lines 11-14), Pfeiffer; M. L. Coletti, Riv. CCM
          4 (1962) 294-303, compares Callimachus with Ovid,
          Heroides 20.17-34 (Acontius and Cydippe).

211       --- Diegeseis on Aetia, Bks. iii-iv, Iambi, Lyrica,
          Hecala, and Hymni i.1, ii.1.   PRIMI 1.18 (I-II,
          Tebtunis).  Quotes many verses from Callimachus,
          Aetia, Iambi, Lyrica, Hecala, and Hymni; refers
          to an Aesopic fable (in diegeseis to Iambus ii), to
          Hipponax as a character (col. 6, line 2), and to
          Ion (col. 9.36); quotes an unidentified lyric poet
          (Diehl, Anth. Lyr. 1$^2$.4.219).  Pfeiffer, Callim.
          1, passim (printed with the passages to which they
          refer), ibid. 2, pp. xii-xiii (bibl.), li, 41, 46;
          Dawson, 153 (bibl.), and passim; Diehl, Hypomn.
          415-18; Gallavotti, Callim. 25-26, and passim.
          Archiv 11.231-45, 12.65-66, 13.87-89; JAW 255.
          93-94.  The editor gives a bibl. through 1935
          (especially, R. Pfeiffer, Sitzb. Münch. Akad.,
          1934, Heft 10); more recent articles include A.
          von Blumenthal, Hermes 71 (1936) 458, Philol. 91
          (1936) 115-16; L. Castiglioni, Rend. Ist. Lomb.
          70 (1937) 55-58; O. Kern, Archiv 12 (1937) 65-66;
          P. Maas, SIFC, NS 14 (1937) 317; K. Mras, WS
          56 (1938) 45-54, Rh. Mus. 87 (1938) 277-84; E. A.
          Barber, CQ 33 (1939) 65-68; S. G. Kapsomenos,
          Byz. neugr. Jahrb. 16 (1939) 1-28; G. Pasquali,
          SIFC, NS 16 (1939) 69-78; B. Snell, Gnomon 15
          (1939) 534-36; E. Delage, Rev. Ét. Anc. 42 (1940)
          93-101; G. Manteuffel, Eos 41 (1940-46) 81-103;
          F. della Corte, Aeg. 21 (1941) 276-82; L. Fruech-
          tel, Phil. Woch. 61 (1941) 189-90; N. Terzaghi,
          Aeg. 31 (1951) 176; J. Andor, Act. Ant. Hung. 1
          (1951-52) 121-25; E. A. Barber, CR, NS 5 (1955)
          241.

212       --- Aetia, Bk. iii, and Libri Incerti.   P. Oxy. 19.
          2213 (II, Oxy.).  Pfeiffer, Callim. 1, frr. 75 (lines
          50-58), 77-78, 80 (4-22), 81, 82 (1-6), 85, 158-74,
          ibid. 2, pp. xiii-xiv, 114-15.  E. A. Barber and P.
          Maas, CQ 44 (1950) 168, restore fr. 85.4-12, Pfeif-
          fer; F. R. Walton, Studies Presented to David
          Moore Robinson 2 (St. Louis 1953) 602-6, on the
          aition of Euthycles.

          --- Aetia, Bks. iii-iv: see No. 186.

213   --- Aetia, Bk. iv, and Libri Incerti.  PSI 11.1218;
P. Oxy. 18.2170 (I-II, Oxy.).  Ed. pr. of PSI 1218:
M. Norsa and G. Vitelli, Ann. Sc. Pisa, Ser. 2.3
(1934) 7-12.  Pfeiffer, Callim. 1, frr. 92 (lines
1-3), 93 (1-18), 95-96, 175-77, ibid. 2, p. xi (bibl.).
Archiv 11.227; E. Diehl, Hermes 71 (1936) 473; Q.
Cataudella, Riv. Fil. 69 (1941) 36-37; E. A. Bar-
ber, CR, NS 5 (1955) 241-42.

214   --- Aetia, Bk. iv (Coma Berenices 44-64).  PSI 9.
1092 (I B.C., Oxy. ?).  Bassi, MIG, No. 110, tav.
XL; Norsa, SLG, tav. 8a.  Pfeiffer, Callim. 1,
fr. 110 (lines 44-64), ibid. 2, p. ix (bibl.)  Ed. pr.:
G. Vitelli, SIFC, NS 7 (1929) 3-12.  Archiv 10.30-
32; JAW 255.147.  F. Ageno, Aeg. 10 (1929) 153-79;
E. Fraenkel, Gnomon 5 (1929) 265-68; W. E. J.
Kuiper, SIFC, NS 7 (1929) 127-29; M. Lenchantin
de Gubernatis, ibid. 113-26; H. W. Prescott, CP
24 (1929) 290-92; E. Diehl, Phil. Woch. 50 (1930)
227-28; R. Pfeiffer, Philol. 87 (1932) 179-228; G.
von Manteuffel, Eos 41 (1940-46) 81-89; L. Pepe,
GIF 3 (1950) 193-99.  Especially on the relation to
Catullus: J. Coman, L'Art de Callimaque et de
Catulle dans le poème "La Boucle de Bérénice"
(Bucarest 1936); E. Bickel, Rh. Mus. 90 (1941)
81-146; Lavagnini, Mimn. Call. 122-27; D. Pieraccioni, AR, NS 3 (1953) 55-56; I. K. Horváth,
Act. Ant. Hung. 10 (1962) 347-56.

215   --- Aetia, Bks. iii, iv, and Iambi 1-4, 12-13.  P. Oxy.
7.1011 (Bodleian Libr., Gr. class. c.72 (P)) (IV,
Oxy.; pap. cod.).  Alludes to an Aesopic fable
(Perry, Aesopica, No. 23) and mentions Hipponax
(Iambus 1.1).  Pfeiffer, CFNR, No. 9; idem, Callim. 1, frr. 75-76, 112,191, 192 (lines 4-17), 193
(1-13, 24-39), 194 (1-12, 22-106), 202 (7-86), 203
(2-66), 204-8; Dawson 157 (bibl.), and passim;
Diehl, Hypomn. 440-41; Gallavotti, Callimn. 31-46,
59-66; Lavagnini, Mimn. Call. 100-110; Winter,
LLP 230-31; A. Dietzler, Die Akontios-Elegie
des Kallimachos (Greifswald 1933).  Archiv 5.543;
JEA 6.123, 8.85.  H. von Arnim, Sitzb. Wien.
Akad. 164 (1910), Abh. 4; R. Ellis, Hermathena
16 (1910) 116-20; A. E. Housman, Berl. Phil. Woch.
30 (1910) 476-77, CQ 4 (1910) 114-20; A. Platt, Berl.
Phil. Woch. 30 (1910) 477; A. Puech, Rev. Ét. Gr.
23 (1910) 255-75; P. Graindor, Mus. Belge 15 (1911)
49-64; R. Herzog, Berl. Phil. Woch. 31 (1911) 29-
30; P. E. Legrand, Rev. Ét. Anc. 13 (1911) 1-32;
G. Pasquali, AR 14 (1911) 165-81; A. D. Knox, CR
27 (1913) 120-21; A. Brinkmann, Rh. Mus. 72 (1917-
18) 473-78; W. Schmid, Phil. Woch. 48 (1928)
1598-99; G. Coppola, Riv. Fil. 58 (1930) 273-91;
E. Lobel, Bodl. Rec. 6 (1930) 138-42, ibid. 7 (1933)
233, Hermes 69 (1934) 167-78, ibid. 70 (1935) 42-45;
G. Coppola, SIFC, NS 10 (1933) 327-32; C. Gallavotti, ibid. 239-45, ibid. 11 (1934) 81-91; M. Pohlenz, Hermes 68 (1933) 323-27; B. Lavagnini, SIFC,
NS 12 (1935) 111-18 (= idem, Mimn. Call. 133-44);
K. Ziegler, Phil. Woch. 55 (1935) 1401-8; H. Zeitz,
Aeg. 16 (1936) 247, on the allusion to an Aesopic
fable (see above); S. G. Kapsomenos, Athena 47
(1937) 28-36; R. Pfeiffer, Philol. 93 (1938) 66-69;
S. G. Kapsomenos, Byz. neugr. Jahrb. 16 (1939)
28-32; F. Wehrli, Hermes 76 (1941) 14-21, on the
relation to Apollonius Rhodius; C. M. Dawson,
AJP 67 (1946) 1-15; N. Terzaghi, Aeg. 31 (1951)
173-74, 176; B. Vazquez, ibid. 32 (1952) 253-56;

E. A. Barber, CR, NS 5 (1955) 241; D. A. Tsirim-
pas, Athena 59 (1955) 150-74; E. Grassi, PP 11 (1956)
207-8; M. Puelma, Philol. 101 (1957) 247-64, on the
epilogue to the Aetia; G. Luck, CQ, NS 9 (1959) 34-37;
B. R. Rees, CR, NS 11 (1961) 1-3, on the identification of the temple in Iambus 1.9; H. Diller, Hermes
90 (1962) 121.

216   --- Aetia, Libri Incerti.  P. Oxy. 11.1362 (Bodleian
Libr., Gr. class. c.77 (P)) (I, Oxy.).  Pfeiffer,
CFNR, No. 8, idem, Callim. 1, frr. 178-83, ibid.
2, p. x (bibl.).  Archiv 7.120; JAW 191.43-45.  L.
Malten, Hermes 53 (1918) 148-79; K. F. W. Schmidt,
Gött. Anz., 1918, 93-94; K. Ziegler, Hermes 80
(1952) 255-56.

217   --- Aetia, Libri Incerti.  P. Oxy. 19.2214 (I B.C.-I,
Oxy.).  Pfeiffer, Callim. 1, fr. 186, ibid. 2, p. ix.
E. A. Barber and P. Maas, CQ 44 (1950) 96;  A.
Swiderek, JJP 4 (1950) 341-47, on the legend of the
Hyperboreans.

  --- Aetia: see also No. 89.

218   --- Iambus 1.  P. Oxy. 11.1363 (Bodleian Libr., Gr.
class. g.60 (P)) (II-III, Oxy.; on the verso of a
document).  Dawson 4, 10-13, 154; Gallavotti, Callim. 32-34; Pfeiffer, CFNR, No. 10, idem, Callim.
1, fr. 191 (lines 5-34), ibid. 2, p. xviii (bibl.).  Archiv 7.122.  R. Pfeiffer, Philol. 93 (1938) 70-71.

219   --- Scholia on Iambus 1.  PSI 9.1094 (II, Oxy.).  The
so-called "Scholia Florentina": ed. pr.: G. Vitelli,
BSAA 24 (1929) 1-4.  Mention Aesop (Perry, Aesopica, No. 26) and Hipponax (?); cite Homer, Il. ii.
469, xvi.259-60.  Dawson 4, 154 (bibl.); Gallavotti,
Callim. 32-34; Pfeiffer, Callim. 1, pp.163, 165,
ibid. 2, p. xvi (bibl.).  Archiv 10.228; JAW 255.
157.  E. Lobel, Bodl. Rec. 6 (1930) 138-42; H. J.
M. Milne, CR 46 (1932) 250.

  --- Iambi 1-4, 12-13: see No. 215.

220   --- Iambi 3-4.  P. Oxy. 19.2215 (II-III, Oxy.).
Pfeiffer, Callim. 1, frr. 193 (lines 5-24), 194 (14-
21), ibid. 2, p. xix.

221   --- Iambi 4-5.  P. Ryl. 3.485 (IV).  Dawson 4, 50-51,
56-57, 156; Gallavotti, Callim. 46-47; Pfeiffer,
Callim. 1, frr. 194 (lines 115-17), 195 (1-7), ibid. 2,
pp. xxi-xxii.  Archiv 14.110-11.  B. Snell, Gnomon
15 (1939) 540.

222   --- Iambi 4-7, 17; Branchus.  PSI 11.1216; P. Oxy.
18.2171-72 (cf. ibid. 18, pp. 183-84, ibid. 19, p.
149) (I-II, Oxy.).  Ed. pr. of PSI 1216, as by Archilochus: AR, Ser. 3.1 (1933) 7-12.  PSI 1216,
line $32_3$ = Archilochus, fr. 109, Bergk (Diehl, Anth.
Lyr. 3.40, fr. 91); lines 33-39 are cited by Ps.-
Gregorius Corinthius as by Callimachus.  Dawson,
4, 50-51, 56-61, 66-69, 155-56 (bibl.), on PSI 1216;
idem 5, 60-61, 68-71, 76-78, 80, 156, on P. Oxy.
2171; Galiano, LG 66-67 (bibl.); Gallavotti, Callim.
46-53, 55, 72-73; Pfeiffer, Callim. 1, frr. 194 (lines
107-17), 195-96, 197 (1-14), 209-14, 229 (1-22), ibid.
2, pp. xi-xii (bibl.).  Archiv 11.227-29; JAW 255.158.
G. Coppola, SIFC, NS 10 (1933) 165-68; G. Pasquali,
ibid. 169-75; R. Pfeiffer, Philol. 88 (1933) 265-71,
identifies PSI 1216; J. Stroux, ibid. 89 (1934) 318-19;
R. Goossens, Chr. Ég. 10 (1935) 375-76; R. Pfeif-

fer, JHS 61 (1941) 1-5, on Callimachus' evidence for the dimensions of Phidias' Zeus; M. F. Galiano, Emérita 11 (1943) 448-49; C. Picard, Rev. Arch., Sér. 6.24 (1945) 129-31; E. A. Barber and P. Maas, CQ 44 (1950) 168; N. Terzaghi, Aeg. 31 (1951) 174-75; E. A. Barber, CR, NS 5 (1955) 242; R. Merkelbach, Archiv 16 (1956) 89-90, on fr. 196, Pfeiffer, and on Callimachus' influence on Caecilius of Caleacte.

223      --- Iambus 7. P. Oxy. 4.661 (cf. ibid. 20, p. 168) (P. Cairo) (II, Oxy.). Roberts, GLH, pl. 16a. Dawson 4, 76-79, 156; Gallavotti, Callim. 53-54; Pfeiffer, Callim. 1, fr. 197 (lines 11-25, 30-51), ibid. 2, p. xvii (bibl.); Powell, CA 194-95. Archiv 3.483. E. Maass, Hermes 58 (1923) 175-86; R. Holland, ibid. 60 (1925) 59-65; R. Pfeiffer, Sitzb. Münch. Akad., 1934, Heft 10, 23-30, identifies the text; E. Diehl, Rh. Mus. 92 (1943) 177-79; E. A. Barber, CR, NS 5 (1955) 242. The additional fragment published in P. Oxy. 20, p. 168, is said to fit into P. Oxy. 2364 (Bacchylides?; No. 184, above): Galiano, LG 144, note 517.

     --- Iambus 9: see No. 1327.

224      --- Iambus 12. P. Oxy. 19.2218 (II-III, Oxy.). Dawson 108-9; Pfeiffer, Callim. 1, fr. 202 (lines 1-6), ibid. 2, p. xix.

225      --- Iambus 12.57-70. C. Bonner, Aeg. 31 (1951) 133-37 (P. Mich. inv. 4967) (II). Pfeiffer, Callim. 2, pp. 118-19 (on fr. 202, lines 57-70). M. Hombert, Chr. Ég. 28 (1953) 154-55.

226      --- Hecala. P. Oxy. 19.2216 (cf. ibid., pp. 145-46) (III, Oxy.; pap. cod.). Pfeiffer, Callim. 1, frr. 238 (lines 1-14, 17-32), 238 a-d, ibid. 2, p. xix. A. Barigazzi, Hermes 82 (1954) 308-17.

227      --- Hecala. T. Gomperz, Raineri M. 6.1-18 (IV; wooden tablet; text on recto, No. 425 on verso). Pfeiffer, CFNR, No. 34; idem, Callim. 1, fr. 260 (lines 1-43, 55-68), ibid. 2, p. xxiv (bibl.).; I. Kapp, Callimachi Hecalae Fragmenta (Berolini 1915), Nos. 58, 60, 62, 64. F. G. Kenyon, CR 7 (1893) 429-30; T. Reinach, Rev. Ét. Gr. 6 (1893) 258-66; R. Ellis, Journ. Philol. 24 (1896) 148-55; W. Weinberger, Philol. 76 (1920) 68-91; E. A. Barber, CQ, NS 2 (1952) 92; A. Barigazzi, Hermes 82 (1954) 317-30; R. Pfeiffer, Festschr. Kapp 95-104; V. Bartoletti, SIFC, NS 33 (1961) 154-62.

228      --- Hecala. P. Oxy. 19.2217 (IV, Oxy.). Pfeiffer, Callim. 1, fr. 260 (lines 44-58), ibid. 2, p. xxi. E. A. Barber, CQ, NS 2 (1952) 92.

229      --- Hecala. P. Oxy. 23.2376 (II, Oxy.). A. Barigazzi, Hermes 86 (1958) 453-71; F. Krafft, ibid. 471-80.

230      --- Hecala. P. Oxy. 23.2377 (III-IV, Oxy.; pap. cod.). See the articles cited under No. 229.

231      --- Hecala. P. Oxy. 24.2398 (II, Oxy.; on the verso of a document). Partially coincides with P. Oxy. 2217 (see No. 228). F. Krafft, Hermes 86 (1958) 472-74; W. S. Barrett, Gnomon 33 (1961) 690-91.

232      --- Hecala. P. Oxy. 25.2437 (II, Oxy.). Parts of some of the same verses as in P. Oxy. 2217 (No. 228) and 2398 (No. 231). H. Lloyd-Jones, CR, NS 11 (1961) 21.

     --- Hecala: see also Nos. 186, 211, 339, 1536.

233      --- Elegia: In Victoriam Nemeaeam (?). P. Oxy. 18.2173 (II, Oxy.). Pfeiffer, Callim. 1, fr. 383, and p. 508, ibid. 2, pp. xvii-xviii. M. F. Galiano, Emérita 11 (1943) 449-50; K. Latte, Philol. 97 (1948) 56-57.

234      --- Elegiae: Sosibi Victoria, etc. P. Oxy. 15.1793 (I, Oxy.). Refers to Archilochus (col. viii. 4). Pfeiffer, Callim. 1, frr. 384-86, 388-91, ibid. 2, p. x (bibl.). Archiv 7.121-22; JAW 255.145-46. E. Cahen, BAGB, April 1924, 5-14; K. F. W. Schmidt, Gött. Anz., 1924, 7-9; G. Coppola, Riv. Fil. 58 (1930) 282-91; R. Pfeiffer, Philol. 87 (1932) 220-28; A. Barigazzi, PP 6 (1951) 410-26.

     --- Sosibi Victoria: see also No. 186.

235      --- Callimachus (?): Elegiac distichs. P. Oxy. 23. 2375 (I, Oxy.). Col. ii. 5 may coincide with Callimachus, fr. 562, Pfeiffer.

236      --- Callimachus (?): Elegiacs in epistolary form. N. Terzaghi, Studi Calderini-Paribeni 2.127-35 (PSI inv. 436) (III-II B.C., Tebtunis). To appear in PSI 15.

     Callimachus: see also Nos. 183, 374, 1205, 1237, 1327, 1338, 1536, 1755, 1782, 1785, 1952, 2069, 2127, 2160, 2172, 2471.

Callinus: see No. 1749.
Callisthenes: On Hermias: see No. 339.
Callistratus of Alexandria: see No. 157.
Cebes: see No. 2089.

237      CERCIDAS: Meliambi, with scholia. P. Oxy. 8.1082; P. Lit. Lond. 59 (Brit. Mus. inv. 2054) (II, Oxy.). Fr. 1, col. 4, lines 5-15 paraphrase, as if by Euripides, Fr. trag. adesp. 151, Nauck (see B. Snell, WS 69₂ 1956, 92). New Chapters 1.2-12; Diehl, Anth. Lyr. 1².3.121-31 (bibl.), ibid. 3³.141-51 (bibl.); Knox, Herodes 189-217; Powell, CA 202-12. Archiv 5.553; JEA 6.124; JAW 174.120-21. P. Maas, Berl. Phil. Woch. 31 (1911) 1011-16; H. von Arnim, WS 34 (1912) 1-27; L. Deubner, Hermes 47 (1912) 480; K. F. W. Schmidt, Gött. Anz., 1912, 634-41; J. U. Powell, CR 27 (1913) 264; G. A. Gerhard, WS 37 (1915) 1-26; Wilamowitz, Sitz. Berl. Akad., 1918, 1138-64; A. D. Knox, CR 38 (1924) 101-4, ibid. 39 (1925) 50-55; M. Gigante, Riv. Fil. 83 (1955) 286-293, on the relation to Philodemus and Horace.

238      --- Cercidas (?): Choliambi. Gerhard, Phoinix 7-10, 156-76; P. Lond. 2.155, verso; P. Lit. Lond. 58 (Brit. Mus. inv. 155, verso) (III, Fayum; on the verso of No. 2374). This text may represent a part of the same verse anthology as No. 1605; see A. D. Knox, The First Greek Anthologist (Cambridge 1923). New Chapters 1.17-18; Diehl, Anth. Lyr. 3³.131-33; Knox, Herodes 228-34; Lesky, GGL 615-16; Powell, CA 213-16. Archiv

5.556; JAW 174.51-53.  H. K. Davids, Mnemos.,
Ser. 3.9 (1941) 238-40.

239    --- Cercidas (?): Choliambi.  Gerhard, Phoinix
       8-9, 159-65 (Bodleian Libr., Gr. class. f.1 (P))
       (II B.C.).  Lines 3-13 are a doublet of lines 13-26
       in P. Lond. 2.155, verso (see No. 238).  The text
       may represent a part of the same verse anthology
       as No. 1605; see Knox, op. cit. under No. 238.
       Ed. pr.: W. Croenert, Archiv 2 (1903) 373-74.
       Diehl, Anth. Lyr. 3³.131-33;  Powell, CA 214-15.
       Archiv 5.557; JAW 174.51-53; New Chapters 1.
       17-18.

       Cercidas: see also No. 1605.

Chaeremon: see Nos. 1613, 2656.
Chamaeleon: see Nos. 1950, 2070, 2290, 2292.

240    CHARES: Sententiae.  G. A. Gerhard, Sitzb. Heid.
       Akad., 1912, Abh. 13 (P. Heid. inv. 434) (III B.C.,
       Hibeh; cart.).  Diehl, Anth. Lyr. 2³.109-13;  Pow-
       ell, CA 223-27;  Young, Theognis 113-17.  Archiv
       7.119;  New Chapters 1.18.

241    CHARITON: Chaereas and Callirhoë ii.3.5-4.2.
       P. Oxy. 7.1019 (Trinity Coll. Libr., Dublin) (II-III,
       Oxy.).  Blake, Char., Praefatio xi-xii.  JAW 170.
       208.  F. Zimmermann, Hermes 63 (1928) 193-224.

242    --- ii.11.5-6, with the colophon of Bk. ii.  P. Mi-
       chael. 1 (II; on the verso are meager fragments
       of an astrological text: see No. 2066).

243    --- iv.2.3-3.2.  P. Fay. 1 (Cambridge Univ. Libr.,
       add. 4070) (II-III, Karanis).  Blake, Char., Prae-
       fatio xi-xii.  Archiv 2.365.

244    --- viii.5.9-7.3, and Chione (?).  U. Wilcken, Ar-
       chiv 1 (1901) 227-64 ("Codex Thebanus deperditus")
       (VI-VII, Thebaid; parch. cod., palimpsest, with
       a Coptic text over the Greek).  Blake, Char., Prae-
       fatio x-xi;  Lavagnini, EGFP 24-27;  Zimmermann,
       GRP, No. 3 (bibl.).  Archiv 1.528-29; R. M. Rat-
       tenbury, New Chapters 3.230-34.  On the Chione
       romance: R. M. Rattenbury, CQ 20 (1926) 181-84;
       F. Zimmermann, Aeg. 11 (1931) 45-56, Hermes 71
       (1936) 236-40; Lavagnini, Studi RG 224-26.

245    CHOERILUS: Persika (title only).  P. Oxy. 11.1399
       (Johns Hopkins Univ. Libr.) (III, Oxy.; on the
       verso of a petition).  Powell, CA 250.  Archiv 7.
       116-17.  K. F. W. Schmidt, Gött. Anz., 1918, 126;
       Lesky, GGL 159.

       Choerilus: see also No. 1612.

246    CHRYSIPPUS: Peri apophatikõn.  P. Pàr. 2 (II B.C.,
       Memphis).  Cites Alcman (?); Anacreon (?);
       Aristophanes, Ranae 1217; Euripides, Andromacha
       204, Auge (fr. 275.3, Nauck), Dictys (fr. 344,
       Nauck), Helena 1261, Iphigenia Aulidensis 28,
       Phoenix (fr. 814.3, Nauck), and Scyrii (?); Iby-
       cus (?); Pindar (Galiano, Pind., Nos. 30, 52); Timo-
       theus, Cyclops; and various unidentified epic,
       lyric, and tragic passages.  Kenyon, Pal. GP, pl.
       XI ("dialectical fragment"); Norsa, SLG, tav. 3b;

Pal. Soc., Ser. 2, vol. 2, pl. 180; Roberts, GLH,
pl. 6a; Thompson, GLP, No. 3 (p. 112).

247    --- Chrysippus (?).  P. Antin. 2.61 (II-III, Antino-
       öpolis).  Evidently alludes to the doctrine that in-
       cest and cannibalism are ethically adiaphora.

248    --- Chrysippus (?): A Stoic fragment.  A. M. Co-
       lombo, PP 9 (1954) 376-81 (P. Univ. Statale di
       Milano) (II).

       Chrysippus: see also Nos. 455, 536, 2089, 2093.

Chrysippus of Cnidus: see Nos. 342, 2088.
Cleanthes: see No. 536.
Clearchus: see No. 2292.
Clidemus: see No. 200.
Clitarchus: see No. 2184.
Clitodemus: see No. 190.
Colluthus: see No. 1835.
Colotes: see No. 2578.
Comanus: see No. 2138.
Corax: see No. 2295.

249    CORINNA: Veroia, Bk. i (?), with prose arguments
       (?).  P. Oxy. 23.2370 (ca. A.D. 200, Oxy.).
       Galiano, LG 122-23; Page, PMG 655.  C. Galla-
       votti, Gnomon 29 (1957) 422-23;  J. Sancho Lasso
       de la Vega, Emérita 28 (1960) 135-42, argues that
       the supposed title "Veroia" is a ghost-word.

250    --- Corinna (?): Orestas (?).  PSI 10.1174 (I-II?,
       Oxy.?).  Ed. pr.: Coppola 231-42.  E. Lobel,
       P. Oxy. 23, p. 60, rejects the attribution to Co-
       rinna.  Diehl, Anth. Lyr. 1².4.200-2; Page, Co-
       rinna 18-28; idem, GLP 1, No. 82; idem, PMG
       690 ("Boeotica incerti auctoris").  Archiv 13.95.
       C. M. Bowra, CQ 30 (1936) 130.

251    --- Fragments with scholia.  BKT 5.2.19-55 (inv.
       13284) (II, Hermupolis Magna).  Schubart, PGB,
       tab. 29a.  Diehl, SL, Nos. 1-2; idem, Anth. Lyr.
       1².4.195-200; Edmonds, LG 3.28-35; Galiano,
       LG 120-21 (bibl.); Lesky, GGL 168; Page, Corin-
       na 9-17; idem, PMG 654.  Archiv 5.549; JAW 144.
       105-6, 178.92-93; JEA 6.123; New Chapters 2.38,
       3.21-30.  W. Croenert, Rh. Mus. 63 (1908) 166-
       76; E. Nachmanson, Glotta 2 (1910) 131-46; J. U.
       Powell, Journ. Philol. 33 (1914) 296-97; L. Bian-
       chi, SIFC 21 (1915) 245-54; W. Vollgraff, Mnemos.
       43 (1915) 318; E. Lobel, Hermes 65 (1930) 357-58;
       P. Maas, Zeitschr. Vergl. Spr. 58 (1931) 268-69;
       G. Bonfante, Riv. Fil. 62 (1934) 535-46; C. M.
       Bowra, Problems in Greek Poetry (Oxford 1953)
       54-65; A. E. Harvey, CQ, NS 5 (1955) 176-80; G.
       M. Bolling, AJP 77 (1956) 282-87; D. L. Page,
       CQ, NS 7 (1957) 109-12.

       Corinna: see also Nos. 1351, 1891-92, 2810.

Crates (the Cynic): see No. 455.
Crates (Cynic or comic poet?): see No. 2078.
Crates (grammarian): see No. 1205.

252    CRATINUS: Hypothesis of the Dionysalexandros.
       P. Oxy. 4.663 (Cambridge Univ. Libr., add. 4415)
       (II-III, Oxy.).  Demiańczuk 31-33; Lesky, GGL 396.
       Archiv 3.485; JAW 152.254 (bibl.); M. Platnauer,
       New Chapters 3.158-61.  M. Croiset, Rev. Et. Gr.

17 (1904) 297-310; A. Koerte, Hermes 39 (1904) 481-98; W. G. Rutherford, CR 18 (1904) 440, on the date of the play; P. Perdrizet, Rev. Ét. Anc. 7 (1905) 109-15; R. C. Flickinger, CP 5 (1910) 1-3, interprets the numeral in the title; G. Norwood, Greek Comedy (London 1931) 118-24: G. Méautis, Rev. Ét. Anc. 36 (1934) 462-66; M. Cervelli, Annali dell' Istituto Superiore "S. Chiara" di Napoli 2 (1950) 109-46.

253   --- Ploutoi.   PSI 11.1212, ibid. 12.1279; P. Mazon, Mél. Bidez 603-12 (Musées Royaux, Bruxelles, inv. E. 6842; further frr. from the same roll) (II, Oxy.). Ed. pr. of PSI 1212: M. Norsa and G. Vitelli, BSAA 29 (1934) 249-56. Lesky, GGL 397; Page, GLP 1, No. 38. Archiv 11.260-62, 16.104 (on PSI 1279, parts of 3 lines from the same roll); JAW 263.2-3. R. Goossens and C. Préaux, Rev. Ét. Anc. 37 (1935) 401-34; R. Goossens, Chr. Ég. 10 (1935) 377-80, ibid. 16 (1941) 106-7, ibid. 18 (1943) 131-34, ibid. 21 (1946) 93-107; M. F. Galiano, Arbor 6 (1946) 133-35; J. Czerniatowicz, Eos 42 (1947) 177-91.

Cratinus: see also Nos. 375, 1186, 1594, 1631, 2121, 2290.

Cratippus: see No. 2189.

254   CRITIAS (or Euripides?): Pirithoüs.   P. Oxy. 17. 2078 (II, Oxy.).   A. W. Pickard-Cambridge, New Chapters 3.148-51; JAW 238.159-60. Attributed to Critias by A. Koerte, Archiv 10.50-53, and A. Vogliano, BFC 34 (1928) 201; A. E. Housman, CR 42 (1928) 9.

Crito: see No. 2089.

255   CTESIAS: Persika.   P. Oxy. 22.2330 (II, Oxy.). A fragment concerning the romance between Stryangaeus, a Mede, and Zarinaea, queen of the Sacae. K. Latte, Gnomon 27 (1955) 497-98; J. W. B. Barns Akten Pap. VIII, 36; R. Merkelbach, Archiv 16 (1956) 109-10, reprints the text and comments on the dialect and style; D. del Corno, Athen., NS 40 (1962) 126-41, and M. Gigante, Riv. Fil., NS 40 (1962) 249-72, analyze the style.

Daïmachus of Plataea: see No. 2189.
Damastes: see No. 2290.
Damoxenus: see No. 1667.
Dares: see No. 1812.
Deinolochus: see No. 359.
Demetrius: see No. 1213.
Demetrius Chlorus: see No. 1327.
Demetrius Magnes: see No. 1333.
Demetrius of Phalerum: see No. 50.
Demetrius of Scepsis: see No. 1203.
Democrates of Sicyon: see No. 2071.
Democritus: see Nos. 2564, 2569, 2578.
Ps.-Democritus: see No. 1998.
Demon: see No. 339.

256   DEMOSTHENES: Olynthiaca i.9, 16, 23-26, ii.1, 10, 13, 17-19, 21-22, 24-27, 30, iii.1, 3, 9-14, 35-36; In Philippum i.2, 4, 7-8, 14-15, 18, 21, 23, 32-41, 43, 45-51; De Pace 16-21.   P. Oxy. 15.1810 (Wellesley Coll.) (II, Oxy.).

257   --- Olynthiaca ii.10, 15.   F. G. Kenyon, CR 6 (1892) 430 (Rossall Sch.)   (I-II, Thebaïd?).

258   --- ii.19.   Mentioned by Schubart, Einführung 475 (P. Berol. inv. 8519) (III).

259   --- iii.33-36.   PSI 11.1205 (II, Oxy.).

--- In Philippum i, 2, 4, etc.: see No. 256.

260   --- In Philippum i.26-29.   P. Genève 3 (inv. 258) (IV-V; parch. cod.?).   Pasquali, Stor. Testo 283-84.

261   --- De Pace 2-5, 7-9.   PSI 2.129 (IV, Oxy.; parch. cod.).

--- 16-21: see No. 256.

262   --- 21, 23.   P. Oxy. 3.460 (Houghton Libr., Harvard Univ.) (II-III, Oxy.).   Archiv 3.283.

263   --- In Philippum ii.1, 5.   P. Amh. 2.24 (IV; parch. cod.).   Archiv 2.361.

264   --- De Halonneso 25.   Mentioned by Schubart, Einführung 475 (P. Berol. inv. 13235) (?).

265   --- 84.   Mentioned by Schubart, Einführung 475 (P. Berol. inv. 8520) (II-III).

266   --- In Philippum iii, 29-34, 61, 62-68.   J. G. Winter, CP 20 (1925) 97-114 (P. Mich. inv. 918) (IV, Panopolis?; parch. cod.).   Pasquali, Stor. Testo 282; Winter, LLP 249, 272.

267   --- 38-40, 43.   P. Fay. 8 (Royal Ontario Mus., Univ. of Toronto) (II, Bacchias).   Archiv 2.360.

268   --- In Philippum iv.10-12.   P. Harris 43 (inv. 180) (II).

--- In Philippum vii: see No. 2128.

269   --- Ad Philippi Epistulam 2-8.   PSI 14.1394 (III, Oxy.).

270   --- De Classibus 40-41.   W. Schubart, Das Buch bei den Griechen und Römern (Berlin u. Leipzig 1921), Abb. 26 (p. 125) (P. Cairo?) (?; parch. cod.).

271   --- Pro Rhodiorum Libertate 194, 198.   Mentioned by Schubart, Einführung 475 (P. Berol. inv. 13274) (V-VI).

272   --- Pro Megalopolitis 8-10, 12-13.   Mentioned by Schubart, Einführung 475 (P. Berol. 13283) (?).

273   --- 204.   Mentioned by Schubart, Einführung 475 (P. Berol. inv. 13264) (V-VI).

274   --- De Corona 1 (written six times).   P. Ryl. 1.59 (III, Oxy.; writing ex.).   E. G. Turner, Mus. Helv. 13 (1956) 236-38, discusses the palaeographical importance of the text, which is not a school exercise.

275  --- 7-8.  P. Oxy. 3.461 (Houghton Libr., Harvard Univ.) (III, Oxy.).  Archiv 3.283.

276  --- 17-18.  P. Oxy. 4.700 (Houghton Libr., Harvard Univ.) (II, Oxy.).  Archiv 3.493.

277  --- 25-28.  P. Oxy. 3.462 (Houghton Libr., Harvard, Univ.) (III, Oxy.).  Archiv 3.283.

278  --- 27-39 (omitting the psephisma and the epistolê). PSI 14.1395 (III, Oxy.; pap. cod.).

279  --- 40-47.  P. Oxy. 2.230 (Johns Hopkins Univ. Libr.) (II, Oxy.).  Archiv 1.523.

280  --- 49-56.  P. Antin. 1.27 (III, Antinoöpolis; parch. cod.).

281  --- 63, 79.  P. Harris 44 (inv. 181 f.) (II-III; on the verso of accounts).

282  --- 85-87.  PRIMI 1.12 (II, Oxy.).

283  --- 163, 169.  P. Ryl. 1.57 (II-III, Theadelphia). Roberts, GLH, pl. 22c.  Pasquali, Stor. Testo 281-82.

284  --- 167-69.  P. Oxy. 11.1377 (P. Princ., AM 9051) (I B.C., Oxy.).  K. F. W. Schmidt, Gött. Anz. 1918, 105.  Pasquali, Stor. Testo 282.

     --- 169: see No. 2498.

285  --- 201-5.  P. Oslo 2.10; P. Harris 45 (inv. 37 c) (I; on the verso of a document).  Ed. pr. of P. Oslo 10: L. Amundsen, SO 4 (1926) 26-28.  Pasquali, Stor. Testo 283 (on P. Oslo 10).  E. G. Turner has noted that these fragments belong to the same papyrus.

286  --- 217-23.  P. Haun. 1.5 (inv. 114) (I-II, Fayum?; on the verso of a document ).  T. Larsen, Actes Pap. V, 249; M. F. Galiano, Emérita 14 (1946) 341-42.

287  --- 227-29.  P. Oxy. 2.231 (Cambridge Univ. Libr., add. 4050) (I-II, Oxy.).  Archiv 1.524.

288  --- 238-42.  O. Montevecchi, Aeg. 23 (1943) 99-105 (P. Med. inv. 10) (II-III).

289  --- 244.  P. Oxy. 1.25 (Johns Hopkins Univ. Libr.) (III, Oxy.).  Archiv 1.116.

     --- 252: see No. 1574.

290  --- 267-324.  P. Ryl. 1.58 (V-VI; sch. ex.; a quire of four pap. sheets).

291  --- De Falsa Legatione 4-7, 12-13.  P. Lond. 5.1814; P. Lit. Lond. 126 (Brit. Mus. inv. 1546 C) (III; pap. cod.).

292  --- 10.  P. Grenf. 2.9 (Bodleian Libr., Gr. class. f.46 (P)) (I-II; on the verso of a document).

293  --- 11-32.  F. G. Kenyon, Journ. Philol. 22 (1894) 247-61; P. Lit. Lond. 127 (Brit. Mus., Add. MS.

34473, art. 1) (II, Fayum?; parch. cod.).

294  --- Commentary on ibid. 40-51, 99-158.  P. Rain. 1.25 (inv. 29795) (III, Fayum; pap. cod.).  Archiv 11.270.

295  --- De Falsa Legatione 53-57.  P. Oxy. 9.1182 (P. Cairo) (II, Oxy.).

296  --- 194-95.  PRIMI 1.13 (II, Tebtunis).

297  --- 274-75, 279-80.  P. Oxy. 8.1094 (Muhlenberg Coll.) (V, Oxy.; parch cod.).  Pasquali, Stor. Testo 283-84.

298  --- 293-95.  P. Tebt. 2.267 (II, Tebtunis).

299  --- Adversus Leptinem 78.  P. Aberdeen 113 (I, Fayum?).  Ed. pr.: E. O. Winstedt, CQ 1 (1907) 263.

300  --- 84-90.  Wilcken, TAGP, Taf. I (P. Berol. inv. 5879) (I-II, Fayum).

301  --- 161-62.  PSI 11.1204 (II, Oxy.).

     --- See also No. 2511.

302  --- In Midiam 33-43.  P. Rain. 1.8 (inv. 29816 a) (IV).

303  --- 41-42.  C. Whitehouse, Proc. Soc. Bibl. Arch. 15 (1892) 86 (when published, in the editor's private collection) (IV-V; pap. cod.).

304  --- 104-5.  P. Heid. Siegmann 207 (inv. 3069) (I).

305  --- 147.  P. Harris 17 (inv. 174 d) (IV: on the verso of accounts).

306  --- 151-54.  P. Oxy. 11.1378 (Christ's Hospital, West Horsham) (III, Oxy.).

     --- 160: see No. 1535.

307  --- Hypothesis and commentary.  P. Lit. Lond. 179 (Brit. Mus. inv. 131, 2, verso) (I, Meir; from the same papyrus as Nos. 163 and 197).  Refers to Aeschines, Contra Timarchum; cites Didymus.  F. G. Kenyon, Athenaion Politeia, 3rd ed., 215-19.

308  --- Lexicon to In Midiam.  C. Wessely, Stud. Pal. 4 (1905) 111-13 (P. Rain. inv. 7) (IV-V, Fayum; pap. cod.).  Quotes Aristotle, Res Publica Atheniensium 53.2-6.  Archiv 3.493.

309  --- Contra Androtionem 8-16.  PSI 11.1203 (II, Oxy.).

     --- 21-23: see No. 2289.

310  --- Commentary on Contra Androtionem.  U. Wilcken, Hermes 42 (1907) 374-418 (P. Strassb. inv. 84) (I-II; on the verso of accounts).  B. Keil, Anonymus Argentinensis (Strassburg 1902), is the ed. pr., published as an historical work.  Archiv 2.362; JAW 142.78-79.  R. Laqueur, Hermes 43 (1908) 220-28, prefers a recapitulation of a work "On Demosthenes"; S. de Ricci, Rev. Ét. Anc.

ll (1909) 30-32;  H. T. Wade-Gery and B. D. Meritt, Hesperia 26 (1957) 163-97, reedit and study in
relation to the Athenian tribute lists;  R. Sealey,
Hermes 86 (1958) 440-46, comments on the readings of Wade-Gery and Meritt.

311    --- Commentary on In Aristocratem 1-18, 209 (?).
       H.' M. Hubbell, Yale Class. Stud. 15 (1957) 181-93
       (Yale Univ. Libr., inv. 1534) (II; pap. cod.).
       Quotes Euripides, Phoenissae 543-44, and part of
       an unidentified verse (?).

312    --- In Aristocratem 51-54.   P. Mich. 3.142 (inv.
       4337) (II).

313    --- 79-80, 82-83.   P. Rain. 1.9 (inv. 26006) (III,
       Fayum; pap. cod.).

314    --- 110-19.   P. Oxy. 3.459 (Columbia Univ. Libr.)
       (III, Oxy.; pap. cod.).   Archiv 3.283.

315    --- 149-50.   P. Oxy. 6.883 (Morgan Libr., New
       York) (III, Oxy.).

316    --- 166-72.   E. M. Husselman, TAPA 76 (1945)
       120-25 (P. Mich. inv. 5472) (II, Karanis).

317    --- Lexicon to In Aristocratem.   BKT 1.78-82 (inv.
       5008) (IV-V, Fayum; pap. cod.).   Ed. pr.: F.
       Blass, Hermes 17 (1882) 148-63.   Quotes or refers
       to Anaximenes of Lampsacus, Philippica, Bk. i
       (?); Aristotle (?), Res Publica Lacedaemoniorum
       (?); Didymus; Ephorus, Bk. xxi (Jacoby, FGH
       2.64); Homer, Il. i.151; Philochorus, Atthis, Bks.
       iii (?) and v; Theopompus, Hellenica and Philip-
       pica (?); Xenophon (?), Res Publica Laconum.

318    --- In Timocratem 53-54, 56-58.   P. Oxy. 2.232;
       P. Lit. Lond. 128 (Brit. Mus. inv. 787) (II-III,
       Oxy.).   Archiv 1.524.

319    --- 63-65.   P. Oxy. 4.701 (Houghton Libr., Harvard
       Univ.) (II-III, Oxy.).   Archiv 3.493.

320    --- 65-66.   P. Aberdeen 120 (II, Fayum?).

321    --- 73-77.   P. Antin. 2.80 (IV, Antinoöpolis; parch.
       cod.).

322    --- 145-46, 150.   P. Oxy. 2.233 (Univ. of Penn-
       sylvania Mus., inv. 2757) (III, Oxy.).   Archiv 1.
       525.

323    --- 183-87.   P. Oxy. 15.1811 (Arch. Inst. of America)
       (III, Oxy.).

       --- See also No. 2300.

       --- In Aristogitonem i.40: see No. 1456.

324    --- ibid. 47-48.   P. Oxy. 6.882 (Yale Univ. Libr.)
       (II, Oxy.).

325    --- 63-67, with scholia.   P. Lit. Lond. 125 (Brit.
       Mus. Add. MS. 34473, art. 2) (V; vellum leaf).

326    --- In Aphobum i.5-7.   PSI 11.1202 (II, Oxy.).

327    --- Contra Phormionem 5-7.   P. Grenf. 2.10
       (Bodleian Libr., Gr. class. f.47 (P)) (II).

       --- 9: see No. 2128.

328    --- Contra Boëtum 7-23.   P. Oxy. 8.1093 (P. Cairo)
       (II, Oxy.).

       --- 10: see No. 2120.

329    --- 52-53.   P. Oxy. 4.702 (Houghton Libr., Har-
       vard Univ.) (II, Oxy.).

330    --- In Stephanum 25-26.   P. Rain. 1.10 (inv. 29824)
       (II).

331    --- Adversus Polyclem 24, 26.   P. Rain. 1.11 (inv.
       29816 b) (IV?).

332    --- De Corona Trierarchiae 7-10.   PSI 6.721 (II;
       text on recto, No. 2627 on verso).

333    --- Contra Dionysodorum 47-50.   M. Papathomo-
       poulos, Recherches Pap. 1 (1961) 37-39 (PIFAO,
       P.S.P. 234) (ca. A.D. 100-150).   C. Préaux, Chr.
       Ég. 36 (1961) 221.

334    --- Contra Theocrinem 15-18.   P. Ryl. 3.550 (II).

335    --- Prooemia 26-29.   P. Oxy. 1.26; P. Lit. Lond.
       129 (Brit. Mus. inv. 744) (II, Oxy.).   Roberts,
       GLH, pl. 19a; Schubart, Gr. Pal., Abb. 83; E.
       G. Turner, GR 21 (1952), pl. CXXII.   Archiv 1.116.
       Pasquali, Stor. Testo 293-94.

336    --- Epistula ii. 18-20, 23-25.   S. Eitrem and L.
       Amundsen, Eranos 54 (1956) 101-8 (P. Oslo inv.
       1471) (II).

337    --- Epistula iii.   Kenyon, Class. Texts 56-62; P.
       Lit. Lond. 130 (Brit. Mus. inv. 133) (I B.C.; from
       the same roll as No. 1234).   Pasquali, Stor. Tes-
       to 294.

       Demosthenes: see also Nos. 339, 458, 2070,
       2078-79, 2126, 2300, 2511.

       Dercylus: see Nos. 89, 196, 205.
       Dexippus of Cos: see No. 2339.

338    DICTYS CRETENSIS: Bellum Troianum.   P. Tebt.
       2.268 (III, Tebtunis; on the verso of revenue re-
       turns).   Archiv 6.260.   Jacoby, FGH 1.279-81;
       New Chapters 3.224-26.   W. Eisenhut, Dictys
       Cretensis (Lipsiae 1958) 134-39, reedits the text.

339    DIDYMUS: Commentary on Demosthenes, Philippica,
       Bk. iii.   BKT i (inv. 9780) (II, Hermupolis Mag-
       na; text on recto, No. 536 on verso).   Cites or
       quotes: Aeschylus, Eleusinioi (col. 14, line 12;
       Galiano, Aesch. 95: bibl.); Anaximenes of Lamp-
       sacus, Philippica vi (6.59), ibid. vii (ll.10-14), On
       Alexander ix (9.51; cf. Jacoby, FGH 2.123); An-
       drotion (passim; see Foucart, op. cit. infra, 159-
       211); Aristophanes, Aves 28 (ll.61), Ranae 237
       (ll.24); Aristotle, Nomima Barbarika iii (4.14),
       Epigram at Delphi (6.36), Paean for Hermias
       (6.18); Bryon, On Theocritus (the sophist of Chios)

(6.44); Callimachus, Hecala (14.33; cf. Pfeiffer, CFNR, No. 35, Callim. 1, fr. 495); Callisthenes, On Hermias (5.64; cf. Jacoby, FGH 2.640); Demon, the paroemiographer (11.64); Ps.-Demosthenes, Epistula Philippi, Or. xii (9.43-45), ibid. xii.23 (10.23-30; cf. Jander 10-11); Ps.-Demosthenes, Ad Philippi Epistulam (11.10-14, attributed to Anaximenes); Dinarchus, Ad Antiphanem de Equo (9.54; cf. Jander 14-15); Duris (12.50; cf. Jacoby, FGH 2.148); Euphorion (14.15; cf. Wilamowitz, Hermes 61, 1926, 289-91); Hermippus, On Aristotle ii (6.51); Homer, Il. xviii.56=437 (14.19), Od. xx.204 (11.22); Marsyas of Philippi (12.55; cf. Jacoby, FGH 2.740); Philemon, Lithoglyphus (9.61; cf. Page, GLP 1, No. 50; JAW 174.236-37); Philochorus (passim; see F. Blass, Archiv 3.288-89, Foucart, op. cit. infra, 159-211, M. Lenchantin de Gubernatis, Aeg. 2, 1921, 23-32, A. E. Raubitschek, Class. Med. 19, 1958, 73-109); Sophocles, Poimenes (14.10); Theopompus (passim; see Jacoby, FGH 2.545, 571-72, 582, 589-90, 598-99; B. P. Grenfell and A. S. Hunt, Hellenica Oxyrhynchia cum Theopompi et Cratippi Fragmentis, Oxonii 1909, Nos. 54, 158-59, 210, 216, 242); Timocles, Ikarioi (10.3), Heroes (9.70; cf. Demiańczuk 71-72, 88-89, Page, GLP 1, No. 51, Schroeder, NCF 60-61); Timosthenes, On Harbors (11.30); and two unknown writers (14.18; 5.52, Hermippus?). Schubart, PGB, tab. 20. Archiv 3.284-92; JAW 142.303-5; F. Leo, Gött. Nachr., 1904, 254-61; A. Koerte, Rh. Mus. 60 (1905) 388-416, especially on the citations of Timocles; W. Croenert, ibid. 62 (1907) 380-89; P. Foucart, MAI, 1909, 27-218, studies the numerous citations.

Didymus: see also Nos. 61, 157, 307, 317, 1205, 1382, 2289, 2292.

340 DINARCHUS: A public oration and In Philoclem 3-4. P. Antin. 2.62 and 81 (III, Antinoöpolis; parch. cod.). The editor suggests that the new public oration is possibly In Aristonicum or In Hagnonidem. H. Lloyd-Jones, CR, NS 11 (1961) 203, on In Philoclem.

Dinarchus: see also Nos. 339, 2128.

341 DIO CHRYSOSTOM: Orationes xiv.1-4, 6, 11; xv.28 (De Servitute et Libertate). H. J. M. Milne, JEA 16 (1930) 187-92 (Brit. Mus. inv. 2823) (IV; pap. cod.). Quotes Homer, Il. xii.326, Od. xii. 184-85 (identified by G. M. Bolling, CP 26, 1931, 315-16; Collart, Od., No. 82). Archiv 11.274.

Dio Chrysostom: see also No. 455.
Dio Chrysostom (?): see No. 2089.

342 DIOCLES OF CARYSTUS (?): Pathos, aetia, therapeia. P. Ryl. 1.39; P. Grenf. 2.7 b (Bodleian Libr., Gr. class. e.63 (P)); G. A. Gerhard, Sitzb. Heid. Akad., 1913, Abh. 13 (P. Heid. inv. 401); P. Hibeh 2.190 (Brit. Mus. inv. 2963) (III B.C., Hibeh; cart.). JEA 2.97; JAW 180.33. A. Koerte, Archiv 7.249-50, queries the attribution (M. Wellmann prefers Chrysippus of Cnidus, Physika theoremata); W. Jaeger, Diokles von Karystos (Berlin 1938) 33-37, accepts Diocles.

Diocles (comicus): see No. 1579.
Diocles (grammaticus): see No. 2069.
Diogenes of Babylon: see Nos. 2088, 2093, 2572.
Diogenes the Cynic: see Nos. 455, 1987-90.
Diogenes or Diogenianus: see No. 2089.
Diogenianus: see No. 2125.

343 DIONYSIUS: Bassarika (and Gigantias?). P. Lond. 2.273; P. Lit. Lond. 40 (Brit. Mus. inv. 273) (III-IV; bound in the same pap. cod. as No. 115). Heitsch, GDRK, fr. XIX; Page, GLP, No. 134. Archiv 2.351, 7.257-58; JEA 11.85, 17.118. F. G. Kenyon, Album Gratulatorium in Honorem Henrici Van Herwerden (Utrecht 1902) 137-42 (ed. pr. in part); J. Bidez, Rev. Phil. 27 (1903) 82, note 6, mistakenly suggested Soterichus as the author; A. Ludwich, Berl. Phil. Woch. 23 (1903) 27-30; H. I. Bell, CR 23 (1910) 223-24; H. J. M. Milne, Archiv 7 (1923) 3-10; Wilamowitz, ibid. 11-16; W. Morel, ibid. 9 (1928) 222-23; R. Keydell, Phil. Woch. 49 (1929) 1101, Hermes 67 (1932) 240-41; P. Maas, Byz. Zeitschr. 29 (1930) 383; A. Wifstrand, Eranos 28 (1930) 102-4, ibid. 29 (1931) 39; E. Orth, Phil. Woch. 52 (1932) 1316-17; Wifstrand, Kallim. Nonn. 178-83.

Dionysius: see also No. 1791.

Dionysius (grammaticus) see No. 2146.
Dionysius of Halicarnassus: see Nos. 1536, 2211.
Dionysius Itycaeus: see No. 2127.
Dionysius Phaselites: see No. 183.
Dionysius Sidonius: see No. 1205.
Dionysius of Syracuse: see No. 2292.

344 DIONYSIUS THRAX: Ars Grammatica. PSI 1.18 (V; a small opisthograph piece of pap., in the same hand as No. 1207).

345 --- Suppl. 4 (Tabulae Flexionum Verbi "typto"). P. Rein. 2.81 (P. Sorbonne inv. 2114) (IV; pap. cod.).

Dionysius Thrax (or Tryphonis?): see No. 2127.

Dionysius Tryphonis: see No. 2297.
Diophil (-?-): see No. 186.

346 DIOSCORIDES: De Materia Medica ii.76. C. Bonner, TAPA 53 (1922) 142-68 (P. Mich. inv. 3) (II). Roberts, GLH, pl. 15c. JEA 10.152.

347 --- iii.130-31. P. Aberdeen 8 (II, Fayum?). Ed. pr.: E. O. Winstedt, CQ 1 (1907) 263-64. Gazza 92.

--- Ibid. v: see No. 1997.

Dioscorides: see also No. 2409.

348 DIOSCORUS OF APHRODITO: Miscellaneous poems. P. Maspero 1.67055, 67097, 67120; 2.67131, 67177, 67179-81, 67183, 67185 verso, 67188; 3.67279 verso, 67315-18, 67338; P. Lit. Lond., p. 68 (bibl.); BKT 5.1.117-26 (inv. 10580, a part of the same pap. as P. Maspero 3.67317) (VI, Aphrodito and Antinoë; some poems on the verso of documents).

Norsa, SLG, tav. 17 (P. Maspero 67097); Schubart, Gr. Pal., Abb. 100 (P. Maspero 67097).
Heitsch, GDRK, fr. XLII, 1-7, 9-11, 13-17, 19-23,
26-28 (bibl.). J. Maspero, Byz. Zeitschr. 19
(1910) 1-6 (ed. pr. of P. Maspero 67055); Preisendanz, PGM 2, p. 202 (P. Maspero 67188, a prayer
for protection from evil spirits). F. della Corte,
Riv. Fil. 64 (1936) 399-404, shows that P. Berol.
10580 belongs to the same papyrus as P. Maspero
3.67317; on this, see Archiv 5.541, and facsimile
in Schubart, Gr. Pal., Abb. 101.

349    --- Panegyric of a Dux of the Thebaid. BKT 5.1.
114-17 (inv. 9799) (VI, Aphrodito; pap. cod.).
Page, GLP 1, No. 141. Archiv 5.540. A. Ludwich, Berl. Phil. Woch. 27 (1907) 495-96.

350    --- An epistle in iambics. R. Keydell, Byz.-neugr.
Jahrb. 10 (1934) 341-45 (P. Berol. inv. 13894) (VI,
Aphrodito?).

351    --- Miscellaneous poems; Greek-Coptic glossary.
P. Lond. 5.1817-21; P. Lit. Lond. 98-101, 188
(= the glossary) (Brit. Mus. inv. 1552, 1733, 1728
+ 1745, 1820, 1727 = the glossary); P. Rein. 2.82
(P. Sorbonne inv. 2070, from the same pap. as
Brit. Mus. inv. 1552) (VI, Aphrodito and Antinoë;
some texts on the verso of documents). Heitsch,
GDRK, fr. XLII, 12, 18, 22, 24-25. Archiv 10.
28-30, 14.111. On the glossary: Coptic Bibl., No.
1840; H. I. Bell and W. E. Crum, Aeg. 6 (1925)
177-226; W. Croenert, Gnomon 2 (1926) 654-66.

352    --- A petition in hexameters, to a poliarchos. G.
Malz, AJP 60 (1939) 172-76 (Walters Art Gallery,
Baltimore, inv. 517) (VI, Aphrodito). Heitsch,
GDRK, fr. XLII, 8. Archiv 14.109.

353    --- A petition in hexameters. G. Malz, AJP 60
(1939) 176-77 (Walters Art Gallery, Baltimore,
inv. 516)-(VI, Aphrodito?). Archiv 14.109.

354    --- Metrological tables and problems. P. Lond.
5.1718, verso (VI, Antinoë; on the verso of a
document).

355    --- Conjugations of poieô, chrysoô, and boaô.
P. Maspero 2.67176, 67275, 3.67351 (VI, Aphrodito?; partly on the verso of a Coptic document).

356    --- Conjugation of poieô. P. M. Meyer, Griechische Papyrusurkunden der Hamburger Staats-
und Universitätsbibliothek 1 (Leipzig-Berlin 1911-
24), No. 68 (P. Hamb. inv 175, verso) (VI, Aphrodito?; on the verso of a document).

Dioscorus: see also No. 2080. For a summary
of his writings, with bibliography, see G. Malz,
Studi Calderini-Paribeni 2.345-56.

Diphilus: see No. 1591.
Dorotheus: see No. 2279.
Duris: see Nos. 339, 2194.
Empedocles: see Nos. 455, 2301, 2569.
Epaphroditus: see No. 186.

357    EPHORUS (?): Historiae, Bk. xii (or xi). P. Oxy.
13. 1610; P. Lit. Lond. 109 (Brit. Mus. inv. 2470)
(II-III, Oxy.). Bilabel, No. 3; Jacoby, FGH 2.
96-97; M. Gigante, Frammenti sulla Penteconta-
ĕtia (P. Oxy. 1610) (Napoli 1948). Archiv 7.229-30.
P. Collart, Rev. Phil. 43 (1919) 57-58; M. Hombert, Chr. Ég. 26 (1951) 432; T. W. Africa, AJP
83 (1962) 86-89, queries the attribution.

358    --- Res Publica Cretensium (?). F. G. Kenyon,
Rev. Phil. 21 (1897) 1-4; P. Lit. Lond. 114 (Brit.
Mus. inv. 187) (II; text on recto, No. 1408 on
verso).

Ephorus: see also Nos. 317, 458, 1205, 2179,
2181-82, 2189.

359    EPICHARMUS: A list of his plays. P. Oxy. 25.2426
(II, Oxy.). Lists the "Promatheus or Pyrrha,"
the "Odysseus Automolos," the "Odysseus Nau-
agos" (?), the "Medea" (perhaps that of Deinolochus, here credited to Epicharmus), and the
"Persai" (?).

360    --- Fragments of various plays. P. Oxy. 25.2427
(II-III, Oxy.). Sixty-seven small fragments, representing the "Promatheus or Pyrrha" (?), the
"Hebas Gamos (?) or the "Mousai" (?), the "Sphinx,"
and possibly other plays.

361    --- Odysseus Automolos. T. Gomperz, Raineri
M. 5.1-10 (II, Arsinoë?). Aristoxenus is mentioned in a scholium. G. Kaibel, Com. Gr. Fr.
1.1.108-9 (fr. 99); Olivieri 31-33; Page, GLP 1,
No. 37; Winter, LLP 223. F. Blass, Neue Jahrb.
139 (1889) 257-62; W. B. Stanford, CP 45 (1950)
167-69; A. Barigazzi, Rh. Mus. 98 (1955) 121-35.

362    --- Commentary on the Odysseus Automolos (and
another play?). P. Oxy. 25.2429 (II, Oxy.).
Mentions Aristoxenus (the poet A. the Selinunti-
an, or a commentator?); quotes Homer, Il. x.
511, Od. xviii.74, xix.446. H. Lloyd-Jones, CR,
NS 11 (1961) 17-18.

Epicharmus: see also Nos. 1623-24, 2898.

363    --- Ps.-Epicharmus (Axiopistus?): Sententiae.
P. Hibeh 1.1; P. Lit. Lond. 56 (Brit. Mus. inv.
1821) (III B.C., Hibeh; cart.). Roberts, GLH, pl.
2b. Demiańczuk 123-24; Olivieri 90-93.

364    --- Idem. P. Hibeh 1.2 (Bodleian Libr., Gr. class.
f.78 (P)) (III B.C., Hibeh; cart.). Olivieri 98;
J. U. Powell, New Chapters 1.18-21, CA 221-22.
Archiv 5.553.

Ps.-Epicharmus: see also Nos. 1567-69, 1572.

Epicurus: see Nos. 2289, 2569, 2574-79.
Erasistratus: see No. 2339.
Eratosthenes: see Nos. 1348, 2069, 2078, 2089,
2188, 2290.

365    ERINNA: Alakata (?). PSI 9.1090 (II, Oxy.).
Ed. pr.: G. Vitelli, BSAA 24 (1929) 9-16. C. M.
Bowra, New Chapters 3.180-85; Diehl, Anth. Lyr.
1².4.207-11 (bibl.); Galiano, LG 127-28; Page,

GLP 1, No. 120. Archiv 10.21-23; JEA 16.121.
L. A. Stella, Rend. Ist. Lomb. 62 (1929) 827-38;
A. Vogliano, Gnomon 5 (1929) 171, 288; P. Maas,
Hermes 69 (1934) 206-9, reedits the text; C. M.
Bowra, Greek Poetry and Life: Essays Presented
to Gilbert Murray... (Oxford 1936) 325-42; J.
M. Edmonds, Mnemos., Ser. 3.6 (1938) 195-203;
A. Vogliano, Athen., NS 21 (1943) 32-37; P. Collart, CRAI, 1944, 183-99; C. M. Bowra, Problems in Greek Poetry (Oxford 1953) 151-68; M.
Cervelli, Annali dell'Istituto Superiore "S. Chiara"
di Napoli 4 (1953) 195-246; K. Latte, Gött. Nachr.,
1953, 79-94; F. Scheidweiler, Philol. 100 (1956)
40-51; D. N. Levin, HSCP 66 (1962) 193-204 (p.
201: bibl.).

Erinna: see also No. 1889.

366   EUCLID: Elementa i, Definitiones 1-10. P. Mich.
3.143 (inv. 925) (III).

367   --- i.39, 41. P. Fay. 9 (Mt. Holyoke Coll.) (II,
Euhemeria). Archiv 2.380.

368   --- ii.5. P. Oxy. 1.29 (Univ. of Pennsylvania Mus.
inv. 2748) (III-IV?, Oxy.). Archiv 1.117; JAW
108.83. E. G. Turner would date this earlier
than saec. III-IV.

Eudemus (or Ecdemus): see No. 2108.
Eudemus: see No. 2346.
Eudorus: see No. 2569.

369   EUDOXUS: Ars Astronomica. P. Par. 1 (II B.C.,
Serapaeum, Memphis?; text combined with documents). Edited by one Leptines; one column, in
iambics, gives the title as an acrostic. Page,
GLP 1, No. 112; Neugebauer, Astron. Pap. Ostr.,
No. 30 (bibl.); Weitzmann, Anc. Bk. Ill. 6 and
fig. 2 ("oldest illustrated Greek papyrus known
today"); idem, Ill. RC 49-50 (bibl.) and pl. 37.

Eudoxus: see also No. 2011.

370   EUPHORION: Arai (?). BKT 5.1.57-66 (inv. 273;
once loaned to the Cairo Mus.) (V, Hermupolis
Magna; parch. cod.). Schubart, PGB, tab. 43b.
Page, GLP 1, No. 121a; J. U. Powell, New Chapters 1.110-11, CA 31, 40. Archiv 5.536. A. Ludwich, Berl. Phil. Woch. 27 (1907) 490; P. Cors-
sen, Philol. 72 (1913) 459-60; A. Barigazzi, SIFC,
NS 24 (1950) 21-27, regards the attribution to the
Arai as certain.

371   --- Thrax and Hippomedon Maior. PSI 14.1390
(II, Oxy.). Hellanicus (?) is mentioned in a
scholium. Ed. pr.: M. Norsa and G. Vitelli,
Ann. Sc. Pisa, Ser. 2.4 (1935) 3-14. Lesky,
GGL 691-92; Page, GLP 1, No. 121b. Archiv 13.
84-86. I. Cazzaniga, Rend. Ist. Lomb. 68 (1935)
769-76; K. Latte, Philol. 90 (1935) 129-55; E.
Lobel, Riv. Fil. 63 (1935) 67-68; P. Maas, Gnomon 11 (1935) 102-4; F. Pfister, Phil. Woch. 55
(1935) 1357-60; A. Barigazzi, Aeg. 27 (1947) 53-
107 (bibl.), Athen. 36 (1948) 34-64; V. Bartoletti, Riv. Fil. 76 (1948) 26-36, on Parthenius'
relation to Euphorion; I. Cazzaniga, Miscellanea
G. Galbiati (Milano 1951) 49-69, reedits the frag-

ments of the Hippomedon, and accepts the view
that it forms a part of the Thrax; P. Treves,
Euforione e la storia ellenistica (Milano-Napoli
1955) 48-54; H. Lloyd-Jones, Gnomon 31 (1959)
111.

372   --- Fragments. P. Oxy. 19.2219 (II, Oxy.; from
the same pap. as No. 2835?). Archiv 16.84.

373   --- Fragments. P. Oxy. 19.2220 (and ibid., p.
146) (I, Oxy.). Archiv 16.84.

374   --- Scholia on the Chiliades (?). P. Oxy. 17.2085
(II, Oxy.). Mention Callimachus, On Rivers
(Pfeiffer, Callim. 1, fr. 457). Archiv 10.228-29;
JEA 22.57.

Euphorion: see also Nos. 339, 1783, 1785, 1858.

375   EUPOLIS: Demoi. G. Lefebvre, Papyrus de
Ménandre; Catalogue général des antiquités égyptiennes du Musée du Caire, 1911, pp. xxi-xxiii
(P. Cairo inv. 43227) (IV-V, Aphroditopolis; from
the same pap. cod. as No. 1301). Fr. 2, recto,
line 7, imitates a line from Cratinus, Euneidae.
Lesky, GGL 401; Page, GLP 1, No. 40; M. Platnauer, New Chapters 3.161-63; Demiańczuk 43-49.
Identified independently by A. Koerte, Berl. Phil.
Woch. 31 (1911) 1546-47, Hermes 47 (1912) 276-313,
and J. van Leeuwen, Mnemos. 40 (1912) 129-36,
207-8. Archiv 6.223; JEA 7.89; JAW 174.176-79,
195.163-65. B. Keil, Gött. Nachr., 1912, 237-55;
A. Mayer, Berl. Phil. Woch. 32 (1912) 830-32;
P. Maas, ibid. 861-62; C. Jensen, Hermes 51
(1916) 321-54; A. Olivieri, Atti Acad. Napoli, NS
11 (1930) 99-110; G. Norwood, Greek Comedy
(London 1931) 179-88; E. Wuest, Philol. 91 (1936)
114-15; J. M. Edmonds, Mnemos., Ser. 3.8 (1939)
1-20, on the plot; W. Schmid, Philol. 93 (1939)
413-29; F. Dornseiff, Hermes 75 (1940) 229-31;
S. Eitrem, SO 26 (1948) 171-73.

376   --- (?). P. Oxy. 10.1240 (P. Cairo) (II, Oxy.).
New Chapters 3.162. Archiv 7.142-43; JAW 174.
179-80. Wilamowitz, Hermes 54 (1919) 69.

377   --- Prospaltioi (?). PSI 11.1213 (I, Oxy.). Lines
14-17 parody Sophocles, Antigone 712-15. Ed. pr.:
M. Norsa and G. Vitelli, BSAA 28 (1933) 137-42.
Norsa, SLG, tav. 9 a. Lesky, GGL 399; Page,
GLP 1, No. 41. Archiv 11.263; JAW 263.4-5.
R. Goossens, Chr. Ég. 10 (1935) 378, ibid. 11
(1936) 516, Rev. Phil., Sér. 3.9 (1935) 333-49;
M. Galiano, Arbor 6 (1946) 132-33; G. Schiassi,
PP 10 (1955) 295-306.

Eupolis: see also Nos. 1186, 1632, 2121, 2126.

378   EURIPIDES: Closing chorus of Alcestis (lines 1155-
1163), Andromacha, etc. P. Hibeh 1.25 (Yale
Univ. Libr.) (III B.C., Hibeh; cart.; sch. ex.?).

--- Alcestis: see also No. 454.

379   --- Andromacha 5-6, 8-28, 30-36, 39-48. P. Oxy.
3.449 (Musées Royaux, Bruxelles, inv. E.5950)
(III, Oxy.; pap. cod.).

--- Andromacha 204: see No. 246.

380 --- 907-14. P. Harris 39 (inv. 181 a) (III).

381 --- 954-1022. P. Oxy. 22.2335 (II, Oxy.).

382 --- 957-59, 988-90, 1239-42, 1273-76. P. Ross. Georg. 1.8 (Libr. of the Hermitage Mus., Leningrad, inv. 15d) (VIII, Sinai?; two strips of parch. used to repair the spine of a cod.).

383 --- 1134-42, 1164-72. G. Manteuffel, JJP 2 (1948) 84-87 (P. Berol. inv. 13418) (V; pap. cod.).

384 --- Bacchae 1, written several times. P. Tebt. 3. 901 (II?, Tebtunis; cart.; sch. ex.).

385 --- 459-71, 496-508 (with parts of twenty-two lines perhaps from the lost portion of the play). P. Antin. 1.24 (V, Antinoöpolis; pap. cod.). E. R. Dodds, Euripides: Bacchae (Oxford 1944), "Introduction," liv-lv, and "Appendix" 230 (first mention).

--- 642: see No. 2291.

--- 968: see No. 1301.

386 --- 1070-91, 1093-1136 (with parts of four lines perhaps from the lost portion of the play). P. Oxy. 19.2223 (II, Oxy.). E. R. Dodds, op. cit. (see (No. 385) liii-liv, 230-31; R. Merkelbach, Rh. Mus. 97 (1954) 373-75, explains line 1104a as an interpolation to clarify the syntax.

387 --- 1154-59, 1183-86. P. Antin. 2.73 (V-VI, Antinoöpolis; pap. cod.). In the same hand as P. Antin. 1.23 (see No. 406). E. R. Dodds, Euripides: Bacchae (Oxford 1960$^2$), "Introduction" lix (first mention).

388 --- Electra, hypothesis of lines 341-584. P. Oxy. 3.420; P. Lit. Lond. 72 (Brit. Mus. inv. 1524) (III, Oxy.). Archiv 3.277.

--- 367-79: see No. 1569.

--- 388-89: see No. 1567.

--- Hecuba 20-21, 503-4: see No. 1571.

--- 254-56: see No. 1567.

389 --- 700-3, 737-40. P. Oxy. 6.876 (P. Princ.) (V, Oxy.; pap. cod.).

390 --- 1252-80. P. Oxy. 6.877 (Univ. of Pennsylvania Mus., inv. E.3075) (III, Oxy.).

391 --- Helena 630-51, 658-74. P. Oxy. 22.2336 (I B.C., Oxy.). K. Latte, Gnomon 27 (1955) 498; G. Zuntz, Mnemos., Ser 4.14 (1961) 122-25, 238; R. Kannicht, ibid. 321-22.

--- 676: see No. 1838.

--- 1261: see No. 246.

--- Hercules 57-59, 1337-39: see No. 455.

392 --- 1092-99. P. Heid. Siegmann 205 (inv. 1120 a) (ca. 250 B.C., Hibeh).

393 --- Hippolytus 1-103. H. Cadell, Recherches Pap. 2 (1962) 25-36 (P. Sorbonne inv. 2252) (III-II B.C., Ghoran; cart.).

394 --- 243-367, 375-430, 492-515. BKT 5.2.88-96 (inv. 5005) (VI, Arsinoë; parch. cod.). JAW 147.100. Pasquali, Stor. Testo 191-92.

--- 403-4, 406-10, 413-23: see No. 1568.

395 --- 579-604. P. Oxy. 19.2224 (II, Oxy.).

396 --- 616-24. BKT 5.2.96-97 (inv. 4758) (II B.C., Thebes; ostr.; sch. ex.). Wilcken, Gr. Ostr. 2.1147.

--- 664-68: see No. 1573.

397 --- 1165-79, 1194-1204. P. Lit. Lond. 73 (Brit. Mus. inv. 2652 B) (III B.C., Philadelphia). JAW 238.115. Roberts, GLH, pl. 3a.

398 --- Hypothesis of the Hippolytus. P. Mil. Vogl. 2.44 (inv. 84) (I; on the verso of a document).

399 --- Ion 732 (quoted in a document). Stud. Pal. 5 (1905), No. 125 (p. 68), fr. 2, line 7.

--- Iphigenia Aulidensis 28: see No. 246.

--- ibid. 790-91: see No. 1571.

400 --- Iphigenia Taurica 174-77, 179-91, 245-55, 272-86, 581-95, 600-27, 629. P. Hibeh 1.24 (Cambridge Univ. Libr., add. 4461) (III B.C., Hibeh; cart.).

401 --- Medea 5-12. P. Didot, pp. 16-18 (II B.C., Serapaeum, Memphis; from the same composite roll as Nos. 31, 1319-20, 1435). F. Blass, Rh. Mus. 35 (1880) 82-83.

402 --- 20-26, 57-63; Orestes 445-1371 (with many lacunae). P. Oxy. 11.1370 (Williams Coll. Libr.) (V, Oxy.; pap. cod.). K. F. W. Schmidt, Gött. Anz., 1918, 100-1. Pasquali, Stor. Testo 192-93.

403 --- Medea 507, 513-17, 545-60. BKT 5.2.97-98 (inv. 13243) (V, Hermupolis Magna; pap. cod.).

404 --- 710-15. P. Oxy. 3.450 (Univ.-Bibl., Graz) (III, Oxy.; on the verso of a document). Archiv 3.277.

405 --- 719-23, 1046-53, 1156-60, 1165-77, 1191-99, 1279-99, 1301-28. P. Harris 38 (Fitzwilliam Mus., MS. Add. 109; formerly P. Harris inv. 179) (II). JEA 24.94. D. Page, CQ 32 (1938) 45-46.

406 --- 825-40, 865-78, with a few scholia. P. Antin. 1.23 (V-VI, Antinoöpolis; pap. cod.). In the same hand as P. Antin. 2.73 (see No. 387).

--- 844-65, etc.: see No. 426.

407    --- 1057-62, 1086-92.  H. J. M. Milne, CR 49
(1935) 14 (University Coll., London) (IV-V, Arsinoe; parch. cod.).

408    --- 1149-63, 1171-90.  P. Oxy. 22.2337 (I, Oxy.;
on the verso of a document).

--- Orestes 6, 9-10: see No. 1592.

409    --- Orestes 53-61, 89-97.  P. Oxy. 13.1616 (P.
Cairo) (V, Oxy.; parch. cod.).

410    --- 205-24, 226-47.  C. W. Keyes, CP 33 (1938)
411-13 (Columbia Univ. Libr., inv. 517 A) (I B.C.).

--- 268-69: see No. 1950.

411    --- 338-43, with musical notation.  K. Wessely,
Raineri M. 5.65-73 (P. Vindob. G. 2315) (ca.
200 B.C., Hermupolis Magna). A. M. Dale, The
Lyric Metres of Greek Drama (Cambridge 1948)
2-3, 197-98; C. Ianus (K. von Jan), Musici
Scriptores Graeci (Lipsiae 1899), No. 1; E. Martin, Trois documents de musique grecque (Paris
1953) 14-24; J. F. Mountford, New Chapters 2.
148-49, 168-69, and passim; Pöhlmann, GMF
20-21, 41; T. Reinach, La Musique grecque
(Paris 1926) 175-76; O. Tiby, La musica in Grecia e a Roma (Firenze 1942) 171-72; R. P. Winnington-Ingram, Mode in Ancient Greek Music
(Cambridge 1936) 31-32. JAW 104.5-8; Chr. Ég.
5 (1930) 279-80. O. Crusius, Philol. 52 (1894)
174-200; C. F. Abdy Williams, CR 8 (1894)
313-17; C. Torr, ibid. 397-98; W. B. Sedgwick,
Class. Med. 11 (1950) 222-24; E. G. Turner,
JHS 76 (1956) 95-96, revises Wessely's dating
(saec. I) to about 200 B.C.; R. P. Winnington-
Ingram, Lustrum 3 (1958) 9; D. D. Feaver, AJP
81 (1960) 1-15; H. Hunger and E. Pöhlmann, WS
75 (1962) 76-78, give a new facsimile and im-
proved transcription; G. A. Longman, CQ, NS
12 (1962) 61-66.

--- 445-1371: see No. 402.

412    --- 754-64.  W. G. Waddell, Ét. Pap. 1 (1932) 15
(No. 7) (P. Cairo inv. 56224) (I-II, Oxy.).

413    --- 1062-85, 1087-90.  J. Nicole, Rev. Phil. 19
(1895) 105-8 (P. Genève inv. 91) (II-III, Fayum).

--- 1155-56: see No. 1576.

414    --- 1313-26, 1335-50, 1356-60.  P. Oxy. 9.1178
(P. Cairo) (I B.C., Oxy.).

--- Phoenissae 3: see No. 1934.

415    --- 31-35.  P. Antin. 2.74 (VI-VII, Antinoöpolis;
sch. ex.?). J. de M. Johnson, JEA 1 (1914) 176
(presumably the first mention).

--- 40, etc.: see No. 455.

416    --- 105-18, 128-40.  H. R. Hall, CR 18 (1904) 2;
P. Lit. Lond. 75 (Egyptian Dept., Brit. Mus.,
inv. 18711) (II B.C.; ostr.; sch. ex.). Archiv
3.484. N. Levitt, AJP 83 (1962) 422-23.

417    --- 171-85, 220-26.  P. Oxy. 9.1177 (Univ. of
Illinois Libr., inv. 1177) (I, Oxy.; on the verso
of a cursive text).

418    --- 307-10, 337-41.  P. Rain. 3.21 (inv. 29769)
(VI-VII; pap. cod.).

419    --- Scholia on 344-1108.  P. Würzb. 1 (inv. 18)
(VI, Hermupolis?; "Privatarbeit eines mittel-
mässigen Schulmeisters"; pap. cod.). Archiv
11.258-59; JAW 259.56. U. Wilcken, Abh. Berl.
Akad., Abh. 6.7-22.

420    --- 446-637, revised (or an original tragedy?).
PSI 13.1303 (II-III, Oxy.; on the verso of ac-
counts). Ed. pr.: M. Norsa and G. Vitelli, Ann.
Sc. Pisa, Ser. 2.4 (1935) 14-16. Page, GLP 1,
No. 33. Archiv 13.102. A. Garzya, Aeg. 32
(1952) 389-98.

--- 529-34: see No. 2642.

--- 543-44: see No. 311.

--- 606: see No. 1356.

421    --- 646-57, 1017-43, 1064-71.  P. Ryl. 3.547; P.
Oxy. 2.224; P. Lit. Lond 76 (Brit. Mus. inv.
783) (II-III, Oxy.). Archiv 1.510. Wilamowitz,
Gr. Versk. 177-78.

422    --- 786-806.  P. Merton 2.54 (II, Arsinoïte nome?;
on the verso of a document; sch. ex.?). J. Bingen, JEA 48 (1962) 54.

423    --- 1027-49.  PSI 11.1193 (II, Oxy.). JAW 259.55-56.

424    --- 1079-95.  G. Manteuffel, JJP 2 (1948) 81-84
(P. Berol. inv. 11868) (II).

425    --- 1097-1107, 1126-37.  W. Weinberger, Raineri
M. 5.74-77 (IV-V; wooden tablet; on the verso
of No. 227). Pasquali, Stor. Testo 193-94.

426    --- 1500-81, 1710-36; Medea 844-65, 977-81, 1087-
1115, 1251-92, 1389-1419; Melanippa Desmotis (?)
(anthology of lyrics from Euripides). W. Croenert, Gött. Nachr., 1922, 17-26 (P. Strassb. WG
304-307) (III B.C.?; cart.; from the same roll
as Nos. 170, 1349, 1592, 1698, 1735). Archiv 7.
256-57, 13.99. N. Lewis, Ét. Pap. 3 (1936) 52
(No. 5); B. Snell, Hermes, Einzelschr. 5 (1937)
69-84. Page, GLP 1, No. 13, queries the attribution to the Melanippa Desmotis.

427    --- Rhesus 48-96.  U. Wilcken, Sitzb. Berl. Akad.,
1887, 813-16; P. Achmîm 4 (now P. Par., Bibl.
Nat., Suppl. grec 1099, 2) (IV-V, Panopolis;
pap. cod.).

428    --- Hypotheses of the Rhesus, Rhadamanthys, and
Scyrii.  PSI 12.1286 (II). Ed. pr.: C. Gallavotti, Riv. Fil. 61 (1933) 177-88. Archiv 11.257-
58; JAW 259.61-62. A. Koerte, Hermes 69

(1934) 1-12, on the Scyrii; E. Bickel, Rh. Mus.
86 (1937) 1-22, on the relation of the Scyrii to
Livius Andronicus, Achilles; V. Steffen, Travaux
de la Société des Sciences et des Lettres de Wroclaw, Seria A, Nr. 54 (1954) 73-78, on the Rhadamanthys; B. Snell, WS 69 (1956) 90.

429 --- Commentary on Troades 9 ff. Sam Eitrem
and L. Amundsen, Studi Calderini-Paribeni 2.
147-50 (P. Oslo inv. 1662) (V, Upper Egypt; on
the verso of a pap. with blank recto). Quotes
Philochorus, Atthis, Bk. v (an error for Bk. iv);
Thucydides i.112.5.

430 --- Troades 876-79. BKT 5.2.98 (inv. 17651) (I;
wooden tablet; sch. ex.).

--- 886: see No. 1456.

--- Aegeus: see Nos. 1186, 1575.

--- Aeolus: see No. 454.

--- Alcmaeon per Corinthum: see No. 2290.

431 --- Alcmaeon. PSI 13.1302 (II, Oxy.). Probably
Alcmaeon in Psophis rather than A. through
Corinth. Archiv 16.103. W. Schadewaldt, Hermes
80 (1952) 46-66 (= idem, Hellas u. Hesperien,
Zürich u. Stuttgart 1960, 316-34).

--- Alcmena: see No. 1704.

432 --- Alexander. W. Croenert, Gött. Nachr., 1922,
1-17 (P. Strassb. WG 2342-2344) (I B.C.). New
Chapters 3.138-40; Archiv 7.255-56; JEA 25.72.
Page, GLP 1, No. 9. B. Snell, Hermes, Einzel-
schr. 5 (1937) 1-68, reedits the text; F. Scheid-
weiler, Philol. 97 (1948) 321-35, on the plot; B.
Menegazzi, Dion., NS 14 (1951) 172-97 (ditto); A.
Pertusi, ibid. 15 (1952) 251-73, on the Trojan
trilogy, to which the play belongs; F. Jouan, Rev.
Ét. Gr. 70 (1957) XV-XVI, on the plot; Lesky,
GGL 360-61.

--- See No. 1456.

--- Antigona: see No. 455.

433 --- Antiopa. P. Petrie 1.1-2; P. Lit. Lond. 70
(Brit. Mus. inv. 485) (III B.C., Gurob; cart.).
Arnim, SE 18-22; A. Nauck, Tragicae Dictionis
Index (Petersburg 1892), pp. xv-xxi; Page, GLP
1, No. 10; A. W. Pickard-Cambridge, New Chapters 3.106-13; H. Schaal, De Euripidis Antiopa
(Berolini 1914). JAW 71.259-67; JEA 8.86. H.
Weil, Rev. Ét. Gr. 3 (1890) 480-85; J. P. Mahaffy, Hermathena 8 (1891) 38-51 (ed. pr.); W.
G. Rutherford and L. Campbell, CR 5 (1891) 123-
26, 401-2; S. Eitrem, Vid. Forh., Christiania,
1906, Avh. 10, 7-8; N. Wecklein, Philol. 79
(1923) 51-69; C. H. Roberts, CQ 29 (1935) 164-66.

--- See No. 1572.

434 --- Archelaus (including a part of the prologue).
P. Hamb. 118 (inv. 639-640) (III-II B.C.; on the
verso of a legal document). Archiv 16.103.

435 --- Archelaus. P. Oxy. 3.419 (Musées Royaux,
Bruxelles; later, Univ. de Louvain: deperdita)
(II-III, Oxy.). New Chapters 3.147. Archiv 3.
277; JAW 147.109-10.

--- See Nos. 1456, 1704.

--- Auge: see No. 246.

436 --- Cresphontes (or extracts from that play?).
P. Oxy. 27.2458 (III, Oxy.). Marginal sigla
suggest an actors' copy.

437 --- Cretenses. BKT 5.2.73-79 (Perg. Berol.
13217) (I-II; parch. cod.). Schubart, PGB, tab.
30a. Arnim, SE 22-24; Hunt, TGFP, No. 5;
Page, GLP 1, No. 11. New Chapters 3.129-31;
Archiv 5.566; JAW 147.97-99. M. Croiset, Rev.
Ét. Gr. 28 (1915) 217-33, on the plot; C. H.
Roberts, CQ 29 (1935) 166-67.

--- See No. 451.

--- Danae: see Nos. 1456, 1576.

--- Dictys: see No. 246.

--- Erectheus: see No. 1536.

438 --- Hypsipyla. P. Oxy. 6.852 (Bodleian Libr.)
(II-III, Oxy.; on the verso of an account). Schu-
bart, Gr. Pal., Abb. 87. Arnim, SE 48-67;
Hunt, TGFP, No. 4; G. Italie, Euripidis Hypsipyla (Berolini 1923); Page, GLP 1, No. 12; O.
Schroeder, Euripidis Cantica (Lipsiae 1910) 174-
77. Archiv 5.567; New Chapters 3.120-29. J.
P. Mahaffy, Hermathena 15 (1909) 347-52; E.
Menozzi, AR 12 (1909) 313-19, SIFC 18 (1910) 1-18,
on the plot; G. Przychocki, WS 31 (1909) 300-5;
C. Robert, Hermes 44 (1909) 376-402, on the
legend; N. Wecklein, Sitzb. Münch. Akad., 1909,
Abh. 8; K. F. W. Schmidt, Gött. Anz., 1910,
643-48; E. Petersen, Rh. Mus. 68 (1913) 584-95,
on the plot; R. Onorato, Atti Acc. Napoli, NS 3
(1915) 193-213; M. T. Colombo, Dion. 11 (1948)
43-51, on the plot; M. F. Galiano, Human. 3
(1950-51) 301-3; U. Scatena, Dion., NS 13 (1950)
3-17; G. Schiassi, Riv. Fil. 81 (1953) 193-208,
on the roles of Euneos and Thoas; idem, ibid.
82 (1954) 1-17, on the role of Hypsipyla.

439 --- P. Petrie 2.49 (c); P. Lit. Lond. 74 (Brit. Mus.
inv. 590) (III B.C., Gurob; cart.). Identified by
F. Petersen, Hermes 49 (1914) 156-58, 623-26.

440 --- (?). P. Petrie 2.49 (d). CC; P. Lit. Lond.
81 (Brit. Mus. inv. 591 A) (III B.C., Gurob; cart.).
C. Haeberlin, Woch. Phil. 13 (1896) 988-89, recognizes, in line 1, Euripides, fr. 403.2 (assigned
by Stobaeus to the Ino), and suggests a florilegium;
H. J. M. Milne, CR 40 (1926) 64, attributes the
whole text to the Hypsipyla; B. Snell, WS 69
(1956) 95, rejects the Hypsipyla, and notes that
lines 5-6 match Euripides, Fab. Incert., fr.
965, Nauck².

--- See No. 1381.

--- Ino: see Nos. 440, 1456, 2642.

441 --- Melanippa Desmotis (?). BKT 5.2.84-87
(inv. 5514) (V, Arsinoë; parch. cod.). Ed. pr.:
F. Blass, Zeitschr. Aeg. Spr. 18 (1880) 37-40.
Schubart, Gr. Pal., Abb. 94; Wilcken, TAGP,
Taf. IV. Arnim, SE 29-31; Page, GLP 1, No.
13. New Chapters 3.113-20; JAW 26.54-56, 147.
99-100. F. Blass, Rh. Mus. 35 (1880) 290-97;
H. Weil, Rev. Phil. 4 (1880) 8-9, 121-24; Wilamowitz, Sitzb. Berl. Akad., 1921, 63-80.

--- See Nos. 426, 1456, 1568, 1625.

442 --- Meleager (?). D. L. Page, CQ 31 (1937) 178-
81 (Ashmolean Mus., Oxford; formerly University Coll., London) (III B.C.; cart.). Page,
GLP 1, No. 27. Archiv 13.99.

--- See No. 1579.

443 --- Oedipus. P. Oxy. 27.2459 (IV, Oxy.; roll
or pap. cod.?).

444 --- Phaethon. BKT 5.2.79-84 (inv. 9771) (III B.C.,
Hermupolis Magna). Schubart, PGB, tab. 4b.
Arnim, SE 69-72; O. Schroeder, Euripidis Cantica (Lipsiae 1910) 172-74. Archiv 5.569; JAW
147.99; New Chapters 3.143-47.

445 --- Phaethon. Mentioned by A. Dain, BAGB, Sér.
4, 1959, 396, and P. Mertens, Chr. Ég. 36 (1961)
430 (P. Par., Bibl. Nat., MS Grec 107 B) (V,
Egypt?; parch. cod.).

--- Phoenix: see Nos. 246, 2295.

--- Phrixus: see No. 1703.

--- Pirithous: see Nos. 254, 1456.

--- Protesilaus: see Nos. 1568, 1573.

--- Rhadamanthys: see No. 428.

446 --- Sciron (?): hypothesis and a few lines. P. Amh.
2.17 (VI-VII; pap. cod.). Steffen, Sat. Gr. Fr.
110. Archiv 2.354; JAW 129.75-76. H. Weil,
Journ. Sav., 1901, 741-43; L. Radermacher,
Rh. Mus. 57 (1902) 138; A. Olivieri, Riv. Ind.
Gr. Ital. 18 (1934) 49-60; G. Zuntz, The Political Plays of Euripides (Manchester 1955) 134,
note 3, queries the attribution to the Sciron.

--- Scyrii: see Nos. 246, 428, 1203.

447 --- Telephus, Prologue. A. Calderini, Aeg. 15
(1935) 239-45 (P. Med.) (II B.C., Memphis).
Norsa, SLG, tav. 4. Page, GLP 1, No. 17;
Srebrny, Stud. Scaen. 8, note 4. Archiv 13.98-
99. R. Goossens, Chr. Ég. 11 (1936) 139-50,
511-15; E. W. Handley and J. Rea, BICSL, Bull.
Supplement 5 (1957) 18-19.

448 --- Telephus. P. Oxy. 27.2460 (I, Oxy.; on the
verso of a tax-register). Ed. pr.: E. W. Handley and J. Rea, BICSL, Bull. Suppl. 5 (1957).
The text partially coincides with No. 447; frr.
18-20 (and 17?) correspond to P. Berol. inv. 9908
(see No. 449), formerly ascribed to Sophocles,

Assembly of the Achaeans. E. Fraenkel, Glotta
37 (1958) 285-87; A. Bataille, Rev. Ét. Gr. 72
(1959) 420-21; F. C. Görschen, Dion., NS 22 (1959)
106-11, joins frr. 12 and 13; H. Strohm, Gnomon
32 (1960) 600-5.

449 --- Telephus. BKT 5.2.64-72 (inv. 9908) (II).
Formerly attributed to Sophocles, Assembly of the
Achaeans, this text coincides with No. 448. Re-
printed in P. Oxy. 27, pp. 97-98. Schubart, PGB,
tab. 30 b. Diehl, SS 29-30; Hunt, TGFP, No. 3;
Jebb-Pearson I, No. 142; Page, GLP 1, No. 3.
Archiv 5.565; JAW 147.95-96. R. Goossens, Chr.
Ég. 18 (1943) 121-31; Srebrny, Stud. Scaen. 11, 21-22,
25-26, 40, queries the new identification.

450 --- Telephus. P. Ryl. 3.482 (II). Formerly attributed to Sophocles, Assembly of the Achaeans, this
text coincides with No. 448, and is reedited by
Handley and Rea, op. cit. (see No. 448), 20-22, 37.
Page, GLP 1, No. 21. Attributed to Sophocles by
T. B. L. Webster, Bull. Ryl. Libr. 22 (1938) 543-
49; A. Koerte, Archiv 14.116-17, regarded the
attribution as certain; B. Snell, Gnomon 15 (1939)
538-40; Srebrny, Stud. Scaen. 11, 26-27.

--- See No. 138.

--- Temenus: see No. 1186.

451 --- Theseus (?) and Cretenses. P. Oxy. 27.2461
(II, Oxy.). H. J. Mette, Hermes 91 (1963) 256,
identifies fr. 4 as from the Cretenses, not the Theseus, as preferred by the editor.

452 --- List of the plays of Euripides. P. Oxy. 27.2456
(II, Oxy.; on the verso of a tax register). Titles
preserved: Temenus, Telephus, Troades, Temenidae, Tennes, Hypsipyla, Phrixus, Phoenix, Philoctetes, Phaethon, Phrixus (sic), Phoenissae, Chrysippus.

453 --- Hypotheses of his plays. P. Oxy. 27.2455 (II,
Oxy.). Medea (?), Melanippa Sapiens, Orestes,
Oedipus, Sisyphus, Stheneboea, Sciron, Syleus,
Temenus, Telephus (?), Troades, Temenidae,
Tennes, Hypsipyla, Phaethon, Phrixus I, Phoenix,
Philoctetes, Phrixus II, Phoenissae, Chrysippus,
Alcmaeon per Corinthum. The order of the Tele-
phus, Troades, and Temenidae is uncertain. Each
hypothesis quotes the first verse of the play in ques-
tion. E. G. Turner, Proc. IX Int. Congr. Pap.
1-17 (first description). B. Snell, Hermes 91 (1963)
120, notes that fr. 4, line 40 (Oedipus) is quoted by
Cicero ap. Plutarchum, Reg. et imp. apophth. 205C.

454 --- Hypotheses of the Alcestis and the Aeolus. P.
Oxy. 27.2457 (II, Oxy.; on the verso of a tax register). Quotes Aeolus, line 1.

Euripides: see also Nos. 92, 237, 1456, 1569, 1574,
1704-5, 1915, 1921, 2087, 2471, 2529, 2593.

Euryphon: see No. 2339.
Euthycles: see No. 1579.

455   FAVORINUS: De Exsilio.   P. Vat. Gr. 11 (ante A.D.
      215?, Marmarica, Libya;  on the verso of land re-
      gisters).  Numerous citations: Aeschylus, Choe-
      phoroe 49 (col. 9, line 42; Galiano, Aesch. 91);
      Alcaeus (9.4; Treu, Alkaios 84); Bacchylides 7.2
      ff. (4.48 ff.;  Galiano, Pind., No. 60); Euripides,
      Antigona, frr. 157-58, Nauck$^2$ (2.39, 17.41; H. Lucas
      Hermes 72, 1937, 239-40), Hercules 57-59, 1337-39
      (15.18-21, 39-41), Phoenissae 40 (17.37), 363 (6.36),
      367-70 (6.19-23), 403 (18.35), 406-7 (6.38), 476 (6.
      29), 531-35 (18.5-9), 536 (18.39), 613 (6.47), and a
      new fragment (2.43); Hesiod, Opera 176 ff. (24.15
      ff.), 640 (24.39), Theogonia 22 ff. (24.43 ff.); Ho-
      mer, Iliad ii.128 (7.34), iii.3 ff. (10.11 ff.), iii.47
      ff. (13.13 ff.), iv.171 (7.3), vi.176, etc. (12.31, note),
      vi.311 (7.14), xiv.308 (13.7), xxii.219 (11.15), xxiii.
      774 (7.12), Odyssey ii.314 ff. (11.27 ff.), iv.502
      (7.12), iv.506 (7.30), v.84, 158 (14.47), v.176, etc.
      (13.20 ff.), x.517 (8.6-18, notes), xi.25, 543 ff. (8.
      6-18, notes), xi.122 ff. (19.37 ff., notes), xiv.222-
      25 (11.11 ff.), xviii.74 (19.13), xx.18 (4.17), xxiii.269
      ff. (19.37 ff.); Menander (23.28 ff.);  Oracle of
      Apollo to Lampon "of Megara" (22.35);  Oracle of
      Apollo to Socrates (22.36); Pindar, Olympia ii.16
      (6.32; Galiano, Pind., No. 3), fr. 88, Schroeder
      (23.13; Galiano, Pind., No. 22); Poetae ignoti
      (6.32, 7.44, 9.26, 11.5; Galiano, Pind., Nos. 53-
      54, 66); proverbs (15.21, 28, 18.40, 41); Sophocles,
      Electra 363-64 (17.30), Tereus (?; 7.44), ibid., fr.
      532.1 ff., Nauck$^2$ (9.25 ff.;  Page, GLP 1, No. 24;
      cf. A. Koerte, Archiv 10.67, P. Maas, DLZ 52,
      1931, 1211, and Galiano, LG 148, note 551), Oedipus
      Coloneus 562-64 (11.18-21), 797-99 (15.6 ff.); The-
      bais, fr. 1, Kinkel (7.3); Xenophon, Cyropaedia
      i.2.8 (20.5 ff.), i.4.11 (25.40). Norsa, SLG, tav.
      13; Roberts, GLH, pl. 18b-c. Archiv 10.64-67;
      Chr. Eg. 8 (1933) 162-64; JAW 272.146-58 (bibl.);
      JEA 18.79, 19.69, 23.84, 24.94. P. Collart, BAGB
      34 (1932) 23-31; G. M. Lattanzi, Riv. Fil. 60 (1932)
      499-500; K. Praechter, Gnomon 8 (1932) 561-72;
      T. Antonini, Rend. Acc. Linc., Ser. 6.10 (1934)
      174-256, on the sources; L. Castiglioni, Acme 1
      (1948) 31-43, studies the "virtues of Odysseus" as
      a Stoic and Cynic commonplace; A. Barigazzi,
      Athen. 38 (1950) 95-115, compares the text with Ps.
      Dio Chrysostom, Or. 37 and 64, ascribed to Favo-
      rinus; idem, SIFC, NS 24 (1950) 187-229, restores
      the names of Chrysippus (col. 1, line 31), Crates (30),
      Dio of Prusa (31), Diogenes (30), and Empedocles
      (24); M. G. Goggin, Yale Class. Stud. 12 (1951)
      149-201, on the prose rhythm.

      Favorinus: see also Nos. 1993, 2087.

456   GALEN: A Neoplatonic commentary on Galen, De
      Sectis ad Tirones, by one Archimedes (or Archon-
      ides?).  E. Nachmanson, Göt. Hösk. Årsskr. 31.2
      (1925) 201-17 (P. Berol. inv. 11739 A-B) (VI, Hermu-
      polis Magna; pap. cod.). Archiv 11.275-76. The
      text shows parallels to the commentaries by Am-
      monius, David, and Elias on Porphyrius' Isagoge.

      Geminus of Rhodes: see No. 2088.
      Glaucon: see No. 2088.
      Glaucus: see No. 2127.

457   Ps.-GREGORIUS CORINTHIUS (Tryphon?):  De
      Tropis iii.218.20, 219.16, Spengel.   P. Rainer
      3.35 (cf. ibid. 4, p. 137) (inv. 29332) (IV-V,
      Hermupolis Magna?; pap. cod.).  Cites Homer,
      Il. i.162, ii.764, ix.38, xxiv.254, Od. xii.172,
      xiii.242-43; Simonides (Diehl, Anth. Lyr. 2$^1$.
      105, No. 113).

      Hagias:  see Nos. 89, 196, 205.

458   HARPOCRATION:  Lexicon in Decem Oratores
      Atticos 171-72, Dindorf.   P. Ryl. 3.532 (II-III).
      Quotes or refers to Demosthenes, In Aristocra-
      tem, Ad Pantaenetum; Ephorus, Historiae, Bk.
      v (?); Lysias, In Andocidem (Or. vi), In Aes-
      chinem Socraticum; Theopompus comicus, Tisa-
      menus, fr. 59 (1.749, Kock). Archiv 14.136. B.
      Snell, Gnomon 15 (1939) 543; M. Naoumides,
      TAPA 92 (1961) 384-88, offers a restoration
      which eliminates the supposed quotation from
      Ephorus.

      Harpocration: see also No. 2091.

      Harpocration (the Platonist?): see No. 2088.
      Hecataeus:  see No. 89.
      Hecataeus of Abdera:  see Nos. 2271, 2488.
      Hedylus:  see No. 1593.
      Hegesander of Delphi:  see No. 2127.
      Hegesippus:  see No. 1601.
      Heliodorus (grammaticus):  see No. 2146.
      Heliodorus (medicus):  see Nos. 2374, 2376-77.

459   HELLANICUS:  Atlantis i.   P. Oxy. 8.1084 (P.
      Princ.) (II, Oxy.).  Archiv 6.242.

      Hellanicus: see also Nos. 371, 2069, 2290, 2810.

      Heracleodorus:  see No. 2339.

460   HERACLIDES LEMBUS:  Epitome of Hermippus the
      Peripatetic, Peri nomothetōn (end of Bk. i, be-
      ginning of Bk. ii).   P. Oxy. 11.1367 (St. Andrews
      Univ. Libr.) (II, Oxy.).  Cites Herodotus iv.161;
      Lasus of Hermione (Page, PMG 705); and Philo-
      chorus. Archiv 7.231-32; JEA 7.91; New Chap-
      ters 2.99-100. K. F. W. Schmidt, Gött. Anz.,
      1918, 99-100; R. Philippson, Rh. Mus. 79 (1930)
      406-10; H. Bloch, TAPA 71 (1940) 33-34; A. A.
      I. Waisglass, AJP 77 (1956) 167-76, on Demonax,
      the lawgiver of Mantinea.

      Heraclides Lembus: see also Nos. 2121, 2127.

      Heraclides: Lingua Barbara, Bk. i: see No. 2127.

461   HERACLIDES OF MILETUS (?):  Peri dysklitōn
      rhēmáton.   P. Rain. 3.33 (cf. ibid. 4, p. 137)
      (inv. 29815 A) (II, Fayum; on the verso of ac-
      counts).  Refers to Homer, Od. xxi.195. Archiv
      14.142.

      Heraclides Ponticus:  see Nos. 136, 2289, 2562.
      Heraclides of Tarentum:  see No. 2377.
      Heraclius:  see No. 2299.
      Hermapias:  see No. 1205.
      Hermarchus:  see No. 1992.
      Hermias:  see No. 1849.

Hermippus the Peripatetic: see Nos. 339, 460, 551, 2292.

Hermippus: Iambi (Iapetus?): see No. 2290.

Hermippus: Stratiotai: see No. 2121.

Hermolaus: see No. 2299.

Herodes or Herodas: see Herondas.

Herodianus: see No. 2299.

Herodicus: see No. 2339.

Herodorus: see No. 1209.

462    HERODOTUS: Historiae i. 9, 11.  P. Oxy. 17. 2095
       (II, Oxy.).  Paap, No. 1.

       --- i. 32: see No. 2120.

463    --- i. 58, 85, 91, 118, 132, 160, 191, 209-14 (with
       lacunae).  P. Oxy. 17. 2096 (II, Oxy.).  Paap,
       No. 2.

464    --- i. 64-65.  P. Oxy. 17. 2097 (III, Oxy.).  Paap,
       No. 3.

465    --- i. 76.  P. Oxy. 1. 19 (II-III, Oxy.; on the verso
       of a document).  Paap, No. 4; Viljoen, No. 1.
       Archiv 1. 114.

466    --- i. 105-6.  P. Oxy. 1. 18; P. Lit. Lond. 102
       (Brit. Mus. inv. 741) (III, Oxy.).  Paap, No. 5;
       Viljoen, No. 2.  Archiv 1. 114.

467    --- i. 105-8.  P. Oxy. 10. 1244 (Musées Royaux,
       Bruxelles, inv. E. 5986) (II, Oxy.).  Paap, No. 6;
       Viljoen, No. 3.

468    --- i. 115-16.  U. Wilcken, Archiv 1 (1901) 471-73
       (P. Monac.) (I-II).  Paap, No. 7; Viljoen, No.
       4.  Archiv 2. 358; JAW 147. 1.

469    --- i. 196, 200-3.  P. Ross. Georg. 1. 15 (Collec-
       tion of G. Zereteli, Tiflis) (III; opisthograph
       roll?).  Paap, No. 8.  JAW 220, 2-3.  S. Linner,
       Eranos 39 (1941) 148.

470    --- i. 196. 4-199. 3.  PSI 10. 1170 (II; on the verso
       of a document).  Paap, No. 9.  JAW 263. 101-2.

471    --- Reminiscences of ii. 28, 171 (?).  P. Lond. 3.
       854; Wilcken, Chrest., No. 117, pp. 147-48 (II;
       in a private letter written by one Nearchos, a
       traveller).

472    --- ii. 96-99, 107-8.  P. Ryl. 1. 55 (II).  Paap, No.
       11; Viljoen, No. 6.  S. Linner, Eranos 39 (1941)
       147.

473    --- ii. 154-75 (with lacunae).  P. Oxy. 8. 1092
       (Bodleian Libr.) (II, Oxy.).  Paap, No. 12; Vil-
       joen, No. 7.  G. Rudberg, Eranos 39 (1941) 145-
       47.

474    --- iii. 26-72.  P. Oxy. 13. 1619 (I-II, Oxy.).  Paap,
       No. 13.  JAW 191. 2-4.  P. Collart, Rev. Phil.
       43 (1919) 58.

       --- iv. 161: see No. 460.

       --- v. 74: see No. 2120.

475    --- v. 77-79.  P. Lit. Lond. 103 (Brit. Mus., Add.
       MS. 34473, art. 5) (III-IV; scrap from a vellum
       leaf).  Paap, No. 14.

476    --- v. 78, 80, 82.  P. Lond. 3. 1109 (a); P. Lit.
       Lond. 104 (Brit. Mus. inv. 1109 A) (I-II).  Paap,
       No. 15; Viljoen, No. 8.  Identified by W. Croe-
       nert, Rh. Mus. 68 (1913) 602.

477    --- v. 104-5.  P. Oxy. 4. 695 (P. Princ.) (III, Oxy.).
       Paap, No. 16; Viljoen, No. 9.  Archiv 3. 487;
       JAW 147. 2.

478    --- v. 113. 2-114. 2.  P. Dura 1 (inv. D. P. 83) (II,
       Dura).  Ed. pr.: C. B. Welles, TAPA 70 (1939)
       203-12.  Paap, No. 17.

       --- vi. 12: see No. 2120.

       --- vii. 148-52, 163: see No. 484.

479    --- vii. 166-67.  P. Oxy. 11. 1375 (P. Cairo) (III,
       Oxy.).  Paap, No. 18.

480    --- vii. 168-73.  P. Oxy. 17. 2098 (III, Oxy.).
       Roberts, GLH, pl. 19b.  Paap, No. 19.

481    --- viii. 22-23.  P. Oxy. 17. 2099 (II, Oxy.).  Paap,
       No. 20.

482    --- viii. 126-27, 129.  P. Harris 40 (inv. 181 b, c)
       (III).  Paap, No. 21.

483    --- Excerpts from Aristarchus' Commentary on
       Herodotus (covering i. 194, 215).  P. Amh. 2. 12
       (III, Hermupolis Magna; on the verso of accounts).
       Paap, No. 10; Viljoen, No. 5.  Lesky, GGL 308;
       Winter, LLP 239.  Archiv 2. 358; JAW 117. 74.  L.
       Radermacher, Rh. Mus. 57 (1902) 139-41; P.
       Viereck, Berl. Phil. Woch. 22 (1902) 716; G.
       Jachmann, Klio 33 (1940) 239.  Quotes Sophocles,
       Poimenes.

484    --- Epitome (by Theopompus?) or history based on
       Herodotus (?).  P. Oxy. 6. 857 (P. Princ.) (IV,
       Oxy.; parch. cod.).  Shows resemblances to
       Herodotus vii. 148-52, 163.  Jacoby, FGH 2. 505.
       Archiv 6. 243.

       Herodotus: see also No. 2289.

Heron of Athens: see No. 1551.

Heron (medicus): see No. 2377.

485    HERONDAS: Mimes.  Kenyon, Class. Texts 1-39,
       Archiv 1 (1901) 379-87; P. Lit. Lond. 96 ("P.
       Egerton" 1: Brit. Mus. inv. 135) (II-III).  Ken-
       yon, Pal. GP, pl. XVIII; Schubart, Gr. Pal.,
       Abb. 82; Wattenbach, SGS, tab. I.  Lesky, GGL
       682-83; Preisendanz, PFF 153-54.  Later edi-
       tions include those of R. Meister, Abh. der
       Königl.-sächs. Gesellschaft der Wissenschaft-
       en zu Leipzig, 1893, Abh. 13; F. Buecheler.
       (Bonn 1892[2]); J. A. Nairn (Oxford 1904); O.
       Crusius (Leipzig 1892, 1914); P. Groeneboom
       (Groningen 1922); W. Headlam and A. D. Knox
       (Cambridge 1922); N. Terzaghi (Torino 1925);
       O. Crusius and R. Herzog (Leipzig 1926); J. A.

Nairn and L. Laloy (Paris 1928); Q. Cataudella (Milano 1948); G. Puccioni (Firenze 1950). The journal literature is extensive; recent articles include G. Puccioni, Ann. Sc. Pisa, Ser 2.19 (1950) 50-52; idem, Maia 3 (1950) 297-99; idem, SIFC, NS 24 (1950) 231-33, on Mime 6.65; A. Leone, Paid. 6 (1951) 301-2, ibid. 10 (1957) 43-44; V. Pisani, ibid. 7 (1952) 89-94; O. Specchia, GIF 5 (1952) 145-48, ibid. 10 (1957) 43-44; B. Marzullo, Maia 6 (1953) 52-67; W. J. Verdenius, Mnemos., Ser. 4.6 (1953) 139; A. Barigazzi, Athen. 42 (1954) 410-21; L. Gil, Emérita 22 (1954) 211-14; J. van Ooteghem, Ét. Cl. 22 (1954) 199-211 (an edition of Mime 3); M. F. Galiano and L. Gil, Studi in onore di Gino Funaioli (Roma 1955) 67-82; A. P. Smotrytsch, Hlk. 1 (1961) 118-26, on Mime 8.

486       --- Mime 8.67-75.   P. Oxy. 22.2326 (II, Oxy.). Listed by the editor as "Scazons in Ionic dialect (Hipponax?)"; identified by A. Barigazzi, Mus. Helv. 12 (1955) 113-14.  Archiv 16.91.

Herondas: see also No. 2339.

Herophilus: see No. 2339.

HESIOD: Opera et Dies 30: see No. 1952.

--- 90-92: see No. 520.

487       --- 111-18, 153-56, 158-61, 169 b-e, 174-82, 210-21. J. Nicole, Rev. Phil. 12 (1888) 113-17 (P. Genève inv. 94) (V, Thebes; pap. cod.). H. Weil, Rev. Phil. 12 (1888) 173-75; H. G. Evelyn-White, CQ 9 (1915) 72; Wilamowitz, Hesiodos' Erga (Berlin 1928) 18-19; M. L. West, CQ, NS 11 (1961) 139-40.

--- 176 ff., 640: see No. 455.

488       --- 199-204, 241-46.  BKT 5.1.46 (inv. 7784) (V-VI; pap. cod.).  JAW 152.12.

--- 210-828: see No. 499.

489       --- 257-89.  P. Oxy. 8.1090 (Liverpool Univ. Libr., Class. Gr. Libr. 420) (I, Oxy.).  JAW 199.21-22.

--- 287: see No. 1567.

490       --- 292-335, 366-69, 373-80.  P. Oxy. 17.2091 (III, Oxy.).

--- 318: see No. 2524.

491       --- 347 (bis).  D. C. Hesseling, JHS 13 (1893) 294-95 (III, Palmyra?; waxed tablets; on the verso of No. 174; sch. ex.).  Ziebarth, No. 16; Ziebarth 2, No. 30.

--- 470: see No. 1186.

--- 486-87: see No. 1327.

--- 765-802: see No. 1692.

492       --- Theogonia 1-7, 28-52, 148-54.  P. Oxy. 17. 2090 (II, Oxy.).  G. Arrighetti, Athen., NS 39 (1961) 236-45 and passim.

493       --- 1-51.  C. C. Edgar, Ann. Serv. 26 (1926) 205-6 (P. Cairo inv. 47269) (II-III, Oxy.; on the verso of an account).  G. Arrighetti, Athen., NS 39 (1961) 256-58 and passim.

--- 22 ff.: see No. 455.

494       --- 75-105, 108-44.  U. Wilcken, Sitzb. Berl. Akad., 1887, 809-13; P. Achmîm 3 (P. Par.: Bibl. Nationale, Suppl. Gr. 1099, 1) (IV-V, Panopolis; pap. cod.; No. 1599 is written in the margin).  G. Arrighetti, Athen., NS 39 (1961) 221-28 and passim; M. L. West, CQ, NS 12 (1962) 177.

--- 116: see No. 78.

495       --- 210-38, 260-70, 296-97.  F. G. Kenyon, Rev. Phil. 16 (1892) 181-83; P. Lit. Lond. 33 (Brit. Mus. inv. 159) (III-IV).  G. Arrighetti, Athen., NS 39 (1961) 230-34 and passim.

496       --- 271-99.  P. Mil. Vogl. 2.38 (inv. 403) (I; on the verso of a document).

--- 378: see No. 186.

497       --- 566-92, 628-41, 652-64, 1016-20.  PSI 11.1191 (II, Oxy.).  G. Arrighetti, Athen., NS 39 (1961) 250-56 and passim; M. L. West, CQ, NS 12 (1962) 178.

498       --- 606-13.  P. Heid. Siegmann 204 (inv. 3070) (II).  G. Arrighetti, Maia 14 (1962) 141-43.

499       --- 626-881; Opera et Dies 210-828; Scutum 1-32, 350-470 (with lacunae).  K. Wessely, Raineri M. 1.73-83, Stud. Pal. 1 (1901), pp. iii-x (P. Rain. inv. 19815) (IV, Fayum; parch. cod.). Archiv 2.347; JAW 152.6-8.  G. Arrighetti, Athen., NS 39 (1961) 228-30 and passim.

500       --- 643-56.  P. Ryl. 1.54 (I B.C. - I, Oxy.). JAW 199.20-21.  G. Arrighetti, Athen., NS 39 (1961) 234-36 and passim.

501       --- 825-53, 868-96.  P. Antin. 2.71 (VI, Antinoöpolis; pap. cod.).  G. Arrighetti, Maia 14 (1962) 143-49; M. L. West, CQ, NS 12 (1962) 180.

502       --- 839-69.  PSI 9.1086 (II?, Oxy.).  G. Arrighetti, Athen., NS 39 (1961) 245-50 and passim; M. L. West, CQ, NS 12 (1962) 180.

503       --- 930-39, 994-1004.  P. Oxy. 6.873 (Yale Univ. Libr.) (III, Oxy.; pap. cod.).  G. Arrighetti, Athen., NS 39 (1961) 258-59 and passim.

--- 984: see No. 186.

--- Scutum 1-32, 350-470: see No. 499.

504       --- Scutum 28-33.  PSI 1.15 (IV-V, Oxy.; parch. fr. written on only one side).  JAW 199.34.

505       --- 207-13.  BKT 5.1.19 (inv. 9774) (I B.C.; text follows No. 962).  JAW 152.11-12, 15.

506 --- 273-89. PSI 9.1087 (II-III, Oxy. ?).

507 --- 466-80. P. Oxy. 4.689 (Wellesley Coll.)
Archiv 3.478; JAW 152.8.

508 --- Catalogus, Bk. i (Unions of noble women with
gods). P. Oxy. 23.2354 (II, Oxy.). Lines 1-2=
Theogonia 1021-22. Merkelbach, Hes., fr. A;
Schwartz, Ps.-Hes. 435-36, 458-59. M. Treu,
Rh. Mus. 100 (1957) 169-86; J. T. Kakridis,
Hellen. 16 (1958-59) 219; M. L. West, CQ, NS
11 (1961) 141; K. Stiewe, Philol. 106 (1962) 291-99.

509 --- Ibid. (Bellerophon). P. Oxy. 3.421 (Houghton
Libr., Harvard Univ.) (II, Oxy.). Merkelbach,
Hes., fr. B; Traversa, Hes. Cat. 48-49. Archiv 3.265; JAW 152.17-18, 199.34. H. G. Evelyn-White, CQ 7 (1913) 217-18, relates this text
to No. 511; K. Stiewe, Hermes 88 (1960) 253-56.

510 --- Ibid. (Mestra and Eurynome). Schwartz, Ps.-
Hes. 265-81 and passim (PIFAO inv. 322) (II).
The text precedes No. 511 and overlaps No. 509.
F. Vian, Rev. Ét. Gr. 74 (1961) 269; M. L.
West, CQ, NS 11 (1961) 142.

511 --- Ibid. (Bellerophon). BKT 5.1.45-46 (inv.
7497) (II). Merkelbach, Hes., fr. B; Traversa,
Hes. Cat. 48-49. Archiv 5.533; JAW 152.14,17,
199.34.

512 --- Ibid. (Tyro). P. Tebt. 2.271 (II-III, Tebtunis).
Quotes Homer, Il. iv.180, Od. xi.249-50. Iden-
tified by W. Schubart, Gött. Anz., 1908, 189-90.
Merkelbach, Hes., fr. C; Traversa, Hes. Cat.
46. Archiv 5.533; JAW 199.35. R. Pfeiffer,
Philol. 92 (1937) 11-14.

513 --- Ibid. (Tyro). PSI 13.1301 (II, Oxy.). Lines 1-9
imitate Homer, Od. xi.281-97. Ed. pr.: M.
Norsa and G. Vitelli, SIFC, NS 12 (1935) 87-91.
Identified by R. Pfeiffer, Philol. 92 (1937) 1-14.
Lesky, GGL 98; Merkelbach, Hes., fr. D;
Schwartz, Ps.-Hes. 372-76; Traversa, Hes.
Cat. 46-48. Archiv 13.79; Chr. Ég. 11 (1936)
555. P. Maas, Ét. Pap. 6 (1940) 37-39; V.
Bartoletti, SIFC, NS 21 (1946) 3-10; L. Alfonsi,
Rev. Phil., Sér. 3.23 (1949) 17-26, studies the
influence on Propertius; M. L. West, CQ, NS
11 (1961) 141.

514 --- Ibid. (Ino-Leucothea; the daughters of Leucon).
PSI 14.1383 (III?; parch. cod.). Ed. pr.: V.
Bartoletti, Aeg. 31 (1951) 263-68; R. Merkelbach,
ibid. 268. Merkelbach, Hes., fr. E 1, E 2 (lines
12-29); Schwartz, Ps.-Hes. 431-35.

515 --- Ibid. (The daughters of Leucon). Merkelbach,
Hes., fr. E 2 (Yale Univ. Libr., inv. 1273) (I-
II). Identified by B. Snell. Republished with
PSI 1383 (see No. 514), with which it partially
coincides. Schwartz, Ps.-Hes. 433-34.

516 --- Ibid. (The children of Althaea, Meleager,
Deianira, Heracles and Deianira, Hypermestra,
the children of Porthaon, Timandra). P. Oxy.
17.2075; PSI 14.1384, from the same roll (II-
III, Oxy.). Ed. pr. of PSI 1384: V. Bartoletti,

Aeg. 31 (1951) 261-62. Coppola 243-49; Merkelbach, Hes., frr. F 1-2, 4-11; Schwartz, Ps.-
Hes. 404-8, 423-28; Traversa, Hes. Cat. 60-
66. Archiv 10.20-21. T. W. Allen, CQ 22 (1928)
73-74, notes that lines 16-23 in P. Oxy. 2075 are
obelized because they partially coincide with Od.
xi.601-4, attributed by the Homeric scholia to
Onomacritus; M. Hombert, Chr. Ég. 28 (1953)
154; M. L. West, CQ, NS 11 (1961) 141.

517 --- Ibid. (The children of Althaea, Meleager,
Deianira). BKT 5.1.22-28 (inv. 9777) (IV; pap.
cod.). Coppola 243-49; Merkelbach, Hes., fr.
F 3-4; Schwartz, Ps.-Hes. 404-8; Traversa,
Hes. Cat. 60-64. Archiv 5.532; JAW 152.12,17,
199.33-34. H. G. Evelyn-White, CQ 7 (1913)
218-19.

518 --- Ibid. (Apollo and Marpessa?). Merkelbach,
Hes., fr. F 3, lines 16-33 (P. Mil. Vogl.) (?,
Tunat-el-Gabal).

519 --- Ibid. (The suitors of Helen). BKT 5.1.28-30
(inv. 9739) (I-II). Ed. pr.: Wilamowitz, Sitzb.
Berl. Akad., 1900, 839-51. Schubart, PGB, tab.
19a. Merkelbach, Hes., fr. G; Schwartz, Ps.-
Hes. 413-15; Traversa, Hes. Cat. 67-70. Archiv 1.507; JAW 152.9-11,12,17, 199.31; New
Chapters 2.190-92.

520 --- Ibid. (The suitors of Helen). BKT 5.1.31-44
(inv. 10560) (III, Hermupolis Magna?; on the
verso). Schubart, PGB, tab. 19b. Merkelbach,
Hes., fr. H; Schwartz, Ps.-Hes. 415-16; Traversa, Hes. Cat. 70-78. Archiv 5.532; JAW
152.12-14, 199.32-33. H. G. Evelyn-White, CQ
9 (1915) 74-75; T. W. Allen, ibid. 26 (1932) 82-
84; D. A. van Krevelen, Aeg. 31 (1951) 327-28;
M. L. West, CQ, NS 11 (1961) 130-36, gives cor-
rected readings and notes that lines 138-40 imitate Hesiod, Opera 90-92.

521 --- Ibid. ? (The genealogy of Io?). C. C. Edgar,
Ann. Serv. 26 (1926) 206-7 (P. Cairo inv. 45624)
(III, Oxy.; on the verso of an account). Mer-
kelbach, Hes., fr. I; Schwartz, Ps.-Hes. 383,
queries the attribution; Traversa, Hes. Cat. 99.
R. Merkelbach, Aeg. 31 (1951) 254-57, attributes
the fragment to Bk. iii (or ii), the genealogy of
Io, not Heracles.

522 --- Ibid. (Europa, the Harpies, the Boreads,
Electra?, Diomedes). P. Oxy. 11.1358 (Cambridge Univ. Libr., add. 6353) (III, Oxy.; on
the verso of a document). Merkelbach, Hes.,
fr. K; Schwartz, Ps.-Hes. 377-79, 385-86;
Traversa, Hes. Cat. 85-88, 90-94, 122-23.
New Chapters 2.194-95. M. L. West, CQ, NS
12 (1962) 181.

523 --- Ibid. (Europa). P. Rein. 2.77 (P. Sorbonne
inv. 2082) (III). The same verses as in P. Oxy.
1358, fr. 1, col. 1, lines 6-13 (see No. 522).
Merkelbach, Hes., fr. K 1 (lines 6-13); Traversa, Hes. Cat. 85-88.

524 --- Ibid. (Pasiphaë). P. Tebt. 3.690 (II B.C.,
Tebtunis; cart.; on the verso of No. 1022).

Merkelbach, Hes., fr. L; Schwartz, Ps.-Hes.
379-80; Traversa, Hes. Cat. 88-89. Archiv 11.
221-22. M. L. West, CQ, NS 11 (1961) 141.

525    --- Ibid. ? (or Atlantis?). P. Oxy. 11.1359 (Cam-
       bridge Univ. Libr., add. 6354) (II-III, Oxy.).
       Merkelbach, Hes., fr. M; Schwartz, Ps.-Hes.
       429-30; Traversa, Hes. Cat. 120-23. Archiv
       7.116; JAW 199.29-31; JEA 6.123; New Chap-
       ters 2.195-96. K. F. W. Schmidt, Gött. Anz.,
       1918, 87-89; C. Robert, Hermes 52 (1917) 477-
       79, prefers Hesiod's Atlantis to the Catalogus;
       Wilamowitz, Hermes 61 (1926) 277-78, queries
       both attributions.

526    --- Ibid. ? (Perseus and Andromeda).   F. della
       Corte, Riv. Fil. 64 (1936) 385-89 (P. Berol. inv.
       9870 + 9871) (?). Traversa, Hes. Cat. 124-26.
       F. della Corte, Riv. Fil. 65 (1937) 42-45, idem,
       Ovidiana: Recherches sur Ovide ... (Paris 1958)
       258-64, on the relation to the accounts of Perseus
       in Ovid, Met. iv-v; S. Abramowicz, Eos 43,
       fasc. 1 (1948-49) 86-96.

527    --- Ibid. (The marriage of Peleus and Thetis).
       R. Reitzenstein, Hermes 35 (1900) 79-80
       (Strassburg: P. Gr. bibl. Argent. inv. 55) (I-II).
       Merkelbach, Hes., fr. O; Traversa, Hes. Cat.
       81-82. Archiv 1.508; JAW 152.8-9.

528    --- Ibid. (Bk. iv?). P. Oxy. 23.2355 (I-II, Oxy.).
       Lines 8-12 = Hesiod, Scutum 1-5. Merkelbach,
       Hes., fr. P.

529    --- Ibid. (Atalanta). P. Petrie 1.3 (3); P. Lit.
       Lond. 32 (Brit. Mus. inv. 486 C) (III B.C.,
       Gurob; cart.). Identified by I. Hopfner, WS 14
       (1892) 154-56. Merkelbach, Hes., fr. Q; Schwartz,
       Ps.-Hes. 365; Traversa, Hes. Cat. 53-54.

530    --- Ibid. (Atalanta). P. Rain. 3.6 (inv. 26768a)
       (III, Soknopaiou Nesos). Traversa, Hes. Cat.
       57-58. Archiv 14.104.

531    --- Ibid. (Atalanta, Amphiaraüs, Lysidice). PSI
       2.130-131 (II-III, Oxy.; on the verso of accounts).
       Merkelbach, Hes., frr. R, N; Schwartz, Ps.-
       Hes. 363 (queries the attribution of PSI 130), 380-
       83; Traversa, Hes. Cat. 54-57, 97-99. Archiv
       7.115-16; JAW 199.35-37; JEA 6.123. Wilamo-
       witz, DLZ 34 (1913) 1865; H. G. Evelyn-White,
       CQ 9 (1915) 76, ibid. 11 (1917) 50-51, identifies
       PSI 131; S. Laser, Hermes 80 (1952) 372-76, com-
       pares PSI 130 with Homer, Il. xxii; M. L. West,
       CQ, NS 11 (1961) 141.

532    --- Ibid. ? (Pirithoüs, Theseus, and Meleager in
       Hades). R. Merkelbach, SIFC, NS 24 (1950)
       255-63, ibid. 26 (1952) 221-22 (P. Ibscher inedi-
       ta) (I B.C.). Merkelbach, Hes., fr. S; Schwartz,
       Ps.-Hes. 27-28, on the attribution. M. L. West,
       CQ, NS 11 (1961) 142.

533    --- Ibid. ? (Aeëtes, Absyrtus, the marriage of
       Jason and Medea?). PSI 14.1389 (IV-V, Oxy.;
       parch. cod.). Ed. pr.: G. Vitelli, BSAA 6.13
       (1928) 294-95. New Chapters 3.258. Attributed
       to Hesiod by W. Croenert, Riv. Fil. 56 (1928)

507-8. Traversa, Hes. Cat. 95-96. V. Bartoletti, Studi Paoli 71-74, rejects Hesiod, prefers
to think of a Hellenistic poem.

534    --- Hesiod (?): Catalogus (?). P. Rain. 3.7
       (inv. 29327) (II-III, Fayum). Archiv 14.107. A.
       Traversa, Proc. IX Int. Congr. Pap. 61, rejects
       this fragment as not Hesiodic.

535    --- Hesiod (?): Catalogus (?). P. Rain. 3.9
       (inv. 26768 B) (V?, Sokopaiou Nesos; pap. cod.).
       Archiv 14.108. Traversa, Hes. Cat. 133-34
       ("Incerti Auctoris").

       --- Catalogus: see also Nos. 1772-73, 1778, 1806,
       1842.

       Hesiod: see also Nos. 89, 186, 1186, 1205, 1209,
       1458, 1772-73, 1950, 2707.

536    HIEROCLES STOICUS: Ethikē stoicheiōsis.   BKT
       4 (inv. 9780, verso) (II-III, Hermupolis Magna;
       on the verso of No. 339). Cites Chrysippus,
       mentions Cleanthes (col. 8, lines 10-13). Ar-
       chiv 6.241; F. W. Hall, New Chapters 1.36-40;
       Winter, LLP 267-68. G. Pasquali, SIFC 16
       (1908) 441-44; F. W. Hall, CQ 10 (1916) 85-86;
       M. Wellmann, Hermes 52 (1917) 130-35, studies
       the sources.

       Hierocles (Stoicus?): see No. 2088.

       Hieronymus (comicus): see No. 138.
       Hieronymus of Cardia: see No. 2203.

537    HIMERIUS: Or. xlvi. 35-49, 79-95 (ed. Colonna).
       S. Eitrem and L. Amundsen, Class. Med. 17
       (1956) 23-30 (P. Oslo inv. 1478) (V; pap. cod.).
       The editors also publish two small fragments
       not identified with speeches of Himerius other-
       wise preserved.

       Hippeus of Rhegium: see No. 1205.
       Hippias of Elis: see Nos. 2089, 2438.

538    HIPPOCRATES: Epidemia iii.1.   PSI 2.116 (II-III,
       Oxy.).

539    --- De Ratione Victus in Morbis Acutis. P. Ryl.
       1.56 (II; on the verso of an illegible text).

540    --- Epistulae 3-6. P. Oxy. 9.1184 (Musées
       Royaux, Bruxelles, inv. E.6010) (I, Oxy.; on
       the verso of a tax-register). JAW 180, 67-68.

541    --- 3-5, 11. BKT 3.5-9 (inv. 7094, verso) (II-III;
       on the verso of No. 2327).

542    --- 5, 11. BKT 3.5-9 (inv. 6934) (III; on the verso
       of a cursive text).

543    --- Prognostica 24-25; Aphorismi 1.1-3. P.
       Antin. 1.28 (III, Antinoöpolis; parch. cod.).

544    --- Aphorismi 5.43-68, 7.36-43, 54-59. P.
       Antin. 2.86 (VI-VII, Antinoöpolis; pap. cod.).

545 --- Aphorismi. P. Fay. 204; P. Cairo G. H. 10244 (II-III, Bacchias; on the verso; sch. ex.). Identified by A. Calderini, Studi della Scuola Papirologica 1 (1915) 3-4. W. G. Waddell, Ét. Pap. 4 (1938) 123-24.

--- Aphorismi: see also No. 2338.

--- De Flatibus: see No. 2339.

Hippocrates: see also Nos. 2339, 2830.

Hippocrates (alius?): see No. 2017.

546 HIPPOLYTUS ROMANUS: Chronica. P. Oxy. 6. 870 (Muhlenberg Coll.) (VI-VII, Oxy.; pap. cod.). Identified by D. Serruys, Rev. Phil. 38 (1914) 27-31. Archiv 6.247. W. Bannier, Philol. 81 (1925) 123-27.

Hippon of Croton: see No. 2339.

547 HIPPONAX: Iambi. P. Oxy. 18.2174 (cf. ibid, 19, pp. 150-51) (II, Oxy.). Diehl, Anth. Lyr. $3^3$. 98, 104-9; Galiano, LG 84-85; Medeiros, frr. 65-96. Archiv 16.88. O. Masson restores fr. 1, col. 2, lines 7-8; see M. Hombert, Chr. Ég. 26 (1951) 172; A. M. Dale, Lustrum 2 (1957) 8.

548 --- P. Oxy. 18.2175 (cf. ibid., p. 184, ibid. 19, pp. 152-53) (II-III, Oxy.). Diehl, Anth. Lyr. $3^3$. 104, 109-15; Galiano, LG 86; Medeiros, frr. 97-109. Archiv 16.88. K. Latte, Philol. 97 (1948) 46-47.

549 --- (?). PSI 9.1089 (II, Oxy.). Ed. pr.: G. Coppola, Riv. Fil. 56 (1928) 500-6. Diehl, Anth. Lyr. $1^2$.3.80-81 (bibl.), ibid. $3^3$.85-86 (bibl.); Knox, Herodes, No. 92; Lavagnini, Mimn. Call. 56-66; Medeiros, frr. 63-64. Archiv 10.44-45; JEA 16.122. G. Pasquali, SIFC, NS 6 (1928) 301-5; G. Coppola, ibid. 7 (1929) 85-88; K. Latte, Hermes 64 (1929) 385-88, queries the attribution; B. Lavagnini, Annali delle Università Toscane 46 (1929) 163-75; O. Masson restores col. 2, lines 10-11: see M. Hombert, Chr. Ég. 26 (1951) 172.

550 --- P. Oxy. 22.2323 (II-III, Oxy.; on the verso of an unidentified prose text).

551 --- Commentary on Hipponax. P. Oxy. 18.2176 (cf. ibid., pp. 184-85; see also under No. 56, above) (II, Oxy.). Cites Aristophanes; Hermippus (?) of Smyrna, On Hipponax; Palamedes of Elea (?); Polemon, Ad Adaeum et Antigonum. Includes quotations from Hipponax (Diehl, Anth. Lyr. $3^3$.115-18). Frr. 3-5 evidently refer to Homer, Il. x.274. Galiano, LG 86-88; Medeiros, frr. 113-14. Archiv 16.88. E. Fraenkel, CQ 36 (1942) 53-56; P. Maas, ibid. 133; K. Latte, Philol. 97 (1948) 37-47; A. Vogliano, Acme 1 (1948) 257-58; O. Masson, Rev. Ét. Gr. 62 (1949) 300-19.

Hipponax: see also Nos. 211, 219, 1573, 1840, 1895, 2131.

552 HOMER: Iliad and Odyssey, many scattered lines from a "Homeromanteion." P. Lond. 1.121 (III-IV). Collart, Il. 101, Od. 27. Preisendanz, PGM, No. 7. Archiv 8.117-18.

553 Iliad, fragments. Mentioned by Breccia, Alexandrea 140 (?).

554 Iliad (or Odyssey?), several verses. Mentioned by Breccia, Alexandrea 142 (?).

555 Iliad i.1. Mon. Epiphan. 2.611 (VI-VII, Thebes; limestone; sch. ex.). Collart 107.

556 i.1. W. G. Waddell, Ét. Pap. 1 (1932) 17 (No. 8) (P. Cairo inv. 56225) (I-III, Oxy.; sch. ex.). Collart 309.

557 i.1-2. Mon. Epiphan. 2.612 (VI-VII, Thebes; limestone; sch. ex.). Collart 108.

558 i.1-8. A. Bataille and P. Collart, Aeg. 11 (1931) 169-70; P. Rein. 2.65 (P. Sorbonne inv. 2089) (III; sch. ex., on the verso of an official letter). Collart 265.

559 i.1-15. P. Oxy. 3.534 (Columbia Univ. Libr.) (III, Oxy.). Collart 109. Archiv 3.259.

560 i.1-16, 37-51, 55-67. P. Hamb. 155 (inv. 383) (I). Lameere 001; Mette, Il. 373.

561 i.1-36, 49-52, 58-60, 69-82, 89-127. O. Bodl. 1 (O. Petrie 399-404, 406-8, 471-72) (Byzantine; ostraca; sch. ex.). Collart 263. W. G. Waddell, Ét. Pap. 1 (1932) 18, identifies O. Petrie 407 as Il. i.49-52.

562 i.8-26, 32-40. P. Mil. Vogl. 2.29 (inv. 152) (III, Tebtunis). Lameere 002.

i.18-20: see No. 1539.

563 i.22 (and passim). Mon. Epiphan. 2.614 (VI-VII, Thebes; limestone; sch. ex.) Collart 110.

564 i.28-38, 58-68. P. Mil. Vogl. 2.30 (inv. 216) (I, Tebtunis; on the verso of a document). Ed. pr.: A. Gianformaggio, Acme 9 (1956) 75-76. Lameere 003.

565 i.32-57, iii.408-22, vi.211-21, x.192-212, xvii.541-50, xviii.209-617 (with lacunae). Mentioned by A. E. R. Boak, Aeg. 4 (1923) 38 (P. Mich. 13, 15, 14, 19, 12, 2 + 2b, ineditae) (frr. of Bk. xviii: II-III). Mette, Il. 374, 394, 412, 426, 444, 445.

566 i.33-50, 59-75. P. Oxy. 15.1815 (III, Oxy.; on the verso of a tax account). Collart 111.

567 i.37-54, 65-67, 72-79, 207-29. Kenyon, Class. Texts 80; P. Lond. 129, verso; P. Lit. Lond. 1 (Brit. Mus. inv. 129, verso). (II; on the verso of accounts). Collart 112.

568 i.39-41. Quoted in a magical text, P. Lond. 1.47 (II-III). Collart 113. Preisendanz, PGM, No. 6. Archiv 8.117.

569    i. 39-55.   PRIMI l.1 (II).   Collart 321.

570    i. 43-59.   P. Oxy. 3.535 (Columbia Univ. Libr.)
       (III, Oxy.).   Collart 114.   Archiv 3.260.

571    i. 44-60.   J. Nicole, Rev. Phil. 18 (1894) 103 (P.
       Genève inv. 95) (II).   Collart 115.   Lameere, pp.
       83-85, reedits the text.

       i. 51: see No. 1217.

572    i. 70-82, 83-104, 114-23, 412-33, 456-65, 494-590.
       BKT 5.1.3 (inv. 6869 + 7492-95) (I-II).   Collart
       116, 117, 129, 133, 135.   Schubart, Gr. Pal., Abb.
       73.

       i. 75-76: see No. 2707.

573    i. 75, 96, ii. 548, iii. 40, iv. 141, xvii. 714.   Quoted
       in a magical text, BGU 4.1204 (inv. 9873) (IV-V,
       Hermupolis Magna; from a papyrus "Aktenbuch").
       Collart 284.   Preisendanz, PGM, No. 22 a.   Ar-
       chiv 8.126.

574    i. 92-99.   H. Gerstinger, Arch. Bibliogr. 1 (1926)
       87 (No. 1) (P. Rain. inv. 26735) (III, Soknopai-
       ou Nesos?; on the verso of a document).   Col-
       lart 272.

575    i. 92-118, 244-61.   P. Ryl. 3.539 (II B.C.; cart.).
       Collart 354.

576    i. 94-112.   P. Iand. 5.73 (inv. 346) (II; on the verso
       of a document).   Collart 273; Gundel 1.

577    i. 107-16.   P. Oxy. 4.748 (Western Reserve Univ.
       Libr.) (II, Oxy.).   Collart 30.   Archiv 3.473.

       i. 117: see No. 1536.

578    i. 121-57, 161-99, 202-41, 244-74, 277-84.   P. Ryl.
       1.43 (III; text on recto, No. 2026 on verso).
       Collart 56.

579    i. 127-47.-   P. Oxy. 3.536 (Columbia Univ. Libr.)
       (III, Oxy.; on the verso of accounts).   Collart
       118.   Archiv 3.260.

580    i. 129-50.   P. Lond. 2.272; P. Lit. Lond. 2 (Brit.
       Mus. inv. 272) (II-III).   Collart 119.

       i. 151: see No. 317.

581    i. 152-66.   Lameere 004 (Bodleian Libr., Gr. class.
       g.16 (P)) (III).

582    i. 160-76.   P. Oxy. 4.749 (P. Cairo) (II, Oxy.).
       Collart 120.   Archiv 3.474.

583    i. 163-75.   P. Univ. Giss. 4.36 (inv. 303) (ca. 100
       B.C., Fayum).   Collart 333; Gundel 2.

584    i. 164-81.   BKT 5.1.4 (inv. 9813) (II-III).   Collart 44.

585    i. 173-87.   P. Freib. 5 (inv. 11 a) (I-II).   Collart
       103.

586    i. 201 (and passim).   Mon. Epiphan. 2.613 (VI-VII,
       Thebes; limestone; sch. ex.).   Collart 121.

587    i. 206.   Wilcken, Gr. Ostr. 2.1149 (VI; ostr.; sch.
       ex.).   Collart 137.

588    i. 209-39.   P. Princ. 3.108 (II).   Mette, Il. 376.

589    i. 215-20, 250-64, 266.   P. Oxy. 3.537 (Columbia
       Univ. Libr.) (III, Oxy.).   Collart 122.   Archiv
       3.260.

590    i. 215-52, 276-312, 337-41, 345-46, 348, 360-65.
       PSI 7.745 (II?, Oxy.).   Collart 123.

591    i. 215-442 (except 265, 375).   J. Schwartz, BIFAO
       54 (1954) 45-62 (No. 23) (P. Strassb. inv. Gr.
       31 + 32) (II; on the verso of documents).   Lameere
       005; Mette, Il. 377.

592    i. 216-37, 574-97.   P. Princ. 3.109 (V; pap. cod.).
       Mette, Il. 378.

593    i. 223-45.   PSI 9.1083 (III?, Oxy.; on the verso
       of accounts).   Collart 124.

594    i. 258-64, 266-78.   C. W. Keyes, AJP 50 (1929)
       255-56 (Columbia Univ. Libr., inv. 472) (III).
       Collart 278.

595    i. 273-97, 318-42.   P. Oxy. 3.538 (Columbia Univ.
       Libr.) (III, Oxy.; pap. cod.).   Collart 61.   Ar-
       chiv 3.260.

596    i. 273-362.   P. Fay. 141; P. Cairo G.H. 10217
       (I-II, Karanis).   Collart 125.   Archiv 2.340.

597    i. 295-319.   P. Harris 113 (inv. 176a) (II; on the
       verso of accounts).   Collart 344.

598    i. 298-333.   Mentioned by F. G. Kenyon, Pal. GP
       139 (Bodleian Libr., Gr. class. e.58 (P)) (I-II).
       Collart 126.

599    i. 308 ff.   J. Schwartz, BIFAO 61 (1962) 147-51
       (No. 33) (P. Mich. inv. 2810) (II, Karanis).
       A. E. R. Boak, JEA 12 (1926) 21 (first mention).
       Mette, Il. 379.

600    i. 311-27.   P. Tebt. 2.425 (II, Tebtunis; on the
       verso of census returns).   Collart 127.

       i. 314: see No. 1467.

601    i. 339-64, 374-75, 377-83, 392, 395-97.   J.
       Schwartz, BIFAO 54 (1954) 63-65 (No. 24) (P.
       Strassb. inv. Gr. 83) (I?).   Lameere 006; Met-
       te, Il. 380.

602    i. 342-90.   J. Schwartz, BIFAO 46 (1947) 30-32
       (No. 1) (P. Soc. Pap. Alex. inv. 230) (III).
       Mette, Il. 381.

603    i. 343-60, 378-95.   H. Gerstinger, Arch. Biblio-
       gr. 1 (1926) 87-88 (No. 2) (P. Rain. inv. 26728)
       (III, Soknopaiou Nesos?; on the verso of a docu-
       ment).   Collart 289.

604 i. 370-405, 428-76. P. Flor. 2.106 (III; pap. cod.). Collart 54.

605 i. 401-6, 437-42, 450-51. J. Schwartz, BIFAO 46 (1947) 32-33 (No. 2) (P. Soc. Pap. Alex. inv. 244) (III?). Mette, Il. 382.

606 i. 404-47. P. Fay. 5 (at one time in the possession of Dr. W. C. Winslow) (II-III, Theadelphia; on the verso of accounts). Collart 19. Archiv 2.340.

607 i. 406-19. BKT 5.1.5 (inv. 10574) (IV; pap. cod.). Collart 128.

608 i. 413, 439-56, 459-79, 492-93, 503-14 (in a confused order). PSI 2.113 (V, Oxy.). Collart 99.

609 i. 449-61. BKT 5.1.4 (inv. 9584) (I). Collart 130.

610 i. 455-84. J. Schwartz, BIFAO 46 (1947) 33-34 (No. 3) (P. Soc. Pap. Alex. inv. 265) (II-III). Mette, Il. 383.

611 i. 468-73. F. G. Kenyon, JHS 29 (1909) 39 (Brit. Mus.) (V; wooden tablet; sch. ex.). Collart 131.

612 i. 471-80, 495-506. P. Ryl. 1.44 (I B.C.). Collart 132.

613 i. 479-82, 484. H. Gerstinger, Arch. Bibliogr. 1 (1926) 88 (No. 3) (P. Rain. inv. 30048) (II, Fayum?). Collart 290.

614 i. 484-94. A. Ludwich, Philol. 63 (1904) 473-75 ("P. Vitelli'' Firenze?) (I, Fayum). Collart 53.

615 i. 485-91. O. Gueraud, Rev. Ég. Anc. 1 (1927) 130-31 (P. Sorbonne inv. 542) (II B.C., El Lahoun; cart.). Collart 266. Del Corno, Il. 141.

  i. 497-98: see No. 1224.

616 i. 506-7, ii. 1-877 (with many lacunae). P. Hawara 24-28 (Bodleian Libr., Gr. class. a.1 (P)) (II?, Hawara). The text includes scholia, giving the variants of Aristarchus. Collart 2. Bassi, MIG, No. 148, tav. LIV; Kenyon, Pal. GP, pl. XX; New Pal. Soc., Ser. 1, vol. 2, pl. 126 (b); Thompson, GLP, No. 18 (p. 142). Ludwich, PC 6-7.

617 i. 522-34. P. Leeds inv 4, inedita (Brotherton Libr., Univ. of Leeds) (?). Information supplied by J. A. Davison.

618 i. 534-46. M. Hombert and C. Préaux, Chr. Ég. 13 (1938) 386 (Musées Royaux, Bruxelles, inv. E.7160) (I). Collart 362. Lameere, pp. 55-64, 265, reedits the text; J. Bingen, Chr. Ég. 36 (1961) 218.

619 i. 539-48, 561-74. P. Tebt. 3.898 (III-II B.C., Tebtunis; cart.). Collart 269. Del Corno, Il. 141.

620 i. 575-83. P. Oxy. 3.539 (Columbia Univ. Libr., but said to be missing) (II-III, Oxy.; text on recto, No. 2023 on verso). Collart 134. Archiv 3.260.

621 i. 580-611. P. Erl. 3 (inv. 117, verso) (III; on the verso of an account). Mette, Il. 384.

622 i. 608-11. P. Lit. Lond. 3 (Brit. Mus. inv. 1862 A) (II). Collart 136.

  ii. 1: see No. 2707.

623 ii. 1-2. P. Flor. 2.259 (II-III, Theadelphia; written in the margin of a private letter: writing exercise?). Collart 286. Roberts, GLH, pl. 22d.

624 ii. 1-20. P. Lit. Goodspeed 5 (inv. 124) (II, Karanis). Ed. pr.: E. J. Goodspeed, CP 1 (1906) 167. Collart 94.

625 ii. 1-42. H. C. Youtie and O. M. Pearl, Papyri and Ostraca from Karanis (AnnArbor 1944: Michigan Papyri, vol. 6), No. 390, pp. 85-86 (P. Mich. inv. 2931) (II, Karanis; a palimpsest: the text under a receipt). Lameere, p. 268.

  ii. 1-877: see No. 616.

  ii. 8: see No. 1216.

626 ii. 10-19, 21-24, 26-31. P. Oslo 3.65 (II, Tebtunis). Collart 336.

627 ii. 12-26. P. Hamb. 156 (inv. 384) (II). Lameere. 007; Mette, Il. 385.

628 ii. 33-37, 46-52, 55-60. P. Tebt. 2.426 (II, Tebtunis). Collart 138.

629 ii. 41-47, 86-92. P. Rain. 1.2 (a) (inv. 29285) (V-VI, Fayum; pap. cod.). Collart 287.

630 ii. 50-58. P. Oxy. 4.686; P. Lit. Lond. 4 (Brit. Mus. inv. 1534) (I B.C.-I, Oxy.). Collart 29. Archiv 3.474.

631 ii. 57-73. P. Oxy. 4.750 (Western Reserve Univ. Libr.) (III, Oxy.). Collart 68. Archiv 3.474.

632 ii. 95-109, 112-15, 121-57, 172-84, 186-87, 197-210. P. Tebt. 1.4 (II B.C., Tebtunis?; cart.). Collart 37. Archiv 3.257. T. W. Allen, CR 17 (1903) 4-5; A. Ludwich, Berl. Phil. Woch. 23 (1903) 1340-42.

633 ii. 101-9. P. Hamb. 136 (inv. 665) (III B.C.; text followed by an obscure comment in prose).

634 ii. 101-494, iii entire, iv. 1-40. Kenyon, Class. Texts 81-92; P. Lond. 126; P. Lit. Lond. 5 (Brit. Mus. inv. 126) (III, Maʿabdeh; pap. cod. containing also No. 1539). Collart 3.

635 ii. 104-12. H. Gerstinger, Arch. Bibliogr. 1 (1926) 88 (No. 4) (P. Rain. inv. 26737) (III, Fayum?). Collart 291.

  ii. 128: see No. 455.

636 ii. 132-62. BKT 5.1.6 (Ägyptische Sammlung, Berlin, inv. 13839) (IV; wooden tablet; sch. ex.). Collart 50.

637    ii. 147-62.   Schubart, Einführung 508 and Taf. iii
       ("Tabula Berol.") (III; wooden tablet; sch. ex.)
       Collart 139. Ziebarth, No. 20; Ziebarth 2, No. 28.

638    ii. 155-209.   PRIMI 1.2 (II).   Collart 322.

639    ii. 158-74.   PSI 2.137 (III, Oxy.).   Collart 140.

640    ii. 174-205, 621-830, iii. 277-371 (with lacunae).
       P. Hibeh 1.19 (Univ.-Bibl., Graz, inv. I + III. 1944)
       (III B.C., Hibeh; cart.). Collart 40. Del Corno,
       Il. 122-29.

641    ii. 188-202.   C. W. Keyes, AJP 50 (1929) 256-57
       (Columbia Univ. Libr., inv. 463 A) (III). Collart
       279.

642    ii. 220-23.   J. G. Milne, Archiv 5 (1913) 379 (I, Ha-
       wara). Collart 141.

643    ii. 251-875 (lacunae), with a prose introduction.   P.
       Ryl. 3.540; P. Lit. Lond. 6 (Brit. Mus. inv.
       1873) (I, Fayum?). The prose introduction quotes
       Il. xxiv. 804, with the line designed to join the Iliad
       and the Aethiopis. Collart, Il. 104, Od. 357. New
       Pal. Soc., Ser. 2, vol. 1, pl. 53. T. W. Allen,
       CQ 23 (1929) 29-30, and The Homeric Catalogue of
       Ships (Oxford 1921), giving a collation of ii. 494-875.

644    ii. 277-80, viii. 274-82, 372-74, with five other frag-
       ments as yet unidentified.  PRIMI 1.8 bis (II,
       Tebtunis). L. Fruechtel, Phil. Woch. 61 (1941)
       383, identifies frr. 1-3.

645    ii. 298, 325, iii. 51, iv. 26, v. 899, vi. 432, ix. 43,
       x. 324, xiii. 734, xix. 107, xxii. 79.   Cited (with
       Od. iii, 115, etc.) in a "Homeromanteion". P. Bon.
       1.3 (inv. 24 b² + 24 f) (II-III; from the same pap.
       cod. as Nos. 1034 and 1801). Ed. pr.: O. Monte-
       vecchi, Aeg. 27 (1947) 183-84. Mette, Il. 386.
       Archiv 16.86. A. Vogliano, Acme 1 (1948) 226-28,
       ibid. 5 (1952) 385-417.

646    ii. 299-312.   P. Oslo 3.66 (I, Oxy.; on the verso of
       an account). Collart 337.

647    ii. 305-19, 338-60, 373-85.   P. Hibeh 2.195 (now P.
       Cairo) (II). Lameere 008; Mette, Il. 387.

648    ii. 327-33.   P. Ryl. 1.45 (II, Oxy.).   Collart 142.

649    ii. 330-336.   P. Mil. Vogl. 2.31 (inv. 151) (III, Teb-
       tunis). Lameere 009.

650    ii. 339-62, 507-652 (with lacunae).   P. Tebt. 2:265
       (II, Tebtunis). Collart 38.

651    ii. 381-92.   G. Lefebvre, BSAA 14 (1912) 191-92 (II,
       Theadelphia). Collart 143.

652    ii. 400-72.   P. Ryl. 3.541 (I).   Collart 358.

653    ii. 436-44.   P. Oxy. 6.944 (Houghton Libr., Harvard
       Univ.) (III, Oxy.). Collart 144.

654    ii. 444-46, 456-67.   P. Oxy. 11.1385 (Uppsala Uni-
       versitets Bibliotek) (V, Oxy.; pap. cod.). Col-
       lart 145.

655    ii. 459-535.   Lameere, No. 010 and pp. 77-81 (Bod-
       leian Libr., Gr. class. d. 41 (P)) (I).

       ii. 469: see No. 219.

656    ii. 484, 494, 511, 517.   O. Bodl. 2.2169 (inv. 1506)
       (II?; ostr.).

657    ii. 484, 527, 536, 546, 557, 559, 569, 581, 591
       (beginnings only). O. Bodl. 2.2170 (inv. 2454)
       (II?; ostr.; written by a schoolboy?).

658    ii. 494-519, 528-76, 594-614, 631-41, 667-78.  P.
       Maspero 2.67172-74 (VI, Aphroditopolis?; pap.
       cod.). Collart 146.

       ii. 504, 766: see No. 1536.

659    ii. 534-53.   BKT 5.1.4 (inv. 9583) (II-III; on the
       verso of a cursive text). Collart 147.

       ii. 548: see No. 573.

660    ii. 577-601.   Lameere 011 (Bodleian Libr., Gr. class.
       e. 126 (P)) (IV).

661    ii. 611-83.   P. Fay. 309; P. Cairo G.H. 10846 (II,
       Theadelphia). Collart 148. Archiv 2.341.

662    ii. 625-85.   PSI 7.746 (III-IV, Oxy.; pap. cod.).
       Collart 149.

663    ii. 648-743.   P. Ross. Georg. 1.2 (Collection of G.
       Zereteli, Tiflis) (II-III). Collart 150.

664    ii. 672-83.   P. Oxy. 3.540 (Columbia Univ. Libr.)
       (III, Oxy.; on the verso of an account). Collart
       151. Archiv 3.260.

665    ii. 687-95.   P. Aberdeen 104 (II, Fayum?; on the
       verso). Ed. pr.: E. O. Winstedt, CQ 1 (1907)
       258. Collart 152.

       ii. 698, 710: see No. 2170.

666    ii. 717-22.   J. Schwartz, BIFAO 46 (1947) 71 (No. 3
       bis) (PIFAO inv. 326) (I; on the verso). Mette,
       Il. 388.

667    ii. 722-41, 753-72.   P. Oxy. 6.945 (P. Cairo inv.
       41085) (V, Oxy.; pap. cod.). Collart 153.

668    ii. 730-828 (with lacunae), iii. 185.   P. Oxy. 1.20;
       P. Lit. Lond. 7 (Brit. Mus. inv. 742) (II, Oxy.).
       Collart 15. Archiv 1.105. New Pal. Soc., Ser. 1,
       vol. 2, pl. 126 (a); Roberts, GLH, pl. 12b.

       ii. 738: see No. 1217.

669    ii. 738-41, 751, 753-54, 759, 765-93. H. Gersting-
       er, Arch. Bibliogr. 1 (1926) 88 (No. 5) (P. Rain.
       inv. 26767) (II, Soknopaiou Nesos?). Collart 292.

670    ii. 745-64.   P. Oxy. 1.21 (Oriental Mus., Univ. of
       Chicago) (I-II, Oxy.). Collart 154. Archiv 1.105.

671    ii. 748-53.   P. Mil. Vogl. 2.32 (inv. 217) (I, Teb-
       tunis). Lameere 012.

672    ii. 754-64, 798-800.   H. Gerstinger, Arch. Bibliogr. 1 (1926) 88 (No. 6) (P. Rain. inv. 26749) (III, Soknopaiou Nesos?).   Collart 293.

ii. 760: see No. 1539.

673    ii. 760-78.   P. Aberdeen 105 (II, Fayum?).   Ed. pr.: E. O. Winstedt, CQ 1 (1907) 258.   Collart 155.

674    ii. 781-94.   P. Ross. Georg. 1. 3 (Collection of G. Zereteli, Tiflis) (II).   Collart 156.

675    ii. 831-39.   P. Harris 114 (inv. 157 r) (I).   Collart 345.

676    ii. 836-52, 864-77.   P. Lond. 3. 886; P. Lit. Lond. 8 (Brit. Mus. inv. 886) (II-III).   Collart 157.

677    ii. 855-67.   P. Flor. 2. 107 (I).   Collart 158.

678    ii. 859-73.   P. Oxy. 3. 541 (Cornell Univ. Libr.) (III, Oxy.).   Collart 159.   Archiv 3. 260.

679    ii. 861-67.   P. Oxy. 6. 946 (Morgan Libr.) (II-III, Oxy.) Collart 160.

iii entire: see No. 634.

iii. 1: see No. 1536.

680    iii. 1-5.   H. Henne, BIFAO 27 (1927) 79-82 (Collection of Wadie Hanna, of the Cairo Mus.) (II-III; ostr.; sch. ex.?).   Collart 161.

iii. 3 ff.: see No. 455.

681    iii. 23-36.   H. J. Mette, Rev. Phil., Sér. 3. 29 (1955) 195 (No. 389) (P. Berol. inv. 13424) (II). Lameere 013.

682    iii. 29-34.   P. Oslo 3. 67 (II, Oxy.; on the verso of a cursive text).   Collart 338.

683    iii. 30-55.   P. Oxy. 4. 751 (P. Cairo) (II-III, Oxy.). Collart 31.   Archiv 3. 474.

684    iii. 33-43.   P. Rein. 2. 66 (P. Sorbonne inv. 2144) (II-III; on the verso of No. 161).   Collart 285.

iii. 40: see No. 573.

iii. 47 ff.: see No. 455.

685    iii. 49-59.   PSI 14. 1374 (II-III; on the verso of a blank recto; sch. ex.?).   Lameere 014.

iii. 51: see No. 645.

686    iii. 59-82.   H. J. Mette, Rev. Phil., Sér. 3. 29 (1955) 195 (No. 390) (P. Berol. inv. 17049) (III). Lameere 015.

687    iii. 106-26.   PRIMI 1. 3 (I, Oxy.; on the verso). Collart 323.

688    iii. 125-32, 134.   H. J. Mette, Rev. Phil., Sér. 3. 29 (1955) 195 (No. 391) (P. Berol. inv. 17054) (II B.C.). Lameere 016.

689    iii. 174-94.   BKT 5. 1. 5 (inv. 10569) (III; leaf of parch., written on one side).   Collart 162.

690    iii. 177-86.   P. Harris 115 (inv. 176 g) (I).   Collart 346.

691    iii. 185, 187-89, 207-16.   P. Oxy. 4. 687; P. Lit. Lond. 9 (Brit. Mus. inv. 1535) (I B.C. -I, Oxy.). Collart 67.   Archiv 3. 474.

iii. 196: see No. 1357.

692    iii. 214-24.   P. Fay. 209; P. Cairo G. H. 10813 (I, Euhemeria).   Collart 163.   Archiv 2. 341.

iii. 229: see No. 2291.

693    iii. 239-51.   H. J. Mette, Rev. Phil., Sér. 3. 29 (1955) 195 (No. 392) (P. Berol. inv. 17039) (III). Lameere 017.

694    iii. 273-85.   F. G. Kenyon, JHS 29 (1909) 39 (Brit. Mus. Add. MS. 33293) (III; wooden tablet; sch. ex.).   Collart 164.   Ziebarth, No. 20.

iii. 277-371: see No. 640.

695    iii. 280-89, 315-18, 320-22, 351-63, 392-98.   BKT 5. 1. 6 (inv. 263) (IV-V; pap. cod.).   Collart 49.

696    iii. 280-398.   H. J. Mette, Lustrum 1 (1956) 9, note 1 (No. 392a) (P. Berol. inv. 13203) (III-IV; pap. cod.).   Lameere 018.

697    iii. 317-37, 345-72, iv. 1-544 (with lacunae).   Kenyon, Class. Texts 93-97; P. Lit. Lond. 11 (Brit. Mus. inv. 136) (III?; on the verso of accounts).   At the end is a colophon, mentioning Euripides, and composed, by one Callinus, in rough iambic trimeters; see H. J. M. Milne, CR 41 (1927) 60; A. Wifstrand, Hermes 68 (1933) 468-72.   Collart 4.

698    iii. 338-63, 386-88, 390-97.   P. Tebt. 2. 427 (II-III, Tebtunis; on the verso of a contract).   Collart 78.

699    iii. 347-51, 354-56, 383-94, iv. 19-22, 55-61, 67-72, 80-83, 86-91, 98-102, 109-13, v. 525-32, 796-803. P. Hibeh 1. 20; P. Grenf. 2. 3; P. Lit. Lond. 10 (Brit. Mus. inv. 1826 + 689 B) (III B.C., Hibeh; cart.).   Collart 41.   Del Corno, Il. 129-31.

700    iii. 361-77.   P. Oxy. 3. 543 (Cornell Univ. Libr.) (II-III, Oxy.; on the verso of a document).   Collart 165.   Archiv 3. 260.

701    iii. 371-88, 390-412, 415-18.   P. Oxy. 3. 542 (Christie Libr., The Victoria Univ. of Manchester) (III, Oxy.; pap. cod.).   Collart 166.   Archiv 3. 260.

702    iii. 384-88, 390-410, 440-61.   P. Hamb. 157 (inv. 385) (I-II).   Lameere 019; Mette, Il. 393.

703    iii. 397-408, 411-22.   P. Flor. 2. 108 (II-III, Theadelphia).   Collart 167.   Roberts, GLH, pl. 22a.

704    iii. 407.   E. J. Knudtzon, Årsb., Lund. 1951-52, 136-37 (Lunds Universitet, inv. 45) (III-IV).

iii. 408-22: see No. 565.

iii. 424-29: see No. 1612.

705    iii. 458 - iv. 1.    P. Oslo 3. 68 (I B.C., Oxy.).    Collart 339.

706    iv. 1-13, 35-39.    BKT 5.1.4 (inv. 7808) (II-III).    Collart 168.

iv. 1-40: see No. 634.

iv. 1-544: see No. 697.

iv. 26: see No. 645.

707    iv. 27-53, 137-238.    BKT 5.1.3 (inv. 7116 + 7117 + 7119) (III).    Collart 42, 169.

708    iv. 33-65.    PSI 7. 747 (II, Oxy.; on the verso).    Collart 170.

709    iv. 50-66.    PSI 1. 11 (IV-V, Oxy.).    Collart 97.

710    iv. 61-70, 72.    P. Fuad 1 (II; on the verso of reports to a strategos).

711    iv. 61-70, 72-73.    J. Schwartz, BIFAO 54 (1954) 65-66 (No. 25) (PIFAO inv. 31 + P. Soc. Pap. Alex. inv. 82) (II or later; on the verso of documents). Lameere 020; Mette, Il. 395.

712    iv. 82-95.    J. Nicole, Rev. Phil. 18 (1894) 103-4 (P. Genève inv. 93) (I-II; on the verso of accounts).    Collart 171.

713    iv. 87-96.    P. Oxy. 4. 752 (Western Reserve Univ. Libr.) (III, Oxy.).    Collart 69.    Archiv 3. 474.

714    iv. 109-20, 163-83, 188-211.    P. Aberdeen 106 (I, Fayum?).    Ed. pr.: E. O. Winstedt, CQ 1 (1907) 258-59.    Collart 173.

iv. 139: see No. 2148.

iv. 141: see No. 573.

iv. 171: see No. 455.

iv. 180: see No. 512.

iv. 182: see No. 136.

715    iv. 182-95, 198.    P. Oxy. 3. 544 (Cornell Univ. Libr.) (III, Oxy.).    Collart 24.    Archiv 3. 260.

716    iv. 191-95, 198-214, 216-19.    P. Cairo G. H. 10443 (II, Fayum).    Collart 172.

717    iv. 199-219, 238-74.    M. Hombert and C. Préaux, Chr. Ég. 13 (1938) 383-86 (Musées Royaux, Bruxelles, inv. E. 7344) (I).    Collart 363.    Lameere, pp. 65-92, 265, reedits the text; J. Bingen, Chr. Ég. 36 (1961) 218.

718    iv. 257-71.    P. Oxy. 11. 1386 (Dulwich Coll., London) (III, Oxy.; on the verso of a document).    Collart 174.

iv. 297-300, 539: see No. 1536.

719    iv. 318-25, 345-52, vii. 205-13, 237-45, xii. 150-202 (with lacunae).    P. Rein. 2. 67 (P. Sorbonne inv. 2132) (IV; parch. cod.).    Collart 283.

720    iv. 328-40, 363-67.    A. Gianformaggio, Acme 9 (1956) 76-77 (P. Univ. Statale di Milano inv. 415) (I B.C.).    Lameere 021.

721    iv. 357-64.    P. Ryl. 1. 46 (I, Oxy.).    Collart 175.

722    iv. 364-68, 370-98.    P. Oxy. 4. 753 (Royal Ontario Mus., Univ. of Toronto) (III, Oxy.; on the verso of an account).    Collart 32.    Archiv 3. 474.

723    iv. 378-84.    P. Princ. 3. 110 (I-II).    Mette, Il. 397.

724    iv. 440-50.    P. Harris 116 (inv. 176 c) (I?).    Collart 347.

iv. 443: see No. 2295.

725    iv. 443-52.    P. Oxy. 6. 947 (Hibbard Libr.) (III, Oxy.).    Collart 176.

726    iv. 444-50.    P. Cairo Crawford 61 (= P. Gradenwitz 133) (Roman).    Lameere 022; Mette, Il. 398.

727    iv. 454-66, 483-88.    P. Iand. 1. 1 (inv. 93) (I B.C.; on a pap. containing traces of an earlier text).    Collart 177; Gundel 3.

728    iv. 455-74, 476-84, 485-505, 507-14.    H. Gerstinger, Arch. Bibliogr. 1 (1926) 88 (No. 7) (P. Rain. inv. 26744) (VI, Fayum?; parch. cod.).    Collart 294.

729    iv. 475-508, viii. 362-99.    J. Schwartz, BIFAO 46 (1947) 34-36, 60-62 (Nos. 4, 13) (P. Soc. Pap. Alex. inv. 245) (II-III; text on recto and verso).    Mette, Il. 399.

730    iv. 476-83, 485-87, 507-17.    PSI 14. 1375 (III-IV; parch. cod.).    Lameere 023.

731    iv. 478-90.    P. Oxy. 3. 545 (Cornell Univ. Libr.) (II-III, Oxy.; on the verso of a document).    Collart 62.    Archiv 3. 261.

iv. 485: see No. 1502.

iv. 521-22: see No. 2297.

732    iv. 532-39.    P. Oxy. 4. 754 (P. Princ.) (I, Oxy.; on the verso of a document).    Collart 70.    Archiv 3. 474.

733    v. 1-41, 43-56, 58-74, 76-278, 284-303, 329-51, 353-74, 397-406, 420-21, 425-42, 544-48, 701-5. P. Oxy. 2. 223 (Bodleian Libr., Gr. class. a. 8 (P)) (III, Oxy.; on the verso of a petition).    Collart 16.    Roberts, GLH, pl. 21a; Thompson, GLP, No. 15 (p. 136).

734    v. 52-55.    P. Tebt. 2. 428 (II-III, Tebtunis).    Collart 178.

735    v. 69-81, 84-93, 103.   BKT 5.1.4 (inv. 8440) (I).
       Collart 80.

       v. 84, 215, 627: see No. 2707.

736    v. 99-909 (with many lacunae, and two plus-verses,
       180a, 522a), vi. 23-30, 61-67, 179-83, 190, 212-26,
       228-29, 233-430 (including 386a), 438-68, 477-507,
       510-29.   P. Bodmer I (inv. 1 + 2) (ca. 250-350,
       Panopolis?; on the verso of accounts;  Bks. v and
       vi belong to separate rolls).  Lameere 024, 034;
       Mette, Il. 400-1.  R. Merkelbach, Gnomon 27
       (1955) 269-75; C. Préaux, Chr. Ég. 30 (1955)
       383-85; A. Traversa, Paid. 12 (1957) 139-41; K.
       J. McKay, AJP 80 (1959) 383-88, on a variant
       reading in v. 785.

       v. 130: see No. 136.

737    v. 130-73.  P. Oxy. 4. 755 (P. Princ.) (III, Oxy.; on
       the verso of a document).  Collart 179.  Archiv 3.
       474.

738    v. 142-62.  J. Schwartz, BIFAO 46 (1947) 36-37 (No.
       5) (PIFAO inv. 94) (III; on the verso of a cursive
       text).  Mette, Il. 402.

739    v. 206-24.  P. Oxy. 11. 1387 (Univ. of Sydney Libr.)
       (II, Oxy.).  Collart 180.

740    v. 216-60.  P. Ryl. 1. 47 (II).  Collart 57.

       v. 253: see No. 157.

741    v. 278-302.   PSI 10. 1167 (III, Oxy.).   Collart 313.

742    v. 287-317.  G. Plaumann, Ber. Berl. Mus., 1913,
       220 (III-IV; from the same wooden tablet as No.
       1180).  Collart 181.

743    v. 289-300.   J. Schwartz, BIFAO 54 (1954) 66-67
       (No. 26) (P. Soc. Pap. Alex. inv. 275) (III?; on
       the verso of an effaced text).  Lameere 025;
       Mette, Il. 403.

744    v. 324-34, 379-90.  P. Oxy. 4. 756 (Yale Univ. Libr.)
       (III-IV, Oxy.; pap. cod.).  Collart 71.  Archiv 3.
       475.

745    v. 365-97.   P. Michael. 3 (II-III).  Lameere 026;
       Mette, Il. 404.

       v. 385-86, 392-93, 395: see No. 2571.

746    v. 385, viii. 424, x. 193, 521, 564, 572.   Quoted in
       the Paris Magical Papyrus: K. Wessely, Denkschr.
       Wien. Akad, 1888, 27-208 (III-IV, Thebes?; pap.
       cod.).  Collart 264.  Preisendanz, PGM, No. 4.
       Archiv 8. 109-15.

       v. 387-91: see No. 1577.

747    v. 406-13, 440-43.  P. Mil. Vogl. 2. 33 (inv. 630)
       (I-II, Tebtunis; pap. cod.).  Ed. pr.: M. Van-
       doni, Acme 14 (1961) 237.  Lameere 027.

748    v. 450-504.   J. Schwartz, BIFAO 46 (1947) 37-41
       (No. 6) (P. Soc. Pap. Alex. inv. 273) (III).  Mette,
       Il. 405.

749    v. 461-583.   Lameere 028 (P. Genève inv. 202)
       (II-III).

750    v. 473-95.   P. Ryl. 3. 542 (III).  Collart 359.

751    v. 481-95.   P. Amh. 2. 22 (II).  Collart 182.  Archiv
       2. 341.

752    v. 486-95.   H. J. Mette, Rev. Phil., Sér. 3. 29
       (1955) 196 (No. 406) (P. Berol. inv. 11645) (I).
       Lameere 029.

753    v. 519-23.   P. Harris 117 (inv. 176 e) (I-II).  Collart
       348.

       v. 525: see No. 1217.

754    v. 529-31, 533-36.  P. Rein. 2. 68 (P. Sorbonne inv.
       2091) (II).  Ed. pr.: A. Bataille and P. Collart,
       Aeg. 11 (1931) 170-71.  Collart 267.

       v. 531: see No. 2524.

755    v. 541-896 (with many lacunae).  H. Gerstinger, Arch.
       Bibliogr. 1 (1926) 88-89 (No. 8) (II-III, Fayum or
       Hermupolis Magna; 21 frr. from the same roll).
       C. Wessely, Stud. Pal. 5. 36-37 (No. 74) is in-
       cluded among these fragments.  Collart 183, 295.
       Archiv 3. 475.

756    v. 578-86.   P. Oxy. 4. 757 (Yale Univ. Libr.)  (I, Oxy.).
       Collart 184.

757    v. 583-96.   P. Oxy. 4. 758 (Yale Univ. Libr.) (II-III,
       Oxy.).  Collart 72.  Archiv 3. 475.

758    v. 648-81, 684-711.  P. Ryl. 1. 48 (III, Oxy.).  Collart
       58.

759    v. 662-82.   P. Oxy. 4. 759 (Musées Royaux, Bruxelles,
       inv. E. 5937) (II-III, Oxy.).  Collart 33.  Lameere,
       pp. 93-97, reedits the text.

760    v. 678-708.   PSI 10. 1168 (II?, Oxy.).  Collart 314.

761    v. 715-18, 720-29.   P. Oxy. 4. 760 (Univ.-Bibl., Graz,
       inv. I. 1928) (I, Oxy.).  Collart 73.  Archiv 3. 475.

762    v. 721-25, 731-43, 815-21, 845-50.  Kenyon, Class.
       Texts 98-99; P. Lit. Lond. 12 (Brit. Mus. inv.
       127 B) (II).  Collart 6.

763    v. 724-35, 744-55.   PSI 7. 748 (IV?; parch. cod.).
       Collart 185.

764    v. 743-48, 786-93.  H. J. Mette, Rev. Phil., Sér.
       3. 29 (1955) 196 (No. 407) (P. Berol. inv. 17009)
       (IV; parch. cod.).  Lameere 030.

       v. 749-50: see No. 1224.

765    v. 762-859.   J. Schwartz, BIFAO 46 (1947) 41-48
       (No. 7.) (P. Soc. Pap. Alex. inv. 242) (II).  Mette,
       Il. 408.

766    v. 824-41.   P. Lit. Goodspeed 6 (inv. 93) (II, Hermu-
       polis Magna?).  Ed. pr.: E. J. Goodspeed, AJP
       21 (1900) 310-14.  Collart 95.  Archiv 1. 507.

767    v. 835-56.    P. Heid. Siegmann 201 (inv. 1968) (II,
       Oxy.).  Lameere 031; Mette, Il. 408a.

768    v. 855-79.    Lameere 032 (Bodleian Libr., Gr. class.
       f. 42 (P)) (I-II?).

769    v. 857-78.    C. W. Keyes, AJP 50 (1929) 386-87
       (Columbia Univ. Libr., inv. 496) (III).  Collart
       280.

       v. 899: see No. 645.

770    vi. 1-15, 25-39.    P. Princ. 3. 111 (III; pap. cod.).
       Mette, Il. 409.

771    vi. 1-21.    P. Mil. Vogl. 2. 34 (inv. 416) (I, Madinet-
       Madi).

772    vi. 1-39.    P. Par. 3 ter (I-II?, Thebes).  Collart 87.

773    vi. 2-347 (with lacunae).    P. Tebt. 3. 899 (II B.C.,
       Tebtunis; cart.).  Collart 270.

774    vi. 4-7.    P. Hibeh 2. 193 (Brit. Mus. inv. 2966) (ca.
       270-230 B.C., Hibeh; cart.).  Line 4 preserves
       a reading "which Aristarchus, on second thoughts,
       admitted into his text."  Lameere 033; Mette, Il.
       410.  Del Corno, Il. 142.

       vi. 23-529: see No. 736.

775    vi. 75-86, 117-27.    H. J. Mette, Rev. Phil., Sér.
       3. 29 (1955) 196 (No. 411) (P. Berol. inv. 11676) (II).
       Lameere 035.

776    vi. 90-107, 111-25.    Kenyon, Class. Texts 98-99; P.
       Lit. Lond. 13 (Brit. Mus. inv. 127 C) (I?).

777    vi. 99-102, 119-22.    PSI 7. 749 (IV?; parch. cod.).
       Collart 186.

778    vi. 121-48, 173-99, 445-529.    P. Oxy. 3. 445; P. Lit.
       Lond. 14 (Brit. Mus. inv. 1190) (II-III, Oxy.).
       Collart 21.  Archiv 3. 258.  A. Ludwich, Berl.
       Phil. Woch. 24 (1904) 380-82.

779    vi. 133-50, 156-60.    P. Oxy. 11. 1388 (Shrewsbury Sch.)
       (I B.C., Oxy.).  Collart 187.

       vi. 146: see No. 1782.

780    vi. 147-49.    P. Oxy. 4. 761 (Houghton Libr., Harvard
       Univ.) (I B.C., Oxy.; on the verso of a document;
       sch. ex.).  Collart 188.  Archiv 3. 475.

781    vi. 156-73, 196-208.    A. Wifstrand, Årsb., Lund
       1934-35, 53-54 (No. 1) (ca. A.D. 200).  Collart
       335.

782    vi. 162-77.    P. Univ. Giss. 4. 37 (inv. 304) (I B.C.,
       Fayum?).  Collart 334; Gundel 4.

       vi. 176: see No. 455.

783    vi. 196-224 (with lacunae), 236-76.    G. Rudberg, SO
       3 (1925) 20-25; P. Oslo 2. 7 (III, Fayum?).  Col-
       lart 189.

       vi. 211-21: see No. 565.

784    vi. 216-28.    C. W. Keyes, AJP 50 (1929) 258 (Colum-
       bia Univ. Libr., inv. 492 B) (II).  Collart 281.

785    vi. 226-309.    J. Schwartz, BIFAO 46 (1947) 48-53
       (No. 8) (P. Soc. Pap. Alex. inv. 213) (II; on the
       verso?).  Mette, Il. 413.

       vi. 234 ff.: see No. 1755.

       vi. 235-36: see No. 1223.

       vi. 268: see No. 89.

786    vi. 269-81.    H. J. Mette, Rev. Phil., Sér. 3. 29
       (1955) 196 (No. 414) (P. Berol. inv. 17153) (III).
       Lameere 036.

       vi. 311: see No. 455.

787    vi. 316-72.    J. Schwartz, BIFAO 46 (1947) 53-56 (No.
       9) (P. Soc. Pap. Alex. inv. 216) (III-IV; on the
       verso?).  Mette, Il. 415.

788    vi. 322-38, 356-74, 386.    PSI 8. 977 (IV?; pap. cod.).
       Collart 190.

789    vi. 326 — xiii. 827 (with many lacunae).    J. Schwartz,
       BIFAO 61 (1962) 151-68 (No. 34) (P. Strassb. inv.
       Gr. 2675) (IV; pap. cod.).

790    vi. 327-53.    J. Nicole, Rev. Phil. 18 (1894) 104 (P.
       Genève inv. 89) (I-II; on the verso of documents).
       Collart 191.

791    vi. 387-410, with a prose exercise based on the text.
       H. Oellacher, Ét. Pap. 4 (1938) 133-35 (P. Rain.
       inv. 26740) (II, Soknopaiou Nesos; sch. ex.).
       Collart 356.

792    vi. 413-43, 445-50.    PSI 11. 1184 (II, Oxy.).  Collart
       327.

       vi. 432: see No. 645.

793    vi. 437-60.    P. Bon. 1. 2 (inv. 5 b) (I-II).  Ed. pr.:
       O. Montevecchi, Aeg. 27 (1947) 172.  Mette, Il.
       416.

       vi. 448-55: see No. 1185.

794    vi. 455-77.    H. J. Mette, Rev. Phil., Sér. 3. 29
       (1955) 197 (No. 417) (P. Berol. inv. 11685) (II).
       Lameere 037.

795    vi. 498-529.    PSI 11. 1185 (II-III, Oxy.; on the verso
       of a document).  Collart 328.

796    vii. 1-30, 32-35.    P. Oxy. 4. 762 (Univ. of Pennsyl-
       vania Mus., inv. 2815) (III, Oxy.; on the verso
       of a list of persons).  Collart 34.  Archiv 3. 475.

797    vii. 4-15.    P. Haun. 1. 1 (inv. 5 n) (II, Fayum?).
       Mette, Il. 418.

       vii. 15-16: see No. 2707.

798    vii. 50-66.    PSI 14. 1376 (I-II).  Lameere 038.

799  vii. 60-68.   P. Aberdeen 107 (II, Fayum?).  Ed.  pr.:
E. O. Winstedt, CQ 1 (1907) 259.  Collart 192.

800  vii. 63-93, 94-124.   Lameere 039 (P. Genève inv.
85) (II).

801  vii. 65-86.   J. Schwartz, BIFAO 46 (1947) 56-57 (No.
10) (PIFAO inv. 312) (IV?, Oxy.).  Mette, Il. 419.

802  vii. 68-134.   P. Oxy. 4. 763 (P. Cairo) (III, Oxy.;
pap. cod.).  Collart 35.  Archiv 3. 475.

803  vii. 117-22, 143-48, 167-74.   Allen, No. 105 (Bodleian Libr., Gr. class. 610 (P): the reference, as
given by Allen, appears incomplete) (II).  Collart
275.

804  vii. 141-58.   P. Hamb. 158 (inv. 83) (I).  Lameere
040; Mette, Il. 420.

vii. 162: see No. 1223.

805  vii. 182-94, 218-30, 250-55, 285-89.   P. Oxy. 11.
1389 (Southern Methodist Univ. Libr.) (IV, Oxy.;
parch. cod.).  Collart 193.

vii. 205-13, 237-45: see No. 719.

806  vii. 223-37, 266-348.   H. Gerstinger, Arch. Bibliogr. 1 (1926) 89-90 (No. 9) (P. Rain. inv. 26730 +
26745) (II-III).  Collart 296.

807  vii. 232-33, 235-49.   PRIMI 1. 4 (III-IV; on the verso of a document).  Collart 324.

808  vii. 237-44, 264-73.   P. Oxy. 3. 546 (Cornell Univ.
Libr.) (II, Oxy.; on the verso of a tax list).  Collart 63.  Archiv 3. 261.

809  vii. 255-59.   M. Vandoni, Acme 15 (1962) 245 (Univ.
Statale di Milano, inv. 419) (II, Madinet-Madi).
Lameere 041.

vii. 264: see No. 2707.

810  vii. 283-98, 313-43 (with lacunae).   J. Schwartz,
BIFAO 46 (1947) 57-60 (No. 11) (P. Soc. Pap. Alex.
inv. 212) (III).  Mette, Il. 421.

811  vii. 324-36, 357-63.   P. Oxy. 3. 547 (Cornell Univ.
Libr.) (II-III, Oxy.).  Collart 194.  Archiv 3. 261.

812  vii. 329-48, 353-68, 370-74.   PSI 7. 750 (IV-V; parch.
cod.).  Collart 195.

813  vii. 355-71.   PSI 2. 114 (V, Oxy.).  Collart 100.

814  vii. 427-441.   S. Daris, Aeg. 39 (1959) 9-10 (P. Med.
inv. 99) (II).  Lameere 042.

vii. 467: see No. 1536.

815  viii. 1, with a coronis.   P. Mil. Vogl. 2. 36 (inv. 414)
(I B. C., Madinet-Madi).  Ed. pr.: M. A. Van-
doni, Acme 11 (1958) 263-64.  Lameere 043.

816  viii. 1-5.   PSI 9. 1085 (?, Oxy.).  Collart, Il. 196,
and Od. 61 (by error).

817  viii. 1-192 (with lacunae).   P. Lond 3. 736 verso; P.
Lit. Lond. 15 (Brit. Mus. inv. 736) (II-III; on the
verso of accounts).  Collart 197.

818  viii. 1-29, 35-68.   P. Lit. Goodspeed 7 (inv. 92) (II,
Karanis).  Ed. pr.: E. J. Goodspeed, AJA, Ser.
2. 2 (1898) 347-56.  Collart 17.  Archiv 1. 105.

819  viii. 17-258 (with lacunae).   P. Heid. Lit. 1 (inv. 1261);
P. Hibeh 1. 21; P. Grenf. 2. 2; P. Lit. Lond. 16
(Brit. Mus. inv. 1827 + 689 A) (III B. C., Hibeh;
cart.).  Collart 7.  Del Corno, Il. 84-93.

820  viii. 41-54, 86-104, 139-56, 173-86.   P. Fay. 210; P.
Cairo G. H. 10814 (II, Euhemeria; on the verso of
accounts).  Collart 198.  Archiv 2. 341.

821  viii. 62-65, 105-14.   P. Flor. 2. 109 (I-II).  Collart 55.

822  viii. 64-75, 96-116.   P. Grenf. 1. 2 (Bodleian Libr.,
Gr. class. d. 20 (P)) (I-II, Fayum).  Collart 20.

823  viii. 109-22.   P. Oxy. 4. 764 (Houghton Libr., Harvard
Univ.) (III, Oxy.).  Collart 199.  Archiv 3. 475.

824  viii. 150-62.   J. Schwartz, BIFAO 46 (1947) 60 (No.
12) (P. Soc. Pap. Alex. inv. 263) (II-III).  Mette,
Il. 422.

825  viii. 169-77, 306-24.   BKT 5. 1. 4 (inv. 7499 + 7502)
(III-IV).  Collart 200-201.  Schubart, Gr. Pal.,
Abb. 93.

826  viii. 198-213.   Lameere 044 (Bodleian Libr., Gr.
class. f. 24 (P)) (III).

827  viii. 216-23, 227-32.   H. Gerstinger, Arch. Bibliogr.
1 (1926) 90 (No. 10) (P. Rain. inv. 26741) (II-III).
Collart 297.

828  viii. 264-76, 278-300.   P. Heid. Siegmann 202 (inv.
1969) (III, Batu-el-Harit).  Lameere 045; Mette,
Il. 422a.

viii. 274-82, 372-74: see No. 644.

829  viii. 312-14, 316-33, 335-38.   PSI 8. 978 (II-III).  Collart 202.

830  viii. 332-36, 362-69.   P. Fay. 4; P. Lit. Lond. 17
(Brit. Mus. inv. 816) (II-I B. C., Bacchias).  Collart 18.  Archiv 2. 342.

viii. 362-99: see No. 729.

viii. 393-94: see No. 1224.

viii. 424: see No. 746.

831  viii. 433-47.   BKT 5. 1. 3 (inv. 6845) (II).  Collart
203; Lameere, pp. 81-83, reedits the text.  Schubart, Gr. Pal., Abb. 76; idem, PGB, tab. 19 c.
J. Bingen, Chr. Ég. 36 (1961) 218.

832  viii. 436-57, 459-61.   H. Gerstinger, Arch. Bibliogr.
1 (1926) 90 (No. 11) (P. Rain. inv. 19768) (I, Karanis).  Collart 298.

833   viii. 451-56, 486-91, xi. 578-81, 607-14, 628-49, 660-
      72, xii. 3-16, 23-47, 53-63, 136-40, 166-70, xiii.
      751-80, 786-813.   PSI 1.10 (IV, Hermupolis Magna;
      pap. cod.).   Collart 96.

834   ix. 1-7.   P. Jouguet and G. Lefebvre, BCH 28 (1904)
      207-8 (PIFAO) (Roman; wooden tablet; sch. ex.).
      Collart 204. Ziebarth, No. 18; Ziebarth 2, No.
      27.

835   ix. 35-41.   P. Hamb. 159 (inv. 696) (I).   Lameere
      046; Mette, Il. 423.

      ix. 43: see No. 645.

836   ix. 103-23, 155-78.   P. Lit. Lond. 18 (Brit. Mus.
      inv. 2037 C) (III-IV; pap. cod.).   Collart 205.

837   ix. 152-61.   H. Gerstinger, Arch. Bibliogr. 1 (1926)
      90 (No. 12) (P. Rain. inv. 26729) (I-II, Soknopaiou
      Nesos?).   Collart 299.

      ix. 169-70: see No. 1223.

838   ix. 181-90.   BKT 5.1.4 (inv. 7803) (I-II).   Collart 206.

839   ix. 186-95.   P. Harris 118 (inv. 176 h) (III; on the ver-
      so).   Collart 349.

840   ix. 198-210.   BKT 5.1.4 (inv. 7806) (II).   Collart 207.

      ix. 230-31: see No. 1221.

841   ix. 235-301.   P. Oxy. 3.548 (Cornell Univ. Libr.)
      (III, Oxy.; pap. cod.).   Collart 64. Archiv 3.261.

842   ix. 277-88, 299-312.   BKT 5.1.4 (inv. 7807) (III-IV).
      Collart 79.

843   ix. 287-96, 325-31.   P. Oxy. 11.1390 (Tonbridge Sch.)
      (V, Oxy.; pap. cod.).   Collart 208.

844   ix. 300-17.   P. Lit. Lond. 19 (Brit. Mus. inv. 1862 F)
      (II).   Collart 209.

845   ix. 320-33.   P. Oxy. 4.765 (Houghton Libr., Harvard
      Univ.) (III, Oxy.).   Collart 74. Archiv 3.476.

      ix. 323-24: see No. 1325.

846   ix. 356-78.   P. Aberdeen 108 (II, Fayum?).  Ed. pr.:
      E. O. Winstedt, CQ 1 (1907) 259-60.   Collart 52.

      ix. 381, 385, 389, 404: see No. 2295.

847   ix. 381-87.   P. Oslo 3.69 (IV).   Collart 340.

848   ix. 401-13, 416-25.   PSI 11.1186 (I-II, Oxy.).   Collart
      329.

849   ix. 480-99.   PSI 11.1187 (II, Oxy.).   Collart 230.

      ix. 568-69: see No. 1184.

850   ix. 575-85, 608-19.   PSI 1.12 (IV, Oxy.; pap. cod.).
      Collart 210.

851   ix. 682-709.   PSI 14.1377  (II).   Lameere 047.

852   x. 1-26.   H. Gerstinger, Arch. Bibliogr. 1 (1926) 90
      (No. 13) (P. Rain. inv. 26753) (I B.C.: on the ver-
      so of a document).   Collart 300.

853   x. 41-57, 76-100, 103-12.   P. Rain. 1.2 b (inv. 19794),
      3.1 (inv. 19791) (cf. ibid. 4, p. 133) (I-II, Karanis;
      on the verso of a document).   Collart 288.

854   x. 82-87.   P. Oslo 3.70 (III-IV, Oxy.).   Collart 341.

855   x. 84-102.   PSI 12.1274 (II, Oxy.).   Lameere 048;
      Mette, Il. 424.

856   x. 106-21.   M. Vandoni, Acme 15 (1962) 245-46 (Univ.
      Statale di Milano, inv. 432) (I-II, Madinet-Madi).
      Lameere 049.

857   x. 123-40.   H. J. Mette, Rev. Phil., Sér. 3.29 (1955)
      197 (No. 425) (P. Berol. inv. 17048) (II).   Lameere
      050.

      x. 192-212: see No. 565.

      x. 193, 521, 564, 572: see No. 746.

858   x. 199-221, 237-57, 262-63.   PSI 1.13 (III, Hermupo-
      lis Magna; pap. cod.).   Collart 98.

859   x. 205-20.   P. Cairo Crawford 59 (= P. Gradenwitz
      131) (Roman).   Lameere 051; Mette, Il. 427.

860   x. 215-26.   H. J. Mette, Rev. Phil., Sér. 3.29 (1955)
      197 (No. 428) (P. Berol. inv. 17152) (II-III).   La-
      meere 052.

861   x. 233-43, 250-55.   P. Oxy. 6.948 (Univ. of Penn-
      sylvania Mus., inv. E. 3076) (III, Oxy.).   Collart
      211.

862   x. 258-81.   J. Schwartz, BIFAO 46 (1947) 62-63 (No.
      14) (P. Soc. Pap. Alex. inv. 224) (III?).   Mette,
      Il. 429.

      x. 274: see No. 551.

863   x. 294-301.   H. J. Mette, Rev. Phil., Sér. 3.29
      (1955) 197 (No. 430) (P. Berol. inv. 17038) (II-III).
      Lameere 053.

      x. 324: see No. 645.

      x. 341: see No. 1539.

864   x. 372-443.   BKT 5.1.5 (inv. 10570) (V; pap. cod.).
      Collart 46.

      x. 394: see No. 89.

865   x. 437-52.   P. Oxy. 6.949 (Univ.-Bibl., Graz, inv.
      I. 1954) (II-III, Oxy.).   Collart 90.

      x. 511: see No. 362.

866   x. 542-47.   P. Oxy. 4.766 (Johns Hopkins Univ. Libr.)
      (III, Oxy.).   Collart 212. Archiv 3.476.

867   x. 550-79.   PSI 11.1188 (II-III, Oxy.; on the verso of
      a document).   Collart 331.

xi. 21: see No. 204.

xi. 34: see No. 1216.

868    xi. 34-42, 69-77.   P. Harris 119 (inv. 79 a) (II?; pap. cod.).   Collart 350.

869    xi. 39-52.   P. Oxy. 3: 549 (Cornell Univ. Libr.) (II-III, Oxy.).   Collart 65.   Archiv 3. 261.

870    xi. 86-96, 121 to end, xii. 1 to xvi. 499.   U. von Wilamowitz-Moellendorff and G. Plaumann, Sitzb. Berl. Akad., 1912, 1198-1219 ("P. Morgan:" Morgan Libr.) (IV; pap. cod.).   Collart 60; Lameere, p. 171. Preisendanz, PFF 256. Schubart, Gr. Pal., Abb. 95. B. Hemmerdinger, SIFC, NS 25 (1951) 85.

871    xi. 101-6.   H. J. Mette, Rev. Phil., Sér. 3. 29 (1955) 197 (No. 431) (P. Berol. inv. 7507) (I).   Lameere 054.

872    xi. 123-52, 154-80, 299-356.   BKT 5.1. 6 (inv. 262) (V-VI; pap. cod.).   Collart 213.

873    xi. 152-62, 185-93.   P. Rein. 2. 69 (P. Sorbonne inv. 2101 + 2118) (V; pap. cod.).   Ed. pr.: A. Bataille and P. Collart, Aeg. 11 (1931) 171-72.   Collart 277.

874    xi. 172-83.   P. Oxy. 4. 688; P. Lit. Lond. 20 (Brit. Mus. inv. 1536) (I B. C.-I, Oxy.).   Collart 214. Archiv 3. 476.

875    xi. 265-89, 678-90, xii. 127-31, 190-98 (with various plus-verses).   P. Hamb. 153 (inv. 649 + 650, frr. 2-4, 7-9, 11) (ca. 200 B. C.; cart. ?).   Lameere 055; Mette, Il. 432.   Del Corno, Il. 135-40.

876    xi. 322-29, 359-402.   P. Oxy. 6. 950 (Morgan Libr.) (III, Oxy.).   Collart 91.

xi. 388: see No. 2148.

877    xi. 449-55, 479-85.   H. Gerstinger, Arch. Bibliogr. 1 (1926) 90-91 (No. 14) (P. Rain. inv. 26751) (IV-V, Fayum?; parch. cod.).   Collart 301.

878    xi. 464-66, 515-17.   PSI 2. 138 (IV, Oxy.; pap. cod.). Collart 215.

879    xi. 502-37.   P. Petrie 1. 3 (4); P. Lit. Lond. 21 (Brit. Mus. inv. 486 D) (III B. C., Gurob; cart.). Collart 8. Del Corno, Il. 93-95.

880    xi. 505-16, 521-47, 555-67, 572-602.   P. Oxy. 3. 550; P. Lit. Lond. 250 (Brit. Mus. inv. 1191) (II, Oxy.). Collart 25. Archiv 3. 261.

881    xi. 533-66.   P. Ryl. 3. 543 (III, Oxy.; on the verso of an account).   Collart 360.

882    xi. 555-61.   P. Oxy. 4. 767 (Johns Hopkins Univ. Libr.) (II, Oxy.).   Collart 216.   Archiv 3. 476.

883    xi. 556-613.   P. Tebt. 2. 266 (II, Tebtunis).   Collart 39.

884    xi. 564-70, 597-602, 608-10, 635-38.   P. Oxy. 11. 1391 (Bibliothèque de l'Université de Louvain, D. 371. 1, deperdita) (V, Oxy.; pap. cod.).   Collart 92. JEA 6. 122. P. Collart, Rev. Phil. 42 (1918) 42-46.

xi. 596: see No. 2707.

885    xi. 652-83, 689-720.   J. Schwartz, BIFAO 61 (1962) 169-71 (No. 35) (P. Strassb. inv. Gr. 1600 a-b + 1624 + 1632 b + 1654 a-b + 1660 b) (IV; pap. cod.).

886    xi. 708-21.   H. Gerstinger, Arch. Bibliogr. 1 (1926) 91 (No. 15) (P. Rain. inv. 26763) (I, Soknopaiou Nesos?).   Collart 302.

887    xi. 712-30.   H. J. Mette, Rev. Phil., Sér. 3. 29 (1955) 197 (No. 433) (P. Berol. inv. 11522) (II). Lameere 056.

888    xi. 734-53, 772-90.   P. Rein. 2. 70 (P. Sorbonne inv. 2104) (VI; pap. cod.).   Collart 355.

889    xi. 736-64.   P. Oxy. 4. 768 (Johns Hopkins Univ. Libr.) (III, Oxy.).   Collart 75.   Archiv 3. 476.

890    xi. 788 to xii. 9.   J. Nicole, Rev. Phil. 18 (1894) 104-11 (P. Genève inv. 90) (II B. C.).   Collart 5.   Del Corno, Il. 78-84.   G. M. Bolling, CP 47 (1952) 87-89.

891    xi. 816-26.   J. Schwartz, BIFAO 54 (1954) 67 (No. 27) (P. Strassb. inv. Gr. 1242) (II-III).   Lameere 057; Mette, Il. 434.

xii. 1 to xvi. 499: see No. 870.

892    xii. 1-3.   P. Harris 120 (inv. 176 d) (II).   Collart 351.

893    xii. 126-34.   P. Harris 121 (inv. 176 b) (II).   Collart 352.

xii. 127-98: see No. 875.

894    xii. 128-40, 176-91, 249-63, 355-68, 370, 374, 399-402, 404-12, 446-58.   P. Lit. Lond. 251 (Brit. Mus. inv. 2722 A); P. Harris 36 (inv. 177), from the same roll (II B. C.).   Collart 217, 342.   Del Corno, Il. 131-135.   T. W. Allen, CQ 22 (1928) 74-75; G. M. Bolling, JEA 14 (1928) 78-81; G. Jachmann, Gött. Nachr., 1949, 169-91; E. Siegmann, P. Hamb., pp. 104-5, reports a new study of P. Lit. Lond. 251.

xii. 150-202: see No. 719.

895    xii. 178-98.   P. Grenf. 1. 4 (Bodleian Libr., Gr. class. e. 21 (P)) (IV, Fayum).   Collart 218.

896    xii. 248-67.   H. Gerstinger, Arch. Bibliogr. 1 (1926) 91 (No. 16) (P. Rain. inv. 26739) (II).   Collart 303.

897    xii. 265-92.   M. Hombert and C. Préaux, Chr. Ég. 13 (1938) 387 (Musées Royaux, Bruxelles, inv. E. 7161) (II-III).   Collart 364. Lameere, pp. 98-104, 265-66, publishes the text in full.

898    xii. 300-13.   H. Gerstinger, Arch. Bibliogr. 1 (1926)
       91 (No. 17) (P. Rain. inv. 26732) (I-II, Soknopaiou
       Nesos?).   Collart 304.

       xii. 326: see No. 341.

       xii. 359-60: see No. 1217.

899    xiii. 2-56, 73-87, 149-775, xiv. 120-293, 332-522 (with
       lacunae).   A. S. Hunt, Journ. Philol. 26 (1899) 25-
       59; P. Lit. Lond. 22 (Brit. Mus. inv. 732) (I).
       Collart 10.   Kenyon, Pal. GP, pl. XIX; Thompson,
       GLP, No. 12 (p. 129).

900    xiii. 26-47, 107-11, 143-73.   P. Par. 3; G. Lumbroso,
       Rend. Acc. Linc., Ser. 5.2 (1893) 831 (P. Vat.)
       (I B.C.-I?, Elephantine?).   Collart 85, 220.   J.
       La Roche, Die Homerische Textkritik im Alterthum
       (Leipzig 1866) 448, evidently refers to P. Par. 3.
       O. Marucchi, Il Museo Egizio Vaticano... (Roma
       1899) 272, reprints P. Vat.

901    xiii. 58-99.   P. Oxy. 3.446 (Houghton Libr., Harvard
       Univ.) (II, Oxy.).   Collart 22.   Archiv 3.261.

       xiii. 64: see No. 197.

902    xiii. 100-27.   P. Bouriant 5 (P. Sorbonne inv. 830)
       (V; on the verso of an account).   Collart 219.

903    xiii. 184-314, 317-41, 345-67.   BKT 5.1.5 (inv. 46;
       once loaned to the Cairo Mus.) (I B.C.; cart.)
       Collart 47.

       xiii. 217: see No. 2463.

904    xiii. 232-831, xiv. 107-61, xvi. 171-293, xx. 106-58,
       xxii. 143-452, xxiii. 495-536 (with lacunae).   PSI
       13. 1298 (V-VI, Antinoöpolis; pap. cod.).   Mette,
       Il. 435.

905    xiii. 297-302.   N. Lewis, Ét. Pap. 3 (1936) 49 (No.
       2) (P. Strassb. inv. Gr. 1876) (II).   Collart 318.

       xiii. 301: see No. 1217.

906    xiii. 308-17, 342-47.   P. Oxy. 4.769 (Johns Hopkins
       Univ. Libr.) (II-III, Oxy.).   Collart 36.   Archiv 3.
       476.

907    xiii. 340-50, 356-75.   P. Tebt. 2.429 (II, Tebtunis).
       Collart 221.

908    xiii. 355-81.   P. Rein. 2.71 (P. Sorbonne inv. 2099)
       (III; cart.).   Collart 274.   Ed. pr.: A. Bataille
       and P. Collart, Aeg. 11 (1931) 173-74.

909    xiii. 372-77, 405-13.   P. Oxy. 4.770 (Chadwick Mus.)
       (II, Oxy.).   Collart 76.   Archiv 3.476.

910    xiii. 496-509.   J. Schwartz, BIFAO 54 (1954) 68 (No.
       28) (P. Strassb. inv. Gr. 2480) (I-II; on the verso
       of a list of names).   In the same hand as No. 1154.
       Lameere 058; Mette, Il. 436.

       xiii. 505: see No. 1221.

911    xiii. 512-27, 545-60.   F. M. Debatin, AJA 35 (1931)
       62 (Washington Univ. Libr.) (IV-V; pap. cod.).
       Collart 308.

912    xiii. 545-59.   Schubart, Einführung 507 and pl. 1
       (P. Berol. inv. 11516) (I).   Collart 222.

913    xiii. 584-640.   Lameere 059 (Bodleian Libr., Gr.
       class. d. 45 (P)) (II).

       xiii. 685: see No. 200.

914    xiii. 762-74.   H. Gerstinger, Arch. Bibliogr. 1 (1926)
       91 (No. 18) (P. Rain. inv. 26752) (II-III, Hermupolis
       Magna).   Collart 305.

       xiii. 763: see No. 2707.

       xiv. 66: see No. 136.

       xiv. 107-61: see No. 904.

915    xiv. 108-26, 162-77.   P. Merton 1.3 (III; pap. cod.).
       Mette, Il. 437.

       xiv. 120-293, 332-522: see No. 899.

       xiv. 129: see No. 1217.

916    xiv. 227-53, 256-68, 270-83.   P. Oxy. 3.551 (P.
       Princ.) (II, Oxy.).   Collart 26.   Archiv 3.261.

917    xiv. 232-51, 291-310.   PSI 10.1169 (III, Oxy.; pap.
       cod.).   Collart 315.

       xiv. 308: see No. 455.

       xiv. 349-50: see No. 1221.

918    xiv. 367-76.   C. W. Keyes, AJP 50 (1929) 259-60
       (Columbia Univ. Libr., inv. 414) (III).   Collart
       282.

919    xiv. 393-410.   Schubart, Gr. Pal., Abb. 90 (P. Berol.
       inv. 11910) (II).   Lameere 060; Mette, Il. 438.

       xv. 208-9: see No. 1539.

920    xv. 301-14.   N. Lewis, Ét. Pap. 3 (1936) 50 (No. 3)
       (P. Strassb. inv. Gr. 1536) (I).   Collart 319.

921    xv. 303-25.   P. Oxy. 11.1392; P. Lit. Lond. 23
       (Brit. Mus. inv. 2446) (III, Oxy.).   Collart 93.

922    xv. 332-70, 386-409.   P. Oxy. 15.1816 (Westminster
       Sch.) (III, Oxy.; on the verso of an account).
       Collart 223.

923    xv. 376-96, 405-25.   H. J. Mette, Rev. Phil., Sér.
       3. 29 (1955) 198 (No. 439) (P. Berol. inv. 17005)
       (VI; pap. cod.).   Lameere 061.

924    xv. 383-90, 421-30.   BKT 5.1.5 (inv. 9968) (III-IV;
       pap. cod.).   Collart 81.

925    xv. 425-82, 539-648, xvii. 101-222, xxiii. 490-511,
       530-52.   BKT 5.1.5 (inv. 230; once loaned to the
       Cairo Mus.) (V; pap. cod.).   Collart 48.

926    xv.540-45, 576-82.  P. Harris 37 (inv. 176 f) (V-VI;
       pap. cod.).  Collart 343.

       xv.563:  see No. 2524.

927    xv.575-94, 623-40.  PSI 7.751 (I?, Oxy.).  Collart
       224.

928    xv.658-73.  P. Ibscher 3 (P. Hamb., p. 130) (I B.C.).
       Lameere 062; Mette, Il. 439a.

929    xv.736-46.  P. Oxy. 4.771 (Christie Libr., The
       Victoria Univ. of Manchester) (II-III, Oxy.).  Col-
       lart 225.  Archiv 3.476.

       xvi.1:  see No. 2436.

930    xvi.1-36.  H. J. Mette, Rev. Phil., Sér. 3.29 (1955)
       198 (No. 440) (P. Berol. inv. 13922) (II).  Lameere
       063.

931    xvi.60-84.  P. Harris 122 (inv. 40 a) (II).  Collart
       353.

932    xvi.157-70, 191-203.  P. Oxy. 11.1393 (Marlborough
       Coll.) (V, Oxy.; parch. leaf).  Collart 226.

       xvi.171-293:  see No. 904.

       xvi.259-60:  see No. 219.

933    xvi.331-49, 372-90.  P. Rain. 3.4 (inv. 30485) (V;
       pap. cod.).

934    xvi.401-5, 418-30.  P. Tebt. 2.430 (I-II, Tebtunis).
       Collart 227.

935    xvi.484-89.  P. Ryl. 1.49 (III B.C., Hibeh?; cart.).
       Collart 59.  Del Corno, Il. 140.

936    xvi.507-18, 530-48.  H. J. Mette, Rev. Phil., Sér.
       3.29 (1955) 198 (No. 441) (P. Berol. inv. 16348)
       (III).  Lameere 064.

937    xvi.611-17, 675-79.  P. Flor. 2.110 (III-IV; pap. cod.).
       Collart 228.

       xvi.631:  see No. 2293.

938    xvi.676-79.  P. Flor. 2.111 (III-IV).  Collart 229.

939    xvi.695-702, 727-33.  H. J. Mette, Rev. Phil., Sér.
       3.29 (1955) 198 (No. 442) (P. Berol. inv. 16970)
       (IV-V; pap. cod.).  Lameere 065.

940    xvi.758-69.  P. Erl. 4 (inv. 55) (II-III).  Mette, Il.
       443.

       xvi.795:  see No. 2291.

       xvi.816:  see No. 1536.

941    xvii.50-761 (with lacunae).  P. Ross. Georg. 1.4
       (P. Golenischeff) (III).  Collart 230.

942    xvii.80-94.  P. Oxy. 3.552 (Houghton Libr., Harvard
       Univ.) (II, Oxy.)  Collart 231.  Archiv 3.262.

943    xvii.101-15.  H. Gerstinger, Arch. Bibliogr. 1 (1926)
       91 (No. 19) (P. Rain. inv. 26742); P. Rain. 3.2
       (II, Soknopaiou Nesos?).  Collart 306.

944    xvii.104, 106-8, 110-11, 142-51.  Raineri F., No.
       533; C. Wessely, Stud. Pal. 20 (1920), No. 299;
       H. Gerstinger, Arch. Bibliogr. 1 (1926) 91 (No. 20)
       (II, Fayum?).  Collart 232.

945    xvii.315-77.  BKT 5.1.4 (inv. 9783) (III-IV).  Collart
       43.

946    xvii.334-46, 368-81.  PSI 7.752 (IV-V; parch. frr.).
       Collart 233.

947    xvii.353-73.  P. Oxy. 4.772 (Bristol Mus.) (II-III,
       Oxy.).  Collart 77.  Archiv 3.476.

948    xvii.379-84, 418-24, xviii.412-14, 455-56, 564-81,
       603-17.  P. Oxy. 15.1817 (Bibl. der Univ. Gent,
       inv. 75) (VI, Oxy.; pap. cod.).  Collart 234.
       Lameere, pp. 175-204, 267, reedits the text.  J.
       Bingen, Chr. Ég. 36 (1961) 219.

       xvii.541-50:  see No. 565.

949    xvii.649-71, 681-83.  C. C. Edgar, Ann. Serv. 26
       (1926) 203; W. G. Waddell, Ét. Pap. 1 (1932) 11
       (P. Cairo inv. 49654) (III, Oxy.; on the verso of
       accounts).  Collart 310.

       xvii.714:  see No. 573.

950    xvii.725-32, with a few marginal scholia.  P. Oxy.
       4.685 (Bodleian Libr., Gr. class. f.75 (P)) (II,
       Oxy.).  Collart 235 and Il., Pap. b.  Archiv 3.477.

951    xvii.729-35.  P. Heid. Siegmann 203 (inv. 1971) (III,
       Oxy.).  Lameere 066; Mette, Il. 444a.

952    xviii.1-617 (with many lacunae).  Kenyon, Class.
       Texts 98-99; P. Lit. Lond. 24 (Brit. Mus. inv.
       127 A) (II).

953    xviii.1-218, 311-617.  P. Lit. Lond. 25 (Brit. Mus.
       inv. 107: the "Harris Homer") (I-II).  Collart 11.
       E. M. Thompson and G. F. Warner, Catalogue of
       Ancient MSS. in the British Museum, Part 1 (Lon-
       don 1881) 1-6.  Pal. Soc., Ser. 2, vol. 1, pl. 64;
       Thompson, GLP, No. 10 (p. 126).

       xviii.56 = 437:  see No. 339.

954    xviii.76-99, 112-35.  PSI 1.14 (IV-V, Oxy.; parch.
       cod.).  Collart 237.

       xviii.112:  see No. 2436.

       xviii.117-18:  see No. 2571.

       xviii.209-617:  see No. 565.

955    xviii.213-23.  V. di Benedetto, Ann. Sc. Pisa, Ser.
       2.26 (1957) 179-80 (PSI, sine numero?) (I, Oxy.).

956    xviii.219-28.  H. J. Mette, Rev. Phil., Sér. 3.29
       (1955) 199 (No. 446) (P. Berol. inv. 11524) (I).
       Lameere 067.

xviii.298, 492: see No. 1536.

957    xviii.395-401, 428-34.  P. Ryl. 1.50 (III; pap. cod.).
       Collart 238.

       xviii.412-14, etc.: see No. 948.

958    xviii.439-617. . J. G. Winter, TAPA 53 (1922) 128-33
       (P. Mich. inv. 2) (II-III).  Collart 239.  Winter,
       LLP 194.

959    xviii.475-99, 518-35, 544-61.  P. Par. 3 bis (II?,
       Thebes).  Collart 86.

960    xviii.483-519, 533-57.  Allen, No. 122 (I-II; marble,
       Museo del Campidoglio, Rome).  "Not included in
       the C.I.G."  Collart 276.

961    xviii.574-79, 615-18.  B. P. Grenfell and A. S. Hunt,
       Mél. Nicole 222-23 (Bodleian Libr., Gr. class.
       g.49 (P)) (IV-V, Hermupolis Magna; pap. cod.).
       Collart 88.

962    xviii.596-608.  BKT 5.1.18-20 (inv. 9774) (I B.C.;
       No. 505 is written after this text).  Collart 51.  A.
       Ludwich, Berl. Phil. Woch. 27 (1907) 486-87.

       xix.21: see No. 1216.

963    xix.41-51.  P. Rein. 1.1 (P. Sorbonne inv. 2010)
       (I?).  Collart 240.  F. Blass, Archiv 3.477, gives
       the date as "Ptolemaïc."

       xix.65: see No. 2436.

964    xix.97-117, 132-33, 135-51.  P. Oxy. 3.553 (Houghton
       Libr., Harvard Univ.) (III, Oxy.; pap. cod.).
       Collart 66.  Archiv 3.262.

       xix.107: see No. 645.

965    xix.121-33.  H. Gerstinger, Arch. Bibliogr. 1 (1926)
       91 (No. 21) (P. Rain. inv. 30049) (III).  Collart 307.

       xix.128-29: see No. 1224.

       xix.222-24: see No. 2297.

966    xix.251-59.  P. Oxy. 3.554 (Univ.-Bibl., Graz) (III,
       Oxy.).  Collart 241.  Archiv 3.262.

967    xix.284-301.  P. Hamb. 160 (inv. 654) (I-II).  Lameere
       068; Mette, Il. 447.

968    xix.365-72.  J. Schwartz, BIFAO 54 (1954) 68-69
       (No. 29) (P. Gabra) (III, Tunat-el-Gabal).  Lameere
       069; Mette, Il. 448.

969    xix.417-21.  P. Oxy. 3.555 (Houghton Libr., Harvard
       Univ.) (III, Oxy.).  Collart 242.  Archiv 3.262.

970    xx.36-110.  P. Fay. 160; P. Cairo G.H. 10218 (I-II,
       Bacchias).  Collart 243.  Archiv 2.342.

       xx.59-60: see No. 2297.

       xx.106-58: see No. 904.

971    xx.205-15, 234-43.  P. Rain. 3.3 (cf. ibid. 4, p. 135)
       (inv. 26469) (IV, Fayum; pap. cod.).

972    xx.241-50.  P. Oxy. 3.556 (Houghton Libr., Harvard
       Univ.) (II-III, Oxy.).  Collart 244.  Archiv 3.262.

       xx.357: see No. 1217.

973    xx.377-87, 418-50.  A. Gianformaggio, Acme 9 (1956)
       77-78 (P. Univ. Statale di Milano inv. 412 + 413) (I).
       Lameere 070.

974    xx.425-37, 470-82.  P. Oxy. 6.951 (P. Princ.) (IV,
       Oxy.; pap. cod.).  Collart 245.

975    xxi.1-26.  P. Aberdeen 109 (III, Fayum?; on the ver-
       so of accounts).  Collart 82.  Ed. pr.: E. O. Win-
       stedt, CQ 1 (1907) 260.

976    xxi.26-41.  P. Fay. 6; P. Cairo G.H. 10764 (I B.C.,
       Euhemeria).  Collart 246.  Archiv 2.342.  Roberts,
       GLH, pl. 9c.

977    xxi.56-73.  PSI 14.1378 (II-III).  Lameere 071.

978    xxi.58-62, 64-65.  P. Aberdeen 110 (III, Fayum?).
       Collart 247.  Ed. pr.: E. O. Winstedt, CQ 1 (1907)
       260-61.

       xxi.180: see No. 1216.

       xxi.198-99: see No. 2435.

       xxi.259: see No. 1217.

979    xxi.302-611, xxii.27-515, xxiii.1-281 (with many la-
       cunae).  P. Heid. Lit. 2 (inv. 1262); P. Hibeh
       1.22; P. Grenf. 2.4 (Bodleian Libr., Gr. class.
       b.3·(P)) (III B.C., Hibeh; cart.).  Collart 12.  G.
       Jachmann, Gött. Nachr., 1949, 217-24; Pasquali,
       Stor. Testo 241-43; Del Corno, Il. 96-121.

980    xxi.359-401, 436-47, 455-66, 474-79, 481-90, 494-
       512, 514-31, 533-51, 557-608; xxii.1-16, 104-11,
       265-83, 420-25, 439-55, 458; xxiii.2.  H. J.
       Mette, Rev. Phil., Sér 3.29 (1955) 199 (No. 449)
       (P. Berol. inv. 16985) (I B.C.).  Lameere 072.

981    xxi.372-82.  P. Oxy. 3.557 (Houghton Libr., Har-
       vard Univ.) (III, Oxy.).  Collart 248.  Archiv 3.
       262.

982    xxi.414-24.  J. Schwartz, BIFAO 46 (1947) 63-64
       (No. 15) (PIFAO inv. 112) (II; on the verso).  Mette,
       Il. 450.

983    xxi.511-24, 526-27.  PSI 7.753 (III, Oxy.).  Collart
       249.

984    xxi.547-76, 580-609; xxii.390-421, 423-54.  BKT
       5.1.3 (inv. 6794) (IV-V; parch.).  Collart 250.
       F. Blass, Zeitschr. Aeg. Spr. 18 (1880) 37 (first
       mention).

985    xxi.608-11, xxii.30-37.  P. Amh. 2.159 (IV; parch.
       cod.).  Collart 251.  Archiv 2.343.

986    xxii.1-17, 22-23, 27-38.  PSI 2.139 (II-III, Oxy.).
       Collart 252.

987    xxii.1-18, 40-57.   P. Oxy. 3.559 (Houghton Libr.,
        Harvard Univ.) (II, Oxy.).  Collart 253.  Archiv
        3.262.

        xxii.1-458: see No. 980.

        xxii.27-515: see No. 979.

        xxii.30-37: see No. 985.

        xxii.79: see No. 645.

988    xxii.109-397 (with lacunae), xxiii.345-70, 383-406.
        P. Oxy. 15.1818 (Musées Royaux, Bruxelles, inv.
        E. 6002 A, B, C) (V-VI, Oxy.; pap. cod.).  Col-
        lart 254.  Lameere, pp. 148-74, 266-67, reedits
        the text.  J. Bingen, Chr. Ég. 36 (1961) 219.

989    xxii.115-34, 143-60.   P. Oxy. 3.558 (Belfast Mus.)
        (II-III, Oxy.).  Collart 27.  Archiv 3.262.

990    xxii.131-62.   P. Mil. Vogl. 2.35 (inv. 223) (I; on the
        verso of an account).  Lameere 073.

991    xxii.140-51, 188-201, 252-53, 277-301.   P. Tebt. 3.
        900 (II B.C., Tebtunis; cart.).  Collart 271.

992    xxii.142-58.   A. Gianformaggio, Acme 9 (1956) 79
        (P. Univ. Statale di Milano, inv. 417) (I-II).  La-
        meere 074.

        xxii.143-452: see No. 904.

        xxii.219: see No. 455.

993    xxii.226-33, 265-72, 300-5.   P. Aberdeen 111 (II,
        Fayum?).  Collart 83.  Ed. pr.: E. O. Winstedt,
        CQ 1 (1907) 261.

994    xxii.239-60.   P. Rein. 2.72 (P. Sorbonne inv. 2090)
        (II-III; on the verso of a document).  Collart 268.
        Ed. pr.: A. Bataille and P. Collart, Aeg. 11 (1931)
        174-75.

995    xxii.253-98, 350-55, 358-65.   P. Fay. 211 (Yale
        Univ. Libr.) (I-II, Euhemeria).  Collart 255.  Ar-
        chiv 2.343.

        xxii.390-421, 423-54: see No. 984.

996    xxii.449-74.   P. Lond. 5.1811; P. Lit. Lond. 26
        (Brit. Mus. inv. 1545) (II-III).  Collart 256.

997    xxiii.1-25, 37-39, 63-68.   P. Michael. 2 (I).  Lameere
        075; Mette, Il. 451.

998    xxiii.1-79, 402-897, xxiv.1-759 (with lacunae).   Ken-
        yon, Class. Texts 100-8; P. Lit. Lond. 27 (Brit.
        Mus. inv. 128) (I).  Scholia cite Philias and Baton
        of Sinope (Jacoby, FGH, Dritter Teil A, p. 79).
        Collart 13.  J. La Roche, WS 14 (1892) 150-54; F.
        G. Kenyon, Journ. Philol. 21 (1893) 296-343, gives
        a full transcription.

        xxiii.1-281: see No. 979.

        xxiii.2: see No. 980.

999    xxiii.22-49, 79-100, 424-47.   F. Blass, Ber. Leip-
        zig, 1904, 211 (Univ.-Bibl., Leipzig) (III; on the
        verso of a document).  Collart 257.  Archiv 3.477.

1000   xxiii.63-88, 93-97, 126-47, 152-56.   PSI 2.140 (III,
        Oxy.; pap. cod.).  Collart 258.

1001   xxiii.81-91.   P. Oxy. 3.447 (Houghton Libr., Harvard
        Univ.) (II, Oxy.).  Collart 23.  Archiv 3.262.

1002   xxiii.91-107.   A. Gianformaggio, Acme 9 (1956) 79-80
        (P. Univ. Statale di Milano, inv. 425) (I B.C.).
        Lameere 076.

1003   xxiii.135-91.   C. C. Edgar, Ann. Serv. 26 (1926) 203;
        W. G. Waddell, Ét. Pap. 1 (1932) 11-12 (P. Cairo
        inv. 47268) (II-III, Oxy.).  Collart 311.

        xxiii.252, 648-49: see No. 1223.

        xxiii.345-70, 383-406: see No. 988.

1004   xxiii.393-98, 405-10.   M. Vandoni, Acme 15 (1962)
        137-38 (Univ. Statale di Milano, inv. 428) (I B.C.,
        Madinet-Madi).

1005   xxiii.400-11, 444-55.   H. J. Mette, Rev. Phil., Sér.
        3.29 (1955) 199 (No. 452) (P. Berol. inv. 11761) (II).
        Lameere 077.

1006   xxiii.451-62.   PRIMI 1.5 (II).  Collart 326.

1007   xxiii.485-91, 499-509.   PSI 2.141 (II-III, Oxy.).  Col-
        lart 259.

        xxiii.495-536: see No. 904.

1008   xxiii.524-55, xxiv.648-81.   PSI 11.1189, 14.1379 (II,
        Oxy.).  Collart 332 (= 1189); Lameere 078 (= 1379).

1009   xxiii.718-32.   BKT 5.1.4 (inv. 9949) (I B.C.).  Col-
        lart 45.

        xxiii.774: see No. 455.

1010   xxiii.775-85, 834-47.   P. Oxy. 3.560 (Royal Ontario
        Mus., Univ. of Toronto) (III, Oxy.).  Collart 28.
        Archiv 3.262.

1011   xxiii.887-97.   PSI 12.1275 (II, Oxy.; on the verso,
        and partly on the recto, at the end of the collema,
        is a medical text: fr. of an elementary manual?).
        Lameere 079; Mette, Il. 453.

        xxiv.1-759: see No. 998.

        xxiv.29: see No. 1201.

1012   xxiv.74-90.   P. Oxy. 6.952 (Peabody Mus., Yale
        Univ.) (III, Oxy.).  Collart 260.

        xxiv.97, 104: see No. 1224.

1013   xxiv.127-804.   P. Lit. Lond. 28 (Brit. Mus. inv. 114)
        (II, Elephantine?).  Collart 14.  Preisendanz, PFF
        96-97.  E. M. Thompson and G. F. Warner, Cata-
        logue of Ancient MSS. in the British Museum, Part
        1 (London 1881) 6.  New Pal. Soc., Ser. 2, vol. 1,

pl. 76; Pal. Soc., Ser. 1, vol. 2, pl. 153; Thompson, GLP, No. 17 (p. 140); Wattenbach, SGS, tab. IV.

1014    xxiv. 169-76.   P. Ryl. 3. 544 (II).   Collart 361.

xxiv. 254: see No. 457.

1015    xxiv. 282, 286, 318-31.   P. Oxy. 3. 561 (Johns Hopkins Univ. Libr.) (III-IV, Oxy.; on the verso of a document).   Collart 261.   Archiv 3. 262.

1016    xxiv. 336-43, 366-74, 377-401.   P. Ryl. 1. 51 (I B.C.).   Collart 84.

1017    xxiv. 373-96.   C. C. Edgar, Ann. Serv. 26 (1926) 203; W. G. Waddell, Ét. Pap. 1 (1932) 12-13 (P. Cairo inv. 45617) (I-II, Oxy.).   Collart 312.

1018    xxiv. 698-747.   BKT 5.1.3 (inv. 5007) (Byzantine; parch.).   Collart 262.

xxiv. 804: see No. 643.

--- Odyssey, many scattered lines, from a "Homeromanteion": see No. 552.

Odyssey i. 1: see No. 1225.

1019    Odyssey i. 1-6, 9-16, 21-23, 32-36.   P. Harris 123 (inv. 176 i) (III; on the verso of a document).   Collart 33.

1020    i. 1-7.   BGU 6. 1470 (O. Berol. inv. 12565) (III-II B.C., Elephantine; ostr., including documents).   Collart 32.   Del Corno, Od. 47-48.

i. 52: see No. 1287.

1021    i. 71-77.   P. Cairo Crawford 60 (= P. Gradenwitz 141) (Roman).   Lameere 080; Mette, Od. 105.

1022    i. 81-94, 96-102.   P. Tebt. 3. 696 (II B.C., Tebtunis; cart.; text on recto, No. 524 on verso).   Collart 22.   Del Corno, Od. 9-10.

1023    i. 131-45.   P. Oxy. 3. 562 (Johns Hopkins Univ. Libr.) (III, Oxy).   Collart 34.   Archiv 3. 263.

1024    i. 145-47, 149-55.   J. Schwartz, BIFAO 46 (1947) 64 (No. 16) (PIFAO inv. 231) (I).   Mette, Od. 106.

1025    i. 239-46.   J. Schwartz, BIFAO 46 (1947) 65 (No. 17) (P. Gabra: in the collection of Prof. Sami Gabra?) (II, Hermupolis Magna).   Mette, Od. 107.

1026    i. 266-76, 296-307.   P. Oxy. 11. 1394 (Merchant Taylors' Sch.) (V, Oxy.; pap. cod.).   Collart 35.

1027    i. 318-33, 344-59, ii. 27-47, 53-73.   H. Gerstinger, Arch. Bibliogr. 1 (1926) 91-92 (No. 22) (P. Rain. inv. 26750) (V, Fayum?; parch. cod.).   Collart 36.

1028    i. 432-44.   P. Oxy. 3. 563 (Johns Hopkins Univ. Libr.) (II-III, Oxy.).   Collart 37.   Archiv 3. 263.

ii. 27-47, 53-73: see No. 1027.

1029    ii. 34-370 (with many lacunae).   P. Lit. Lond. 29 (Brit. Mus. inv. 127 D) (I).   Collart 38.

1030    ii. 127-40, 152-66.   Described by V. Bérard, Introduction à l'Odyssée 1 (Paris 1924) 65 (P. Genève inédite) (II-III).   Collart 39.

1031    ii. 304-12, 339-57, 362-74, 386-406, 408-10.   P. Oxy. 4. 773 (Musées Royaux, Bruxelles, inv. E. 5938) (IV, Oxy.).   Collart 1.   Archiv 3. 477.   Lameere, pp. 113-47, 266, reedits the text; J. Bingen, Chr. Ég. 36 (1961) 219.

ii. 314 ff.: see No. 455.

1032    ii. 315-27.   P. Oxy. 3. 564 (Johns Hopkins Univ. Libr.) (II-III, Oxy.).   Collart 40.   Archiv 3. 263.

1033    ii. 404-6, 408-16, 431-34, iii. 1.   P. Merton 2. 52 (I B.C.).   Lameere 081.   J. Bingen, JEA 48 (1962) 178.

1034    iii. 115, xi. 80, xiii. 344, xiv. 162, xviii. 416, xix. 307, 406 (?).   Cited (with Iliad ii. 298, etc.) in a "Homeromanteion": P. Bon. 1. 3 (inv. 24 b$^2$ + 24 f) (I-II; see Nos. 645, 1801).   A. Vogliano, Acme 5 (1952) 385-417.

1035    iii. 169-79.   J. Schwartz, BIFAO 61 (1962) 172 (No. 36) (P. Strassb. inv. Gr. 2462 a + 2489) (II; on the verso of a document).

1036    iii. 178-86.   PSI 9. 1084 (?, Oxy.).   Collart 41.

1037    iii. 179-90.   H. Gerstinger, Arch. Bibliogr. 1 (1926) 92 (No. 23) (P. Rain. inv. 26731) (II).   Collart 42.

1038    iii. 226-31.   P. Oxy. 4. 774 (Johns Hopkins Univ. Libr.) (III, Oxy.).   Collart 2.   Archiv 3. 477.

1039    iii. 267-496 (with lacunae).   F. G. Kenyon, Journ. Philol. 22 (1894) 238-46; P. Lit. Lond. 30 (Brit. Mus. inv. 271); H. Gerstinger, Arch. Bibliogr. 1 (1926) 92-93 (No. 24) (P. Rain. inv. 26746 + 26754-60) (I, Soknopaiou Nesos?).   There are a few scholia, mentioning Ammonius, Apion, and Zenodotus.   Collart 3, 43.   Ludwich, PC 20-22.   Kenyon, Pal. GP, pl. XV; Pal. Soc., Ser. 2, vol. 2, pl. 182; Thompson, GLP, No. 8 (p. 123).

1040    iii. 338-59.   H. J. Mette, Rev. Phil., Sér. 3. 29 (1955) 200 (No. 108) (P. Berol. inv. 11762) (IV; parch. cod.).   Lameere 082.

1041    iii. 364-75, 384-402.   J. Nicole, Rev. Phil. 18 (1894) 101-3 (P. Genève inv. 92) (?, Soknopaiou Nesos?).   Collart 21.

1042    iii. 435-49.   PSI 2. 122 (I, Oxy.).   Collart 44.

iii. 490: see No. 1225.

1043    iv. 87-105.   P. Rein. 2. 73 (P. Sorbonne inv. 2100) (II-III).   Collart 45.   Ed. pr.: A. Bataille and P. Collart, Aeg. 11 (1931) 175-76.

1044   iv. 97-100, 197-204, 222-24, 248-61.   P. Oxy. 6. 953
       (Bibl. de l'Univ. de Louvain, inv. 218, deperdita)
       (II, Oxy.).   Collart 23.

1045   iv. 146-50, 187-88.   O. Guéraud, Rev. Ég. Anc. 1
       (1927) 131 (P. Sorbonne inv. 543) (II B.C., El La-
       houn; cart.).   Collart 46.   Del Corno, Od. 48.

1046   iv. 166-76.   PSI 7. 754 (II-III?, Oxy.).   Collart 47.

1047   iv. 201-11, 220-33.   P. Harris 124 (inv. 178) (I).   Col-
       lart 48.

1048   iv. 292-302.   P. Oxy. 3. 565 (Johns Hopkins Univ. Libr.)
       (II-III, Oxy.).   Collart 4.   Archiv 3. 263.

1049   iv. 382-96 (including 391a).   PSI 14. 1380 (II).   Lameere
       083.

1050   iv. 388-98, 400.   P. Oxy. 4. 775 (Univ. of Pennsylvania
       Mus. inv. 2821) (III, Oxy.).   Collart 5.   Archiv 3. 477.

       iv. 389: see No. 1205.

1051   iv. 450-81.   Mentioned by A. E. R. Boak, Aeg. 4 (1923)
       38 (P. Mich. inv. 16) (?).   Mette, Od. 109.

1052   iv. 483-92.   G. Rudberg, SO 6 (1928) 55-56; P. Oslo
       2. 8 (III-IV, Fayum?; on the verso of a document).
       Collart 49.

       iv. 502: see No. 455.

       iv. 506 ff.: see No. 455.

1053   iv. 520-29.   P. Oxy. 4. 776 (Univ. of Pennsylvania
       Mus., inv. 2817) (I-II, Oxy.).   Collart 50.   Ar-
       chiv 3. 477.

1054   iv. 685-708.   P. Oxy. 3. 566 (Johns Hopkins Univ.
       Libr.) (III, Oxy.).   Collart 51.   Archiv 3. 263.

1055   iv. 757-65.   P. Oxy. 3. 567 (Johns Hopkins Univ.
       Libr.) (III, Oxy.).   Collart 52.   Archiv 3. 263.

1056   iv. 796-812, v. 6-264 (with lacunae).   P. Tebt. 3. 697
       (II B.C., Tebtunis).   Collart 30.   Del Corno, Od.
       10-21; Lameere, p. 243.

1057   iv. 840-47.   P. Ross. Georg. 1. 5 (collection of G.
       Zereteli, Tiflis) (II).   Collart 53.

       iv. 841: see No. 1216.

       v. 6-264: see No. 1056.

1058   v. 7-17, 34-44.   P. Oxy. 4. 777 (P. Cairo) (IV, Oxy.;
       pap. cod.).   Collart 54.   Archiv 3. 477.

       v. 84, 158, 176, etc.: see No. 455.

1059   v. 106-13.   PSI 1. 8 (I, Oxy.).   Collart 29.

       v. 116-24: see No. 2642.

1060   v. 139-45, 180-91, 197-204, 210-21, 248-70.   PSI 11.
       1190 (II, Oxy.).   Collart 56.

1061   v. 346-53.   P. Grenf. 1. 3 (Bodleian Libr., Gr. class.
       g. 7 (P)) (III, Fayum).   Collart 57.

1062   vi. 146-71.   P. Hal. 5 b (inv. 5) (II).   Collart 58.

1063   vi. 190-91, 199-201, 204, 206-8, 236-75.   P. Merton
       1. 1 (II B.C., Oxy. ?).   Mette, Od. 110.

1064   vi. 201-3, 205-9, 255-56, 258-63, 286-300, 325-28.
       P. Fay. 7; P. Lit. Lond. 31 (Brit. Mus. inv. 817)
       (I B. C., Euhemeria).   Collart 6.   Archiv 2. 343.
       Roberts, GLH, pl. 9b.

       vi. 222: see No. 2524.

1065   vi. 250-59, 273-82, 310-21, viii. 491-508.   P. Hamb.
       161 (inv. 617 + 659 + 661) (I B.C.).   Lameere 084;
       Mette, Od. 111.

1066   vi. 264-75, 294-305.   P. Oxy. 11. 1395 (Dominion Mus.,
       Wellington, New Zealand) (IV, Oxy.; parch.).
       Collart 59.

       vi. 268: see No. 1216.

       vii. 1: see No. 2707.

1067   vii. 67-126.   F. Blass, Ber. Leipzig, 1904, 211-12
       (Univ.-Bibl., Leipzig) (IV; parch. cod.).   Collart
       26.   Archiv 3. 477.

1068   vii. 111-24.   P. Univ. Giss. 4. 38 (inv. 364) (I B.C.,
       Fayum?).   Collart 60; Gundel 6.

       vii. 294: see No. 1536.

1069   viii. 168-76.   A. Traversa, Studi Calderini-Paribeni
       2, 357-62 (Università di Genova, inv. 1192) (I).
       Lameere 085.

       viii. 170-71: see No. 2526.

       viii. 186-87: see No. 1221.

1070   viii. 214-30.   N. Lewis, Ét. Pap. 3 (1936) 51 (No. 4)
       (P. Strassb. inv. Gr. 1827) (I).   Collart 63.

1071   viii. 348-50.   BKT 5. 1. 4 (inv. 7805) (II).   Collart 64.

       viii. 360-62: see No. 1217.

       viii. 491-508: see No. 1065.

1072   viii. 501-11.   J. Schwartz, BIFAO 46 (1947) 65-66
       (No. 18) (PIFAO inv. 266) (I B. C. -I).   Mette, Od.
       112.

1073   viii. 537-54.   PSI 7. 755 (III?, Oxy.).   Collart 65.

       viii. 553: see No. 2519.

       ix. 5-6, 11: see No. 1539.

       ix. 5-11: see No. 77.

1074   ix. 41-65, 94-101.   P. Rein. 2. 74 (P. Sorbonne inv.
       2092) (IV; pap. cod.).   Collart 66.   Ed. pr.: A.
       Bataille and P. Collart, Aeg. 11 (1931) 176-78.

1075    ix. 73-93.   J. Schwartz, BIFAO 54 (1954) 69-70 (No.
        30) (PIFAO inv. 330) (II B.C. ?).  Lameere 086;
        Mette, Od. 113.  Del Corno 49-50.

1076    ix. 75-92.   BKT 5.1.5 (inv. 40) (I).  Collart 67.

1077    ix. 119-26, 128-31.   P. Harris 125 (inv. 79 j) (I-II; on
        the verso of a document).  Collart 68.

1078    ix. 122-50.   P. Ryl. 3.545 (III; sch. ex. ?).  Collart
        69.

        ix. 124: see No. 1502.

1079    ix. 139-231.   H. J. Mette, Rev. Phil., Sér. 3.29
        (1955) 200 (No. 114) (P. Berol. inv. 13874) (II-III).
        Lameere 087.

1080    ix. 194-235.   P. Iand. 5.74 (inv. 238; now lost or
        destroyed) (II).  Collart 70; Gundel 7.

1081    ix. 212-566 (with lacunae), x.1-13, 26-96.  O. Gue-
        raud, Rev. Ég. Anc. 1 (1927) 88-130 (P. Sorbonne
        inv. 2245) (III B.C., Ghoran; cart.; palimpsest:
        written over an expunged non-literary text).  Col-
        lart 31.  Del Corno, Od. 21-42.

        ix. 355: see No. 1539.

1082    ix. 358-61, 364, 405-8, 410-12.   P. Oxy. 11.1396
        (P. Princ., AM. 9049) (V, Oxy.; pap. cod.).  Col-
        lart 71.

        ix. 455: see No. 2519.

1083    x. 3-12, xi. 244-323, 414-26, 428-32, xii. 1-4.   P.
        Oxy. 15.1819 (Johns Hopkins Univ. Libr.) (II, Oxy.).
        Collart 72.

1084    x. 26-50.   P. Oxy. 4.778 (Univ. of Pennsylvania
        Mus., inv. 2818) (II-III, Oxy.).  Collart 7.  Archiv
        3.478.

1085    x. 124-30.   P. Oxy. 4.779 (P. Cairo) (II-III, Oxy.).
        Collart 73.  Archiv 3.478.

1086    x. 217-68.   H. J. Mette, Rev. Phil., Sér 3.29 (1955)
        200 (No. 115) (P. Berol. inv. 11754) (VI; pap. cod.).
        Lameere 088.

1087    x. 260-64, 266-69.   J. Schwartz, BIFAO 54 (1954) 70
        (No. 31) (PIFAO inv. 274) (I).  Lameere 089; Met-
        te, Od. 116.

1088    x. 284-94.   H. J. Mette, Rev. Phil., Sér. 3.29 (1955)
        200 (No. 117) (P. Berol. inv. 16084) (II-III).  La-
        meere 090.

1089    x. 287-99.   P. Rein. 2.75 (P. Sorbonne inv. 2119)
        (I; on the verso of a document).  Collart 74.

1090    x. 291-99.   P. Ross. Georg. 1.6 (Collection of G.
        Zereteli, Tiflis) (III; on the verso of a list of
        names).  Collart 75.

1091    x. 329-41, 343-45.   H. J. Mette, Rev. Phil., Sér.
        3.29 (1955) 201 (No. 118) (P. Berol. inv. 16083) (II).
        Lameere 091.

1092    x. 366-67, 373-80, 399-402.   P. Fay. 157 (Houghton
        Libr., Harvard Univ.) (I-II, Bacchias).  Collart
        8.  Archiv 2.344.

        x. 517: see No. 455.

        xi: Lines attributed to Bk. xi by Julius Africanus:
        see No. 53.

1093    xi. 1-20.   P. Oxy. 3.568 (Johns Hopkins Univ. Libr.)
        (III, Oxy.).  Collart 76.  Archiv 3.263.

        xi. 25, 543 ff.: see No. 455.

        xi. 80: see No. 1031.

1094    xi. 110-12, 126-34.   P. Schubart 1 (P. Berol. inv.
        11678) (III-II B.C.).  Mette, Od. 119.  Del Corno,
        Od. 50.

        xi. 122: see No. 455.

        xi. 131: see No. 1223.

1095    xi. 145-209.   H. Gerstinger, Arch. Bibliogr. 1 (1926)
        93 (No. 25) (P. Rain. inv. 26764) (II-III; on the
        verso of a document).  Collart 77.

        xi. 164-203: see No. 1173.

1096    xi. 195-208.   P. Oxy. 3.569 (Johns Hopkins Univ.
        Libr.) (II, Oxy.; on the verso of a cursive ac-
        count?).  Collart 9.  Archiv 3.264.

        xi. 249-50: see No. 512.

        xi. 281-97: see No. 513.

        xi. 311: see No. 2131.

1097    xi. 424-30, 457-63.   PSI 14.1381 (VI; pap. cod.).
        Line 428 is supplied by a later hand.  Lameere
        092.

1098    xi. 425-30.   P. Aberdeen 112 (I, Fayum?).  Mette,
        Od. 121.

1099    xi. 428-40.   P. Tebt. 2.431 (I-II, Tebtunis).  Collart
        78.

1100    xi. 471-93, 523-45.   P. Oxy. 4.780 (Trinity Coll.
        Libr., Dublin, Pap. F.12) (II?, Oxy.).  Collart
        10.  Archiv 3.478.

        xi. 475-76: see No. 2614.

1101    xi. 492-511.   P. Ryl. 1.52 (II-III; on the verso of a
        document).  Collart 79.

1102    xi. 557-73, 588-610.   P. Fay. 310 (Univ. of Pennsyl-
        vania Mus., inv. 2772) (I-II, Theadelphia).  Col-
        lart 11.  Archiv 2.344.

        xi. 601-4: see No. 516.

        xi. 609-10: see No. 2471.

1103   xi. 628 — xii. 1.   P. Mil. Vogl. 2. 37 (inv. 212) (I B.C.,
       Madinet-Madi).   Ed. pr.: M. A. Vandoni, Acme
       11 (1958) 263-64.   Lameere 093.

       xii. 1: see No. 1103.

       xii. 1-4: see No. 1083.

1104   xii. 31-57.   P. Iand. 5. 75 (inv. 347) (ca. A. D. 100).
       Collart 80; Gundel 8.

1105   xii. 119-32, 152-65.   H. Gerstinger, Arch. Bibliogr.
       1 (1926) 93 (P. Rain. inv. 26743) (V; parch. cod.).
       Collart 81.

       xii. 184-85: see No. 341.

1106   xii. 275-446, xiii. 1-440, xiv. 8-509, xv. 2-400, xviii.
       103-401, xix. 1-604, xx. 26-392, xxi. 1-434 (with
       many lacunae), xxi-xxiv entire.   P. Ryl. 1. 53
       (III; parch. cod.).   Collart 28.   New Pal. Soc.,
       Ser. 2, vol. 1, pl. 54; Schubart, Gr. Pal., Abb.
       97.   M. H. A. L. H. van der Valk, Textual Criti-
       cism of the Odyssey (Leiden 1949) 77-80.

       xii. 330: see No. 1217.

1107   xii. 344-52.   P. Hal. 5 a (inv. 30) (Ptolemaïc).   Col-
       lart 83.   Del Corno, Od. 49.

1108   xii. 379-83.   P. Rein. 2. 76 (P. Sorbonne inv. 2135)
       (II; on the verso of a document).   Collart 84.

       xii. 417: see No. 2301.

       xii. 432-33: see No. 1287.

       xiii. 1: see No. 1225.

       xiii. 1-440: see No. 1106.

       xiii. 106: see No. 89.

1109   xiii. 110-26, 137-54.   BKT 5. 1. 6 (inv. 264) (V-VI; pap.
       cod.).   Collart 85.

1110   xiii. 341-61.   C. C. Edgar, Ann. Serv. 26 (1926) 203;
       W. G. Waddell, Ét. Pap. 1 (1932) 13 (P. Cairo inv.
       49655) (III, Oxy.; on the verso of a cursive text).
       Collart 86.

       xiii. 344: see No. 1031.

       xiv. 8-509: see No. 1106.

1111   xiv. 15-24, 35-60, 71-86, 374-81, 407-10, 430-41.
       BKT 5. 1. 4 (inv. 7517) (VI-VII, Fayum?; pap. cod.).
       Collart 12.

1112   xiv. 50-72.   P. Oxy. 3. 570 (Johns Hopkins Univ. Libr.)
       (II, Oxy.).   Collart 87.   Archiv 3. 264.

       xiv. 214-25: see No. 2297.

       xiv. 222-25: see No. 455.

1113   xiv. 299-303, 328-332.   P. Oxy. 6. 954 (Stanford Univ.
       Libr.) (IV-V, Oxy.; parch. cod.).   Mette, Od. 122.

       xiv. 345: see No. 1216.

       xiv. 463-66: see No. 1456.

       xv. 2-400: see No. 1106.

1114   xv. 161-81, 189-210.   P. Amh. 2. 23 (III-IV; parch.
       cod.).   Collart 13.   Archiv 2. 344.

1115   xv. 194-210, 228-43, xvii. 40-111.   PSI 13. 1299 (VI-VII,
       Antinoöpolis; pap. cod.).   Mette, Od. 123.   Norsa,
       SLG, p. 36 and tav. 18 a (first publication of xv.
       228-43).

1116   xv. 216-31, 239-53.   P. Cairo G. H. 10397; P. Cairo
       Goodspeed 1 (II).   Collart 14.   Archiv 3. 264.

1117   xv. 324-27, 356-60.   H. J. Mette, Rev. Phil., Sér.
       3. 29 (1955) 201 (No. 124) (P. Berol. inv. 17008)
       (III-IV; parch. cod.).   Lameere 094.

1118   xv. 329-33, 362-66.   PSI 1. 9 (IV-V, Oxy.; parch. cod.).
       Collart 91.

1119   xv. 531-53.   H. J. Mette, Rev. Phil., Sér. 3. 29 (1955)
       201 (No. 125) (P. Berol. inv. 11759) (I-II).   Lameere
       095.

1120   xv: a fragment.   Mentioned by A. H. Sayce, The
       Academy, 12 May 1894, 401 (?, Fayum).   Collart
       89.

1121   xvi. 1-8.   P. Oxy. 3. 571 (Johns Hopkins Univ. Libr.)
       (I-II, Oxy.).   Collart 15.   Archiv 3. 264.

1122   xvi. 153-67, 175-76, 176 a-c, 177-78.   P. Hamb. 154
       (inv. 603 + 663) (II B.C.).   Lameere 096; Mette,
       Od. 126.   Del Corno, Od. 44-46.

1123   xvi. 243-56, 288-301.   P. Oxy. 4. 781 (Univ. of Penn-
       sylvania Mus., inv. 2819) (III, Oxy.; pap. cod.).
       Collart 92.   Archiv 3. 478.

       xvi. 300, 302-3: see No. 1223.

       xvi. 317: see No. 89.

1124   xvi. 415-28.   PSI 14. 1382 (II, Oxy.).   Lameere 097.

       xvii. 40-111: see No. 1115.

1125   xvii. 137-48, 182-93.   P. Oxy. 4. 782 (Univ. of Penn-
       sylvania Mus., inv. 2816) (III, Oxy.; pap. cod.).
       Collart 16.   Archiv 3. 478.

1126   xvii. 200-9, 228-34, 301-8, 324-32.   S. de Ricci,
       CRAI, 1905, 215-17 (Acad. des Inscr. et Belles-
       Lettres, Paris) (IV, Lyconpolis; parch. cod.).
       Collart 93.

1127   xvii. 331-35, 356-64.   J. Schwartz, BIFAO 46 (1947)
       66-67 (No. 19) (PIFAO inv. 75) (I?).   Mette, Od.
       127.

1128    xvii. 331-55.  C. W. Keyes, AJP 50 (1929) 387-89
        (Columbia Univ. Libr., inv. 514) (II).  Collart 94.

1129    xvii. 357-63, 365-68, xix. 400-404, 407-8, 411-13.
        P. Hibeh 2.194 (Brit. Mus. inv. 2967) (ca. 280-240
        B.C., Hibeh; cart.).  Lameere 098; Mette, Od.
        128.  Del Corno, Od. 46-47.

1130    xvii. 410-28.  P. Oxy. 4.783 (Edinburgh Univ. Libr.)
        (I B.C., Oxy.).  Collart 17.  Archiv 3.478.

1131    xvii. 601-6, xviii. 27-40.  P. Oxy. 6.955 (Yale Univ.
        Libr.) (III, Oxy.; pap. cod.).  Collart 95.

1132    xviii. 1-35, 56-93.  P. Oxy. 3.572 (Johns Hopkins
        Univ. Libr.) (III, Oxy.).  Collart 18.  Archiv 3.264.

        xviii. 27-40: see No. 1131.

1133    xviii. 55-80, 95-121, 137-63, 178-205.  P. Oxy. 15.
        1820 (P. Cairo) (VI-VII, Oxy.; pap. cod.).  Collart
        96.

        xviii. 74: see Nos. 362, 455.

        xviii. 79: see No. 1567.

1134    xviii. 103-11, 113, 128-30, 132-39.  P. Ross. Georg.
        1.7 (Collection of G. Zereteli, Tiflis) (IV; parch.
        cod.).  Collart 98.

        xviii. 103-401: see No. 1106.

        xviii. 130: see No. 2156.

1135    xviii. 171-83.  P. Haun. 1.2 (inv. 101) (III, Fayum?).
        Mette, Od. 129.

        xviii. 385-86: see No. 1205.

        xviii. 416: see No. 1031.

        xix. 1-604: see No. 1106.

1136    xix. 7-17.  J. Schwartz, BIFAO 61 (1962) 172 (No. 37)
        (P. Strassb. inv. Gr. 2408 a ) (I).

        xix. 40, 136: see No. 1223.

1137    xix. 51-272 (with lacunae).  H. J. Mette, Rev. Phil.,
        Sér. 3.29 (1955) 201 (No. 130) (P. Berol. inv. 11635)
        (II-III).  Lameere 099.

1138    xix. 215-28.  PSI 8.979 (III B.C.).  Collart 99.  Del
        Corno, Od. 43-44.

        xix. 307, 406: see No. 1031.

        xix. 446: see No. 362.

1139    xix. 452-71.  P. Oxy. 3.573 (Musées Royaux, Bruxelles,
        inv. E.5949) (III, Oxy.; on the verso of a document).
        Collart 100.  Archiv 3.264.  Lameere, pp. 105-11,
        266, reedits the text.

        xix. 471: see No. 1740.

1140    xix. 534-99.  BKT 5.1.5 (inv. 10568) (IV-V; parch.
        cod.).  Collart 25.

1141    xx. 1 — end (?).  H. J. Mette, Rev. Phil., Sér. 3.
        29 (1955) 202 (No. 131) (P. Berol. inv. 17209) (II).
        Lameere 0100.

        xx. 18: see No. 455.

        xx. 26-392: see No. 1106.

1142    xx. 29-32.  J. Schwartz, BIFAO 46 (1947) 67 (No. 20)
        (PIFAO inv. 311) (Roman).  Mette, Od. 132.

1143    xx. 41-68.  P. Hibeh 1.23 (Morgan Libr.) (III B.C.,
        Hibeh).  Collart 19.  Del Corno, Od. 5-9.

        xx. 204: see No. 339.

        xx. 245: see No. 1539.

        xxi — xxiv: see No. 1106.

1144    xxi. 1-4, 31-34.  P. Hamb. 162 (inv. 25) (II-IV; parch.
        cod.).  Lameere 0102; Mette, Od. 133.

1145    xxi. 1-21, 432-34, xxii. 1.  Lameere, pp. 15-53, 264-
        65, and No. 0101 (Bibl. de l'Université de Louvain,
        P. gr. inv. 1 = "P. Lefort") (III B.C.).  J. Bingen,
        Chr. Ég. 36 (1961) 216-18;  D. del Corno, Gnomon
        33 (1961) 537-38.

        xxi. 1-434: see No. 1106.

        xxi. 195: see No. 461.

1146    xxi. 327-42.  P. Merton 2.53 (II-III; on the verso of
        a document).  Lameere 0103.

1147    xxi. 356-67.  P. Oxy. 11.1398 (St. Paul's Sch.) (III,
        Oxy.).  Collart 101.

        xxi. 390-91: see No. 2131.

        xxii. 1: see No. 1145.

        xxii. 5: see No. 2291.

1148    xxii. 31-47, 80-93, 111-48, 182-96, 230-317, xxiii.
        185-94, 230-42.  P. Oxy. 3.448 (Cornell Univ.
        Libr.) (III, Oxy.; on the verso of a prose literary
        text, erased and illegible).  Collart 20.  Archiv 3.
        264.

1149    xxii. 243-74.  J. Schwartz, BIFAO 46 (1947) 67-69
        (No. 21) (PIFAO inv. 21) (I; on the verso).  Mette,
        Od. 134.

1150    xxiii. 74-80, 93-103.  H. J. Mette, Rev. Phil., Sér.
        3.29 (1955) 202 (No. 135) (P. Berol. inv. 16087)
        (IV; parch. cod.).  Lameere 0104.

        xxiii. 185-94, 230-42: see No. 1148.

        xxiii. 269 ff.: see No. 455.

        xxiii. 278: see No. 1223.

1151    xxiii. 309-26, 342-56.  P. Oxy. 6.956 (Western Re-
        serve Univ. Libr.) (II-III, Oxy.).  Collart 24.

xxiv.11-12: see No. 78.

xxiv.62: see No. 197.

xxiv.74: see No. 1381.

1152   xxiv.141-50.   J. Schwartz, BIFAO 46 (1947) 69-70 (No. 22) (P. Soc. Pap. Alex., inv. 221) (II-III). Mette, Od. 136.

1153   xxiv.421-45.   PSI 2.115 (II-III, Oxy.).   Collart 102.

1154   xxiv.430-33.   J. Schwartz, BIFAO 61 (1962) 173 (No. 38) (P. Strassb. inv. Gr. 2479 b) (I). In the same hand as No. 910.

1155   xxiv.459-72.   P. Ryl. 3.546 (II).   Collart 103.

1156   xxiv.501-8.   P. Tebt. 2.432 (II, Tebtunis).   Collart 104.

Homer: see also Nos. 1535, 1948, 2087, 2564.

1157   Homerica: Prose summary of the beginning of the Iliad. P. Bon. 1.6 (inv. 10 a) (III-IV; from a school manual?). Ed. pr.: O. Montevecchi, Aeg. 27 (1947) 173. Mette, Il., Pap. K. Archiv 16.121.

1158   Paraphrase of Il. i.1-6, 8-12. U. Wilcken, Sitzb. Berl. Akad., 1887, 818-19 (P. Berol. inv. 5014) (V, Panopolis?; an opisthograph leaf; sch. ex.). F. Blass, Zeitschr. Aeg. Spr. 18 (1880) 35-36 (partial ed. pr.). Collart, Il., Pap. e, Pap. k. Ziebarth, No. 23; Ziebarth 2, No. 29. A. Erman and F. Krebs, Aus den Papyrus der Königlichen Museen (Berlin 1899) 232-33; Wilamowitz, Hermes 23 (1888) 142-47; A. Calderini, Aeg. 2 (1921) 311-13.

1159   Commentary and paraphrase of Il. i.1-21. U. Wilcken, Sitzb. Berl. Akad., 1887, 816-18; P. Achmîm 2 (Bibliothèque Nationale, Paris, Suppl. Gr. 1099, 3) (III-IV, Panopolis; pap. cod.). Collart, Il. 106. Ludwich, PC 2-4. Wilamowitz, Hermes 23 (1888) 142-47, discusses this along with No. 1158; A. Calderini, Aeg. 2 (1921) 310.

1160   Vocabulary for Il. i.5-24. P. Oslo 2.12 (II, Theadelphia?; sch. ex.; text on recto, No. 2148 on verso). Collart, Il., Pap. y. Archiv 10.225.

1161   Glossary to Il. i.10-12. J. Schwartz, BIFAO 54 (1954) 70-71 (No. 32) (PIFAO inv. 105) (III?; on the verso). Lameere 0105; Mette, Il., Pap. L.

1162   Glossary to Il. i.58-128. P. Oxy. 24.2405 (II-III, Oxy.) Lameere 0106.

1163   Lexicon to Il. i.151-361. R. Reitzenstein, Hermes 35 (1900) 611-21 (P. Strassburg inv. Gr. 33) (III, Fayum; on the verso of an account; sch. ex.). Collart, Il., Pap. f. Ludwich, PC 4-6. Archiv 1.536. A. Calderini, Aeg. 2 (1921) 309.

1164   Commentary on Il. i.263-64, 399. P. Oxy. 3.418 (Houghton Libr., Harvard Univ.) (I-II, Oxy.). Collart, Il., Pap. a. Archiv 3.263. A. Ludwich, Berl. Phil. Woch. 24 (1904) 317-20.

1165   Glossary to Il. i.266-72. P. Schubart 2 (P. Berol. inv. 7501) (III; on the verso of a document; sch. text). Mette, Il., Pap. M. Archiv 16.121.

1166   Lexicon to Il. i.338-50. BKT 5.1.6 (inv. 10577) (?). Collart, Il., Pap. g.

1167   Glossary to Il. i.464-69, 480-86. P. Antin. 2.70 (III, Antinoöpolis; pap. cod.).

1168   Scholia on Il. i.525-51. M. Vandoni, Acme 14 (1961) 238-39 (Università Statale di Milano, inv. 613) (II; on the verso of a document).

1169   Prose paraphrase of Il. i.528-48. P. Erl. 5 (inv. 3) (II). Mette, Il., Pap. N. Archiv 14.100, 16.121.

1170   Scholia on Il. ii.45-57. Mentioned by P. Collart, Atti Pap. IV, 71 (P. Rein. inv. 2088) (?). Collart, Il., Pap. w.

1171   Scholia on Il. ii.414-21, xviii.412-77, 552-603. P. Maspero 3.67331 (?, Antinoë?; pap. cod.). Mette, Il., Pap. O.

1172   Paraphrase of Il. ii.617-38, 639-70. PSI 12.1276 (I B.C.; on the verso are traces of a horoscope). Ed. pr.: V. Bartoletti, Aeg. 19 (1939) 177-86. Mette, Il., Pap. P. Archiv 16.120.

1173   Commentary on Il. ii.751-827. P. Oxy. 8.1086; P. Lit. Lond. 176 (Brit. Mus. inv. 2055) (I B.C., Oxy.; text on recto, No. 2409 on verso). Refers to Alcaeus (Lobel, Alcaeus 48; Lobel-Page, PLF, p. 266); Aristarchus; Homer, Od. xi.164-203; Pindar, fr. 92, Schroeder (Galiano, Pind., No. 23); Praxiphanes, De poetis (?). Collart, Il., Pap. c. Archiv 6.252.

1174   Commentary on Il. iii.59 (= vi.333). BKT 5.1.6 (inv. 9960)(I-II). Collart, Il., Pap. h.

1175   Scholia on Il. iv.306-7. P. Ryl. 1.24 (I, Oxy.). Refers to one Apollonius: A. Koerte, Archiv 6.254, prefers Apollonius the son of Chaeris to A. Rhodius. Collart, Il., Pap. i.

1176   Prose paraphrase of Il. iv.349-63; Il. iv.364-73, with explanations. M. Hombert and C. Préaux, Ann. Inst. Ph. H. O. 11 (1951; = Mél. H. Grégoire) 161-68 (Bodleian Libr., Greek Inscriptions 3017; now in the Ashmolean Mus.) (II-III; wooden tablet; sch. ex.). The explanations often agree with the Homeric scholia. Lameere 0107; Mette, Il., Pap. Q and No. 396.

1177   Paraphrase of Il. iv. Phil. Anzeiger 14 (1884) 414 (P. Rain.; later published?) (?, Fayum). Collart, Il., Pap. j.

1178   Glossary to Il. v.5-11, 37-53. P. Ryl. 3.537 (IV, Oxy.; an opisthograph sheet probably not from a pap. cod.; sch. ex.?). Archiv 14.141.

1179   Commentary on Il. v.88-254. O. Plasberg, Archiv 2 (1903) 196-206 (P. Strassb. inv. Gr. 1015) (II; sch. ex.). Collart, Il., Pap. l. A. Ludwich, Berl. Phil. Woch. 24 (1904) 348-50; A. Calderini, Aeg. 2 (1921) 405.

1180    Lexicon to Il. v. 265-89.   G. Plaumann, Ber. Berl.
        Mus., 1913, 220 (P. Berol. inv. 11636) (III-IV;
        wooden tablet, including No. 742; sch. ex.).   Met-
        te, Il., Pap. R.   A. Calderini, Aeg. 2 (1921) 309-10.

1181    Scholia minora on Il. v. 670-710.   P. Lit. Lond. 177
        (Brit. Mus. inv. 113 (14 b)) (IV; sch. ex.).   Collart,
        Il., Pap. z.   Archiv 10. 226.

1182    Scholia on Il. vi. 1-48.   P. Haun. 1. 3 (inv. 314) (III,
        Fayum?; on the verso of a document).   Mette, Il.,
        Pap. S.   Archiv 16. 121.

1183    Scholia on Il. vi. 84-98, 130-40 (?).   PSI 2. 135 (I-II,
        Oxy.; small opisthograph fr.; sch. ex.).   Collart,
        Il., Pap. m.   Archiv 7. 245.   Wilamowitz, DLZ 34
        (1913) 1863, regards the text as a stylistic exercise
        based on this passage.

1184    Commentary on Il. vi. 236, 252-85.   W. G. Waddell,
        Mél. Maspero 1. 148-51 (P. Cairo inv. 60566) (II,
        Oxy.).   Quotes Homer, Il. ix. 568-69.   Archiv 13.
        119.

1185    Prose summary of Il. vi, quoting vi. 448-55.   N.
        Lewis, Ét. Pap. 3 (1936) 46 (No. 1) (P. Strassb. inv.
        Gr. 2374) (III B.C.; on the verso of a letter or re-
        port; sch. ex.).   Collart, Il. 317; Mette, Il., Pap.
        T.   Archiv 13. 121.   Del Corno, Il. 141.

1186    Commentary on Il. vii. 75-83.   P. Oxy. 8. 1087 (P.
        Cairo) (I, Oxy.).   Quotes or refers to Aeschylus,
        Phineus (Galiano, Aesch. 110; Mette, FTA, fr. 434;
        Murray, Aesch. 96); Alcaeus (Lobel, Alcaeus 66;
        Lobel-Page, PLF, p. 285); Ananius; Antimachus,
        Thebais, Bk. i (Powell, CA 249; Wyss, Thebais,
        fr. 11); Archilochus; Cratinus, Malthaci; Euripi-
        des, Aegeus, Temenus (B. Snell, WS 69, 1956, 90);
        Eupolis; Hesiod, Opera 470, op. incert. (Merkel-
        bach, Hes. Fr., Z 1-2); Ps.-Hesiod, Ceÿcis Nup-
        tiae (New Chapters 2. 197); "Leandrius"(Meandrius
        of Miletus?); Leucon, Phrateres; Lycophron (?);
        Pindar (Galiano, Pind., No. 37); Simonides, fr.
        32, Bergk (G. Perrotta, Maia 5, 1952, 262); So-
        phocles, Phineus Primus; Stesichorus, Oresteia
        (Page, PMG 214); and Xenophanes, Silli, Bk. v.
        Collart, Il., Pap. d.   Schubart, Gr. Pal., Abb. 78.
        Archiv 6. 253.

1187    Lexicon to Il. ix. 58-93.   M. Manfredi, SIFC, NS 27-28
        (1956) 50-52 (PSI, sine numero?) (VII, Tebtunis;
        pap. cod.).   Lameere 0108.

1188    Commentary on Il. ix. 447.   P. Lond. 5. 1816 c; P.
        Lit. Lond. 142 (Brit. Mus. inv. 1605 C) (II).   Mette,
        Il., Pap. U.   Archiv 10. 235.   Identified by R.
        Pfeiffer, Philol. 92 (1937) 16-18.

1189    Glossary to Il. ix. 454-68.   B. A. van Groningen,
        Mnemos., Ser. 3. 5 (1937) 62-68 (Collection of E.
        von Scherling, Leiden, inv. G 99) (I-II, Oxy.?; on
        the verso of a petition?).   Archiv 13. 120; Chr. Ég.
        12 (1937) 265-66; P. Collart, Mél. Boisacq, 191-93.

1190    Summary of Il. x — xvii.   Mentioned by Winter, LLP
        195 (P. Mich. inv. 1315). (II).

1191    Lexicon to Il. xi. 136-263.   BKT 5. 1. 6 (inv. 10511)
        (II; waxed tablet; sch. ex.).   Collart, Il., Pap. n.
        A. Calderini, Aeg. 2 (1921) 308-9.

1192    Lexicon to Il. xi. 558-601.   P. Amh. 2. 19 (VII; parch.
        cod.; sch. ex.).   Collart, Il. 89.   Ludwich, PC
        7-8.   Archiv 2. 344; A. Calderini, Aeg. 2 (1921)
        313.

1193    Narrative based on Il. xi. 575 ff.   P. Oxy. 3. 574,
        verso (Bodleian Libr., Gr. class. f. 74 (P)) (II,
        Oxy.; on the verso of a list of tax payments; sch.
        ex.).   Collart, Il., Pap. p.

1194    Commentary on Il. xi. 677-754 and xviii. 219.   P.
        Iand. 1. 2 (inv. 1) (I B.C.).   Collart, Il., Pap. o;
        Gundel 5.

1195    Lexicon to Il. xiii. 198-227, 317-24, 415-35, 530-62.
        P. Ryl. 3. 536 (III; pap. cod.).   Archiv 14. 141.

1196    Lexicon to Il. xiii. 634 ff.   BKT 5. 1. 6 (inv. 10510) (II;
        waxed tablet; sch. ex.).   Collart, Il., Pap. q.

1197    Zetemata Grammatika on Il. xiv, by Apollodorus of
        Athens (a subscriptio).   PRIMI 1. 19 (II, Tebtunis).
        Mette, Il., Pap. V.   Archiv 13. 118-19.   E. G. Turn-
        er, Akten Pap. VIII, 54, note 2, suggests that
        "Sōsuou" may refer to the Sosii, the famous Roman
        publishers.

1198    Lexicon to Il. xiv. 227-521.   BKT 5. 1. 6 (inv. 10508)
        (II; waxed tablet; sch. ex.).   Collart, Il., Pap. r.
        A. Calderini, Aeg. 2 (1921) 306-7.

1199    Lexicon to Il. xv. 17-180.   BKT 5. 1. 6 (inv. 10509) (II;
        waxed tablet; sch. ex.).   Collart, Il., Pap. s.
        A. Calderini, Aeg. 2 (1921) 307-8.

1200    Collection of similes from Homer (Il. xvi. 642-46,
        751-70, 818-29, xvii. 1-7, 18-23).   W. G. Waddell,
        Mél. Maspero 1. 145-48 (P. Cairo inv. 60565) (I-II,
        Oxy.).   Collart, Il. 320.   Archiv 13. 121.

1201    Commentary on Il. xvii. 4 (?), 112 (?), 481 ff. (?),
        520 (?), 693 ff.   P. Oxy. 24. 2397 (I, Oxy.).
        Quotes Homer, Il. xxiv. 29 (?), and Callimachus,
        Hymni i. 50 (?); refers to Ptolemaeus (the Ascal-
        onite?) and one (...) dius.   Lameere 0109.

1202    Lexicon to Il. xviii. 373-86.   P. Ryl. 1. 25 (II, Oxy.;
        on the verso of a document; sch. ex.).   Collart,
        Il., Pap. t.   Archiv 6. 254; A. Calderini, Aeg. 2
        (1921) 305.

1203    Scholia on Il. xix. 326, xx. 53 (?), 146 ff. (?) (or
        hypothesis to the Scyrii of Euripides or Sophocles?).
        P. Schubart 21 (V; parch. cod.).   Listed by Schu-
        bart as a commentary on Sophocles, Scyrii (?);
        L. Alfonsi, Aeg. 33 (1953) 299-303, prefers a com-
        mentary on the Scyrii of Euripides, or else a mytho-
        logical compilation; B. Snell, ap. Schubart, sug-
        gests Homeric scholia; R. Merkelbach, Archiv 16
        (1956) 117-18, concurs with Snell, and notes a re-
        ference to Demetrius of Scepsis.

1204 Commentary on Il. xx. 144-50. J. Nicole, Rev. Phil. 17 (1893) 109-15 (P. Genève) (?, Philadelphia). Collart, Il., Pap. u.

1205 Scholia on Il. xxi. 1-363, by one Ammonius (?). P. Oxy. 2. 221; P. Lit. Lond. 178 (Brit. Mus. inv. 1184) (II, Oxy.; on the verso of No. 2172). Quotes or refers to Aeschylus (?; Fritsch, No. 6); Alcaeus (Edmonds, LG 1. 388; Lobel, Alcaeus 62; Lobel-Page, PLF, p. 281); Anacreon (?), Partheneia (?; C. M. Bowra, New Chapters 3. 66-67; B. Snell, Philol. 73, 1938, 438, reads Paroenia; Galiano, Pind., No. 59; Gentili, Anacr. 100, fr. 190; Page, PMG 501); Archilochus (seen in fr. e by F. Lasserre, Mus. Helv. 5, 1948, 6-15, along with Hesiod, fr. 235, Rzach; rejected by B. Snell, Philol. 97, 1948, 336); Aristarchus; Aristonicus; Aristophanes of Byzantium; Aristotle, Aporemata Homerica (?), Hist. Animal. vi. 16. 570a, viii. 2. 592a, ix. 32. 618b. 28; Athenocles (?); Callimachus, Epigr. 55. 3; Crates grammaticus; Didymus; Dionysius Sidonius; Ephorus, Hist., Bk. ii; Hermapias (?); Hesiod (?; Traversa, Hes. Cat. 130); Hippeus of Rhegium (?); Homer, Od. iv. 389, xviii. 385-86; Istrus (a follower of Callimachus); Megaclides, On Homer; Philetas (?); Phrynichus, Phoenissae (restored in col. 3 by H. Diels, Rh. Mus. 56, 1901, 29-36); Pindar, Paeans (?; Galiano, Pind., Nos. 17, 38; Turyn, fr. 71); Protagoras (of Abdera, or a grammarian?); Ptolemaeus of Ascalon; Seleucus (quoted by error for Panyasis; Page, GLP 1. 118; Powell, CA 248); Solon, Laws; Sophocles (?); Stesichorus (Page, PMG 273); Zenodotus; and an unknown epic passage (Powell, CA 79). On these citations see, further, Wilamowitz, Gött. Anz., 1900, 40-44; Galiano, Aesch. 123, note 337. Collart, Il., Pap. v. Lesky, GGL 74; Ludwich, PC 8-20; O. Muller, Uber den Papyruskommentar zum ῷ der Ilias (Diss. Munchen 1913). Archiv 1. 533-34. T. W. Allen, W. G. Rutherford, A. Platt, CR 14 (1900) 14-20.

1206 Brief summaries of Il. xxii-xxiii and Od. ii-iii. P. Antin. 2. 69 (II-III, Antinoöpolis; on recto and verso).

1207 Catechism on the Iliad. PSI 1. 19 (V; sch. ex.; in the same hand as No. 344). Mette, Il., Pap. Y. Archiv 7. 245.

1208 Epitome of Odyssey iii and vi. P. Ryl. 1. 23 (II; sch. ex.). Collart, Pap. a. Archiv 6. 254.

1209 Scholia on Od. iii. 4, 91, xi. 321-22, 326, 519, 582, xii. 70, 85, xiii. 96, 259, xiv. 327. PSI 10. 1173 (III; pap. cod.). Refers to Asclepiades; Herodorus (?); Hesiod; Lycophron; and Pherecydes (?). Collart, Pap. b. Archiv 13. 119-20. R. Pfeiffer, Philol. 92 (1937) 14-16.

1210 Memoranda (?) on Od. ix. 1-3, 39-40. J. Schwartz, BIFAO 61 (1962) 173-74 (No. 39) (II, Deir-el- Medineh; ostr.). B. Bruyere, Fouilles de l' Inst. Fr. d'Arch. Or. du Caire 20, fasc. 2 (1952) 25 (first mention).

1211 Scholia minora on Od. xv. 1-521. P. Amh. 2. 18; O. Plasberg, Archiv 2. 206-8 (P. Strassb. inv. Gr. 162) (II; on the verso of accounts; for school use?). Collart, Od., Pap. d. Ludwich, PC 22-24. Archiv 2. 345. A. Ludwich, Berl. Phil. Woch. 24 (1904) 316-17; A. Calderini, Aeg. 2 (1921) 305.

1212 Scholia minora on Od. xviii. 67, 70. P. Oxy. 11. 1397 (P. Princ. AM. 9050) (V, Oxy.). Collart, Pap. i.

1213 Commentary on Od. xxi. 218-34. P. Fay. 312; P. Cairo G. H. 10848 (I-II, Theadelphia). One Demetrius is mentioned. Collart, Pap. e. Archiv 2. 347.

1214 Dialogue on the Odyssey. P. Lit. Lond. 160 (Brit. Mus. inv. 1874) (I B. C.). From the same composition, but not the same papyrus, as No. 1215. Collart, Pap. h. Archiv 10. 224-25.

1215 Dialogue on the Odyssey. P. Univ. Giss. 4. 39 (inv. 361) (ca. 200 B. C., Fayum?). From the same composition as No. 1214. Collart, Pap. h; Gundel 9. Archiv 13. 117-18.

1216 Homeric glosses, by Apion. P. Ryl. 1. 26 (I, Oxy.). Cite Homer, Il. ii. 8, xi. 34, xix. 21, xxi. 180, Od. iv. 841, vi. 268, xiv. 345. Archiv 6. 254.

1217 Homeric lexicon, by Apollonius Sophista. E. W. B. Nicholson, CR 11 (1897) 390-93 (Bodleian Libr., Gr. class. e. 44 (P)) (I). Cites Homer, Il. i. 51, ii. 738, v. 525, xii. 359-60, xiii. 301, xiv. 129, xx. 357 (?), xxi. 259 (?), Od. viii. 360-62, xii. 330.

1218 Homeric glossary (words in en-). C. C. Edgar, Ann. Serv. 26 (1926) 203; W. G. Waddell, Mél. Maspero 1. 152-54 (P. Cairo inv. 50208) (III, Oxy.). Mette, Il., Pap. Z. Archiv 13. 121.

1219 Alphabetical lexicon of Homeric words. P. Freib. 1 c, verso (inv. 12) (I B. C.; on the verso of Nos. 1577 and 2658). Mette, Il., Pap. Z.¹ Archiv 7. 244.

1220 Glosses, partly Homeric (words in omicron). P. Hibeh 1. 5 verso; P. Ryl. 1. 16 a; P. Lit. Lond. 186 (Brit. Mus. Inv. 1823, v.) P. Bad. 6. 180, verso; P. Heid. Siegmann 200 (inv. 406, v.) (ca. 200 B. C., Hibeh; cart.; on the verso of No. 1660). Mette, Il., Pap. Z.² Archiv 14. 121-24.

1221 Explanations of Homeric words (or commentary on an unknown poetic text?). P. Hamb. 137 (inv. 657) (III-II B. C.). Quotes Homer, Il. ix. 230-31, xiii. 505, xiv. 349-50, Od. viii. 186-87, and perhaps refers to Il. ii. 848a (cf. P. Oxy. 221, col. 6, lines 20-21). Archiv 16. 118.

1222 Homeric glossary. P. Mich. inv. 1585, inedita (?).

1223 Allegorical interpretations of Homer (Plutarch?). P. Lond. 3. 734, verso; P. Lit. Lond. 175 (Brit. Mus. inv. 734, v.) (III; on the verso of a land register). Quotes Homer, Il. vi. 235-36, vii. 162, ix. 169-70, xxiii. 252, 648-49, Od. xi. 131, xvi. 300, 302-3, xix. 40, 136, xxiii. 278. Mette, Il., Pap. Z.³ Archiv 10. 225. F. della Corte, Riv. Fil. 66 (1938) 40-49, attributes the text to Plutarch, Homerikai Meletai.

1224 On Homeric cosmology (or philosophy?). M. Hombert and C. Préaux, Mél. Boisacq 493-97 (Musées Royaux, Bruxelles, inv. E. 7162) (I-II). Cites Homer, Il. i. 497-98, v. 749-50 (= viii. 393-94), xix. 128-29, xxiv. 97, 104. Collart, Il. 365; Mette,

Il., Pap. Z⁴. A. Koerte, Archiv 14.139-40, suggests as the author an opponent of Leogoras of Syracuse; F. della Corte, Riv. Fil. 67 (1939) 36-42, prefers a philosophical treatise.

1225   Discussion of the days of the Odyssey.   P. Schubart 3 (P. Berol. inv. 9571, recto) (II-III; written on the·recto beneath a document, No. 1381 on verso). Cites Homer, Od. i.1, iii.490, xiii.1.   Schubart, Einfuhrung 397 (first mention).   Mette, Od., Pap. k.   M. F. Galiano, PP 8 (1953) 65-70; idem, Emérita 28 (1960) 95-98; R. Merkelbach, Archiv 16 (1956) 118-19, revises the text.

1226   Homeric commentary (?).   P. Aberdeen 119 (II, Fayum?).   Ed. pr.: E₆O. Winstedt, CQ 1 (1907) 264. Mette, Il., Pap. Z⁶.

1227   Homeric scholia.   Mentioned by Breccia, Alexandrea 140 (?).   Mette, Il., Pap. W.

1228   Scholia minora on Homer.   Mentioned by A. E. R. Boak, Aeg. 4 (1923) 38 (P. Mich. inv. 9, inedita) (II-III).   Mette, Il., Pap. X.

1229   Fragment of a dialogue (?) on Homer.   P. Schubart 4 (III).   Mentions Peisandros, perhaps as author of the Kypria; P. Maas, Gnomon 23 (1951) 243. Mette, Il., Pap. Z⁵ Archiv 16.119.

1230   Fragment mentioning "Homer the poet."   O. Bodl. 2.2179 (inv. 163) (II; ostr.).   The rest of the text is now illegible.

Homerica: see also Nos. 633, 1287, 1844, 1925, 2453-2454, 2456, 2614, 2642, 2644, 2724-25.

Homeric Hymn to Demeter, ii.8-423: see No. 1774.

1231   Ibid. ii.402-7.   P. Oxy. 23.2379 (III, Oxy.).   R. Merkelbach, Stud. Jachmann 155-56.

1232   Homer (?): Margites (?).   P. Oxy. 22.2309 (I B.C.-I, Oxy.).   Ends of 21 lines, alternating hexameters and iambic trimeters.   Archiv 16.84.   K. Latte, Gnomon 27 (1955) 492-93; J. A. Davison, CR, NS 8 (1958) 13-14, attributes the text to a later, non-Homeric "Margites"; H. Langerbeck, HSCP 63 (1958) 59-63; M. Forderer, Zum homerischen Margites (Amsterdam 1960) 5-7, rejects the attribution; W. Ludwig, Gnomon 33 (1961) 448-52.

Ps.-Homer: Thebais: see No. 455.

Hyginus: see No. 2452.

1233   HYPERIDES: Pro Lycophrone, Pro Euxenippo, In Demosthenem.   J. G. Kenyon, Hyperidis Orationes et Fragmenta (Oxonii 1906), pp. iii-iv; P. Lit. Lond. 132 (Brit. Mus. inv. 108 + 115); P. Iand. 5.80 (inv. 213) (II, Gournou).   Gundel 21 (P. Iand. 80).   Kenyon, Pal. GP, pl. XVI (small frr. of P. Lit. Lond. 132 donated to the Rossall Sch.); Pal. Soc., Ser. 1, vol. 2, pl. 126; Roberts, GLH, pl. 13b; Thompson, GLP, No. 9 (p. 124); Wattenbach, SGS, tab. II.   Archiv 10.218; JAW 161.186-210 (a bibl. of Hyperides).   H. L. Hudson-Williams, Fifty Years Cl. Schol. 199-200, 211; Lesky, GGL

563; Winter, LLP 250-55.   F. Zucker, Gnomon 7 (1931) 509 (on P. Iand. 80).   G. Colin, Le discours d' Hyperide contre Démosthène sur l'argent d' Harpale (Paris 1934; see p. 50 on P. Iand. 80); V. de Falco, Iperide: Le orazioni in difesa di Eussenippo e contro Atenogene (Napoli 1947) 45-141, 203-19.   The bibl. of Hyperides is of course extensive; the reader is referred to the volumes of Marouzeau-Ernst, L'Année philologique.

1234   --- In Philippidem.   J. G. Kenyon, Hyperidis Orationes et Fragmenta, p. iv; idem, Class. Texts 42-55; P. Lit. Lond. 134 (Brit. Mus. inv. 134) (II-I B.C.; from the same roll as No. 337).   H. van Herwerden, Mnemos. 19 (1891) 397-404; H. Weil, Rev. Et. Gr. 5 (1892) 1-6.

1235   --- In Athenogenem.   F. G. Kenyon, Hyperidis Orationes et Fragmenta, p. iv (P. Par.: Musee du Louvre inv. 9331) (II B.C., Panopolis?).   Kenyon, Pal. GP, pl. XII; Schubart, Gr. Pal., Abb. 70; Thompson, GLP, No. 4 (p. 114).   H. Diels, Sitzb. Berl. Akad., 1889, 663-66; E. Revillout, Rev. Ét. Gr. 2 (1889) 1-16; H. Weil, ibid. 5 (1892) 157-88; P. Vogt, WS 16 (1894) 168-217; V. de Falco, op. cit. (see No. 1233), 145-97, 220-36.

1236   --- Epitaphios.   F. G. Kenyon, Hyperidis Orationes et Fragmenta, pp. iv-v; P. Lit. Lond. 133 (Brit. Mus. inv. 98) (II, Upper Egypt; on the verso of a horoscope).   Ed. pr.: C. Babington, The Funeral Oration of Hyperides over Leosthenes ... (Cambridge 1858).   Wattenbach, SGS, tab. III.

Hyperides: see also Nos. 2070, 2128, 2499-2502, 2546.

Hypsicrates: see No. 2091.

1237   IBYCUS: Fragments.   P. Oxy. 15.1790, 17.2081 f. (I B.C., Oxy.).   Quotes Callimachus or Lysimachus (?), On Teucer (Pfeiffer, Callim. 1, p. 498, favors Lysimachus).   On the false attribution of the text to Stesichorus, see Galiano, LG 131, 133. Schubart, Gr. Pal., Abb. 75.   C. M. Bowra, New Chapters 3.30-36; Diehl, Anth. Lyr. 2¹.49-53; Edmonds, LG 2.114-19; J. G. Griffith, Fifty Years Cl. Schol. 51-52; Lavagnini, Aglaia 210-14; Page, PMG 282, Wilamowitz, Pindaros 508-13.   Archiv 7.133-34; G. Vitale, Aeg. 3 (1922) 133-39; K. F. W. Schmidt, Gött. Anz., 1924, 5-6; B. Snell, Philol. 96 (1944) 290-92; D. L. Page, Aeg. 31 (1951) 158-72; J. P. Barron, CR, NS 11 (1961) 185-87, supports the ascription to Ibycus.

Ibycus: see also Nos. 246, 2471.

Ion of Chios: see Nos. 211, 1707, 1739, 2290.
Iophon: see No. 157.

1238   ISAEUS: De Nicostrati Hereditate 16-18.   P. Rain. 1.12 (inv. 29768) (III).

1239   --- Adversus Elpagoram et Demophanem.   P. Oxy. 3.415 (Univ.-Bibl., Graz) (II, Oxy.).   Jander 9-10. Archiv 3.293.

Isaeus: see also Nos. 2504-5.

1240 ISIDORUS: Four hymns to Isis-Hermouthis. A.
Vogliano, Primo Rapporto degli scavi condotti
dalla Missione Archeologica d'Egitto della R.
Università di Milano nella zona di Madinet-Madi
(Milano 1936) 27-51 (?, Madinet-Madi; inscribed
on pilasters at the south entrance to the temple-
precinct). A. Vogliano, Atti Pap. IV, 488, 491-96,
reprints the text; idem, Supplementum Epigraphi-
cum Graecum 8, fasc. 2 (1938), Nos. 548-51; F.
Bilabel, Sammelbuch griechischer Urkunden aus
Aegypten 5 (Heidelberg 1934), Nos. 8138-41, gives
the text; M. Vandoni, Prolegom. 2 (1953) 105-22;
R. Keydell, ibid. 123-24, on the meter.

1241 ISOCRATES: Ad Demonicum 8-12. P. Ross. Georg.
1.16 (Collection of G. Zereteli, Tiflis) (IV; pap.
cod.).

1242 --- 10-11. P. Rein. 2.79 (P. Sorbonne inv. 2146)
(II).

1243 --- 12-14. A. Wifstrand, Årsb., Lund, 1934-35,
57-58 (No. 3) (III; on the verso of a document).

1244 --- 18-52. Drerup, No. 9 (P. Berol. inv. 8935)
(II; on the verso of an inventory).

1245 ---. 26-28. P. Lond. 2.230, verso; P. Lit. Lond.
255 (Brit. Mus. inv. 230) (III-IV, Fayum?; on the
verso of a Psalter, P. Lit. Lond. 207; sch. ex. ?).
Syllables are marked off, as if for an exercise in
reading or shorthand.

1246 --- 33-34. E. M. Husselman, TAPA 76 (1945) 118-
20 (P. Mich. inv. 5299) (I-II, Karanis).

1247 --- 34-35, 44. P. Ibscher 4 (P. Hamb., pp. 130-31)
(IV; parch. cod.).

1248 --- 39, 41, 50. Drerup, p. viii (P. Berol. inv.
7426) (II-III; on the verso of accounts).

--- 39, etc.: see No. 1992.

1249 --- 40-45. P. Oxy. 15.1812 (P. Cairo) (V-VI, Oxy.;
pap. cod.).

1250 --- 40-46. P. Oxy. 8.1095 (Muhlenberg Coll.)
(IV, Oxy.; pap. cod.).

1251 --- 45. R. Reitzenstein, Hermes 35 (1900) 607-8
(P. Strassb. inv. Gr. 92) (III; text on recto, No.
1993 on verso). Drerup, No. 6. Archiv 1.522.

1252 --- 50-53. P. Amh. 2.25 (I-II). Drerup, No. 7.
Archiv 2.359.

1253 --- Ad Nicoclem 1-6, 8-9. PSI 11.1198 (II, Oxy.).

1254 --- 1-30. A. Schoene, Mél. Graux 481-504 (Musée
Arch. du Chateau Borelly, Marseille) (III-IV?;
roll cut to form a codex?). Drerup, No. 1 (bibl.).

1255 --- 2-4. Raineri M. 4.136-39 (IV, Fayum). Drerup,
No. 3. JAW 152.127.

1256 --- 9-11. P. Lit. Goodspeed 1 (inv. 103) (III, Karanis). Ed. pr.: E. J. Goodspeed, CP 1 (1906) 167.

1257 --- 12-13. P. Erl. 8 (inv. 5, verso) (III; on the
verso of No. 2235). Formerly listed as a philosophical fragment; identified by C. H. Roberts,
JJP 9-10 (1955-56) 135-36.

1258 --- 32-36. G. Björck, SO 14 (1935) 68-72 (Uppsala
Universitets Bibliotek, inv. 114) (III-IV; pap. cod.).

1259 --- 47-51. PSI 1.16 (V, Oxy.; pap. cod.).

1260 --- A paraphrase of the speech. Mentioned by
Schubart, Einführung 480 (P. Berol. inv. 7426)
(II). Drerup, No. 10 (?).

1261 --- Panegyricus 1-54 (with lacunae). P. Oslo 3.71
(I-II, Oxy.?).

1262 --- 18-22. P. Iand. 5.79 (inv. 211) (ca. A.D. 200).
Gundel 20.

1263 --- 19-116. P. Oxy. 5.844 (Houghton Libr., Harvard
Univ.) (II, Oxy.).

1264 --- 37-39. Mentioned by Breccia, Alexandrea 140
(?).

1265 --- 78-82. PSI 7.762 (IV, Oxy.; parch. cod.).
BSAA 6 (1928) 295-96. Identified by F. Heichelheim,
Hermes 60 (1925) 372; J. Keil, Archiv 9 (1928) 61.

1266 --- 95-96. P. Antin. 2.84 (III, Antinoöpolis; parch.
cod.).

1267 --- 125-31. PSI 9.1088 (II, Oxy.).

1268 --- 189; De Pace 1-3. P. Oxy. 8.1096 (Libr. of the
Princeton Theological Seminary, inv. 6) (IV, Oxy.;
parch.).

1269 --- Philippus 40, 42. P. Rain. 3.40 (inv. 19892 A)
(V, Fayum; parch. cod.).

1270 --- 114-17. Raineri M. 2.74-76 (I-II, Fayum).
Drerup, No. 2. JAW 152.127.

1271 --- De Pace 1. PSI 11.1199 (II, Oxy.).

--- 1-3: see No. 1268.

1272 --- 13-145. H. I. Bell, Journ. Philol. 30 (1907)
1-83; P. Lit. Lond. 131 (Brit. Mus. inv. 132) (I-II).
Drerup, No. 4. JEA 8.87; JAW 152.128; M. L.
W. Laistner, CQ 15 (1921) 78-84.

1273 --- 43-44, 56-61. P. Heid. Siegmann 208 (inv.
3073) (ca. A.D. 100).

1274 --- A criticism of the Evagoras. Raineri M.
2.79-82 (I-II, Fayum). Cites Evagoras 53-54.
Jander 38-39. JAW 152.127.

1275 --- Helena 23-24, 26. P. Rain. 3.42 (inv. 806)
(cf. ibid. 4, p. 137) (IV-V, Fayum; pap. cod.).
Identified independently by W. Schmid, in a letter
to the Vienna editors, and by H. Herter, Rh. Mus.
89 (1940) 240.

1276 --- 61-63. P. Antin. 2.82 (IV, Antinoöpolis; parch.
cod.).

1277    --- Panathenaïcus 29-34.    P. Antin. 2.83 (IV, Anti-
        noöpolis; parch. cod.).

1278    --- In Sophistas 1-3.    C. W. Keyes, AJP 50 (1929)
        262-63 (Columbia Univ. Libr., inv. 458) (II; on the
        verso of a register).

1279    --- 16-18.    P. Oxy. 4.704 (Univ. of Pennsylvania
        Mus.) (III, Oxy.).    Drerup, No. 8.    Archiv 3.492.

1280    --- De Antidosi 16-18.    P. Princ. 3.113 (II).

1281    --- 83, 87.    P. Oxy. 1.27 (Oriental Institute, Univ.
        of Chicago) (I-II, Oxy.).    Drerup, No. 5.    Archiv
        1.115.

1282    --- Trapeziticus 44-48.    P. Oxy. 9.1183 (P. Princ.)
        (I, Oxy.).

        Isocrates: see also Nos. 2080-81, 2205.

        Istrus: see No. 1205.

1283    JOSEPHUS: Bellum Iudaïcum ii.20.6-7.    P. Rain.
        3.36 (inv. 29810) (cf. ibid. 4, p. 137) (III; pap. cod.).

        Lasus of Hermione: see Nos. 460, 2444.
        Leogoras: see No. 1224.
        Leonidas of Tarentum: see Nos. 1593, 1595-96.
        Leontiscus: see No. 2337.
        Leptines: see No. 369.
        Leucon: see No. 1186.

1284    LIBANIUS: Or. 18.4-6, 7-8.    A. Traversa, Aeg. 35
        (1955) 185-88 (P. Med. inv. 71) (VIII-IX; pap. cod.).

        Lucian: see Nos. 2087, 2101.
        Lucillus of Tarrha: see No. 2298.

1285    LYCOPHRON: Alexandra 586-92, 924-39, 1345-79.
        P. Oxy. 17.2094 (II, Oxy.).

1286    --- 1108-28, 1154-63.    A. Hartmann, Philol. 76
        (1920) 228-33 (P. Monac. inv. 156) (I?, Arsinoë).
        JEA 7.87.

1287    --- Scholia on Alexandra 744-46.    PSI 6.724 (III).
        The text quotes Homer, Od. i.52, xii.432-33 (Col-
        lart, Pap. g). Fritsch, No. 11. JEA 9.100. A.
        Koerte, Archiv 7.244-45, prefers scholia on the
        Odyssey; G. Vitelli, Aeg. 3 (1922) 141-42, re-
        prints the text, credits Wilamowitz with the attri-
        bution; G. Méautis, Revue Belge 32 (1928) 87-90,
        suggests a commentary on Sophocles, Teucer; E.
        Harrison, CR 51 (1937) 38.

        Lycophron: see also Nos. 1186, 1209, 1707, 2861.

1288    LYCURGUS: Contra Leocratem 22-23.    P. Ryl.
        3.551 (II, Oxy.).

1289    --- Contra Menesaechmum Delatio (a fragment).
        W. Croenert, Gött. Nachr., 1922, 45-46 (P. Berol.
        inv. 11748) (II-III).  F. Durrbach, Lycurgue: Contre
        Léocrate, Fragments (Paris 1932) 91.  Archiv 7.
        225.

1290    LYSIAS: Pro Eratosthene 47-48; Pro. Eryximacho
        (fragments).    H. J. M. Milne, JEA 15 (1929) 75-77
        (Brit. Mus. inv. 2852); P. Ryl. 3.489 (III-IV, Oxy.;
        pap. cod.).  New Chapters 3.258-59.  Archiv 10.
        217-28, 14.134; Chr. Ég. 5 (1930) 130-31; U. Al-
        bini, SIFC 27-28 (1956) 6-7; idem, Maia, NS 11
        (1959) 65-66.

1291    --- Epitaphius 75-79.    PSI 11.1206 (II, Oxy.).

1292    --- Pro Antiphontis Filia, and fragments of other
        speeches.    P. Rain. 1.13 (inv. 29816) (cf. ibid. 3,
        p. 93) (II-III).  New Chapters 3.259.  Archiv 11.
        268, 270.

1293    --- Contra Hippothersem, Contra Theomnestum, and
        four unknown orations.    P. Oxy. 13.1606 (Bodlei-
        an Libr., Gr. class. b.19 (P)) (II-III, Oxy.).  T.
        W. Lumb, New Chapters 1.153-55. Lesky, GGL
        547. Archiv 7.156-58; JEA 8.87, 10.151; P. Col-
        lart, Rev. Phil. 43 (1919) 49-54; T. Reinach, Rev.
        Et. Gr. 32 (1919) 443-50, on the argument of Contra
        Hippothersem; P. Cloché, Rev. Ét. Anc. 23 (1921)
        28-36, on the same subject.

1294    --- In Theozotidem.    P. Hibeh 1.14 (Bodleian Libr.,
        Gr. class. d.78 (P)) (III B.C., Hibeh; cart; text
        on recto, No. 1569 on verso).  Jander 7-8;  New
        Chapters 1.154-55.  Archiv 6.236; A. Wilhelm,
        WS 52 (1934) 52-56.

        Lysias: see also Nos. 458, 2070, 2087, 2289,
        2502-4, 2637.

        Lysimachides: see No. 2130.
        Lysimachus: see Nos. 1237, 2206.
        Lysippus: see No. 2290.
        Magnes: see No. 1626.

1295    MANETHO:  Fragment of an Epitome of Manetho.
        P. Bad. 4.59 (V, Harara; on the verso of docu-
        ments?).  Bilabel, No. 11 (ed. pr.); Jacoby, FGH,
        Dritter Teil C, 97.  New Chapters 2.71-72.  Ar-
        chiv 7.232-33.

        Manetho: see also Nos. 1767, 1875, 2488.

        Marsyas of Philippi: see No. 339.

1296    MAXIMUS THE "DECURION": The Vision (a poem in
        Sotadeans).    J. P. Mahaffy and J. B. Bury, BCH
        18 (1894) 149-51, 154-57 (I-II, Talmis, Ethiopia;
        inscribed on a temple wall).  The author gives his
        name as an acrostic.  Manteuffel, Opusc., Appen-
        dix, No. 1, pp. 198-99.  A. H. Sayce and H. Weil,
        Rev. Et. Gr. 7 (1894) 284-91; G. Kaibel, Sitzb.
        Berl. Akad., 1895, 781-89; E. Rohde, Philol. 54
        (1895) 11-15; G. Manteuffel, Eos 31 (1928) 181-86.

        Meandrius of Miletus: see No. 1186.
        Megaclides: see No. 1205.
        Melanippides: see No. 1948.
        Meleager: see No. 1598.
        Menaechmus: see No. 2181.

1297 MENANDER: Titles of the plays of Menander. P.
Oxy. 27.2462 (II, Oxy.; on the verso of a land
register). The titles in order: Androgynoi, Agroi-
kos, Aspis, Anepsioi, Halieus, Apistos, Heauton
Penthon, Adelphoi I, Adelphoi II, Andria, Heauton
Timoroumenos, Achaioi ē Peloponnesioi, Halaeis,
Auletrides ē Arrhephoros, Boiotia, Georgos, Dys-
kolos, Demiourgos, Deisidaimon.

1298 --- Dyscolus. V. Martin, Papȳrus Bodmer IV:
Mēnandre, Le Dyscolos (Cologny-Genève 1958; ed.
pr.) (III, Panopolis?; eleven leaves from a pap.
cod.). An hypothesis in verse (attributed to Aristophanes of Byzantium), a didascalia, and a list of
the dramatis personae precede the play.
A complete bibl. to June 1960: J. T. McDonough,
Jr., The Classical World 53 (1960) 277-80, 296-98
(reviews of the ed. pr., editions, translations, and
articles). Another bibl.: A. Traversa, Paideia
14 (1959) 344-46, ibid. 15 (1960) 327-30, ibid. 16
(1961) 324-25. A "Forschungsbericht": W. Kraus,
Anz. AW 15 (1962) 1-12.
Critical editions: R. Cantarella (Mazara 1959);
C. Gallavotti (Napoli 1959); B. Marzullo (Torino
1959); N. B. Sphyroeras (Athenai 1959); J. Bingen
(Leiden 1960, revised ed. 1963); C. Diano (Padova
1960); O. Foss (Copenhagen 1960); B. A. van
Groningen (Leiden, Brill, 1960); idem, Verhandelingen der Koninklijke Nederlandse Akad. van Weten-
schappen, Afd. Letterkunde, Nieuwe Reeks, Deel
67, No. 3 (Amsterdam 1960); W. Kraus, Sitzb.
Wien. Akad. 234 (1960), Abh. 4; idem (Zürich 1960);
H. Lloyd-Jones (Oxonii 1960); H. J. Mette (Götting-
en 1960); M. Treu (München 1960); J. Martin
(Paris 1961). Editions by W. E. Blake, E. W.
Handley, P. Lekatsas, F. H. Sandbach, and A.
Thierfelder have been reported as promised or
forthcoming.
V. Martin, Aeg. 37 (1957) 271-73; idem, CRAI,
1957, 283-88; idem, Gnomon 29 (1957) 560; M. H.
Rocha Pereira, Human., NS 6-7 (1957-58) 200-1;
G. T. W. Hooker, GR, Ser. 2.5 (1958) 105-7;
Lesky, GGL 597-98; V. Martin, Mus. Helv. 15
(1958) 209-14; idem, PP 13 (1958) 365-75; P. J.
Photiades, GR, Ser. 2.5 (1958) 108-22; G. d'Anna,
Riv. CCM 1 (1959) 298-306; A. Ardizzoni, Sic.
Gymn. 12 (1959) 177-84; A. Barigazzi, Athen. 47
(1959) 184-95; idem, PP 14 (1959) 365-76; idem,
Riv. Fil., NS 37 (1959) 119-47; J. Bingen, Chr. Ég.
34 (1959) 86-90, ibid. 141-46, 300-4; W. E. Blake,
"Emendations and Restorations to Menander's
Dyskolos" (Ann Arbor 1959; privately distributed);
S. Boscherini, SIFC, NS 31 (1959) 247-53; R.
Cantarella, Rend. Ist. Lomb. 93 (1959) 77-114; D.
del Corno, Dion. 22 (1959) 132-35; C. Corbato,
IFC Trieste 6 (1959) 15-39; C. B. Dedouses, Platon
11 (1959) 399-404; C. Diano, Maia, NS 11 (1959)
326-41; idem, Note in margine al Dyskolos di
Menandro (Padova 1959); S. Eitrem, SO 35 (1959)
131-38; R. Flacelière, Rev. Ét. Gr. 72 (1959) 370-
76; O. Foss, Class. Med. 20 (1959) 30-46; C.
Gallavotti, Riv. CCM 1 (1959) 227-79; K. D. Geor-
goules, Platon 11 (1959) 223-29; P. K. Georgountzas,
ibid. 210-17; M. Gigante, PP 14 (1959) 211, 337-58;
G. P. Goold, Phoenix 13 (1959) 139-60; F. C. Gor-
schen, Dion., NS 22 (1959) 101-5; B. A. van
Groningen, Mnemos., Ser. 4.12 (1959) 224-32,
289-97; P. W. Harsh, Gnomon 31 (1959) 577-86;

(Menander: Dyscolus, continued)
H. L. Herter, Rh. Mus. 102 (1959) 96, on the set-
ting; J.-M. Jacques, BAGB, Sér. 4.2 (1959) 200-15;
J. C. Kamerbeek, Mnemos., Ser. 4.12 (1959) 113-
28; R. Kassel, Mus. Helv. 16 (1959) 172-73; idem,
Rh. Mus. 102 (1959) 247-49; S. N. Koumanoudis,
Platon 11 (1959) 90-93; W. Kraus, Anz. AW 12 (1959)
149-53 (bibl.); idem, Rh. Mus. 102 (1959) 146-56;
J. Lanowsky, Eos 50 (1959-60), fasc. 2, 70-89; H.
Lloyd-Jones, CR, NS 9 (1959) 183-92; O. Luschnat,
Philol. 103 (1959) 154-56; B. Marzullo, Riv. CCM
1 (1959) 280-97; G. Monaco, SIFC, NS 31 (1959)
236-46; A. Oguse, Bull. de la Faculté des Lettres
de Strasbourg 38, No. 2 (1959) 135-53; E. Paratore,
Riv. CCM 1 (1959) 310-25, on the flutist in the D.
and in Plautus, Pseudolus; G. Pascucci, AR, NS
4 (1959) 102-5; P. J. Photiades, Chr. Ég. 34 (1959)
305-26; eadem, GR, Ser. 2.6 (1959) 89; C. Préaux,
Acad. Royale de Belgique, Bull. de la classe des
Lettres, Ser. 5.45 (1959) 245-73; eadem, Chr. Ég.
34 (1959) 327-41; C. Questa, Riv. CCM 1 (1959)
307-9, on the relation to the lost Dyscolus of Plautus; W. Richter, Philol. 103 (1959) 317-19; W.
Schmid, Rh. Mus. 102 (1959) 157-82, 263-66, on
the D. and the Timon legend; R. K. Sherk, AJP
80 (1959) 400-1; I. Skardasis, Platon 11 (1959) 460-
64; L. Strzelecki, GIF 12 (1959) 305-8, on the
relation to Plautus' Dyscolus; A. Thierfelder, Rh.
Mus. 102 (1959) 141-46; E. G. Turner, BICSL 6 ·
(1959) 61-72; idem, Bull. Ryl. Libr. 42 (1959)
242-58; E. Vogt, Rh. Mus. 102 (1959) 192, on the
concluding verses; G. Zuntz, Mnemos., Ser. 4.12
(1959) 298-300.
L. Alfonsi, Aeg. 40 (1960) 73-76, suggests that
Ovid, Ars Am. iii.332, may echo the Dyscolus;
W. E. Blake, CP 55 (1960) 174-76; C. Brescia,
Menandrea 113-24; M. Brožek, Meander 15 (1960)
39-46; G. Brugnoli, Menandrea 59-70, on the
form of the codex; R. Cantarella, ibid. 55-58, on
the date; Q. Cataudella, ibid. 29-34, 199-201; A.
della Casa, ibid. 153-57; E. Cavaignac, BAGB,
Sér. 4.3 (1960) 367-72; M. Coccia, Menandrea
159-94, on the meter; F. della Corte, Maia, NS
12 (1960) 83-88; C. Gallavotti, Riv. Fil., NS 38
(1960) 1-31; M. Gigante, Menandrea 71-78; J. G.
Griffith, CQ 54 (1960) 113-17, on the distribution of
the roles; B. A. van Groningen, Verhandelingen
der Kon. Nederl. Akad. van Wetenschappen, Nieuwe
Reeks 67, No. 3 (1960); K. Kerényi, Streifzuge
eines Hellenisten (Zürich 1960) 99-104; V. Longo,
Menandrea 195-98; T. Mantero, ibid. 125-52; V.
Martin, Script. 14 (1960) 3-15; B. Marzullo, Rend.
Acc. Linc. 15 (1960) 62-70; R. Merkelbach, Mus.
Helv. 17 (1960) 171-74; A. Oguse, Bull. de la Faculté des Lettres de Strasbourg 38, No. 7 (1960)
347-51; A. Pastorino, Menandrea 79-106, on the
religious aspects; M. Pope, Act. Class. 3 (1960)
40-52, on the changes of speaker; L. A. Post,
TAPA 91 (1960) 152-61; C. Préaux, Chr. Ég. 35
(1960) 222-39, on legal points; G. Rambelli, Menandrea 35-54, on the staging; A. Salač, Philol.
104 (1960) 145-46; P. Steinmetz, Rh. Mus. 103
(1960) 185-91, on the relation to Theophrastus; F.
Stoessl, Gymnas. 67 (1960) 204-9; idem, Sitzb.
Wien. Akad. 234 (1960), Abh. 5, on the changes of
speaker; J. Taillardat, Chr. Ég. 35 (1960) 240-43;
A. Thierfelder, Menandrea 107-12; A. Traversa,
ibid. 9-28; T. B. L. Webster, Studies in Menander

(Menander: Dyscolus, continued)

(Manchester 1960$^2$) 221-34; F. Zucker, Sitzb. Berl. Akad., 1960, Nr. 5.

W. E. Blake, Classical Journal 56 (1961) 338-43; S. Eitrem, SO 37 (1961) 153-58; A. Garzya, Studi su Euripide e Menandro (Napoli 1961) 118-35 (= Le Parole e le Idee 1, 1959, 150-60); W. Görler, Philol. 105 (1961) 299-307, on the relation to Terence, Eunuchus; B. A. van Groningen, Recherches Pap. 1 (1961) 95-112; H. Juhnke, Hermes 89 (1961) 122-27, on the codicology; J. Lanowski, Eos 51 (1961) 275-94, compares the play as discovered with earlier attempts to reconstruct it; B. Marzullo, Hlk. 1 (1961) 153-59; idem, Rend. Acc. Linc. 16 (1961) 320-29; U. E. Paoli, Iura 12 (1961) 194-97, on line 41; idem, Mus. Helv. 18 (1961) 53-62, on points of law; L. A. Post, AJP 82 (1961) 94-104; L. Strzelecki, Eos 51 (1961) 261-73, on the meter.

M. Gigante, Riv. Fil., NS 40 (1962) 185; H. Kupiszewski, Eos 52 (1962) 47-66, on the relation to Attic law; J. H. Quincey, Mnemos., Ser. 4.15 (1962) 44-46; V. Steffen, Eos 52 (1962) 39-45; F. Stoessl, Philol. 106 (1962) 126-32; O. Vicenzi, Gymnas. 69 (1962) 406-26.

C. Gallavotti, Riv. Fil. 91 (1963) 72-81; M. Gigante, PP 88 (1963) 54-55; W. Görler, Hermes 91 (1963) 268-87, on the character of Cnemon; R. B. Lloyd, AJP 84 (1963) 146-61, compares the prologue with that of Plautus, Rudens; H.-J. Newiger, Hermes 91 (1963) 127-28; L. A. Post, AJP 84 (1963) 36-51.

1299  --- Dyscolus 140-49, 169-74. B. P. Grenfell and A. S. Hunt, Mél. Nicole 220-22 (Bodleian Libr., Gr. class. g.50 (P)) (III, Hermupolis Magna; parch. cod.). Identified by C. H. Roberts. M. Treu gives the text in his edition of the Dyscolus (München 1960) 122-23.

1300  --- Dyscolus 263-72, 283-90. P. Oxy. 27.2467 (III, Oxy.). Identified by E. G. Turner and used in the edition of H. Lloyd-Jones (Oxonii 1960) before publication in P. Oxy.

1301  --- Heros, Epitrepontes, Samia, Periciromene, and Fabula Incerta. G. Lefebvre, Papyrus de Ménandre (Catalogue général des antiquités Égyptiennes du Musée du Caire; Le Caire 1911) (P. Cairo inv. 43227) (IV-V, Aphroditopolis; from the same pap. cod. as No. 375). New Pal. Soc., Ser. 1, vol. 2, pl. 127; Norsa, SLG, tav. 16 (Samia). Jensen, pp. vii-xx, xl-xlvii, and passim; Koerte, Men., pp. viii-xvi, xxv, and passim. Archiv 6.224; JAW 174.186-89; Preisendanz, PFF 214-15. C. Jensen, Hermes 49 (1914) 382-432; C. Robert, Hermes 49 (1914) 433-46, on the Epitrepontes; idem, ibid. 633-34, sees in Epitrepontes 88 a reminiscence of Euripides, Bacchae 968; P. E. Sonnenburg, Rh. Mus. 69 (1914) 80-86, on the plot of the Heros; E. Schwartz, Hermes 50 (1915) 312-15, on the Epitrepontes; Wilamowitz, Sitzb. Berl. Akad., 1916, 66-86, on the plot of the Samia; A. Kolar, WS 39 (1917) 18-25 (ditto); E. Wuest, Philol. 78 (1922) 189-202 (ditto); K. Kunst, WS 43 (1922-23) 147-56 (ditto); R. Taubenschlag, Sav. Zeitschr. 46 (1926) 68-82 (= idem, Opera Minora 1, Warszawa 1959, 623-39) on Attic law in the Epitrepontes; E. J. Kuiper, Mnemos.

57 (1929) 235-44, on the Fabula Incerta; A. Koerte, Hermes 72 (1937) 50-73 (ditto); idem, ibid. 78 (1943) 285-86, on Epitrepontes 571; G. Rambelli, SIFC 22 (1947) 241-50, on the scene of the Periciromene; V. de Falco, Human. 2 (1948-49) 268-70, on the Epitrepontes; idem, Emérita 17 (1949) 153-57; C. Brescia, GIF 3 (1950) 1-14; E. Honigmann, Mém. de l'Acad. Royale de Belgique, Classe des Lettres 46, fasc. 2 (1950), on the lost end of the Epitrepontes; J. M. Edmonds, Phoenix, Suppl. Vol. 1 (1952) (= Studies in Honour of Gilbert Norwood) 127-32, presents readings seen by infra-red photography; U. E. Paoli, Aeg. 32 (1952) 265-69, 282-85; A. Barigazzi, Athen. 44 (1956) 325-40, on the Heros; W. J. Verdenius, Mnemos., Ser. 4.9 (1956) 231; Lesky, GGL 597; E. W. Whittle, CQ, NS 9 (1959) 57-58, on Periciromene 87-88; O. Schroder, Hermes 88 (1960) 124-28; A. Barigazzi, Studi Castiglioni 1.43-49, on the Epitrepontes; R. Harder, Kleine Schriften (München 1960) 247-56 (ditto); B. Marzullo, Rh. Mus. 104 (1961) 224-29, having photographed a part of the papyrus by infra-red, reports negative results; T. Williams, WS 74 (1961) 43-58, studies the Epitrepontes in relation to Greek marriage-contracts from Egypt; J. Martin, BAGB, Sér. 4.1 (1962) 120-21, on Edmonds' readings.

1302  --- Epitrepontes. P. Oxy. 10.1236 (P. Cairo) (IV, Oxy.; parch.). Jensen, pp. xxi, 37-40; Koerte, Men., pp. xvii-xviii, etc. Archiv 7.145; JAW 174. 190. F. G. Allinson, AJP 36 (1915) 185-202.

1303  --- Periciromene. A. Koerte, Ber. Leipzig, 1908, 145-75 (Univ.-Bibl., Leipzig, inv. 613) (III, Antinoopolis?; parch. cod.). Jensen, pp. xxx-xxxi, 58-61, 63-66; Koerte, Men., pp. xxv-xxvi. Archiv 6.226; JAW 174.193.

1304  --- P. Oxy. 2.211 (Houghton Libr., Harvard Univ.) (I-II, Oxy.). Jensen, pp. xxix-xxx, 66-69; Koerte, Men., pp. xxvi-xxvii, etc. Archiv 1.513. H. van Herwerden, Mnemos. 28 (1900) 118-22; E. Eitrem, Vid. Forh., Christiania, 1906, Avh. 10, 8-13.

1305  --- G. A. Gerhard, Sitzb. Heid. Akad., 1911, Abh. 4 (P. Heid. inv. 219) (II). Jensen, p. xxxi, etc.; Koerte, Men., p. xxvii, etc. Archiv 6.226; JAW 174.193.

1306  --- Georgus. J. Nicole, Le Laboureur de Ménandre (Genève 1898) (P. Genève inv. 155) (V-VI; pap. cod.). Jensen, pp. xlvii-xlviii, 88-92; Koerte, Men., pp. xlii-xliii, 91-95; Sudhaus 79-84. Archiv 1.111. K. Dziatzko, Rh. Mus. 54 (1899) 497-525, on the plot; C. Brescia, GIF 3 (1950) 14. New Pal. Soc., Ser. 1, vol. 1, pls. 74-75.

1307  --- PSI 1.100 (IV, Upper Egypt?; pap. cod.). Jensen, pp. xlviii, 92-93; Koerte, Men., pp. xliii, 96-97; Sudhaus 82-83. Archiv 6.225; JAW 174.189-90.

1308  --- H. J. M. Milne, JEA 16 (1930) 192-93 (Brit. Mus. inv. 2823 A) (IV; pap. cod.). Koerte, Men., pp. xliv, 97-98. Archiv 11.263-64.

1309 --- Theophoroumene (?). PSI 12.1280 (I-II, Oxy.).
Ed. pr.: M. Norsa and G. Vitelli, Ann. Sc. Pisa,
Ser. 2.4 (1935) 1-3. Norsa, SLG, tav. 9 d. Koerte,
Men., pp. xlv-xlvi, 101-2; Page, GLP 1, No. 55.
Archiv 13.102; JAW 263.5-6. R. Goossens, Chr.
Ég. 10 (1935) 378; A. Koerte, Hermes 70 (1935)
431-38; A. Lesky, ibid. 72 (1937) 123-27; M. F.
Galiano, Arbor 6 (1946) 138-39; A. Garzya, Dion.,
NS 16 (1953) 64-75.

1310 --- Citharista (?). BKT 5.2.115-22 (inv. 9767) (I
B.C.). Schubart, Gr. Pal., Abb. 72; idem, PGB,
tab. 11 a. Jensen, pp. xlix-l, 96-100; Koerte, Men.,
pp. xlvi-xlvii, 104-8; Sudhaus 85-88. Archiv 6.
225; JAW 174.191-92. G. Manteuffel, Charist.
Przychocki 117-18; idem, Eos 42 (1947) 63-73.

1311 --- Colax. P. Oxy. 3.409 (Bodleian Libr., Gr.
class. c.55 (P)) (II, Oxy.). Jensen, pp. li, 102-4;
Koerte, Men., pp. xlvii-xlviii, 110-13, 115-17; Sudhaus 89-94. Archiv 3.277. F. Leo, Gött. Nachr.,
1903, 673-92; G. Coppola, Aeg. 4 (1923) 137-48;
W. E. J. Kuiper, Mnemos. 59 (1932) 165-83; O.
Schröder, Hermes 88 (1960) 128.

1312 --- P. Oxy. 10.1237 (Bodleian Libr., Gr. class. f.95
(P)) (III, Oxy.). Jensen, pp. li-lii, 104-8; Koerte,
Men., pp. xlviii, 113-15; Sudhaus 89-94. Archiv
7.145-46; JAW 174.192; New Chapters 3.170.

1313 --- Coneazomenae. P. Ross. Georg. 1.10 (Collection of G. Zereteli, Tiflis) (II; on the verso of
accounts). Jensen, pp. liv-lv, 110-111; Koerte,
Men., pp. l, 120-21; Sudhaus 95-96. Archiv 6.226;
JAW 174.192, 234.164-65. U. E. Paoli, Aeg. 32
(1952) 270-79.

1314 --- Misumenus. P. Oxy. 7.1013 (P. Cairo) (V-VI,
Oxy.; pap. cod.). Jensen, pp. lv, 113-15; Koerte,
Men., pp. li, 123; Sudhaus 97-98. Archiv 6.266;
JAW 174.192. C. Brescia, GIF 3 (1950) 14-15; A.
Barigazzi, Studi Castiglioni 1.50-57.

1315 --- Wilamowitz, Sitzb. Berl. Akad., 1918, 747-49
(P. Berol. inv. 13281) (III; pap. cod.). Jensen, pp.
lv, 112-13; Koerte, Men., pp. li, 122-23; Page,
GLP 1, No. 52; P. Schubart 22 (fr. I) gives a revised text. Archiv 7.146. G. Vitale, Aeg. 2 (1921)
84-86.

1316 --- P. Oxy. 13.1605 (P. Cairo) (III, Oxy.). Jensen,
pp. lv-lvi, 116; Koerte, Men., pp. li, 126. G.
Coppola, SIFC, NS 3 (1923) 49-62.

1317 --- Perinthia. P. Oxy. 6.855 (Bodleian Libr., Gr.
class. e.99 (P)) (III, Oxy.). Jensen, pp. lvii-lviii,
120-21; Koerte, Men., pp. lii-liii, 130-31; Sudhaus
99-100. Archiv 6.227; JAW 174.193-94. F. Leo,
Hermes 44 (1909) 143-46; A. Koerte, ibid. 309-13;
K. F. W. Schmidt, Gött. Anz., 1910, 648-49; F.
Schoell, Sitzb. Heid. Akad., 1912, Abh. 7, on the
relation of the play to Terence, Andria; C. Brescia, GIF 3 (1950) 15-16.

1318 --- "Comoedia Florentina" (Epiclerus?); Misumenus.
PSI 2.126; P. Schubart 22, fr. II, a fragment of
the Misumenus from the same cod. (V, Panopolis
or Hermupolis?; parch. cod.). Menander quotes

Carcinus the younger (Com. Flor. 74-76). Schubart, Gr. Pal., Abb. 99. Jensen, pp. lx-lxi, 128-
31; Koerte, Men., pp. lvi-lvii, 138-42; Page, GLP
1, No. 54. Archiv 7.146-48, 16.104; JAW 174.245,
195.187; New Chapters 3.170-71. R. Herzog, Hermes 51 (1916) 315-16; F. G. Allinson, TAPA 52 (1921)
69-81; G. Coppola, Riv. Ind. Gr. Ital. 6 (1922) 35-
48; E. Ulbricht, Kritische u. exegetische Studien
zu Menander (Leipzig 1933) 1-4; G. Ghedini, Aeg.
24 (1944) 159-60; C. Brescia, GIF 3 (1950) 16; L.
A. Post, AJP 77 (1956) 217, on the Misumenus; G.
G. Schiassi, Dion., NS 19 (1956) 253-63, favors the
Coneazomenae over the Epiclerus; O. Schröder,
Hermes 88 (1960) 128.

1319 --- Menander (?): Fragment (Epitrepontes? First
Adelphoe?). P. Didot 2-15 (II B.C., Serapaeum,
Memphis; from the same composite roll as Nos.
31, 401, 1320, 1435). Attributed by the editor to
Euripides, Temenidae. Jensen, pp. 132-33; Koerte,
Men., pp. lx-lxiii, 143-44, including the history of
the earlier attributions; Page, GLP 1, No. 34, lists
as an anonymous tragic fragment. Lesky, GGL 599,
rejects the Epitrepontes. JAW 17.34-43. F. Blass,
Rh. Mus. 35 (1880) 75-82; E. Holzner, WS 11 (1889)
170-71, emends the subscription; D. S. Robertson,
CR 36 (1922) 106-9, argues for the Epitrepontes, and
defends his position in Hermes 61 (1926) 348-50; A.
Koerte, ibid. 134-56, 350-51, favors Menander; H.
J. M. Milne, CR 39 (1925) 117, supports Robertson;
H. Lucas, Phil. Woch. 58 (1938) 1101-4, suggests
Menander, First Adelphoe; A. Barigazzi, Athen.
43 (1955) 278-326, seeks to integrate the fragment
with Epitrepontes, Act IV; W. Bühler, Hermes 91
(1963) 345-51, rejects Menandrian authorship, following Wilamowitz, Herakles 1.42, note 82.

1320 --- Menander (Hypobolimaeus?) or Ariston (?). P.
Didot 25-28 (II B.C., Serapaeum, Memphis; from
the same composite roll as Nos. 31, 401, 1319, 1435).
Kock, CGF 3.420-21; Koerte, Men., pp. lxiii-lxiv, 145;
Page, GLP 1, No. 53. JAW 263.9; New Chapters
3.168. For the earlier attributions (Philemon, Alexis,
Theognetus), see F. Blass, Rh. Mus. 35 (1880) 88-90,
T. Bergk, ibid. 255-58, and T. Kock, ibid. 277-78.
R. Herzog, Philol. 89 (1934) 185-96; G. Rambelli,
SIFC, NS 19 (1942) 25-34, doubts that the fragment
is a prologue; A. Barigazzi, Athen. 43 (1955) 267-
77; B. Hemmerdinger, Rev. Ét. Gr. 66 (1953), p.
XI, and Aeg. 36 (1956) 24, attributes the fragment
to Ariston, regarding the last words as a subscription; G. Zuntz, Proc. Brit. Acad. 42 (1956) 239-41.

1321 --- Arguments of the Hiereia and the Imbrioi. P.
Oxy. 10.1235 (P. Cairo) (II, Oxy.). Jensen, pp. 1-5;
Koerte, Men., pp. lxiv, 146-50. JAW 174.190-91;
New Chapters 3.171. A. Koerte, Archiv 7.149, and
Berl. Phil. Woch. 38 (1918) 787-91, suggests Sellius
as the author; idem, Hermes 75 (1940) 106-16, on the
Hiereia; W. E. J. Kuiper, Mnemos., Ser. 3.8 (1940)
283-93 (ditto).

1322 --- Sententia 371 (Meineke), with a Coptic version.
W. E. Crum, Short Texts from Coptic Ostraca and
Papyri (Oxford 1921), No. 403 (?). Identified by E.
Lobel; see S. Gaselee, CR 36 (1922) 138-39.

--- Sententiae: see also Nos. 1570, 1574, 1582-91,
2643, 2713.

1323    --- Empimpramene (title only, on a sillybos).  Z.
        Aly, Et. Pap. 8 (1957) 163-67 (P. Cairo?) (?, Oxy.).

1324    --- Menander (?): A fragment.  P. Hibeh 2.180 (Brit.
        Mus. inv. 2953) (ca. 270-240 B.C., Hibeh; cart.).
        Line 20 is possibly Menander, fr. 768 Kock = 482
        Koerte-Thierfelder.

        Menander:  see also Nos. 455, 1568-69, 1580 (Nomo-
            thetes), 1642-59, 1663, 1952, 2087, 2126 (Enchiri-
            dium, Georgus, Phanium, Philadelphoe, Synaris-
            tosae), 2291 (Cecryphalus), 2643 (Heros), 2759 (a
            list of his plays).

        Menecrates of Syracuse:  see No. 2339.
        Menodorus:  see No. 2377.
        Menon:  see No. 2339.
        Mesatus:  see No. 46.
        Metrodorus:  see No. 2574.
        Mimnermus:  see Nos. 82, 89, 195-96.
        Mnaseus of Patara:  see No. 2290.
        Moschus of Lampsacus:  see No. 2071.
        Musaeus of Ephesus:  see No. 1751.

1325    MUSONIUS RUFUS:  Fr. 15.A (ed. Hense):  Ei panta ta
        gînomena tekna threpteon.  P. Harris 1 (inv. 3) (III).
        Musonius quotes Homer, Il. ix. 323-24.  Identified
        by M. P. Charlesworth, and republished by J. E.
        Powell, Archiv 12 (1937) 175-78; ibid. 13.112; B.
        Snell, Gnomon 13 (1937) 578; C. E. Lutz, Yale Class.
        Stud. 10 (1947) 6, 98; L. Alfonsi, Aeg. 28 (1948)
        126-28.

        Neophron:  see No. 1709.

1326    NICANDER:  Theriaca 333-44.  A. S. F. Gow and A.
        F. Scholfield, Nicander:The Poems and Poetical
        Fragments (Cambridge 1953) 14, 50-51, 176 (P. Oxy.
        inedita) (II-III, Oxy.).

1327    --- Commentary on Theriaca 377-95 (by Theon or
        Demetrius Chlorus?).  P. Oxy. 19.2221 (I, Oxy.;
        on the verso are some medical prescriptions, as
        yet unedited).  Quotes Callimachus, Iambi ix (Daw-
        son 92-93; Pfeiffer, Callim. 1, fr. 199); Hesiod,
        Opera 486-87; Nicander (new); Sophocles, Poemen-
        es (fr. 507, Jebb-Pearson, plus a new line).  A. S.
        F. Gow and A. F. Scholfield, op. cit. (see under
        No. 1326) 11, 14, 52-55, 177-78.  Archiv 16.118.  A.
        Colonna, Aeg. 34 (1954) 3-26, reedits the text and
        rejects Theon in favor of Demetrius Chlorus as the
        author of the commentary.

1328    --- Commentary on Theriaca 526-29.  P. Mil. Vogl.
        2.45 (inv. 608) (I, Tebtunis).  Quotes Sophron, fr.
        165, Kaibel, and two new fragments of Nicander (?).
        Ed. pr.: I. Cazzaniga, SIFC, NS 27-28 (1956) 83-
        101.  J. Bingen, Chr. Ég. 33 (1958) 142.

        Nicander:  see also Nos. 1755, 1858.

        Nicanor:  see Nos. 1473, 1890, 2297.
        Niceratus:  see No. 2388.
        Nicocrates:  see No. 2180.
        Nicolaus of Damascus:  see No. 2214.
        Nicomachus:  see No. 1710.
        Nigrinus:  see No. 2089.
        Ninyas:  see No. 2339.

1329    NONNUS:  Dionysiaca xiv. 386-419, 434-37, xv. 1-415,
        xvi. 1-30 (with lacunae).  BKT 5.1.94-106 (inv. 10567)
        (VI-VII; pap. cod.).  Schubart, PGB, tab. 44 b.  A.
        Ludwich, Berl. Phil. Woch. 27 (1907) 494-95.  R.
        Keydell, Nonni Panopolitani Dionysiaca (Berolini
        1959), "Prolegomena" 11-12.

        Nonnus:  see also Nos. 1611, 1833.

        Olympius Isidorianus:  see No. 2519.
        Onomacritus:  see No. 516.

1330    OPPIAN:  Halieutica iv. 412-38.  C. C. Edgar, Ann.
        Serv. 26 (1926) 209-10 (P. Cairo inv. 45623) (III, Oxy.;
        on the verso of No. 2910).

1331    --- v. 104-19, 142-57.  BKT 5.1.80-81 (inv. 240; once
        loaned to the Cairo Mus.) (IV, Hermupolis Magna;
        pap. cod.).

1332    ORACULA SIBYLLINA v. 498-505, 517-23 (plus a new
        verse after 502).  P. Flor. 3.389 (IV, Hermupolis
        Magna; parch. cod.).  Ed. pr.: AR 7 (1904) 354-56.
        Archiv 3.479.

1333    PALAEPHATUS:  Peri apistôn historiôn.  F. Blass,
        Archiv 3 (1906) 500 (?; copy of a leaf of parch. or
        paper; modern forgery?).  The text includes no-
        tices on three writers of this name, with a reference
        to Demetrius Magnes, Peri homonymôn.

        Palamedes of Elea:  see No. 551.
        Pamphilus:  see No. 78.

1334    PAMPREPIUS PANOPOLITANUS (?):  Idyll, with a
        prologue in iambics; Verse encomium, to the patri-
        cian Theagenes; Epic fragments.  H. Gerstinger,
        Sitzb. Wien. Akad., 1928, Abh. 3 (P. Vindob. Gr.
        inv. 29788 A-C) (V-VI; pap. cod.).  Heitsch, GDRK,
        fr. XXXV; Page, GLP 1, No. 140 a-b; Wifstrand,
        Kallim. Nonn. 190-93.  Archiv 10.25-28; JAW 230.
        122-23.  R. Asmus, Byz. Zeitschr. 22 (1913) 320-47,
        on Pamprepius in general; P. Graindor, Byz. 4
        (1927-28) 469-75, queries the attribution to P.;  H.
        Grégoire, BAGB, No. 24 (July 1929) 33-38, on P.
        generally; R. Keydell, Byz. Zeitschr. 29 (1929-30)
        290-93; P. Maas, Gnomon 5 (1929) 250-52; O.
        Schissel, Phil. Woch. 49 (1929) 1073-80; P. Ber-
        nardini Marzolla, Maia 7 (1955) 125-27.

1335    PANCRATES:  Hadrian and Antinous.  P. Oxy. 8.1085
        (Bodleian Libr., Gr. class. d. 113 (P)) (II, Oxy.).
        Heitsch, GDRK, fr. XV; Page, GLP 1, No. 128.
        Archiv 5.539; JAW 216.6.  J. P. Postgate, CR 25
        (1911) 172; B. A. Mueller, Berl. Phil. Woch. 36
        (1916) 671-72; L. Radermacher, ibid. 833-34, would
        identify Pancrates with the "Pachrates" mentioned
        in the Paris Magical Papyrus (Preisendanz, PGM,
        No. 4, lines 2445 ff.); I. Opelt, Rh. Mus. 103 (1960)
        48.

1336    --- P. Lond. 3.1109 (b); P. Lit. Lond. 36 (Brit. Mus.
        inv. 1109 B) (II).  Archiv 10.24-25.

        Panyasis:  see Nos. 89, 1205.

1337 PARTHENIUS: Epicedium on Timander. P. Lit.
Lond. 64 (Brit. Mus., Add. MS. 34473, art. 4)
(III-IV; parch. cod.). Archiv 10.41; New Chapters
3.186-87. I. Cazzaniga, PP 16 (1961) 124-26, on the
relation to Catullus 68.94-100.

1338 --- Parthenius (?): Arete (?). J. Nicole, Rev. Ét.
Gr. 17 (1904) 215-29 (P. Geneve inv. 97) (IV-V?;
parch. cod.). Pfeiffer, CFNR, No. 5; idem, Callim. 2, pp. xxv-xxvi, rejects Callimachus; Wilamowitz, Hellenistische Dichtung (Berlin 1924) 2.
174-76, queries the attribution to Callimachus,
Aetia; R. Pfeiffer, CQ 37 (1943) 23-32, suggests
Parthenius, Arete.

Parthenius: see also Nos. 1754, 1783.

Persaeus of Citium: see No. 2088.
Petron of Aegina: see No. 2339.
Phaselas of Tenedos: see No. 2339.
Phavorinus: see Favorinus.
Pherecrates: see No. 1568.

1339 PHERECYDES: Pentemychos. P. Grenf. 2.11 (Bodleian Libr., Gr. class. f.48 (P)) (III).

Pherecydes: see also Nos. 78, 1209.

1340 PHILEMON: Fr. 89.1, Kock. W. G. Waddell, Ét.
Pap. 1 (1932) 17 (No. 9) (P. Cairo inv. 56226) (I-III,
Oxy.; sch. ex. ?).

1341 --- Fr. 233.1, Kock. P. Jouguet and G. Lefebvre,
BCH 28 (1904) 208 (Inst. Fr. d'Arch. Or. du Caire)
(Byzantine; from the same wooden tablet as No.
1843; sch. ex.). Ziebarth, No. 28 a; Ziebarth 2,
No. 42 a. Archiv 3.486.

Philemon: see also Nos. 339, 1456, 1577, 1579,
1588, 1592, 1660-63, 2296, 2643, 2721.

Philetas: see Nos. 186, 196, 1205, 2129, 2471.
Philiadas: see No. 1601.
Philias: see No. 998.

1342 PHILICUS: Hymn to Demeter. PSI 12.1282 (III B.C.).
Ed. pr. in part: M. Norsa, SIFC, NS 5 (1927) 87-92;
ed. pr. in full: C. Gallavotti, ibid. 9 (1931) 37-60.
Page, GLP 1, No. 90. Archiv 8.255-56; New Chap-
ters 2.61-62. P. Maas, Gnomon 3 (1927) 439; A.
Koerte, Hermes 66 (1931) 442-54; K. Latte, Mus.
Helv. 11 (1954) 1-19.

Philicus: Epigram on the tragedian Philicus: see
No. 1764.

Philinna: see Nos. 1871-72.
Philiscus: see No. 1640.
Philistion: see No. 2339.

1343 PHILISTUS: De Sicilia, Bk. v (?). PSI 12.1283 (II).
Ed. pr.: G. Coppola and A. Momigliano, Riv. Fil.
58 (1930) 449-66, 467-70. Subject of the fragment:
the Athenians' first Sicilian expedition, 427-425
B.C. Jacoby, FGH III B, pp. 679-80. A. Koerte,
Archiv 10.67-69, accepts the attribution; R. Laqueur, RE 19.2.2417, rejects it. G. Perrotta, SIFC,
NS 8 (1931) 311-15; V. Bartoletti, ibid. 24 (1950) 159-
60.

Philistus: see also Nos. 2193, 2266.

1344 PHILO JUDAEUS: Fragments of De Ebrietate, De
Posteritate Caini, Sacrarum Legum Allegoriae,
Quod Deterius Potiori Insidiari Soleat, De Mer-
cede Meretricis, and other treatises. PSI 11.1207;
P. Oxy. 9.1173, 11.1356, 18.2158; P. Haun. 1.8
(inv. 322) (III, Oxy.; pap. cod.). On Philo's citation of Sappho (P. Oxy. 1356), see Diehl, Anth. Lyr.
1².4.84; Lobel, Sappho 55; Treu, Sappho 100; A.
Turyn, Eos 31 (1928) 236. K. F. W. Schmidt, Gött.
Anz., 1918, 81-83; L. Freuchtel, Phil. Woch. 58
(1938) 1437-39.

1345 --- Quis Rerum Divinarum Heres Sit; De Sacrificiis
Abelis et Caini. V. Scheil, MIFAO 9, fasc. 2
(1893) (Bibliothèque Nationale, Paris, P. Gr. 1120,
Supplément grec 2) (VI, Coptos; pap. cod.).

1346 --- Philo: De Deo (or Hermetica?). K. Stahlschmidt,
Aeg. 22 (1942) 161-76 (P. Berol. inv. 17027) (IV-V,
Hermupolis Magna; pap. cod.). K. Aland, Theologische Literaturzeitung 68 (1943) 169-70, identifies
fr. D as from the Hermetica (cf. Rev. Et. Gr. 61,
1948, 233); L. Alfonsi, Aeg. 23 (1943) 262-69, approves the attribution to Philo, and notes the influence of Posidonius, De Deo.

Philochorus: see Nos. 317, 339, 429, 460, 2069.
Philocles: see No. 157.
Philolaus of Croton: see No. 2339.

1347 PHILOSTRATUS: Eikones (end, with title). K. Stahlschmidt, Archiv 14 (1941) 1-23 (P. Berol. inv. 17013)
(IV, Hermupolis Magna; pap. cod.). Archiv 16.125.

Philostratus of Alexandria: see No. 1736.
Philoxenus: see No. 1948.
Philoxenus of Alexandria: see No. 2377.

1348 PHLEGON OF TRALLES (?): Chronica (?) (Fragment
on the tyranny of Lachares). P. Oxy. 17.2082 (II,
Oxy.). Jacoby, FGH 2.1194-96. Winter, LLP 246-
47; E. M. Walker, New Chapters 2.73-75. A.
Koerte, Archiv 10.69-70, regards the attribution as
certain; G. de Sanctis, Riv. Fil. 56 (1928) 53-77,
prefers Eratosthenes, Olympionikai; W. S. Fergu-
son, CP 24 (1929) 1-31; L. A. Post, ibid. 25 (1930)
183-84.

Phlegon of Tralles: see also No. 2188.

1349 PHOENIX OF COLOPHON (?): Choliambics. Knox,
Herodes 253-59 (II-I B.C. ?; on the verso of Nos.
426, etc.). Mentioned by W. Croenert, Gött. Nachr.,
1922, 31, and B. Snell, Hermes, Einzelschr. 5 (1937)
89, 91.

Phoenix of Colophon: see also Nos. 125, 1605.

Phrynicus (comicus): see No. 1640.
Phrynicus (grammaticus): see No. 2291.
Phrynicus (tragicus): see Nos. 1205, 1707, 2290.
Phylarchus: see No. 2121.

1350   PINDAR: "The Complete Works of Pindar" (title, on
       a sillybos).   P. Antin. 1.21 (III, Antinoöpolis; parch.).
       C. H. Roberts, in S. R. K. Glanville, The Legacy
       of Egypt (Oxford 1942) 258 (first mention).   Galiano,
       Pind., No. 51.

1351   --- A life of Pindar.   P. Oxy. 26.2438 (II-III, Oxy.).
       Mentions Corinna (Page, PMG 695 A) and Simonides;
       quotes Pindar, Olympia ii.94-97 and fr. 116.   D. M.
       Lewis, CR, NS 12 (1962) 201, notes the evidence for
       the archon, Archias; B. Snell, Hermes 90 (1962) 5.

1352   --- Olympia i.106-16, ii.1-17, 21-44, vi.71-95, vii.
       6-20.   P. Oxy. 13.1614 (Cambridge Univ. Libr.,
       Add. 6366) (V-VI, Oxy.; pap. cod.).   Wilamowitz,
       Pindaros 309.   Galiano, Pind., No. 1.

       --- ii.1-17, 21-44: see No. 1352.

       --- ii.16: see No. 455.

1353   --- ii.16-28, 42-94.   P. Oxy. 17.2092 (II, Oxy.).
       Galiano, Pind., No. 2.

       --- ii.94-97: see No. 1351.

1354   --- v.6-25.   P. Antin. 2.76 (III, Antinoöpolis; parch.
       cod.).

       --- vi.71-95: see No. 1352.

1355   --- vi.103-5, vii.1-10.   PSI 12.1277 (II).   Ed. pr.:
       D. Pieraccioni, Maia 1 (1948) 287-88.   Galiano,
       Pind., No. 3 bis.

       --- vii.1-10: see No. 1355.

       --- vii.6-20: see No. 1352.

       --- xiii.18: see No. 1381.

1356   --- Scholia on Pythia i.46-66.   P. Rain. 1.23 (inv.
       29817) (cf. ibid. 3, p. 96) (VI; pap. cod.).   Cites
       Euripides, Phoenissae 606.   Galiano, Pind., No.
       5.   Archiv 11.245-46.

1357   --- Commentary on Pythia ii.17-19.   Wilamowitz,
       Sitzb. Berl. Akad., 1918, 749-50 (P. Berol. inv.
       13419) (III-IV; on the verso).   Cites Homer, Il. iii.
       196, and a tag from an unknown poet (line 8); refers
       to an unknown historian, perhaps Timaeus (line 19).
       Galiano, Pind., Nos. 6, 35.   Archiv 7.138-39.

1358   --- Commentary on Isthmia i, iv, vi-viii and unidentified
       Pindaric texts.   P. Oxy. 26.2451 (I-II, Oxy.).   Fr.
       17 perhaps refers to the oschophorika known to have
       been composed by Pindar.

1359   --- Isthmia viii.7-14 and three other fragments.
       P. Oxy. 26.2439 (I, Oxy.).   The three additional
       fragments are possibly from Isthmian Odes not
       otherwise extant.   On the verso are a few words of
       a literary (?) text.

1360   --- Fragments of the Hymns, Paeans, and other poems.
       P. Oxy. 26.2442 (III, Oxy.).   Fr. 14 partially co-
       incides with P. Oxy. 841 (see No. 1361).   B. Snell,
       Hermes 90 (1962) 1-2, 4-6.

1361   --- Fragments of Paeans i-x, with scholia.   P. Oxy.
       5.841; P. Lit. Lond. 45 (Brit. Mus. inv. 1842, v.)
       (II, Oxy.; on the verso of a list of persons and a
       land survey).   The scholia refer to Aristarchus (?);
       Aristophanes of Byzantium (?); Chrysippus (?; pu-
       pil of Zenodotus); Theon (?; grammarian); and
       Zenodotus (?).   Roberts, GLH, pl. 14.   Galiano,
       Pind., No. 8 (bibl.); idem, LG 152, note 570 (bibl.);
       Radt 1-11, 13-197.   Bowra, Pindar, Nos. 35-43, 45;
       Diehl, SL, Nos. 1-10; Snell, Pindarus, frr. 52 a-l;
       Turyn, frr. 41-52, 55-62.   Archiv 5.549.   H. Ju-
       renka, Philol. 71 (1912) 173-210; C. Robert, Hermes
       49 (1914) 315-19; B. Snell, ibid. 73 (1938) 428-39;
       R. Hampe, Hermes 76 (1941) 136-42, on Paean ii;
       M. F. Galiano, Human. 3 (1950-51) 304-12, on Paean
       vii; E. G. Turner, GR 21 (1952), pl. CXXI (Paean
       v, ad fin.); E. Thummer, Gnomon 31 (1959) 725-28;
       B. Snell, Hermes 90 (1962) 1.

1362   --- Paeans vi-vii (with lacunae).   PSI 2.147 (II, Her-
       mupolis Magna; pap. cod.).   Galiano, Pind., No.
       9; Radt 11-12, 83-195, 197-99.   Diehl, SL, Nos. 5-6;
       Snell, Pindarus, fr. 52 f-g (pp. 216-19); Turyn, frr.
       46 (lines 45-51, 76-83, 92-115, 126-35), 47 (lines
       1-13); Wilamowitz, Pindaros 134.   Archiv 7.136.
       B. Snell, Hermes 73 (1938) 425-28.

1363   --- Paeans vi, xii, xiii (?; with lacunae).   P. Oxy.
       15.1792 (cf. ibid. 26, pp. 13-25: corrections and
       additional frr.) (II, Oxy.).   Galiano, Pind., No.
       10 (bibl.); Radt 12, 83-195, 197-99.   Bowra, Pin-
       dar, No. 47; Page, GLP 1, No. 83 b; Snell, Pin-
       darus, frr. 52 m, 52 n (a), lines 8-10; Turyn, frr.
       46 (lines 99 ff.), 53, 54 (lines 8-10), 63-65; Wila-
       mowitz, Pindaros 518-19.   Archiv 7.137-38.   B.
       Snell, Hermes 73 (1938) 431-32.

1364   --- Paean viii (a fragment).   P. Oxy. 15.1791 (I,
       Oxy.).   Galiano, Pind., No. 11.   Bowra, Pindar,
       No. 46; Page, GLP 1, No. 83 a; Snell, Pindarus,
       fr. 52 i (pp. 222-23); Turyn, fr. 49 (lines 16-35);
       Wilamowitz, Pindaros 507.   Archiv 7.136-37.   K.
       F. W. Schmidt, Gött. Anz., 1924, 6-7; B. Snell,
       Hermes 73 (1938) 432, identifies the text as from
       Paean viii.

1365   --- Paean xiii.   Bowra, Pindar, No. 343 (P. Berol.
       inv. 13411) (II).   Ed. pr.: G. Zuntz, Aeg. 15 (1935)
       282-96, preferring Bacchylides or Simonides.
       Galiano, Pind., No. 12 (bibl.); idem, LG 155.
       Page, PMG 652 (iii), queries the attribution to
       Simonides; Snell, Pindarus, fr. 52 n; Turyn, fr.
       54.   A. Koerte, Archiv 13.93, regards the attri-
       bution to Pindar as certain; B. Snell, Hermes 75
       (1940) 185-91, notes coincidences with P. Oxy. 1792
       (see No. 1363).

1366   --- Paeans (meager fragments).   P. Oxy. 26.2440
       (II, Oxy.).   The texts partially coincide with P.
       Oxy. 841 (see No. 1361), 1791 (see No. 1364), and
       possibly 2442 (see No. 1360).   B. Snell, Hermes
       90 (1962) 2-5.

       --- Paeans: see also No. 1205.

1367   --- Dithyrambs i-iii (frr. 70 a-c, Schroeder[5]), with
       marginalia.   P. Oxy. 13.1604 (II, Oxy.).   Galiano,
       Pind., No. 13 (bibl.).   Bowra, Pindar, Nos. 60-62;

Snell, Pindarus, fr. 70 a-c; Turyn, frr. 86, 89-90; Wilamowitz, Pindaros 341-45. Archiv 7.134-35. W. H. D. Rouse, CR 34 (1920) 67; K. F. W. Schmidt, Gött. Anz., 1922, 90-92.

1368 --- Dithyrambs (?) and other fragments. P. Oxy. 26.2445 (II, Oxy.). B. Snell, Hermes 90 (1962) 6.

1369 --- Fragments (dithyrambs?). P. Oxy. 26.2450 (I-II, Oxy.).

--- Dithyrambs: see also Nos. 1381, 2154.

1370 --- Fragments (Prosodia?). P. Oxy. 26.2441 (II, Oxy.).

1371 --- Partheneia (frr. 104 c-d, Schroeder[5]) and an Ode. P. Oxy. 4.659; P. Lit. Lond. 44 (Brit. Mus. inv. 1533) (I B.C., Oxy.; text on recto, No. 1595 on verso). Galiano, Pind., No. 15 (bibl.). Bowra, Pindar, Nos. 83-84; Diehl, SL, Nos. 11-12; Snell, Pindarus, fr. 94 a-b; Turyn, frr. 105-6. Archiv 3.480. Wilamowitz, Gött. Anz., 1904, 670-72; O. Schroeder, Berl. Phil. Woch. 24 (1904) 1476-79; F. Sbordone, Athen., NS 18 (1940) 26-50.

1372 --- Hyporchemata. P. Oxy. 26.2446 (II-III, Oxy.).

1373 --- Threnoi (frr. 140 a-b, Schroeder[5]). P. Oxy. 3. 408 (Yale Univ. Libr., inv. 44) (I-II, Oxy.). Galiano, Pind., No. 27 (bibl.). Bowra, Pindar, Nos. 124-25; Diehl, SL, No. 13 a-b; Snell, Pindarus, fr. 140 a-b; Turyn, frr. 192, 222; Wilamowitz, Pindaros 500-2. Archiv 3.266. W. H. Willis, AJP 63 (1942) 87-90.

1374 --- Threnoi (?). P. Oxy. 26.2447 (II, Oxy.).

1375 --- Pindar (?): Lyric fragment. P. Ryl. 1.14 (II-III, Oxy.). Galiano, Pind., No. 28. Snell, Pindarus, fr. 173. Archiv 5.551.

1376 --- Pindar (?): Lyric fragment. P. Harris 21 (inv. 174 h) (III-IV). E. Lobel, P. Oxy. 26, p. 10, note 1, would date this papyrus to saec. II. Galiano, Pind., No. 31 (bibl.); idem, LG 156. Snell, Pindarus, fr. 260. B. Snell, Gnomon 13 (1937) 582, suggests Pindar; A. Koerte, Archiv 13.93-94, approves; B. Snell, Hermes 73 (1938) 438.

1377 --- Fragments. P. Oxy. 26.2448 (II-III, Oxy.). "Uncertain category." B. Snell, Hermes 90 (1962) 6.

1378 --- Pindar (or Simonides?): Epinician Ode. E. Egger, CRAI, 1877, 92-95 (P. Louvre inv. 7734) (Roman). Galiano, Pind., No. 39 (bibl.). Schroeder[5], p. 558; Snell, Pindarus, fr. 333 (under "Fragmenta Dubia"); Turyn, fr. 237. F. Blass, Rh. Mus. 32 (1877) 450-58, attributes the poem to Pindar; Wilamowitz, Gött. Abh., Neue Folge 4, Abh. 3 (1900) 48, prefers Simonides; Page, PMG 652 (i), queries the attribution to Simonides.

1379 --- Pindar (?): A fragment. PSI 2.145 (II-III, Oxy.; pap. cod.). Galiano, Pind., No. 40; Snell, Pindarus, fr. 334 (under "Fragmenta Dubia"); Turyn, fr. 152; Wilamowitz, Pindaros 134. Archiv 7.138;

assigned to Pindar by Wilamowitz, DLZ, 1913, p. 1862.

1380 --- Pindar (?): A fragment. PSI 2.146 (III, Oxy.). Galiano, Pind., No. 41. Snell, Pindarus, fr. 335 (under "Fragmenta Dubia"); Turyn, fr. 194; Wilamowitz, Pindaros 134-35. Archiv 7.138.

1381 --- Commentary on Pindar, Dithyrambs (or treatise on the dithyramb?). W. Schubart, Archiv 14 (1941) 24-29 (P. Berol. inv. 9571, verso) (III; on the verso of No. 1225 and a document). Cites Euripides, Hypsipyla, fr. 752, Nauck; Homer, Od. xxiv.74; Pindar, Olympia xiii.18, Dithyrambs (Bowra, Pindar, No. 61.6 ff.); and refers to Simonides (?). Galiano, Pind., Nos. 4, 14, 56. Archiv 16.119.

1382 --- Commentary on Pindar (?). G. Zuntz, CR 49 (1935) 4-7 (P. Berol. inv. 13875) (II). Quotes Pindar (Turyn, fr. 291); refers to Simonides (Page, PMG 607). Galiano, Pind., No. 45; idem, LG 150. Snell, Pindarus, frr. 339, 339 a ("Fragmenta Dubia"). A. Koerte, Archiv 13.94-95, doubts that Didymus is the author, as suggested by Zuntz.

1383 --- Commentary on Pindar (?). P. Oxy. 26.2449 (II-III, Oxy.).

1384 --- Pindar (?): A fragment. Snell, Pindarus, fr. 343 (Ashmolean Mus., inv. 20) (?). Under "Fragmenta Dubia."

1385 --- Pindar (?): A fragment. Snell, Pindarus, fr. 344 (PSI inv. 557, inedita) (?). Under "Fragmenta Dubia." Galiano, LG 156. Archiv 16.98.

Pindar: see also Nos. 147, 179, 185, 200, 246, 455, 1173, 1186, 1205, 1351, 1400, 1449, 1536, 1904-7, 1909, 1919, 1949, 2172, 2868.

Pisander: see No. 1229.

1386 PLATO: Euthyphro 2 A-C. PSI 14.1392 (I-II, Oxy.).

1387 --- Apologia Socratis 40B - 41C. W. Schubart, JJP 4 (1950) 83-87 (P. Berol. inv. 13291) (I-II, Soknopaiou Nesos). Schubart, Einführung 483 (first mention). M. Hombert, Chr. Ég. 26 (1951) 414-15.

1388 --- Phaedo 67E - 69A, 79C - 81D, 82A - 84B. P. Petrie 1.5-8; P. Lit. Lond. 145 (Brit. Mus. inv. 488) (III B.C., Gurob; cart.). Kenyon, Pal. GP, pl. X; Pal. Soc., Ser. 2, vol. 2, pl. 161; Thompson, GLP, No. 2 (p. 110). Lesky, GGL 17. G. Coppola, Aeg. 5 (1924) 213-18.

1389 --- 75A - 117C (with lacunae). P. Oxy. 18.2181 (II, Oxy.). R. Stark, Philol. 106 (1962) 290.

1390 --- 96 D-E. PSI 14.1393 (I-II, Oxy.).

1391 --- 102E - 103C. P. Oxy. 15.1809 (II, Oxy.).

1392 --- 109 C-D. P. Oxy. 2.229; P. Lit. Lond. 146 (Brit. Mus. inv. 786) (II, Oxy.). Archiv 1.522.

--- See also Nos. 2120, 2560-61.

1393 --- Commentary on Theaetetus 142D - 158A. BKT 2
(inv. 9782) (II, Hermupolis Magna). New Pal. Soc.,
Ser. 1, vol. 1, pl. 103; Schubart, PGB, tab. 31;
Thompson, GLP, No. 13 (p. 132). Pasquali, Stor.
Testo 254-55. Archiv 3.494-95; JAW 129.123-24.
P. Shorey, CP 24 (1929) 409-10.

1394 --- Theaetetus 143 C-E, 144D - 145A. P. Antin.
2.78 (VI, Antinoöpolis; parch. cod.).

1395 --- Sophista 223E. 4 - 224A. 2, 224B.1-3. P. Hibeh
2.228 (now in the Brit. Mus.) (ca. 270-230 B.C.,
Hibeh; cart.). E. G. Turner, Rh. Mus. 98 (1955)
97-98.

1396 --- Politicus 257B, 261D - 262C. P. Oxy. 27.2468
(II, Oxy.).

1397 --- 280E - 282E. P. Oxy. 10.1248 (St. Andrews
Univ. Libr.) (II, Oxy.). G. Coppola, Aeg. 5 (1924)
225.

1398 --- 308E - 309B. P. Oslo 2.9 (II, Oxy.?). Ed. pr.:
G. Rudberg, SO 8 (1929) 92-94.

1399 --- Symposium 200B - 223D. P. Oxy. 5.843 (P.
Cairo inv. 41082) (II, Oxy.). Schubart, Gr. Pal.,
Abb. 88.

1400 --- Phaedrus 227A - 230E. P. Oxy. 7.1016 (Toledo
Mus. of Art) (III, Oxy.; on the verso of a document).
Plato quotes Pindar, Isthmia i.2 (Galiano, Pind.,
No. 7). Roberts, GLH, pl. 20a. Pasquali, Stor.
Testo 256. C. Diano, PP, fasc. 5 (1947) 189-92.

1401 --- 238C - 240D, 245A - 251B. P. Oxy. 7.1017; P.
Lit. Lond. 147 (Brit. Mus. inv. 2048) (II-III, Oxy.).
Pasquali, Stor. Testo 255-56. G. Coppola, Aeg.
5 (1924) 224-25.

1402 --- 242D --244E. P. Oxy. 17.2102 (II, Oxy.). Plato
quotes Stesichorus, Palinode to Helen (in 243A).
Pasquali, Stor. Testo 256-57. R. Stark, Philol.
106 (1962) 289-90.

1403 --- 257D. P. Antin. 2.77 (II-III, Antinoöpolis).

1404 --- Commentary on Phaedrus 265 C-D (or treatise
on dialectics?). BKT 2.52-53 (inv. 8) (II, Theadelphia). Archiv 3.499. K. Praechter, Hermes 42
(1907) 150-53, identifies a quotation of Plato, Phi-
lebus 16D - 17A. F. della Corte, Riv. Fil. 64 (1936)
389-92.

1405 --- Phaedrus 266B, D. C. W. Keyes, AJP 50 (1929)
260-62 (Columbia Univ. Libr., inv. 492 A) (II).

1406 --- 267B - 268C. PRIMI 1.9 (II-III, Oxy.).

1407 --- Alcibiades i.107C. P. Harris 12 (inv. 174 c)
(II). Identified by P. Maas; see JEA 24.94. B.
Snell, Gnomon 13 (1937) 578-79.

1408 --- Laches 181B - 182A. P. Lond. 2.187, verso; P.
Lit. Lond. 144 (Brit. Mus. inv. 187, v.) (II-III;
on the verso of No. 358).

1409 --- Laches 189D - 192A. P. Petrie 2.50 (Bodleian
Libr., Gr. class. d.22-23 (P)) (III B.C., Gurob;
cart.). Pasquali, Stor. Testo 262-63. J. G.
Smyly, Hermathena 10 (1899) 407-8; G. Coppola,
Aeg. 5 (1924) 219-20.

1410 --- 197A - 198A. P. Oxy. 2.228 (Bodleian Libr.,
Gr. class. d.64 (P)) (II, Oxy.). Archiv 1.521.

1411 --- Lysis 208 C-D. P. Oxy. 6.881, verso (Cambridge Univ. Libr., add. 5884, v.) (III, Oxy.; on
the verso of No. 1412).

1412 --- Euthydemus 301E - 302C. P. Oxy. 6.881 (Cambridge Univ. Libr., add. 5884, r.) (II-III, Oxy.;
text on recto, No. 1411 on verso).

1413 --- Protagoras 337-57. P. Oxy. 13.1624 (Trinity
Coll. Libr., Dublin) (III, Oxy.). Plato discusses
a scolion of Simonides (in 339A - 347A). G. Coppola, Aeg. 5 (1924) 225-27.

1414 --- Gorgias 447 B-C, 468 A-D. PSI 11.1200 (II, Oxy.).

1415 --- 504B - 505A. Raineri M. 2.76-78 (III, Fayum;
pap. cod.).

1416 --- 507B - 508E, 522-26. P. Oxy. 3.454 (Bodleian
Libr., Gr. class. c.54 (P)); PSI 2.119 (II, Oxy.;
on the verso of an account in Latin). Archiv 3.294.

1417 --- 522 C-D. P. Fuad 1.2 (II).

--- Meno 94C: see No. 2290.

1418 --- Res Publica iii. 406 A-B. P. Oxy. 3.455 (III,
Oxy.). Archiv 3.294.

1419 --- iv.422D. P. Oxy. 3.456 (II-III, Oxy.). Archiv
3.294.

1420 --- vi.485D - 486C. PRIMI 1.10 (III?, Oxy.; pap.
cod.).

1421 --- viii.546B - 547D. P. Oxy. 15.1808 (II, Oxy.).

1422 --- x.607-8. P. Oxy. 1.24 (Yale Univ. Libr.) (III,
Oxy.).

--- Leges ii. 672C, v.747D: see No. 2120.

1423 --- vii.797A. P. Harris 42 (inv. 174 a) (III).

1424 --- viii.832E - 835E. BKT 2.53-54 (inv. 9766)
(III, Oxy.?). Archiv 3.496; JEA 7.90. F. della
Corte, Riv. Fil. 64 (1936) 404-6, states that this
papyrus is in the same hand as No. 1425.

1425 --- ix.862-63. P. Oxy. 1.23 (Cambridge Univ.
Libr., add. 4030) (III, Oxy.; in the same hand as
No. 1424?). Archiv 1.114.

1426 --- Timaeus 19C - 20A. PSI 11.1201 (II, Oxy.).

--- Timaeus: various passages: see No. 2339.

--- Commentary on the Timaeus: see No. 2569.

1427 --- Ps.-Plato: De Iusto 372A. P. Antin. 2.79
(III, Antinoöpolis).

1428    --- Ps.-Plato: De Virtute 376 B-C.   J. G. Milne, Archiv 5 (1913) 379 (II, Hawara).

1429    --- Ps.-Plato: Eryxias 405E; Demodocus 380A. H. Hunger, WS 74 (1961) 40-42 (P. Vindob. Gr. inv. 39846) (IV; parch. cod.).

Plato: see also Nos. 2049, 2087, 2205, 2563.

Plato (comicus): see No. 1568.

1430    PLUTARCH: Pelopidas 7.1-5.   P. Heid. Siegmann 209 (inv. 51) (ca. A.D. 180).  F. Bilabel, Actes Pap. V, 80 (first mention).

1431    --- Vita Caesaris 33-35, 59-61 (with lacunae).  V. Martin, Aeg. 31 (1951) 138-47 (P. Genève inv. 272 a-b) (III).  M. Hombert, Chr. Ég. 28 (1953) 155.

1432    --- Ps.-Plutarch: Epitome de placitis philosophorum (scattered fragments of Bks. ii-v: Diels, Doxographi Graeci, pp. 352-435).  P. Antin. 2.85 (III, Antinoopolis; pap. cod.).

Plutarch: see also No. 1223.

Polemon: Ad Adaeum et Antigonum: see No. 551.
Polemon of Ilium: see No. 2290.
Pollio, Valerius: see No. 2091.

1433    POLYBIUS: Historia xi.13.8-16.8.  P. Ryl. 1.60; U. Wilcken, Archiv 1 (1901) 388-95 (P. Berol. inv. 9570) (II, Fayum).  Archiv 2.362.

Polybius: see also Nos. 2212, 2265.

Polybus: see No. 2339.
Polyphradmon: see No. 46.

1434    POSIDIPPUS COMICUS: Apokleiomenē (the last thirteen verses, with a subscription).  P. Heid. Siegmann 183 (inv. 1269) (ca. 200 B.C.).  P. Maas, Glotta 35 (1956) 301; E. Vogt, Rh. Mus. 102 (1959) 192, compares the stereotyped concluding verses with those of Menander's Dyscolus.

1435    POSIDIPPUS OF PELLA: Epigrams on the Pharos at Alexandria and the temple of Arsinoë-Aphrodite Zephyritis.  P. Didot 28-34 (II B.C., Serapaeum, Memphis; from the same composite roll as Nos. 31, 401, 1319-20).  Page, GLP 1, No. 104; F. Freiherr H. v. Gaertringen, Historische Griechische Epigramme (Lietzmann's Kleine Texte, Nr. 156; 1926), Nos. 92, 95.  F. Blass, Rh. Mus. 35 (1880) 90-93.

1436    POSIDIPPUS (of Thebes or of Pella?): Elegy.  H. Diels, Sitzb. Berl. Akad., 1898, 847-56 (Tabula cerata Berol. 14283) (I-II; waxed tablet; the author's autograph or a schoolboy's copy?).  Schubart, PGB, tab. 17.  Heitsch, GDRK, fr. I; Page, GLP 1, No. 114.  Archiv 1.517.  R. Ellis, AJP 21 (1900) 76-77; W. Schubart, Symbolae Philologicae O. A. Danielsson Dicatae (Uppsala 1932) 290-98; C. A. Trypanis, CR, NS 2 (1952) 67-68, argues from a Delphic inscription that the elegy is a copy of an authentic poem of Posidippus of Pella.

Posidippus: see also Nos. 196, 1593, 1598, 1600-1, 1605, 2642.

Posidonius: see Nos. 2089, 2093.
Praxiphanes of Mitylene: see Nos. 196, 1173.
Protagoras of Abdera: see No. 1205.
Ptolemaeus: see No. 79.
Ptolemaeus of Ascalon: see Nos. 1201, 1205.
Ptolemaeus of Megalopolis: see No. 2210.

1437    PTOLEMY: Episēmōn poleōn kanōn.  P. Ryl. 3.522 (III, Fayum?; pap. cod.; on the verso of No. 2028).

Ptolemy: see also No. 2026.

Ptolemy Euergetes: see No. 2206.
Ptolemy Soter: see No. 2197.
Rhianus: see No. 2861.
Rhinthon: see No. 1623.
Salustius: see No. 186.

1438    SAPPHO: Bk. i.1.  P. Oxy. 21.2288 (II?, Oxy.). Galiano, LG 95-96 (bibl.).  Lobel-Page, PLF 2-3; Page, SA 3-18 (on fr. 1).  D. Pieraccioni, Maia 5 (1952) 130-31; A. Colonna, Paid. 10 (1955) 308-9; V. Pisani, ibid. 244; J. C. Kamerbeek, Mnemos., Ser. 4.9 (1956) 97; A. Luppino, PP 11 (1956) 361; D. Pieraccioni, Maia 8 (1956) 59-62; W. J. Verdenius, Mnemos., Ser. 4.9 (1956) 102; A. J. Beattie, CQ, NS 7 (1957) 180-83; V. Pisani, Paid. 12 (1957) 121-24; G. M. Bolling, AJP 82 (1961) 153-54.

1439    --- Bk. i.  PSI 13.1300 (II B.C.; ostr.).  Ed. pr.: M. Norsa, Ann. Sc. Pisa, Ser. 2.6 (1937) 8-15. Norsa, SLG, tav. 5 b.  Galiano, LG 94 (bibl.); J. G. Griffith, Fifty Years Cl. Schol. 42-43.  Lobel-Page, PLF 4-5; Page, GLP 1, No. 81; Page, SA 34-44 (bibl.); Treu, Sappho 26.  Archiv 13.90-91; JEA 23.122-23, 24.93, 25.72.  R. Pfeiffer, Philol. 92 (1937) 117-25; C. Theander, ibid. 465-69; V. Bartoletti, SIFC, NS 15 (1938) 75-77; W. Schubart, Hermes 73 (1938) 297-303; E. Siegmann, ibid. 76 (1941) 417-22; C. Gallavotti, SIFC, NS 18 (1942) 175-202; A. Turyn, TAPA 73 (1942) 308-18; A. Setti, SIFC, NS 19 (1943) 125-42; L. Alfonsi, Aeg. 26 (1946) 1-17; W. Theiler and P. von der Mühll, Mus. Helv. 3 (1946) 22-25; L. Righini, SIFC, NS 22 (1947) 101-4; A. Rivier, Mus. Helv. 5 (1948) 227-39; W. Schubart, Philol. 97 (1948) 312-13; Lavagnini, Mimn. Call. 21-38; M. F. Galiano, Anales de filología clásica 5 (Buenos Aires 1950-52) 81-90; idem, Emérita 24 (1956) 66-71; J. C. Kamerbeek, Mnemos., Ser. 4.9 (1956) 97-98; D. Pieraccioni, Maia 8 (1956) 63-67; K. Matthiessen, Gymnas. 64 (1957) 554-64; R. Merkelbach, Philol. 101 (1957) 26-29; G. Lanata, SIFC, NS 32 (1960) 64-90; V. Pisani, Paid. 15 (1960) 245-46; E. Heitsch, Rh. Mus. 105 (1962) 284-85; E. Risch, Mus. Helv. 19 (1962) 197-201.

1440    --- Bk. i.  BKT 5.2.9-10 (inv. 5006) (VII, Arsinoë?; parch.).  Ed. pr.: F. Blass, Zeitschr. Aeg. Spr. 18 (1880) 36-37.  Diehl, Anth. Lyr. $1^2$.4.16-17; Edmonds, LG 1.202-5; Lobel-Page, PLF 6; Treu, Sappho 30, 32.  F. Blass, Rh. Mus. 35 (1880) 287-90.

1441    --- Bk. i. 3-4.  P. Oxy. 3.424 (Univ.-Bibl., Graz,
I.1926) (III, Oxy.).  Edmonds, LG 1.204; Lobel,
Sappho 1; Lobel-Page, PLF 6-7; Treu, Sappho
32.  Archiv 3.268.  J. M. Edmonds, CR 35 (1921)
139-41.

1442    --- Bk. i.5.  P. Oxy. 1.7; P. Lit. Lond. 43 (Brit.
Mus. inv. 739) (III, Oxy.).  Diehl, Anth. Lyr.
$1^2$.4.17-19 (bibl.); idem, SL, No. 1; Edmonds, LG
1.204-7; Lavagnini, Aglaia 125-26; Lobel, Sappho
2-3; Lobel-Page, PLF 8-9; Treu, Sappho 32.  H.
Diels, Sitzb. Berl. Akad., 1898, 497; Wilamowitz,
Gött. Anz., 1898, 697-98; J. M. Edmonds, CQ 3
(1909) 249-53; H. I. Bell, CR 34 (1920) 63; J. M.
Edmonds, ibid. 4-6; E. Lobel, CQ 15 (1921) 163-
65; C. M. Bowra, CR 48 (1934) 126; W. Schubart,
Philol. 97 (1948) 313-14; A. W. Gomme, JHS 77
(1957) 258-59.

1443    --- Bk. i (including i. 3.5-18? and i. 6.4-8).  P. Oxy.
21.2289 (II?, Oxy.).  Galiano, LG 91.  Lobel-Page,
PLF 8-13; Page, SA 45-51; Treu, Sappho 18, 32,
36.  A. Colonna, Paid. 10 (1955) 309-10.

1444    --- Bk. i.  PSI 2.123 (II-III, Oxy.).  A marginal
note refers to Ni(canor?).  Edmonds, LG 1.210;
Lavagnini, Aglaia 129-30; Lobel, Sappho 4-5;
Lobel-Page, PLF 14-15; Page, SA 58-62; Treu,
Sappho 36.  Archiv 7.126.  H. Jurenka, WS 36
(1914) 207-10; R. Merkelbach, Philol. 101 (1957)
23-25.

1445    --- Bk. i.  P. Oxy. 10.1231 (Bodleian Libr., Gr.
class. c.76 (P)), 17.2081 (c), 18.2166 (a) (II, Oxy.).
See further P. Oxy. 21, pp. 122-26.  Galiano, LG
91-92 (bibl.); J. G. Griffith, Fifty Years Cl. Schol.
42.  Diehl, Anth. Lyr. $1^2$.2.19-30 (bibl); idem, SL,
Nos. 4-17; Edmonds, LG 1.194, 206-18; Lavagnini,
Aglaia 126-30; Lobel, Sappho 3-14; Lobel-Page,
PLF 13-31; Page, SA 52-57; Treu, Sappho 21, 34, 36,
38, 40, 42, 44, 46.  Archiv 7.124-26.  T. L. Agar,
CR 28 (1914) 189-90; L. Castiglioni, AR 17 (1914)
233-46; J. M. Edmonds, CR 28 (1914) 73-75, ibid.
30 (1916) 98-102, ibid. 33 (1919) 125-27; A. S. Hunt,
ibid. 28 (1914) 127; H. Jurenka, WS 36 (1914) 203-7,
210-14, 329; S. Reinach, Rev. Arch. 24 (1914) 336-
37; Wilamowitz, Neue Jahrb. 33 (1914) 226-29; E.
Bignone, BFC 22 (1915) 12-16; J. U. Powell, CQ 9
(1915) 142-43; N. Terzaghi, Riv. Ind. Gr. Ital. 1,
fasc. 2 (1917) 37-38; G. Pesenti, Aeg. 3 (1922) 49-
54; A. Vogliano, BFC 32 (1926) 36-38; H. J. M.
Milne, Aeg. 13 (1933) 176-78; idem, Hermes 68
(1933) 475-76; C. M. Bowra, Hermes 70 (1935) 240;
C. Theander, Eranos 41 (1943) 139-56; W. Schubart,
Philol. 97 (1948) 314-15; R. Hampe, Mus. Helv. 8
(1951) 144-46; D. Pieraccioni, Maia 5 (1952) 136;
C. Gallavotti, Aeg. 33 (1953) 161-63; D. Pieraccioni,
AR, NS 3 (1953) 53-54; J. C. Kamerbeek, Mnemos.,
Ser. 4.9 (1956) 99; A. W. Gomme, JHS 77 (1957)
258-59; H. Eisenberger, Philol. 103 (1959) 130-35;
J. D. Meerwaldt, Mnemos., Ser. 4.13 (1960) 106-10.

1446    --- Five small fragments.  P. Oxy. 23.2357 (II, Oxy.).
Fr. 1 may be from Bk. i.

1447    --- Bk. ii.  P. Oxy. 10.1232 (Bodleian Libr., Gr.
class. c.75 (P)) (III, Oxy.).  Diehl, Anth. Lyr.
$1^2$.4.35-39; idem, SL, Nos. 19-20; Edmonds, LG
1.226-30; Lavagnini, Aglaia 130-34; Lobel, Sappho
20-22; Lobel-Page, PLF 35-37; Page, SA 63-74;
Treu, Sappho 50, 52, 54.  Archiv 7.126-27.  L.
Castiglioni, AR 17 (1914) 246-52; J. M. Edmonds,
CR 28 (1914) 75, ibid. 33 (1919) 127; H. Jurenka,
WS 36 (1914) 214-20; Wilamowitz, Neue Jahrb. 33
(1914) 229-30; B. Snell, Hermes 66 (1931) 73, 368;
G. Tarditi, Riv. Fil. 84 (1956) 237-43; B. Mar-
zullo, Studi di poesia eolica (Firenze 1958) 115-94;
A. Massimi, GIF 12 (1959) 26-29; E.-M. Voigt,
Hermes 89 (1961) 251-53.

1448    --- Bk. ii, with scholia.  P. Oxy. 17.2076 (II, Oxy.).
Lobel, Sappho 78; Lobel-Page, PLF 36-37; Treu,
Sappho 52, 54.  Archiv 10.45-46.

1449    --- Bk. iv.  P. Oxy. 15.1787 (cf. ibid. 21, pp. 134-39),
18.2166 (d); P. Hal. 3 (inv. 18) (III, Oxy.).  Galiano, LG 92-93 (bibl.).  Diehl, Anth. Lyr. $1^2$.4.
43-54; idem, SL, No. 21; Lobel, Sappho 25-42;
Lobel-Page, PLF 41-65; Page, PMG 918 (b-c);
Treu, Sappho, 18, 58, 60, 62, 64-69.  Archiv 7.
127-28.  E. Lobel, Bodl. Rec. 3 (1923) 290, attributes P. Oxy. 1787, fr. 8 to Pindar rather than to
Sappho (cf. Bowra, Pindar, No. 344; Galiano,
Pind., No. 67); E. Bignone, BFC 30 (1924) 66-67;
F. Stiebitz, Phil. Woch. 46 (1926) 1259-62; B.
Snell, Hermes 73 (1938) 438, rejects Lobel's attri-
bution (see above); E. Fraenkel, CQ 36 (1942) 56.

1450    --- Bk. iv (?).  P. Oxy. 21.2290 (II-III, Oxy.).
Lobel-Page, PLF 66-67; Treu, Sappho 8.

1451    --- Bk. v.  BKT 5.2.10-18 (inv. 9722); Lobel, Sappho
79-80 (2 additional frr. of the same manuscript)
(VII; parch. cod.).  Galiano, LG 93 (bibl.).  Diehl,
Anth. Lyr. $1^2$.4.57-63; idem, SL, Nos. 22-25;
Edmonds, LG 1.238-47; Lavagnini, Aglaia 136-44;
Lobel, Sappho 1-2, 42-45; Lobel-Page, PLF 74-
80; Page, SA 75-96; Treu, Sappho 72, 74, 76, 78.
Archiv 2.351; Winter, LLP 205-6.  J. M. Edmonds,
CR 30 (1916) 129-33, ibid. 35 (1921) 139-41; A. Turyn,
Eos, Supplementa 6 (1929) 58-69; G. Zuntz, Mnemos.,
Ser. 3.7 (1939) 81-110, reedits the text and gives the
ed. pr. of the verso (ibid. 109-10); A. Vogliano,
Athen., NS 20 (1942) 114-18; W. Schubart, Philol.
97 (1948) 315-16; Lavagnini, Mimn. Call. 9-15; B.
Marzullo, Maia 5 (1952) 85-92; J. C. Kamerbeek,
Mnemos., Ser. 4.9 (1956) 99-101; A. W. Gomme,
JHS 77 (1957) 260; G. M. Bolling, AJP 82 (1961) 155.

1452    --- Bk. v.  C. Gallavotti, Riv. Fil. 69 (1941) 161-68
(Fr. A = P. Haun. inv. 301; fr. B = P. Univ. Statale di Milano) (I-II).  A. Vogliano, Philol. 93 (1939)
277-86 (ed. pr. of P. Milano); idem, Sappho: Una
nuova ode della poetessa (Milano 1941; ed. pr. of
P. Haun. and revised ed. of P. Milano); P. Mil.
Vogl. 2.40: both frr. republished, with bibl.  Galiano, LG 95 (bibl.).  Archiv 14.111-12.  Lobel-Page,
PLF 80-81; Page, SA 97-103 (bibl.); Treu, Sappho
78, 80.  F. Cumont, Ant. Class. 8 (1939) 181-82;
C. Gallavotti and G. Pugliese Carratelli, SIFC, NS
18 (1942) 161-74, reedit the text, with notes on the
historical background, and would restore the name
of Alcaeus in line 18 (this is queried by A. Vogliano,

ibid. 203-4); A. Ardizzoni, AR 45 (1943) 37-40, studies the meter; V. Steffen, Eos 43, fasc. 1 (1948-49) 68-77; S. Srebrny, ibid. 138-42; E. Grassi, SIFC 25 (1951) 189-90; A. Vogliano, Prolegom. 1 (1952) 27-33, 35-42; W. Schadewaldt, Studies Presented to David Moore Robinson 2 (St. Louis 1953) 499-506; J. C. Kamerbeek, Mnemos. Ser. 4.9 (1956) 101-2; G. M. Bolling, AJP 80 (1959) 276-87, ibid. 82 (1961) 156; E. A. Hahn, ibid. 81 (1960) 73-75.

1453    --- Commentary on Sappho. P. Oxy. 21.2292 (II, Oxy.). Galiano, LG 97. Treu, Sappho 10, 12. C. Gallavotti, Aeg. 33 (1953) 164-65.

1454    --- Commentary on Sappho (Bk. iv?). P. Oxy. 21. 2293 (II, Oxy.). Lobel-Page, PLF 68-73; Treu, Sappho 12, 14.

1455    --- Stichometrical and other details about the Books of Sappho's poems. P. Oxy. 21.2294 (II, Oxy.). Galiano, LG 98. Lobel-Page, PLF 84-85, 110; Page, SA 116-19, suggests that lines 1-13 refer to Bk. viii, the Epithalamia (lines 17-20) constituting the ninth and last book; Treu, Sappho 14, 16. D. Pieraccioni, Maia 5 (1952) 132-33; C. Gallavotti, Aeg. 33 (1953) 165.

Sappho: see also Nos. 59, 67, 246, 1344, 1898-1903, 2070, 2143, 2172.

1456    SATYRUS: Bion anagraphe, Bk. vi (Life of Euripides). P. Oxy. 9.1176; P. Lit. Lond. 122 (Brit. Mus. inv. 2070) (II, Oxy.). Cites Aristophanes, Thesmophoriazusae 335-37 (fr. 39, col. 12, lines 8-15), ibid. 374-75 (39.12.1-7), Fabulae Incertae (8.2. 17-19; 39.9.25-28); Demosthenes, In Aristogitonem i. 40 (39.8.17-33); Euripides, Alexander (?; 38.2. 7-30), Archelaus (?; 39.17.30-39; see Q. Cataudella, AR 41, 1939, 41-46), Danae (?; 39.6.4-15; see R. Goossens, Chr. Ég. 16, 1941, 109-10), Ino (39.17.1-6), Melanippa Desmotis (39.11), Pirithous (37.2.19-28), Troades 886 (37.3.26-29), Fabulae Incertae (see index of citations, P. Oxy. 9, ad fin.; Page, GLP 1, No. 18; B. Snell, WS 69, 1956, 91-94); Homer, Od. xiv. 463-66 (restored in fr. 9 by F. Leo, Hermes 49, 1914, 152-53); Philemon (39.7. 32-36); Timotheus (biographical material, 39.22; see Edmonds, LG 3.282-83); Old Comedy (39.16. 6-17; attributed to Aristophanes, Gerytades, by K. Kuiper, Mnemos. 41, 1913, 238-42; cf. JAW 174.128-29), Old Comedy (39.4.1-15), New Comedy (39.5.12-27), Doric Comedy (Rhinthon?; 39.17. 10-13); anonymous authorities for Macedonian history (39.20.29 ff.; Jacoby, FGH, Dritter Teil C, 771). Arnim, SE 3-9; New Chapters 1.144-52; Winter, LLP 261-62. F. Leo, Gött. Nachr., 1912, 273-90; K. F. Smith, AJP 34 (1913) 62-73, on the Hystaspes episode in 39.14; K. F. W. Schmidt, Gött. Anz., 1914, 608-10; M. L. de Courten, AR 18 (1915) 127-37, on the dialogue form used by Satyrus; H. Gerstinger, WS 38 (1916) 54-71; A. Dihle, Gött. Abh., Ser. 3.37 (1956) 105-7. Many of the citations are reprinted in Demiańczuk and in Page, GLP 1.

1457    --- On the Demes of Alexandria. P. Oxy. 27.2465 (II, Oxy.).

Seleucus: see No. 1205.
Seleucus of Alexandria: see No. 2091.
Sellius: see No. 1321.
Semonides of Amorgos: see No. 1581.
Sextius Niger: see No. 2412.

1458    SIMIAS OF RHODES (?): Apollo (?). J. G. Winter, TAPA 53 (1922) 133-36 (ed. pr.); P. Mich. 3.139 (inv. 11) (II). Assigned by the editor to Hesiod, Catalogus. Traversa, Hes. Cat. 130-31. Archiv 8.251-54; New Chapters 2.196-97; Winter, LLP 198-99. R. Merkelbach, Aeg. 31 (1951) 257-60, rejects Hesiod, suggests Simias of Rhodes.

Simon Socraticus: see No. 2089.

1459    SIMONIDES: Remarks on expenditure. P. Hibeh 1.17 (Bodleian Libr., Gr. class. d.79 (P)) (III B.C., Hibeh; cart.). Edmonds, LG 2.252-55. Archiv 6.240; New Chapters 2.93.

1460    --- Name and title on a label. P. Oxy. 25.2433 (II, Oxy.; a small, rectangular piece of pap.). "Commentary on sayings of (or: passages from) Simonides" (?).

Simonides: see also Nos. 184, 457, 1186, 1351, 1365, 1378, 1381-82, 1413, 1750, 1908-12, 1951, 2070, 2172, 2290, 2810.

Socrates: see Nos. 1575, 2584.
Sodamus of Tegea: see No. 2292.
Solon: see Nos. 163, 1205.
Sophilus: see No. 1667.

1461    SOPHOCLES: Ajax 51-66, 266-76, 291-307. P. Oxy. 17.2093 (II-III, Oxy.).

1462    --- 694-705, 753-64. P. Oxy. 13.1615 (Wellesley Coll.) (IV, Oxy.; pap. cod.).

1463    --- Antigona 242-46. P. Oxy. 6.875 (Western Reserve Univ. Libr.) (II, Oxy.).

--- 689-90: see No. 1571.

--- 712-15 (parodied): see No. 377.

1464    --- Electra 16-24. P. Antin. 2.72 (VI-VII, Antinoöpolis; parch., with blank verso).

--- 363-64: see No. 455.

1465    --- 993-1007. P. Oxy. 4.693 (P. Princ.) (III, Oxy.). Archiv 3.484.

1466    --- Oedipus Rex 102-974 (with lacunae). P. Oxy. 18.2180 (II, Oxy.; perhaps from the same roll as No. 1467). H. J. Rose, CR 57 (1943) 5, suggests that line 531, omitted in the papyrus, comes from a stage copy.

1467    --- 179-200, with scholia. PSI 11.1192 (II, Oxy.). The scholia quote Homer, Il. i. 314.

1468    --- 375-85, 429-41. P. Oxy. 1.22; P. Lit. Lond. 69 (Brit. Mus. inv. 743) (IV-V, Oxy.; pap. cod.). Archiv 1.110.

1469    --- 688-97, 708-10, 731-40, 751-53, 775-84, 819-27,
        1304-10, 1351-58.  P. Oxy. 11.1369 (Southern Metho-
        dist Univ. Libr.) (V-VI, Oxy.; pap. cod.).  K. F.
        W. Schmidt, Gött. Anz., 1918, 100.

1470    --- Oedipus Coloneus 136-45.  P. Mich. 3.140 (inv.
        35) (II-III).  Winter, LLP 220-21.

        --- 562-64, 797-99: see No. 455.

        --- 892: see No. 1640.

1471    --- Trachiniae 12-1276 (with lacunae).  P. Oxy. 15.
        1805 (II, Oxy.).  Cursive annotations cite Aristo-
        phanes of Byzantium (?).  A. Dain, Actas PCEEC
        182.

        --- Achaion syllogos: see Nos. 448-50.

        --- Achilleos erastai: see Nos. 47, 1739.

        --- Chryses: see No. 1708.

1472    --- Eurypylos.  P. Oxy. 9.1175, 17.2081 (b); P.
        Lit. Lond. 66 (Brit. Mus. inv. 2069) (II, Oxy.).
        Diehl, SS 21-28; Hunt, TGFP, No. 2; Jebb-
        Pearson 1, Nos. 206-22; Page, GLP 1, No. 4;
        Srebrny, Stud. Scaen. 28-33.  Archiv 5.563.  A.
        C. Pearson, CR 26 (1912) 211-12; K. F. W. Schmidt,
        Gött. Anz., 1914, 608; G. Brizi, Aeg. 8 (1927)
        3-39.

1473    --- Ichneutai.  P. Oxy. 9.1174, 17.2081 (a); P. Lit.
        Lond. 67 (Brit. Mus. inv. 2068) (II, Oxy.).
        Variant readings are recorded, of which some are
        referred to Aristophanes of Byzantium (?), Ni(ca-
        nor?), and Theon.  Diehl, SS 3-20; Hunt, TGFP,
        No. 1; Jebb-Pearson 1, No. 314; Page, GLP 1,
        No. 7; Steffen, Sat. Gr. Fr. 60-85; R. J. Wal-
        ker, The Ichneutae of Sophocles (London 1919).
        Archiv 5.558; A. Dain, Actas PCEEC 181-82;
        JAW 277.48-55; A. W. Pickard-Cambridge, New
        Chapters 3.87-95.  F. R. Walton, HSCP 46 (1935)
        167-89; E. Bignone, AR 41 (1939) 77-91; D. Fer-
        rante, GIF 3 (1950) 352-58; idem, Dion., NS 16
        (1953) 103-14.

1474    --- Inachos.  P. Oxy. 23.2369 (I B.C.-I, Oxy.).
        W. M. Calder, GRBS 1 (1958) 137-55, suggests
        that the play is a tragedy, not a satyr play, and
        studies the dramaturgy; R. Pfeiffer, Sitzb. Münch.
        Akad., 1958, Heft 6; A. M. Dale, CR, NS 10 (1960)
        194-95; R. Kassel, Gnomon 32 (1960) 180-82.

1475    --- Inachos.  P. Tebt. 3.692 (II B.C., Tebtunis;
        cart.).  Fritsch, No. 7; Page, GLP 1, No. 6;
        Steffen, Sat. Gr. Fr. 56-59.  Archiv 11.252-57;
        JAW 259.124-29, 277.53.  R. Pfeiffer, Sitzb.
        Münch. Akad., 1938, Heft 2, 23-62.

        --- Iphigeneia: see No. 1702.

        --- Kophoi: see No. 46.

        --- Nauplios Pyrkaeus: see No. 1736.

1476    --- Niobe (?).  P. Hibeh 1.11 (Bodleian Libr., Gr.
        class. g.54 (P)) (III B.C., Hibeh; cart.).  Fritsch,
        No. 9.  Archiv 5.571; JAW 147.108-9.  According
        to F. Blass, this is from the same papyrus as No.
        1477.

1477    --- Niobe (?).  P. Grenf. 2.6 a; P. Lit. Lond. 68
        (Brit. Mus. inv. 690 A) (III B.C., Hibeh; cart.).
        Jebb-Pearson 2, Nos. 442-45; Page, GLP 1, No.
        22.  F. Blass, Lit. Zentralbl., 1897, 333-34, Rh.
        Mus. 55 (1900) 96-101.  From the same papyrus as
        No. 1476 (?).

        --- Niobe: see No. 1700.

        --- Phineus: see No. 1186.

        --- Phrixos: see No. 1703.

        --- Poimenes: see Nos. 46, 339, 483, 1327.

        --- Polyidos vel Manteis: see No. 1739.

        --- Polyxene: see No. 1710.

        --- Salmoneus: see No. 2121.

1478    --- Skyrioi.  P. Oxy. 17.2077 (II-III, Oxy.).  Fritsch,
        No. 10; Page, GLP 1, No. 5.  Archiv 10.48-49;
        JAW 259.132-33; New Chapters 3.95-97.  C. M.
        Bowra, CR 42 (1928) 132; R. Pfeiffer, Philol. 88
        (1933) 1-15.

        --- Skyrioi: see No. 1203.

        --- Tantalos: see No. 1700.

        --- Tereus: see No. 455.

        --- Teukros: see No. 1287.

1479    --- Theseus.  P. Oxy. 27.2452 (II, Oxy.).  A mar-
        ginal note refers to Aristophanes of Byzantium (or
        Aristarchus?).

        --- Thyestes: see No. 2092.

1480    --- Tyro (?).  P. Hibeh 1.3 (Bodleian Libr., Gr.
        class. e.89 (P)) (III B.C., Hibeh; cart.).  Jebb-
        Pearson 2, No. 649; Page, GLP 1, No. 25.  Ar-
        chiv 5.565; JAW 147.102-4.

        Sophocles: see also Nos. 449-50, 455, 1205, 1710,
        2168, 2295, 2524, 2564, 2741, 2865.

1481    SOPHRON: Mimoi gynaikeioi (title only, on a sillybos).
        P. Oxy. 2.301; P. Lit. Lond. 95 (Brit. Mus. inv.
        801) (I-II, Oxy.).  Archiv 1.510.

1482    --- Fragments of a mime ("The Sorceresses").
        PSI 11.1214 (I, Oxy.).  Ed. pr.: G. Vitelli and M.
        Norsa, SIFC, NS 10 (1933) 119-24, 247-53.  Bassi,
        MIG, No. 111, tav. XL; Norsa, SLG, tav. 9 b.
        Page, GLP 1, No. 73.  S. Eitrem, SO 12 (1933)
        10-29, on the relation to Theocritus, Pharmakeutriai;
        C. Gallavotti, Riv. Fil. 61 (1933) 459-76; A. S. F.
        Gow, CR 47 (1933) 113-15, 168-69; K. Latte, Philol.
        88 (1933) 259-64, 467-69; P. E. Legrand, Rev. Ét.

Anc. 36 (1934) 25-31; P. Chantraine, Rev. Phil.,
Sér. 3.9 (1935) 22-32; R. Goossens, Chr. Ég. 10
(1935) 378-79; M. F. Galiano, Arbor 6 (1946) 148-
50; G. Perrotta, SIFC, NS 22 (1947) 93-100, on the
meter; U. Albini, Maia, NS 13 (1961) 126-30, on the
meter, in relation to Sophron, fr. 24, Kaibel.

Sophron: see also Nos. 1328, 1621, 1981.

1483   SORANUS OF EPHESUS: De morbis muliebribus.
PSI 2.117 (IV, Upper Egypt?; pap. cod.).

Soranus: see also Nos. 2339, 2347.

Sosibius: see No. 81.
Sosiphanes: see Nos. 78, 81.
Sositheus: see No. 1710.
Sostratus: see No. 2377.

1484   SOSYLUS: Hannibal, Bk. iv. U. Wilcken, Hermes
41 (1906) 103-41, ibid. 42 (1907) 510-12 (P. Wurzb.)
(II B.C.). Bilabel, No. 10; Jacoby, FGH 2.903-5.
JAW 142.82-83; New Chapters 1.143; Winter, LLP
245. F. Ruehl, Rh. Mus. 61 (1906) 352-59; H.
Bengtson, Historia 3 (1955) 301-7; G. Manganaro,
PP 14 (1959) 283-90.

Sotades: see No. 2752.
Soterichus: see Nos. 343, 1849.
Speusippus: see No. 2205.
Stasicles: see No. 78.

1485   STESICHORUS (?): Syotherai (?). P. Oxy. 23.2359
(II, Oxy.). Galiano, LG 131-32. Page, PMG 222.
D. L. Page, CR, NS 7 (1957) 192; B. Snell, Hermes
85 (1957) 249-51.

1486   --- Stesichorus (?): Nostoi (?). P. Oxy. 23.2360
(I, Oxy.). On Telemachus' departure from Sparta,
as in Homer, Od. xv. Galiano, LG 132. Page,
PMG 209. W. Peek, Philol. 102 (1958) 169-77.

Stesichorus: see also Nos. 1186, 1205, 1237, 1402,
1950, 2290, 2471.

Straton: see No. 2642.
Telesilla: see No. 1487.
"Testamentum Salomonis": see No. 2038.
Themison: see No. 2088.

1487   THEOCRITUS: Fragments of Idylls i-ii, v, x, xii-xv,
xvii-xviii, xxii, xxiv, xxvi, xxviii-xxxi (including
some new lines), with scholia. A. S. Hunt and
John Johnson, Two Theocritus Papyri (London 1930)
(V-VI, Antinoë; pap. cod.). A marginal note at
xv.60 (p. 46) mentions Telesilla (Galiano, LG 126-
27; Lesky, GGL 170; Page, PMG 726). From its
relation to the text of Theocritus it has been con-
jectured that she may have written a poem on the
marriage of Zeus and Hera. Gesch. der Text-
uberlief. 248-49; Lesky, GGL 660. Archiv 10.
23-24; JEA 17.118, 18.78. C. Gallavotti, Riv. Fil.
58 (1930) 498-503, proposes a different reconstruction of the codex; P. Maas, Gnomon 6 (1930)
561-64; K. Latte, Gött. Nachr., 1949, 225-32.

1488   --- Fragments of Idylls i, iv-v, xiii, xv-xvi, xxii,
xxvi. K. Wessely, WS 8 (1886) 221-30; Raineri
M. 2.78-79 (V-VI, Fayum; parch. cod.).

1489   --- Fragments of Idylls i, iii, iv-viii, with scholia.
A. S. Hunt and John Johnson, Two Theocritus Pa-
pyri (London 1930) 3-19 (P. Oxy. 2064) (II, Oxy.).
P. Maas, Gnomon 6 (1930) 561-64.

1490   --- Idylls v.53-65, 81-93, 110-37, 139-50, vii.4-13,
68-117, xv.38-47, 51-57, 59-80, 84-100. P. Oxy.
13.1618 (Bodleian Libr., Gr. class. d.128 (P)) (V,
Oxy.; pap. cod.). JAW 191.64; JEA 7.88. F.
Garin, Riv. Fil. 47 (1919) 434-38, on the relation
to the text tradition.

1491   --- Idylls xi.20-24, xiv.59-63. BKT 5.1.55 (inv.
5017) (VI-VII?; parch. cod.). JAW 178.111.

1492   --- Idylls xiii.19-34. P. Oxy. 4.694 (P. Princ.)
(II, Oxy.). Archiv 3.479.

--- Idylls xiv.59-63: see No. 1491.

--- Idylls xv.38-100: see No. 1490.

1493   --- Idylls xvii.94-107, xxviii.1-13. Described by
Gow 257 (P. Oxy. inedita) (IV?, Oxy.; pap. cod.).

1494   --- Idylls xviii.12-43. Described by Gow 257 (P.
Oxy. inedita) (IV, Oxy.; pap. cod.).

1495   --- Idylls xxii.8, 38-39, 40-84. P. Oxy. 15.1806
(I, Oxy.).

--- Idylls xxviii.1-13: see No. 1493.

1496   --- Scholia on Idylls v.38-49. BKT 5.1.56 (inv.
7506) (I-II). Archiv 6.256; JAW 178.111.

Theodectes: see Nos. 1568, 2290.
Theodoridas: see No. 1600.

THEOGNIS: Elegiae 25: see No. 1567.

1497   --- 254-78. P. Oxy. 23.2380 (II-III, Oxy.; on the
verso of a document). A. Garzya, Teognide:
Elegie (Firenze 1955) 34-35. C. Gallavotti, Gnomon 29 (1957) 424-25; A. Luppino, Riv. Fil. 85
(1957) 234, note 1; J. Carrière, Rev. Ét. Gr. 75
(1962) 37-44, observes that the papyrus is damag-
ing to the theory that the Theognidea are a late
compilation.

--- 425-27: see No. 77.

1498   --- 434-38. P. Viereck, Racc. Lumbroso 254-55
(P. Berol. inv. 12310) (III B.C., Philadelphia; from
the same ostr. as No. 1697).

Theognis (tragicus): see No. 138.
Theon: see Nos. 82, 186, 1327, 1361, 1473.

1499   THEOPHRASTUS: De aqua. P. Hibeh 1.16 (III B.C.,
Hibeh; cart.). Archiv 6.238.

1500   --- Characteres xxv-xxvi. P. Oxy. 4.699 (Trinity
Coll. Libr., Dublin, Pap. F.11) (III, Oxy.). Archiv 3.496.

1501    --- Theophrastus (?): De animalibus.  P. Lit. Lond.
        164 (Brit. Mus. inv. 2242) (II-III?).  Ed. pr.: H.
        J. M. Milne, CR 36 (1922) 66-67.  JEA 9.99.  A.
        Koerte, Archiv 7.248-49, regards the text as "ein
        leichtfertiger Auszug aus Aristoteles ..."

1502    --- Theophrastus (?): Peri lexeos, Bk. i (?).  P.
        Hamb. 128 (inv. 650 + 650, fr. 16) (ante 250 B.C.;
        cart. ?).  Refers to a metaphor (from tragedy?)
        cited by Aristotle, Poetics 21.1457b.25 (lines 42-43);
        Homer, Il. iv. 485 (48-49), Od. ix.124 (43-44).
        Cites phrases from unknown poets (49, 55-56; Page,
        PMG 927).  The content is related to Aristotle,
        Poetics 20-21.  Archiv 16.107-8.

        Theophrastus: see also Nos. 89, 1574, 2089, 2289-90,
        2296, 2862.

1503    THEOPOMPUS: An epitome of Philippica, Bk. xlvii
        (on events of 340 B.C.).  P. Ryl. 1.19 (II).  Bi-
        label, No. 6; B. P. Grenfell and A. S. Hunt,
        Hellenica Oxyrhynchia cum Theopompi et Cratippi
        Fragmentis (Oxonii 1909), No. 211; Jacoby, FGH
        2.581.  Archiv 6.243; New Chapters 2.71.

        Theopompus: see also Nos. 186, 317, 339, 484,
        2189, 2191-92, 2204, 2289, 2496.

        Theopompus (comicus): see No. 458.
        Thersagoras: see No. 2091.
        Thessalus: see No. 2088.
        Thrasybulus: see No. 2070.
        Thrasymachus: see No. 2339.

1504    THUCYDIDES: Historia i.2-3, 28-29.  P. Hamb.
        163 (inv. 646 + 666 recto) (III B.C. or I?; No.
        1770 is on the verso of inv. 666).  E. G. Turner,
        JHS 76 (1956) 96-98, revises the editors' dating
        (saec. I) to saec. III B.C., and shows that this
        does not belong to the same roll as No. 1505; A.
        et R. Calderini, Proc. IX Intr. Congr. Pap., 141,
        note 5, doubt which dating is right; H. T. Wade-
        Gery and B. D. Meritt, Hesperia 26 (1957) 194-95.

1505    --- i.3.3-4.  W. G. Waddell, Ét. Pap. 1 (1932) 15
        (No. 6) (P. Cairo inv. 47993 a) (I, Oxy.).

1506    --- i.11-14.  P. Oxy. 13.1620 (Libr. of the Univ.
        of Melbourne) (II-III, Oxy.).  Hemmerdinger,
        Thucyd. 22.

1507    --- i.49.6-50.2.  A. Wifstrand, Årsb., Lund, 1934-
        35, 54-56 (No. 2) (II).

1508    --- i.52-54.  P. Harris 41 (inv. 181 d-e) (II-III).

1509    --- i.71.4-73.2.  PSI 11.1195 (II, Oxy.).

        --- i.112.5: see No. 429.

        --- i.136: see No. 2289.

1510    --- i.139.4-141.3.  P. Oxy. 10.1245 (P. Cairo) (IV,
        Oxy.).

1511    --- ii.2-5, 13, 15.  P. Genève 2 (inv. 257); P. Ryl.
        3.548 (III; pap. cod.).  Fischer, No. 2.

1512    --- ii.7-8.  P. Oxy. 1.17 (Johns Hopkins Univ. Libr.)
        (II-III, Oxy.).  Fischer, No. 3.  Archiv 1.114.

1513    --- ii.11.5-9, 35.1.  P. Oxy. 13.1621; P. Lit. Lond.
        106 (Brit. Mus. inv. 2471) (IV, Oxy.; parch. cod.).

        --- ii.22: see No. 2289.

1514    --- ii.22-25.  P. Oxy. 6.878 (Musées Royaux,
        Bruxelles, inv. E.5941) (I, Oxy.).  Fischer, No.
        4.  Hemmerdinger, Thucyd. 22.

1515    --- ii.59-60.  Fischer, No. 5 (P. Giss. inv. 12)
        (IV-V, Antinoöpolis; parch. cod.).  Gundel 16.
        In 1945 the script was virtually effaced by damp.

1516    --- ii.65.6-82.1 (with lacunae).  A. H. Salonius,
        Fin. Vet. Soc. 2.2 (1927) 1-16 (P. Berol. inv. 13236)
        (II-III, Hermupolis Magna; pap. cod.).  O. Lusch-
        nat, Philol. 98 (1954) 37-38.

1517    --- ii.65.13, 67.1-2.  P. Oxy. 13.1622 (Kongelige
        Biblioteket, København, Oxy. 1) (II, Oxy.).  Norsa,
        SLG, tav. 8 c; Schubart, Gr. Pal., Abb. 80.
        Hemmerdinger, Thucyd. 20.  P. Collart, Rev.
        Phil. 43 (1919) 58-60.

1518    --- ii.73.1-74.1.  V. Bartoletti, Studi Castiglioni 1,
        61-66 (P. Univ. Statale di Milano) (II; on the verso
        of a document).

1519    --- ii.73.3, 74.1.  P. Oxy. 3.451 (Royal Ontario
        Mus., Univ. of Toronto) (III, Oxy.).  Fischer, No.
        6.  Archiv 3.281.

1520    --- ii.90.5-6, 91.1-2.  P. Oxy. 2.225; P. Lit. Lond.
        105 (Brit. Mus. inv. 784) (I, Oxy.).  Fischer, No.
        7.  Archiv 1.519.

1521    --- iii.7-9.  P. Oxy. 13.1623 (P. Cairo) (V-VI, Oxy.;
        parch. cod.).

        --- iii.49.4: see No. 2120.

1522    --- iii.58-59.  P. Oxy. 6.879 (P. Cairo inv. 41084)
        (III, Oxy.).

1523    --- iv.15-16, v.4, 18, 42-43, 72-73, viii.6, 20, 23-
        25, 52-54, 81, 96, 103.  P. Oxy. 17.2100 (II, Oxy.).
        Hemmerdinger, Thucyd. 59; Pasquali, Stor. Testo
        321-23.

1524    --- iv.28-41.  P. Oxy. 1.16, 4.696 (Univ. of Penn-
        sylvania Mus.) (I, Oxy.).  Archiv 3.488.  Hemmer-
        dinger, Thucyd. 19-22.

1525    --- iv.87.5-6.  P. Oxy. 3.452 (II-III, Oxy.).  Ar-
        chiv 3.281.

        --- v.4-73: see No. 1523.

1526    --- v.32-34, 40, 96-98, 103-5, 111.  P. Oxy. 6.880
        (Univ.-Bibl., Graz, inv. II.1948) (II, Oxy.).

1527    --- v.60.3-63.1.  P. Oxy. 9.1180 (Univ. of Illinois
        Libr., inv. 1180) (III, Oxy.).

1528    --- vi.32.2-3.  P. Oxy. 3.453 (I-II, Oxy.).  Archiv
        3.282.

--- vi. 80. 4: see No. 2120.

1529  --- vii. 36. 4, 57. 11.  P. Mich. 3. 141 (inv. 42); P.
Hamb. 164 (inv. 653; from the same roll?) (II).
Winter, LLP 240.

1530  --- vii. 38. 1.  P. Oxy. 10. 1246 (Muhlenberg Coll.)
(II, Oxy.).

1531  --- vii. 54-68. 2, 72-73, 78. 5-6, 79. 5-82. 4.  P. Oxy.
11. 1376; P. Lit. Lond. 107 (Brit. Mus. inv. 2445)
(II-III, Oxy.).  Hemmerdinger, Thucyd. 27, 47;
Pasquali, Stor. Testo 321-23.  K. F. W. Schmidt,
Gött. Anz., 1918, 103-5; P. Focardi, Aeg. 35 (1955)
43-62, studies this and other papyri of Thucydides
in their bearing on the text tradition.

--- vii. 60: see No. 2126.

--- viii. 6-103: see No. 1523.

1532  --- viii. 8. 3-11. 2.  P. Oxy. 10. 1247 (Toledo Mus. of
Art) (II, Oxy.).  Hemmerdinger, Thucyd. 22, 47,
59.

1533  --- viii. 80. 1-82. 1.  P. Antin. 1. 25 (III, Antinoöpolis;
parch. cod.).  Hemmerdinger, Thucyd. 20, 22.

1534  --- viii. 91-92.  K. Wessely, WS 7 (1885) 116-22 (P.
Rain. inv. 200) (V-VI, Arsinoe; parch. cod.).
Pasquali, Stor. Testo 326.  H. Landwehr, Philol.
44 (1885) 743-45, would date the codex to saec. VII;
O. Luschnat, ibid. 98 (1954) 39-41.

1535  --- Commentary on i. 1-9.  H. Gerstinger, Denkschr.
Wien. Akad., 1925, Abt. 2 (P. Vindob. inv. Gr.
29247) (III, Fayum; pap. cod.).  Refers to Aelius
Aristides, Prooemia; Homer (?); Demosthenes,
In Midiam 160.  Archiv 8. 264-65.  O. Rossbach,
Phil. Woch. 46 (1926) 513-14; K. F. W. Schmidt,
Gnomon 3 (1927) 61; O. Luschnat, Philol. 98 (1954)
29-31.

1536  --- Commentary on ii. 1-45.  P. Oxy. 6. 853 (P. Cairo)
(II, Oxy.; on the verso of a composite roll).  Cites
or refers to Callimachus, Hecala, and a new fragment (Pfeiffer, CFNR, Nos. 37-38; idem, Callim.
1, fr. 305); Dionysius of Halicarnassus, De Thucydide; Euripides, Erechtheus (B. Snell, WS 69, 1956,
89); Homer, Il. i. 117, ii. 504, 766, iii. 1, iv. 297-300
(?), 539, vii. 467, xvi. 816 (?), xviii. 298, 492, Od.
vii. 294; and Pindar, fr. 110, Schroeder (Galiano,
Pind., No. 25).  Roberts, GLH, pl. 17a; Schubart,
Gr. Pal., Abb. 86.  Fischer, No. 1.  Archiv 6. 256.
W. Rhys Roberts, CR 23 (1910) 82; O. Luschnat,
Philol. 98 (1954) 25-29; G. B. Alberti, Maia, NS
15 (1963) 129-31.

Thucydides: see also Nos. 2070, 2190, 2293.

Timaeus: see Nos. 1357, 2193, 2268.
Timocles: see Nos. 339, 1579.
Timocreon: see No. 2298.
Timosthenes: see No. 339.

1537  TIMOTHEUS: Persae.  Wilamowitz, Timotheos: Die
Perser (Leipzig 1903) (P. Berol. inv. 9875) (IV B. C.,
Abusir).  New Pal. Soc., Ser. 1, vol. 1, pl. 22;
Norsa, SLG, tav. 1 a; Roberts, GLH, pl. 1; Schubart, Gr. Pal., Abb. 64; idem, PGB, tab. 1;
Thompson, GLP, No. 1 (p. 106); Wilamowitz, Der
Timotheos-Papyrus: Lichtdruck-Ausgabe (Leipzig
1903).  Diehl, Anth. Lyr. $2^1$. 138-50; Edmonds, LG
3. 308-25; Page, PMG 791.  Archiv 3. 268-69; JAW
125. 52-54, 133. 245-58, 144. 4-7, 110-11, 178. 99-101;
Lesky, GGL 14, 392; C. J. Ellingham, New Chapters 1. 59-65; Winter, LLP 211-13.  S. Sudhaus, Rh.
Mus. 58 (1903) 481-99; O. A. Danielsson, Eranos
5 (1903-4) 1-39, 98-128; H. L. Ebeling, AJP 46
(1925) 317-31; G. A. Privitera, Maia 5 (1952) 82-84,
ibid. 6 (1953) 214-19; G. A. Longman, CR, NS 4
(1954) 208-9; C. del Grande, Filologia minore
(Milano-Napoli 1956) 187-94, 351-52.

1538  --- Timotheus (?): Lyric fragments.  P. Grenf.
2. 8 (a); P. Lit. Lond. 49 (Brit. Mus. inv. 693);
P. Bad. 6. 178 (two additional fragments) (III B. C.,
Hibeh; cart.).  Attributed to Timotheus by the
editor of P. Bad.  Page, GLP 1, No. 89; idem, PMG
925 (under lyric adespota).  Archiv 14. 113-14.  H.
Oellacher, Gnomon 16 (1940) 507-9.

Timotheus: see also Nos. 246, 1456, 1948, 2564.

Timotheus of Metapontum: see No. 2339.
Tisias: see No. 2295.

1539  TRYPHON: Ars Grammatica.  Kenyon, Class. Texts
109-16; P. Lit. Lond. 182 (Brit. Mus. inv. 126)
(III-IV?, Ma'abdeh; from the same pap. cod. as
No. 634).  Quotes Homer, Il. i. 18-20, ii. 760, x.
341, xv. 208-9, Od. ix. 5, 6, 11, 355, xx. 245.

1540  --- On the Spartan Dialect (title on a sillybos).  P.
Oxy. 24. 2396 (II, Oxy.; strip of parch.).  "Tryphon, son of Ammonius, on the Spartan dialect, in
two (?) books: Bk. i (?)."

Tryphon: see also Nos. 457, 2143.

Tyrannion: see No. 82.

1541  TYRTAEUS: Elegiae.  Wilamowitz, Sitzb. Berl.
Akad., 1918, 728-36 (P. Berol. inv. 11675) (III B. C.;
cart.).  Diehl, Anth. Lyr. $1^2$. 1. 6-11, ibid. $1^3$. 4-7.
Archiv 7. 119; JAW 191. 37-38; C. M. Bowra, New
Chapters 3. 62-66.  A. Calderini, Aeg. 2 (1921) 75-
78; A. Gercke, Hermes 56 (1921) 346-54; J. Sitzler,
Phil. Woch. 45 (1925) 27-29; V. de Falco, Riv.
Ind. Fil. Ital. 10 (1926) 63-76; idem, Human. 2
(1948-49) 265-67.

Xenophanes: see No. 1186.

XENOPHON: Anabasis ii. 1. 6, v. 4. 29: see No. 2126.

1542  --- vi. 5. 12-15.  PSI 11. 1196 (II, Oxy.).

1543  --- vi. 6. 9-24.  P. Oxy. 3. 463 (Bodleian Libr., Gr.
class. a. 7 (P)) (II-III, Oxy.).  Persson 18-19.  Archiv 3. 281; JAW 142. 345.

1544   --- vii.1.40. P. Oxy. 9.1181 (Muhlenberg Coll.) (III, Oxy.). Persson 20.

    --- Cyropaedia i.2.8, 4.11: see No. 455.

1545   --- i.4.15, 17-20, 6.3. P. Oxy. 17.2101 (III, Oxy.). JAW 230.21.

1546   --- i.6.3-11, ii.1.30. P. Oxy. 4.697 (Trinity Coll. Libr., Dublin, Pap. E.9) (III, Oxy.; pap. cod.). Persson, 20-28, 40. Archiv 3.489; JAW 142.345-46.

1547   --- i.6.6-8, 9-10, iv.5.41-42, 47-48, v.2.35, 3.2-3, vii.2.6-8, 12-15. P. Varsov. 1; P. Ryl. 3.549 (III, Fayum?; pap. cod.). G. Manteuffel, Charist. Przychocki 108-15 (ed. pr. of P. Varsov.).

1548   --- i.6.27-29. P. Oxy. 7.1018 (P. Ryl. inv. 450) (III, Oxy.; on the verso of an account). Persson 28-29.

1549   --- i.6.45 — ii.1.1. P. Oxy. 4.698 (Wellesley Coll.) (III, Oxy.). Persson 30. Archiv 3.490; JAW 142.346.

1550   --- iv.5.41-44. J. G. Milne, Archiv 5 (1913) 378 (II, Hawara). Persson 30-31.

1551   --- v.2.3-4, 6-7, 22, 24-25, 28, 3.1-9, 12-17, 19-26. Raineri M. 6.81-97 (II, Hermupolis Magna). A marginal note on v.2.4 contains a doubtful reference to Heron of Athens. Pasquali, Stor. Testo 304-5; Persson 31-40. K. Münscher, Philol., Suppl. 13.2 (1920) 180-81.

1552   --- Hellenica i.2.2-5.8 (with lacunae). Raineri M. 6.97-113 (III, Soknopaiou Nesos or Karanis; on the verso of a tax roll). Persson 40-45.

    --- i.6.5: see No. 2289.

1553   --- i.6.30, 34, 36-38, 7.30, 32. P. Princ. 3.112 (IV; parch.).

1554   --- iii.1.3-7. P. Oxy. 1.28 (St. Andrews Univ. Libr.) (II, Oxy.). Persson 45. Archiv 1.115.

1555   --- v.4.43-44, 47-54, vi.1.11-13. PSI 11.1197 (II, Oxy.).

1556   --- vi.5.7-9. P. Oxy. 2.226 (Columbia Univ. Libr.) (I-II, Oxy.). Persson 45-46. Archiv 1.519.

1557   --- Memorabilia i.3.7-13. P. Heid. Siegmann 206 (inv. 435) (ca. 280 B.C.; text on recto, No. 1963 on verso). Gesch. der Textüberlief. 271. R. Merkelbach, Stud. Jachmann 157-62.

1558   --- i.3.15, 4.1-3. P. Grenf. 2.13; P. Lit. Lond. 149 (Brit. Mus. inv. 695 B) (III-IV). Identified by H. Diels, Sitzb. Berl. Akad., 1897, 144. Persson 46-47.

1559   --- ii.1.5-16. PSI 2.121 (I-II, Oxy.). Persson 47-48.

1560   --- iii.1.4-7. C. C. Edgar, Ann. Serv. 26 (1926) 207-8 (P. Cairo inv. 45612) (IV, Oxy.; parch. cod.).

1561   --- iv.2.1-4. P. Lond. 5.1814 (b); P. Lit. Lond. 150 (Brit. Mus. inv. 1546 B) (II). JAW 230.23.

1562   --- Cynegeticus 13.5-74. P. Rein. 2.78 (P. Sorbonne inv. 2098) (II).

1563   --- Oeconomicus 8.17-9.2. P. Oxy. 2.227; P. Lit. Lond. 151 (Brit. Mus. inv. 785) (I-II, Oxy.). Persson 48-49. Archiv 1.520.

1564   --- Symposium 4.51-55, 64 (?), 5.1-3. P. Antin. 1.26 (II?, Antinoöpolis; parch. roll). JEA 1 (1914) 177 (first mention). J. Bingen, Chr. Ég. 37 (1962) 334-37.

1565   --- 8.6-9, 15-18. P. Lond. 2.184; P. Lit. Lond. 152 (Brit. Mus. inv. 184); P. Giss. 1.1 (inv. 175) (II-III). H. J. M. Milne, Aeg. 4 (1923) 41-42, identifies P. Lond. Ed. pr. of P. Giss.: E. Kornemann, Philol. 67 (1908) 321-24. Archiv 2.368; JAW 142.346, 203.32. Persson 50. J. Bingen, Chr. Ég. 37 (1962) 334, notes 2-3.

1566   --- De vectigalibus 1.5-6. U. Wilcken, Archiv 1 (1901) 473-75 (P. Monac.) (II). Persson 50-51. Archiv 2.359.

    --- Agesilaus 6.8: see No. 2289.

Xenophon: see also Nos. 317, 2087.

Xenophon (Gaius Stertinius Xenophon): see No. 2088.
Zeno: see No. 2127.
Zenodotus: see Nos. 1039, 1205, 1361, 2184.
Zopyrus: see No. 2184.

## B. ADESPOTA

### 1. POETRY

#### Anthologies

1567   Anthology. Wilamowitz, Sitzb. Berl. Akad., 1918, 742-43 (O. Berol. inv. 12319) (III; ostr.; sch. ex.?). Contents in order: Ps.-Epicharmus (New Chapters 1.18-21; Page, GLP 1, No. 102 b; Powell, CA 222-23); three unidentified comic fragments; Euripides, Electra 388-89, Hecuba 354-56; Theognis 25; Homer, Od. xviii. 79 (Collart 97); Hesiod, Opera 287; two prose sententiae (with the second, S. G. Mercati, Biblica 3, 1922, 453-54, compares Heraclitus, fr. 13, Bywater, and ii Peter 2:22). Archiv 7.152-53; JAW 191.40. M. Calderini Mondini, Aeg. 2 (1921) 80-81.

1568   Anthology of tragedy and comedy. BKT 5.2.123-28 (inv. 9772) (II B.C.). Contents in order: Plato comicus (Demiańczuk 82; Page, GLP 1, No. 43); Pherecrates (Demiańczuk 71; Page, GLP 1, No. 39); Menander (?); Theodectes (?); Ps.-Epicharmus (JAW 152.231-32; Demiańczuk 124-25; New Chapters 1.18-21; Olivieri 106-7; Page, GLP 1, No. 102 a; Powell, CA 222); Antiphanes, fr. 253, Kock; Euripides, Melanippa Desmotis (Arnim, SE 32-33; Hunt, TGFP, No. 6; Page, GLP 1, No. 13), Protesilaus, fr. 658.2-4, Nauck, Hippolytus 403-4, 406-7, 407a-10, 413-23; Apollodorus (of Carystus?;

Page, GLP 1, No. 58).   Schubart, PGB, tab. 6 c.
Archiv 6.233;  JAW 147.100-2.

1569   Gnomic anthology.   P. Hibeh 1.7 (Bodleian Libr., Gr.
class. d.78 (P)) (III B.C., Hibeh; cart.; on the
verso of No. 1294).  Euripides, Electra 367-79
(J. D. Denniston, Euripides: Electra, Oxford 1939,
pp. xlii-xliii);  Ps.-Epicharmus; Menander (or
Euripides?), as quoted by St. Paul, i Cor. 15:34.
Archiv 6.233.

1570   Anthology of tragedy and comedy (?).   P. Schubart
27 (II-III; on the verso of a document).  Includes
Menander, Sententiae 26 (?).

1571   Tragic anthology (?).   F. M. Heichelheim, AJP 61
(1940) 209-10 (Fitzwilliam Mus., inv. 2) (I-II).
Contents (doubtful, as only a few letters of each
line are preserved): Euripides, Hecuba 503-4,
20-21, Iphigenia Aulidensis 790-91; Sophocles,
Antigona 689-90.

1572   Anthology.   P. Petrie 1.3 (1); P. Lit. Lond. 57 and
71 (Brit. Mus. inv. 486A) (III B.C., Gurob; cart.).
Ps.-Epicharmus (Olivieri 108); Euripides, Antiopa,
fr. 198, Nauck.

1573   Anthology: selections on women.   BKT 5.2.129-30
(inv. 9773) (II B.C.).  Contents in order: Euripides, Protesilaus, fr. 658.2-4, Nauck; Anaxandrides;
Euripides, Hippolytus 664-68 (JAW 147.100-2); Antiphanes (the name only); unknown verse (five lines);
two choliambics (Hipponax?); Medeiros, pp. XLVIII-
XLIX).  Archiv 6.234.

1574   Anthology: selections on Tyche, in verse and prose.
J. Barns, CQ 44 (1950) 126-32 (Egypt Exploration
Society, London) (II B.C., Medinet-el-Fayum; sch.
text).  Includes Euripides, fr. 1017, Nauck² (?);
Menander, Sententiae 306 (?); many new iambic
sententiae, chiefly from New Comedy; a prose sententia attributed to "Theophrastus or Anaximenes"
(cf. Stobaeus, Eclogae ii.346); Demosthenes, De
Corona 252.  Archiv 16.105.  J. Barns, CQ 44 (1950)
132-37, ibid., NS 1 (1951) 1-19, discusses this and
other gnomic anthologies; O. Masson, Rev. Ét. Gr.
64 (1951) 441-42.

1575   Anthology: verse and prose.   P. Viereck, Racc.
Lumbroso 255-57 (P. Berol. inv. 12311) (III B.C.,
Philadelphia; ostr.; sch. ex.).  Contents: Euripides, Aegeus, fr. 11, Nauck; paraphrase of a
sententia of Socrates; New Comedy (two lines).

1576   Anthology from Euripides.   P. Ross. Georg. 1.9
(Collection of G. Zereteli, Tiflis) (II B.C.).  Contents: Euripides, Danae, fr. 324, Nauck, Orestes
1155-56.

1577   Anthology: Schoolbook.   P. Freib. 1 (b), recto (inv.
12) (II-I B.C.; from the same pap. as No. 2658;
on the verso, No. 1219).  Contents: eight comic
trimeters (Philemon?); Page, GLP 1, No. 69); a
simile from epic (Antimachus?; Page, GLP 1, No.
119; Powell, CA 251); Agon Homeri et Hesiodi
205-6; Homer, Il. v.387-91 (Collart 102).  Archiv
7.152; JAW 207.124.

1578   Verse anthology (?).   P. Oxy. 11.1401 (Williams Coll.)
(V, Oxy.; pap. cod.).  Perhaps from the same
papyrus as No. 402.  Classified by the editor as
tragedy (?).  Archiv 7.142.  E. Fraenkel, CQ, NS
2 (1952) 186, sees Aristophanes Aves 382, 460-61,
in two of the four fragments.

1579   Comic anthology.   P. Schubart 28 (II B.C.; on the
verso is a prose text).  Contents: a line from
Diocles (or Euthycles, Timocles?); Euripides,
Meleager, fr. 529, Nauck, as if by Philemon;
Antiphanes, Fab. Incert., fr. 265, Kock (= fr. 50,
Meineke).  Archiv 16.106.  L. Alfonsi, Aeg. 33
(1953) 310-14, observes (inter alia) that Philemon
may have parodied Euripides.

1580   Comic anthology.   K. Kalbfleisch, Racc. Lumbroso
29-35 (Univ.-Bibl., Giessen, inv. 152) (ca. 100
B.C., Fayum?; text on recto, No. 1984 on verso).
Contents: comedy, unidentified (ten lines); Menander, Nomothetes.  Gundel 11.  Archiv 8.258-59.

1581   Anthology (?).   P. Lond. 5.1812; P. Lit. Lond. 53
(Brit. Mus. inv. 1568 C) (III-IV; pap. cod.).
Iambics attributed in P. Lit. Lond. to Semonides
of Amorgos (?).  Diehl, Anth. Lyr. 3³.68-70 (under
"Anonymorum Iambi").  A. Koerte, Archiv 10.44,
suggests a Hellenistic poet; A. D. Knox, JEA 15
(1929) 140, prefers a tragic anthology.

1582   Gnomic anthology.   Mon. Epiphan. 2.615 (VI-VII?,
Thebes; limestone; sch. ex.).  Contents: Menander, Sententiae 27, 67, 64, 93, 98, 128, 214, 219,
194, 203, 230, 270 (?), 328, 340, 350, 371, 403,
ed. Meineke (in that order), plus one found in P.
Bouriant 1 (see No. 2643), plus about thirteen unknown.

1583   Fragments of a gnomic anthology, with Coptic translations.   O. Marucchi, Il Museo Egizio Vaticano
descritto ed illustrato (Roma 1899) 296-303 (VI?;
four opisthograph frr.; sch. ex.?).  Contents
(arranged acrostically, alpha to gamma): Menander, Sententiae 596, 648, 26, 4, 11, 19, 74, 67,
69, 71, 60, 90, 96, 83, 91, 86, ed. Meineke (in
that order), and nine others not in Meineke.  Ed.
pr.: E. Sarti et V. Puntoni, Gnomologii acro-
stichi fragmentum Graeca una cum metaphrasi
Copto-Sahidica (Pisis 1883).  Coptic Bibl., Nos.
1799, 1805.

1584   Gnomic anthology.   P. Rain. 3.24 (inv. 19999 A)
(cf. ibid. 4, p. 136) (I, Soknopaiou Nesos; on the
verso of a document).  Twenty-five lines, including Menander, Sententiae 137, 139, 191, 226, 239,
374, 394, 472, ed. Meineke.  Archiv 14.125-27.

1585   Gnomic anthology.   O. Bodl. 1.150 (O. Petrie 449)
(Byzantine; ostr.; sch. ex.).  Menander, Sententiae 232, 263, ed. Meineke, and other verse
maxims.

1586   Gnomic anthology.   J. G. Milne, JEA 8 (1922) 156-57
(II; ostr.; sch. ex.).  Twelve iambic trimeters,
arranged acrostically; line 9 resembles Menander,
Sententiae 257, ed. Meineke.  Archiv 8.259-61.
Manteuffel, Opusc., No. 40.

1587    Gnomic anthology.   O. Bodl. 1.144 (O. Petrie 405)
        (Byzantine; ostr.; sch. ex.). Menander, Senten-
        tiae 270, 272, 276, 278, 294, ed. Meineke, and
        other verse maxims, unidentified.  Chr. Eg. 8
        (1933) 164-66;  P. Collart, BIFAO 30 (1931) 419-23;
        W. G. Waddell, Ét. Pap. 1 (1932) 18.

1588    Gnomic anthology.  P. Schubart 29 (P. Berol. inv.
        16136) (II, Dime; on the verso of an account).
        Contents: Menander, Sententiae 640, 319, 383
        (Philemon, fr. 202, Kock), 410, 313, 315; Menan-
        der, fr. 659. 2, Kock; parts of four other verse
        maxims. Ed. pr.: G. Manteuffel, JJP 2 (1948)
        87-91.  Archiv 16.106.

1589    Anthology: Epigrams on women.  O. Plasberg, Ar-
        chiv 2 (1903) 185-96 (P. Strassb. inv. Gr. 1016) (II).
        Forty-seven lines, including Menander, Sententiae
        361, 334, 700, 353, ed. Meineke.

1590    Anthology.   P. Rain. 3.25 (inv. 19999 B) (cf. ibid.
        4, p. 136) (I, Soknopaiou Nesos; on the verso of
        documents).  Contents: a comic dialogue; Menan-
        der, Sententia 422, ed. Meineke; and an unidentified
        prose text. Archiv 14.127.  M. F. Galiano, Arbor
        6 (1946) 141-42.

1591    Gnomic anthology.  P. Iand. 5, 77 (inv. 348) (II-III,
        Fayum).  Ten lines: Menander, Sententia 752, ed.
        Meineke; Diphilus, fr. 114, Kock; two maxims
        known from other sources, and six new maxims.
        Ed. pr.: K. Kalbfleisch, Hermes 63 (1928) 100-3.
        Gundel 10.  Archiv 10.56.  Page, GLP 1, No. 56.

1592    Anthology.  B. Snell, Hermes, Einzelschr. 5 (1937)
        89-92 (P. Strassb. WG 305-307, verso) (II-I B.C.?;
        cart.; from the verso of the same roll as Nos. 170,
        426, 1349, 1698, 1735).  Contents: Philemon (?),
        fr. 89, Kock; Paean to the wind Eurus (Page, PMG
        858); adaptation of Euripides, Orestes 9, 10, 6;
        unidentified verses.  Archiv 13.95-96.

1593    Anthology: "Miscellaneous Epigrams" (by Hedylus or
        Posidippus?), beginning with an epithalamium for
        Arsinoë.  P. Petrie 2.49 (a); P. Lit. Lond. 60
        (Brit. Mus. inv. 589 A) (ca. 250 B.C., Gurob;
        cart.).  Diehl, Anth. Lyr. 2¹.238.  New Chapters
        3.187.  O. Crusius, Philol. 53 (1894) 12; W. Peek,
        RE 22.1.439.  F. Lasserre, Rh. Mus. 102 (1959)
        222-47, reedits the recto, gives the ed. pr. of the
        verso, reading the names of Leonidas (?), Hedylus
        (?), and Anyte (?) as well as Posidippus, and sug-
        gests that the epithalamium serves as a proem to
        the "Symmeikta Epigrammata" offered by Hedylus
        or Posidippus as a wedding-present to Arsinoë;
        idem, ibid. 103 (1960) 191-92.

1594    Anthology of epigrams.   P. Petrie 2.49 (b) (III B.C.,
        Gurob; cart.).  Nine epigrams on various literary
        compositions, including works by Aristarchus,
        Astydamas, and Cratinus.  R. Reitzenstein, Berl.
        Phil. Woch. 14 (1894) 155-59.

1595    Anthology of epigrams.   P. Oxy. 4.662; P. Lit. Lond.
        61 (Brit. Mus. inv. 1533) (I B.C.-I, Oxy.; on the
        verso of No. 1371).  Contents: Leonidas of Taren-
        tum, Anth. Pal. vii.163; Antipater of Sidon, ibid.
        164 (Page, GLP 1, No. 107); Amyntas, two epigrams

        (J. U. Powell, Aeg. 14, 1934, 468-72; A. Wifstrand,
        Lunds Universitets Årsskrift, NF 23, Nr. 3, 1927,
        33-39, identifies the second epigram as an imitation
        of Anth. Pal. vii.723); Leonidas, two epigrams
        (A. S. F. Gow, CR, NS 4, 1954, 6); and Antipater
        (new).  Archiv 3.484; New Chapters 3.188.   A. S.
        F. Gow, The Greek Anthology: Sources and Ascrip-
        tions (Society for the Promotion of Hellenic Studies,
        Supplementary Paper No. 9, London 1958) 15.

1596    Collection of first lines of epigrams.   Wilcken, Gr.
        Ostr. 2.1488 (II B.C., Thebes?; ostr.; sch. ex.).
        Included are Leonidas, Anth. Pal. ix.322 (recto,
        line 7), ibid. vi.13 (verso, line 6).

1597    Anthologia Palatina ix.538, with a cipher alphabet.
        Mon. Epiphan. 2.616 (VI-VII?, Thebes; wood).

1598    Anthology of epigrams.   BKT 5.1.75-76 (inv. 10571);
        Wilamowitz, Sitzb. Berl. Akad., 1918, 750-51 (I).
        Anth. Pal. xii.76 (Asclepiades or Posidippus), 77
        (Asclepiades or Posidippus), 78 (Meleager), ix.15, xii.106 (Melea-
        ger), v.151 (Meleager), xii.19 (A. Wifstrand, Lunds
        Universitets Årsskrift, NF 23, Nr. 3, 1927, 10-12,
        identifies ix.15 and xii.19).  Archiv 5.547; JAW
        178.162.  A. Ludwich, Berl. Phil. Woch. 27 (1907)
        492; A. S. F. Gow, The Greek Anthology: Sources
        and Ascriptions (see No. 1595, above) 15-16.

1599    Anthologia Palatina xiv.100.  U. Wilcken, Sitzb. Berl.
        Akad., 1887, 819-20; P. Achmîm 5 (identified and
        republished) (IV-V, Panopolis; written on the mar-
        gin of No. 494).  Wilamowitz, Hermes 22 (1887)
        635-36.

1600    Anthology of epigrams.   P. Freib. 4 (inv. 10 c) (I
        B.C.).  Posidippus, Anth. Pal. xvi.119; Theo-
        doridas, ibid. ix.743; and a part of the same epi-
        gram on Homer as in BKT 5.1.78-79 (see No. 1758).
        Archiv 7.123;  JAW 178.162.  K. Fuhr, Berl. Phil.
        Woch. 35 (1915) 863-64, identifies the epigram by
        Theodoridas; A. Wifstrand, op. cit. (see No.
        1598, above) 30-33, recognizes the epigram on
        Homer.

1601    Anthology of Epigrams.   P. Tebt. 1.3 (I B.C., Teb-
        tunis or Kerkeosiris; cart.).  Contents: On the
        death of Phaethon; Alcaeus of Messene, Anth. Pal.
        ix.588; on a literary work by Posidippus (or Hege-
        sippus?; W. Peek, RE 22.1.438); on the Spartan
        woman who slew her cowardly son (Asclepiades,
        Philiadas?).  Archiv 3.276.

1602    Anthology of epigrams.   P. Harris 56  (I B.C.).
        First published as a magical text; redated and
        identified by C. H. Roberts, JJP 4 (1950) 215-17.
        Fr. a, recto, is an epigram referring to the painter
        Apelles; on the verso are some lines from tragedy
        (?).  M. Hombert, Chr. Ég. 26 (1951) 415-16; T.
        B. L. Webster, JJP 5 (1951) 237; A. Barigazzi,
        Hermes 80 (1952) 494-95.

1603    Anthology of epigrams.   E. G. Turner, JJP 4 (1950)
        235-38 (P. Petrie, now at University Coll., London)
        (ca. 100 B.C., Hawara).  An epitaph for a dog; an
        epigram to Artemis.  Archiv 16.91.  M. Hombert,
        Chr. Ég. 26 (1951) 415; A. Barigazzi, Hermes 80
        (1952) 495-96.

1604 Anthology. P. Oxy. 6.864 (Univ. of Illinois Libr., inv. 864) (III, Oxy.). Five hexameters; twenty iambic verses from a Hellenistic tragedy, perhaps on Hero and Leander (L. Malten, Rh. Mus. 93, 1949, 68-69). Archiv 6.235.

1605 Anthology: Ethical choliambics. Gerhard, Phoinix 1-7, 11-155 (P. Heid. inv. 310) (II B.C.; cart.). Contents: choliambics on base gain (lines 1-73; Cercidas?; Diehl, Anth. Lyr. $1^2$.3.111-16, ibid. $3^3$.134-36; Powell, CA 216-19); Phoenix of Colophon (lines 75-97, with title; Diehl, Anth. Lyr. $1^2$.3.104-6, ibid. $3^3$.124-26; Powell, CA 235-36); choliambics on pederasty (lines 98-132; but this section may include quotations from comedy, as shown by the rhythm of line 127). The section by Phoenix is addressed to one Posidippus (P. of Pella?). Knox, Herodes 228-29, 234-39; New Chapters 1.12-17; A. D. Knox, The First Greek Anthologist (Cambridge 1923), holds that this text comes from an extensive anthology, composed by Cercidas himself, and used by Gregory of Nazianzus. Archiv 5.555-56; JAW 174.51-53. P. Vallette, Rev. Phil. 37 (1913) 162-83, and D. Serruys, ibid. 183-90, write especially on the personality of Phoenix; Q. Cataudella, Riv. Fil. 59 (1931) 509-11, ibid. 61 (1933) 71-74.

1606 Anthology. P. Tebt. 1.1 (II-I B.C., Kerkeosiris; cart.; from a papyrus containing also decrees of Ptolemy II Euergetes; in the same hand as No. 1607). Contents: Helen's Lament, a monody (Manteuffel, Opusc., Nos. 31-32; Powell, CA 185; Winter, LLP 216); lyric: description of a woodland solitude (Diehl, Anth. Lyr. $2^1$.296-97; New Chapters 1.56-57, 2.62-63; Powell, CA 185; Winter, LLP 217); three couplets on love; a prose (?) obscenity. Roberts, GLH, pl. 7c. Page, GLP 1, No. 92. Archiv 3.275.

1607 Anthology. P. Tebt. 1.2 (II-I B.C., Kerkeosiris; cart.; in the same hand as No. 1606). Frr. a-c: the same contents as the first three parts of No. 1606, but in a fuller form; fr. d, verso: a paraklausithyron (from a mime?; Manteuffel, Opusc., No. 20; New Chapters 1.56; Winter, LLP 216-17). Archiv 3.275.

1608 Anthology of epigrams. PSI 1.17 (III, Hermupolis Magna; opisthograph pap., not from a cod.). Six epitaphs, apparently for real persons. Page, GLP 1, No. 117. Archiv 7.124.

1609 Fragment from a collection of epigrams (?). P. Rain. 3.14 (inv. 29282) (cf. ibid. 4, p. 136) (II-III, Fayum; pap. cod.). P. Maas, according to the editors, prefers a didactic poem on medicine; A. Koerte, Archiv 14.109-10, following H. Oellacher, thinks rather of an erotic paignion.

1610 Two verse maxims. P. Ross. Georg. 1.12 (Libr. of the State Hermitage Mus., Leningrad) (II-III; wooden tablet; sch. ex.). Ed. pr.: G. Zereteli, Mél. Chatelain 113-15. Ziebarth 2, No. 18.

1611 Epigrams. G. A. Gerhard and O. Crusius, Mél. Nicole 615-24 (P. Heid. inv. 1271) (VI; pap. cod.). Six epigrams in hexameters, with titles. P. Collart, Rev. Ét. Gr. 49 (1936) 429-39, terms the author a "Nonnien fervent"; W. Morel, Hermes 87 (1959) 379.

1612 Verse anthology: Iambics and hexameters. P. Michael. 5 (III B.C.). Perhaps extracts made for private use, including Homer, Il. iii. 424-29, in a version differing from the vulgate (Del Corno, Il. 143), and possibly an extract from Choerilus of Samos, Persika.

1613 Gnomic anthology. P. Hibeh 2.224 (now in the Brit. Mus.) (ca. 280-250 B.C., Hibeh; cart.). Parts of hexameters and iambic trimeters. The name Chaeremon appears (a heading, referring to C's Kentauros?).

1614 Epideictic epigrams. P. Oxy. 4.671 (Wellesley Coll.) (III, Oxy.). The remains are too exiguous for a fuller description. Archiv 3.484.

1615 Anthology dealing with astrology. P. Ryl. 3.488 (II; on the verso of an account or list of names). Hexameters and elegiacs of astrological content. Archiv 14.110. Neugebauer-Van Hoesen, Astrol. Pap. Ostr., No. 132.

1616 Anthology (?). P. Ryl. 3.497 (I, Oxy.). Parts of thirteen lines, including some iambic verses. E. Lobel suggests an anthology.

1617 Anthology: Scolia (arranged as an acrostic). P. Oxy. 15.1795 (I, Oxy.). Diehl, Anth. Lyr. $2^3$.114-16; Heitsch, GDRK, fr. VII; Manteuffel, Opusc., No. 27; Page, GLP 1, No. 125; Powell, CA 199-200; Young, Theognis 119-21. Archiv 7.140; Winter, LLP 217-18. P. Maas, Berl. Phil. Woch. 42 (1922) 581-82; K. F. W. Schmidt, Gött. Anz., 1924, 10; A. Dihle, Hermes 82 (1954) 184.

1618 Anthology: Epigrams (arranged as an acrostic). P. Oxy. 1.15 (Glasgow Univ. Libr.) (III, Oxy.). Heitsch, GDRK, fr. VIII; Manteuffel, Opusc., p. 179; Young, Theognis 122-23. Archiv 1.113. Wilamowitz, Gr. Versk. 364; idem, Gött. Anz., 1898, 695-96.

1619 Anthology: Legend and myth. H. Weil, Mél. Perrot 331-32 (in Paris?) (III-IV, Memphis?; waxed tablet; sch. ex.). Ten iambic trimeters forming five distichs: the stories of Ajax, Palamedes, Helen, Daphne, and Icarus. Ziebarth, No. 27; Ziebarth 2, No. 45.

1620 Anthology: Hymns to Aphrodite, Apollo, Dionysus, and Artemis-Hecate. P. Lit. Goodspeed 2 (inv. 101) (II-III; on the verso of accounts). Ed. pr.: E. J. Goodspeed, JHS 23 (1903) 237-47. Powell, CA 82-89. New Chapters 1.110. J. U. Powell, Journ. Philol. 34 (1915) 106-28, identifies and republishes the text.

1621 Verse anthology. P. Hamb. 121 (inv. 633, verso) (II B.C.; on the verso of documents). Hexameters from a bucolic poem (?); iambics (Sophron?); Aratus, Phaenomena 480-94 (Martin, Texte d'Aratos 210). Archiv 16.106.

1622    Anthology of epigrams (?).    P. Hamb. 125 (inv. 82)
        (I-II).  Meager remains of distichs.

        Verse anthologies:  see also Nos. 171, 425, 440,
        1706, 1961, 2642.


                            Drama


Comedy

1623    Doric Comedy (Epicharmus or Rhinthon?).    P. Heid.
        Siegmann 181 (inv. 416, verso) (ca. 250 B.C., Hi-
        beh; on the verso).  H. Lloyd-Jones, Gnomon 29
        (1957) 425:  M. Gigante, PP 13 (1958) 277-78, sug-
        gests Rhinthon, Amphitryon.

1624    Doric comedy (Epicharmus?).    P. Oxy. 25.2428 (II,
        Oxy.).

1625    Comedy (Aristophanes?).    P. Grenf. 2.12; P. Lit.
        Lond. 86 (Brit. Mus. inv. 695 A) (III).  Demiańc-
        zuk 94.  JAW 116.303.  F. Blass, Lit. Zentralbl.,
        1897, 334, suggests the Thesmophoriazusae Se-
        cundae; O. Crusius, Mél. Weil 81-90, prefers the
        Gerytades.  The editors suggested Euripides, Mel-
        nippe Desmotis.

1626    Old Comedy, with marginal scholia (Aristophanes?).
        P. Amh. 2.13 (III).  The scholia mention Magnes,
        the comic poet.  Demiańczuk 90-91.  Archiv 2.355.
        Weitzmann, Ill. RC, p. 119 and pl. 106.

1627    Old Comedy (Aristophanes?).    P. Oxy. 11.1403 (P.
        Princ., AM 9048) (V, Oxy.; pap. cod.).  Archiv
        7.143.

1628    Old Comedy (Aristophanes?).    PSI 7.846 (II-III?).
        Archiv 8.257; JAW 207.122, 234.120.

1629    Old Comedy (Aristophanes?).    P. Ryl. 3.483 (II).
        Archiv 14.118.

1630    Scholia on a comedy (Aristophanes?).    P. Oxy. 11.
        1402 (P. Princ., AM 9047) (V, Oxy.; pap. cod.)
        Archiv 7.143.  G. Zuntz, Byz. 13 (1938) 687-90.

1631    Old Comedy (Cratinus?).    P. Rain. 3.23 (inv. 29413)
        (IV-V; pap. cod.).  Archiv 14.118-19.  T. T. M.
        F. Pieters, Cratinus: Bijdrage tot de Geschiedenis
        der vroeg-attische Comedie (Leiden 1946) 97, sug-
        gests Cratinus.

1632    Old Comedy (Eupolis?).    P. Oxy. 6.863 (P. Cairo)
        (III, Oxy.).  Demiańczuk 117; Page, GLP 1, No.
        40 (under Eupolis, Demi); Schroeder, NCF 65-67.
        Archiv 6.232; JAW 174.179.

1633    Old Comedy: Fragment with Spartan words.    B.
        Snell, Hermes, Einzelschr. 5 (1937) 103-5 (P.
        Strassb. inv. Gr. 2345) (III B.C.?).  Archiv 7.
        257; JAW 207.123-24; New Chapters 3.164.  W.
        Croenert, Gött. Nachr., 1922, Heft 1.27-31 (ed.
        pr. of the first two fragments).

1634    Old Comedy.    PSI 2.143 (III, Oxy.; opisthograph roll
        or separate sheet?).  Archiv 7.143-44; JAW 174.
        245; New Chapters 3.164.

1635    Old Comedy (?).    P. Lit. Lond. 254 (Brit. Mus. inv.
        488 B) (III B.C.).

1636    Old (?) Comedy.    PSI 12.1281 (II, Oxy.).  Archiv 16.
        105.

1637    Old (?) Comedy.    PSI 14.1388 (II, Oxy.).  Ed. pr.:
        V. Bartoletti, SIFC, NS 27-28 (1956) 45-48.

1638    Old Comedy (or fragment of a political treatise?).
        P. Heid. Siegmann 182 (inv. 1119 a-b) (III B.C.,
        Hibeh; on the verso is No. 2337, a metrological
        text).  The editor sees trochaic tetrameters, and
        suggests Old Comedy; M. Gigante, Maia 9 (1957)
        68-74, regards the text as a fragment of a political
        treatise of the fifth century B.C., comparable to
        Ps.-Xenophon, Res Publica Atheniensium.

1639    Middle (?) Comedy (Alexis, Lemnia?).    P. Bad. 6.
        175 (I).  A. Koerte, Archiv 14.124, prefers New
        Comedy.

1640    Middle Comedy (Philiscus? Phrynichus?).    PSI 10.
        1175 (I).  The fragment mentions Sophocles, perhaps
        citing Oedipus Coloneus 892.  Ed. pr.: M. Norsa
        and G. Vitelli, BSAA 25, Suppl. (1930).  Page, GLP 1,
        No. 47.  Archiv 10.55-56; JAW 234.118-19, 263.
        6-7; M. Platnauer, New Chapters 3.164-66.  C.
        Gallavotti, Riv. Fil. 58 (1930) 209-15, and A. Koerte,
        Hermes 65 (1930) 472-76, and RE 19.2.2382, favor
        Philiscus, Dios gonai; G. Vitelli prefers Phryni-
        chus, Kronos; M. F. Galiano, Arbor 6 (1946) 135-36;
        M. Cervelli, Annali dell' Istituto Superiore "S.
        Chiara" di Napoli 3 (1951) 195-274 (inaccessible).

1641    Middle Comedy (Alexis?).    Wilamowitz, Sitzb. Berl.
        Akad., 1918, 743-47 (P. Berol. inv. 11771) (III B.C.;
        cart.).  Page, GLP 1, No. 48.  Archiv 7.144-45;
        JAW 195.172; New Chapters 3.166-67.  G. Vitale,
        Aeg. 2 (1921) 82-84; G. Norwood, Greek Comedy
        (London 1931) 56-58; G. Zuntz, Mnemos., Ser. 3.
        5 (1937) 53-61, revises the text; C. Ferrari, Dion.
        11 (1948) 177-84, on the interest of the fragment for
        the comic chorus; G. Zuntz, Aeg. 31 (1951) 329-31.

1642    New Comedy (Menander?: Misogynes, Karchedonios,
        or Proenkalon?).    P. Antin. 2.55 (IV, Antinoö-
        polis; parch. cod.).  E. G. Turner, Bull. Ryl.
        Libr. 42 (1959) 241-42 (first mention).  Reedited
        by H. J. Mette, in his ed. of the Dyscolus (Göt-
        tingen 1961[2]).  C. Préaux, Chr. Ég. 36 (1961)
        209-10; K. Latte, Gnomon 34 (1962) 152-54, rejects
        the Misogynes; T. Williams, Rh. Mus. 105 (1962)
        193-225, suggests Menander, Proenkalon.

1643    New Comedy (Menander, Cecryphalus?).    P. Hamb.
        120 (inv. 656) (III B.C.).  Archiv 16.104.  U. E.
        Paoli, Studi Calderini-Paribeni 2.117-25; D. del
        Corno, Dion. 36 (1962) 136-45, studies the allusion
        to the gynaikonomoi and interprets the sign "XNX"
        as a stage-direction.

1644    New Comedy (Menander?).    P. Harris 11 (inv. 174 b)
        (IV?; pap. cod.).  Archiv 13.104.

1645    New Comedy (Menander, Perinthia?).    P. Hibeh 2.
        181 (Brit. Mus. inv. 2954) (ca. 260-230 B.C.,
        Hibeh; cart.).  A. Barigazzi, Hermes 88 (1960)
        379-82, suggests Menander, Perinthia.

1646 New Comedy (Menander?). P. Oxy. 1.11; P. Lit.
Lond. 94 (Brit. Mus. inv. 740) (I-II, Oxy.). Demiańczuk 111-13; Page, GLP 1, No. 62; Schroeder,
NCF 38-42. Archiv 1.113; JAW 174-246; New Chapters 3.174. Wilamowitz, Gott. Anz., 1898, 694-95.

1647 New Comedy (Menander?). P. Oxy. 10.1238 (P. Cairo)
(I, Oxy.). Schroeder, NCF 56-57. Archiv 7.150.

1648 New Comedy (Menander?). P. Oxy. 10.1239 (P. Cairo)
(III, Oxy.). Schroeder, NCF 57-58. Archiv 7.149-
50.

1649 New Comedy (Menander?). P. Oxy. 15.1824 (III, Oxy.).
Archiv 7.151; JAW 207.121-22.

1650 New Comedy (Menander?). P. Oxy. 22.2329 (II-III,
Oxy.). Archiv 16.105. K. Latte, Gnomon 27 (1955)
497; A. Barigazzi, Athen. 44 (1956) 340-61, suggests Menander, Georgus; R. Stark, Rh. Mus. 100
(1957) 129-39.

1651 New Comedy (Menander?). P. Rain. 3.26 (inv.
30486) (I-II; sch. ex.). Archiv 14.125.

1652 New Comedy (Menander?). P. Ryl. 3.498 (III, Oxy.;
small pap. cod.).

1653 New Comedy (Menander?). PRIMI 1.8 (II, Tebtunis).
Archiv 13.102-3.

1654 New Comedy (Menander?). PSI 1.99 (II, Oxy.).
Schroeder, NCF 49-51. Archiv 6.232; JAW 174.
244-45. G. Coppola, Aeg. 4 (1923) 49-56.

1655 New Comedy (Menander?). A. Wifstrand, Årsb.,
Lund, 1934-35, 58-59 (No. 4) (I-II). Archiv 13.
103-4.

1656 New Comedy (Menander?). P. Jouguet, BCH 30
(1906) 103-23 (P. Sorbonne inv. 72) (III B.C.,
Ghoran; cart.). Demiańczuk 99-102; Page, GLP
1, No. 66; Schroeder, NCF 20-29. Archiv 6.229;
JAW 174.239-40, 195.187-88, 207.153-54. G. Capovilla, BSAA 4.17 (1919) 193-205, favors Menander.

1657 New Comedy (Menander?). P. Jouguet, BCH 30
(1906) 123-49 (P. Sorbonne inv. 72) (III-II B.C.,
Ghoran; cart.). Demiańczuk 104-10; Page, GLP
1, Nos. 65, 72; Schroeder, NCF 29-38, 63-65.
Archiv 6.230; JAW 174.240-41, 195.187-88; M.
Platnauer, New Chapters 3.172-73. G. Capovilla,
BSAA 4.17 (1919) 205-29, suggests Menander, Dis
exapaton.

1658 New Comedy (Menander?). Mentioned by Schubart,
Einführung 482 (P. Berol. inv. 13281) (III-IV).

1659 New Comedy (Menander? Apollodorus?). P. Antin.
1.15; P. Schubart 23 (III-IV, Antinoöpolis; pap.
cod.). The end of a play or act, followed by a list
of characters and the beginning of a new (?) play
or act. Archiv 16.105. T. B. L. Webster, CR,
NS 2 (1952) 57-60, attributes both fragments to
Act IV of the same comedy, and prefers Apollodorus to Menander; W. Morel, Philol. 107 (1963)
145-50, reedits and cites evidence favoring Menander.

1660 New Comedy (Philemon?). P. Ryl. 1.16 (a); P. Bad.
6.180; P. Hibeh 1.5; P. Lit. Lond. 91 (Brit. Mus.
inv. 1823); P. Heid. Siegmann 184 (inv. 406)
(III B.C., Hibeh; cart.; text on recto, No. 1220
on verso). Bassi, MIG, No. 150, tav. LIV (P. Ryl.
16); Norsa, SLG, tav. 10 c (ditto). Demiańczuk
98-99; Schroeder, NCF 11-29; Page, GLP 1, No.
64. Archiv 6.227-28, 14.121-24; JAW 174.242-43;
New Chapters 3.176-77. F. Leo, Hermes 41 (1906)
629-32; F. Blass, Rh. Mus. 62 (1907) 102-7, and
W. E. J. Kuiper, Mnemos., Supplementum 2 (1940)
122-25, hold that P. Hibeh 5 is from a play by Philemon, the original of Plautus, Aulularia; W. E. J.
Kuiper, Mnemos., Ser. 3.9 (1940-41) 44-50, studies
P. Hibeh 5 with P. Petrie 1.4 (see No. 1662); H.
Oellacher, Gnomon 16 (1940) 509-10; M. F. Galiano,
Arbor 6 (1946) 145-46; M. Treu, Philol. 102 (1958)
228-39, on the role of the mageiros in P. Heid.
Siegmann 184. Nos. 1660 and 1661 are not from the
same papyrus.

1661 New Comedy (Philemon?). P. Grenf. 2.8 (b); P.
Lit. Lond. 91 (Brit. Mus. inv. 694) (III B.C., Hibeh?).
Page, GLP 1, No. 64; Schroeder, NCF 11-20. New
Chapters 3.176-77. Not from the same papyrus as
No. 1660; see G. A. Gerhard, P. Bad. 6.180, and
Archiv 14.121-24.

1662 New Comedy (Philemon?). P. Petrie 1.4 (1); P.
Lit. Lond. 90 (Brit. Mus. inv. 487 A) (III B.C.,
Gurob; cart.). Demiańczuk 113-14; Schroeder,
NCF 11-20, holds that this text is from the same
play as No. 1661.

1663 New Comedy (Menander? Philemon?). PSI 10.1176
(I; on the verso of accounts). Ed. pr.: G. Vitelli,
SIFC, NS 7 (1929) 235-42. Norsa, SLG, tav. 11 a.
Page, GLP 1, No. 61. Archiv 10.56-61; JAW 234.
117-18, 263.7; New Chapters 3.174-75. A. Vogliano,
Gnomon 6 (1930) 113-15, favors Menander; A. Koerte,
Hermes 72 (1937) 73-77, suggests Philemon, ex-
cluding Menander on metrical grounds; M. F.
Galiano, Arbor 6 (1946) 142-44, believes that this
fragment is from the same play as No. 1668.

1664 New Comedy (or Old Comedy: Aristophanes?). P.
Erl. 6 (inv. 97) (V; pap. cod.). Archiv 16.105.
W. Morel, Aeg. 42 (1962) 133-35, prefers Aristo-
phanes.

1665 New Comedy (?): a prose paraphrase. P. Univ. Giss.
4.41 (inv. 302) (II, Fayum?). Gundel 12.

1666 New Comedy. P. Hibeh 1.6; P. Lit. Lond. 89 (Brit.
Mus. inv. 1824) (III B.C., Hibeh; cart.). Roberts,
GLH, pl. 2a. Demiańczuk 102-4; Page, GLP 1,
No. 63; Schroeder, NCF 3-11. Archiv 6.228; JAW
174.244.

1667 New Comedy (?). P. Lond. 3.691 (b); P. Lit. Lond.
93 (Brit. Mus. inv. 691 B) (III B.C.). Line 4, as
read by Croenert, refers to Sophilus, perhaps the
writer of Middle Comedy; line 9 refers to Damoxenus (?), a comic poet (or a mageiros?). Archiv
10.61.

1668    New Comedy.   P. Rain. 3.22 (inv. 29811) (cf. ibid.
        4, p. 136) (III B.C.).   Archiv 14.119-21.  W. Schu-
        bart, Gnomon 16 (1940) 43.

1669    New Comedy.   PSI 6.723 (IV-V, Oxy.; pap. cod.?).
        Archiv 7.151; JAW 207.122.

1670    New Comedy.   PSI 7.847 (I-II?).  Archiv 8.257-58;
        JAW 207.122, 234.120.  Weitzmann, Anc. Bk. Ill.,
        p. 64 and fig. 72 (a few traces of a miniature).

1671    A prologue from New Comedy.  G. Kaibel, Gott.
        Nachr., 1899, 549-55 (P. Strassb. inv. Gr. 53)
        (I). Demiańczuk 96-97; Page, GLP 1, No. 60;
        Schroeder, NCF 45-48.  Archiv 1.514; JAW 174.
        238.  R. Reitzenstein, Hermes 35 (1900) 622-26;
        H. Weil, Rev. Ét. Gr. 13 (1900) 427-31; A. Oli-
        vieri, Riv. Fil. 30 (1902) 435-38; G. Rambelli,
        SIFC, NS 19 (1942) 35-41; O. Bianco, Riv. CCM
        3 (1961) 97.

1672    Comedy.   P. Antin. 1.16 (III-IV, Antinoöpolis; pap.
        cod.). Archiv 16.105.  W. Morel, Philol. 107
        (1963) 151, conjectures that this belongs to the same
        comedy as P. Antin. 15 (see No. 1659).

1673    Comedy.   BKT 5.2.113-14 (inv. 9941) (I B.C.; cart.).
        Demiańczuk 97-98; Page, GLP 1, No. 67; Schroe-
        der, NCF 43-45.  Archiv 6.231; JAW 174.238-39.
        J. M. Edmonds, Mnemos. 2 (1935) 51-54.

1674    Comedy.   P. Hibeh 1.12 (Bodleian Libr., Gr. class.
        g.55 (P)) (III B.C., Hibeh; cart.).  Schroeder,
        NCF 51-52.  Archiv 6.231; JAW 174.244.

1675    Comedy.   P. Lond. 2.484 (d); P. Lit. Lond. 88
        (Brit. Mus. inv. 484 D) (II).  Archiv 10.61.

1676    Comedy.   P. Lit. Lond. 92 (Brit. Mus. inv. 2294)
        (III-II B.C.).  Archiv 10.61.

1677    Comedy.   P. Oxy. 1.10 (Yale Univ. Libr.) (II-III,
        Oxy.).  Demiańczuk 110-11; Page, GLP 1, No. 68;
        Schroeder, NCF 48-49.  Archiv 1.113.

1678    Comedy (?).   P. Oxy. 3.428 (Houghton Libr., Har-
        vard Univ.) (II-III, Oxy.).  Archiv 3.278; JAW
        147.121.

1679    Comedy.   P. Oxy. 3.429 (Manchester Mus.) (III,
        Oxy.).  Schroeder, NCF 52-53.  Archiv 3.278.

1680    Comedy.   P. Oxy. 3.430 (Houghton Libr., Harvard
        Univ.) (II-III, Oxy.; on the verso of accounts).
        Schroeder, NCF 53.  Archiv 3.279.

1681    Comedy.   P. Oxy. 3.431 (Houghton Libr., Harvard
        Univ.) (II-III, Oxy.).  Schroeder, NCF 54.  Archiv
        3.279.

1682    Comedy.   P. Oxy. 3.432 (Univ.-Bibl., Graz, inv.
        I.1929) (III, Oxy.; on the verso of accounts).  Ar-
        chiv 3.279.

1683    Comedy.   P. Oxy. 4.677 (Wellesley Coll.) (I-II, Oxy.).
        Demiańczuk 116-17; Page, GLP 1, No. 70; Schroe-
        der, NCF 54-55.  Archiv 3.486.

1684    Comedy.   P. Oxy. 4.678 (Wellesley Coll.) (II, Oxy.).
        Schroeder, NCF 59.  Archiv 3.486.

1685    Comedy.   P. Oxy. 6.862 (P. Cairo) (III, Oxy.).
        Schroeder, NCF 55-56.  Archiv 6.232.

1686    Comedy (?).   P. Oxy. 11.1400 (P. Cairo) (II-III, Oxy.;
        on the verso of a tax list).  Archiv 7.151.

1687    Comedy.   P. Oxy. 15.1825 (V?, Oxy.; pap. cod.).
        Archiv 7.150-51; JAW 207.122.

1688    Comedy.   P. Ryl. 1.16 (II-III, Theadelphia).  Roberts,
        GLH, p. 22b.  Schroeder, NCF 58-59.  Archiv 6.
        232.

1689    Comedy.   P. Ryl. 3.484 (I-II; on the verso of ac-
        counts).  Archiv 14.124-25.

1690    Comedy (?).   P. Ryl. 3.515 (III B.C.; cart.).

1691    Comedy (?).   P. Schubart 20 (III-IV; on the verso of
        a document; sch. ex.?).  Archiv 16.104.

1692    Comedy.   P. Schubart 24 (III B.C.).  Refers to
        Hesiod, Opera 765-802 (?).

1693    Comedy.   P. Schubart 25 (I, Oxy.; on the verso of a
        document).

1694    Argument of a comedy (?).   P. Schubart 26 (II-III;
        on the verso of a document).  Archiv 16.105.

1695    Comedy.   P. Tebt. 3.693 (III B.C., Tebtunis; cart.;
        on the verso of a document).  Page, GLP 1, No. 49.
        Archiv 11.265-66; JAW 263.8.

1696    Comedy (?).   B. Snell, Hermes, Einzelschr. 5 (1937)
        102 (P. Strassb. inv. Gr. 1348) (?).

1697    Comedy.   P. Viereck, Racc. Lumbroso 254-55 (P.
        Berol. inv. 12310) (III B.C., Philadelphia; from
        the same ostracon as No. 1498).

1698    Hellenistic Comedy (?) (Encomium of an officer).
        W. Croenert, Gött. Nachr., 1922, 31-32 (P. Strassb.
        WG 307, verso) (II-I B.C.?; from the verso of the
        same roll as Nos. 170, 426, 1349, 1592, 1735).
        Page, GLP 1, No. 111.  Archiv 7.257; JAW 207.
        124;  New Chapters 3.178.

        Comedy: see also Nos. 1456, 1567, 1574-75, 1577,
        1580, 1590, 1605, 1726, 1729, 1741, 1966, 2121,
        2289, 2605, 2642, 2721, 2819, 2860, 2909.


Tragedy

1699    Tragedy (Aeschylus?).   P. Heid. Siegmann 186 (inv.
        420 a-b) (ca. 200 B.C., Hibeh?).  Galiano, Aesch.
        102.  M. Gigante, PP 11 (1956) 449-56, suggests
        Aeschylus, Danaïdes.

1700    Tragedy (Aeschylus, Niobe or Phorkides? Sophocles,
        Niobe or Tantalos?).   P. Oxy. 2.213 (Yale Univ.
        Libr.) (II, Oxy.; on the verso of an account; sch.
        ex.).  Galiano, Aesch. 83-84, gives the history of
        the attributions.  Jebb-Pearson 2, Nos. 574-75,

assigned to the Tantalos; Page, GLP 1, No. 23. Archiv 1.510; JAW 125.182-83, 259.134-37. N. Wecklein, Berl. Phil. Woch. 20 (1900) 508, favors Aeschylus, Niobe; C. Robert, Hermes 49 (1914) 624-26, prefers Aeschylus, Phorkides; K. Reinhardt, ibid. 69 (1934) 233-61, prefers Aeschylus, Niobe, and studies the play as a whole.

1701 Tragedy (Aeschylus?). PSI 11.1210 bis (II, Oxy.; in the same hand as Nos. 27, 29, 36, etc.).

1702 Tragedy (Sophocles, Iphigeneia?). P. Petrie 1.3 (2); P. Lit. Lond. 79 (Brit. Mus. inv. 486 B) (III-II B.C.). Fritsch, No. 8. JAW 259.129-31; New Chapters 3.155.

1703 Tragedy (Sophocles or Euripides, Phrixos?). G. Vitelli, Rev. Eg., NS 1 (1919) 47-49 (PSI?) (II-III). Page, GLP 1, No. 32, queries the attributions; A. W. Pickard-Cambridge, New Chapters 3.97-100, is also sceptical. A. Koerte, Archiv 10.49-50, considers the attribution to Euripides, Phrixos, almost certain; JAW 277.70. A. Vogliano, Riv. Fil. 54 (1926) 206-17, ibid. 55 (1927) 79, suggests Euripides, Phrixos; Wilamowitz, ibid., prefers the Phrixos of Sophocles; W. Schadewaldt, Hermes 63 (1928) 1-14.

1704 Tragedy (Euripides?: Archelaos or Alkmene?). P. Hamb. 119 (inv. 648) (III-II B.C.). Archiv 16.103.

1705 Choral lyric or monody from tragedy (Euripides?). P. Rain. 3.18 (inv. 29774) (cf. ibid. 4, p. 136) (II-III, Fayum). Page, PMG 930. Archiv 14.117-18.

1706 Two tragic texts (from an anthology?) with musical notation. S. Eitrem, L. Amundsen, and R. P. Winnington-Ingram, SO 31 (1955) 1-87 (P. Oslo inv. 1413 A-B) (ca. A.D. 80-120, Oxy.?). A (lines 1-15) = anapaests, B (lines 15-19) = trimeters. Winnington-Ingram, op. cit. 29-87, studies the music, comparing it with that of the other extant musical texts. Pöhlmann, GMF 27, 42-43. A. M. Dale, Lustrum 2 (1957) 8; R. P. Winnington-Ingram, ibid. 3 (1958) 7-8; V. Pappalardo, Dion., NS 22 (1959) 220-34; G. B. Pighi, Aeg. 39 (1959) 280-89.

1707 Fragment of an historical tragedy: Gyges and Candaules. P. Oxy. 23.2382 (with bibl.) (II-III, Oxy.). Ed. pr.: E. Lobel, Proc. Brit. Acad. 35 (1949) 207-16. Phrynichus, suggested by the editor, is now generally rejected. Archiv 16.104. M. F. Galiano, Est. Clás. 1 (1950) 119; K. Latte, Eranos 48 (1950) 136-41; A. Lesky, Anz. AW 3 (1950) 216-17; P. Maas, Gnomon 22 (1950) 142-43; D. L. Page, CQ 44 (1950) 125; idem, A New Chapter in the History of Greek Tragedy (Inaugural Lecture, Cambridge 1951); R. Cantarella, Dion., NS 15 (1952) 3-31, thinks of a versified novella of the Hellenistic age; P. Chantraine, Rev. Ét. Gr. 65 (1952), pp. XV-XVI; M. Gigante, PP 7 (1952) 5-17, suggests Lycophron; J. C. Kamerbeek, Mnemos., Ser. 4.5 (1952) 108-15, thinks of a Hellenistic tragedy; V. Martin, Mus. Helv. 9 (1952) 1-9; A. Traversa, GIF 5 (1952) 169-70; J. T. Kakridis, Hellen. 12 (1952-53) 1-14, 372, regards the fragment as post-Herodotean; H. Lloyd-Jones, Proceedings of the Cambridge Philological Society 182 (1952-53) 33 ff.

(inaccessible); I. Cazzaniga, PP 8 (1953) 381-98; A. Lesky, Hermes 81 (1953) 1-10, compares the technique with that of Ezechiel tragicus, Exagoge; T. B. L. Webster, Fifty Years Cl. Schol. 75; A. Raubitschek, Classical Weekly 48 (1954-55) 48-50 (text, bibl., discussion); J. A. Davison, CR, NS 5 (1955) 129-32; J. A. S. Evans, Athen. 43 (1955) 333-36, argues for a post-Herodotean dating; M. Gigante, Dion., NS 18 (1955) 7-8, favors Lycophron; E. Bickel, Rh. Mus. 100 (1957) 141-52; Q. Cataudella, Studi Calderini-Paribeni, 2.103-16, argues that the author was some obscure poet earlier than Herodotus' time; Lesky, GGL 307, 681; A. Raubitschek, Rh. Mus. 100 (1957) 139-40, suggests Ion of Chios.

1708 Tragedy (post-Classical?). P. Hibeh 1.4; P. Grenf. 2.1; P. Lit. Lond. 80 (Brit. Mus. inv. 688 + 1822) (III B.C., Hibeh; cart.). Arnim, SE 38-40; Page, GLP 1, No. 28. A. W. Pickard-Cambridge, New Chapters 3.154, observes that the stage direction chorou melos "dates the play later than the fifth century." Archiv 5.570; JAW 147.105-7; Lesky, GGL 582. O. Rossbach, Berl. Phil. Woch. 19 (1899) 1630-31, thinks of Sophocles, Chryses.

1709 Tragedy (post-Classical?). P. Lond. 2.186, verso; P. Lit. Lond. 77 (Brit. Mus. inv. 186, verso) (II-III; on the verso of No. 2402). D. L. Page, Euripides: Medea (Oxford 1938), p. xxxii, note 6, rejects the attribution to Neophron; A. W. Pickard-Cambridge, New Chapters 3.152-53. W. Croenert, Archiv 3 (1906) 1-5, suggests Neophron, Medea; JAW 147.110-12; S. Eitrem, Vid. Forh., Christiania, 1906, Avh. 10, 3-7; S. Mekler, Philol. 70 (1911) 492-98.

1710 Tragedy (Antiphon, Nicomachus, Sositheus, Sophocles?). E. Lobel, Greek Poetry and Life: Essays Presented to Gilbert Murray ... (Oxford 1936) 295-98 (Bodleian Libr., sine numero?) (I). Page, GLP 1, No. 30. Archiv 13.100-2; A. von Blumenthal, JAW 277.62-64, suggests Sophocles, Polyxene; W. Morel, Phil. Woch. 57 (1937) 558-60, suggests the play by Antiphon imitated by Ennius in his Andromacha Aechmalotis; J. C. Kamerbeek, Mnemos., Ser. 3.6 (1938) 335-49, suggests a Hellenistic tragedy by Sositheus or Nicomachus.

1711 Hellenistic (?) tragedy: Hercules Oetaeus. P. Oxy. 27.2454 (II, Oxy.).

1712 Tragedy (an Iphigenia at Aulis?). P. Lit. Lond. 78 (Brit. Mus. inv. 2560) (II). New Chapters 3.154-55. A. Koerte, Archiv 10.53-54, thinks of a post-classical composition.

1713 Tragedy: Fragment of a Medea. P. Schubart 18 (II; on the verso of a document?).

1714 Tragedy: Commentary on an Oedipus (?). P. Rain. 1.24 (inv. 29779) (IV-V; pap. cod.). Archiv 11. 259-60.

1715 Tragedy: Fragment of a Philoctetes (?). P. Schubart 19 (II B.C., Hermupolis). Archiv 16.104.

1716    Tragedy.   P. Aberdeen 115 (II-III, Fayum?).   Ed. pr.:
        E. O. Winstedt, CQ 1 (1907) 262.  JAW 147.122.

1717    Tragedy.   P. Grenf. 2.6 (b);  P. Lit. Lond. 83 (Brit.
        Mus. inv. 691 A) (III B.C., Hibeh;  cart.).

1718    Tragedy.   P. Grenf. 2.6 (c);  P. Lit. Lond. 82 (Brit.
        Mus. inv. 690 B) (III B.C., Hibeh;  cart.).

1719    Tragedy.   P. Hibeh 1.10 (Bodleian Libr., Gr. class.
        f.79 (P)) (III B.C., Hibeh;  cart.).  JAW 147.107-8.

1720    Tragedy (?).   P. Hibeh 2.178 (Brit. Mus. inv. 2951)
        (III B.C., Hibeh;  cart.).

1721    Tragedy (?).   P. Lond. 5.1813;  P. Lit. Lond. 84
        (Brit. Mus. inv. 1707) (II).  Archiv 10.54.

1722    Tragedy.   P. Oxy. 4.676 (Wellesley Coll.) (III, Oxy.).
        Archiv 3.485; JAW 147.121.

1723    Tragedy (?).   P. Oxy. 6.861 (Newton Theological
        Institute) (III, Oxy.).  Archiv 5.572.

1724    Tragedy.   P. Oxy. 15.1823 (I B.C., Oxy.).  Archiv
        7.142.

1725    Tragedy (?).   P. Rain. 3.20 (inv. 29423) (V, Fayum;
        pap. cod.).  Archiv 14.118.

1726    Tragedy (or comedy?).   P. Ross. Georg. 5.1 (Col-
        lection of G. Zereteli, Tiflis) (I).

1727    Tragedy (?).   P. Ryl. 3.495 (II, Oxy.).  Archiv 14.
        118.

1728    Tragedy (?).   P. Ryl. 3.496 (II B.C.;  cart.).

1729    Tragedy (or comedy?).   PSI 2.134 (I-II, Oxy.).  A.
        Koerte, Archiv 7.142, thinks of a parodic passage
        from a comedy.

1730    Tragedy (or gnomic verses?).   PSI 2.136 (II).  A.
        Koerte, Archiv 7.119-20, prefers "paränetische
        Iamben."

1731    Tragedy (or mime?).   PSI 2.149, recto (IV-V, Hermu-
        polis Magna; text on recto, No. 1833 on verso).  O.
        Crusius, Herondae Mimiambi (Lipsiae 1914⁵) 122,
        regards the text as a mime.

1732    Tragedy.   PSI 2.150 (III, Oxy.; on the verso).  Ar-
        chiv 7.142.

1733    Tragedy.   M. Norsa and G. Vitelli, BSAA 28 (1933)
        121 (evidently not published in PSI) (II?, Oxy.).

1734    Tragedy.   W. Croenert, Gött. Nachr., 1922, 27 (P.
        Strassb. inv. Gr. 1917) (II-III).  Archiv 7.257.

1735    Tragedy (?).   B. Snell, Hermes, Einzelschr. 5 (1937)
        92 (II-I B.C.?; cart.; from the same composite
        roll as Nos. 170, 426, 1349, 1592, 1698).  Archiv
        7.257.

1736    Tragedy: Scholia on a tragedy (?).   PSI 12.1287 (II).
        The text mentions Sophocles, Nauplios Pyrkaeus,
        and Philostratus of Alexandria, Peri tôn tou Sopho-
        kleous klopôn.  Archiv 16.117.

1737    Tragedy: List of scenes from the Trojan and Theban
        cycles (?).   O. Bodl. 2.2171 (inv. 2950) (II, Ele-
        phantine;  ostr.).

1738    Tragedy: Drawing of a scene from a tragedy (?).
        A. Hartmann, Festschrift für Georg Leidinger ...
        (München 1930) 103-8 (P. Monac. inv. 128) (IV; a
        leaf of pap.; drawing, but no writing, on the recto,
        a document of saec. VI on the verso).

        Tragedy: see also Nos. 171, 237, 246, 1602, 1604,
            1915-16, 1964, 2170, 2868.

Satyr Plays

1739    Satyr play: Fragments (Sophocles: Polyidos vel
        manteis, and other plays?).   P. Oxy. 8.1083,
        27.2453 (Cambridge Univ. Libr., MS. Add. 5895)
        (II, Oxy.).  P. Oxy. 2453 now adds fragments from
        Sophocles, fab. cit.  The references which follow
        apply to P. Oxy. 1083.  Bassi, MIG, No. 113, tav.
        XL; Schubart, Gr. Pal., Abb. 74.  Hunt, TGFP,
        No. 7; Page, GLP 1, No. 31; Steffen, Sat. Gr.
        Fr. 146-50.  Archiv 5.570;  New Chapters 3.101-2.
        P. Maas, Berl. Phil. Woch. 32 (1912) 1426-29,
        suggests Sophocles; A. Koerte, Neue Jahrb. 39
        (1917) 290, suggests Ion of Chios or Achaeus;  V.
        Steffen, Eos 41 (1940-46) 114-22, suggests Sopho-
        cles, Achilleos erastai.

1740    Satyr play (?).   P. Hibeh 2.179 (Brit. Mus. inv. 2952)
        (ca. 280-240 B.C., Hibeh;  cart.).  The text on the
        verso possibly quotes Homer, Od. xix.471.

1741    Satyr play (or Old Comedy?).   P. Iand. 5.76 (inv.
        694) (I).  Gundel 13.  Archiv 10.54-55.

1742    Satyr play (?).   P. Ibscher 1 (P. Hamb., pp. 127-28)
        (I B.C.).  Archiv 16.104.

Mimes

1743    Verse mime ("Alexandrian Erotic Fragment").   P.
        Grenf. 1.1 (cf. ibid. 2, "Appendix," pp. 209-17);
        P. Lit. Lond. 50 (Brit. Mus. inv. 605) (II B.C.,
        Thebaïd; on the verso of contracts).  O. Crusius,
        Herondae Mimiambi (Lipsiae 1914⁵) 124-27;  Man-
        teuffel, Opusc., No. 18; Powell, CA 177-80, and
        New Chapters 1.54-55; Winter, LLP 215-16.  JAW
        104.144-45.  O. Crusius, Philol. 55 (1896) 353-84;
        Wilamowitz, Gött. Nachr., 1896, 209-32; W. Voll-
        graff, Mnemos. 50 (1922) 86; N. Russo, AR 7
        (1926) 286-88; M. Gigante, PP 2 (1947) 300-8.

1744    Verse mime: Lament for a cock.   P. Oxy. 2.219
        (Yale Univ. Libr.) (I, Oxy.).  O. Crusius, Heron-
        dae Mimiambi (Lipsiae 1914⁵) 131-33; Manteuffel,
        Opusc., No. 23 (bibl.); Page, GLP 1, No. 75;
        Powell, CA 182-84.  Archiv 1.518;  New Chapters
        1.56.  W. Croenert, Rh. Mus. 64 (1909) 443-44;
        H. W. Prescott, CP 5 (1910) 158-68, on the meter.

1745 Mime (the Chariton mime) and farce. P. Oxy. 3.
413 (Bodleian Libr., Gr. class. b.4 (P)) (II, Oxy.).
O. Crusius, Herondae Mimiambi (Lipsiae 1914[5])
101-9; G. Knoke, De Charitio Mimo Oxyrhynchio
(Kiel 1908); Manteuffel, Opusc., Nos. 13-14; Page,
GLP 1, Nos. 76-77. Lesky, GGL 735-36; New
Chapters 1.120-23, 2.215-22; Winter, LLP 236-37.
E. Hultzsch, Hermes 39 (1904) 307-11; S. Sudhaus,
ibid. 41 (1906) 247-77; L. D. Barnett, JEA 12 (1926)
13-15; H. Lyngby, Eranos 26 (1928) 52-58; G.
Manteuffel, Eos 32 (1929) 40-42; idem, Hermes
65 (1930) 123-25; A. Swiderek, Eos 47 (1954) 68-70.

1746 Verse mime. T. Reinach, Mél. Perrot 291-96; P.
Rein. 1, pp. 5-12, 239 (P. Sorbonne inv. 2223)
(II-I B.C., Thebes; ostr.). O. Crusius, Heron-
dae Mimiambi (Lipsiae 1914[5]) 137-38; Manteuffel,
Opusc., No. 22; Page, GLP 1, No. 74; Powell,
CA 181-82. Archiv 3.280. Wilamowitz, Gött. Anz.,
1905, 715-17.

1747 Verse mime or dramatic lyric (?). P. Lit. Lond.
52 (Brit. Mus. inv. 2208) (III, Oxy.). Heitsch,
GDRK, fr. IX; Manteuffel, Opusc., No. 21; Page,
GLP 1, No. 79. Archiv 10.62-63; JAW 230.152-54.
E. Wuest and W. Croenert, Philol. 84 (1928) 153-
72; W. Schubart, Gnomon 4 (1928) 398-99; A. D.
Knox, JEA 15 (1929) 140-41; G. Manteuffel, Eos 32
(1929) 33-40.

1748 Libretto for a mime (?). P. Giss. 3 (inv. 20) (A.D.
117, Apollinopolis). Fourteen lines, in verse and
prose, celebrating the accession of Hadrian. The
text was injured by damp in 1945. Gundel 19. Ed.
pr.: E. Kornemann, Klio 7 (1907) 278-88. Roberts,
GLH, pl. 15a. Heitsch, GDRK, fr. XII; Manteuffel,
Opusc., No. 12. Archiv 5.249; JAW 230.152. R.
Reitzenstein, Neue Jahrb. 21 (1908) 365-67, suggests
the proclamation of a festival; W. Croenert, Racc.
Lumbroso 460-70, prefers a mime.

Verse mimes: see also Nos. 1607, 1731, 1922, 1930.

For prose mimes, see Nos. 2434-37.

## Elegy and Epigram

1749 Elegy: Fragments (Callinus?). B. Snell, Hermes,
Einzelschr. 5 (1937) 93-97 (P. Strassb. WG 2340)
(III B.C.; cart.?). Ed. pr.: W. Croenert, Rh.
Mus. 68 (1913) 596-602. Diehl, Anth. Lyr. 1[3].
139-41. Archiv 13.87.

1750 Fragments of early elegy (Simonides?). P. Oxy.
22.2327 (II, Oxy.). Galiano, LG 62. Archiv 16.
88. A. Barigazzi, Mus. Helv. 20 (1963) 61-76,
argues for Simonides.

1751 Hellenistic elegy (Musaeus?). Wilamowitz, Sitzb.
Berl. Akad., 1918, 736-39 (P. Hamb. inv. 381)
(III B.C.; cart.). P. Hamb., pp. 126-27 (bibl.
and notes). Diehl, Anth. Lyr. 2[1].236-37; Page,
GLP 1, No. 110; Powell, CA 131-32. Archiv 7.
122-23; JAW 191.51; New Chapters 1.106-7. J. U.
Powell, CR 33 (1919) 90, suggests Musaeus of
Ephesus; idem, JHS 45 (1925) 143; M. Calderini
Mondini, Aeg. 2 (1921) 78-79; A. Momigliano,

BFC 36 (1929) 151-55; V. Bartoletti, SIFC, NS 34
(1962) 25 ff.; W. Peek, Maia, NS 15 (1963) 199-210;
W. Richter, ibid. 93-117, reedits, suggesting that
the poem was addressed by Musaeus to Attalus I
of Pergamon.

1752 A Hellenistic (?) epigram on the daughters of Lycambes.
G. W. Bond, Hermathena 80 (1952) 3-11 (Trinity
Coll. Libr., Dublin, inv. 193 a) (III B.C.). Iambic
tetrameters, not elegiacs. Evidently not by Archilochus. Galiano, LG 67-68. Treu, Archil. 130,
251-52. Archiv 16.89. W. Peek, Philol. 99 (1955)
46-49.

1753 Fragment of a Hellenistic elegy (?). P. Schubart 13
(II B.C.; ostr.). The subject, a victory in a box-
ing match (?). Archiv 16.91.

1754 Alexandrian elegy. P. Iand. 5.78 (inv. 515) (II, Fayum?). Gundel 14. Archiv 10.42-43. A. Barigazzi,
Maia 3 (1950) 25, rejects Parthenius and Euphorion
in favor of "un epigono abbastanza tardo."

1755 Alexandrian elegy: Description of the Golden Age
(Nicander?). P. Oxy. 1.14 (Edinburgh Univ. Libr.)
(II, Oxy.). Pfeiffer, Callim. 1, p. 498, favors
Nicander over Callimachus; Powell, CA 130-31.
E. Lobel, on P. Oxy. 19.2221 (see No. 1327), and
A. S. F. Gow and A. F. Scholfield, Nicander: The
Poems and Poetical Fragments (Cambridge 1953)
220, adduce evidence in favor of Nicander. Archiv
1.113; JAW 133.165-66; New Chapters 1.107. Wila-
mowitz, Gött. Anz., 1898, 695. Lines 2-3 refer
to Homer, Il. vi.234 ff.

1756 Elegy: On Meleager and the Calydonian boar. M.
Papathomopoulos, Recherches Pap. 2 (1962) 99-111
(P. Sorbonne inv. 2254) (II B.C.; cart.). (In-
formation from A. Bataille).

1757 Elegy. P. Ryl. 3.499 (II B.C.; cart.). Archiv 14.
110.

1758 Epigram on Homer's birthplace. BKT 5.1.78-79
(inv. 4758) (II B.C., Thebes; ostr.; sch. ex.).
Schubart, PBG, tab. 8 a. Wilcken, Gr. Ostr. 2.
1148.

1759 Epigram on Agesilaus. O. Bodl. 2.2172 (inv. 930)
(I B.C.; ostr.; sch. ex.). Ed. pr.: B. P. Grenfell, JEA 5 (1918) 16-17. Manteuffel, Opusc., No.
41. New Chapters 1.108.

1760 Epigram on Agesilaus (a duplicate of No. 1759). O.
Bodl. 2.2173 (inv. 1205) (I B.C.; ostr.; sch. ex.).
B. P. Grenfell, JEA 5 (1918) 17, note (first men-
tion).

1761 Two epitaphs for Zenon's hunting dog, Tauron. C.
C. Edgar, Ann. Serv. 19 (1920) 101-4; P. Cairo
Zen. 4.59532 (III B.C., Philadelphia). New Pal.
Soc., Ser. 2, vol. 2, pl. 116; Norsa, SLG, tav. 2.
G. Herrlinger, Antike Tier-Epikedien (Tübingen
1929) 52-53; Manteuffel, Opusc., "Appendix" No.
2; Page, GLP 1, No. 109. Archiv 6.453-54, 7.80;
New Chapters 1.107-8. C. Gorteman, Chr. Ég.
32 (1957) 116-18.

1762   Epigram in honor of Augustus at Actium.   F. G.
       Kenyon, Rev. Phil. 19 (1895) 177-79;  P. Lit. Lond.
       62 (Brit. Mus. inv. 256) (I, Fayum?; from a com-
       posite roll containing also documents and, on the
       verso, No. 2515).  Page, GLP 1, No. 113.  Archiv
       1.117;  New Chapters 3.189-90.  H. Weil, Rev. Phil.
       19 (1895) 180-81;  R. Keydell, Hermes 69 (1934) 420-
       25;  L. Alfonsi, Aeg. 30 (1950) 72-76;  C. I. Gatti,
       PP 7 (1952) 149-57;  L. Alfonsi, Aevum 28 (1954)
       552-54;  I. Opelt, Rh. Mus. 103 (1960) 46.

1763   Epigram on a statue.  BKT 5.1.77-78 (inv. 9812) (III
       B.C.).  Page, GLP 1, No. 108.  Archiv 5.547;  JAW
       178.202.

1764   Epigram on the tragedian Philicus.   Wilamowitz,
       Sitzb. Berl. Akad., 1912, 547-50 (P. Hamb. inv.
       312) (III B.C.;  cart.).  P. Hamb., p. 126 (bibl.
       and notes).  Page, GLP 1, No. 106;  F. Schramm,
       Tragicorum Graecorum Hellenisticae Quae Dicitur
       Aetatis Fragmenta ... (Münster 1929) 20.  Archiv
       5.547;  JAW 178.202;  New Chapters 1.107, 3.200.

1765   Epigram: Conundrum.   H. Diels, Sitzb. Berl. Akad.,
       1898, 857-58;  P. Lit. Lond. 63 (Egyptian Depart-
       ment, Brit. Mus., inv. 29527) (II-III;  waxed tablet;
       sch. ex.).  Ziebarth 2, No. 20.

1766   Votive epigram to Pan Euagros, as the Egyptian Min.
       F. W. Householder, Jr., and D. W. Prakken, TAPA
       76 (1945) 108-16 (Collection of C. J. Kraemer, Jr.,
       New York Univ.).  (III B.C., Upper Egypt?;  sand-
       stone).

1767   Astrological epigrams.   P. Oxy. 3.464 (Bodleian
       Libr., Gr. class. d.75 (P)) (III, Oxy.;  on the verso
       of No. 2295).  Closely related to Manetho.  Neuge-
       bauer-Van Hoesen, Astrol. Pap. Ostr., No. 122
       (bibl. and restorations).  Archiv 3.279.  A. E.
       Housman, CR 17 (1903) 385-86.

1768   Elegiac poem on astrology.  P. Schubart 16 (P. Berol.
       inv. 7508) (III).  Neugebauer-Van Hoesen, Astrol.
       Pap. Ostr., No. 105.

1769   Epitaph of Anubion, son of Chaeremon, age twenty.
       P. Ross. Georg. 1.14 (Collection of M. Maximova,
       Tiflis?) (III;  wooden tablet, of the sort attached to
       a mummy).  Archiv 8.261.

1770   Elegy (?): Fragments of distichs.   P. Hamb. 124
       (inv. 666, verso) (III-II B.C.;  on the verso of a
       part of P. Hamb. 163: see No. 1504).

1771   Humorous epitaph for one Clitorius.  P. Viereck,
       Racc. Lumbroso 257-59 (O. Berol. inv. 12309)
       (III B.C., Philadelphia;  ostr.;  written by a school-
       boy?).

       Elegy and Epigram: see also Nos. 1809, 1924, 1963,
       1968, 1978, 2642, and further under Verse Antho-
       logies, passim.

Epic, Pastoral, Hymnic and
Didactic Poetry

1772   Epic fragments (Hesiod?  Cyclic epic?).   P. Rain.
       3.5 (inv. 26762) (cf. ibid. 4, p. 135) (II, Soknopaiou
       Nesos).  Traversa, Hes. Cat. 132-33 ("Incerti
       Auctoris").  Assigned by editors to Hesiod, Cata-
       logus;  A. Koerte, Archiv 14.104, prefers a cyclic
       epic.

1773   Epic (Hesiod or Hellenistic epic?).   P. Rain. 3.8
       (inv. 29409) (cf. ibid. 4, p. 135) (IV, Soknopaiou
       Nesos;  pap. cod.).  Traversa, Hes. Cat. 49-50,
       assigns the fragment to the story of Bellerophon
       and the Solymi.  Attributed by the editors to Hesiod,
       Catalogus;  A. Koerte, Archiv 14.104-5, prefers a
       Hellenistic epic.

1774   Epic: Paraphrase of a poem on the rape of Persephone.
       BKT 5.1.7-18 (inv. 13044, verso) (I B.C., Abusir-
       el-Malaq;  cart.;  on the verso of Nos. 2068 and
       2099).  Quotes the Homeric Hymn to Demeter, ii.
       8-12, 17-36, 54-56, 248-49, 256-62, 418, 420-23.
       O. Kern, Orphicorum Fragmenta (Berolini 1922)
       119-25.  Archiv 5.534.  T. W. Allen, CR 21 (1907)
       97-100;  A. Ludwich, Berl. Phil. Woch. 27 (1907)
       483-86;  idem, ibid. 39 (1919) 999-1008, 1028-32;
       A. Krueger, Hermes 73 (1938) 352-55.

1775   Alexandrian (?) epic: On the estate of Diomedes.
       BKT 5.1.67-74 (inv. 10566) (IV, Hermupolis Magna;
       from the same pap. cod. as No. 1851).  Powell, CA
       72-76.  Archiv 5.537;  New Chapters 1.109-10.  A.
       Ludwich, Berl. Phil. Woch. 27 (1907) 490-92.

1776   Alexandrian epic (Antimachus, Thebaïs?).  P. Oxy.
       6.859 (Liverpool Univ. Libr., Class. Gr. Libr.
       418) (III, Oxy.).  Powell, CA 249;  Wyss, No. 151
       (under "Fragmenta Dubia").  A. Koerte, Archiv
       5.535, favors the attribution.

1777   Fragment of a Thebaïs (Antimachus?).   P. Schubart
       6 (III, Hermupolis Magna;  pap. cod.).

1778   Epic (?): Hexameters (Antimachus, Thebaïs, or
       Hesiod, Catalogus?).  P. Hamb. 122 (inv. 645)
       (III-II B.C.).  Archiv 16.85.

1779   Epic (Antimachus?).   PSI 14.1385 (II-III).  H. Lloyd-
       Jones, Gnomon 31 (1959) 109-10.

1780   Epic: Lines from a Thebaïs.  P. Hibeh 2.177 (Brit.
       Mus. inv. 2950) (III B.C., Hibeh;  cart.).

1781   Alexandrian epic (?).  E. Visser, Jaarbericht van
       het Voorziatisch-Egyptisch Gezelschap "Ex
       Oriente Lux" 6 (1939) 60-62 (P. Berol. inv. 16352)
       (II B.C., Abusir-el-Malaq?;  cart.).

1782   Alexandrian epyllion (Callimachus?).  P. Oxy. 15.
       1794 (II, Oxy.;  on the verso of a document).
       Page, GLP 1, No. 122;  Pfeiffer, Callim. 1, fr.
       387;  Powell, CA 78-79.  Archiv 7.117-18.  E.
       Cahen, BAGB, April, 1924, 14-17;  K. F. W. Schmidt,
       Gött. Anz., 1924, 9-10;  W. Morel, Phil. Woch. 46
       (1926) 351;  G. Méautis, Chr. Ég. 7 (1932) 256-57,
       suggests a disciple of Callimachus, and notes that
       line 10 imitates Homer, Il. vi.146;  H. J. Mette,
       83 (1955) 500-2, on the relation to Catullus.

1783   Epyllion on Hero and Leander (Euphorion? Parthenius?). P. Ryl. 3.486 (I; on the verso of accounts). Page, GLP 1, No. 126. Archiv 14.105-6. B. Snell, Gnmon 15 (1939) 540-42, favors Euphorion or his circle; A. Colonna, SIFC, NS 22 (1947) 231-39, suggests Parthenius of Nicaea; G. Pasquali, ibid. 259-60, rejects Parthenius; L. Malten, Rh. Mus. 93 (1949) 66-68.

1784   Fragment of a Hellenistic epic. P. Schubart 5 (III-IV, Hermupolis Magna; pap. cod.).

1785   Fragment of a Hellenistic epic (Euphorion? Callimachus?). P. Schubart 7 (I B.C.-I; cart.). Archiv 16.84. P. Maas, Gnomon 23 (1951) 243; A. Barigazzi, SIFC, NS 26 (1952) 149-68, suggests Euphorion.

1786   Two epic fragments. P. Antin. 1.17 (III, Antinoöpolis; pap. cod.). Possibly aetia or founding legends: the meeting between Telamon and Odysseus (?); the rivalry of the Sirens and the Muses. Archiv 16.84-85.

1787   Alexandrian epic. P. Hal. 2 (inv. 4) (IV). Powell, CA 81.

1788   Alexandrian epic (?). P. Haun. 1.4 (inv. 323 a) (I, Fayum?; sch. ex.?). Perhaps a quotation from a commentary in prose. Archiv 16.85. P. Maas, Class. Med. 8 (1947) 220-21.

1789   Alexandrian epic (?): On Hercules. P. Lit. Lond. 41 (Brit. Mus., Add. MS. 34473, art. 3) (IV-V; parch. cod.). Archiv 10.24.

1790   Hellenistic epic (?). P. Rain. 3.10 (inv. 29809) (III; roll or cod.?). Traversa, Hes. Cat. 134-35 ("Incerti Auctoris"). Archiv 14.107.

1791   Hellenistic or late epic (?): A storm at sea (Dionysius?). P. Rain. 3.11 (inv. 29805) (cf. ibid. 4, p. 135) (III). Archiv 14.107-8. Heitsch, GDRK, fr. XIX, 28, includes this among the "Fragmenta Dubia" of Dionysius (cf. No. 343).

1792   Alexandrian epic (?): On Telephus. P. Oxy. 2.214; P. Lit. Lond. 39 (Brit. Mus. inv. 1181) (III, Oxy.; pap. cod.?). Heitsch, GDRK, fr. XVIII; Page, GLP 1, No. 133; Powell, CA 76-78. Archiv 1.516; New Chapters 1.110. A. Platt, CR 13 (1899) 439-40; G. M. Bolling, AJP 22 (1901) 63-69.

1793   Epic (?). P. Amh. 2.16, recto (II; text on recto, No. 99 on verso). Archiv 2.349.

1794   Epic: A single hexameter. P. Cairo Zen. 4.59535 (III B.C., Philadelphia; sch. ex.). Roberts, GLH, pl. 4c.

1795   Epic. BKT 5.2.145-46 (inv. 1969) (Byzantine).

1796   Epic (?). BKT 5.2.146 (inv. 10562) (II). Archiv 5.539.

1797   Epic: On Thebes. BKT 5.2.147 (inv. 5226) (VII; on the verso of documents). Heitsch, GDRK, fr. XL. Archiv 5.541.

1798   Epic (?). BKT 5.2.146 (inv. 13239) (IV; pap. cod.). Archiv 5.542.

1799   Epic. BKT 5.2.147 (inv. 5227) (VII). Heitsch, GDRK, fr. XLI. Archiv 5.542.

1800   Epic (magic?). BGU 2.597 (P. Berol. inv. 6987) (A.D. 75, Fayum; a hexameter quoted in a private letter). Heitsch, GDRK, fr. XIV. A. Calderini, Riv. Ind. Gr. Ital. 1.2 (1917) 39-42.

1801   Epic: An Orphic (?) description of the Lower World. P. Bon. 1.4 (inv. 24 a-f) (III-IV; from the same pap. cod. as Nos. 645 and 1034). Ed. pr.: G. B. Pighi, Aeg. 27 (1947) 175-83. Archiv 16.85. R. Merkelbach, Mus. Helv. 8 (1951) 1-11, reedits the text as an Orphic (?) katabasis; O. Montevecchi, Aeg. 31 (1951) 76-79; A. Vogliano, Acme 5 (1952) 385-417; R. Keydell, ibid. 418, on the meter; A. Vogliano, Prolegom. 1 (1952) 100-7; M. Treu, Hermes 82 (1954) 24-51, studies the relation to Vergil; R. Turcan, Rev. de l'hist. des religions 150 (1956) 136-72.

1802   Epic (?). P. Cairo G.H. 10578 (I-II).

1803   Epic: On Achilles and Polyxena. P. Flor. 3.390 (IV-V, Hermupolis Magna; pap. cod.). Ed. pr.: G. Vitelli, AR 7 (1904) 356-57. Heitsch, GDRK, fr. XXXVII. Archiv 3.480.

1804   Epic. P. Goth. 98 (inv. 98) (?).

1805   Epic. P. Grenf. 2.5 (Bodleian Libr., Gr. class. f. 45 (P)) (III B.C., Hibeh?; cart.).

1806   Epic: On the marriage of Peleus and Thetis (?) (Hesiod, Catalogus, or a Hellenistic poem?). P. Hamb. 123 (inv. 658) (III-II B.C.). Archiv 16.85.

1807   Epic: A Titanomachy (?). P. Harris 3 (inv. 173 d) (I-II). Traversa, Hes. Cat. 135-36 ("Incerti Auctoris"). Archiv 13.80. B. Snell, Gnomon 13 (1937) 579-80.

1808   Epic (?). P. Harris 4 (inv. 173 j) (I?). Archiv 13.86. B. Snell, Gnomon 13 (1937) 580, suggests a dilettante's epitaph for Patroclus.

1809   Epic (or elegy?). P. Harris 5 (inv. 182 j) (I-II). Archiv 13.86.

1810   Epic (?). P. Harris 7 (inv. 181 g) (I?). Archiv 13.86. P. Maas, Gnomon 13 (1937) 581, sees hexameters.

1811   Epic. P. Hibeh 1.8 (Musées Royaux, Bruxelles, inv. E.5952) (III B.C., Hibeh; cart.). Archiv 5.539.

1812   Epic. P. Hibeh 1.9 (Houghton Libr., Harvard Univ.) (III B.C., Hibeh; cart.). Perhaps related to the source of the Latin Dares. Archiv 5.539.

1813   Epic. P. Lond. 5.1816 b; P. Lit. Lond. 37 (Brit. Mus. inv. 1605 B) (II; on the verso). Archiv 10.30.

1814    Epyllion or hymn (?).  P. Lond. 3.970; P. Lit. Lond.
        38 (Brit. Mus. inv. 970) (III).  A. Koerte, Archiv
        10.30, suggests an epithalamium.

1815    Epic.  P. Lit. Lond. 252 (Brit. Mus. inv. 2722 B)
        (II B.C.; used for backing No. 894).

1816    Epic (?).  P. Lond. 3.1109 c; P. Lit. Lond. 257
        (Brit. Mus. inv. 1109 C) (II).

1817    Epic.  P. Mil. Vogl. 2.39 (inv. 218) (I).

1818    Epic: Sibylline (?) oracles.  P. Oslo 2.14 (I-II).
        Archiv 10.25.  S. Eitrem, SO 5 (1927) 38; W. Croe-
        nert, ibid. 6 (1928) 57-59.

1819    Epic.  P. Oxy. 3.422 (Houghton Libr., Harvard Univ.)
        (III, Oxy.).  Powell, CA 80.  Archiv 3.265.

1820    Epic.  P. Oxy. 3.423 (Houghton Libr., Harvard Univ.)
        (III, Oxy.).  Archiv 3.265.

1821    Epic (a threnos or an epitaphios?).  P. Oxy. 3.434
        (Houghton Libr., Harvard Univ.) (III, Oxy.).  Ar-
        chiv 3.276.

1822    Epic.  P. Oxy. 4.672 (Wellesley Coll.) (I, Oxy.).
        Archiv 3.479.

1823    Epic.  P. Oxy. 15.1821 (III, Oxy.).  Archiv 7.118.

1824    Epic (?).  P. Rain. 1.31 (inv. 29383) (I, Fayum).

1825    Epic (?).  P. Rain. 3.12 (inv. 29833) (IV-V; pap. cod.).
        Archiv 14.108.

1826    Epic (?).  P. Rain. 3.13 (inv. 29479) (VI; pap. cod.).
        Archiv 14.108-9.

1827    Epic (or prose text with verse citations?).  P. Rain.
        3.15 (inv. 29333) (II-III, Fayum; on the verso of a
        document).  Archiv 14.108.

1828    Epic: On Phineus.  Mentioned in Phil. Anzeiger, 14
        (1884) 477 (P. Rain.; since published?) (?).

1829    Epic: Epithalamium.  P. Ryl. 1.17 (IV, Hermupolis
        Magna; "a small complete sheet of papyrus").
        Heitsch, GDRK, fr. XXV; Manteuffel, Opusc.,
        No. 34; Page, GLP 1, No. 139.  Archiv 5.541;
        JEA 7.89.

1830    Epic (?).  P. Ryl. 1.32 (I B.C.).  Archiv 5.539.

1831    Epic: Odysseus' vengeance on the suitors.  P. Ryl.
        3.487 (III-IV; pap. cod.?; sch. ex.?).  Heitsch,
        GDRK, fr. XXI; Page, GLP 1, No. 137.  Archiv
        14.106-7; JAW 272.16.

1832    Epic: On the return of Persephone (?).  P. Ryl.
        3.494 (II, Oxy.).  Archiv 14.108.

1833    Epic: Panegyric (?) (or mime?).  PSI 2.149, verso
        (IV-V, Hermupolis Magna; on the verso of No.
        1731).  Heitsch, GDRK, fr. XXXIII.  Archiv 7.119;
        JEA 7.88.  P. Collart, Rev. Phil. 43 (1919) 36-38,
        suggests a poet of the school of Nonnus.

1834    Epic: On Achilles and Hector.  PSI 6.722 (III).  Ar-
        chiv 7.118; JEA 8.84.  G. Vitale, Aeg. 2 (1921)
        37-42.

1835    Epic (Colluthus?).  PSI 7.845 (V-VI; pap. cod.).
        Heitsch, GDRK, fr. XXXIX; Page, GLP 1, No. 147.
        Archiv 8.255.  R. Keydell, Hermes 69 (1934) 420-
        25, suggests Colluthus.

1836    Epic (from a cyclic epic?).  PSI 14.1386 (I B.C.-I,
        Oxy.).  H. Lloyd-Jones, Gnomon 31 (1959) 110,
        prefers an epic of the Hesiodic type.

1837    Epic.  M. Manfredi, SIFC, NS 27-28 (1956) 49-50
        (PSI inedita?) (II).

1838    Epic: On Penelope, Paris, and Helen.  P. Schubart
        8 (I B.C.-I).  Line 9 is reminiscent of Euripides,
        Helena 676.

1839    Epic.  P. Schubart 9 (II-I B.C.).  Two fragments,
        perhaps from different poems: the first lyric
        (Alcman?); the second, hexameters.

1840    Epic: Fragment with scholia.  P. Schubart 10 (II-III).
        The scholia cite Hipponax (Medeiros, fr. 131).

1841    Epic: On the creation.  W. Kroll, Analecta Graeca
        (Wissenschaftliche Beilage zum Vorlesungsver-
        zeichnis der Universität Greifswald) 3-5 (IV,
        Hermupolis Magna).  A. Gercke, op. cit. 15-16,
        suggests a hymn to Urania.  Heitsch, GDRK, fr.
        XLVI.  Archiv 2.349.

1842    Epic (Hesiod, Catalogus?).  C. C. Edgar, Ann. Serv.
        26 (1926) 203 (P. Cairo inv. 47270) (?, Oxy.).
        Traversa, Hes. Cat. 131-32.

1843    Epic: Apostrophe of the shade of Achilles to the
        Achaeans.  P. Jouguet and G. Lefebvre, BCH 28
        (1904) 208-9 (Institut Fr. d'Arch. Orientale du
        Caire) (Byzantine; from the same wooden tablet
        as No. 1341; sch. ex.).  Heitsch, GDRK, fr.
        XXXVIII; Ziebarth, No. 28 b; Ziebarth 2, No.
        42 b.  Archiv 3.480.  O. Crusius, Philol. 64
        (1905) 144-46.

1844    Epic: Homeric themes.  C. Graves, Hermathena
        5 (1885) 237-57 (Collection of the editor, Limerick,
        Eire) (IV, Thebes?; pap. cod.; sch. ex.).  Heitsch,
        GDRK, fr. XXVI.  Identified by R. Reitzenstein,
        Hermes 35 (1900) 103-5.

1845    Epic: On the myth of Leda.  J. Nicole, Mél. Weil
        291-97 (P. Geneve inv. 96) (late).  Archiv 1.109.

1846    Epic.  Mentioned by Gerhard, Phoinix, 1, note 2
        (four frr. of P. Heid. inv. 310; published?) (II
        B.C.).

1847    Epic: Panegyric on the gymnasiarch Theon.  P. Oxy.
        7.1015 (P. Cairo) (III, Oxy.).  Heitsch, GDRK, fr.
        XVI; Manteuffel, Opusc., "Appendix" No. 3; Page,
        GLP 1, No. 130.  Archiv 5.540.  E. G. Turner,
        JEA 38 (1952) 85; idem, Akten Pap. VIII, 142 and
        pl. 2.

1848   Epic on the wars of Diocletian, and late Imperial
history.   R. Reitzenstein, Zwei religionsgeschicht-
liche Fragen (Strassburg 1901) 47-50 (P. Strassb.
inv. Gr. 480) (IV, Gizeh; pap. cod.).   Heitsch,
GDRK, fr. XXII; Page, GLP 1, No. 135.   Archiv
2.350.   F. Cumont, Rev. Ét. Anc. 4 (1902) 36-40.

1849   Epic: Hermes founds a city.   R. Reitzenstein, op.
cit. (see No. 1848) 53-58 (P. Strassb. inv. Gr. 481)
(IV, Gizeh; pap. cod.; evidently by the same author
as No. 1848).   Heitsch, GDRK, fr. XXIV; Jacoby,
FGH, Dritter Teil C, 184-85; Page, GLP 1, No.
136.   Archiv 2.350.   J. Bidez, Rev. Phil. 27 (1903)
81-85, suggests Soterichus, Patria Oaseos; R.
Keydell, Hermes 71 (1936) 465-67, conjectures that
this is from the text recast into iambics by Hermias
in his Patria tês Hermoupoleos; T. Zielinski,
Sixième Congrès International d'Études Byzantines,
Alger 1939 (Paris 1940) 63-64, on Hermetic elements;
B. Wyss, Mus. Helv. 6 (1950) 194, notes imitations
by Gregory of Nazianzus, and suggests Antimachus
of Heliopolis, Kosmopoiia.

1850   Panegyric of the Dux Heraclius (?).   PSI 3.253 (V,
Hermupolis Magna).   Heitsch, GDRK, fr. XXXIV;
Page, GLP 1, No. 144; Wifstrand, Kallim. Nonn.
199-200.   R. Keydell, DLZ 55 (1934) 448, and Byz.-
neugr. Jahrb. 12 (1936) 8-11, suggests a poem on
the campaigns of Heraclius of Edessa against the
Vandals.

1851   Epicedia on professors of Berytus.   BKT 5.1.82-93
(inv. 10558-59) (IV, Hermupolis Magna; from the
same pap. cod. as No. 1775).   Schubart, PGB, tab.
44 a.   Heitsch, GDRK, frr. XXX-XXXI; Page, GLP
1, No. 138.   Archiv 5.547; JAW 174.103.   A. Ludwich, Berl. Phil. Woch. 27 (1907) 493; F. Schem-
mel, Phil. Woch. 43 (1923) 236-40.

1852   Panegyric on the victory of Germanus over the Blem-
myes.   BKT 5.1.108-14 (inv. 5003) (V, Thebes;
pap. cod.).   Wilcken, TAGP, Taf. V.   Heitsch,
GDRK, fr. XXXII; Page, GLP 1, No.142; Wifstrand, Kallim. Nonn. 183-85.   F. Buecheler, Rh.
Mus. 39 (1884) 277-82; K. Wessely, WS 7 (1885)
77-78; A. Ludwich, Berl. Phil. Woch. 27 (1907)
495; J. Draeseke, Woch. Phil. 33 (1916) 15-21, on
the historical background.

1853   Encomium of one Maximus, a Tyrian.   P. Rain. 1.5 a
(inv. 29788 a) (cf. ibid. 3, pp. 90-93) (IV; from the
same pap. cod. as No. 1888).   Heitsch, GDRK, fr.
XXVIII; Page, GLP 1, No. 132.   Archiv 11.224-25;
JAW 272.15.   K. F. W. Schmidt, Gött. Anz., 1936,
248-49.

1854   Epic: Appeal to a Roman general.   P. Flor. 2.114
(V, Hermupolis?; pap. cod.).   Ed. pr.: G. Vi-
telli, AR 53 (1903) 149-58.   Heitsch, GDRK, fr.
XXXVI; Page, GLP 1, No. 143.   Archiv 3.266.   G.
Vitelli, SIFC 16 (1908) 452-64.

1855   Late epic.   P. Antin. 2.57 (V-VI, Antinoöpolis; pap.
cod.).   K. Latte, Gnomon 34 (1962) 154.

1856   Late epic.   P. Antin. 2.58 (IV-V; Antinoöpolis; parch.
cod.).   The editor suggests a precursor of Nonnus.
K. Latte, Gnomon 34 (1962) 154.

1857   Late (?) epic.   P. Antin. 2.59 (VI, Antinoöpolis;
parch. cod.).

Epic poetry: see also Nos. 246, 1205 (ad fin.),
1577, 1604, 1957, 1962, 1977-78, 2292, 2370,
2460, 2464, 2655.

1858   Pastoral: Pan and his pipe (or hymn to Pan?).   P.
Rain. 1.4 (inv. 29801) (cf. ibid. 3, pp.89-90, 4,
pp. 133-34) (III-IV; pap. cod.).   C. Gallavotti,
Theocritus Quique Feruntur Bucolici Graeci (Romae
1946) 221-24, reedits as "Anonymi Panis Epyllium";
Heitsch, GDRK, fr. XVII; Page, GLP 1, No. 123.
Lesky, GGL 689; New Chapters 3.208-9.   P. Collart, Rev. Ét. Gr. 46 (1933) 168-80, assigns the
text to Euphorion; R. Keydell, Byz.-neugr. Jahrb.
12 (1936) 8; K. F. W. Schmidt, Gött. Anz., 1936,
247-48: "vielleicht Euphorion"; R. Keydell, JAW
272 (1941) 13-15; A. Koerte, Archiv 11.222-24,
queries the attribution to Euphorion; C. Gallavotti,
Riv. Fil. 69 (1941) 233-58, suggests Bion, and L.
Alfonsi, BFC 48 (1942) 97-98, approves; H. Oellacher, Mnemos., Ser. 3.12 (1942) 1-33; idem,
SIFC, NS 18 (1942) 113-50, suggests Nicander; A.
Barigazzi, Athen. 34 (1946) 7-27, rejects Euphorion; J. C. Kamerbeek, Mnemos., Ser. 4.4 (1951)
80, compares line 12 with Propertius i.9.23; A.
S. F. Gow and A. F. Scholfield, Nicander: The
Poems and Poetical Fragments (Cambridge 1953)
219, doubt the ascription to Nicander.

Pastoral Poetry: see also No. 1621.

1859   Hymnic Poetry: Hymn to Demeter (?).   P. Harris
6 (inv. 173 e) (II-III).   Archiv 13.80-81.   B. Snell,
Gnomon 13 (1937) 580-81.

1860   Hymn (?).   P. Oxy. 4.670 (Wellesley Coll.) (III, Oxy.).
Powell, CA 80-81 and "Addendum," 245.   Archiv 3.
479.   R. Ganszyniec, ARW 21 (1922) 498-99, suggests a hymn on the release of Hera when entrapped
by Hephaestus in a magic chair.

1861   Hymn to Dionysus.   P. Ross. Georg. 1.11 (Collection
of G. Zereteli, Tiflis) (III, Fayum?; on the verso
of a document).   Heitsch, GDRK, fr. LVI; Page,
GLP 1, No. 129.   Archiv 8.254-55; JAW 230.84-86.
L. Castiglioni, Aeg. 7 (1926) 228-34; D. A. Tsi-
rimpas, Platon 5 (1953) 33-80.

1862   Hymn to Isis (?).   PSI 7.844 (III?).   Heitsch, GDRK,
fr. XLVIII.   Archiv 8.255.   First published as an
encomium of a philosopher, reedited by E. Heitsch,
Mus. Helv. 17 (1960) 185-88, as a hymn to Isis.

1863   Magical hymns to Apollo, Helios, and Apollo-Helios.
In magical texts: Preisendanz, PGM, Nos. 1-2
(IV-V).   Archiv 8.106-8 (bibl.).   H. Riesenfeld,
Eranos 44 (1946) 153-60.   Heitsch, GDRK, fr. LIX,
4: the hymn to Helios, with its variations found
in other magical texts.

1864   Hymns to Helios and the Pantocrator.   In a magical
text: K. Wessely, Denkschr. Wien. Akad. 36
(1888) 139-48 (P. Louvre inv. 2391) (III-IV).   Heitsch,
GDRK, fr. LIX, 2, 5; Preisendanz, PGM, No. 3
(lines 198-228, 549-58).   Archiv 8.108-9 (bibl.).
E. Heitsch, Hermes 88 (1960) 150-58.

1865    Hymns (partly in hexameters) to Typhon, Hecate,
        Helios, Selene, Artemis, Selene-Artemis and
        Aphrodite.  In the "Paris Magical Papyrus". Prei-
        sendanz, PGM, No. 4 (Bibliothèque Nationale,
        Paris, Suppl. Gr. 574) (III-IV, Thebes?). Heitsch,
        GDRK, fr. LIX, 3, 4, 6, 7, 9-14. Archiv 8.109-15
        (bibl.).

1866    Hymn to Hermes.  In a magical text: P. Lond. 1.46;
        K. Wessely, Denkschr. Wien. Akad. 36 (1888) 127-
        39  (IV; pap. cod.). Preisendanz, PGM, No. 5
        (lines 400-19).  Archiv 8.116-17 (bibl.).

1867    Hymn to Helios-Apollo.  In a magical text: P. Lond.
        1.47; K. Wessely, Denkschr. Wien. Akad. 36
        (1888) 149-50 (II-III). Preisendanz, PGM, No. 6.
        Archiv 8.117 (bibl.).

1868    Hymn to Hermes.  In a magical text: P. Lond. 1.121;
        Preisendanz, PGM, No. 7 (III-IV). Gazza, p. 97.
        Archiv 8.117-18 (bibl.).

1869    Hymn to the Pantocrator.  In a magical text: A.
        Dieterich, Jahrbücher für klass. Philol., Supple-
        mentband 16 (1888) 778-79 (Rijksmuseum van Oud-
        heden, Gr. P. J 384) (III-IV; pap. cod.). Heitsch,
        GDRK, fr. LIX, 1; Preisendanz, PGM, No. 12
        (lines 244-52).

1870    Hymn to Hermes.  In a magical text: O. Plasberg,
        Archiv 2 (1903) 208-17 (P. Strassb. inv. Gr. 1179)
        (III; on the verso of accounts). Heitsch, GDRK,
        fr. LIX, 8; Preisendanz, PGM, No. 17 b. Archiv
        8.125 (bibl.). E. Heitsch, Philol. 103 (1959) 223-36.

        On the magical hymns in general, see Heitsch,
        GDRK, fr. LIX (bibl. and texts); idem, Philol.
        103 (1959) 215-22.

        Hymnic poetry: see also Nos. 1620, 1814, 1858,
        1943, 2481.

1871    Didactic poetry: Charms against inflammation and
        headache (in hexameters).  P. Amh. 2.11; BKT
        5.2.144 (inv. 7504) (I B.C.-I). The "Philinna
        Papyrus". two of the charms are ascribed in the
        text to a "Thessalian Philinna" and a "Syrian woman
        of Gadara." Page, GLP 1, No. 146; Preisendanz,
        PGM, No. 20. Archiv 2.363, 5.542, 8.125. A.
        Abt, Philol. 69 (1910) 150-52, conjectures that the
        Berlin and Amherst papyri belong to the same roll;
        P. Maas, JHS 62 (1942) 33-38, confirms this and
        reconstructs the whole text; C. Bonner, Hesperia
        13 (1944) 349-51; S. Eitrem, SO 29 (1952) 129-31;
        L. Koenen, Chr. Ég. 37 (1962) 167-74, interprets
        the allusion to the myth of Horus.

1872    Charms against inflammation and headache.  P. Maas,
        JHS 62 (1942) 36-37 (P. Oxy. inedita) (IV, Oxy.).
        From the text ascribed to "Philinna" (cf. No. 1871).
        R. Merkelbach, Archiv 16.85-86, gives a revision.

1873    Poem on Egyptian botany (in hexameters).  P. Oxy.
        15.1796 (II, Oxy.; on the verso of property lists).
        Heitsch, GDRK, fr. LX; Page, GLP 1, No. 124.
        Archiv 7.118; New Chapters 2.35. K. F. W.
        Schmidt, Gött. Anz., 1924, 10-11.

1874    Poem on astronomy (?).  P. Oxy. 15.1822 (II, Oxy.;
        on the verso of accounts).  Archiv 7.118.

1875    Verses on astrology (hexameters and elegiacs).  PSI
        3.157 (III?, Oxy.).  Similar to Manetho, Apoteles-
        mata.  Neugebauer-Van Hoesen, Astrol. Pap. Ostr.,
        No. 135.

        Didactic poetry: see also Nos. 1609, 2170.

                    Gnomic Poetry and Verse Fable

1876    An anecdote about Anacharsis (in trimeters).  P.
        Jouguet and G. Lefebvre, BCH 28 (1904) 201-5 (P.
        Cairo?) (II, Thebes?; ostr.; sch. ex.). Man-
        teuffel, Opusc., No. 39; Page, GLP 1, No. 115;
        Ziebarth, No. 24; Ziebarth 2, No. 44. Archiv 3.
        486. O. Crusius, Philol. 64 (1905) 142-43; F. Leo,
        Hermes 40 (1905) 159-60; T. Reinach, BCH 29
        (1905) 257-58, 575; A. van Hove, Ant. Class. 13
        (1944) 119-25.

1877    Verse fable (Babrius?).  H. Weil, Rev. Ét. Gr. 3
        (1890) 309-10 (?, Deirut).

1878    Gnomic couplet: Response of an oracle (?).  P.
        Aberdeen 14 (III?, Fayum?; a narrow strip of pap.).
        Archiv 14.111.

1879    Two verse sententiae.  P. Oxy. 6.966 (P. Cairo)
        (III, Oxy.; on the verso of an account; sch. ex.).

1880    Gnomic verse: On behavior proper for small boys.
        Quoted in an official letter: P. Oxy. 9.1185 (P.
        Ryl. inv. 454) (ca. A.D. 200, Oxy.). Manteuffel,
        Opusc., No. 38.

1881    Gnomic verse.  PSI 4.280 (IV-V, Oxy.; sch. ex.).
        Page, GLP 1, No. 36.

1882    A verse maxim.  P. Ross. Georg. 1.13 (Libr. of the
        State Hermitage Mus., Leningrad) (III; waxed tab-
        let; sch. ex.). Ed. pr.: G. Zereteli, Mél. Chate-
        lain 115-17. Ziebarth 2, No. 13.

1883    Gnomic verse: On the trials of a farmer's life.  G.
        Parthey, Abh. Berl. Akad., 1865, 140 (Tabula
        cerata Berol. 29) (IV, Athribis; waxed tablet; by
        a student?). U. Wilcken, Archiv 1 (1901) 428-29,
        rejects the editor's identification as an invocation
        to St. George and reedits the text as verses on a
        farmer's life; H. Leclercq, Bulletin d'ancienne
        littérature et d'archéologie chrétiennes 3 (1913)
        209-12, thinks of a student's theme on this subject.

1884    Verse maxim.  E. J. Goodspeed, Mél. Nicole 181-82
        (No. 6) (Mus. of the New York Historical Society)
        (?, Abusir; wooden tablet; sch. ex.). E. Cougny,
        Epigrammatum Anthologia Palatina (Paris 1890)
        3.406, 433; Ziebarth, No. 10; Ziebarth 2, No. 16.

1885    A moral maxim.  E. J. Goodspeed, Mél. Nicole 182
        (No. 7) (Mus. of the New York Historical Society)
        (?, Abusir; wooden tablet; sch. ex.). E. Cougny,
        op. cit. (see No. 1884), 405-6, 433; Ziebarth, No.
        8; Ziebarth 2, No. 14.

.886   A moral maxim (the same as No. 1885).   E. J.
       Goodspeed, Mél. Nicole 182-83 (Mus. of the New
       York Historical Society) (?, Abusir; wooden tab-
       let; sch. ex.). Ziebarth, No. 9; Ziebarth 2, No.
       15.

1887   A verse maxim.   W. G. Waddell, Ét. Pap. 1 (1932)
       16, 18 (No. 10) (P. Cairo inv. 56227) (I-III, Oxy.;
       sch. ex.).

1888   Encomium (?) in iambics.   P. Rain. 1.5 b (cf. ibid.
       3, pp. 90-93, 4, p. 135) (inv. 29788 b) (IV; from
       the same pap. cod. as No. 1853).  Perhaps from
       a prolalia to the Encomium of Maximus (see No.
       1853). Heitsch, GDRK, fr. XXVII. Archiv 11.225.
       K. F. W. Schmidt, Gött. Anz., 1936, 249-50.

       Gnomic verse: see also Nos. 1569, 1582-89, 1591,
       1605, 1610, 1730, 2643, 2713, 2720, 2731, 2737,
       2750.


                        Lyric Poetry

1889   A lyric fragment (Alcman, Partheneion? Erinna,
       Alakata?).   P. Oxy. 1.8 (Houghton Libr., Harvard
       Univ.) (I-II, Oxy.). Diehl, Anth. Lyr. 2¹.157-58;
       Edmonds, LG 3.420-21; Manteuffel, Opusc., No.
       35.2, p. 190; J. U. Powell, CA 186-87.  Archiv
       1.110; New Chapters 1.53-54, 3.184-85. H. Diels,
       Sitzb. Berl. Akad., 1898, 497, and Wilamowitz,
       Gött. Anz., 1898, 696-97, regard the text as an
       imitation of Alcman; F. Blass, Neue Jahrb. 3
       (1899) 80, suggests Erinna; H. Jurenka, WS 22
       (1900) 25-28, favors Alcman.

1890   Choral lyric in Doric (Alcman?).   P. Oxy. 24.2394
       (II-III, Oxy.). Marginalia refer to one Ni(canor?).
       Page, PMG 162.

1891   Boeotian lyric.   P. Oxy. 23.2371 (ca. A.D. 200, Oxy.).
       Not by Corinna, according to the editor.  Page, PMG
       691.

1892   Boeotian lyric, with marginalia.   P. Oxy. 23.2372
       (II, Oxy.). The editor doubts that the verses are
       by Corinna.  Fr. 36 is possibly a list of titles of
       poems with their first lines. Galiano, LG 123.
       Page, PMG 692.

1893   Boeotian lyric.   P. Oxy. 23.2373 (II-III, Oxy.).
       Perhaps in the same hand as PSI 9.1090 (see No.
       365). Page, PMG 693.

1894   Boeotian verse, with comments.   P. Oxy. 23.2374
       (II, Oxy.). Galiano, LG 123-24.  Page, PMG 694.

1895   Lyric: Epodes, with a few scholia (Archilochus?
       Hipponax?).   R. Reitzenstein, Sitzb. Berl. Akad.,
       1899, 857-64 (the "Strassburg Epodes:" P. Strassb.
       inv. Gr. 3 a-b) (II), Galiano, LG 79-83 (bibl.).
       Diehl, Anth. Lyr. 1².3.35-37, 3³.34-36, SL, Nos.
       2-3; F. Lasserre, Les Épodes d'Archiloque (Paris
       1950) 274-85; Lavagnini, Aglaia 112-13; Medeiros,
       pp. LV-LIX and frr. 181-83; Treu, Archil. 76, 78,
       225-27. Archiv 1.508; C. M. Bowra, New Chap-
       ters 3.58-60; Lesky, GGL 106.  G. Coppola, SIFC,
       NS 7 (1929) 155-68, suggests a Hellenistic poet;

G. Pasquali, ibid. 307-11, argues for Archilochus;
G. Perotta, ibid., NS 15 (1938) 3-41, ibid. 16 (1940)
177-88, assigns both epodes to Hipponax; U. Galli,
AR 40 (1938) 157-75, ibid. 42 (1940) 255-67, assigns
I to Archilochus; A. D. Knox, SIFC, NS 15 (1938)
193-96, replies to Perotta; N. Terzaghi, ibid. 17
(1940) 217-35, sides with Perotta; R. Cantarella,
Aeg. 24 (1944) 1-112, assigns I to Archilochus and
II to Hipponax; O. Masson, Rev. Ét. Gr. 59-60
(1946-47) 8-27, accepts the attribution of II to Hipponax; C. del Grande, GIF 1 (1948) 255-57, assigns
I to the post-Euripidean epoch; V. Klinger, Eos
43, fasc. 1 (1948-49) 40-47; R. Cantarella, Aevum
23 (1949) 208-9, ibid. 24 (1950) 415-17; O. Masson,
Rev. Ét. Gr. 64 (1951) 427-41, reedits the text and
attributes both poems to Hipponax, rejecting the
hypothesis of an anthology; D. Pieraccioni, AR,
NS 3 (1953) 56-57; F. Lasserre, Archiloque:
Fragments (Paris 1958), p. XCI, attributes both
poems to Hipponax; G. Kirkwood, TAPA 92 (1961)
267-82, assigns I to Archilochus, II to Hipponax,
defending the assumption of an anthology.

1896   Ionic verses (Archilochus?).   P. Oxy. 22.2324 (II,
       Oxy.). Iambic trimeters or trochaic tetrameters.
       Galiano, LG 119 (Anacreon?). W. Peek, Philol.
       100 (1956) 24-25.

1897   Ionic verses (Archilochus?).   P. Oxy. 22.2325 (II,
       Oxy.). W. Peek, Philol. 100 (1956) 24-25.

1898   Lyric fragments (Alcaeus or Sappho?).   PRIMI 1.7
       (III B.C.; cart.). Lobel-Page, PLF, p. 297, re-
       ject Alcaeus and Sappho; Page, PMG 920; Treu,
       Sappho 21. Archiv 13.91.  B. Snell, Gnomon 15
       (1939) 531, approves Alcaeus as the author.

1899   Lyric fragments (Alcaeus or Sappho?).   P. Rain.
       1.6 a-b (inv. 29777 a-b) (IV, Hermupolis; pap.₂
       cod.?). Galiano, LG 100. Diehl, Anth. Lyr. 1²
       4.214; Lobel-Page, PLF 297 ("Incertum utrius
       auctoris fragmenta"); Treu, Sappho 16.  Archiv
       11.245.

1900   Aeolic verses (Alcaeus or Sappho?).   E. Lobel and
       D. Page, CQ, NS 2 (1952) 1-3 (P. Fuad inv. 239)
       (II-III). Galiano, LG 100, 107. Lobel-Page, PLF
       237; Page, SA 261-65; Treu, Sappho 6, 162-64.

1901   Aeolic lyric (Alcaeus or Sappho?).   P. Oxy. 21.2291
       (III, Oxy.; on the verso of an account). Galiano,
       LG 96-97. Lobel-Page, PLF 82-83 (as Sappho,
       Bk. v); Treu, Sappho 10, 165. Archiv 16.91.  C.
       Gallavotti, Aeg. 33 (1953) 163-64, favors Alcaeus;
       B. Snell, Hermes 81 (1953) 118-19, and A. W. Gomme,
       JHS 77 (1957) 260-61, also prefer Alcaeus.

1902   Aeolic (?) verses.   P. Oxy. 21.2308 (II-III, Oxy.).
       Parts of five lines. Lobel-Page, PLF 296 ("In-
       certum utrius auctoris fragmenta"); Treu, Sappho
       18.

1903   Lyric verses in the Aeolic dialect, with marginalia.
       P. Oxy. 23.2378 (I-II, Oxy.). Page, PMG 919,
       rejecting Alcaeus and Sappho. C. Gallavotti, Gno-
       mon 29 (1957) 419-20; M. Treu, Philol. 102 (1958)
       13-20, attributes the text to Alcaeus.

1904    Lyric (Pindar?).    P. Harris 8 (inv. 173 i) (II).   Galiano, Pind., No. 43.   Snell, Pindarus, fr. 337
("Fragm. dub.").  Archiv 13.94.   Gnomon 13 (1937)
581.

1905    Lyric (Pindar?).    P. Oxy. 4.674 (Trinity Coll. Libr.,
Dublin, Pap. F.11) (I-II, Oxy.).  Galiano, Pind.,
No. 44 (bibl.).   Snell, Pindarus, fr. 338 ("Fragm.
dub.").   Archiv 3.482.

1906    Lyric (Pindar or Bacchylides?).   Bowra, Pindar,
No. 342 (P. Berol. inv. 16139) (I-II).   Lines 1-7
partially coincide with P. Oxy. 23.2364 (see No.
184).  Galiano, LG 141; idem, Pind., No. 42 (bibl.).
Snell, Pindarus, fr. 336 ("Fragm. dub.").  A. Turyn,
Gnomon 12 (1936) 367, rejects Pindar; B. Snell,
Hermes 75 (1940) 183-84, prefers Pindar to Bacchy-
lides; E. Lobel, on P. Oxy. 23.2364, prefers
Bacchylides.

1907    Lyric (Pindar or Bacchylides?).   Bowra, Pindar,
No. 341 (P. Berol. inv. 16140) (I-II).   Galiano,
Pind., No. 62 (bibl.).   Snell, Bacchyl. 13, 103-5
("Fragm. dub.").   A. Turyn, Gnomon 12 (1936)
367, rejects Pindar; B. Snell, Hermes 75 (1940)
177-83, rejects Pindar, suggests Bacchylides.

1908    Lyric (Simonides or Bacchylides?).   PSI 10.1181
(II-III, Oxy.; on the verso of a document).  Galiano, LG 131 and note 404 (once falsely attributed
to Stesichorus?), 140; idem, Pind., No. 64 (bibl.).
Page, GLP 1, No. 84; idem, PMG 652 (ii); Snell,
Bacchyl. 13, 100-2 ("Fragm. dub.").  JEA 19.69.
Lesky, GGL 177-78.   H. J. M. Milne, CR 47 (1933)
62; J. A. Davison, ibid. 48 (1934) 205-7, suggests
Simonides; A. Koerte, Archiv 13.92-93, approves
this attribution, E. Lobel, P. Oxy. 25, p. 45, note
2, queries it.

1909    Lyric (Pindar, Simonides, or Bacchylides?).   B.
Snell, Hermes, Einzelschr. 5 (1937) 98-101 (P.
Strassb. WG 1406-1409) (II).  Galiano, LG 136; idem,
Pind., No. 65.   Page, PMG 921.   Archiv 13.91-92.
E. Lobel, P. Oxy. 25, p. 45, note 2, and p. 87,
doubts that Simonides is the author; B. Gentili,
Riv. CCM 2 (1960) 116-17, rejects Simonides and
Pindar in favor of Bacchylides.

1910    Lyric: Fragments of choral lyric in the Doric dialect
(Simonides?).   P. Oxy. 25.2430 (I-II, Oxy.).   165
small fragments.   Page, PMG 519.   H. Lloyd-Jones,
CR, NS 11 (1961) 18-19.

1911    Lyric (Simonides: Epinician Odes?).   P. Oxy. 25.
2431 (II, Oxy.).   Page, PMG 511.   B. Gentili, Riv.
CCM 2 (1960) 113-23.

1912    Lyric (Simonides or Bacchylides?).   P. Oxy. 25.2432
(I B.C.-I, Oxy.).   Page, PMG 541 (as by Simonides).
M. Treu, Rh. Mus. 103 (1960) 319-36, accepts the
attribution to Simonides; H. Lloyd-Jones, CR, NS
11 (1961) 19, prefers Bacchylides; C. M. Bowra,
Hermes 91 (1963) 257-67 (ditto).

1913    Choral lyric (Bacchylides?).    P. Oxy. 23.2365 (III,
Oxy.).   Galiano, LG 145.

1914    Lyric (?) (Bacchylides: Hymni?).    P. Oxy. 23.2366
(II-III, Oxy.; on the verso of a document).   Galiano,
LG 145-46.

1915    Dithyramb (?) or choral song from tragedy (Euripides?).
P. Rain. 3.19 (inv. 29819) (cf. ibid. 4, p. 136) (II,
Hermupolis; opisthograph roll).   Page, PMG 931.
Archiv 14.115.

1916    Lyric (or tragic?) fragment with musical notation.
P. Cairo Zen. 4.59533 (III B.C., Philadelphia; a
separate strip of papyrus?).   Norsa, SLG, tav. 3 a.
Pohlmann, GMF 23, 27, 40.   J. F. Mountford,
New Chapters 3.260-61; R. P. Winnington-Ingram,
Mode in Ancient Greek Music (Cambridge 1936)
32-33.   C. del Grande, Atti Pap. IV, 369-82; J.
F. Mountford, JHS 51 (1931) 91-100; O. J. Gombosi,
Die Tonarten u. Stimmungen der antiken Musik
(Copenhagen 1939) 127-28; H.-I. Marrou, Rev.
Phil., Sér. 3.13 (1939) 308-20; W. B. Sedgwick,
Class. Med. 11 (1950) 222.   JAW 246.26, 259.139.

1917    Choral lyric.   P. Oxy. 24.2395 (III, Oxy.).   Page,
PMG 924.   W. S. Barrett, Gnomon 33 (1961) 690.

1918    Choral lyric.   P. Oxy. 26.2443 (II, Oxy.).

1919    Choral lyric (or Pindar: Hymni?).   P. Oxy. 26.2444
(I-II, Oxy.).

1920    Ritual song or choral lyric from tragedy (?).   P.
Hibeh 2.176 (Brit. Mus. inv. 2949) (ca. 270-250
B.C., Hibeh; cart.).

1921    Hellenistic lyric or choral song from tragedy (Euripides?).   P. Schubart 17 (III-II B.C.).   Page, PMG
1023 (as lyric).   Archiv 16.103-4.   L. Alfonsi, Aeg.
33 (1953) 297-99; R. Merkelbach, Mus. Helv. 10
(1953) 125-27.

1922    Monody on Phaethon (or mime?).   P. Lit. Lond. 51
(Brit. Mus. inv. 2103) (II; on the verso of a list
of persons; sch. ex. ?).   Heitsch, GDRK, fr. X;
Manteuffel, Opusc., No. 33.   Archiv 10.46-47;
JAW 230.152.   W. Croenert, Philol. 84 (1928) 170-
72; W. Schubart, Gnomon 4 (1928) 397-98, prefers
a mime.

1923    Lyric (or Gnostic hymn?).   P. Fay. 1.2; P. Lit.
Lond. 240 (Brit. Mus. inv. 1192) (II, Karanis).
Heitsch, GDRK, fr. LVIII; Manteuffel, Opusc.,
No. 9; Page, GLP 1, No. 94.   Archiv 2.357.
Wilamowitz, Gött. Anz., 1901, 34-35; A. Swoboda,
WS 27 (1905) 299-301, holds that the text comes from
the Gnostic hymn quoted in part by Hippolytus, Re-
futatio v.10; D. S. Robertson, CR 57 (1943) 70;
S. Eitrem, SO 30 (1953) 108-9.

1924    Two scolia and an elegy.   BKT 5.2.56-63 (inv. 13270)
(III B.C., Elephantine).   Schubart, PGB, tab. 3.
Galiano, LG 119-20.   Edmonds, LG 3.580-81; Page,
GLP 1, Nos. 86, 103; idem, PMG 917; Powell,
CA 190-92.   Archiv 5.552, 7.66; New Chapters 1.
58.   The scolia: Diehl, Anth. Lyr. $2^1$.189-90;
Manteuffel, Opusc., No. 26; Winter, LLP 214.
The elegy: Diehl, Anth Lyr. $2^1$.237-47 (bibl.);
Manteuffel, Opusc., No. 25; H. Jurenka, WS 29
(1907) 326; A. Taccone, Riv. Fil. 38 (1910) 23-24.

1925     Lyric: Praise of Homer, and oracle of Cassandra. BKT 5.2.131-39 (inv. 9775) (I B.C.-I). Schubart, PGB, tab. 11 b. Diehl, Anth. Lyr. 2¹. 310-13; Manteuffel, Opusc., Nos. 36-37; Page, GLP 1, No. 93; Powell, CA 187-90. Archiv 5.557; JAW 178.107; New Chapters 1.57. K. F. W. Schmidt, Woch. Phil. 25 (1908) 460-62; S. Eitrem, SO 30 (1953) 109.

1926     A lyric hymn to Fortune. BKT 5.2.142-43 (inv. 9734) (III; on the verso of No. 2170). Diehl, Anth. Lyr. 2¹. 313-14; Edmonds, LG 3.482-83; Heitsch, GDRK, fr. LV; Manteuffel, Opusc., No. 1; Page, GLP 1, No. 99; Powell, CA 196. Archiv 5.557; JAW 178.107; New Chapters 1.59. K. F. W. Schmidt, Woch. Phil. 25 (1908) 462-63.

1927     A song of boatmen on the Nile. P. Oxy. 3.425 (Musées Royaux, Bruxelles, inv. E.5928) (II-III, Oxy.; sch. ex.). O. Crusius, Herondae Mimiambi (Lipsiae 1914⁵) 134; Heitsch, GDRK, fr. III; Manteuffel, Opusc., No. 28; Page, GLP 1, No. 97; Powell, CA 195. Archiv 3.276; New Chapters 1. 58-59. Wilamowitz, Gött. Anz., 1904, 670; O. Crusius, Philol. 66 (1907) 315; W. Croenert, Rh. Mus. 64 (1909) 444-45; P. Maas, Philol. 68 (1909) 445-46; J. U. Powell, CQ 5 (1911) 177; Wilamowitz, Gr. Versk. 135, 374; S. Eitrem, SO 17 (1937) 104-5; A. Dihle, Hermes 82 (1954) 184-85.

1928     A paean. P. Oxy. 4.675 (Univ.-Bibl., Graz, inv. I.1922) (I, Oxy.). Page, PMG 1035. Archiv 3.484.

1929     A sailor's song, to the Rhodian winds. P. Oxy. 11. 1383 (Princeton Univ. Libr., AM 9053) (III, Oxy.). Heitsch, GDRK, fr. IV; Manteuffel, Opusc., No. 29; Page, GLP 1, No. 98; Powell, CA 195-96; Preisendanz, PGM, No. 29. Archiv 7.141, 8.127; JEA 7.89; New Chapters 1.59. H. Draheim, Woch. Phil. 35 (1918) 310-11; K. F. W. Schmidt, Gött. Anz., 1918, 123-25; L. Deubner, Sitzb. Heid. Akad., 1919, Abh. 17, 11-13; K. Preisendanz, Berl. Phil. Woch. 40 (1920) 1130-32; Wilamowitz, Gr. Versk. 374; idem, Hermes 60 (1925) 314-15; W. Croenert, Philol. 84 (1928) 159; A. Dihle, Hermes 82 (1954) 185-87.

1930     Lyric (or mime?): A maiden's lament. P. Ryl. 1. 15 (II, Fayum; on the verso of a tax account). Heitsch, GDRK, fr. XI; Manteuffel, Opusc., No. 19; Powell, CA 200-1. Archiv 5.558; JAW 178. 107; New Chapters 1.55.

1931     Barbarous verses on the Labors of Hercules, with three caricatures (the "gryllus papyrus"). P. Oxy. 22.2331 (III, Oxy.; for school use?). A poetic dialogue, between Hercules and a challenger (fragment on the Nemean Lion). Archiv 16.98. Weitzmann, Anc. Bk. Ill., p. 53 and fig. 59. K. Latte, Gnomon 27 (1955) 498; A. von Salis, Mus. Helv. 12 (1955) 173-80, studies the sketches; D. L. Page, CR, NS 7 (1957) 189-91, identifies the sketches as "grylli" and reedits the text; K. Weitzmann, AJA 61 (1957) 84 and pl. 33, fig. 1; P. Maas, GR, Ser. 2.5 (1958) 171-73 and pl. 7, reedits the text; N. C. Conomis, Act. Class. 4 (1961) 49-50.

1932     Lyric: Myths regarding flowers and plants (?). F. Bilabel, Philol. 80 (1925) 332-39 (P. Heid. inv. 222) (II-III). Heitsch, GDRK, fr. VI; Page, GLP 1, No. 95. Archiv 8.256-57; New Chapters 3.201.

1933     A Sarapis aretalogy in Phalaecean verses. A. Abt, ARW 18 (1915) 257-68 (P. Berol. inv. 10525) (III). Manteuffel, Opusc., No. 5; Page, GLP 1, No. 96; O. Weinreich, Neue Urkunden zur Sarapis-Religion (Tübingen 1919) 13-18. Archiv 7.140-41; JAW 178. 202-3, 230.151; Wilamowitz, Gr. Versk. 150-51; G. Manteuffel, Eos 31 (1928) 186-92.

1934     Lyric hymn to Helios-Horos (or to one of the Ptolemies?). O. Edfu 3.326 (pp. 331-32) (Ptolemaic, Edfu; ostr.). Sung by a choir of school-children (?). Euripides, Phoenissae 3, appears as a refrain. Ed. pr.: G. Manteuffel, JJP 3 (1949) 102-3. Archiv 16.125.

1935     Lyric hymn to Sarapis. P. Rain. 3.28 (inv. 29248 B) (cf. ibid. 4, p. 137) (I; on the verso of accounts; sch. ex.). Archiv 14.115-16.

1936     Song of a chorus of initiates (?). B. Snell, Hermes, Einzelschr. 5 (1937) 106-11 (P. Strassb. inv. Gr. 1313) (III). Ed. pr.: W. Croenert, Gött. Nachr., 1922, 27. Heitsch, GDRK, fr. LVII. Archiv 7. 257, 13.96. A. M. Dale, Lustrum 2 (1957) 8.

1937     Lyric (?) fragment. P. Harris 9 (II).

1938     A paean. P. Oxy. 4.660 (Univ.-Bibl., Graz, inv. I.1923) (I-II, Oxy.). Page, PMG 922. Archiv 3. 483.

1939     Lyric (Bacchylides?). P. Oxy. 4.673 (Musées Royaux, Bruxelles; later, Bibl. de l'Univ. de Louvain: deperdita) (III, Oxy.). Snell, Bacchyl. 13, 103 ("Fragm. dub."). Archiv 3.482.

1940     Lyric. P. Oxy. 6.860 (Bodleian Libr., Gr. class. f.88 (P)) (I-II, Oxy.). Snell, Bacchyl. 13, 102-3 ("Fragm. dub."). Archiv 5.551.

1941     Lyric (Anacreontics?). P. Ryl. 1.34 (I, Oxy.). Archiv 5.558.

1942     Lyric. P. Tebt. 3.691 (III B.C., Tebtunis; cart.). Page, PMG 923. Archiv 11.248.

1943     A hymn to Demeter. C. H. Roberts, Aeg. 14 (1934) 447-51 (P. Berol. inv. 11793) (III B.C.; cart.). In alternating dactylic hexameters and tetrameters. Page, GLP 1, No. 91. Archiv 13.89-90; Chr. Ég. 21 (1936) 171-72.

1944     Lyric: A fragment on the songs of birds. W. G. Waddell, Ét. Pap. 4 (1938) 121-22 (P. Cairo inv. 67860) (II-III, Oxy.). Heitsch, GDRK, fr. V; Page, PMG 1036. JAW 272.59-60. R. Goossens, Chr. Ég. 21 (1946) 107-11.

1945     A schoolboy's valedictory, in Anacreontics. G. Vitelli, SIFC 12 (1904) 320 (P. Med.?) (IV, Hermupolis Magna). Heitsch, GDRK, fr. XIII; Manteuffel, Opusc., No. 30; Page, GLP 1, No. 100. Archiv 3.487; New Chapters 3.208. G. Vitelli, SIFC 14 (1906) 126; Wilamowitz, Gr. Versk. 611; W. Croenert, Gnomon 2 (1926) 663: E. Orth, Phil. Woch. 52 (1932) 1316.

1946    Lyric (?) fragment.    O. Bodl. 2.2174 (inv. 2105)
        (II; ostr.).

1947    A fragment of late lyric.    H. C. Youtie, TAPA 81
        (1950) 111-13 (O. Skeat 13, now in the Kelsey Mus.
        of Arch., Univ. of Michigan) (I-II, Thebes?; ostr.).
        Page, PMG 1038 (II).

1948    Commentary on a dithyramb or choral ode.    P. Rain.
        1.22 (inv. 19996 a-b) (cf. ibid. 3, pp. 95-96, 4, p.
        135) (I B.C.-I, Soknopaiou Nesos).    The text in-
        cludes quotations from the dithyramb or ode (Page,
        PMG 929) and from Timotheus (?); mentions Homer,
        Melanippides, and Philoxenus (?).    Page, GLP 1,
        No. 87.    Archiv 11.246-48;  New Chapters 3.209-10.
        J. U. Powell, CR 46 (1932) 262-63;  W. Croenert,
        SO 14 (1935) 133, assigns fr. b 2, col. 1 to the Odys-
        seus of Timotheus;  K. F. W. Schmidt, Gött. Anz.,
        1936, 252-53.

1949    Commentary on choral verses (of Pindar or Bacchyli-
        des?).    PSI 14.1391 (II, Oxy.).    In the same hand
        as the Florence Euphorion (see No. 371).    First
        mention: G. Vitelli and M. Norsa, Ann. Sc. Pisa,
        Ser. 2.4 (1935) 14;  ed. pr.: V. Bartoletti, SIFC
        27-28 (1956) 39-44.    Galiano, LG 151.    H. Lloyd-
        Jones, Gnomon 31 (1959) 111-12.

1950    A commentary on the melic poets.    Page, PMG 10,
        13 b-d, 193, 217 (?, Oxy.).    To appear in P. Oxy.,
        Part 29.    Mentions Aeschylus, Chamaeleon, and
        Hesiod; quotes Alcman, Euripides, Orestes 268-69,
        and Stesichorus.

1951    Commentary on lyric verses (of Simonides?).    P.
        Oxy. 25.2434 (II, Oxy.).    Mentions Simonides (?).
        Page, PMG 608.

1952    Commentary on a poetic work.    P. Antin. 2.60 (II-III,
        Antinoöpolis; pap. cod.).    Quotes Hesiod, Opera
        30 (?); mentions Aristophanes, Callimachus, and
        Menander (?).

        Lyric Poetry: see also Nos. 66, 166, 211, 246,
            1606-7, 1617, 1747, 1839, 1948, 1960, 2172, 2439.


                        Unidentified Verse

1953    Fragments: Hexameters (Hesiod: Catalogus?).    P.
        Aberdeen 114 (I, Fayum?).    Attributed to Hesiod
        by Traversa, Hes. Cat. 126.

1954    Verse (?).    P. Aberdeen 140 (II, Fayum?).

1955    Verse (?).    P. Aberdeen 141 (II, Fayum?).

1956    Verse (?).    P. Aberdeen 146 (II-III, Fayum?).

1957    Hellenistic (?) hexameters.    P. Antin. 2.56 (III,
        Antinoöpolis; pap. cod.).

1958    Verse: iambic trimeters.    P. Hamb. 126 (inv. 664) (I).

1959    Verse: trimeters (?).    P. Hamb. 127, frr. a-h (inv.
        650, frr. 5, 10, 13, 12, 14, 15, 17, 18) (ca. 200 B.C.;
        cart. ?).

1960    Verse (lyric?).    P. Harris 35 (inv. 183 e) (I B.C.-I).
        Archiv 13.96;  Gnomon 13 (1937) 582.

1961    Verse (Anthology?).    P. Heid. Siegmann 187 (inv.
        409 c, recto) (ca. 250 B.C., Hibeh; text on recto,
        No. 1962 on verso).

1962    Verse (hexameters).    P. Heid. Siegmann 188 (inv.
        409 c, verso) (ca. 250 B.C., Hibeh; on the verso
        of No. 1961).

1963    Verse (Hellenistic elegy?).    P. Heid. Siegmann 189
        (inv. 435, verso) (III-II B.C.; on the verso of No.
        1557).    H. Lloyd-Jones, Gnomon 29 (1957) 426.

1964    Verse (?) (tragedy?).    P. Hibeh 2.222 (now in the
        Brit. Mus.) (ca. 270-240 B.C., Hibeh; cart.).

1965    Verse (?).    P. Hibeh 2.223 (now in the Brit. Mus.)
        (ca. 300-280 B.C. ?, Hibeh; cart.).

1966    Iambic verses (New Comedy?).    P. Leeds inv. 3,
        inedita (Brotherton Libr., Univ. of Leeds) (?).
        Information from J. A. Davison.

1967    Verse (?).    P. Lit. Lond. 65 (Brit. Mus. inv. 589 B)
        (III B.C., Gurob?; cart.).    A. Koerte, Archiv 10.
        64: "anscheinend Verse."

1968    Elegiacs (or commentary on a poem?).    P. Lit. Lond.
        195 (Brit. Mus. inv. 1862 B) (I B.C.).    Archiv 10.
        236.    A. D. Knox, JEA 15 (1929) 139.

1969    Dramatic verse (?) (or "Acta Alexandrinorum"?).
        P. Oslo 3.170, verso (III).    Musurillo, No. XVII,
        pp. 76, 228 ("Fragm. Dubia vel Incerta").

1970    Verse (?).    P. Oslo 3.173 (I-II?).

1971    Verse (?).    P. Oslo 3.175 (II).

1972    Verse (?).    P. Oslo 3.176 (II).

1973    Verse (?).    P. Rain. 3.53 (inv. 29361) (II, Soknopaiou
        Nesos).

1974    Verse.    P. Rain. 3.55 (inv. 31490) (IV-V; parch. cod.).
        Archiv 14.116.

1975    Verse (?).    P. Rain. 3.56 (inv. 26748) (II B.C., Sok-
        nopaiou Nesos).

1976    Verse (?).    P. Ryl. 3.500 (III, Oxy.).

1977    Verse (hexameters?).    P. Ryl. 4.552 (II B.C.).

1978    Verse (hexameters or elegiacs?).    P. Schubart 11
        (III, Hermupolis).

1979    Verse (?).    P. Schubart 14 (II B.C.; ostr.).

1980    Verse (?).    P. Schubart 43 (II, Dime).

1981    Verse (?): Fragment in the Doric dialect (Sophron?).
        PSI 14.1387 (and Addendum, ibid., p. XVI) (II,
        Oxy.).

1982 Verse (?). D. G. Hogarth, JHS 25 (1905) 118 (Ash-molean Mus., G.141.1) (II-I B.C., Naucratis?; ostr.). Page, PMG 1038 (I). D. L. Page, JHS 67 (1947) 134-35, identifies the text as literary, and probably verse.

1983 Iambic trimeters. P. Mur. 108b and pl. LXXXI (I, Murabba'at, Judaea; papyrus). Listed by the editor as a philosophical (?) text; J. Bingen, Chr. Ég. 36 (1961) 410-11, discovers that the text is in iambics.

1984 Verse fragments. K. Kalbfleisch, Racc. Lumbroso 29-35 (Univ.-Bibl., Giessen, inv. 152, verso) (I B.C., Fayum?; on the verso of No. 1580).

Unidentified verse fragments: see also Nos. 166, 311, 455, 1357, 1502, 2176, 2292, 2460, 2662, 2707, 2713, 2720-21, 2731, 2737, 2826, 2850.

## 2. PROSE

### Agriculture

1985 Agricultural manual (?): On the culture of the almond. P. Hibeh 2.187 (Brit. Mus. inv. 2960) (ca. 280-240 B.C., Hibeh; cart.).

1986 Instructions for viticulture (copied by Zenon). PSI 6.624 (III B.C.).

### Anthologies

1987 Sayings of Diogenes. C. Wessely, Festschr. Gomperz 67-74 (P. Rain.) (I B.C., Fayum?; sch. ex.). Archiv 2.369-70.

1988 Sayings of Diogenes. H. Thompson, Proc. Soc. Bibl. Arch. 34 (1912) 197 (in the editor's private collec-tion) (III-IV, Thebes; ostr.; sch. ex.). F. Prei-sigke, Sammelbuch griechischer Urkunden aus Aegypten 1 (Strassburg 1913), No. 5730. W. A. Oldfather, Aeg. 14 (1934) 496-97.

1989 Sayings of Diogenes and others. P. Rain. 3.32 (inv. 19766) (cf. ibid. 4, p. 137) (II; on the verso of docu-ments; sch. ex.). Archiv 14.137-38.

1990 Sayings of Diogenes and Aristotle (?). P. Rein. 2. 85 (P. Sorbonne, inv. 2150) (III; sch. ex.?). Ar-chiv 14.138.

1991 Collection of prose maxims (?). A. Vogliano, Acme 1 (1948) 230-31 (P. Bon. inv. 5) (III-IV; pap. cod.).

1992 Anthology of maxims. A. Brinkmann, Rh. Mus. 71 (1916) 581-84 (P. Berol. inv. 7426) (II-III; on the verso). Sententiae from Isocrates, Ad Demonicum 39, etc.; a maxim ascribed to one Hermarchus (cf. Stobaeus iv. 34. 66).

1993 Philosophical maxims. R. Reitzenstein, Hermes 35 (1900) 608-11 (P. Strassb. inv. Gr. 92) (III; on the verso of No. 1251). The name of Favorinus stands at the head of the second section.

1994 Maxims. PSI 2.120 (IV, Oxy.). Archiv 7.156; New Chapters 2.99.

1995 Anecdotes (?). P. Oxy. 3.441 (Musées Royaux, Bruxelles, inv. E.5930) (III, Oxy.). Archiv 3. 282.

1996 Prose anthology. PRIMI 1.20 (II, Tebtunis). Con-tents: On the phoenix; Hercules excluded from the Eleusinian Mysteries; On exile; On the flower named after Antinous; On a style of himation worn by philo-sophers and orators. A. Koerte, Archiv 13.116-17, regards the text as "das Machwerk eines namenlosen Schulmeisters"; B. Snell, Gnomon 15 (1939) 536.

Prose anthologies: see also Nos. 76, 2853.

### Alchemy and Chemistry

1997 Treatise on chemistry. C. Leemans, Papyri Graeci Musei Antiquarii Publici Lugduni-Batavi 2 (Lugdu-ni Batavorum 1885) 199-259 (Rijksmuseum van Oud-heden, Leiden, inv. 10) (III-IV, Thebes; pap. cod.). Contains excerpts from Dioscorides, De Materia Medica, Bk. v. H. Diels, Antike Technik (Leipzig 1920$^2$) 139-49. JEA 6.127.

1998 Treatise on chemistry. P. Holm. (III-IV, Thebes?; pap. cod.). Cites "Aphrikianos"(Africanus?); Anaxi-laus; Ps.-Democritus. Schubart, Gr. Pal., Abb. 96. H. Diels, Antike Technik (Leipzig 1920$^2$) 139-49; R. J. Forbes, Studies in Ancient Technology 1 (Leiden 1955) 135, 137 (on No. 1997 also); J. R. Viellefond, Jules Africain: Fragments des Cestes (Paris 1932), "Introduction," pp. xxii-xxiii. JEA 2.97. K. Tittel, Berl. Phil. Woch. 34 (1914) 676-79; I. H. Jensen, Historisk-filologiske Meddelelser udgivne af det Kgl. Danske Videnskabernes Selskab 4 (1921), No. 2, p. 41 and passim; M. Wellmann, Abh. Berl. Akad., 1928, Nr. 7, 68-77, on the sources of this and No. 1997.

1999 On alchemy. P. Oxy. 3.467 (Bodleian Libr., Gr. class. f.73 (P)) (I-II, Oxy.). Archiv 3.298.

2000 Recipes for dyeing furs or hides, and wood to resemble ebony. C. Gallavotti, Riv. Fil. 67 (1939) 252-57 (PSI sine numero?) (?).

2001 Recipes for colors. P. Iand. 3.85 (inv. 212) (ca. A.D. 100). Gundel 47.

### Astronomy and Astrology

2002 Treatise on astronomy (?). P. Aberdeen 12 (II-III, Fayum?; on the verso of a document). Ed. pr.: E. O. Winstedt, CQ 1 (1907) 266. "Concerning northern constellations, probably part of an Aratus commentary ..." (Neugebauer, Astron. Pap. Ostr., No. 1).

2003 From a treatise on predictions of events from the moon and the planets. P. Mich. 3.148 (inv. 4) (I). Neugebauer-Van Hoesen, Astrol. Pap. Ostr., No. 117.

2004    Astronomical tables.    P. Aberdeen 128 (I, Fayum?).
        Neugebauer, Astron. Pap. Ostr., No. 2.

2005    Planetary table, with positions of the planets for four
        years.    O. Neugebauer, Chr. Ég. 32 (1957) 269-72
        (Bodleian Libr., Gr. class. f.7 (P)) (I; fragment
        of a wooden tablet).    For the years 60-63 (?).    Neu-
        gebauer, Astron. Pap. Ostr., No. 4.

2006    Treatise on the rising of Sirius.    O. Bodl. 2.2176
        (inv. 2897, now in the Ashmolean Mus., Oxford)
        (III; ostr.).    "Treatise concerning a 40-year cycle
        of the Alexandrian date of the rising of Sirius in
        relation to new moons ..." (Neugebauer, Astron.
        Pap. Ostr., No. 5).

2007    Tables of solar or lunar longitudes.    O. Bodl. 2.2177
        (inv. 1604, now in the Ashmolean Mus., Oxford)
        (III; ostr.).    Neugebauer, Astron. Pap. Ostr. No.
        6.

2008    An astronomical table.    Mentioned by Neugebauer,
        Astron. Pap. Ostr., No. 7 (Brooklyn Mus., Brook-
        lyn, New York) (?).    Meager fragments.    Identified
        by C. H. Roberts.

2009    Astronomical ephemeris.    P. Harris 60 (inv. 184 e)
        (III).    P. Ryl. 3.526 (see No. 2314) is possibly from
        the same text.    Neugebauer, Astron. Pap. Ostr.,
        No. 11.

2010    Astronomical ephemeris for A.D. 345-346 to 348-349.
        O. Neugebauer, Historisk-filologiske Meddelelser
        udgivne af det Kgl. Danske Videnskabernes Selskab,
        36, No. 4 (1956) (P. Heid. inv. 34) (IV; pap. cod.).
        F. Bilabel, Actes Pap. V, 82 (first mention).    J.
        J. Burckhardt, Osiris 13 (1958) 79-87, 91-92, shows
        that the calculations were made with the aid of
        Ptolemy's "Handy Tables"; O. Neugebauer, ibid.
        112. Neugebauer, Astron. Pap. Ostr., No. 12, adds
        some corrections to his ed. pr.

2011    Festival calendar and parapegma for years near 300
        B.C.    P. Hibeh 1.27 (Trinity Coll. Libr., Dublin)
        (III B.C., Hibeh; cart.; sch. text).    Based on the
        theories of Eudoxus.    Schubart, Gr. Pal., Abb. 66.
        Archiv 4.180-81.    Jacoby, FGH, Dritter Teil C,
        266-68.    Neugebauer, Astron. Pap. Ostr., No. 14.
        F. Bilabel, Neue Heidelb. Jahrb., 1929, 13-14 (from
        a study including various other festival calendars);
        A. Rehm, Abh. Münch. Akad. 19 (1941) 30-33.

2012    Treatise on spherical astronomy.    P. Iand. 5.84
        (inv. 533) (II).    Gundel 45.    Neugebauer, Astron.
        Pap. Ostr., No. 15.    Archiv 10.234-35.

2013    Concordance of the Julian and Alexandrian month names
        H. G. Gundel, Archiv 16 (1956) 13-19 (P. Iand. inv.
        654) (VI-VII; on the verso of a private letter?).
        Neugebauer, Astron. Pap. Ostr., No. 16.

2014    Astronomical tables ("Handy Tables").    O. Neuge-
        bauer and T. C. Skeat, Osiris 13 (1958) 93-113
        (Brit. Mus.) (ca. A.D. 200; pap. cod.).    P. Lond.
        3.1278 (first description).    Neugebauer, Astron.
        Pap. Ostr., No. 17.

2015    Lunar tables.    E. J. Knudtzon and O. Neugebauer,
        Årsb., Lund, 1946-47, 77-84 (inv. 35a) (II).
        Neugebauer, Exact Sc. 163-64 and pl. 2.    "Lunar

        tables, probably from Nero 6 to Trajan 12, i.e.
        from A.D. 59 to 108" (Neugebauer, Astron. Pap.
        Ostr., No. 18).

2016    Planetary ephemeris.    E. J. Knudtzon and O. Neu-
        gebauer, Årsb., Lund, 1946-47, 85-88 (inv. 35b)
        (II).    Perhaps from the same text as P. Tebt. 2.
        274 (see No. 2034).    "Planetary ephemeris for
        Hadrian 4 (i.e., A.D. 119/120)" (Neugebauer, As-
        tron. Pap. Ostr., No. 19).

2017    Astrological-astronomical treatise.    P. Mich. 3.149
        (inv. 1) (II).    Col. 16, line 2, refers to one Hippo-
        crates.    Ed. pr.: F. E. Robbins, CP 22 (1927)
        1-45.    A. E. Housman, ibid. 257-63; E. Honigmann,
        P. Mich. 3, pp. 301-21; O. Neugebauer, Trans.
        Amer. Philos. Soc., NS 32, Part 2 (1942) 255-58;
        Neugebauer, Astron. Pap. Ostr., No. 20; Neuge-
        bauer-Van Hoesen, Astrol. Pap. Ostr., No. 118
        (the authors doubt that "Hippocrates" is the Pre-
        Socratic mathematician of that name).

2018    Astronomical table.    P. Mich. 3.150 (inv. 3823) (III-
        IV).    O. Neugebauer, Trans. Amer. Philos. Soc.,
        NS 32, Part 2 (1942) 251-52.    "Full moons for one
        year ..." (Neugebauer, Astron. Pap. Ostr., No.
        21).

2019    Astronomical table.    P. Mich. 3.151 (inv. 924) (III).
        O. Neugebauer, Historisk-filologiske Meddelelser
        udgivne af det Kgl. Danske Videnskabernes Selskab
        39.1 (1960), adds another fragment from the same
        roll (P. Heid. inv. 4144).    O. Neugebauer, Trans.
        Amer. Philos. Soc., NS 32, Part 2 (1942) 260-62.
        "... arithmetical progressions related to zodiacal
        signs" (Neugebauer, Astron. Pap. Ostr., Nos. 13,
        22).

2020    An astronomical ephemeris for the year A.D. 467.
        H. D. Curtis and F. E. Robbins, Publ. Obs. U.M.
        6, No. 9 (1937) 77-100 (P. Mich. inv. 1454) (A.D.
        467; pap. cod.).    JEA 24.96; Chr. Eg. 11 (1936)
        177-78.    J. K. Fotheringham, CR 49 (1935) 242;
        R. W. Sloley, JEA 22 (1936) 218-19; J. J. Burck-
        hardt, Osiris 13 (1958) 79-80, 87-92, shows that
        the "Handy Tables" of Ptolemy were used for the
        calculations; Neugebauer, Astron. Pap. Ostr.,
        No. 23, gives some new interpretations of details.

2021    Astronomical treatise.    P. Oslo 3.73 (I-II).    Ed. pr.:
        S. Eitrem, Aeg. 13 (1933) 479-86.    M. Pieper, SO
        13 (1934) 65-67; L. Borchardt, ibid. 14 (1935) 73-
        76; O. Neugebauer, ibid. 17 (1937) 49-53; S. Ei-
        trem, ibid. 103.    "Treatise on the determination
        of the apparent diameter of the sun, mentioning a
        waterclock and an instrument with a ruler" (Neu-
        gebauer, Astron. Pap. Ostr., No. 24).

2022    Treatise on lunar motion.    P. Oxy. 2.303 (Bodleian
        Libr., Gr. class. g.48 (P)) (I, Oxy.).    Only lines
        4-5 are published in P. Oxy. 303; Neugebauer,
        Astron. Pap. Ostr., No. 26, gives a complete
        transcription.

2023    Treatise (?).    P. Oxy. 3.539, verso (Columbia Univ.
        Libr., but now missing) (II-III, Oxy.; on the verso
        of No. 620).    Neugebauer, Astron. Pap. Ostr.,
        No. 28, suspects that this is from the same roll as
        P. Ryl. 1.27 (see No. 2026).

2024    Fragments of a Royal Canon (Cyrus to Philippus Arabs, A.D. 249) and of an astronomical treatise. P. Sattler, Studien aus dem Gebiet der Alten Geschichte (Wiesbaden 1962) 39-50 (Egypt Exploration Society, London, inv. 7 B/1959) (III-IV, Oxy.; pap. cod.). Neugebauer, Astron. Pap. Ostr., No. 29 (first mention).

2025    Astronomical fragment. P. Petrie 3.134 (III, B.C., Gurob). On the 36 decans and feasts in Thoth, Tybi, and Pachon. Neugebauer, Astron. Pap. Ostr., No. 31.

2026    Treatise on lunar theory. P. Ryl. 1.27 (III; on the verso of No. 578). Cites Ptolemy and includes a Royal Canon, from Antoninus Pius to Trebonianus Gallus (col. 3, lines 75 ff.). Neugebauer, Exact. Sc. 164, 187; idem, Astron. Pap. Ostr., No. 32. O. Neugebauer, Historisk-filologiske Meddelelser udgivne af det Kgl. Danske Videnskabernes Selskab 32.2 (1949), shows that the text gives "rules for the computation of dates and longitudes of the moon." B. L. van der Waerden, Centaurus 5 (Copenhagen 1958) 177-91.

2027    Fragment of an astronomical treatise. P. Ryl. 3. 464 (cf. "Addenda and Corrigenda," p. xvii) (III; on the verso of a document). Neugebauer, Astron. Pap. Ostr., No. 33.

2028    Astronomical tables. P. Ryl. 3.523 (III, Fayum?; pap. cod.; text on recto, No. 1437 on verso). Neugebauer, Astron. Pap. Ostr., No. 34.

2029    Method of finding "lunar" new moons, and table of equivalents. P. Ryl. 4.589 (inv. 666) (ca. 180 B.C., Philadelphia?; text follows eight columns of accounts). Ed. pr.: E. G. Turner and O. Neugebauer, Bull. Ryl. Libr. 32 (1949) 80-96. Neugebauer, Astron. Pap. Ostr., No. 36.

2030    Introduction to the use of tables. Mentioned by Neugebauer, Astron. Pap. Ostr., No. 37 (I-II). To appear as PSI 15.1491. "Probably concerning the equations due to the eccentricities of the deferents."

2031    Astronomical table. Mentioned by Neugebauer, Astron. Pap. Ostr., No. 38 (II). To appear as PSI 15.1492. "Auxiliary table for the computation of the daily motion of Saturn."

2032    Astronomical table. Described by Neugebauer, Astron. Pap. Ostr., No. 39 (Roman period). To appear as PSI 15.1493.

2033    Fragments of planetary tables. Described by Neugebauer, Astron. Pap. Ostr., No. 41 (P. Strassb. inv. Gr. 1097) (?). "... probably concerning the entry of Mars or Venus into the zodiacal signs."

2034    Planetary ephemeris for A.D. 107 to 115. P. Tebt. 2.274 (II, Tebtunis). Perhaps from the same text as P. Lund. inv. 35 b (see No. 2016). Neugebauer, Astron. Pap. Ostr., No. 42; idem, Trans. Amer. Philos. Soc., NS 32.2 (1942) 241-43 and pl. 27.

2035    Astronomical calendar. P. Tebt. 2.449 (II, Tebtunis). "Daily motion of the moon during the month of Mekheir" (Neugebauer, Astron. Pap. Ostr., No. 43).

2036    Treatise on astronomy (including weather signs). C. Wessely, Sitzb. Wien. Akad., 1900, 1-41 (Institut für Österreichische Geschichtsforschung, Wien) (III B.C., Fayum). Neugebauer, Astron. Pap. Ostr., No. 44. Archiv l.536-38. A. Rehm, Berl. Phil. Woch. 22 (1902) 513-16; O. Neugebauer, Sitzb. Wien. Akad. 240 (1962), Abh. 2, 29-44 reedits the text.

2037    An ephemeris for the year A.D. 348 or 424. H. Gerstinger and O. Neugebauer, Sitzb. Wien. Akad. 240 (1962), Abh. 2, 5-25 (P. Vindob. inv. Gr. 29370 + 29370 b) (ca. A.D. 350-450; pap. cod.). Hemerologion of the Roman, Hellenic-Macedonian, and Alexandrian calendars, and of some fourth calendar. Neugebauer, Astron. Pap. Ostr., No. 45.

2038    Astrology: "Testamentum Salomonis" 18.34-40. K. Preisendanz, Eos 48.3 (= Symbolae R. Taubenschlag Dedicatae 3) (1957) 161-67 (P. Vindob. inv. Gr. 330) (VI). Fragment of a pseudonymous work, of medico-astrological interest, known hitherto only from late manuscripts.

2039    Fragment of an astrological treatise. P. Erl. 14 (inv. 129) (III-IV; pap. cod.). From the same work, but not the same papyrus, as No. 2055. Neugebauer-Van Hoesen, Astrol. Pap. Ostr., No. 112. Archiv 14.100.

2040    Fragment of an astrological treatise. P. Iand. 1.3 (inv. 10) (II, Fayum?; on the verso). Neugebauer-Van Hoesen, Astrol. Pap. Ostr., No. 113.

2041    Classification of the signs of the zodiac. P. Oslo 3. 74 (II, Tebtunis; on the verso of an account). Neugebauer-Van Hoesen, Astrol. Pap. Ostr., No. 121.

2042    Fragment of a work on apotelesmatika. P. Merton 2.56 (II). Neugebauer-Van Hoesen, Astrol. Pap. Ostr., No. 115.

2043    Fragment on prognostications. P. Merton 2.57 (II). A name on the verso may be that of the author: (...)ychides. Neugebauer-Van Hoesen, Astrol. Pap. Ostr., No. 116.

2044    Rules for a board game, with their mythological and astrological motivations; the construction of a waterclock. P. Oxy. 3.470 (Trinity Coll. Libr., Dublin, Pap. F. 8 (III, Oxy.; pap. cod.). Neugebauer, Astron. Pap. Ostr., No. 27; Neugebauer-Van Hoesen, Astrol. Pap. Ostr., No. 124. Archiv 3.299. L. Borchardt, Die altägyptische Zeitmessung (Berlin 1920) 10-14 and pls. 7-8, on the waterclock; M. Pieper, Zeitschr. für ägyptische Sprache und Altertumskunde 66 (1931) 29-30, on the board game.

2045    Fragment of an astrological treatise. P. Rain. 1.26 (inv. 29826) (III, Fayum?). Neugebauer-Van Hoesen, Astrol. Pap. Ostr., No. 127. Archiv 11.280-81.

2046    Fragment of an astrological treatise. P. Rain. 1.27 (inv. 31572) (I-II, Philadelphia?). Neugebauer-Van Hoesen, Astrol. Pap. Ostr., No. 128. Archiv 11.281.

2047    Astrological fragment.    P. Rein. 1.6 (P. Sorbonne
        inv. 2015) (II).  Neugebauer-Van Hoesen, Astrol.
        Pap. Ostr., No. 129, suggest restorations.  Ar-
        chiv 3.500-1.

2048    Fragment of an astrological treatise.    P. Ross. Georg.
        5.2 (Collection of G. Zereteli, Tiflis) (II).  Neuge-
        bauer-Van Hoesen, Astrol. Pap. Ostr., No. 130.

2049    Astrological dialogue.    P. Ryl. 2.63 (III; on the verso
        of an account).  An imaginary dialogue between Plato
        and an Egyptian prophet.  Neugebauer-Van Hoesen,
        Astrol. Pap. Ostr., No. 131.

2050    Treatise (in dialogue form?):  Influence of the positions
        of the planets.  P. Ryl. 3.527 (III, Oxy.; on the
        verso of No. 2933).  Neugebauer-Van Hoesen, As-
        trol. Pap. Ostr., No. 133.  Archiv 14.147.

2051    Effects (apotelesmata) of the positions of the planets.
        P. Tebt. 2.276 (II-III, Tebtunis).  Neugebauer-
        Van Hoesen, Astrol. Pap. Ostr., No. 143.

2052    Fragment of a treatise on astrology.    P. Tebt. 2.277
        (III, Tebtunis; on the verso of a land survey).
        Neugebauer-Van Hoesen, Astrol. Pap. Ostr., No.
        144.

2053    From a treatise on the planets.    PSI 3.158 (III?, Oxy.;
        pap. cod.).  Neugebauer-Van Hoesen, Astrol. Pap.
        Ostr., No. 136.

2054    From an astrological manual.    PSI 12.1289 (II, Oxy.).
        It is said that the papyrus has been returned to
        Cairo and is now lost.  Ed. pr.: V. Bartoletti,
        Aeg. 19 (1939) 186-92.  Neugebauer-Van Hoesen,
        Astrol. Pap. Ostr., No. 138.

2055    Fragment on medical astrology (?).    P. Lit. Lond.
        172 (Brit. Mus. inv. 2397, verso) (III; on the verso
        of No. 2358).  Neugebauer-Van Hoesen, Astrol.
        Pap. Ostr., No. 114, restore col. II.  Archiv 10.
        235.

2056    Astrological calendar.    P. Oxy. 3.465; P. Lit. Lond.
        173 (Brit. Mus. inv. 1526, verso) (II, Oxy.; on the
        verso of a list of persons).  Neugebauer-Van Hoesen,
        Astrol. Pap. Ostr., No. 123 (detailed discussion).
        Archiv 3.296.

2057    Astrological (?) fragment.    P. Aberdeen 127 (II-III,
        Fayum?).  Neugebauer-Van Hoesen, Astrol. Pap.
        Ostr., No. 101, doubt whether the text is astro-
        logical.

2058    Fragment of an astrological treatise.    P. Ryl. 3.528
        (II-III).  Neugebauer-Van Hoesen, Astrol. Pap.
        Ostr., No. 134.  Archiv 14.147.

2059    Fragment of a treatise on judicial astrology, with
        geographical data.  PSI 6.727 (IV?, Oxy.).  Neu-
        gebauer-Van Hoesen, Astrol. Pap. Ostr., No. 137.
        Archiv 7.254.

2060    Fragment of a treatise.    E. Rabel, Gött. Abh., Neue
        Folge 16, Abh. 3 (1917) 74 (Univ.-Bibl., Basel, inv.
        36, verso) (III; on the verso of a document).  Neu-
        gebauer-Van Hoesen, Astrol. Pap. Ostr., No. 104:
        "... from treatise concerning sun and moon in

        quartile or octile with respect to some planet. "
        JAW 243.65.  F. Boll, Gött. Abh. 16, Abh. 3
        (1917) 85-88.

2061    Astrological fragment.    F. Boll, Archiv 1 (1901) 500-1
        (P. Monac. inv. 92) (II).  Neugebauer-Van Hoesen,
        Astrol. Pap. Ostr., No. 119.  Archiv 2.375.

2062    Astrological fragment.    F. Boll, Archiv 1 (1901) 492-
        500 (Bayerische Staatsbibliothek, München, cod.
        Graec.610, No. 5) (III, Egypt?; parch.).  Neuge-
        bauer-Van Hoesen, Astrol. Pap. Ostr., No. 120,
        revise the dating: saec. III, not VII-VIII.  Archiv
        2.375.

2063    Astrology: A horoscope.    P. Ryl. 3.524 (III, Fayum?).
        Archiv 14.146.  Regarded by the editors as a frag-
        ment of an astronomical treatise, this has been
        identified as a horoscope by O. Neugebauer and H.
        B. Van Hoesen, Aeg. 32 (1952) 333-35; as such, it
        no longer falls within the scope of the present list.

2064    Astrological fragment.    O. Bodl. 2.2178 (inv. 2755)
        (III?; ostr.).  Neugebauer-Van Hoesen, Astrol.
        Pap. Ostr., No. 109.

2065    Astrological fragment.    O. Strassb. 1.811 (inv. 469)
        (II; ostr.).  Neugebauer-Van Hoesen, Astrol. Pap.
        Ostr., No. 141.

2066    Astrological text.    P. Michael. 1 (II; on the verso of
        No. 242).  Neugebauer-Van Hoesen, Astrol. Pap.
        Ostr., No. 118a.

2067    An astrological portion of the "Paris Magical Papyrus. "
        Preisendanz, PGM, No. 4, lines 835-49 (pp. 102-3)
        (Paris, Bibl. Nat., Suppl. Gr. 574) (IV; pap. cod.).
        Neugebauer-Van Hoesen, Astrol. Pap. Ostr., No.
        126.


        Poems on astrology: see Nos. 1615, 1767-68, 1874-75.
        Astronomy and astrology: see also Nos. 96, 186,242,
        2213.


                        Biography

2068    Famous men.    H. Diels, Abh. Berl. Akad., 1904,
        Abh. 2 (P. Berol. inv. 13044) (II-I B.C., Abusir-
        el-Malaq; cart.; from the same papyrus as No.
        2099; No. 1774 on the verso).  The "Laterculi
        Alexandrini": brief notices of lawgivers, painters,
        sculptors, architects, etc.  Schubart, PGB, tab.
        7 b.  Archiv 3.492.

2069    Famous men.    P. Oxy. 10.1241 (Trinity Coll. Libr.,
        Dublin) (II, Oxy.).  Notices of sculptors, painters,
        grammarians, librarians, inventors of weapons;
        important for the librarianship, at Alexandria, of
        Apollonius Rhodius.  Cites Aristotle (?); Hellani-
        cus (Jacoby, FGH 1.150); Philochorus.  Archiv 7.
        242-43; JEA 6.127.  Jacoby, FGH 2.1011, on Era-
        tosthenes of Cyrene; J. Tolkiehn, Woch. Phil. 32
        (1915) 1143-46, on the grammarian Diocles; V.
        Gardthausen, Zeitschr. Deutsch. Ver. Buchw. 5
        (1922) 76, on the absence of Callimachus from the
        list of librarians; C. Wendel, Handbuch der Biblio-
        thekswissenschaft ... herausgegeben von G. Leyh
        3.1 (Wiesbaden 1955) 74.

2070    Writers and heroes.   P. Oxy. 15.1800, 17.2081 h
(II-III, Oxy.).  Biographies of Sappho, Simonides,
Aesop. Thucydides, Demosthenes, Aeschines, Thra-
sybulus, Hyperides, Leucocomas (a hero of romance)
Abderus (the eponym of Abdera), and perhaps Lysias.
Cites the grammarian Chamaeleon.  For the life of
Sappho, see Lobel-Page, PLF 106-7; Treu, Sappho
110.  For that of Aesop, see Zeitz 25-26, and Aeg.
16 (1936) 248-50; Perry, Aesopica, No. 25; A.
Wiechers, Aesop in Delphi (Meisenheim-Glan 1961)
16, 24, 33, 44.  A. Calderini, Rend.
Ist. Lomb. 55 (1922) 261-66; K. F. W. Schmidt,
Gött. Anz., 1924, 12-13.

2071    A list of tragedians.   P. Tebt. 3.695 (III B.C., Tebtunis; cart.).  Names, birthplaces, and number of
plays written by each; those preserved: Amymon
of Sicyon, Democrates of Sicyon, and Moschus of
Lampsacus.  Archiv 11.277.

2072    A life of Aesop.   PSI 2.156 (IV, Upper Egypt; pap.
cod. ?).  The text corresponds to Vita Aesopi 1-3
in Perry, Aesopica.  Perry, Studies 40-45; Zeitz
3-6.  Identified by O. Crusius, Lit. Zentralbl. 1913,
1725-26; P. Collart, Rev. Phil. 43 (1919) 38-46.

2073    A life of Aesop.   P. Oxy. 17.2083 (IV-V, Oxy.; pap.
cod.).  The text corresponds to Vita Aesopi 60-62
in Perry, Aesopica.  Perry, Studies 45-52; Zeitz
6-10.  Archiv 10.233.

2074    A life of Aesop.   Zeitz 11-14 (P. Berol. inv. 11628)
(II-III).  Schubart, Gr. Pal., Abb. 89.  The text
corresponds to Vita Aesopi 121-24 in Perry, Aesopica.  Perry, Studies 53-58.

2075    A life of Aesop.   H. Weil, Rev. Phil. 9 (1885) 19-24;
P. Ross. Georg. 1.18 (P. Golenischeff, State Mus.
of Fine Arts, Moscow) (VI-VII, Fayum?; pap.
cod.).  The text corresponds to Vita Aesopi 125-33
in Perry, Aesopica.  Perry, ibid., p. 13; idem,
Studies 58-70; Zeitz 15-25.  Archiv 8.271-72.  G.
Zereteli, in a memorial volume for B. I. Lamanskii
(Petrograd 1907) 41-54 (in Russian); L. Castiglioni,
Aeg. 7 (1926) 226-27; C. F. Kumaniecki, ibid. 13
(1933) 51-52.

2076    Fragment of a saying of Aesop.   Wilcken, Gr. Ostr.
2.1226 (Late Roman; ostr.; sch. ex.).

2077    Life of Alcibiades.   P. Oxy. 3.411; P. Lit. Lond. 123
(Brit. Mus. inv. 1523) (V, Oxy.; parch. cod.).
Archiv 3.282.

2078    Life of Demosthenes (or fragment of a grammatical
treatise?).   PSI 2.144 (II, Oxy.).  Refers to Crates
(the comic poet or the Cynic?); Eratosthenes (?).
Wilamowitz, DLZ 34 (1913) 1863, prefers a treatise
on accentuation or etymology; A. Koerte, Archiv
7.243, prefers a grammatical treatise.

2079    An encomium of Demosthenes (?).   W. E. Blake,
TAPA 57 (1926) 275-95 (P. Mich. inv. 10)  (II).
Archiv 10.219-20; New Chapters 2.73; Winter,
LLP 249-50.

2080    Life of Isocrates (Dioscorus of Aphrodito?).   P.
Maspero 2.67175 (VI-VII?, Aphrodito; sch. text?).

2081    A saying of Isocrates.   Wilcken, Gr. Ostr. 2.1310
(Late Roman; ostr.; sch. ex.).

2082    An anecdote about Pyrrhus.   P. Mil. Vogl. 2.48 (inv.
225) (II-III; on the verso).  Ed. pr.: M. Vandoni,
Acme 8, fasc. 2-3 (1955) 137-38.  The same anecdote as in Plutarch, Vita Pyrrhi 8.

2083    Life of the philosopher Secundus.   P. Ross. Georg.
1.17 (State Hermitage Mus., Leningrad) (II-III; sch.
ex. ?).  H. Sauppe, Philol. 17 (1861) 149-54; L.
Castiglioni, Aeg. 7 (1926) 227-28.

2084    Life and sayings of Socrates.   P. Hibeh 2.182 (Brit.
Mus. inv. 2955) (ca. 280-250 B.C., Hibeh; cart.).
One of the anecdotes reappears, in a condensed
version, in Diogenes Laertius ii. 34.

2085    A biographical reference book.   Mentioned by Winter,
LLP 262-63 (P. Mich. inv. 25) (II-III).

2086    Sayings (like those of Diogenes?).   Mentioned by
Winter, LLP 269 (P. Mich. inv. 41) (?).

Biography: see also Nos. 1351, 1987-90, 2292
(apophthegms of the Seven Sages), 2643 (sayings of Diogenes).

### Book Catalogues

2087    Book catalogue.   M. Norsa and R. Sabbadini, Aeg.
2 (1921) 17-22 (PSI sine numero?) (III, Oxy.; on
the verso of a property list).  The text lists: Aris-
tophanes; Aristotle (?), Eudemus; Euripides,
Opera Omnia (?); Favorinus (?); Homer, Opera
Omnia (?); Lucian (?), Anacharsis; Lysias (?),
Ad Calliclem;  Menander, Opera Omnia (?);
Plato (many titles); Xenophon, Agesilaus, Anabasis, Cynegeticus, Cyropaedia, Symposium.
Archiv 7.112, 247-48.  C. H. Oldfather, The Greek
Literary Texts ... 72-75.  V. Gardthausen, Zeitschr.
Deutsch. Ver. Buchw. 5 (1922) 92; H. Gerstinger,
WS 50 (1932) 187-88; C. Wendel, Zentralblatt für
Bibliothekswesen 54 (1937) 586-87, rejects the re-
storation of "Favorinus," and suggests an inven-
tory of books on hand, not a list of desiderata nor
of required readings; E. G. Turner, JEA 38 (1952)
90-91; C. Wendel, Handbuch der Bibliothekswissen-
schaft ... herausgegeben von G. Leyh 3.1 (1955) 73.

2088    Book catalogue.   G. Manteuffel, Aeg. 13 (1933) 367-73
(P. Varsov. inv. 5) (III, Fayum?; a rectangular
leaf of papyrus; on the verso of accounts).  Lists
the philosophers Antipater (?) of Tarsus; Diogenes
of Babylon; Geminus (of Rhodes?); Harpocration
(the Platonist?); Hierocles; Persaeus of Citium
(?); (--?--) Socraticus; and the physcians Chrysippus, Glaucon, Themison, Thessalus, Xenophon
(Gaius Stertinius Xenophon?).  Archiv 11.277, 13.
125-26.  G. Manteuffel, Eos 34 (1932-33) 197-98.

2089    Catalogue of a library(?).   Wilcken, Chrest., No.
155; P. Ross. Georg. 1.22 (Public Libr., Leningrad) (III, Memphis).  The text lists: Aelius
(Aelius Aristides?); Anthestius (?), Sokratikon
Epistolon Synagogai; Apion; Archimedes; Aristotle, Peri aretes, Politeia Athenaion, Politeia

Neapoliton; Cebes Socraticus; Chrysippus (?),
Techne logon kai tropon, Bk. i; Crito (?); Diogenes (or Diogenianus?); Dion (?), Peri apistias;
Eratosthenes (?), Peri alypias; Eucri--(?); Hippias; Nigrinus, Apologiai; Posidonius, Peri orges,
Bk. i; Simon Socraticus; Theophrastus, Peri so-
phrosynes. Ed. pr.: J. Zuendel, Rh. Mus. 21
(1866) 431-37. Archiv 2.163; New Chapters 2.214-
15. E. Kurtz, Byz. Zeitschr. 11 (1902) 219, regards
the text as an inventory of business documents and
literary works; V. Gardthausen, Zeitschr. Deutsch.
Ver. Buchw. 5 (1922) 91-92; L. Castiglioni, Aeg.
7 (1926) 224; H. Gerstinger, WS 50 (1932) 186-87.

2090    Book catalogue (or index to an author?).    P. Flor.
3.371, recto (III).    Line 12 matches Plato, Res
Publica vii.540 C.    Ed. pr.: G. Vitelli, AR 7 (1904)
178-79.    Archiv 3.492.    V. Gardthausen, Zeitschr.
Deutsch. Ver. Buchw. 5 (1922) 78-79; F. Lasserre,
Aeg. 37 (1957) 243-49, regards the text as a Pinax
listing the works of one writer, and restores the
titles, "Concerning Dionysius," "On the Dry Style,"
and "On the Beautiful Style."

2091    A letter concerning books.    P. Oxy. 18.2192 (II, Oxy.).
The writer desiderates copies of Hypsicrates,
Komodoumenoi, Bks. vi-vii, and mentions Harpo-
cration, Seleucus, "Polion," and "prose epitomes
of Thersagoras' work on the myths of tragedy." E.
G. Turner, JEA 38 (1952) 91-92, identifies the Har-
pocration mentioned as the well known lexicographer
(cf. No. 458, above), and the "Polion" as Valerius
Pollio of Alexandria, the author of a Synagoge
Attikon lexeon; idem, Akten Pap. VIII, 143; F.
Zucker, Archiv 16 (1958) 252; B. Hemmerdinger,
Rev. Ét. Gr. 72 (1959) 107-9, discusses the floruit
of Harpocration, and suggests that the Seleucus
in question is the grammarian S. of Alexandria.

2092    A list of payments for copying manuscripts.    H. I.
Bell, Aeg. 2 (1921) 281-88 (Brit. Mus. inv. 2110)
(II, Oxy.?; from an account).    Mentions Aristo-
phanes, Plutus; Sophocles, Thyestes Tertius.
JEA 8.85; New Chapters 3.100-1.    E. G. Turner,
JEA 38 (1952) 90.

2093    Private letter, containing a list of books.    PRIMI
1.11 (II, Oxy.).    Lists titles for Antipater, Boëthus,
Chrysippus, Diogenes, and Posidonius.    Archiv
12.80-81; JEA 23.92.    E. G. Turner, JEA 38 (1952)
91; K. Reinhardt, RE 22.1, 568, 768, on Posidonius,
Peri tou protrepesthai.

Book catalogues: For book catalogues recorded in
inscriptions, see A. Maiuri, Nuova silloge epi-
grafica di Rodi e Cos (Firenze 1925), No. 11; C.
Wendel, Die griechisch-römische Buchbeschreib-
ung (Halle 1949) 44, 71; idem, Handbuch der
Bibliothekswiss. ... herausg. von G. Leyh 3.1
(Wiesbaden 1955) 72, 97.    For lists of Biblical,
Patristic, and Christian works, see C. Wessely,
Festschrift zu Ehren Emil von Ottenthals (Inns-
bruck 1925) 184-85; H. Gerstinger, WS 50 (1932)
185-92; and C. H. Roberts, Zeitschrift für die
neutestamentliche Wissenschaft 37 (1938) 185-88.

## Botany and Zoology

2094    On the medical properties of plants.    P. Tebt. 2.679
(II, Tebtunis).    The colored illustrations include
one for Pseudo-Dictamnum.    Weitzmann, Anc. Bk.
Ill. 11 and fig. 10.    JAW 180.68.    J. DeM. Johnson,
Arch. Gesch. N.T. 4 (1913) 403-8.

2095    On the properties of plants (symphyton and phlommos).
C. Singer, JHS 47 (1927) 31-33 ("P. Johnson": Egypt
Exploration Society, London?) (ca. A.D. 400, Antinoë).    Illustrations.    Weitzmann, Anc. Bk. Ill.
11-12 and fig. 11.

2096    On natural history (?).    P. Tebt. 2.675 (II, Tebtunis).

A poem on botany: see No. 1873.

Zoology: see No. 1501.

## Cooking

2097    Cooking: Opsartytika (two Greek fragments and a
Latin fragment).    F. Bilabel, Sitzb. Heid. Akad.,
1919, Abh. 23; idem, Philol. 80 (1925) 340-41 (P.
Heid. inv. 1001 a-b) (III-V; cart.).    JEA 10.152.
C. Giarratano and F. Vollmer, Apicii De Re
Coquinaria (Lipsiae 1922) 87-91.    The Latin frag-
ment: Cavenaile, CPL 318; Lowe, CLA 8.1220;
Marichal 291.

## Dialogue

2098    A Socratic (?) dialogue: The importance of oratory
in a democracy.    PSI 11.1215 (I-II, Oxy.).    Ed. pr.:
BSAA 8, No. 28 (1933) 133-34.    Archiv 11.272.    M.
Gigante, Aeg. 28 (1948) 195-98, ibid. 29 (1949) 51-
55; R. Merkelbach, ibid. 56-58; V. Bartoletti,
SIFC, NS 31 (1959) 100-3.

2099    Dialogue of Alexander and the Gymnosophists.    U.
Wilcken, Sitzb. Berl. Akad., 1923, 160-83 (P. Berol.
inv. 13044) (II-I B.C., Abusir-el-Malaq; cart.;
from the same roll as No. 2068; No. 1774 on the
verso).    Jacoby, FGH 2.827-28; Manteuffel, Opusc.,
No. 11; Merkelbach, Quellen 104, 113-18; Robinson,
Hist. Alex. 273-74.    Archiv 7.234; New Chapters
3.220-21; Winter, LLP 261.    G. Zuntz, Hermes 87
(1959) 436-40.

2100    Dialogue of Alexander and the Gymnosophists (Greek
text in Latin characters).    PSI 7.743 (I-II).    Identified by G. Vitelli, Aeg. 4 (1923) 314-15.    Calderini,
PL, No. 14; Cavenaile, CPL 69; Collart, PLL 1;
Marichal 68.

2101    Dialogue on the deification of Alexander; Dialogue
between Antipater and Cassander.    P. Freib. 2
a-b (inv. 7, 8) (II; a, on the verso of an inventory
of jewelry in Latin; b, on the verso of documents?;
sch. ex.).    Jacoby, FGH 2.825-26; Robinson, Hist.
Alex. 271-73.    Archiv 7.238-39; JAW 211.83-85;
JEA 8.86, 10.150; New Chapters 2.106-11.    W.
Bannier, Rh. Mus. 72 (1917-18) 230-31; L. Deubner, Hermes 56 (1921) 314-19, on the relation to
Lucian, Demosthenis Encomium 26; W. Croenert,
Gött. Nachr., 1922, 32-45; R. Reitzenstein, ibid.
189-96.

2102    Rhetorical dialogue on the trial of Demades.   BKT
7.13-34 (inv. 13045) (I B.C., Abusir-el-Malaq;
cart.; from the same roll as No. 2570). Schubart,
Gr. Pal., Abb. 71. Archiv 7.236-38; JAW 211.
85-86; JEA 11.86; New Chapters 2.111-14, 122-23.
H. von Arnim, WS 43 (1922-23) 86-90, 213-15.

2103    Socratic (?) dialogue: On Eros. P. Erl. 7 (inv. 4)
(ca. A.D. 200). Archiv 14.100. R. Merkelbach,
Archiv 16 (1956) 107, reprints the text, and doubts
that it comes from Aeschines Socraticus, Alcibiades.

     Dialogue: see also Nos. 1214-15, 2049-50, 2249,
2444, 2539, 2560, 2562, 2593, 2596, 2652, 2811-12,
2842.

     For catechisms, see Nos. 1207, 2277, 2287-88,
2340-43, 2601, 2644.

### Divination

2104    Treatise on divination. P. Amh. 2.14 (III-IV; pap.
cod.). Archiv 2.374-75. E. M. Husselman, Aeg.
19 (1939) 3-10.

2105    Treatise on divination. P. Oxy. 6.885 (Musées Royaux, Bruxelles, inv. E.5973) (II-III, Oxy.). The
interpretation of lightning bolts which strike statues.

2106    Treatise on types of divination (?). PSI 10.1179 (II-III,
Oxy.). Archiv 13.130.

2107    Treatise on hepatoscopy. PSI 10.1178 (II). Archiv
13.130.

2108    Treatise on hieroscopy. P. Ross. Georg. 1.21 (P.
Golenischeff, State Mus. of Fine Arts, Moscow)
(II). Mentions, apparently as an authority, one
Eudemus or Ecdemus. L. Castiglioni, Aeg. 7
(1926) 225.

2109    Numerology: A list of isopsephisms. T. C. Skeat,
Mizraim 3 (1936) 23-25 (VI; wooden tablet; on the
verso of No. 2316).

2110    Treatise on palmomancy. P. Flor. 3.391 (III). Ed.
pr.: G. Vitelli, AR 7 (1904) 32-42. Archiv 3.296-
97.

2111    Fragment on palmomancy. P. Oslo 3.76 (IV, Oxy.).
S. Kyriakides, SO 15-16 (1936) 138-39.

2112    Treatise on palmomancy. P. Ryl. 1.28 (IV; pap. cod.).

2113    Treatise on palmomancy. PSI 6.728 (IV; pap. cod.?).
Archiv 7.254.

     Divination: see also Nos. 552, 645, 1031 ("Homero-
manteia"). On the omission of the magical texts,
see the Introduction, p.

### Epistolography

2114    An Alexander romance in epistolary form. PSI 12.
1285 (II, Oxy.; on the verso of a document). Two
letters from Darius to Alexander, two from Alexander to Darius, and one from Polyidus to Darius;
of these, two are found in Ps.-Callisthenes. Ed.
pr.: D. Pieraccioni, Lettere del ciclo di Alessan-
dro in un papiro egiziano (Firenze 1947). Merkelbach, Quellen 1, 201-6. Archiv 16.111. R. Merkelbach, Aeg. 27 (1947) 144-58; S. Mariotti, Ann. Sc.
Pisa, Ser. 2.17 (1948) 223-28; C. Préaux, Chr.
Ég. 23 (1948) 197-98; A. Barigazzi, Acme 3 (1950)
435-38; idem, Athen., NS 34 (1956) 167-69; Lesky,
GGL 700.

2115    An anthology of fictitious letters. P. Hamb. 129 (inv.
605) (I B.C.). Nine letters preserved: four from
the epistolary Alexander romance (cf. No. 2114); a
letter from Hannibal to the Athenians; a correspondence between Philip and the Spartans. According
to the subscription, the entire roll contained 170
letters. R. Merkelbach, Aeg. 27 (1947) 144, 153
(first mention). Merkelbach, Quellen 1-2, 195,
199-201, 216; P. H. Thomas, Incerti Auctoris
Epitoma Rerum Gestarum Alexandri ... (Lipsiae
1960), pp. XI, 17-18. Archiv 16.111. J. Bingen,
Chr. Ég. 31 (1956) 173-74.

2116    A letter of the Emperor Hadrian to Antoninus. P.
Fay. 19 (II, Bacchias; on the verso of a tax list;
sch. ex.).

2117    Epistolary models, in Latin and Greek. P. Bon. 1.5
(inv. 1) (III-IV). Edd. pr.: G. B. Pighi, Aeg. 27
(1947) 162-70 (partial publication); A. Vogliano and
L. Castiglioni, Acme 1 (1948) 199-216; Vogliano,
ibid. 407-8, reports suggestions by P. Maas. R.
Merkelbach, Archiv 16 (1956) 127-28. Cavenaile,
CPL 279 (the Latin portion). R. Marichal, Pauli
Sent. Fr. Leid., p. 34, dates the Latin script to
saec. III-IV.

2118    A model letter, from a collection (?). P. Schubart
40 (III).

     Epistolography: see also Nos. 236, 2203-4, 2259,
2726.

### Glossaries and Word-Lists

2119    Fragments of the "Cyrillus-glossary." P. Colt 8
(VII, Nessana, Palestine; a part of the pap. cod.
containing also P. Colt 9, the Twelve Chapters on
Faith ascribed to Gregory Thaumaturgus). In the
tradition of Hesychius and the Suda lexicon. Identified by P. Maas, Byz. Zeitschr. 44 (1951) 409.

2120    A glossary of words in alpha. P. Oxy. 17.2087 (II,
Oxy.). Cites Aeschines Socraticus, Peri ploutou
xxii (line 29); Aristotle, Historia Animalium
ix.40.624a.34 (43-44), Res Publica Atheniensium
54.2 (1-10); Demosthenes, Contra Boëtum 10 (32-33);
Herodotus i.32 (31), vi.12 (28), v.74 (41); Plato,
Leges 747D (26), Phaedo (22) (by error for Leges
ii.672C; see O. Immisch, Phil. Woch. 48, 1928,
908); Thucydides iii.49.4 (25), vi.80.4 (12). Archiv 10.230-31.

2121    Comic lections (words in beta).   P. Oxy. 15.1801 (I, Oxy.; text on recto, No. 2149 on verso). Cites Alexis, Hesione (line 50; restored, so as to refer to Antiphanes, by O. Weinreich, Sitzb. Wien. Akad., 1942, Abh. 4, 123-38); Aristophanes, Acharnenses 345 (46), Lysistrata 354 (detected in line 16 by S. Kurz, apud Weinreich, op. cit.), Polyidus (21), Vespae 1530 (?) (40), Fabula Incerta (59); Cratinus (?), Satyrs (17), Thressae (?) (34); Eupolis (removed from line 15 by Kurz, loc. cit.); Hermippus, Stratioati (?) (57); Phylarchus, Historiae, Bk. iv (44; Jacoby, FGH 2.164; idem, Hermes 58, 1923, 239-40 = Abhandlungen zur griech. Geschichtschreibung, Leiden 1956, 352-53, where it is also suggested that a citation of Heraclides Lembus has been lost); Sophocles, Salmoneus (?) (10).   Archiv 7.246; JAW 216.8.

2122    Fragments with words in delta and epsilon.   P. Hibeh 2.175 (Brit. Mus. inv. 2948) (ca. 260-240 B.C., Hibeh; cart.).

2123    Fragment of a word-list (words in zeta).   P. Michael. 6 (Byzantine).

2124    Fragment including a gloss on neleites.   P. Oxy. 22. 2328 (I-II, Oxy.).   Treu, Archil. 21.

2125    Words in phy-- (Diogenianus?).   PSI 8.892 (IV?; pap. cod.).   A. Koerte, Archiv 10.231-32, suggests Diogenianus, Lexis pantodapé, a source for Hesychius.

2126    Words in sigma.   P. Oxy. 15.1803 (VI, Oxy.; pap. cod.).   Cites Aristophanes, Equites 655-56, and Geras; Demosthenes, In Dionysodorum; Eupolis, Chrysoun Genos; Menander, Enchiridium, Georgus, Phanium, Philadelphoe, Synaristosae; Thucydides vii.60; Xenophon, Anabasis ii.1.6, v.4.29 (?). Archiv 7.247; JAW 207.121.   K. F. W. Schmidt, Gött. Anz., 1924, 15-16.

2127    Rare words.   P. Oxy. 15.1802 (II-III, Oxy.; on the verso of No. 2195).   Cites Andron (historian of Halicarnassus?); Antenor (historian of Crete ?); Anticlides (historian of Athens?); Apollodorus (of Athens?; Jacoby, FGH 2.1045); Aristotle, Historia Animalium ix.13.615b.24, ix.41.627b-628a, Res Publica Soleorum, Res Publica Thessalorum (?); Asclepiades (?); Autoclides, Exegeticum (?); Callimachus, Hypomnemata (Pfeiffer, Callim. 1, fr. 462); Dionysius (Thrax or Tryphonis?); Dionysius (?) Itycaeus; Glaucus (a geographer; Jacoby, FGH Dritter Teil C, 843); Hegesander (of Delphi?); Heraclides (Lembus?); Heraclides, Lingua Barbara, Bk. i; --?--, On Babylon (bis), On Rivers, Scythica, Bk. iii (Jacoby, FGH, Dritter Teil C, 931); Zeno (grammarian of Myndus?).   Archiv 7. 245-46.   K. F. W. Schmidt, Gött. Anz., 1924, 13-15.

2128    Lections from oratory.   P. Oxy. 15.1804 (III, Oxy.). Cites Aeschines, De Falsa Legatione 158; Demosthenes, Contra Phormionem 9, In Philippum vii; Dinarchus, Adversus Polyeuctum; Hyperides, Contra Autoclem.   Archiv 7.246-47.   K. F. W. Schmidt, Gött. Anz., 1924, 16.

2129    A poetical onomasticon   (Philetas, Glôssai ataktoi?). P. Hibeh 2.172 (Brit. Mus. inv. 2945) (ca. 270-230 B.C., Hibeh; cart. ?).   A non-alphabetical list of compound adjectives, poetic epithets.   Galiano, LG 142.   Page, PMG 928.

2130    An etymological fragment on the festival of the Scirophoria (Lysimachides?).   P. Merton 2.55 (II). Possibly from a glossary; refers to Apollonius (of Acharnae?).

2131    Glossary.   Wilamowitz, Sitzb. Berl. Akad., 1918, 739-42 (O. Berol. inv. 12605) (III B.C.; ostr.; sch. ex.).   Quotes Antimachus, Lyde (Diehl, Anth. Lyr. 1².1.100-1; Powell, CA 250; Wyss, No. 159); Hipponax (Diehl, Anth. Lyr. 1².3.88, ibid. 3³.93, fr. 42 A; Medeiros, pp. LXI-LXII and fr. 62); and Homer, Od. xi.311, xxi.390-31 (Collart, Pap. f; Mette, Od. 120; Del Corno, Od. 50-51).   Archiv 7.243-44; JEA 8.84.   J. U. Powell, CR 33 (1919) 90-91; A. Calderini, Aeg. 2 (1921) 79-80; A. Humpers, Rev. Phil. 45 (1921) 90-92, queries the identification as glosses to Homer, Od. xxi.390-91.

2132    Greek-Coptic glossary.   L. Galante, SIFC 9 (1901) 194-98 (Museo Egiziano, Firenze) (III-IV, Thebes?; ostr.).

2133    Greek-Coptic glossary (words in omicron).   J. Krall, Raineri M. 4 (1888) 126-35 (Late; pap. cod.).   Coptic Bibl., No. 1836.

2134    Greek-Coptic glossary (?): A list of bird names. Mon. Epiphan. 2.621 (VI-VII?, Thebes).   The right side of the leaf, not preserved, probably gave the Coptic equivalents.

2135    Glossary (?).   P. Dura 3 (inv. D. Pg. 33) (II, Dura; parch.).

2136    Manual of conversation (?): Greek text in Armenian script.   G. Cuendet, Mél. Boisacq 219-26 (VII?, Fayum?; a leaf of papyrus, now lost, but the editor gives a facsimile).   Regarded by the editor as a magical formula or school exercise; M. Leroy, Byz. 13 (1938) 513-37, and C. Préaux, Chr. Ég. 14 (1939) 187-88, prefer a manual of conversation.

2137    List of words and phrases (or notes on reading?). P. Cairo Zen. 4.59534 (III B.C., Philadelphia). Rare, poetic, or literary words.

        Glossaries: see also Nos. 85, 168, 308, 317, 351.

        Homeric glossaries: see Nos. 1158, 1160-62, 1165-67, 1178, 1180, 1187, 1189, 1191-92, 1195-96, 1198-99, 1202, 1216-22.

        Greek-Demotic glossary: see No. 2157.

        Latin-Greek Glossaries: see Nos. 3003-8.

        Greek glosses on Gaius: see No. 2953.

Grammar and Metrics

2138 Elementary grammatical definitions. H. M. Hubbell, CP 28 (1933) 189-98 (Yale Univ. Libr., inv. 446) (I; on the verso of a tax record). Archiv 11.276-77. The editor suggests Comanus, a contemporary of Aristarchus, as the author; on the identity of Comanus, see F. Solmsen, CP 40 (1945) 115-16; V. di Benedetto, Ann. Sc. Pisa, Ser. 2.27 (1958) 186, queries the attribution and notes divergences from the techne of Dionysius Thrax.

2139 Grammar: Definitions. PSI 7.761 (V-VI, Oxy.; parch.; sch. ex.). Definitions of verb, article, etc.

2140 Summary of elementary grammatical terms. P. Antin. 2.68 (IV, Antinoöpolis).

2141 Elementary rules of grammar. P. Oxy. 3.469 (Oriental Institute, Univ. of Chicago) (III, Oxy.; on the verso of official correspondence; sch. ex.). Archiv 3.299. Ziebarth 2, No. 24. V. di Benedetto, Ann. Sc. Pisa, Ser. 2.27 (1958) 190.

2142 Collection of rules of grammar. P. Amh. 2.21 (III-IV, Hermupolis Magna; on the verso of official correspondence; sch. ex.). Archiv 2.381. V. di Benedetto, Ann. Sc. Pisa, Ser. 2.27 (1958) 190.

2143 Treatise on the dialects (?). P. Bouriant 8 (P. Sorbonne inv. 833) (II). Cites Alcaeus (Diehl, Anth. Lyr. 1².4.94; Lobel, Alcaeus 75; Lobel-Page, PLF 263-64, 267; Treu, Alkaios 62, 84); Sappho (Diehl, Anth. Lyr. 1².4.75; Treu, Sappho 92). A. Koerte, Archiv 8.267-70, suggests Tryphon as the author; E. Lobel, ibid. 10.1-4.

2144 Treatise on grammar. BKT 3.27-29 (inv. 8439) (II). Quotes or mentions Apollonius of Rhodes, On Antimachus; Antimachus (Powell, CA 250; Wyss, No. 158); Aristotle, Historia Animalium ii.14.505b.18, viii.3.593a.3. Archiv 6.258. F. della Corte, Riv. Fil. 64 (1936) 395-99.

2145 Treatise (?). P. Harris 59 (inv. 172 b + 182 h) (II; pap. cod.). Chiefly on prepositions and adverbs; on the verso, a list of authors, with the number of books written by each: of these, only Alcimus is recognizable. Archiv 13.123-24. B. Snell, Gnomon 13 (1937) 582-86.

2146 Treatise. P. Heid. Siegmann 197 (inv. 1893) (I?). Mentions several grammarians: Heliodorus, Dionysius, Apollonius (?). V. di Benedetto, Ann. Sc. Pisa, Ser. 2.27 (1958) 186-87.

2147 Treatise. P. Iand. 1.5 (inv. 2) (VI-VII, Oxy.?; parch. cod.; injured by damp in 1945). On the perfect tense of -mi verbs, and reduplication. Gundel 23.

2148 Lecture based on an Ars Grammatica (?). P. Oslo 2.13 (II, Theadelphia?; on the verso of No. 1160). Definition of sound and letter. Quotes Homer, Il. iv.139, xi.388. Archiv 10.229-30.

2149 Fragment of a treatise. P. Oxy. 15.1801, verso (I-II, Oxy.; on the verso of No. 2121). On the declension of Drakon, and words like aster, bater.

2150 Fragment of a treatise. P. Rain. 1.19 (inv. 29772) (I B.C.-I, Fayum). On the middle and passive participles. Archiv 11.277.

2151 Fragment of a treatise. P. Ryl. 1.35 (II-III; on the verso of an account). Mentions Anacreon. Archiv 6.259.

2152 Fragment of a treatise. V. di Benedetto, Ann. Sc. Pisa, Ser. 2.26 (1957) 180-85 (PSI, sine numero?) (I). Definitions and examples of gender and number in nouns, compound nouns, etc. Uses the name "Homeros" as an example.

2153 Examples of amphibolia in Demosthenes, etc. P. Mil. Vogl. 2.49 (inv. 171) (VII; parch. cod.). Ed. pr.: I. Cazzaniga, Acme 8, fasc. 2-3 (1955) 67-71. Col. iv mentions "tetrameters" (though none appears) and quotes an unidentified prose passage (oratory?) to illustrate kyriologia (?).

2154 On synaloepha (or scholia on an unknown poet?). P. Ryl. 3.535 (I-II). Quotes Pindar, Dithyrambi, fr. 78, Schroeder (Galiano, Pind., No. 19; Turyn, fr. 94). B. Snell, Gnomon 15 (1939) 543, and A. Koerte, Archiv 14.141, prefer scholia on an unknown poet.

2155 Fragment of a treatise. PSI 7.849 (II; pap. cod.). Archiv 8.270.

2156 Fragment on grammar (?). P. Tebt. 2.270 (II-III, Tebtunis). Cites Homer, Od. xviii.130. Archiv 6.259.

2157 Treatise on grammar (recto); Greek-Demotic glossary (verso). Mentioned by F. Bilabel, Actes Pap. V, 79-80 (P. Heid. inv. 414) (III B.C., Hibeh; cart.). Prepositions; definitions of case, noun, and verb.

2158 Fragment on the noun. P. Heid. Siegmann 198 (inv. 201 a, verso) (II-III; on the verso of a document).

2159 Fragment on possessive pronouns and prepositions. H. Gundel, Aeg. 19 (1939) 210-14 (P. Iand. inv. 664) (II, Fayum?). Gundel 25. Archiv 14.142-43.

2160 Fragment on the form ar(t)idakrys. P. Oxy. 20.2259 (I-II, Oxy.). Quotes Callimachus, fr. 700, Pfeiffer, and refers to Aeschylus (Mette, FTA, fr. 600; B. Snell, Gnomon 25, 1953, 434). Archiv 16.119.

2161 Forms of the verbs boao and chrysoo. P. Rain. 3.34 (inv. 29770) (V-VI; pap. cod.). Archiv 14.144.

2162 Conjugation of grapho. G. Zalateo, Aeg. 20 (1940) 8-11 (PSI, sine numero) (III, Oxy.; sch. ex.?).

2163 Conjugation of phoneo. A. Oguse, Aeg. 37 (1957) 77-88 (P. Strasb. inv. Gr. 364 + 16) (II-III; on the verso of a document). The editor studies this and similar texts in their relation to Theodosius, Kanones eisagogikoi peri rhêmatôn (saec. IV-V).

2164 Conjugation of pleo. P. Ryl. 3.534 (III-IV; pap. cod.). Archiv 14.143-44.

2165 Conjugation of poieo. P. Hamb. 166 (inv. 175, verso) (VI; on the verso of a document). The editors analyze similar papyrus texts.

2166    Conjugation of poieo.    P. Ryl. 3.533 (IV).   Archiv
        14.144.

2167    Conjugation of typto.    P. Rain. 3.33 (inv. 29815 B)
        (II, Fayum).  Archiv 14.144.

2168    Grammar (or scholia?).    P. Rain. 1.35 (inv. 29293)
        (V, Hermupolis Magna;  pap. cod.).  Mentions
        Sophocles.  Archiv 11.278.

        Grammar:  see also Nos. 2078, 2173, 2642-44,
        2659-61, 2698, 2705-6, 2711-12, 2714, 2732,
        2735, 2738.

2169    Metrics:  Fragment of a treatise on prosody.    P.
        Antin. 2.67 (IV, Antinoöpolis;  parch. cod.).  On
        the accentuation of adjectives derived from place-
        names.  The editor suggests that the work "shared
        a common source with Herodian. "

2170    Rules on meter.    BKT 5.2.140-42 (P. Berol. inv.
        9734) (III;  text on recto, No. 1926 on verso).  The
        treatise, like that of Terentianus Maurus, is itself
        in meter.  Cites as model verses Homer, Il. ii.
        698, 710;  and a passage from tragedy (Nauck, Frr.
        Adespota 138).  Heitsch, GDRK, fr. LXI;  Page,
        GLP 1, No. 131.  Archiv 5.540;  JAW 144.80.  A.
        Koerte, Rh. Mus. 65 (1910) 474-75;  Wilamowitz,
        Gr. Versk. 69, 380-81.

2171    Treatise on metrics.    P. Univ. Giss. 4.43 (inv. 151)
        (II-I B.C., Fayum?).  Gundel 15.  Archiv 13.125.

2172    Treatise on metrics.    P. Oxy. 2.220;  P. Lit. Lond.
        185 (Brit. Mus. inv. 1184) (I-II, Oxy.;  text on rec-
        to, No. 1205 on verso).  Mentions Aeschylus, Alc-
        man, Pindar, and Simonides.  Cites Aeschylus
        (Pyrkaeus or Lyomenos?);  Mette, FTA, fr. 337);
        Anacreon, frr. 62.1, 92.1, Bergk;  Callimachus,
        Epigrams 37.1;  Pindar, fr. 178 b, Schroeder
        (Galiano, Pind., No. 29);  Sappho, fr. 53, Bergk
        (Lobel, Sappho 73-74);  and several unidentified
        lyric passages (Diehl, Anth. Lyr. 1$^2$.4.214-15, 219;
        Lobel-Page, PLF 295;  Page, GLP 1, No. 85;
        Powell, CA 193-94).  Galiano, Aesch. 108, on col.
        xii.3-6 (Aeschylus or lyric?);  Gallavotti, Callim.
        66, on col. viii, line 9 (Callimachus, Iambus xiv?).
        Mentions the "Cyrenaïc meter," perhaps invented
        by Callimachus (cf. Pfeiffer, CFNR, No. 58).
        Archiv 1.532-33;  JAW 125.8-11.  O. Hense, Rh.
        Mus. 56 (1901) 111-12;  Wilamowitz, Gr. Versk. 153,
        426.

2173    Metrical and grammatical problems.    P. Rain. 1.20
        (inv. 29773) (V-VI, Soknopaiou Nesos;  pap. cod.).
        Archiv 11.278.

2174    Fragment on metrics.    P. Rain. 1.21 (inv. 29249)
        (V;  pap. cod.).  Archiv 11.278.

2175    Fragment on metrics.    P. Ryl. 3.505 (V-VI;  pap.
        cod.).  Archiv 14.143.

2176    Fragment on metrics.    P. Varsov. 1.3 (III, Fayum?).
        Verses are perhaps quoted as examples in lines 5,
        8, and 13.  Archiv 13.125;  Eos 34 (1932-33) 199.

        Metrics:  see also Nos. 2301, 2644, 2812.

## History and Geography

2177    Fragment on the suppression of early tyrannies in
        Sicyon and Athens.    P. Ryl. 1.18 (II B.C.;  in the
        same hand as No. 2444).  Bilabel, No. 1;  Jacoby,
        FGH 2.504.  Archiv 6.245;  E. M. Walker, New
        Chapters 2.65-66.  N. G. L. Hammond, CQ, NS
        6 (1956) 45-53;  D. M. Leahy, Bull. Ryl. Libr. 38,
        No. 2 (1956) 406-35, regards the text as part of an
        epitome on the Seven Sages, after the school of
        Dicaearchus;  M. White, Phoenix 12 (1958) 2-14,
        dates the Orthagorid tyranny at Sicyon 615-610 to
        515-510 B.C.;  D. M. Leahy, ibid. 13 (1959) 31-37.

2178    Fragment on the travels of Solon.    P. Oxy. 4.680
        (Manchester Mus.) (III, Oxy.).  Archiv 3.491;  JEA
        10.151.  Identified by K. Fuhr, Berl. Phil. Woch.
        24 (1904) 1438-39, and E. Lobel, Bodl. Rec. 4
        (1923) 96.

2179    Fragment on Polycrates of Samos (Ephorus?).  Men-
        tioned by F. Bilabel, Actes Pap. V, 80-81 (P. Heid.
        inv. 1740) (I;  on the verso of No. 2577).  F. Bilabel,
        Neue Heidelb. Jahr., 1934, 156-59.

2180    Fragment of Boeotian history (or periegesis?).    C.
        Bonner, TAPA 72 (1941) 26-35 (P. Mich. inv. 4913)
        (II-III).  Cites Nicocrates, On Boeotia, and perhaps
        another treatise of his (col. III, ad init.).  Archiv
        16.112.  M. Gigante, Aeg. 28 (1948) 3-16, suggests
        a periegesis of Boeotia.

2181    On the history of Sicyon (Aristotle, Ephorus, Menae-
        chmus?).    P. Oxy. 11.1365;  P. Lit. Lond. 111
        (Brit. Mus. inv. 2444) (III, Oxy.).  Bilabel, No.
        2;  Jacoby, FGH 2.504-5.  Archiv 7.230-31;  JEA
        6.126, 7.90.  K. F. W. Schmidt, Gött. Anz., 1918,
        98;  M. Lenchantin de Gubernatis, BFC 25 (1918-19)
        127-30, suggests Menaechmus, Sikyonika;  A. Mo-
        migliano, AR 10 (1929) 145-53.

2182    On the Persian wars (Ephorus?).    P. Ryl. 3.492 (V;
        pap. cod.).  Archiv 14.133.  M. Gigante, Aeg. 29
        (1949) 45-50, suggests Ephorus or an epitome of
        Ephorus.

2183    Treatise on Nomima Barbarika (Aristotle?).    P.
        Petrie 1.9;  P. Lit. Lond. 112 (Brit. Mus. inv. 480)
        (III B.C., Gurob;  cart.).  H. Diels, Sitzb. Berl.
        Akad., 1891, 837, suggests Aristotle;  O. Crusius,
        Philol., Suppl. 6 (1891-93) 295-300;  F. Blass,
        Neue Jahrb. 145 (1892) 580;  S. Mekler, WS 24 (1902)
        457-61.

2184    On the customs of a barbarian people.    P. Oxy. 2.
        218;  P. Lit. Lond. 113 (Brit. Mus. inv. 1183) (III,
        Oxy.).  Jacoby, FGH 2.630-31, 751;  Robinson,
        Hist. Alex. 44, 181.  Archiv 1.529.  Mentions Ar-
        chelaus (?);  Clitarchus (the historian of Alexander?);
        Zenodotus (?);  Zopyrus (the historian from Colo-
        phon or Clazomenae?).

2185    Periegesis of Attica.    P. Hawara 28-29 (loaned by
        the editor to U. Wilcken:  still in Leipzig?) (I-II,
        Hawara).  Regarded by the editor as from a history
        of Sicily;  identified as a periegesis of Attica and
        reedited by U. Wilcken, Genethliakon Carl Robert..
        (Berlin 1910) 191-225.

2186 List of early Athenian archons (Areïphron to Apsan-
drus). P. Oxy. 13.1613 (Musées Royaux, Bruxelles,
inv. E.5998) (II, Oxy.). Jacoby, FGH 2.1197. Archiv 7.234-35.

2187 Fragment of an Atthis (?). P. Schubart 31 (II; on the
verso).

2188 List of Olympic victors, Olympiads 96 and 75-83
(Eratosthenes, Phlegon of Tralles?). P. Oxy. 2.
222; P. Lit. Lond. 124 (Brit. Mus. inv. 1185); P.
Oxy. 23.2381 (Brit. Mus. inv. 2932) (III, Oxy.; on
the verso of an account). A. S. Hunt, JEA 1 (1914),
pl. viii (opposite p. 84). Jacoby, FGH 2.656. Archiv 1.531-32; New Chapters 2.73-75; Winter, LLP
209-10. C. Robert, Hermes 35 (1900) 141-95, suggests Phlegon; H. Diels, ibid. 36 (1901) 72-80,
queries this attribution; J. Jüthner, Philostratos
über Gymnastik (Leipzig u. Berlin 1909) 63-64,
believes that the text is related to Phlegon, but not
directly dependent upon him; W. Janell, Klio 21
(1927) 344-39; G. de Sanctis, Riv. Fil. 56 (1928)
70-77, prefers Eratosthenes.

2189 "Hellenica Oxyrhynchia." P. Oxy. 5.842; P. Lit.
Lond. 110 (Brit. Mus. inv. 1843) (II-III, Fayum or
Oxy.; on the verso of a land register). Roberts,
GLH, pl. 17b. B. P. Grenfell and A. S. Hunt,
Hellenica Oxyrhynchia (Oxonii 1909); Jacoby, FGH
2.17-35; E. Kalinka, Hellenica Oxyrhynchia (Lip-
siae 1927; bibl. to 1926); C. Ricci (and members
of his seminar), Publicaciones del Instituto de
Investigaciones Históricas de la Universidad Nacio-
nal 63 (Buenos Aires 1934; text and detailed study);
M. Gigante, Le Elleniche di Ossirinco (Roma 1949).
JAW 142.36-43; H. Bloch, HSCP, Special Volume
(1941) 304 (detailed bibl.); G. T. Griffith, Fifty
Years Cl. Schol. 160-62; Lesky, GGL 576. Attributed to Cratippus by J. H. Lipsius, Cratippi
Hellenicorum Fragmenta Oxyrhynchia (Lietzmann's
Kleine Texte, Nr. 138; Bonn 1916); A. von Mess,
Rh. Mus. 63 (1908) 370-91; L. Pareti, SIFC 19
(1912) 398-517 (= Studi minori di storia antica 2, Roma
1961, 285-401); V. Bartoletti, Hellenica Oxyrhyn-
chia (Lipsiae 1959; bibl.). Attributed to Daïmachus
of Plataea by F. Jacoby, Gött. Nachr., 1924, 13-18.
Attributed to Ephorus by E. M. Walker, The Hellenica Oxyrhynchia; Its Authorship and Authority
(Oxford 1913), and New Chapters 1.124-33; Winter,
LLP 240-42 (bibl.); W. Judeich, Rh. Mus. 66
(1911) 94-139. Attributed to Theopompus by E. Meyer,
Theopomps Hellenika (Halle 1909); A. Koerte, Archiv 6.242; G. Busolt, Hermes 43 (1908) 255-85;
U. Wilcken, ibid. 475-77. Recent articles: P.
Frassinetti, GIF 3 (1950) 180-82; F. Jacoby, CQ
44 (1950) 1-8 (= Abhandlungen zur griech. Geschichtschreibung, Leiden 1956, 322-33), discusses the
problem of authorship in the light of the new fragments (see No. 2190); M. Hombert, Chr. Ég. 26
(1951) 432-34; K. L. McKay, CR, NS 3 (1953) 67;
A. W. Gomme, CQ, NS 4 (1954) 53-55, discusses
the identity of Cratippus; I. A. F. Bruce, CQ, NS
11 (1961) 166-70; idem, Emérita 30 (1962) 63-69, on
the political terminology; Q. Cataudella, Hlk. 1
(1961) 310-11.

2190 "Hellenica Oxyrhynchia." PSI 13.1304 (II, Oxy.).
Five fragments from the same work, but not the
same papyrus, as No. 2189. Fr. A, col. ii, re-
fers to Thucydides (?). V. Bartoletti, Hellenica
Oxyrhynchia (Lipsiae 1959) VII-VIII, XI-XIV, XXVII-
XXXIV (bibl.), 1-5; M. Gigante, Le Elleniche di
Ossirinco (Roma 1949) LVI-LXXV, 1-11. A. Calderini, Aeg. 28 (1948) 222-23; A. Vogliano, Acme
1 (1948) 393-99; Chr. Ég. 24 (1949) 348-50; M.
Gigante, Maia 2 (1949) 208-31; S. Accame, Riv.
Fil. 78 (1950) 30-49; F. Jacoby and P. Maas, CQ
44 (1950) 8-11, give the text; A. Fuks, ibid. 45
(1951) 155; M. Treu, Gymnas. 59 (1952) 302-19;
A. Vogliano, Prolegom. 1 (1952) 93-99; Q. Catau-
della, Hlk. 1 (1961) 309-10.

2191 Fragment on the history of the fourth century B.C.
(Theopompus?). C. Wessely, Beiträge zur Alten
Geschichte: Festschrift Hirschfeld (Berlin 1903)
100-3 (P. Rainer) (II, Soknopaiou Nesos or Karanis).
Bilabel, No. 5; Jacoby, FGH 2.505. Archiv 3.
282, 491; E. M. Walker, New Chapters 2.68-69.

2192 Anonymi Philippica (events of 340-337 B.C.). P.
Ryl. 3.490 (III B.C.). Archiv 14.129. M. Gigante,
PP 1 (1946) 127-37, suggests an epitome of Theo-
pompus, Philippica.

2193 Epitome of a history of Sicily. P. Oxy. 4.665 (Libr.
of Victoria Coll., Toronto) (II, Oxy.). Jacoby,
FGH, III B, p. 679. Archiv 3.490; JAW 142.70.
F. Blass, as noted by the editors, suggests an epitome of Timaeus; G. de Sanctis, Riv. Fil. 33 (1905)
66-73, prefers an argumentum of Philistus, Sicili-
ca, Bk. iv; F. M. Heichelheim, SO 31 (1955) 88-95.

2194 On the history of Sicily under Agathocles (Duris?).
P. Oxy. 24.2399 (I B.C., Oxy.). Events of 310
B.C. W. S. Barrett, Gnomon 33 (1961) 691-92.

2195 On Alexander the Great. P. Oxy. 15.1798, 17.2081 g.
(II, Oxy.; text on recto, No. 2127 on verso). Bi-
label, No. 7; Jacoby, FGH 2.816-18; Robinson,
Hist. Alex. 262-63. Archiv 7.66, 233; E. M.
Walker, New Chapters 2.70-71.

2196 On Alexander. P. Hamb. 130 (inv. 652) (I B.C.).
The battle at the Granicus; how Clitus saved the
life of Alexander; the losses of the Persians and
Macedonians. Archiv 16.110.

2197 On Alexander's campaign in India. C. C. Edgar,
Ann. Serv. 26 (1926) 208-9 (P. Cairo inv. 49653)
(I, Oxy.). The editor suggests the history by
Ptolemy Soter.

2198 On the campaigns of Alexander (?). P. Oxy. 4.679
(Musées Royaux, Bruxelles; later, Bibliothèque
de l'Univ. de Louvain: deperdita) (I B.C., Oxy.).
Archiv 3.491.

2199 Prayer of Alexander to Sarapis. PRIMI 1.21 (I B.C.,
Oxy.). Merkelbach, Quellen 29. Archiv 13.129.
R. Merkelbach, ibid. 17 (1960) 108-9.

2200 On Alexander (?). P. Lond. 5.1815; P. Lit. Lond.
115 (Brit. Mus. inv. 1778) (I; on the verso of an
account). Archiv 10.70.

2201    "Last Days and Will of Alexander." P. Rain. 1.7
        (inv. 31954) (I B.C.-I). Merkelbach, Quellen, 54,
        110, 123, 137, 151, 243-44; P. H. Thomas, Incerti
        Auctoris Epitoma Rerum Gestarum Alexandri Magni
        cum Libro de Morte Testamentoque Alexandri (Lip-
        siae 1960), pp. XII, 43-44. G. de Sanctis, Mel.
        Glotz 1.315-18; H. Fuhrmann, Archiv 11 (1933) 107-
        9, and M. Segrè, Riv. Fil. 61 (1933) 225-26, iden-
        tify the text; K. F. W. Schmidt, Gött. Anz., 1936,
        250.

2202    From a history of the Diadochi (Arrian?). PSI 12.
        1284 (II, Oxy.; on the verso is a fragment of a
        shorthand manual). Archiv 16.110.

2203    Letter to a king of Macedon. P. Oxy. 1.13 (Columbia
        Univ. Libr.) (II-III, Oxy.). Jacoby, FGH 2.824.
        Archiv 1.116. F. Ruhl, Rh. Mus. 54 (1899) 152-55;
        G. de Sanctis, Riv. Fil. 59 (1931) 330-34, suggests
        Hieronymus of Cardia, History of the Diadochi.

2204    Letter to a king of Macedon on principles of govern-
        ment. (Aristotle, Theopompus?). P. Oxy. 2.217
        (Cambridge Univ. Libr., add. 4049) (III, Oxy.).
        Archiv 1.525.

2205    Chronological work on the years 355-315 B.C. P.
        Oxy. 1.12 (Cambridge Univ. Libr., add. 4029)
        (III, Oxy.). Includes biographical data on Isocrates,
        Plato, and Speusippus. Bilabel, No. 12; Jacoby,
        FGH 2.1153-56. Archiv 1.118; Winter, LLP 244.
        W. Soltau, Philol. 58 (1899) 558-76.

2206    Account of the Third Syrian War (Lysimachus, Ptolemy
        III Euergetes?). P. Petrie 2.45, 3.144 (Dublin?)
        (III B.C., Gurob; cart.). Attributed by the editors
        to Ptolemy III. Bilabel, No. 9; Jacoby, FGH 2.
        885-87; Wilcken, Chrest., No. 1. J. U. Powell,
        New Chapters 1.142-43; Winter, LLP 243-44. U.
        Koehler, Sitzb. Berl. Akad., 1894, 445-60, regards
        the text as the report of a nauarchos; Wilamowitz,
        Hermes 49 (1914) 447-53; M. Holleaux, Rev. Ét.
        Anc. 18 (1916) 153-65, favors Ptolemy III; A. G.
        Roos, Mnemos. 51 (1923) 262-78, prefers Lysima-
        chus; W. Croenert, Racc. Lumbroso 441-60, sug-
        gests a letter of Ptolemy III to Berenice.

2207    On the siege of Rhodes by Demetrius Poliorcetes, 304
        B.C. H. von Gaertringen, Sitzb. Berl. Akad.,
        1918, 752-62 (P. Berol. inv. 11632) (II). Schubart,
        Gr. Pal., Abb. 92. Bilabel, No. 8. Archiv 7.234;
        New Chapters 2.66-68. G. Vitale, Aeg. 2 (1921)
        207-9.

2208    On the Seleucids (?). P. Ryl. 3.510, verso (II-III;
        on the verso of No. 2608). Archiv 14.131.

2209    Chronological list of the Ptolemaic kings. P. Oxy.
        19.2222 (I, Oxy.). From Ptolemaeus VII Neos
        Philopator to Ptolemaeus XIII, the older brother
        of Cleopatra. Archiv 16.110.

2210    From a work on Ptolemaic history (or biographies of
        the Ptolemies?): Events of 246-221 B.C. (Ptole-
        maeus of Megalopolis?). P. Haun. 1.6 (inv. 311)
        (II, Fayum?). Archiv 16.110. M. Segrè, Rend.
        della Pontificia Accad. Romana di Arch. 19 (1942-
        43) 269-80, suggests a series of brief biographies

of the Ptolemies; A. Momigliano and P. Fraser,
CQ 44 (1950) 108-18, discuss the evidence for the
date of the battle of Andros; E. Manni, Athen. 40
(1952) 182-89, suggests that there were two battles
of Andros; F. W. Walbank, A Historical Commentary on Polybius 1 (Oxford 1957) 564.

2211    The story of Coriolanus. P. Antin. 1.19 (V, Antino-
        öpolis; parch. cod.). Possibly from the lost
        abridgment of Dionysius of Halicarnassus, Anti-
        quitates Romanae, made by the author himself.
        Archiv 16.110.

2212    On the Second Punic War: The Peace of 203 B.C.
        (Polybius?). P. Ryl. 3.491 (II B.C., Fayum). A.
        Koerte, Archiv 14.129-31, suggests a "vorpolybi-
        anischer Autor"; W. Hoffmann, Hermes 76 (1941)
        270-82; A. Klotz, WJA 1 (1946) 153-54, removes
        a possible objection to Polybius; M. Gigante, Aeg.
        30 (1950) 77-92, prefers "un ignoto scrittore"; M.
        Treu, ibid. 33 (1953) 30-56, rejects Polybius.

2213    Royal canon from Augustus to Decius, A.D. 250. P.
        Oxy. 1.35, verso (Univ. of Pennsylvania Mus., inv.
        2749) (III, Oxy.; on the verso of a proclamation).
        Neugebauer, Astron. Pap. Ostr., No. 25.

2214    On a Roman expedition against the Ethiopians (Nico-
        laus of Damascus? a document?). P. Mil. Vogl.
        2.46 (inv. 718) (I-II). An expedition led by C.
        Petronius, prefect of Egypt 25-21 B.C. Ed. pr.:
        A. Vogliano, Un papiro storico greco della raccolta
        Milanese e le campagne dei Romani in Etiopia
        (Milano 1940). Archiv 14.131-32. E. G. Turner,
        JRS 40 (1950) 57-59, regards the text as a document
        or a private letter; J. Stroux, Sitzb. Berl. Akad.,
        1952, Nr. 2, studies the historical content, admit-
        ting the possibility of a document.

2215    "Acta Alexandrinorum" (or translation of a document?)
        (The "Boulê-Papyrus."). PSI 10.1160 (I). C. P.
        Jud. 2.150 (bibl.); Musurillo, No. I, pp. 1-3, 83-
        92 (bibl.). Archiv 9.253-56. E. Breccia, BSAA,
        NS 7 (1929) 352-54 (bibl.); J. H. Oliver, Aeg. 11
        (1931) 161-68, compares the Acta Pauli et Antonini,
        of the reign of Hadrian (see Nos. 2228-29); W.
        Schubart, BIFAO 30 (1931) 407-15, thinks that the
        "Kaisar" is Claudius rather than Octavian; M.
        Norsa and G. Vitelli, BSAA, NS 8 (1932) 1-16, reply
        to Oliver and Schubart; H. I. Bell, JEA 35 (1949)
        167-69; E. G. Turner, JRS 45 (1955) 119-20, holds
        that the Caesar in question is Augustus and the text
        a translation of an official document in Latin.

2216    "Acta Alexandrinorum" (?): A speech of Germanicus
        to the Alexandrians (recto); Alexander and Timo-
        xenus before Augustus in Rome (verso). P. Oxy.
        25.2435 (I, Oxy.; on recto and verso). E. Vol-
        terra, Iura 11, Parte 2 (1960) 262-64; J. Barns,
        JHS 81 (1961) 179-80; C. Questa, Riv. CCM 3 (1961)
        126-27.

2217    "Acta Alexandrinorum" (Audience of Isidorus and
        Dionysius with the Prefect Flaccus). P. Oxy. 8.
        1089 (Bodleian Libr., Gr. class. d.101 (P)) (III,
        Oxy.; on the verso of a land survey). C. P. Jud.
        2.154 (bibl.); Musurillo, No. II, pp. 4-7, 93-104
        (bibl). Archiv 14.132-33. A. von Premerstein,
        Philol., Suppl. 16, Heft 2 (1923) 4-14.

2218    "Acta Alexandrinorum" (The "Gerousia Acta. "). P.
        Univ. Giss. 5.46 (inv. 308) (II-III, Fayum?). C.
        P. Jud. 2.155 (bibl.); Musurillo, No. III, pp. 8-17,
        104-16 (bibl.). Gundel 31. Archiv 14.132-33; Chr.
        Ég. 15 (1940) 151-53. K. F. W. Schmidt, Phil. Woch.
        61 (1941) 266-69.

2219    "Acta Alexandrinorum" (Isidorus and Lampon before
        Claudius). BGU 2.511 (P. Berol. inv. 7118); T.
        Reinach, Revue des études juives 31 (1895) 161-78,
        ibid. 34 (1897) 296-98 (P. Cairo inv. 10448) (ca.
        A.D. 200; on the verso of accounts). C. P. Jud.
        2.156a, 156d (bibl.); Musurillo, No. IV, pp. 18-
        26, 117-40 (bibl.). U. Wilcken, Hermes 30 (1895)
        481-98 (ed. pr. of BGU 511), Abh. Leipzig, 1909,
        800-6, and Chrest., No. 14; A. von Premerstein,
        Philol., Suppl. 16, Heft 2 (1923) 15-27; R. Matta,
        Didask., NS 4 (1926) 71-106; H. I. Bell, Archiv
        10 (1931) 12-14; J. C. Naber, Aeg. 12 (1932) 329-
        32.

2220    "Acta Alexandrinorum" (Acta Isidori). Woldemar,
        Graf Uxkull-Gyllenband, Sitzb. Berl. Akad. 28
        (1930) 664-79 (P. Berol. inv. 8877) (II-III; on the
        verso of an account). C. P. Jud. 2.156c; Musurillo,
        No. IV, pp. 18-26, 117-40 (bibl.). A. Momigliano,
        Rend. della Pontificia Accad. Romana di Arch.,
        Ser. 3.7 (1932) 119-27; A. von Premerstein, Her-
        mes 67 (1932) 174-96, on the date of the hearing;
        A. Stein, Aeg. 13 (1933) 130-31.

2221    "Acta Alexandrinorum" (Acta Isidori). H. I. Bell,
        Archiv 10 (1931) 5-16 (Brit. Mus. inv. 2785) (III,
        Panopolis?). C. P. Jud. 2.156b; Musurillo, No.
        IV, pp. 18-26, 117-40 (bibl.). A. Neppi Modona,
        Aeg. 12 (1932) 333-38.

2222    "Acta Alexandrinorum" (Acta Diogenis?). P. Oxy.
        20.2264 (II, Oxy.; on the verso of a land register).
        Musurillo, No. V A, pp. 27-30, 141-46 (ed. pr.).
        Archiv 16.111.

2223    "Acta Alexandrinorum" (?) (Vespasian's reception
        in Alexandria). P. Fuad 8 (inv. 150) (I). For-
        merly regarded as a document, the text is thought
        to have affinities with the "Acta." C. P. Jud. 2.
        418 (bibl.); Musurillo, No. V B, pp. 30-31. P.
        Jouguet, Mél. Ernout 201-10; idem, Bull. de
        l'Institut d'Égypte 24 (1942) 21-32; idem, La Do-
        mination romaine en Égypte (Alexandrie 1947) 44-
        46; A. Stein, Die Präfekten von Ägypten (Bernae
        1950) 38; P. Derchain and J. Hubaux, Latomus 12
        (1953) 47-52; E. G. Turner, JRS 44 (1954) 61;
        R. Merkelbach, Archiv 16 (1956) 111-12, gives text,
        bibl., and commentary.

2224    "Acta Alexandrinorum" (Hermias before Titus). C.
        H. Roberts, JRS 39 (1949) 79-80 (P. Harris, un-
        edited) (III?; on the verso of an account). Musu-
        rillo, No. VI, pp. 32, 147-49.

2225    "Acta Alexandrinorum" (Acta Maximi: Trial of C.
        Vibius Maximus, prefect of Egypt). P. Oxy. 3.
        471 (Bodleian Libr., Gr. class. a. 10 (P)) (II, Oxy.).
        Musurillo, No. VII, pp. 33-38, 150-59. Archiv 4.
        381-82; New Chapters 2.122. S. de Ricci, Rev.
        Ét. Gr. 18 (1905) 333; A. von Premerstein, Philol.,
        Suppl. 16, Heft 2 (1923) 3, suggests that the text

belongs to the "Acta"; J. Mussehl, Hermes 61
(1926) 111-12; O. W. Reinmuth, Klio, Beih. 34
(1935) 3.

2226    "Acta Alexandrinorum" (Acta Maximi). P. Schubart
        42 (II). Musurillo, No. VII, pp. 39-40, 150-55,
        159-60.

2227    "Acta Alexandrinorum" (Hermaïscus and others before
        Trajan). P. Oxy. 10.1242; P. Lit. Lond. 117
        (Brit. Mus. inv. 2436) (II-III, Oxy.; on the verso
        of documents). C. P. Jud. 2.157 (bibl.); Musu-
        rillo, No. VIII, pp. 44-48, 161-78 (bibl.). Archiv
        7.236. W. Weber, Hermes 50 (1915) 47-92; R.
        Matta, Didask., NS 4 (1926) 49-63.

2228    "Acta Alexandrinorum" (Paulus and Antoninus before
        Hadrian). P. Par. 68 (P. Louvre inv. 2376 bis);
        P. Lond. 1, pp. 229-30; P. Lit. Lond. 118 (Brit.
        Mus. inv. 1) (II; opisthograph roll). C. P. Jud.
        2.158a (bibl.); Musurillo, No. IX, pp. 49-58, 179-
        94 (bibl.). U. Wilcken, Abh. Leipzig, 1909, 807-21;
        A. von Premerstein, Hermes 57 (1922) 268-302;
        A. Fuks, JRS 51 (1961) 103.

2229    "Acta Alexandrinorum" (Paulus and Antoninus). BGU
        1.341 (P. Berol. inv. 8111) (II-III, Fayum). C. P.
        Jud. 2.158b (bibl.); Musurillo, No. IX, pp. 58-59,
        179-88, 194 (bibl.). U. Wilcken, Abh. Leipzig,
        1909, 821-22; A. von Premerstein, Hermes 57
        (1922) 302-16.

2230    Fragment on Jewish disturbances ("Acta Alexandri-
        norum" or a document?). P. Mil. Vogl. 2.47
        (inv. 701) (II, Tebtunis). Ed. pr.: I. Cazzaniga,
        Mel. Boisacq 159-67. P. Mil. Vogl. 47 gives a
        bibl. and new discussion. C. P. Jud. 2.435 (bibl.);
        Musurillo, No. IX C, pp. 59-60, 194-95 (bibl.).
        C. Préaux, Chr. Ég. 14 (1939) 180-81; H. I. Bell
        (?), JEA 25 (1939) 79, queries the attribution to
        the "Acta" and suggests an edict of the prefect of
        Egypt (M. Rutilius Lupus?).

2231    "Acta Alexandrinorum" (Athenodorus before Trajan
        or Hadrian?). P. Oxy. 18.2177 (III, Oxy.). The
        text is reprinted under P. Schubart 42. Musurillo,
        No. X, pp. 61-64, 196-204 (bibl.). A. D'Ors,
        Emérita 11 (1943) 452-54, favors Trajan as the em-
        peror concerned.

2232    "Acta Alexandrinorum" (Appianus before Commodus).
        P. Oxy. 1.33; P. Lit. Lond. 119 (Brit. Mus. inv.
        2435); C. B. Welles, TAPA 67 (1936) 7-23 (Yale
        Univ. Libr., inv. 1536) (III, Oxy.; on the verso
        of documents). C. P. Jud. 2.159 (bibl.); Musu-
        rillo, No. XI, pp. 65-70, 205-20 (bibl.). Archiv
        13.114, 14.200-1. U. Wilcken, Abh. Leipzig, 1909,
        822-25; A. von Premerstein, Philol., Suppl. 16,
        Heft 2 (1923) 28-45; R. Matta, Didask., NS 4
        (1926) 64-84; M. Hombert, Chr. Ég. 14 (1939) 185-
        86; A. G. Roos, Mnemos. Ser. 3.6 (1938) 172-74;
        G. Bjoerck, Eranos 46 (1948) 72-74.

2233    "Acta Alexandrinorum" (?) (Reception of Alexandrian
        envoys by a Roman emperor). BGU 2.588 (P.
        Berol. inv. 7362) (II-III, Fayum). Musurillo, No.
        XII, pp. 71, 221-22. U. Wilcken, Abh. Leipzig,
        1909, 825-26.

2234    "Acta Alexandrinorum" (or a document?).   P. Fay.
        217 (Musées Royaux, Bruxelles, inv. E.5966) (II-
        III; on the verso of an account).   Musurillo, No.
        XIII, pp. 73, 224.

2235    "Acta Alexandrinorum" (?).   P. Erl. 16 (inv. 5, recto)
        (II; text on recto, No. 1257 on verso).   Musurillo,
        No. XIV, pp. 73, 224.

2236    "Acta Alexandrinorum" (?).   P. Aberdeen 136 (II,
        Fayum?).   Musurillo, No. XV, pp. 74, 225.

2237    "Acta Alexandrinorum" (?).   P. Bouriant 7 (P. Sor-
        bonne, inv. 832) (II-III; on the verso of a document).
        Musurillo, No. XVI, pp. 75, 226-27.   Archiv 8.
        265.

2238    "Acta Alexandrinorum" (?) (An audience of Caracalla
        in Alexandria).   P. Benoît and J. Schwartz, Et.
        Pap. 7 (1948) 17-33 (PIFAO) (III?, Hermupolis
        Magna).   C. B. Welles, AJP 71 (1950) 109-10, sug-
        gests the "Acta." Musurillo, No. XVIII, pp. 77-79,
        229-32 (bibl.), thinks rather of a copy of an official
        protocol of a trial.

2239    "Acta Alexandrinorum, " document or letter (?).   P.
        Ryl. 2.437 (I).   Musurillo, No. XIX, pp. 80, 233.

2240    "Acta Alexandrinorum" (?).   Musurillo, No. XX, pp.
        81, 234 (P. Harris, unedited) (II; on the verso of
        a document).   Mentions one Archias, perhaps an
        Alexandrian.

2241    "Acta Alexandrinorum" (?) (Acta Maximi?).   Musu-
        rillo, No. XXI, pp. 82, 234 (P. Harris, unedited)
        (II).

2242    "Acta Alexandrinorum" (Acta Maximi?).   H. Musu-
        rillo, JRS 47 (1957) 185-90 (P. Mich. inv. 4800)
        (I, Karanis).   H. Musurillo, Acta Alexandrinorum
        (Lipsiae 1961), No.. XXII.   J. Bingen, Chr. Ég. 33
        (1958) 279-80.

        "Acta Alexandrinorum": see also Nos. 1969, 2483.

2243    Fragment of a chronicle (on the years 251-270, 306,
        312-317, 325-338).   H. Lietzmann, Quantulacumque:
        Studies Presented to Kirsopp Lake ... (London
        1937) 339-48 (P. Berol. inv. 13296) (IV-V; parch.
        cod.).   JEA 24. 97.

2244    World history.   A. Bauer and J. Strzygowski, Denkschr.
        Wien. Akad., 1906, 1-118 (P. Golenischeff, State
        Mus. of Fine Arts, Moscow) (V; pap. cod., with
        crude miniatures).   Bilabel, No. 13.   Archiv 3.491.
        Weitzmann, Ill. RC, p. 114 and pl. 101.

2245    History (or biography, oratory?).   P. Antin. 2.63
        (V-VI, Antinoöpolis; pap. cod.).   Refers to a battle
        fought by "Augoustos" (Octavian at Actium?).

2246    Historical fragment.   P. Bouriant 6 (P. Sorbonne,
        inv. 831) (II-I B.C.).   Archiv 8.265.

2247    History.   P. Groning. 21 (inv. 10) (III).

2248    History (or romance?).   P. Harris 13 (inv. 174 g)
        (II).   Archiv 13.113.

2249    History (or oratory, dialogue?).   P. Harris 14 (inv.
        161 d) (I).

2250    History (or a document?).   P. Harris 15 (inv. 49 b)
        (II).

2251    History (?).   P. Harris 16 (inv. 173 h) (II).

2252    History (?).   P. Heid. Siegmann 195 (inv. 2048) (II?,
        Oxy.).

2253    History (?).   P. Lit. Lond. 116 (Brit. Mus. inv. 1847
        B) (IV, Fayum?; parch. cod.).   Archiv 10.70.

2254    History.(Xenophon, Hellenica?).   P. Oxy. 2.302
        (Bodleian Libr., Gr. class. g. 47 (P)) (I, Oxy.).
        Archiv 1.530-31.   Persson 40.

2255    History.   P. Oxy. 3.436 (Yale Univ. Libr.) (III, Oxy.).
        Archiv 3.282.

2256    History.   P. Oxy. 6.866 (Muhlenberg Coll.) (I, Oxy.).
        Archiv 6.246.

2257    History.   P. Oxy. 6.867 (Univ. of Illinois Libr.,  G.
        P. 867) (III, Oxy.).   Jacoby, FGH 2.507.   Archiv
        6.246.

2258    History.   P. Oxy. 7.1014 (Musées Royaux, Bruxelles,
        inv. E.5977) (III, Oxy.; on the verso of a survey
        list).   Jacoby, FGH 2.507.   Archiv 6.246.

2259    History (or romance, literary epistle?).   P. Oxy.
        27.2466 (III, Oxy.).   How the Egyptians repulsed
        a band of invading Arabs commanded by one Webêlis.

2260    History (?).   P. Rain. 3.43 (inv. 29263) (VI).   Archiv
        14.134.

2261    History (or oratory?).   P. Rain. 3.60 (inv. 29311)
        (V; pap. cod.).   Archiv 14.137.

2262    History: On Persian fiscal policy.   P. Ryl. 1.20
        (I B.C.).   Archiv 6.240.

2263    History.   P. Ryl. 1.30 (I B.C.).   Archiv 6.246.

2264    History.   P. Ryl. 1.31 (I B.C.).   Archiv 6.246.

2265    History (Polybius?).   P. Ryl. 3.501 (II B.C., Fayum;
        cart.).   Archiv 14.133.

2266    History (Philistus?).   P. Ryl. 3.504 (II-III).   A.
        Koerte, Archiv 14.133-34, regards the attribution
        to Philistus as only a "remote possibility. "

2267    History (or oratory?).   Bilabel, No. 14 (P. Berol.
        inv. 13361) (II).   Jacoby, FGH 2.505-6.   Archiv 7.
        235; New Chapters 2.72.

2268    History (Timaeus?).   O. Montevecchi, Aeg. 23 (1943)
        90-92 (P. Med. inv. 36) (III, pap. cod.).   Archiv
        16. 126.   L. Alfonsi, Aeg. 23 (1943) 92-98, suggests
        Timaeus.

2269    A miscellany of graffiti of historical interest, in Greek
        and Latin.   J. Baillet, MIFAO 42 (1926), 2 vols.:
        Texte, Planches (III B.C. - VI; graffiti on the

tombs, "Syringes, " in the Valley of the Kings, Thebes). The homonyms of many classical authors appear, but most are suspect. For the Greek poems, in various meters, see Baillet's "Index carminum, " p. 598. For the signatures of prefects and other administrators of Egypt (e.g., C. Vibius Maximus, No. 1356), see Baillet, vol. 1, pp. XXXV-XXXIX. A. Bataille, Les Memnonia (Le Caire 1952) 168-78.

2270    A miscellany of graffiti, in Greek and Latin. A.-J. Letronne, MAI 10 (1833) 249-359 (I-II; graffiti on the Colossus of "Memnon, " Amenhotep III, Thebes). A. Bataille, Les Memnonia (Le Caire 1952) 152-68 (bibl.); ibid. 164, for references to the graffiti in verse.

History: see also Nos. 310, 1357, 1456, 2127, 2468, 2496, 2506-7, 2545, 2550, 2554, 2558, 2597, 2630, 2784, 2870, 2872.

2271    Geography (?): A fragment on the district of Canopus (Hecataeus?). P. Michael. 4 (II). Ed. pr.: J. Drescher, BSAA, No. 38 (1949) 17-20. R. Merkelbach, Archiv 16 (1956) 112-14, reedits the text, and suggests Hecataeus of Abdera as the author.

2272    Geography: An ethnographical fragment. P. Hibeh 2.185 (Brit. Mus. inv. 2958) (ca. 280-250 B.C., Hibeh; cart.; text on verso of a blank recto?).

2273    Geography (or history?). P. Oxy. 4.681 (Johns Hopkins Univ. Libr.) (II, Oxy.). Archiv 3.491.

2274    Geography: Towns and localities in Egypt, Palestine, and Asia Minor. C. A. Noordegraaf, Mnemos., Ser. 3.6 (1938) 273-310 (Collection of E. von Scherling, Leiden, inv. G 110) (V, Panopolis?). Chr. Eg. 13 (1938) 410-11.

Geography: see also Nos. 2059, 2127 (On Rivers), 2642.

## Hunting and Wrestling

2275    Work on hunting (?). P. Fay. 313 (Bodleian Libr., Gr. class. d.71 (P)) (III, Theadelphia; on the verso of accounts). Archiv 2.366.

2276    Directions for wrestling (?). P. Oxy. 3.466 (Columbia Univ. Libr.) (II, Oxy.). Archiv 3.298. J. Jüthner, Philostratos über Gymnastik (Leipzig u. Berlin 1909) 26-30.

Wrestling: P. Oxy. 6.887 (Archiv 8.126), regarded by the editors as a treatise on wrestling, is identified by A. Abt, Philol. 69 (1910) 147-50, as a magical text (see Preisendanz, PGM, No. 24 b).

## Law

2277    Commentary on points of Roman law, in the form of a catechism. E. Schönbauer, Aeg. 13 (1933) 621-43 (P. Berol. inv. 11866 A-B) (V-VI; pap. cod.). Mentions the jurisconsults Paulus and Sabinus, and one Anatolius, perhaps a professor of law at Berytus. Collart, PLL 40. E. Schönbauer, Sav. Zeitschr. 53 (1933) 451-64 (a second edition).

2278    Juridical fragment. PSI 13.1349 (VI?; parch. cod.). Cites Paulus.

2279    Greek summary of Digesta ii. 8.12-14, 9.1, 11.2.8-9, 11.4 pr., 1-5. PSI 13.1350 (VI; pap. cod.). Marichal, No. 319. G. La Pira, BIDR 38 (1930) 151-74 (ed. pr.), suggests Dorotheus as the author. F. Pringsheim, Sav. Zeitschr. 53 (1933) 488-91.

2280    Juridical fragments, in Greek and Latin. P. Ryl. 3. 475 (V, Thebaid?; pap. cod.). Cites the jurist Vivianus (lines 11-12); Sab(--), the jurist Sabatius or a scholiast (16). Cavenaile, CPL 95; Collart, PLL 33. Archiv 14.149-50.

2281    Fragment on Longi Temporis Praescriptio (?). W. Schubart, Münchener Beiträge zur Papyrusforschung und antiken Rechtsgeschichte 35 (1945) (=Festschr. für Leopold Wenger 2) 184-90 (P. Berol. inv. 16976 + 16977) (V?; pap. cod.). In Greek, with some Latin words. Mentions Paulus, cites one Comous (?), a jurist. R. Regler, Tijdschr. v. Rechtsg. 20 (1952) 330-34. E. Schönbauer, Studi in onore di V. Arangio-Ruiz 3 (Napoli 1953) 501-19, holds that the subject is rather "praescriptiones temporis. "

2282    A register of imperial constitutions, in Greek and Latin. P. Ryl. 3.476 (IV-V; pap. cod.). Cavenaile, CPL 91; Collart, PLL 15; Lowe, CLA 2. 225. Archiv 14.150.

2283    Legal fragment (or prose maxims, or private letter?). A. Vogliano, Acme 1 (1948) 260 (Musei del Castello Sforzesco, Milano) (?, Crocodilopolis; opisthograph fr.). Quotes one Gaius (?), the jurist or a generic designation for the Romans (?).

2284    Fragments of a juristic text. P. Colt 11 (VI-VII, Nessana, Palestine; pap. cod.).

2285    Fragment on the law of inheritance (?). P. Colt 12 (VII, Nessana, Palestine; pap. cod.).

2286    Juridical fragment. P. Rain. 3.38 (inv. 29291) (V, Fayum; opisthograph fr.). Archiv 14.142. Regarded by the editors as scholia on an unknown text; identified as a juridical fragment by A. Christopoulos, Sav. Zeitschr. 63 (1943) 414-15.

Law: for legal texts primarily in Latin, see Nos. 2953 ff.

## Literary Criticism and Rhetoric

2287    Catechism in rhetoric. PSI 1.85 (III, Oxy.; on the verso of a document). Includes a definition of the chria. Archiv 7.228-29.

2288    Rhetorical catechism. H. Oellacher, WS 55 (1937) 68-78 (P. Vindob. inv. Gr. 754) (VI; pap. cod.). Archiv 13.117.

2289    Treatise on literary composition. P. Oxy. 7.1012 (Toledo Mus. of Art) (III, Oxy.; on the verso of a cursive document). Quotes or mentions Aeschines, De Falsa Legatione 10, Contra Timarchum

165; Aristippus; Aristophanes; Caecilius Calactinus (?); Demosthenes, In Androtionem 21-23; Didymus; Epicurus (?); Heraclides Ponticus (?); Herodotus; Lysias; Theophrastus, Peri kairôn; Theopompus, Philippica, Bk. vi (Jacoby, FGH 2. 571); Thucydides i.136, ii.22; Xenophon, Agesilaus 6.8, Hellenica i.6.5 (?); and an unknown comic poet (in fr. 9, col. 2, line 3). Archiv 6.257.

2290   A work on literary criticism (?).   P. Oxy. 13.1611 (Bodleian Libr., Gr. class. b.17 (P)) (III, Oxy.). Quotes or cites Acusilaus of Argos (see Jacoby, FGH 1.53; P. Maas, Zeitschr. für das Gymnasialwesen 73, 1919, 191-93; J. T. Kakridis, CR 61, 1947, 77-80); Arctinus (or Achaeus?); Aristarchus (?); Aristophanes; Chamaeleon (D. Holwerda, Mnemos., Ser. 4.5, 1952, 228-31); Cratinus, Ploutoi; Damastes (E. Lobel, Bodl. Rec. 4, 1923, 48); Eratosthenes (?); Euripides, Alkmaion dia Korinthou (Page, GLP 1, No. 8; B. Snell, WS 69, 1956, 87); Hellanicus, Ktiseis (Jacoby, FGH 1.124); Hermippus, Iapetus (Wilamowitz, Pindaros 449, reads Iambi); Ion, Omphale (Lesky, GGL 386; Page, GLP 1, No. 19; Steffen, Sat. Gr. Fr. 118); Lysippus, Bacchae; Mnaseus of Patara, On Oracles; Phrynichus (?); Plato, Meno 94 C; Polemon of Ilium (?); Simonides (?); Stesichorus; Theodectes (?), Orestes; Theophrastus, Peri basileias, Bk. ii. Archiv 7.240-42. L. Deubner, Sitzb. Heid. Akad., 1919, Abh. 17, 3-8, suggests that the text belongs to the lyseis-literature.

2291   Treatise on literary criticism (?) (Phrynichus?). P. Lond. 3.885; P. Lit. Lond. 183 (Brit. Mus. inv. 885) (II). Refers to Euripides, Bacchae 642; Homer, Il. iii.229, xvi.795, Od. xxii.5; Menander, Cecryphalus (?). W. Croenert, according to the editor, suggests Phrynichus, Peri onomatôn kai rhêmatôn Attikôn. Archiv 10.229.

2292   Treatise on gnomic literature (Didymus?).   PSI 9. 1093 (II, Oxy.). Quotes or cites Chamaeleon (?); Clearchus, On Proverbs (?); Dionysius of Syracuse, fr. 6, Nauck; Hermippus (?), On Aristotle, Bk. i; Sodamus of Tegea (?); two apophthegms of the Seven Sages; and two or more hexameters on Chilon, by an unknown poet (Page, GLP 1, No. 127). Ed. pr.: G. Vitelli, BSAA 24 (1929) 4-8. Archiv 10.223-24. B. Snell, Festschr. Kapp 105-11, notes that lines 1-23 are in hexameters, and attributes them to the fifth century B.C.

2293   On the use of set speeches by historians.   P. Harris 22 (inv. 175 c) (II; on the verso of a list of names). Quotes Homer, Il. xvi.631; mentions Thucydides. Archiv 13.123.

2294   On the myth.   J. G. Winter, TAPA 53 (1922) 137-41 (P. Mich. inv. 6) (III; opisthograph fr.). Title on the verso, "Peri mythou." Mentions the mythos Aisopeios; refers to the Aesopic fable of the dog and the meat (No. 233, Halm). Archiv 8.265-66; JEA 10.147.

2295   Treatise on oratory.   P. Oxy. 3.410 (Bodleian Libr., Gr. class. d.75 (P)) (II, Oxy.; text on recto, No. 1767 on verso). Quotes Euripides, Phoenix, fr. 809.7-8, Nauck; Homer, Il. iv.443, ix.381, 385,

389, 404; Sophocles, Fabula Incerta (JAW 147.120). Archiv 3.294; New Chapters 2.116-17. W. Rhys Roberts, CR 18 (1904) 18-21, sees reminiscences of the rhetorical techne of Tisias and Corax.

2296   Treatise on poetry and poetic diction (Theophrastus?). P. Hibeh 2.183 (Brit. Mus. inv. 2956) (ca. 270-230 B.C., Hibeh; cart.). Mentions Philemon (?).

2297   De Tropis.   P. Würzb. 2 (inv. 19) (II; on the verso of an account). Quotes or cites Dionysius (Tryphonis?), (De Tropis, Ars Grammatica?); Homer, Il. iv.521-22, xix.222-24, xx.59-60, Od. xiv.214-25; and three proverbs. Archiv 11.276. F. della Corte, Riv. Fil. 64 (1936) 406-9, suggests Marcus Seius Nicanor as the author.

2298   On the proverb.   PSI 11.1221 (II, Oxy.). Illustrates the ainos Kyprios and the ainos Sybaritikos; quotes Aristophanes, Vespae 1435-40, and Timocreon, Carmen in Themistoclem (?; Galiano, LG 134; Page, PMG 730). A. Koerte, Archiv 13.122-23, suggests Lucillus of Tarrha, Peri paroimiôn.

2299   Rhetorical treatise.   P. Flor. 2.116 (III). Discusses the figure hypobaton; cites or quotes Athenocles (of Cyzicus?); one "Heraclius rhetor"; Hermolaus; Herodianus (?).

2300   Rhetorical treatise.   P. Oxy. 17.2086, verso (III, Oxy.; on the verso of No. 2860). Refers to Demosthenes, In Philippum (?), Contra Timocratem. Archiv 10.220.

2301   Fragment on the lengthening and shortening of syllables (metrics?).   P. Ibscher 2 (P. Hamb., pp. 128-29) (III-II B.C.). W. Morel, Hermes 87 (1959) 379-80, recognizes Homer, Od. xii.417 in line 5; the text quotes also two tags of verse, of which the second is Empedocles, fr.115.6, Diels-Krantz, identified by M. L. West, CR, NS 12 (1962) 120.

2302   Rhetoric (or oratory?).   P. Hamb. 131 (inv. 643) (III B.C.). On the evidential value of statements taken from slaves under torture; on the epilogue. Archiv 16.114.

2303   Rhetorical treatise (or private letter?).   P. Harris 48 (inv. 183 d) (V-VI).

2304   Fragment on rhetoric (?).   P. Oslo 3.167 (IV).

2305   Fragment on rhetoric (?).   P. Ryl. 3.506 (III).

Epistolary models: see No. 2117.

Rhetoric: see also Nos. 2564, 2784, 2807, 2851.

## Mathematics and Metrology

2306   Mathematical tables.   P. Cairo G.H. 10758   (VI, Panopolis; pap. cod. with a leather cover). Ed. pr.: J. Baillet, Mémoires publiés par les membres de la Mission Arch. Française au Caire 9 (1892) 1-89. M. Cantor, Zeitschr. Math. Phys. 38 (1893) 81-87; J. G. Smyly, Hermathena 19 (1920-22) 105-14.

2307     Multiplication table.  PSI 8.958 (IV, Antinoe; three sheets of papyrus, inscribed on recto and verso).

2308     Tables of division and problems in arithmetic.  P. Michael. 62 (VI?; wooden tablet).  Ed. pr.: D. S. Crawford, Aeg. 23 (1953) 222-40.  M. Hombert, Chr. Ég. 30 (1955) 145-47.

2309     Table of fractions and arithmetical problems.  P. Mich. 3.145 (inv. 4966) (II).

2310     Table of fractions.  P. Mich. 3.146 (inv. 621) (IV, Fayum).  Ed. pr.: F. E. Robbins, CP 18 (1923) 328-33.  L. C. Karpinski, Isis 5 (1923) 20-25; Q. Vetter, CP 20 (1925) 309-12.

2311     Table of fractions.  P. Mich. 3.147 (inv. 1460) (II; sch. ex.?).

2312     Table of fractions.  H. Thompson, Ancient Egypt 1 (1914) 52-54 (University Coll., London) (Byzantine; wooden tablets).  Carved on the back are the words "Phoibamn Daueit" (name of the schoolboy owner?).

2313     On fractional numbers.  P. Hamb. 139 (inv. 697) (I-II).

2314     Mathematical or astronomical table.  P. Ryl. 3.526 (III, Fayum?).  P. Harris 60 (see No. 2009) is possibly from the same text.  Neugebauer, Astron. Pap. Ostr., No. 35, interprets as an astronomical ephemeris.

2315     Treatise on elementary arithmetic and geometry.  PSI 7.763 (I B.C.).  Norsa, SLG, tav. 5 a.

2316     Problems in arithmetic.  T. C. Skeat, Mizraim 3 (1936) 18-22 (Brit. Mus.) (VI; wooden tablet; No. 2109 is on the verso).  Measurement of a well, a paved court, a heap of grain, and an arch.

2317     A fragment on elementary geometry, with diagrams.  Neugebauer, Exact Sc. 179 and pl. 12 (P. Cornell inv. 69, unedited) (?).

2318     On the mensuration of land.  P. Lit. Goodspeed 3 ("P. Ayer," Chicago Natural History Mus.) (I-II, Hawara?).  Ed. pr.: E. J. Goodspeed, AJP 19 (1898) 25-39.  Archiv 1.118-19.  Weitzmann, Ill. RC, p. 48 and pl. 36.

2319     Problems in geometry.  W. Schubart, Ber. Berl. Mus., 1916, 161-70 (P. Berol. inv. 11529) (II; on the verso; sch. ex.).  Archiv 7.254.  Weitzmann, Ill. RC, p. 48 and pl. 35.

2320     Problems.  PSI 3.186 (IV, Oxy.; on recto and verso; sch. ex.).  To find the number of spectators that can be accommodated in a theater of given dimensions; to find the number of artabs contained in a vessel of given dimensions.  J. G. Smyly, Hermathena 19 (1920-22) 105-14; E. G. Turner, Akten Pap. VIII, 141.

2321     A demonstration in geometry, with a figure.  P. Harris 50 (inv. 183 c) (III; sch. ex.?).

2322     Problems in solid geometry, with diagrams.  P. Rain. 1.1 (inv. 19996) (I B.C., Soknopaiou Nesos; school text?).  Archiv 11.279-80.  Weitzmann, Anc. Bk. Ill., p. 5 and fig. 1.  F. Zucker, Gnomon 9 (1933) 649-50; K. F. W. Schmidt, Gött. Anz., 1936, 242-47; J. Mau and W. Muller, Archiv 17 (1960) 10.

2323     Problems in solid geometry, with diagrams.  J. Mau and W. Müller, Archiv 17 (1960) 1-10 (O. Berol. inv. 11999, 12002, 12007, 12008, 12609, 12611) (III B.C., Elephantine; six ostraca, all in the same hand).  E.g., to inscribe a regular icosahedron in a sphere of given diameter.

2324     Algebraic problems.  P. Mich. 3.144 (inv. 620) (II).  Ed. pr.: F. E. Robbins, CP 24 (1929) 321-29.  L. C. Karpinski and F. E. Robbins, Science 70 (1929) 311-14; K. Vogel, CP 25 (1930) 373-75.

2325     Mathematical treatise (?).  P. Ryl. 3.525 (IV; pap. cod.).  Archiv 14.146.

       Mathematics: see also Nos. 2109, 2642, 2657-58, 2739.

2326     Metrology.  On the conversion of artabs from one standard into another.  P. Lond. 2.265 (I).

2327     Discussion and comparison of dry measures.  K. Kalbfleisch, Papyri Graecae Musei Britannici et Musei Berolinensis (Vorlesungsverzeichnis, Rostock 1902) 9-14 (P. Berol. inv. 7094) (II; text on recto, No. 541 on verso).  Archiv 2.379-80; JAW 158.193.

2328     On liquid measures.  P. Oxy. 13.1609, verso (Edinburgh Univ. Libr., Ox. P. 13) (II-III, Oxy.; on the verso of No. 2569; sch. ex.).

2329     On various measures of length and area.  P. Oxy. 4.669 (P. Cairo) (III, Oxy.; on the verso of accounts).

2330     Table of linear measures.  P. Ryl. 2.64 (IV-V; sch. ex.?).

2331     Table of the Roman monetary system.  P. Ryl. 4.538 (II; sch. ex.?).  Archiv 14.147.

2332     List of names of the Attic and Macedonian months.  P. Par. 4 (?).

2333     List of the Coptic months.  Mon.Epiphan. 2.617 (VI-VII?, Thebes; on wood).

2334     List of days of the week.  Mon. Epiphan. 2.618 (VI-VII?, Thebes; limestone).

2335     Symbols for the numbers 1,000 — 10,000.  PSI 3.250 (III-IV, Oxy.).

2336     List of the ordinal numbers from 1 to 18.  Mon. Epiphan. 2.619 (VI-VII?, Thebes; limestone; sch. ex.).

2337     Metrological fragment.  P. Heid. Siegmann 199 (inv. 1119 a-b, verso) (ca. 200 B.C., Hibeh; on the verso of No. 1638).  Mentions one Leontiscus (as an authority?).

Metrology: see also Nos. 2403, 2642 (Macedonian months), 2664, 2728.

## Medicine and Surgery

2338    Medical aphorisms.  P. Ryl. 3.530 (III; pap. cod.). Some are from the Aphorismi of Hippocrates, but in a different order.  Archiv 14.145.

2339    "Anonymi Londinensis Iatrica" (Soranus of Ephesus?). H. Diels, Anonymi Londinensis ex Aristotelis Iatricis Menoniis et Aliis Medicis Eclogae (Supplementum Aristotelicum 3.1); F. G. Kenyon, Sitzb. Berl. Akad., 1901, 1319-21; P. Lit. Lond. 165 (Brit. Mus. inv. 137) (I-II).  Includes an extract from Menon, Iatrika (J. Jüthner, Philostratos über Gymnastik, Leipzig u. Berlin 1909, 10-11). Refers to the following physicians or philosophers (see Jones, op. cit. infra, pp. 14-16): Abas (or Aias?), Aegimius of Elis, Alcamenes of Abydus, Alexander Philalethes, Aristotle (in reference to Menon's work), Asclepiades, Dexippus of Cos, Erasistratus, Euryphon, Heracleodorus, Herodicus (of Cnidus), Herodicus (of Selymbria), Herophilus, Hippon of Croton, Hippocrates, Menecrates of Syracuse, Ninyas the Egyptian, Petron of Aegina, Phaselas of Tenedos, Philistion, Philolaus of Croton, Plato (many passages of the Timaeus), Polybus, Thrasymachus of Sardis, and Timotheus of Metapontum.  H. Beckh and F. Spaet, Anonymus Londinensis (Berlin 1896); W. H. S. Jones, The Medical Writings of Anonymus Londinensis (Cambridge 1947).  Archiv 2.375-76; JAW 79.284-86; Lesky, GGL 532; E. T. Withington, New Chapters 2.183-88, queries the attribution.  F. G. Kenyon, CR 6 (1892) 237-40 (first mention); H. Diels, Hermes 28 (1893) 407-34; F. Spaet, Münchener medicinische Wochenschrift 43 (1896) 57-60; F. von Oefele, ibid. 132-33; M. Wellmann, Hermes 57 (1922) 396-429, ibid. 61 (1926) 329-34, suggests Soranus, Eisagoge; K. Schubring, Gnomon 24 (1952) 416-19.  On the supposed excerpt from Ps.-Hippocrates, De Flatibus, see F. Blass, Hermes 36 (1901) 405-10; F. Steckerl, CP 40 (1945) 166-80.

2340    Catechism for medical students.  PRIMI 1.15 (II?, Oxy.; pap. cod. ?).  Mentions Asclepiades of Bithynia, a physician.  Archiv 13.126-27.  B. Snell, Gnomon 15 (1939) 532.

2341    Catechism on anatomy.  A. Wifstrand, Årsb., Lund, 1934-35, 64-65 (No. 7) (III-IV; pap. cod.).  Archiv 13.127.

2342    Catechism on the eye (?).  P. Aberdeen 11 (II, Fayum?; on the verso of an account).  Ed. pr.: E. O. Winstedt, CQ 1 (1907) 266.  Archiv 14.145.

2343    Catechism on ophthalmology.  P. Ross. Georg. 1.20 (P. Golenischeff, State Mus. of Fine Arts, Moscow) (II).  Col. 2, lines 14-18, resembles Ps.-Galen, Horoi (19.435, ed. Kuehn).  JAW 180.68-69.  C. Kappus, Berl. Phil. Woch. 32 (1912) 266-67.

2344    Fragment on ophthalmology.  J. W. B. Barns, CQ 43 (1949) 3-4 (No. 2) (Egypt Exploration Society, London) (II B.C., Fayum).

2345    Anatomy: Names of parts of the male pudenda.  P. Iand. 5.82 (inv. 349) (I B.C.).  Archiv 10.235.

2346    Treatise on physiology.  P. Ryl. 1.21; BKT 3.10-19 (inv. 9770); P. Rein. 1.2 (P. Sorbonne inv. 2011) (I B.C.).  Schubart, Gr. Pal., Abb. 69.  Archiv 6.261; JAW 180-68.  M. Wellmann, RE 6.904, suggests Eudemus.

2347    On gynaecology.  A. Bäckström, Archiv 3 (1906) 158-62 (P. Golenischeff, State Mus. of Fine Arts, Moscow) (III).  JAW 158.163.  The editor suggests Soranus of Ephesus as the author.

2348    Obstetrical (?) fragment.  P. Hibeh 2.191 (Brit. Mus. inv. 2964) (ca. 260-230 B.C., Hibeh; cart.; on the verso of an official letter-book).  Gazza, p. 89.

2349    Medical treatise.  P. Aberdeen 9 (I-II, Fayum).  Ed. pr.: E. O. Winstedt, CQ 1 (1907) 264.

2350    Prescription for a plaster.  P. Aberdeen 10 (I, Fayum?).  Ed. pr.: E. O. Winstedt, CQ 1 (1907) 265.  Gazza, p. 91.

2351    Medical fragment.  P. Aberdeen 123 (III, Fayum?).

2352    Medical fragment.  P. Aberdeen 124 (II, Fayum?).

2353    Medical fragment (?).  P. Aberdeen 125, verso (III-IV, Fayum?; on the verso of No. 2786).

2354    Treatise on the study of medicine.  BKT 3.22-26 (inv. 9764) (I).  Gives the view of Archibius, a physician.  Archiv. 6.262.

2355    Treatise of the Empirical School.  BKT 3.29-30 (inv. 9015) (I-II; pap. cod. ?).  Archiv 6.261.

2356    Medical treatise (?).  P. Cairo G.H. 10160; P. Cairo Goodspeed 2 (II).  Archiv 3.298.

2357    Medical treatise (?).  P. Hamb. 140 (inv. 650, frr. 1 + 6) (ca. 200 B.C.; cart. ?).  Archiv 16.122.

2358    De ossibus.  P. Lit. Lond. 167 (Brit. Mus. inv. 2397) (II-III; text on recto, No. 2055 on verso).  Archiv 10.235.

2359    Treatise on surgery (?).  P. Oxy. 3.437 (Musées Royaux, Bruxelles, inv. E.5929) (III, Oxy.).  Archiv 3.295.

2360    Medical treatise (a fragment on dysouria).  P. Oxy. 3.468 (Edinburgh Univ. Libr.) (III, Oxy.).  Archiv 3.298.

2361    Treatise based on a neuron-pneuma theory.  PRIMI 1.14 (II).  Archiv 13.126.  B. Snell, Gnomon 15 (1939) 531-32.

2362    Medical treatise.  P. Rain. 3.57 (inv. 29368) (IV; pap. cod.).  Archiv 14.145.

2363    Medical fragment (on alopecia?).  PSI 2.132 (III, Oxy.; on the verso of a document).  Archiv 7.250.

2364    Medical treatise.  PSI 3.252 (III).

2365 Medical treatise. P. Tebt. 2.272 (II, Tebtunis; on the verso of accounts). On the treatment of thirst in fever. Archiv 6.262.

2366 Medical treatise. P. Tebt. 2.676 (II, Tebtunis).

2367 Medical treatise (?). P. Tebt. 2.677 (II, Tebtunis).

2368 Medical treatise. P. Tebt. 2.678 (II, Tebtunis).

2369 Medical treatise (?). P. Tebt. 2.689 (I-II, Tebtunis).

2370 Medical treatise (a fragment on apoplexy). J. W. B. Barns, CQ 43 (1949) 4-5 (No. 3) (Egypt Exploration Society, London) (II B.C., Fayum; palimpsest: of the original text three lines, perhaps epic verse, are legible).

2371 Medical treatise. K. Kalbfleisch, Papyri Graecae Musei Britannici et Musei Berolinensis (Vorlesungs-verzeichnis, Rostock 1902) 8-9 (P. Berol. inv. 9095) (I-II). Archiv 2.378; JAW 158.193.

2372 Fragment of a treatise. N. Lewis, Ét. Pap. 3 (1936) 90-92 (P. Strassb. inv. Gr. 1187) (I-II). Archiv 13.128.

2373 Definitions of surgical terms. J. Nicole, Archiv 2 (1903) 1-3 (P. Genève inv. 111) (II-III; on the verso of a document; sch. ex. ?). Archiv 2.377.

2374 On surgery (Heliodorus?). P. Lond. 2.155; K. Kalb-fleisch, Papyri Graecae Musei Britannici et Musei Berolinensis (Vorlesungsverzeichnis, Rostock 1902) 3-8; P. Lit. Lond. 166 (Brit. Mus. inv. 155) (II, Fayum; text on recto, No. 238 on verso). Archiv 2.375-76; JAW 158.193. W. Croenert, Archiv 2 (1903) 475-82, suggests Heliodorus.

2375 On facial surgery. P. Univ. Giss. 4.44 (inv. 153) (ca. 100 B.C., Fayum?). Archiv 13.127. Gundel 26.

2376 On surgery: Treatment of a fractured shoulder (Heliodorus?). P. Ryl. 3.529 (III; pap. cod.). Archiv 14.145.

2377 On optical surgery (Heliodorus?). P. Cairo Craw-ford 1 (III). Ed. pr.: J. Nicole and J. Ilberg, Archiv 3 (1908) 269-83. Ilberg suggests Heliodorus, Cheirourgoumena, Bk. ii. Cites, as authorities, Heraclides of Tarentum, Heron, Menodorus, Philo-xenus of Alexandria, and Sostratus of Alexandria. JAW 158.170.

2378 On constipation. BKT 3.19-21 (inv. 9095) (I). Gazza, p. 90.

2379 On diseases of the eye. C. (K.) Kalbfleisch, Papyri Argentoratenses Graecae (Programm, Rostock 1901) 4-8 (P. Strassb. inv. Gr. 90) (II). Gazza, p. 92. Archiv 2.378-79; JAW 158.192-93.

2380 Medical treatise: On fever (Agathinus?). C. (K.) Kalbfleisch, Papyri Argentoratenses Graecae (Pro-gramm, Rostock 1901) 8-12 (P. Strassb. inv. Gr. 1) (III-IV). The editor suggests Agathinus of Lace-daemon. Archiv 2.377; JAW 158.192-93.

2381 On diseases of the scalp.(?). P. Flor. 2.117 (I). Gazza, p. 91. Archiv 6.262.

2382 Prescription for falling hair. S. Moeller, Griechische Papyri aus dem Berliner Museum (Göteborg 1929) 81-82 (No. 13) (P. Berol. inv. 11317) (III-IV, Hermu-polis Magna). Gazza, p. 97.

2383 On diet and exercise for invalids. H. Oellacher, Miscellanea Giovanni Galbiati 2 (Milano 1951) 179-82 (P. Monac. inv. Gr. 123) (I). Archiv 16.122.

2384 On diet for epilepsy and paraplexy. P. Oslo 3.72 (II).

2385 Fragment of a treatise (on the common cold?). P. Princ. 3.114 (II-III).

2386 On pharmacology (Apollonius Mys?). A. Wifstrand, Arsb., Lund, 1934-35, 60-64 (No. 6) (II). Gazza, p. 92.

2387 On pharmacology. PRIMI 1.16 (II). Gazza, p. 94. Archiv 13.128.

2388 Veterinary (?) medicine: On the therapeutic proper-ties of asphalt. G. A. Gerhard, SIFC, NS 12 (1935) 93-94 (PSI, sine numero?) (III). Cites Ni-ceratus (?) of Athens, and others (names not clear). Gazza, pp. 96-97. Archiv 13.128.

2389 Medicine (or philosophy?). P. Rain. 1.32 (inv. 29250) (III; pap. cod.).

2390 Five medical prescriptions. P. Antin. 2.64 (VI, Antinoöpolis; pap. cod.).

2391 Magico-medical prescriptions. P. Antin. 2.66 (V, Antinoöpolis).

2392 On the preparation of ox tallow. BKT 3.30-31 (inv. 9765) (II). Gazza, p. 92. Archiv 6.263.

2393 Medical prescriptions. BKT 3.32-33 (inv. 7763) (V-VI; parch. cod.). Gazza, p. 98. Archiv 6.264.

2394 Prescriptions. BKT 3.33-34 (inv. 9776) (I B.C.). Gazza, p. 90. Archiv 6.262.

2395 Prescription (?). P. Univ. Giss. 4.45 (inv. 154) (I B.C., Fayum?). Gundel 29. Gazza, p. 90.

2396 Prescription (?). P. Grenf. 1.52 (Bodleian Libr., Gr. class. f. 31 (P)) (III). Regarded by the editor as an account of sums spent on medicinals. Gazza, pp. 95-96, 101 (note 2).

2397 Prescription (medical or magical?). P. Harris 46 (inv. 175 b) (I). Gazza, p. 91.

2398 Prescription (medical or magical?). P. Harris 47 (inv. 182 e) (I-II). Gazza, p. 92.

2399 Prescriptions. P. Hibeh 2.192 (Brit. Mus. inv. 2965) (ca. 270-250 B.C., Hibeh; cart.; from a pap. with accounts on recto and verso). Gazza, p. 89.

2400 Veterinary prescription. P. Iand. 5.86 (inv. 695) (III). Gundel 30. Gazza, p. 96.

2401   Prescriptions.   P. Lit. Goodspeed 4 (inv. 108) (II-III, Karanis; on the verso of accounts). Ed. pr.: E. J. Goodspeed, AJP 24 (1903) 327-29. Gazza, p. 95.

2402   Prescriptions (?).   P. Lond. 2.186 (Brit. Mus. inv. 186) (II?; text on recto, No. 1709 on verso). P. Lit. Lond. 77 described this text as metrological rather than medical. Gazza, p. 95.

2403   Prescriptions.   P. Lit. Lond. 169 (Brit. Mus. inv. 113 (15 b)) (V-VI; opisthograph fr.). Gazza, pp. 98-99.

2404   Prescriptions.   P. Lit. Lond. 170 (Brit. Mus. inv. 2559) (I). Gazza, p. 91.

2405   Prescriptions.   P. Lit. Lond. 171 (Brit. Mus. inv. 2558) (III; on the verso of an account or property list). Gazza, p. 95.

2406   Prescription.   P. Maspero 2.67141 (VI, Aphrodito; written at the foot of a page of accounts). Gazza, p. 99.

2407   A letter to a physician.   P. Merton 1.12 (A.D. 58). Mentions the plaster invented by the physician Archagathus. Gazza, pp. 91-92, 101.

2408   Prescription.   P. Oxy. 2.234 (II-III, Oxy.; on the verso of a document). Gazza, p. 93.

2409   Prescriptions.   P. Oxy. 8.1088; P. Lit. Lond. 168 (Brit. Mus. inv. 2055) (I, Oxy.; on the verso of No. 1173). Gives examples from Dioscorides and Galen. Gazza, pp. 91-92. Archiv 6.262; JAW 180.67.

2410   Prescriptions.   P. Oxy. 11.1384 (Glasgow Univ. Libr.) (V, Oxy.; from the same pap. as two theological texts). Gazza, p. 98. K. F. W. Schmidt, Gött. Anz., 1918, 125-26.

2411   Prescriptions.   P. Rain. 3.58 (inv. 29288) (V?, Fayum; pap. cod.). Gazza, p. 97. Archiv 14.146.

2412   Prescriptions (Sextius Niger?).   P. Ross. Georg. 1.19 (P. Golenischeff, State Mus. of Fine Arts, Moscow) (II). Gazza, p. 93. JEA 10.152. L. Castiglioni, Aeg. 7 (1926) 225.

2413   Prescription.   P. Ross. Georg. 5.57 (Collection of G. Zereteli, Tiflis) (III; on the verso of a list of persons). Gazza, p. 96.

2414   Prescriptions.   P. Ryl. 1.21, verso; BKT 3.10-19, verso (inv. 9770, verso) (I B.C.-I). Gazza, p. 90.

2415   Prescriptions.   P. Ryl. 1.29 (III; parch., from a short roll?). Gazza, p. 96. Archiv 6.263.

2416   Prescriptions.   P. Ryl. 1.29 a (II). Gazza, p. 94. Archiv 6.263.

2417   Prescriptions.   P. Ryl. 1.29 b (II). Gazza, p. 94. Archiv 6.263.

2418   Prescriptions.   P. Ryl. 3.531 (III-II B.C.). On the medical use of otters' kidneys. Gazza, p. 90. Archiv 14.146.

2419   Prescription.   PSI 4.297 (V?, Hermupolis Magna; on the verso of a letter to a physician). Gazza, p. 98.

2420   Prescription.   PSI 6.718 (IV-V, Oxy. ?; a scrap of parch.). Gazza, p. 97.

2421   Prescriptions.   PSI 10.1180 (II, Tebtunis). Gazza, pp. 94, 100 (possible names of pharmacists). Archiv 13.128.

2422   Prescriptions.   P. Tebt. 2.273 (II-III, Tebtunis; on the verso of a document). Gazza, p. 95. Archiv 6.263.

2423   Prescription (?).   Mon. Epiphan. 2.622 (VI-VII?, Thebes; ostr.).

2424   Prescription.   O. Bodl. 2.2181 (inv. 1251) (II-III; ostr.). C. Préaux, Chr. Ég. 31 (1956) 136-39.

2425   Prescription.   O. Bodl. 2.2182 (inv. 1366) (II-III; ostr.). C. Préaux, Chr. Ég. 31 (1956) 139-41.

2426   Prescription.   O. Bodl. 2.2183 (inv. 1221) (IV; ostr.). C. Préaux, Chr. Ég. 31 (1956) 141-42.

2427   Prescription.   O. Bodl. 2.2184 (inv. 923) (IV?; ostr.). C. Préaux, Chr. Ég. 31 (1956) 142-43.

2428   Prescription.   O. Bodl. 2.2185 (inv. 1418) (IV?; ostr.). C. Préaux, Chr. Ég. 31 (1956) 143-44.

2429   Prescription.   O. Bodl. 2.2186 (inv. 1567) (IV?; ostr.). C. Préaux, Chr. Ég. 31 (1956) 144-46.

2430   Prescription.   O. Bodl. 2.2187 (inv. 1763) (III?; ostr.). C. Préaux, Chr. Ég. 31 (1956) 146.

2431   Prescription (or household account?).   O. Bodl. 2. 2188 (inv. 2549) (IV?; ostr.). C. Préaux, Chr. Ég. 31 (1956) 146-47.

2432   Prescription (?).   O. Bodl. 2.2189 (inv. 2554) (IV?; ostr.).

2433   Prescription (?).   O. Bodl. 2.2564 (inv. 992 + 993) (Byzantine; ostr.). The text is now effaced.

Medical astrology: see No. 2055.
Medical charms in hexameters: see Nos. 1871-72.
Medicine: see also Nos. 1011, 1327, 1871-72, 2038, 2542, 2846, 2877-78. For a list of medical reports, see O. Nanetti, Aeg. 21 (1941) 301-2.

# Mimes

2434   A prose farce.   A. Koerte, Archiv 6 (1913) 1-8; P. Lit. Lond. 97 (Brit. Mus. inv. 1984) (II, Fayum?). A cursive jotting on the verso says that Herakleides copied (?) this from the library of Praxias (?). O. Crusius, Herondae Mimiambi (Lipsiae 1914[5]) 117-21; Manteuffel, Opusc., No. 15; Page, GLP 1, No. 78. Archiv 7.153; New Chapters 1.123. L. de Stefani, Berl. Phil. Woch. 34 (1914) 253; S. Srebrny, Eos 30 (1927) 401-12; G. Manteuffel, Hermes 65 (1930) 126-28.

2435 Fragment of a mime. P. Varsov. 2 (II, Fayum?).
Contains a possible citation of Homer, Il. xxi.198-
99 (Collart 316). Archiv 11.268. G. Manteuffel,
Charist. Przychocki 115-17 (ed. pr).

2436 Fragment of a mime. Manteuffel, Opusc., No. 16
(P. Berol. inv. 13876, recto) (II). Quotes Homer,
Il. xvi.1, xviii.112, xix.65. Archiv 10.61-62.

2437 Notes for the performance of a mime. G. Manteuffel,
Eos 32 (1929) 27-33 (P. Berol. inv. 13927) (V-VI).
Inventory of stage-properties for a "variety num-
ber" entitled "Leucippe" and seven dramatic sketches
Manteuffel, Opusc., No. 17. Archiv 10.63-64. I.
Cazzaniga, Stud. Cl. Or. 7 (1958) 7-19.

Mimes: for verse mimes, see Nos. 1743-48.

## Music

2438 On the moral effects of music (Hippias of Elis?). P.
Hibeh 1.13 (Univ. of Pennsylvania Mus., inv. E.3068)
(III B.C., Hibeh; cart.). Jander 18-20. Archiv
6.238; JAW 144.2-4; New Chapters 2.91-92, 181-
83. C. E. Ruelle, Rev. Phil. 31 (1907) 235-40; W.
Croenert, Hermes 44 (1909) 503-21, suggests one
of the earliest members of the school of Isocrates;
Wilamowitz, Gr. Versk. 66.

2439 Texts with musical notation. W. Schubart, Sitzb.
Berl. Akad., 1918, 763-68 (P. Berol. inv. 6870)
(II-III, Contrapollinopolis?; on the verso of a Latin
military document). A "Music Lovers' Library:"
a paean to Apollo (Heitsch, GDRK, fr. LII); an
instrumental piece; an address to Ajax after his
suicide (Aeschylus, Hoplon Krisis?); and two other
short passages. O. J. Gombosi, Tonarten und
Stimmungen der antiken Musik (Copenhagen 1939)
133-35; Pöhlmann, GMF 21, 28, 45-46. Archiv
7.139-40; JAW 191.63, 193.1-7; New Chapters 2.
150-53, 172-76. T. Reinach, Rev. Arch., Ser. 5.10
(1919) 11-27; O. Schroder, Berl. Phil. Woch. 40
(1920) 350; R. Wagner, Philol. 77 (1921) 256-310;
C. Préaux, Chr. Ég. 5 (1930) 280-83; C. del
Grande, ibid. 6 (1931) 441-50; G. B. Pighi, Aeg.
23 (1943) 169-243; F. M. Heichelheim, SO 34 (1958)
15-18, suggests that fr. C (the address to Ajax after
his suicide), P. Oxy. 2256, fr. 71 (see No. 46), and
P. Oxy. 2255, fr. 5 (see No. 45), belong to the
same chorus of Aeschylus (Hoplon Krisis?); R. P.
Winnington-Ingram, Lustrum 3 (1958) 10-11.

2440 A monody with musical notation. P. Oxy. 25.2436
(II, Oxy.; on the verso is a magical text). Perhaps
a lyric from a satyr play rather than a "Hellenistic
or Roman music-hall scena" or a dithyramb. Page,
PMG 1024; Pöhlmann, GMF 27, 43-44. H. Lloyd-
Jones, CR, NS 11 (1961) 20-21.

2441 Tragic and comic fragments, with musical notation.
H. Hunger and E. Pöhlmann, WS 75 (1962) 51-76
(P. Vindob. Gr. inv. 29825 a-f) (late III B.C.;
frr. a-b are written on both recto and verso).
Pöhlmann, GMF 79. O. Crusius, Philol. 52 (1893)
200, mentions unedited musical papyri in this collection. H. Gerstinger, Atti Pap. IV, 309.

2442 Text with musical notation. Mentioned by R. P.
Winnington-Ingram, Lustrum 3 (1958) 7, note 2,
and Pöhlmann, GMF 79 (P. Mich. inv. 2958) (II).
To be published by O. M. Pearl.

2443 From a treatise on music. P. Tebt. 3.694 (III B.C.,
Tebtunis; cart.). Archiv 11.279.

2444 Treatise on music (or philosophical dialogue?). P.
Rein. 1.5 (P. Sorbonne inv. 2014); BKT 2.55 (inv.
9869) (II B.C.; in the same hand as No. 2177).
Cites Lasus of Hermione (?). Discovered by W.
Schubart that P. Rein. and BKT belong to the same
papyrus; see F. della Corte, Riv. Fil. 64 (1936)
392-95. Archiv 3.499, 500.

2445 Musical treatise, with notation (?). P. Hibeh 2.231
(Brit. Mus.) (ca. 250 B.C., Hibeh; cart.). Meager fragments.

Music: see also Nos. 411 (Euripides, Orestes, with
musical notation), 1706 (tragic texts with musical
notation), 1916 (fragment with musical notation).
For a Christian hymn with musical notation, see
P. Oxy. 15.1786, and G. B. Pighi, Aeg. 21 (1941)
189-220 (detailed study, with bibl.), Pöhlmann,
GMF 80 (bibl.), and R. P. Winnington-Ingram,
Lustrum 3 (1958) 10.

## Mythography and Religion

2446 Mythological fragment. P. Rein. 1.3 (P. Sorbonne
inv. 2012) (I?). Archiv 3.500.

2447 Artemis destroys the Aloadae. P. Rain. 1.17 (inv.
29784) (III). Archiv 11.278-79. R. Pfeiffer, Philol.
92 (1937) 16, note 25.

2448 Adventures of Hercules. P. Petrie 2.49 f; P. Lit.
Lond. 190 (Brit. Mus. inv. 592) (III B.C., Gurob;
cart.).

2449 On an adventure of Hercules and Jason. P. Hibeh
2.186 (Brit. Mus. inv. 2959) (ca. 250-220 B.C.,
Hibeh; cart.). On the verso of Fr. a are a few
lines about "first discoverers" (prōtoi heuretai):
no names preserved.

2450 On the legendary wars of Thebes. PSI 9.1091 (I-II,
Oxy.). In the Doric dialect. Norsa, SLG, tav.
9 c. Archiv 10.232.

2451 Mythology (?): The death of Tiresias. PSI 14.1398
(II, Oxy.; on the verso of accounts). S. Daris,
Aeg. 39 (1959) 21-22; H. Lloyd-Jones, Gnomon
31 (1959) 113-14, identifies the subject: the death
of Tiresias near the fountain of Telphussa.

2452 The consorts of the Muses; the victors at the funeral
games for Pelias (extracts from, or source of
Hyginus?). J. Schwartz, Studi Calderini-Paribeni
2.151-56 (P. Strasb. W.G. 332) (II). Perhaps
from the original Hyginus, in Greek, not Latin.
S. Daris, Aeg. 39 (1959) 18-21.

2453    Preliminaries to the Trojan War.   N. Lewis, Ét.
        Pap. 3 (1936) 87-90 (P. Strassb. inv. Gr. 2493,
        verso) (I-II).   Archiv 13.125.

2454    Catalogue of the Ships; Story of Philoctetes.    P.
        Haun. 1.7 (inv. 300) (I, Fayum?).   Archiv 16.126.

2455    From the story of Philoctetes.    P. Oxy. 6.865 (Newton
        Theological Institute) (III, Oxy.).   Archiv 6.246;
        JEA 11.87.   E. Lobel, Bodl. Rec. 4 (1924) 172, iden-
        tifies the subject.

2456    On Achilles.    P. Tebt. 2.683, recto (I-II, Tebtunis;
        sch. ex.; text on recto, No. 2665 on verso).

2457    Events at Troy after the death of Achilles.    P. Ryl.
        1.22 (I, Oxy.; on the verso of an account).   Jacoby,
        FGH 1.182-83.   Archiv 6.260.

2458    Mythological fragment.    P. Univ. Giss. 4.42 (inv.
        306) (I B.C., Fayum?).   Gundel 31.   Archiv 13.125.

2459    From a mythological treatise (?).   P. Ryl. 1.40 (II).
        Archiv 6.260.

2460    Mythological fragment (or commentary on an epic
        poem?).    P. Bad. 6.176; P. Heid. Siegmann 176
        (inv. 1891) (III B.C., Philadelphia; from the Zenon
        archive).   Quotes eight hexameters from an unknown
        poet.   Archiv 14.140.

2461    Mythological fragment (?).    P. Rain. 3.44 (inv.
        29381) (cf. ibid. 4, p. 137) (III; pap. cod.).   Archiv
        14.140.

2462    Mythological fragment (?).    PSI 7.850 (II-III?; pap.
        cod.).   Archiv 8.270.

2463    Mythological fragment.    PSI 8.1000 (IV; ostr.).
        Quotes Homer, Il. xiii.217 (or xiv.116).   Archiv 10.
        233.

        Mythography: see also Nos. 2646, 2649, 2723,
            2861, 2868, 2911.

2464    Religion: Orphic (?) text: Ritual of the Mysteries.
        P. Gurob 1 (III B.C., Gurob; cart.).   Contains
        several tags of hexameters.   O. Kern, Orphicorum
        Fragmenta (Berolini 1922) 101-4.   Archiv 7.250;
        JEA 9.100.   M. Tierney, CQ 16 (1922) 77-87; A.
        Olivieri, Atti. Acc. Napoli, NS 8 (1924) 273-305,
        notes resemblances to Clement of Alexandria,
        Protrepticus; O. Schuetz, Rh. Mus. 87 (1938)
        241-67.

2465    On the legend of Orpheus.   W. Schubart, in A. Gercke
        and E. Norden, Einleitung in die Altertumswissen-
        schaft (Leipzig 1927³) 1.9, p. 42 (P. Berol. inv.
        13426) (II).   E. Orth, Phil. Woch. 47 (1927) 1469-71.

2466    The ritual of the Eleusinian Mysteries (or romance?).
        P. Antin. 1.18 (II, Antinoöpolis).   Triptolemus,
        identified with Osiris as judge of the dead, is ad-
        dressed.   Archiv 16.123-24.   A. Delatte, Bull.
        Acad. Belg., Sér. 5.38 (1952), 194-208; idem, CRAI,
        1952, 251-58.

2467    Religion (?): A fragment mentioning Zeus and Posei-
        don.   P. Mil. Vogl. 2.43 (inv. 213) (II, Tebtunis).
        Ed. pr.: A. Vogliano, A. Cinotti, A. M. Colombo,
        Studi in onore di Vincenzo Arangio-Ruiz 2 (Napoli
        1953) 515-18.

2468    An Apollo aretalogy.   W. Schubart, Hermes 55 (1920)
        188-95 (P. Berol. inv. 11517) (II; on the verso of
        accounts).   Manteuffel, Opusc., No. 6.   Archiv 7.
        252-53; JEA 7.87.   S. Eitrem, SO 26 (1948) 175-76,
        quotes W. Croenert's opinion that the text is the
        work of a Hellenistic historian, on the affairs of
        Delphi; S. Eitrem, Dragma Martino P. Nilsson ...
        Dedicatum (Skrifter utgivna av Svenska Institutet
        i Rom, Ser. 2.1; Lund och Leipzig 1939) 170-80.

2469    On ancient cult statues.   P. Schubart 34 (I B.C.-I).
        Archiv 16.125.

2470    On the names of the gods.   Wilcken, TAGP, Taf. II
        (II-III).

2471    Fragment on the epithets of Athena (Apollodorus?),
        or commentary on a poetic text (?).   P. Oxy. 20.
        2260 (II, Oxy.).   Quotes Callimachus, fr. 37,
        Pfeiffer; Euripides (B. Snell, WS 69, 1956, 94);
        Homer, Od. xi.609-10; Ibycus (Page, PMG 298;
        idem, CR, NS 3, 1953, 1-2); Philetas (L. Alfonsi,
        Aeg. 34, 1954, 211-14, attributes the quotation to
        Philetas' Demetra); the Phoronis; and Stesichorus
        (Page, PMG 233).   B. Snell, Gnomon 25 (1953) 433-
        34; R. Merkelbach, Archiv 16 (1956) 115-17, suggests
        Apollodorus of Athens, Peri theôn.

2472    Oath of an initiate.   PSI 10.1162 (III?, Oxy.).   U.
        Wilcken, Archiv 10 (1931) 257-59, and O. Kern,
        ibid. 12 (1937) 66-67, think of the cult of the Ca-
        biri; F. Cumont, Harv. Theol. Rev. 26 (1933)
        151-60, reedits the text, querying Wilcken's hypo-
        thesis; A. Momigliano, Aeg. 13 (1933) 179-86,
        favors the cult of Sarapis; R. Merkelbach, Ann.
        Univ. Sarav. 8 (1959) 51-52, suggests the mysteries
        of Isis and Osiris.

2473    Oath of an initiate.   PSI 12.1290 (I, Oxy.).   From the
        same text, but not the same papyrus, as No. 2472.
        Ed. pr.: V. Bartoletti, Ann. Sc. Pisa, Ser. 2.6
        (1937) 143-52.   O. Schuetz, Archiv 13 (1939) 210-12,
        regards the text as Orphic.

2474    Religious fragment (or romance?).   P. Oxy. 3.417
        (Smithsonian Institution) (III, Oxy.).   Lavagnini,
        EGFP 31-32.   Archiv 3.296; New Chapters 3.245-
        46.   B. A. Mueller, Rh. Mus. 71 (1916) 359, suggests
        a romance; F. Zimmermann, Archiv 11 (1935) 175-
        82, prefers a treatise on religion.

2475    A list of Greek festivals.   P. Harris 49 (inv. 183 b)
        (III-IV; on the verso of accounts).

2476    Dream of Nectanebus.   U. Wilcken, Mél. Nicole
        579-96 (P. Leid.) (II B.C., Serapaeum, Memphis).
        Ed. pr.: C. Leemans, Papyri Graeci Musei ...
        Lugduni Batavi 1 (Lugduni Batavorum 1843) 122-29.
        Manteuffel, Opusc., No. 10; Lavagnini, EGFP
        37-42; Wilcken, UPZ 1, No. 81.

2477    Invocation of Isis.  P. Oxy. 11.1380 (Bodleian Libr.,
        Gr. class. b.16 (P)) (II, Oxy.; text on recto, No.
        2479 on verso).  Manteuffel, Opusc., No. 2; B.
        A. van Groningen, De Papyro Oxyrhynchita 1380
        (Groningen 1921).  Archiv 7.251; JEA 6.127, 9.101,
        10.154.  G. Lafaye, Rev. Phil. 40 (1916) 55-108;
        K. F. W. Schmidt, Gött. Anz., 1918, 106-17; G.
        P. Wetter, Eranos 18 (1918) 134-59; G. Manteuffel,
        Rev. Phil. 53 (1928) 161-67; C. H. Roberts, JEA
        39 (1953) 114.

2478    Polemic against the anthropomorphic portrayal of
        Osiris and Isis.  G. Michaelides, BIFAO 49 (1950)
        23-43 (II, Achmîm; inscribed on a vase in the
        editor's collection in Cairo).  Archiv 16.108.

2479    Invocation of Imouthes-Asklepios.  P. Oxy. 11.1381
        (Bodleian Libr., Gr. class. b.16 (P), verso) (II,
        Oxy.; on the verso of No. 2477).  E. J. and L.
        Edelstein, Asclepius: A Collection and Interpreta-
        tion of the Testimonies 1 (Baltimore 1945), No. 331;
        Manteuffel, Opusc., No. 3.  Archiv 7.251-52.  K.
        F. W. Schmidt, Gött. Anz., 1918, 117-22; G. P.
        Wetter, Eranos 18 (1918) 114-34; G. Manteuffel,
        Eos 31 (1928) 192-94.

2480    Aretalogy of Sarapis.  P. Oxy. 11.1382 (Crozer Theo-
        logical Seminary) (II, Oxy.; on the verso of an
        account).  Manteuffel, Opusc., No. 4; O. Wein-
        reich, Neue Urkunden zur Sarapis-Religion
        (Tübingen 1919) 13-18.  Archiv 7.252.  K. F. W.
        Schmidt, Gött. Anz., 1918, 123.

2481    Fragment of a Sarapis aretalogy.  P. Schubart 12
        (III; written on the recto, under a document;  on
        the verso, a text on a cult practice).  Includes
        portions of a hymn to the god (Heitsch, GDRK, fr.
        L).

2482    On the myth of Horus.  H. Lietzmann, Gött. Nachr.,
        1912, 320 (Philol. Seminar der Univ. Jena) (III;
        text from a pap. of Irenaeus).

2483    Egyptian prophecy (?).  PSI 8.982 (III; on the verso
        of a document).  Archiv 10.25; Chr. Eg. 10 (1935)
        410.  G. Manteuffel, Mél. Maspero 119-24, regards
        the text as similar to the "Acta Alexandrinorum";
        C. H. Roberts, P. Oxy. 22, p. 89, note 4, thinks
        rather of Greco-Egyptian prophecy akin to the
        "Oracle of a Potter" (see No. 2486).

2484    Treatise (?) on Egyptian priests and temples.  V. B.
        Schuman, Harv. Theol. Rev. 53 (1960) 159-70
        (Washington Univ. Libr., inv. 138) (II, Oxy.; on
        recto and verso).

2485    On the sacred animals of the Egyptians.  K. Hanell,
        Årsb., Lund, 1937-38, 137-42 (Sept. 4, A.D. 98).

2486    "Oracle of a Potter to King Amenopis."  C. Wessely,
        Denkschr. Wien. Akad, 1893, Abh. 2, 3-6 (P. Rain.
        inv. 19813 + "P. Graf") (II-III; on the verso of an
        account).  Manteuffel, Opusc., No. 7 (bibl.).  R.
        Reitzenstein, Gött. Nachr., 1904, 309-32; U.
        Wilcken, Hermes 40 (1905) 544-60; H. Gerstinger,
        WS 44 (1924-25) 219-20, reedits P. Rain.

2487    "Oracle of a Potter to King Amenopis."  P. Oxy. 22.
        2332 (III, Oxy.; on the verso of a legal document).
        From the same text, but not the same papyrus, as
        No. 2486; the ed. pr. discusses the relation to
        No. 2486, with a bibliography.  J. T. Kakridis,
        Hellen. 14 (1955-56) 440-42; R. Merkelbach, Ar-
        chiv 16 (1956) 124, contributes parallels to the
        thought.

2488    Religion (or history?).  C. H. Roberts, P. Oxy. 22,
        p. 92 and note 3 (Trinity Coll. Libr., Dublin) (III
        B.C.).  Regarded by the editor as possibly related
        to the "Oracle of a Potter" (see Nos. 2486-87); A.
        D. Nock, ad loc., prefers to think of a historical
        text, e.g. Manetho or Hecataeus.

2489    Aretalogy of the deified Amenothes (Amenhotep).  O.
        Gueraud, BIFAO 27 (1927) 121-25; A. Bataille, Et.
        Pap. 4 (1938) 125-31, adds the second fr. (P. Cairo
        inv. 67300) (III B.C., Deir-el-Bahari; ostr. in two
        frr.).  One Polyaratos records his gratitude for a
        miraculous cure.

2490    A graffito referring to Amenothes.  P. Jouguet, Mél.
        Glotz 2.493-500 (?, the "Holy Rock," near Thebes;
        graffito).  Includes a verse maxim.  A. Bataille,
        BIFAO 38 (1939) 141-77, adds other graffiti of re-
        ligious interest.

2491    Prayer to a pagan deity, perhaps Sarapis.  P. Oxy.
        6.923 (P. Ryl. inv. 451) (II-III, Oxy.).

2492    Question to the oracle of Zeus-Helios-Sarapis:  Should
        Menandros marry?  P. Oxy. 9.1213 (Cambridge
        Univ. Libr., add. 5900) (II, Oxy.).

2493    Appeal to the god Souchos for an oracle.  F. Cenderelli,
        Athen. 35 (1947) 171-74 (P. Mil. Vogl.) (?, Tebtunis).

        For other questions to oracles, see Preisendanz,
        PGM, Nos. 30-31, and A. Wilhelm, Archiv 15
        (1953) 71-74.

2494    Religious (?) fragment.  P. Rain. 3.31 (inv. 29812)
        (I; sch. ex.).  Mentions Souchos, Helios, Hermes,
        and Tyche.  Archiv 14.148.

        Religion: see also Nos. 455 (oracles of Apollo),
        1774 (Orphic text), 1818 (oracles), 1878 (oracular
        response), 1933 (aretalogy of Sarapis), 1935
        (hymn to Sarapis), 1936 (initiates' song), 2639
        (prophecy?).

## Oratory

2495    Accusation of one of the admirals at Arginusae (?).
        E. Egger, Mémoires d'histoire ancienne et de
        philologie, 1863, 175-96 ("P. Dugit:" Paris?) (I,
        Thebes).  Ed. pr.: idem, Rev. Arch. 6 (1862)139-
        52.  Jander 26-30.  New Chapters 2.120.

2496    A speech by an Athenian general.  P. Hibeh 1.15; P.
        Lit. Lond. 136 (Brit. Mus. inv. 1825) (III B.C.,
        Hibeh; cart.).  Jacoby, FGH 2.506-7; Jander 31-33.
        New Chapters 2.117.  A. Koerte, Archiv 6.237,
        suggests that the speech is placed in the mouth of
        an Athenian general by a historian, Anaximenes
        or Theopompus.

2497    A declamation against Alcibiades.   N. Lewis, Ét.
        Pap. 3 (1936) 79-87 (P. Strassb. inv. Gr. 2346)
        (V; pap. cod.).   Archiv 13.114-15.

2498    A speech against Demosthenes.   P. Oxy. 6.858
        (Muhlenberg Coll.) (II-III, Oxy.; on the verso of
        a cursive document; sch. ex.?).   Paraphrases
        Demosthenes, De Corona 169.   Jander 36-38.   Ar-
        chiv 6.237; New Chapters 2.121.

2499    An Attic forensic speech (Hyperides?).   P. Oxy. 27.
        2464 (III, Oxy.).

2500    A speech in behalf of Lycophron (Hyperides?).   P.
        Oxy. 13.1607; P. Lit. Lond. 135 (Brit. Mus. inv.
        2468) (II-III, Oxy.).   A. Koerte, Archiv 7.158-60,
        and Hermes 58 (1923) 230-37, rejects the attribu-
        tion to Hyperides on stylistic grounds.

2501    A private oration (Hyperides?).   Brief mention by D.
        G. Hogarth and B. P. Grenfell, Egypt Exploration
        Fund: Archaeological Report, 1895-96, p. 16 (II,
        Karanis).   Perhaps covered by some other item in
        this list.

2502    Fragment of an Attic orator (Hyperides or Lysias?).
        P. Oxy. 11.1366 (Bibliotheek der Universiteit Gent,
        inv. 51) (III, Oxy.; on the verso of accounts).   In-
        cludes part of a hypothesis, and a title: ... ogenous.
        A. Koerte, Archiv 7.160, suggests Hyperides, In
        Athenogenem, or Lysias, In Diogenem; K. F. W.
        Schmidt, Gött. Anz., 1918, 98-99.

2503    Political oration (Lysias or a rhetorical exercise?).
        P. Hamb. 132 (inv. 405) (III-IV; pap. cod.).   Pre-
        sumably on events of 404 B.C.   Mentions Lysander,
        the Lacedaemonians, and Lycurgus.   Archiv 16.114.
        E. G. Turner, Symbolae R. Taubenschlag Dedicatae
        2 (Eos 48, fasc. 2, 1956) 143-46, rejects Lysias,
        and suggests a rhetorical exercise.

2504    Fragment of an Attic orator (Lysias or Isaeus?).   P.
        Bad. 6.177 (II, Oxy.).   Archiv 14.136.

2505    From a legal plea (Isaeus?).   P. Iand. 5.81 (inv. 214)
        (ca. A.D. 300; pap. cod.).   Gundel 22.   Archiv
        10.219.

2506    From an Athenian political oration (or history?).
        PSI 14.1396 (II-III, Oxy.).   Ed. pr.: A. Perosa,
        SIFC, NS 12 (1935) 95-97.   Norsa, SLG, tav. 10 b.
        Archiv 13.113; Chr. Ég. 11 (1936) 555.   G. de
        Sanctis, Riv. Fil. 14 (1936) 134-52, 253-73;   P.
        Roussel, Mélanges Desrousseaux (Paris 1937)
        429-34.

2507    A eulogy of the Thebans (oratory or history?).   P.
        Schubart 32 (I).   Archiv 16.126.

2508    Speech by an Athenian orator on a letter of Philip of
        Macedon.   P. Oxy. 2.216 (Yale Univ. Libr.) (I,
        Oxy.).   Roberts, GLH, pl. 10a.   Jacoby, FGH 2.
        826-27; Jander 33-34; Robinson, Hist. Alex. 273.
        Archiv 1.526; New Chapters 2.119.   A rhetorical
        exercise (?).

2509    Declamation on the campaigns of Alexander (?).   P.
        Rain. 3.29 (inv. 26747) (I, Soknopaiou Nesos; sch.
        ex.).   Archiv 14.136-37.

2510    A suasoria urging resistance to Alexander.   P. Lond.
        3.884; P. Lit. Lond. 139 (Brit. Mus. inv. 884) (II).
        Archiv 10.221.

2511    A speech by Leptines (exercise based on Demosthenes,
        Adversus Leptinem).   BKT 7.4-13 (inv. 9781) (III
        B.C., Hermupolis Magna).   Contains many verbal
        echoes of Demosthenes.   Schubart, Gr. Pal., Abb.
        68.   Archiv 7.227;  New Chapters 2.120-21.

2512    A political declamation.   BKT 7.31-34 (inv. 13045)
        (III-IV; on the verso of accounts).   Schubart, Gr.
        Pal., Abb. 91.   Archiv 7.227-28;  JAW 211.86.

2513    From a forensic speech (?).   PSI 12.1288 (III, Oxy.).
        Archiv 16.114.

2514    From a forensic speech.   P. Schubart 33 (I-II).   One
        Pythodorus is a principal in the case.   Archiv 16.
        114.

2515    Parts of three legal pleas.   F. G. Kenyon, Mel. Weil
        243-48; P. Lit. Lond. 138 (Brit. Mus. inv. 256)
        (I, Fayum?; on the verso of No. 1762 and docu-
        ments; perhaps from a school of rhetoric).   Jander
        23-25.   Archiv 1.117-18, 10.221;   New Chapters 2.
        121-22.

2516    Plea in a case of disinheritance.   P. Lit. Lond. 140
        (Brit. Mus. inv. 1546 A) (II).   Archiv 10.219.

2517    Oration on the cult of Caesar.   P. Oxy. 13.1612
        (Bibliotheek der Univ. Ghent, inv. 63 (III, Oxy.).
        Archiv 7.226-27.   L. Deubner, Sitzb. Heid. Akad.,
        1919, Abh. 17, 8-11.

2518    Draft of a speech in honor of one Appion.   PSI 14.1399
        (V-VI; large sheet of pap., with two columns).
        Ed. pr.: M. Norsa, Aeg. 1 (1920) 154-58.   JEA
        7.87, 8.87-88, 9.100.   B. Lavagnini, Aeg. 2 (1921)
        192-99 (= idem, Studi RG 159-68), suggests a ro-
        mance; M. Norsa, SIFC, NS 2 (1922) 202-8, prefers
        as before; scholia on an known text; Jacoby, FGH
        1 (1923), pp. 521-22, classifies the text as a romance
        about Troy; V. Bartoletti, Studi Paoli 74-80, pre-
        fers an outline of an address in honor of one Appion
        (perhaps the praefectus praetorio per Orientem of
        the early sixth century).

2519    Oration translated from the Latin, by one Olympius
        Isidorianus.   P. Ryl. 2.62 (III; on the verso of
        a document).   Quotes Homer, Od. viii.553, ix.
        455.   Collart, PLL 56.   R. Calderini, Aeg. 33
        (1953) 344.

2520    Forensic speech against a certain Zoïlus.   P. Hamb.
        133 (inv. 16, recto) (I-II; text on recto, No. 2817
        on verso).   Archiv 16.114.

2521    Legal plea in defense of one Hermione.   P. Oxy. 3.
        472 (Morgan Libr.) (II, Oxy.).   New Chapters 2.
        122.

2522    A speech to an emperor in defense of one Didymus.
PSI 11.1222 (II-III, Oxy.). Ed. pr.: T. Bolelli,
Ann. Sc. Pisa, Ser. 2.3 (1934) 15-17. Archiv 13.
115-16.

2523    A protreptic speech.   P. Petrie 1.10;  P. Lit. Lond.
137 (Brit. Mus. inv. 490) (III B.C., Gurob; cart.).
Jander 21-22. New Chapters 2.117-18.

2524    Sophistic discourses.   P. Lit. Lond. 193 (Brit. Mus.
inv. 2239) (II; on the verso of a tax register).
Contents: praise of modesty; account of a bird
(the phoenix?). Quotes Homer, Il. v.531, xv.563,
Od. vi.222; Hesiod, Opera 318; and possibly an
iambic passage from Sophocles (?). Archiv 10.
220; New Chapters 2.123-24, 3.251-53.

2525    Sophistic encomia of Minos, Rhadamanthys, and Tydeus.
I. Cazzaniga, SIFC, NS 29 (1957) 133-73 (P. Univ.
Statale di Milano) (III B.C.).

2526    Fragment of an encomium.   P. Rain. 1.15 (cf. ibid.
3, pp. 94-95) (inv. 29792) (V-VI, Hermupolis Magna; pap. cod.). The subscription quotes Homer,
Od. viii.170-71 (Collart 62). Archiv 11.271-72. K.
F. W. Schmidt, Gött. Anz., 1936, 251-52.

2527    Encomium on the fig.   P. Oxy. 17.2084 (III, Oxy.).
Manteuffel, Opusc., No. 24. Archiv 10.221-22.

2528    Collection of rhetorical exercises.   H. Gerstinger,
Mitteilungen des Vereines Klass. Philologen in
Wien 4 (1927) 35-47 (P. Rain. inv. 29789) (III-IV,
Soknopaiou Nesos; pap. cod.). Parts of three
progymnasmata, two ethopoeiae, and an encomium.
Archiv 10.222.23.

2529    List of subjects for declamations.   P. Oxy. 24.2400
(III, Oxy.; on the verso of a tax register). Includes Euripides placed on trial for impiety because
he showed Heracles going mad.

2530    Logos stephanõtikos, addressed to an emperor.   P.
Rain. 3.62 (inv. 29328 + 29791) (IV-V; pap. cod.).
Archiv 14.137.

2531    Panegyric on an emperor, possibly Julian.   P. Rain.
1.14 (cf. ibid. 3, p. 94) (inv. 29834 A-D + 29292 +
29504) (IV-V, Soknopaiou Nesos; pap. cod.). The
editors reject Libanius as the author because of the
clausulae. Archiv 11.270-71. K. F. W. Schmidt,
Gött. Anz., 1936, 250-51.

2532    Commentary on an oration (?): The trial of Phidias
(?).   J. Nicole, Procès de Phidias dans les
Chroniques d'Apollodore (Genève 1910) (P. Geneve
inv. 263 + 264) (III, Hermupolis Magna?). The
editor's attribution to Apollodorus is rejected by
A. Koerte, Archiv 6.244, and F. Jacoby, Berl.
Phil. Woch. 30 (1910) 1148-56. L. Pareti, Mittheilungen des K.-D. Arch. Instituts, Roem. Abt.
24 (1909) 271-316 (= idem, Studi minori di storia
antica 2, Roma 1961, 133-77); P. Ducati, AR 14
(1911) 9-21; S. Witkowski, Berl. Phil. Woch. 32
(1912) 1766-68; C. Robert, Sitzb. Berl. Akad.,
1914, 806-13, thinks of an epitome or commentary
on a speech; W. Judeich, Hermes 60 (1925) 50-58.

2533    Oratory (?).   P. Aberdeen 118 (II, Fayum?). Ed.
pr.: E. O. Winstedt, CQ 1 (1907) 265.

2534    Oratory (or collection of sayings?).   P. Bon. 1.7
(inv. 11 d) (III-IV; pap. cod.?). Edd. pr.: G. B.
Pighi, Aeg. 27 (1947) 173-74, and A. Vogliano,
Acme 1 (1948) 230-31.

2535    Oratory.   P. Freib. 3 (inv. 9) (II-I B.C.). Archiv
7.226.

2536    Oratory (?).   P. Freib. 6 (inv. 35 i) (II B.C.). Archiv 7.226.

2537    Attic oratory (?).   P. Heid. Siegmann 191 (inv. 1976)
(III, Oxy.; on the verso of a document).

2538    Attic oratory (?).   P. Heid. Siegmann 192 (inv. 1132)
(ca. 250 B.C.).

2539    Attic oratory (or philosophical dialogue?).   P. Heid.
Siegmann 193 (inv. 1103 a) (III B.C., Hibeh).

2540    Oratory (?).   P. Lond. 3.878, verso (IV; on the
verso of a document). Evidently not in P. Lit.
Lond.

2541    Encomium (?).   P. Lond. 5.1816 a; P. Lit. Lond.
141 (Brit. Mus. inv. 1605 A) (III; on the verso of
a document). Archiv 10.222.

2542    Oratory (or medicine?).   P. Lit. Lond. 196 (Brit.
Mus. inv. 1862 C) (II). Archiv 10.236.

2543    Encomium of Athens (?).   P. Oxy. 3.442 (Trinity
Coll. Libr., Dublin, Pap. E.8) (?, Oxy.). Jander
21. Archiv 3.296.

2544    Oratory.   P. Oxy. 3.443 (Univ.-Bibl., Graz, I.1927)
(II, Oxy.). Jander 17. Archiv 3.293.

2545    Oratory (or history?).   P. Oxy. 3.444 (Yale Univ.
Libr.). (II, Oxy.). Mentions Philip and the Macedonians. Archiv. 3. 282.

2546    Oratory (Hyperides?).   P. Oxy. 4.682 (Edinburgh
Univ. Libr.) (II-III, Oxy.). Jander 17. Archiv 3.
494.

2547    Oratory.   P. Oxy. 15.1799 (II, Oxy.). Perhaps a
vindication of the policy of Demosthenes. Archiv
7.228; New Chapters 2.72-73, 121.

2548    Oratory.   P. Oxy. 15.1827 (III, Oxy.). Archiv 7.160.

2549    Oratory (?).   P. Ryl. 3.509 (II). Archiv 14.136.

2550    Oratory (or history?).   PSI 2.128 (II-III, Oxy.; pap.
cod.). The speakers are kybernetai under the
orders of Lysander. Archiv 7.228.

2551    Oratory.   PSI 2.148 (III, Hermupolis Magna). Archiv 7.226.

2552    Oratory.   PSI 2.153 (II-III, Oxy.; pap. cod.?). Archiv 7.160

2553    Oratory (?).   PSI 2.154 (I-II, Oxy.). Archiv 7.228.

2554     Oratory (or history?).    PSI 14.1397 (II, Oxy.).

2555     Oratory: On the observance of the law.  F. Blass, Ber. Leipzig, 1904, 205-11 (Univ.-Bibl., Leipzig) (I-II; on the verso of a composite roll; from a school of rhetoric?).  Jander 34-36.  Archiv 3.494.

2556     Oratory.  E. Egger, MAI, 1870, Partie 2, 47-48 ("P. Henri Pereire," Bibliothèque Nationale, Paris, Suppl. Gr. 1324, IV) (I-II?).  Jander 18.

2557     Oratory (?).  C. Gallavotti, Riv. Fil. 67 (1939) 257-59 (PSI sine numero?) (II B.C.).

2558     Oratory (or history?).  C. Gallavotti, Riv. Fil. 67 (1939) 259-60 (PSI sine numero?) (I B.C.).

2559     Oratory (or a document?).  H. Oellacher, Mnemos., Ser. 3.8 (1939) 45-48 (P. Vindob. Gr. inv. 29451) (VI; on the verso of a document).

       Oratory: see also Nos. 2182, 2249, 2261, 2267, 2295, 2570, 2572, 2630, 2634, 2637, 2785, 2811, 2818-19, 2842-43, 2866, 2870, 2872, 2874, 2897.

### Philosophy

2560     Philosophical dialogue (?).  U. Wilcken, Archiv 1 (1901) 475-79 (P. Monac.) (III B.C., Fayum). Archiv 2.367.  The editor notes a relation to Plato, Phaedo 106 B-C; G. Coppola, Aeg. 5 (1924) 221-23, regards the text as a commentary on the Phaedo.

2561     Philosophical treatise (commentary on Plato, Phaedo 92-93?).  Mentioned by F. Bilabel, Actes Pap. V, 78-79 (P. Heid.) (III B.C., Hibeh; cart.).

2562     Dialogue on government (Heraclides Ponticus?).  P. Oxy. 4.664 (P. Cairo) (III, Oxy.).  New Chapters 2.104-6.  F. Blass, Archiv 3.497-99, suggests Heraclides Ponticus.

2563     Fragments from the later Platonism (?): On the Platonic doctrine of Ideas.  H. Oellacher, Ét. Pap. 4 (1938) 182-96 (P. Rain. inv. 29800) (I, Fayum).  Group b, fr. 2, line 2 mentions Plato (?).  Archiv 13.111-12.

2564     Fragments on aesthetics or literary criticism (Aristotle?).  T. Gomperz, Raineri M. 1.84-88 (ed. pr. in part); P. Rain. 1.16 (inv. 26008 + 29329) (cf. ibid. 3, p. 95; 4, p. 135) (III, Fayum; frr. of two rolls).  Contains reminiscences of Aristotle; mentions Democritus; refers to Homer, Sophocles, and Timotheus, "in the threnos of Odysseus" (Scylla?).  Archiv 11.274-75.  H. Oellacher, Ét. Pap. 4 (1938) 135-81, suggests Aristotle, Pragmateia tês poiētikês technēs;  A. Rostagni, Riv. Fil. 66 (1938) 295-97, proposes Aristotle, Peri poiētôn, or a disciple of Aristotle, for Group a.

2565     Fragment on Aristotelian (or Neoplatonic?) physics. PSI 14.1400 (VII-VIII; pap. cod.).  Evidently bears some relation to Aristotle, Metaphysics xi.  Ed. pr.: M. Norsa, Ann. Sc. Pisa, Ser. 2.7 (1938) 1-12. Norsa, SLG, tav. 19.  Archiv 13.110.  A. Barigazzi, Aeg. 29 (1949) 59-75, sees a Neoplatonic fragment.

2566     Treatise on logic.  P. Harris 2 (inv. 175 a) (II-III). Gives definitions of the terms apophasis and kataphasis.  Archiv 13.113.  B. Snell, Gnomon 13 (1937) 579.

2567     Treatise on logic.  PSI 9.1095 (III, Oxy.).  Archiv 10.223. R. Philippson, Riv. Fil. 57 (1929) 495-506; F. Solmsen, ibid. 507-10; A. Vogliano, ibid. 511-12.

2568     On forms of propositions in logic.  P. Hibeh 2.189 (Brit. Mus. inv. 2962) (270-240 B.C., Hibeh; cart.; an exercise?).

2569     On images in mirrors (Eudorus?).  P. Oxy. 13.1609 (Edinburgh Univ. Libr., Ox. P. 13) (II, Oxy.; text on recto, No. 2328 on verso).  The author refers to a commentary of his own on Plato's Timaeus, and mentions the views of Democritus, Empedocles, and Epicurus.  Archiv 7.249.

2570     A comparison of various political constitutions (philosophy or oratory?).  BKT 7.13-34 (inv. 13045) (I B.C., Abusir-el-Malaq; cart.; from the same papyrus as No. 2102).  Archiv 7.240.

2571     A Stoic (?) treatise on resignation (or dialogue?).  P. Rein. 2.82 (P. Sorbonne inv. 2093) (II).  Cites Homer, Il. v.385-86, 392-93, 395, xviii.117-18 (Collart 366 and Pap. X).  Archiv 14.140.

2572     On Athena (Diogenes of Babylon?).  N. Festa, Archiv 3 (1906) 151-57 (Museo Egiziano Vaticano) (I-II).  M. Adler, Charisteria Alois Rzach ... dargebracht (Reichenberg 1930) 5-10, regards the text as oratorical rather than philosophical.

2573     On kingly virtues, chiefly temperance and self-control.  J. Bidez, Rev. Phil. 30 (1906) 161-72 (ed. pr.); P. Lit. Lond. 163 (Brit. Mus. inv. 275) (III; pap. cod.). According to Bidez, T. Gomperz assigns the text to Antisthenes, Cyrus; C. Haeberlin, Rh. Mus. 62 (1907) 154, suggests Apollonius Syrus.

2574     An Epicurean gnomologion.  A. Vogliano, SIFC, NS 13 (1937) 267-81 (P. Berol. inv. 16369) (II, Egypt). Includes six Epicurean sententiae, of which three are new, and three known (Epicurus, fr. 181, Usener, and Metrodorus; see loc. cit. for full references).  Archiv 13.110-11.

2575     Philosophy (Epicurus?).  P. Grenf. 2.7 a; P. Lit. Lond. 158 (Brit. Mus. inv. 692) (III B.C., Hibeh; cart.). H. Diels, Sitzb. Berl. Akad., 1916, 900-1, suggests Epicurus.

2576     Philosophy (Epicurus?).  P. Oxy. 2.215; P. Lit. Lond. 157 (Brit. Mus. inv. 1182) (I B.C.-I, Oxy.). Subject: the popular fear of the gods.  Archiv 1. 527; JEA 6.127; New Chapters 2.97-98. H. Diels, Sitzb. Berl. Akad., 1916, 886-901, suggests Epicurus; A. Barigazzi, Acme 8, fasc. 2-3 (1955) 37-55.

2577     Epicurean treatise.  E. Siegmann, Festschr. Bruno Snell (München 1956) 167-72 (P. Heid. inv.1740) (I; text on recto, No. 2179 on verso).  Ed. pr. of Fr. a: R. Philippson, Ét. Pap. 6 (1940) 41-44; ed. pr.

of Fr. b: F. Bilabel, Neue Heidelb. Jahrb., 1934, 156-59, and Actes Pap. V, 80-81.

2578 Epicurean (?) fragment. P. Flor. 2.115 (I-II; pap. cod.). Apostrophizes Democritus. Archiv 6.240. W. M. Edwards, New Chapters 2.98-99, suggests Colotes as the author.

2579 Treatise on optics (Epicurus?). K. Wessely, WS 13 (1891) 312-23 (Musée du Louvre, Paris, inv. 7733) (III-II B.C., Memphis; text on recto, No. 2911 on verso). E. Egger, CRAI, 1870, 241 (first mention); A. Olivieri, Riv. Fil. 29 (1901) 73-76; W. Croenert, Rh. Mus. 62 (1907) 123-32, suggests Epicurus, Peri physeôs, Bk. xi or xii; L. Denon, Athen. 35 (1947) 34-54, rejects Epicurus.

2580 Collection of Cynic diatribes. V. Martin, Mus. Helv. 16 (1959) 77-115 (P. Genève inv. 271 (II). An interview between Alexander the Great and the Indian sage, Dandamis (cols. 1-8); Ps.-Heraclitus, Ep. vii (cols. 9-15; pp. 283 ff., ed. R. Hercher, Epistolographi Graeci). P. Photiades, Mus. Helv. 16 (1959) 116-39; J. D. M. Derrett, Class. Med. 21 (1960) 66, 76, and passim; J. T. Kakridis, Mus. Helv. 17 (1960) 34-36, restores the names of Hesiod (col. 15.5) and Archilochus (col. 15.14); idem, PP 16 (1961) 383-86.

2581 Philosophy. P. Amh. 2.15 (II-III, Fayum?). Archiv 2.369.

2582 Philosophy. P. Fay. 311; P. Cairo G.H. 10847 (II, Theadelphia; opisthograph fr.). Archiv 2.369.

2583 On the gods. P. Fay. 337; P. Cairo G.H. 10858 (II, Theadelphia). Archiv 2.367.

2584 On education. P. Flor. 2.113 (II). Mentions Antisthenes and Socrates. Archiv 6.238; New Chapters 2.93-94.

2585 Philosophy. P. Hal. 4 (inv. 16) (I).

2586 Philosophy (?): On the "battle of the elements." P. Heid. Siegmann 194 (inv. 1977) (II, Oxy.).

2587 Doctrines and terms of an unnamed philosopher. P. Hibeh 2.188 (Brit. Mus. inv. 2961) (ca. 270-240 B.C., Hibeh; cart.).

2588 Moral precepts. P. Oxy. 1.79; P. Lit. Lond. 162 (Brit. Mus. inv. 756) (III, Oxy.; on the verso of a document; sch. ex.?).

2589 Philosophy. P. Oxy. 3.438 (Yale Univ. Libr.) (II, Oxy.; on the verso of an account). Archiv 3.295.

2590 Philosophy. P. Oxy. 3.439 (Chadwick Mus.) (III, Oxy.; on the verso of an account). Archiv 3.295.

2591 Advice for dealings with sovereigns. P. Oxy. 4.684 (Johns Hopkins Univ. Libr.) (III, Oxy.). Archiv 3.499.

2592 Philosophy. P. Oxy. 6.869 (Toledo Mus. of Art) (III, Oxy.). Archiv 6.242.

2593 Philosophical dialogue: On the kinship of mankind (Theophrastus?). P. Petrie 2.49 (e); P. Lit. Lond. 159 a (Brit. Mus. inv. 591 B) (III B.C., Gurob; cart.; text on recto, No. 2862 on verso). C. Gorteman, Chr. Ég. 33 (1958) 79-101, reedits the text and attributes it to Theophrastus, Peri eusebeiãs, suggesting that "the poet" in col. ii.10 is Euripides.

2594 On kingship. P. Schubart 35 (I B.C.). Archiv 16.125.

2595 Philosophy (?): On athletic contests. P. Schubart 37 (II-III). Archiv 16.126.

2596 On old age. P. Schubart 38 (I-II). Cites Anacreon (Page, PMG 503) and perhaps another verse. Uncertain whether a discussion or a dialogue. Archiv 16.108.

2597 Moral lessons from the careers of the Diadochi (philosophy or history?). P. Schubart 39 (I). Line 9 quotes one Arist(...): L. Alfonsi, Aeg. 33 (1953) 303-9, reads Arist(on of Chios) instead of Arist(oteles); R. Merkelbach, Archiv 16.108, and Mus. Helv. 10 (1953) 127.

2598 Ethical and aesthetic disquisitions (?). PSI 7.744 (II?).

2599 Ethical fragment. PSI 7.851 (II-III; on the verso of an unidentified text). Archiv 8.266-67.

2600 Philosophy. P. Tebt. 2.269 (II, Tebtunis). Archiv 6.242.

2601 Elementary catechism in philosophy. F. Bilabel, Philol. 80 (1925) 339-40 (P. Heid. inv. 1716) (II; on the verso of a document or letter). Archiv 8.266.

2602 Ethical treatise: Eros and philanthropia. D. Comparetti, Festschr. Gomperz 80-89 (PSI) (II-III, Fayum?). Mentions the Stoa. Archiv 2.368.

2603 Precepts addressed to men in high place. E. Kuehn, Ber. Berl. Mus. 42 (1920-21) 102-4; idem, Aeg. 3 (1922) 87-88 (P. Berol. inv. 12318) (III B.C., Philadelphia; ostr.; sch. ex.). JEA 8.92.

2604 Philosophy (?). P. Aberdeen 122 (III, Fayum?). Ed. pr.: E. O. Winstedt, CQ 1 (1907) 266.

2605 Philosophy (or comedy?). P. Hibeh 1.18 (Bodleian Libr., Gr. class. f.80 (P)) (III B.C., Hibeh; cart.). Archiv 6.240.

2606 Philosophy (?). P. Lond. 2.208 c; P. Lit. Lond. 161 (Brit. Mus. inv. 208 C) (I). Mentions the Stoics (line 5). Archiv 10.223.

2607 Philosophy (?). P. Prin. 3.115 (II-III; palimpsest?).

2608 On the relation of the whole to its parts. P. Ryl. 3.510, recto (II-III; text on recto, No. 2208 on verso). Archiv 14.131.

2609 Philosophy (?). P. Ryl. 3.511 (II).

2610 Philosophy (?). P. Ryl. 3.512 (II).

2611    Philosophy.   PSI 2.152 (II).   Archiv 7.155; New Chap-
        ters 2.99.

2612    Philosophy (?).   PSI 7.852 (II-III).   Archiv 8.267.

2613    Philosophy (?).   P. Tebt. 3.896 (II B.C., Tebtunis;
        cart.).

2614    Philosophy (or Homeric commentary?).   G. Lefebvre,
        BSAA 14 (1912) 192-94 (I, Theadelphia).   Quotes Ho-
        mer, Od. xi.475-76 (Collart, Pap. c).   Archiv 7.
        245.

2615    Philosophy.   Mentioned by Schubart, Einführung 483
        (?).   Perhaps now covered by another item in this
        list.

        Philosophy: see also Nos. 1224, 2389, 2539, 2843,
        2851, 2853, 2862, 2995.


                            Romance

2616    Adventure of Ninus.   U. Wilcken, Hermes 28 (1893)
        161-93 (P. Berol. inv. 6926) (I, Soknopaiou Nesos
        or Karanis?).   New Pal. Soc., Ser. 2, vol. 1, pl.
        27; Roberts, GLH, pl. 11a; Schubart, PGB, tab.
        18.   Lavagnini, EGFP 1-15; Zimmermann, GRP,
        No. 1 (bibl.).   Lesky, GGL 780; R. M. Rattenbury,
        New Chapters 3.213-23.   G. Vitelli, SIFC 2 (1894)
        297-98, on the writer's avoidance of hiatus;   L.
        Levi, Riv. Fil. 23 (1895) 1-22; B. A. Mueller, Rh.
        Mus. 72 (1917-18) 198-216; L. Castiglioni, BFC 33
        (1926) 147; F. Zimmermann, Hermes 67 (1932) 91-
        116; L. Herrmann, Chr. Ég. 15 (1940) 273-75; R.
        Jenistova, Listy Fil., NS 1 (1953) 30-54, 210-28,
        319 (English summary); L. Piotrowicz, Meander
        8 (1953) 197-98.

2617    A fragment of the Ninus Romance.   PSI 13.1305 (I,
        Oxy.).   From the same romance, but not the same
        papyrus, as No. 2616.   Ed. pr.: M. Norsa, Scritti
        Rosellini 191-98.   Archiv 16.122.   Lavagnini, Studi
        RG 221-22, on the relation to a mosaic from Antioch;
        R. Jenistova, Listy Fil., NS 1 (1953) 38-39;   F.
        Zimmermann, Wissenschaftliche Zeitschr. der
        Univ. Rostock, Sprachwiss. Reihe 3 (1953-54), Heft
        2, 175-81.

        Ninus Romance: see also No. 2647.

2618    Story of Tefnut.   P. Lond. 2.274; P. Lit. Lond. 192
        (Brit. Mus. inv. 274) (II-III).   R. M. Rattenbury,
        New Chapters 3.226-29.   Identified by R. Reitzen-
        stein, Sitzb. Heid. Akad., 1923, Abh. 2.

2619    Story of King Sesonchosis.   P. Oxy. 15.1826 (III-IV,
        Oxy.; pap. cod.).   Jacoby, FGH, Dritter Teil
        C, 272; Zimmermann, GRP, No. 2.   Archiv 7.253-
        54; New Chapters 3.223-24.   F. Zimmermann,
        Rh. Mus. 85 (1936) 165-76.

2620    Adventures of Glaucetes.   P. Oxy. 11.1368 (P. Cairo)
        (III, Oxy.; on the verso of a document).   Lavagnini,
        EGFP 33-34.   Archiv 7.253; New Chapters 3.246-
        47; K. F. W. Schmidt, Gött. Anz., 1918, 100.

2621    Herpyllis Romance.   J. G. Smyly, Hermathena 11
        (1901) 322-30 ("P. Dublin" inv. C 3: Royal Irish
        Academy?)   (II, Arsinoë?; on the verso of ac-
        counts).   Lavagnini, EGFP 16-20; Zimmermann,
        GRP, No. 8.   Archiv 1.268-71, 2.365-66;   R. M.
        Rattendury, New Chapters 3.234-37.   J. P. Mahaf-
        fy, Rend. Acc. Linc., Ser. 5.6 (1897) 91-96 (ed.
        pr.).

2622    Metiochus and Parthenope Romance.   F. Zimmermann,
        Aeg. 13 (1933) 53-61 (P. Berol. inv. 7927 + 9588)
        (II, Soknopaiou Nesos or Karanis?; on the verso
        of a document).   Ed. pr. of P. Berol. inv. 7927:
        F. Krebs, Hermes 30 (1895) 144-50.   Lavagnini,
        EGFP 21-24; Zimmermann, GRP, No. 6.   Archiv
        1.264-67, 11.283;   R. M. Rattenbury, New Chapters
        3.237-40.   F. Zimmermann, Archiv 11 (1933) 114-16,
        and Aeg. 15 (1935) 277-81, 405-14; Lavagnini, Studi
        RG 222-24, on the relation to a mosaic from Antioch.

2623    Metiochus and Parthenope Romance (?).   P. Oxy. 3.
        435 (Yale Univ. Libr.) (II-III, Oxy.).   Lavagnini,
        EGFP 28-29; Zimmermann, GRP, No. 6 c.   Ar-
        chiv 3.282; New Chapters 3.245.   F. Garin, SIFC,
        NS 1 (1920) 179-80; F. Zimmermann, Philol. 90
        (1935) 194-205.

2624    Romance.   PSI 2.151 (III, Oxy.; on the verso of ac-
        counts).   Jacoby, FGH, Dritter Teil C, 544-45;
        Lavagnini, EGFP 32-33; Zimmermann, GRP, No.
        5.   Archiv 7.253; New Chapters 3.248-49.   B. A.
        Mueller, Rh. Mus. 71 (1916) 358-63, identifies the
        text as a romance.

2625    Romantic narrative (a Milesian Tale?).   PSI 11.1220
        (II-III, Oxy.).   Ed. pr.: BSAA 28 (1933) 135-37.
        A. Koerte, Archiv 11.282-83, suggests a Milesian
        Tale.

2626    Romance.   PSI 6.725 (III-IV; on the verso of a docu-
        ment).   Lavagnini, EGFP 36-37; Zimmermann,
        GRP, No. 11.   Archiv 7.253; New Chapters 3.248.
        F. Zimmermann, SO 15-16 (1936) 101-10.

2627    Romance.   PSI 6.726 (II-III; on the verso of No. 332).
        Lavagnini, EGFP 20-31; Zimmermann, GRP, No.
        9.   Archiv 7.253; New Chapters 3.247-48.

2628    Romance.   PSI 8.981 (II, Oxy.).   Zimmermann, GRP,
        No. 4.   Archiv 8.271; R. M. Rattenbury, New
        Chapters 3.240-44.   F. Zimmermann, Phil. Woch.
        55 (1935) 1211-16, on the relation to Lucian, Toxaris.

2629    Romance.   C. Bonner, Aeg. 13 (1933) 203-7 (P. Mich.
        inv. 3378) (II).   Archiv 11.283.

2630    Romance (or history, oratory?).   P. Oxy. 6.868
        (Muhlenberg Coll.) (I, Oxy.).   Lavagnini, EGFP
        27-28.   Archiv 6.246; New Chapters 3.250.   W.
        Croenert, Woch. Phil. 26 (1909) 119, suggests a
        romance; K. Muenscher, JAW 149 (1910) 180; B.
        A. Mueller, Rh. Mus. 71 (1916) 360, and F. Zimmer-
        mann, Archiv 11 (1935) 182-88, prefer a historical
        fragment.

2631    Romance.   Zimmermann, GRP, No. 7 (P. Berol. inv.
        10535) (II-III).   F. Zimmermann, FF 11 (1935) 319-
        20, and Atti Pap. IV, 383-93 (ed. pr.).   Archiv
        13.129.

2632 Romance (?). P. Fuad 1.4 (IV).

2633 Romance (?). P. Harris 18 (inv. 174 f) (I). Archiv 13.129.

2634 Romance (or oratory?). P. Harris 19 (inv. 174 j) (I-II). Archiv 13.129.

2635 Romance (?). P. Harris 20 (inv. 173 a, b, c) (III; on the verso of accounts). Archiv 13.129-30.

2636 Romance (?): A description of magical powers. C. Bonner, TAPA 52 (1921) 111-18 (P. Mich. inv. 5) (II, Fayum). Preisendanz, PGM 2, No. 34. Archiv 8.128, 16.122-23; JEA 10.156. E. R. Dodds, Phoenix, Supplementary Vol. 1 (1952; = Studies in Honour of Gilbert Norwood) 133-38, favors a romance.

2637 Romance (or oratory?). P. Lit. Lond. 194 (Brit. Mus. inv. 1847 A) (IV; parch.). Zimmermann, GRP, No. 13. Archiv 10.234; New Chapters 3. 250-51. A. D. Knox, JEA 15 (1929) 139, prefers "a speech of Lysias."

2638 Romance (?). P. Lit. Lond. 245 (Brit. Mus. inv. 2037 D) (VI; parch. cod.). Zimmermann, GRP, No. 12. New Chapters 3.251.

2639 Romance (or prophecy?). PSI 7.760 (III-IV; on the verso of a document). Manteuffel, Opusc., No. 8. New Chapters 3.251. C. H. Roberts, P. Oxy. 22, p. 89, note 4, regards this as Greco-Egyptian prophecy akin to the "Oracle of the Potter" (see Nos. 2486-87).

2640 Romance (or magical text?), with illustrations. P. Lond. 113.15 c; P. Lit. Lond. 198 (Brit. Mus. inv. 113 (15 c)) (V-VI, Fayum). A. Bauer and J. Strzygowski, Denkschr. Wien. Akad., 1906, Abh. 2, 177.

2641 Romance, with illustrations. Mentioned by A. Bauer and J. Strzygowski, Denkschr. Wien. Akad., 1906, Abh. 2, 174 (Bibliothèque Nationale, Paris, Suppl. Gr. 1294) (I-II). New Chapters 3.253. Weitzmann, Anc. Bk. Ill., p. 100 and fig. 107; idem, Ill. RC, pp. 51-52 and pl. 40. K. Weitzmann, AJA 61 (1957) 84 and pl. 33, fig. 2.

Romance: see also Nos. 244, 2248, 2259, 2466, 2474, 2647, 2811, 2827, 2869, 2902.

## School Exercises and Writing Exercises

2642 A manual for study in the schools. Guéraud-Jouguet (P. Cairo inv. 65445) (III B.C., Fayum?). Contents: syllabaries; list of the Macedonian months; list of numbers to 25; names of divinities; list of rivers; proper names in two, three, four, and five syllables (Roberts, GLH, pl. 5a); a verse anthology (see below); squares of numbers (Neugebauer, Exact Sc. 25-26 and pl. 5); subdivisions of the drachma. Quotes Euripides, Ino, fr. 420, Nauck[2] (lines 126-29), Phoenissae 529-34 (115-25); Homer, Od. v.116-24 (131-39; Collart 55; Del Corno, Od. 48-49); Straton, Phoenicides (185-215; Page, GLP 1, No. 57; Roberts, GLH, pl. 5b);

two comic monologues, spoken by mageiroi (162-69, 170-84; for the first, see Page, GLP 1, No. 59; on the second, see R. Goossens, Chr. Ég. 16, 1941, 108, ibid. 17, 1942, 113); an epigram on a fountain (140-54; Posidippus?; Page, GLP 1, No. 105); and an elegy celebrating the dedication of a temple to Homer (155-61). Actes Pap. V, 174-91 (first description). Archiv 13.104-9. W. Schubart, Gnomon 15 (1939) 101-3; K. F. W. Schmidt, Phil. Woch. 59 (1939) 833-37; J. Barns, CQ 44 (1950) 135-37; M. Treu, Philol. 102 (1958) 215-28, studies the role of the mageiros in the first of the two comic monologues (see above).

2643 A pupil's notebook. P. Bouriant 1 (P. Sorbonne inv. 826) (IV; eleven leaves, once bound to form a notebook). Contents: exercises in syllabification; sayings of Diogenes; verse maxims, including Menander, Heros, fr. 210.2, Kock, Sententiae 74, 186, 204, 231, 267, 317, 360, 368, 400, 434, 472, 515, 526, 553, and Philemon, fr. 147.2, Kock; Babrius, Fables, Prologue 1-11; and the pupil's postscript. Page, GLP 1, No. 116; Ziebarth, No. 29; idem 2, No. 46; idem, Gr. Schulwesen 127-28. P. Jouguet and P. Perdrizet, Stud. Pal. 6 (1906) 148-61 (an earlier ed.); O. Immisch, Rh. Mus. 79 (1930) 153-69, compares the text of Babrius (see above) with the Codex Athoüs.

2644 A school text. J. Schwartz, Ét. Pap. 7 (1948) 93-109 (PIFAO, inv. 320) (Byzantine; seven leaves from a parch. cod.). Contents: causes of the Trojan War; catechism on the Iliad; metrical definitions; phonology of vowels and consonants. Chr. Ég. 24 (1949) 350-51. Archiv 16.121.

2645 An exercise in logic (?). P. Hibeh 2.184 (Brit. Mus. inv. 2957) (ca. 300-280 B.C., Hibeh; cart.; exercise by an advanced student?).

2646 From a mythological genealogy. P. Cornell 55 (I; on the verso of an account). The parentage of Rhadamanthys, Musaeus, Eumolpus, and Trophonius.

2647 A student's theme (?). O. Edfu 2.306 (I, Apollinopolis Magna; ostr.). C. Bonner suggests a fragment of the Ninus Romance; cf. line 2: Nino(..).

2648 Description of a temple (?). P. Fuad 1.3 (I; sch. ex. ?).

2649 Story of Adrastus. P. Oxy. 1.124 (Winchester Coll.) (II-III, Oxy.; on the verso of an account).

2650 On the preparations for the Trojan War. P. Rain. 1.18 (inv. 29790) (I, Hermupolis Magna; a separate sheet of papyrus?). Archiv 11.278.

2651 Fragment of a theme, or notes, on the Trojan legend. J. Schwartz, BIFAO 61 (1962) 174 (No. 40) (P. Strasb. inv. Gr. 1352) (Roman; perhaps written by a pupil).

2652 Dialogue between a cat and a mouse. P. Rain. 3.30 (inv. 29813-14) (cf. ibid. 4, p. 137) (I; on the verso). Archiv 14.138.

2653   Riddle of the bat.  P. Rein. 2.84 (P. Sorbonne inv.
       2188) (II; ostr.).  Ed. pr.: P. Collart, Mél. Mas-
       pero 213-17.  Chr. Ég. 11 (1936) 501, 554.

2654   List of traders or artificers;  Tale of a lost garment
       (nursery rhyme?).  P. Tebt. 2.278 (I, Tebtunis).
       Ziebarth 2, No. 41.

2655   Paraphrase of an epic poem (?) on Hercules.  J. W.
       B. Barns, CQ 43 (1949) 1-3 (No. 1) (Egypt Explora-
       tion Society, London) (II B.C., Fayum).  Archiv 16.
       120-21.

2656   Text citing Chaeremon, Achilles Thersictonus (as if
       by Euripides).  P. Collart, CRAI, 1945, 249-58
       ("O. Clermont-Ganneau") (II, Elephantine; ostr.).

2657   Addition table.  P. Lond. 3.737 (I-III).  Evidently not
       in P. Lit. Lond.

2658   Exercises in fractions.  P. Freib. 1 a, recto (inv. 12)
       (II-I B.C.; from the same papyrus as No. 1577; on
       the verso, No. 1219).

2659   School text for article and pronouns.  P. Iand. 5.83
       (inv. 555) (III, Fayum?; on the verso of a document).
       Gundel 24.  Archiv 10.230.

2660   Model conjugation of poieō.  P. Rein. 2.86 (P. Sor-
       bonne inv. 2120) (VI).  Archiv 14.144.

2661   Declension of toioutos, etc.  P. Rein. 2.87 (P. Sor-
       bonne inv. 2190) (II-III; on the verso: recto erased).

2662   Fragment from the end of an acrostic (iambics?).  P.
       Ryl. 1.41 (VI).  For the letters phi-omega.

2663   Writing exercise (?).  P. Ryl. 2.443 (III; written
       across the fibres).

2664   Sums of drachmas in multiples of a thousand, with
       symbols.  PSI 3.250 (III-IV, Oxy.).

2665   Alphabet.  P. Tebt. 2.683, verso (I-II, Tebtunis; on
       the verso of No. 2456).

2666   Spelling exercise (?).  P. Varsov. 6 (III, Fayum?;
       on the verso of accounts).  Archiv 13.130; Eos 34
       (1932-33) 200.

2667   Writing exercise (?).  P. Varsov. 7 (II, Fayum?).
       Eos 34 (1932-33) 200.

2668   School exercise (?).  O. Bodl. 1.46 (O. Bodleian
       Libr., inv. 280) (I B.C.; ostr.).

2669   School exercise (?).  O. Bodl. 1.80 (O. Ashmolean
       Mus., inv. 105) (?; ostr.).

2670   Copying exercise.  O. Bodl. 1.144 (O. Petrie inv. 411)
       (Byzantine; ostr.).

2671   Alphabet, alpha to pi.  O. Bodl. 1.144 (O. Petrie inv.
       412) (IV?; ostr.).

2672   Copying exercise (?).  O. Bodl. 1.145 (O. Petrie inv.
       413) (Byzantine; ostr.).

2673   School exercise (?).  O. Bodl. 2.2190 (inv. 911) (?;
       ostr.).

2674   Alphabet.  O. Bodl. 2.2191 (inv. 1975) (I B.C.-I; ostr.).

2675   Writing exercise (?).  O. Bodl. 2.2192 (inv. 2686)
       (?; ostr.).  Only seven letters remain from five
       lines.

2676   School exercise (?): A syllabary.  O. Bodl. 2.2193
       (inv. 2925) (IV-V; ostr.).

2677   Writing exercise (?).  O. Bodl. 2.2194 (inv. 1008)
       (IV?; ostr.).

2678   Writing exercise (?).  O. Bodl. 2.2195 (inv. 542) (?;
       ostr.).  Only two letters remain.

2679   School exercise.  O. Bodl. 2.2565 (inv. 82) (Byzan-
       tine; ostr.).

2680   School exercise (?).  O. Edfu 1.229 (?, Apollinopolis
       Magna; ostr.).

2681   Beginning of a student's theme (?); Exercise in pro-
       nunciation (?).  O. Edfu 2.305 (Ptolemaic, Apol-
       linopolis Magna; ostr.).  The content is "fort
       énigmatique."

2682   Exercise in syllabification.  O. Edfu 2.307 (I, Apol-
       linopolis Magna; ostr.).

2683   An apostrophe of the Erinys.  O. Edfu 2.308 (I, Apol-
       linopolis Magna; ostr.).

2684   School exercise (?).  O. Edfu 3.327 (pp. 331-32)
       (Ptolemaic, Edfu; ostr.).

2685   List of divinities.  O. Mich. 1.656 (III, Karanis; ostr.).

2686   Copy of an inscription (?).  O. Mich. 1.657-58 (III-
       IV, Karanis; ostr.).

2687   Name "Antoni," with the letters alpha-epsilon in re-
       verse order.  O. Mich. 1.659 (III-IV, Karanis;
       ostr.).  H. C. Youtie, TAPA 72 (1941) 453-56.

2688   Name "Babylonians" or "Of Babylon."  O. Mich. 1.
       661 (III, Karanis; ostr.).

2689   Names Palmyrenes," "Alemanni" (?).  O. Mich. 1.
       662 (III-IV, Karanis; ostr.).

2690   Writing exercise.  O. Mich. 1.672 (Roman, Karanis;
       ostr.).

2691   Writing exercise (?).  O. Mich. 1.693 (III-IV, Kara-
       nis; ostr.).

2692   Part of an alphabetical list of words.  Hall, CGT, pl.
       13 (inv. 27432) (VII-VIII?; ostr.).  Words begin-
       ning with upsilon, phi, and chi.

2693   Syllabic abecedarium.  Hall, CGT, pl. 28 (inv. 31387)
       (VII-VIII?; ostr.).

2694   Abecedarium.  Hall, CGT, pl. 28 (inv. 31663) (VII-
       VIII?; ostr.).

2695 Writing exercises. Hall, CGT, pl. 29 (inv. 19082 + 18816, 18798 + 18972) (VII-VIII?; ostr.).

2696 Alphabet. Hall, CGT, pl. 29 (inv. 21247) (VII-VIII?; ostr.).

2697 Abecedarium and copybook. Hall, CGT, pl. 29 (inv. 26739) (VII-VIII; ostr.).

2698 Forms of didasko, with Coptic equivalents. Hall, CGT, pl. 31 (inv. 14222) (VII-VIII?; ostr.). Coptic Bibl., No. 1837. H. Leclercq, Bull. d'ancienne litt. et d'arch. chretiennes 3 (1913) 212.

2699 Names of persons and places, chiefly from the New Testament. Hall, CGT, pl. 32 (inv. 26210 + 26211 + 26215) (VII-VIII?; ostr.).

2700 Name "Agamemnon." Hall, CGT, pl. 34 (inv. 33187) (VII-VIII, Deir-el-Bahari; ostr.).

2701 Alphabet. O. Strassb. 1.805 (inv. 60) (Roman, Upper Egypt; ostr.).

2702 Alphabet. O. Strassb. 1.806 (inv. 210) (Roman?; ostr.).

2703 Alphabet. O. Strassb. 1.807 (inv. 958) (VI-VII?; ostr.).

2704 Alphabet, and ornament or diagram. O. Strassb. 1. 808 (inv. 955) (VI-VII?; ostr.).

2705 Declensions of nouns and adjectives. G. Zalateo, Aeg. 20 (1940) 7 (PSI) (V-VI, Antinoë).

2706 Declensions of sophos, Priamos, and Hekabe. G. Zalateo, Aeg. 20 (1940) 12-14 (PSI) (V-VI, Antinoë; on recto and verso).

2707 Lines of verse, as writing exercises. PSI 12.1293 (II-III, Oxy.). Homer, Il. i.75-76, ii.1, v.84, 215, 627, vii.15-16, 264, xi.596, xiii.763 (Mette, Il., No. 375), Od. vii.1; a "Hesiodic" hexameter; and an iambic trimeter otherwise unknown. Ed. pr. of fr. b: S. Cammelli, Aeg. 20 (1940) 15-16.

2708 Syllabary. A. E. R. Boak, CP 16 (1921) 189-91 (Mich. Tablet No. 1) (IV?; wooden tablet). JEA 8.92.

2709 Exercises in writing, and in the cardinal numerals to 9,000. A. E. R. Boak, CP 16 (1921) 191-92 (Mich. Tablet No. 2) (IV?; wooden tablet).

2710 Writing exercise (?). D. C. Hesseling, JHS 13 (1892-93) 296, note 11 (Bodleian Libr., Gr. Inscr. 4) (?; waxed tablet). Ziebarth, No. 17; Ziebarth 2, No. 26.

2711 A sentence for practice in grammatical agreement; Optative and participles of nikao. F. G. Kenyon, JHS 29 (1909) 29-31 (Brit. Mus. Add. MS. 37516) (III; wooden tablet). The sentence relates to Pythagoras. Ziebarth 2, Nos. 22, 37. A. Brinkmann, Rh. Mus. 65 (1910) 151-55.

2712 School notebook. F. G. Kenyon, JHS 29 (1909) 32-39 (Brit. Mus. Add. MS. 37533) (III; 8 tablets, forming a cod.). Contents: a list of 207 verbs; phonetic classification of letters of the alphabet; gnomic questions and answers; notes on the uses of conjunctions; classification of nouns; and rules for the use of cases with verbs. Ziebarth, No. 30.

2713 School exercise. F. G. Kenyon, JHS 29 (1909) 39-40; P. Lit. Lond. 253 (Brit. Mus. Add. MS. 34186) (II?; waxed tablet). Contents: two iambic lines as a writing exercise; multiplication table; list of words divided into roots and suffixes. Written first by the teacher, then copied twice by the pupil. Line 1 = Menander, Sententiae 476, Meineke. Ziebarth, No. 14; Ziebarth 2, No. 11.

2714 Names of the cases, and portrait of teacher (?). F. G. Kenyon, JHS 29 (1909) 39-40 (Brit. Mus. Add. MS. 33368) (IV-V; eight waxed tablets).

2715 Alphabet, in boustrophedon arrangement. J. G. Milne, JHS 28 (1908) 121 (No. I) (Royal Ontario Mus., Toronto) (II, Upper Egypt; ostr.). Ziebarth, No. 1; Ziebarth 2, No. 1.

2716 Illustrative list of familiar names. J. G. Milne, JHS 28 (1908) 122 (No. II) (Bodleian Libr.) (II, Upper Egypt; ostr.). Ziebarth, No. 2; Ziebarth 2, No. 8.

2717 Syllabary. J. G. Milne, JHS 28 (1908) 122-23 (No. III) (Brit. Mus.) (IV-V, Oxy.; ostr.). Ziebarth, No. 5.

2718 Two lists of common nouns. J. G. Milne, JHS 28 (1908) 123-24 (Nos. IV-V) (No. IV: Royal Ontario Mus., Toronto; No. V: Bodleian Libr.) (II, Upper Egypt; ostraca). Ziebarth, No. 3; Ziebarth 2, No. 7.

2719 Symbols for numerals. J. G. Milne, JHS 28 (1908) 125 (No. VI) (Royal Ontario Mus., Toronto) (II, Upper Egypt; ostr.).

2720 An iambic trimeter as a model for copying. J. G. Milne, JHS 28 (1908) 126 (No. VII) (Bodleian Libr.) (II, Upper Egypt; ostr.). Ziebarth, No. 13; Ziebarth 2, No. 10.

2721 Text for copying (Philemon?). J. G. Milne, JHS 28 (1908) 126-27, 130-31 (Nos. VIII and XV) (Bodleian Libr.) (II, Thebes; two ostraca). J. G. Milne, JHS 43 (1923) 40-43, shows that Nos. VIII and XV join, and adds a second ostracon containing the same text. Ziebarth 2, No. 39. JAW 207.122-23. E. Fraenkel, Hermes 59 (1924) 362-68.

2722 Text for copying: Duties of a citizen (?). J. G. Milne, JHS 28 (1908) 127 (No. IX) (Bodleian Libr.) (II; Upper Egypt; ostr.).

2723 Student's theme: The story of Philoctetes. J. G. Milne, JHS 28 (1908) 128 (No. X) (Royal Ontario Mus., Toronto) (III, Upper Egypt; ostr.). Ziebarth 2, No. 40.

2724 An Homeric theme. J. G. Milne, JHS 28 (1908) 129 (No. XI) (Bodleian Libr.) (II, Upper Egypt; ostr.).

2725    Catalogue of deities, with reference to Iliad xx.    J.
        G. Milne, JHS 28 (1908) 129 (Nos. XII-XIII) (Royal
        Ontario Mus., Toronto) (II, Upper Egypt; ostr.).
        Milne, JHS 43 (1932) 42-43, joins Nos. XII and XIII
        with a third fragment of the same ostracon.

2726    Letter of Alexander to the Carthaginians.    J. G. Milne,
        JHS 28 (1908) 130 (No. XIV) (Bodleian Libr.).    (II,
        Upper Egypt; ostr.).

2727    Ordinal numbers from first to twelfth.    J. G. Milne,
        JHS 28 (1908) 131 (No. XVI) (Royal Ontario Mus.,
        Toronto) (III-IV, Upper Egypt; ostr.).    Ziebarth
        2, No. 9.

2728    Exercise in coinage and in fractions of the aroura.
        J. G. Milne, JHS 28 (1908) 132 (No. XVII) (Bodlei-
        an Libr.) (I B.C., Upper Egypt; ostr.).

2729    Tag from a school exercise.    N. Lewis, Ét. Pap. 3
        (1936) 105 (No. 23) (P. Cairo inv. 64847) (II-III, Oxy.;
        ostr.).

2730    A schoolboy's notebook (alphabets, accounts, etc.).
        F. Lenormant, Rev. Arch. 8, Partie 2 (1852) 461-
        70 (?, Memphis; eight waxed tablets forming a
        cod.).

2731    Copying exercises.    W. Froehner, Annales de la
        Société Française de Numismatique et d'Archéo-
        logie 3 (1868) lxviii-ix (Musée du Chateau Borelly,
        Marseille) (III-IV; six wooden tablets).    A maxim
        in two iambic trimeters; the story of Agamemnon
        and Iphigenia.    Ziebarth, No. 11 a-b; Ziebarth 2,
        No. 17 a-b.

2732    List of pronouns; verb paradigms; paraphrase of
        Iliad i.1-16; arithmetic tables.    W. E. Crum, Mél.
        Maspero 1.73-74 (Bodleian Libr., Gr. Inscr. 3019)
        (III, Thebes?; seven wooden tablets).

2733    A hexameter as an exercise in syllabification.    O.
        Crusius, Philol. 64 (1905) 146 (first mention); P.
        Bad. 4.111 (?; wooden tablet).    Ziebarth, No. 19;
        Ziebarth 2, No. 21; idem, Gr. Schulwesen 128.

2734    Syllabary.    Wilcken, Chrest., No. 139 (Univ.-Bibl.,
        Leipzig) (I?; ostr.).    Ziebarth 2, No. 4.

2735    Fifteen school exercises.    K. Wessely, Stud. Pal. 2
        (1902) xlii-lviii (Nos. 1, 7-15: III-VII, Fayum; Nos.
        2-6: Hermupolis Magna).    Alphabets, syllabaries,
        writing exercises, and conjugation of grapho.    Zie-
        barth, Nos. 4, 6-7, 21; Ziebarth 2, Nos. 3, 5, 6,
        19, 23.

2736    Copying exercise as a penalty.    A. Erman and F.
        Krebs, Aus den Papyrus der Königlichen Museen
        (Berlin 1899) 233 (Tabula Berol. 13234) (?; wooden
        tablet).    Ziebarth, No. 15; Ziebarth 2, No. 12;
        idem, Gr. Schulwesen 129.    Chr. Ég. 11 (1936) 495.

2737    Exercises in writing, spelling, and adding; sacred
        symbols; a verse sententia.    G. Plaumann, Ber.
        Berl. Mus., 1913, 214-19 (Tabula Berol. 14000) (IV-
        V; nine waxed tablets, forming a cod.).    Ziebarth
        2, No. 48.    Chr. Ég. 11 (1936) 499.

2738    Declensions of nouns and adjectives of the three
        genders.    G. Plaumann, Ber. Berl. Mus., 1913,
        219 (Collection of R. Blanckertz) (?; four waxed
        tablets forming a cod.).    Ziebarth 2, No. 49.

2739    Exercises in arithmetic.    G. Plaumann, Ber. Berl.
        Mus., 1913, 221-23 (Tabula Berol. 16717) (VII;
        wooden tablet).    Ziebarth 2, No. 51.

2740    Writing exercise (?).    P. M. Meyer, Griechische
        Texte aus Ägypten (Berlin 1916) 203 (No. 83) (Roman,
        Thebes; ostr.).    The name "Kametis," with seven
        letters of the alphabet.

2741    School exercise.    BGU 7.1688 (P. Berol. inv. 11609)
        (IV, Philadelphia).    Line 2 is possibly Sophocles,
        fr. 749, Nauck.

2742    Vowels and syllables.    C. Leemans, Papyri Graeci
        Musei Antiquarii Publici Lugduni-Batavi (Lugduni
        Batavorum 1885) 260-61 (II B.C., Serapaeum).    Re-
        garded by the editor as a magical text, but identi-
        fied by Wilcken, UPZ 1, No. 147, as a school
        exercise written by young Apollonius, the son of
        Glaucias; see Preisendanz, PMG 2.177, note 1.
        Archiv 8.129.

2743    Alphabet.    Mon. Epiphan. 2.620 (VI-VII?, Thebes;
        ostr.).

2744    School exercise (?): List of miscellaneous proper
        names.    E. J. Knudtzon, Årsb., Lund, 1951-52,
        134-36 (inv. 9) (III-IV?).

2745    Writing exercise.    P. Mich. 8.1099 (inv. 9598)
        (Ptolemaic, Karanis; ostr.).    The Greek alphabet,
        in capitals.

2746    Writing exercise.    P. Mich. 8.1100 (inv. 9353) (III,
        Karanis; ostr.).    Includes the statement "Homer
        a god, not a man."

2747    Writing exercise (or cryptogram?).    P. Oxy. 1.90
        (II, Oxy.; written beneath a receipt).

2748    Writing exercise.    P. Oxy. 2.285, verso (I, Oxy.;
        (written beneath and on the verso of a petition).

2749    Writing exercise in Greek and Latin.    PSI 13.1307,
        verso (I; on the verso of a military document).
        Greek: two iambic trimeters (?); Latin: "Iuli,"
        then "Aeneas Dardaniae" (bis).    Cavenaile, CLP
        61.

2750    Writing exercise.    K. Kalbfleisch, Archiv 15 (1953)
        107 (P. Univ. Giss. inv. 132) (II, Fayum; on the
        recto, under a contract).    Includes a verse maxim
        in two iambic trimeters.

2751    Writing exercise.    A. Bataille, Studi Calderini-
        Paribeni 2.277-83 (P. Sorbonne inv. 2249) (II-III).
        Recto: the name Appianus Antonianus (dative)
        written repeatedly in Greek; verso: a formula of
        leave-taking in Latin, and a date (?).

        School exercises: see also the List of Texts, passim,
            as indicated by the abbreviation "sch. ex."

## Scoptic Literature

2752    Collection of satirical sketches or "characters."
        P. Bad. 6.179 (inv. 1129); P. Heid. Siegmann 190
        (inv. 1103 b-c + 1169 + 413 a-b) (250-210 B.C., Hibeh;
        cart.; on recto and verso). E. Diehl, Anth. Lyr.
        (1942), "Addenda addendis," pp. 66-68, saw verses
        and ascribed the text to Sotades; the editor of P.
        Heid. Siegmann 190 regards it as a collection of
        "characters" in prose. Archiv 14.114-15. H. Oel-
        lacher, Gnomon 16 (1940) 510-11; R. Kassel, Rh.
        Mus. 99 (1956) 242-45, thinks rather of a joke book;
        H. Lloyd-Jones, Gnomon 29 (1957) 426-27, suggests
        a rhetorical handbook such as was used by Pollux.

## Shorthand

2753    Fragments of syllabaries. Milne, Gr. Shorthand
        Man., p. 6 (IV-V, mostly from Hermupolis Magna;
        papyri and waxed tablets). Ed. pr.: C. Wessely,
        Denkschr. Wien. Akad., 1896, Abh. 4.

2754    Fragments of the "Syllabary." Milne, Gr. Shorthand
        Man., 7, 9, 13-14 (P. Antin. inv. 6) (IV-V, Antinoë;
        pap. cod.).

2755    Fragments of the "Commentary." Milne, Gr. Short-
        hand. Man. 6 (?). Ed. pr.: K. Wessely, Stud.
        Pal. 2 (1902) 51.

2756    Fragment of the "Commentary" in a different version.
        Milne, Gr. Shorthand Man. 7, 9, 68 (P. Antin. inv.
        5) (IV, Antinoe; pap. cod.).

2757    The "Commentary." Milne, Gr. Shorthand Man. 6-7
        (ca. A.D. 250). Ed. pr.: A. S. Hunt, Rec. Cham-
        pollion 713-20.

2758    The "Commentary," signs 1-785, 1-446, 278-579
        (each repeated four times). Milne, Gr. Shorthand
        Man. 7-8 (Brit. Mus., Add. MS. 33270) (III-IV;
        seven waxed tablets). F. W. G. Foat, JHS 21 (1901)
        238-67 (useful for Greek shorthand generally).

2759    The "Commentary," signs 5-637. Milne, Gr. Short-
        hand Man. 7-8, 21-56 (Brit. Mus. inv. 2562) (III-IV;
        a quire of eighteen double leaves). Includes a list
        of plays by Menander (folio 9 recto, tetrades 330-34)
        see J. Stroux, Philol. 90 (1935) 88-89.

2760    The "Commentary," signs 1-810. Milne, Gr. Short-
        hand Man. 7-8, 57-67 (Brit. Mus. inv. 2561) (III-IV;
        a quire of twelve leaves and one single leaf).

2761    Fragments of the "Syllabary"; scattered signs from
        the "Commentary." Milne, Gr. Shorthand Man.
        7-9, 15-18, 69-70 (P. Antin. inv. 1) (IV-V, Antinoë;
        a double leaf plus four small fragments).

2762    Seven scattered signs from the "Commentary."
        Milne, Gr. Shorthand man. 7, 9 (P. Antin. inv. 2)
        (?, Antinoë; pap. cod.).

2763    Fifteen scattered signs from the "Commentary."
        Milne, Gr. Shorthand Man. 7, 9 (P. Antin. inv. 3)
        (III, Antinoë; pap. cod.).

2764    Seventeen scattered signs from the "Commentary."
        Milne, Gr. Shorthand Man. 7, 9 (P. Antin. inv.
        4) (V, Antinoë; pap. cod.).

2765    Remains of two lines in shorthand. P. Antin. 2.97
        (VI, Antinoë; on the verso of a document).

2766    Faint traces of a text in shorthand. P. Antin. 2.105
        (VI, Antinoë; on the verso of a document).

2767    Fragments with tachygraphic writing. C. J. Kraemer,
        Jr., Excavations at Nessana 3: Non-Literary Pa-
        pyri (Princeton 1958), Nos. 44, 195 (P. Colt) (?,
        Nessana, Palestine).

2768    Fragment of a manual. Mentioned by H. C. Youtie,
        TAPA 91 (1960) 244, note 23 (Columbia Univ. Libr.
        inv. 551, evidently unedited) (?).

2769    Signs. P. Erl. 148 (inv. 35) (Byzantine).

2770    Tachygraphic fragment. P. Erl. 149 (inv. 67) (By-
        zantine).

2771    Sign for some form of nikesas. P. Harris 51 (inv.
        183 f) (I?). Milne, Gr. Shorthand Man. 26. Ar-
        chiv 13.126.

2772    Fragment of the "Syllabary" or the "Commentary."
        Gundel 66 (P. Iand. inv. 67, inedita) (VI?; opis-
        thograph. pap.). H. G. Gundel, Proc. IX Int.
        Congr. Pap. 361 (first mention). To be published
        by H. Boge.

2773    Syllabary. A. Mentz, Archiv 8 (1927) 34-59, ibid.
        13 (1939) 61-70 (P. Hal.) (?; seven waxed tablets,
        forming a cod.).

2774    Syllabary. A. Mentz, Archiv 8 (1927) 34-59 (P.
        Hal.) (?; two waxed tablets).

2775    Syllabary. A. Mentz, Archiv 8 (1927) 34-59 (P.
        Berol. inv. 5464) (Byzantine; opisthograph fr.).

2776    Tachygraphic fragment. A. Mentz, Archiv 11 (1933)
        64-69 (P. Berol. inv. 6755 + 6756) (?; sch. ex. ?).

2777    Fragments of the End-Signs, Syllabary, and Com-
        mentary. A. Mentz, Byz. Zeitschr. 43 (1950)
        1-9 (P. Ibscher, inedita) (VI-VII; pap. cod. ?).

2778    Fragment of a manual. G. Zalateo, Aeg. 20 (1940)
        3-4 (PSI) (V, Antinoë). A. Mentz, Rh. Mus. 90
        (1941) 158-60.

2779    From a manual: Symbols for pronouns. G. Zalateo,
        Aeg. 20 (1940) 5-6 (PSI) (V-VI, Antinoë; opistho-
        graph fr.). A. Mentz, Rh. Mus. 90 (1941) 156-58.

        Shorthand: for a short Christian text written in
        shorthand, see A. Mentz, Archiv 13 (1939) 71-72.
        A bibl. of Mentz' studies in Greek shorthand: H.
        G. Gundel, Proc. IX Int. Congr. Pap. 360-62.

Unidentified Prose

2780    Prose (?).    O. Bodl. 1.46 (Bodleian Libr., inv. 279)
        (I B.C. ?; ostr.).

2781    Prose (?).    O. Bodl. 1.171 (Cambridge Univ. Libr.,
        inv. 123) (Byzantine; ostr.).

2782    Prose.    O. Bodl. 2.2175 (inv. 2722) (Roman; ostr.).

2783    Prose (document?).    P. Aberdeen 116 (I B.C. -I).    Ed.
        pr.: E. O. Winstedt, CQ 1 (1907) 265.

2784    Prose (rhetoric or history?).    P. Aberdeen 117 (I,
        Fayum?).

2785    Prose (oratory?).    P. Aberdeen 121 (I-II, Fayum?).

2786    Prose (?).    P. Aberdeen 125, recto (III-IV, Fayum?;
        text on recto, No. 2353 on verso).

2787    Prose (?).    P. Aberdeen 134 (I B.C. -I, Fayum?).

2788    Prose (?).    P. Aberdeen 135 (I B.C. -I, Fayum?).

2789    Prose (?).    P. Aberdeen 137 (I B.C. -I, Fayum?).

2790    Prose (?).    P. Aberdeen 138 (II, Fayum?).

2791    Prose (?).    P. Aberdeen 139 (II, Fayum?).

2792    Prose (literary?).    P. Aberdeen 142 (II, Fayum?).

2793    Prose (?).    P. Aberdeen 143 (I-II, Fayum?).

2794    Prose (?).    P. Aberdeen 144 (I-II, Fayum?).

2795    Prose (?).    P. Aberdeen 145 (I-II, Fayum?).

2796    Prose (?).    P. Aberdeen 146 a (I, Fayum?).

2797    Prose.    P. Amh. 2.160 (VI; parch.).    Archiv 2.366.

2798    Prose (literary?).    P. Bon. 1.8 (inv. 5 a, verso)
        (III-IV).    Ed. pr.: G. B. Pighi, Aeg. 27 (1947)
        170-72.

2799    Prose.    P. Cairo G.H. 10166 (III B.C.).

2800    Prose.    P. Dura 4 (inv. 44) (II, Dura, Mesopotamia).

2801    Prose.    P. Dura 5 (inv. 89) (II, Dura).

2802    Prose.    P. Dura 6 (inv. 87) (II, Dura).

2803    Prose.    P. Dura 7 (inv. 111) (III, Dura).

2804    Prose.    P. Dura 8 (inv. 92) (III, Dura).

2805    Prose.    P. Dura 9 (inv. 64) (III, Dura).

2806    Prose (?).    P. Erl. 9 (inv. 6) (Ptolemaic).

2807    Prose (treatise on rhetoric?).    P. Erl. 10 (inv. 88)
        (III).

2808    Prose (?).    P. Erl. 12 (inv. 8) (III).

2809    Prose (?).    P. Erl. 13 (inv. 7) (VII; pap. cod.).

2810    Scholia on an unidentified text.    P. Univ. Giss. 4.40
        (inv. 307) (ca. A.D. 100, Fayum?; on the verso
        of an unidentified literary text).    Mentions Acusi-
        laus of Argos (?), Hellanicus (?), and Simonides.
        Gundel 18.    Archiv 13.124.    Page, Corinna 43-45,
        sees a citation of Corinna in col. ii, line 2;    K.
        Latte, Eranos 54 (1956) 65, note 2, proposes a
        reading which would eliminate the relation with
        Corinna.

2811    Prose (letter, dialogue, speech, or romance?).    P.
        Hamb. 134 (inv. 11) (I; a leaf of papyrus, not from
        a roll?).    Archiv 16.125.

2812    Prose (dialogue on metrics?).    P. Hamb. 135 (inv.
        662) (III-II B.C.).    Two paragraphoi indicate chan-
        ges of speaker.

2813    Prose.    P. Hamb. 138 (inv. 382) (II).    Quotes Homer,
        Od. xi.548-50.

2814    Prose (a Christian text?).    P. Hamb. 141 (inv. 699)
        (III; pap. cod.).

2815    Prose.    P. Hamb. 142 (inv. 651) (I).

2816    Prose.    P. Hamb. 143 (inv. 647) (I B.C.).

2817    Prose.    P. Hamb. 144 (inv. 16, verso) (II-III; on the
        verso of No. 2520).

2818    Prose (from a forensic speech?).    P. Hamb. 145 (inv.
        380) (I-II).

2819    Prose (?): Attic oratory or comedy (?).    P. Hamb.
        146 (inv. 694) (II).

2820    Prose.    P. Hamb. 147 (inv. 693) (ca. A.D. 200).

2821    Prose.    P. Hamb. 148 (inv. 698) (II).

2822    Prose.    P. Hamb. 149 (inv. 700) (I; on the verso of
        a document).

2823    Prose.    P. Hamb. 150 (inv. 701) (II).

2824    Prose (or verse?).    P. Hamb. 151 (inv. 660) (II B.C.).

2825    Prose (or verse?).    P. Hamb. 152 (inv. 695) (II-III).

2826    Commentary on a poetic work (?).    P. Harris 10 (inv.
        173 f) (II).    Prose, with some poetic words.

2827    Prose (romance?).    P. Harris 23 (inv. 47 a) (I).    Ar-
        chiv 13.130.

2828    Prose (?).    P. Harris 24 (inv. 174 i) (I).

2829    Prose.    P. Harris 25 (inv. 175 d) (II-III).

2830    Prose.    P. Harris 26 (inv. 79 b) (III; on the verso of
        a cursive text).    Mentions Hippocrates (?).

2831    Prose.    P. Harris 27 (inv. 174 e) (I-II?).

2832    Prose (?).   P. Harris 28 (inv. 182 f) (III).

2833    Prose (?).   P. Harris 29 (inv. 173 g) (I-II).

2834    Prose (literary?).   P. Harris 30 (inv. 182 g) (III).

2835    Prose.   P. Harris 32 (inv. 182 b) (II; perhaps from the same papyris as No. 372).

2836    Prose (?).   P. Harris 33 (inv. 182 c) (III?).

2837    Prose (?).   P. Harris 34 (inv. 182 a) (II?).

2838    Prose.   P. Heid. Siegmann 196 (inv. 1108, verso) (III B.C., Hibeh; on the verso of an unpublished literary text).

2839    Prose.   P. Hibeh 2.221 (now in the Brit. Mus.) (ca. 270-240 B.C., Hibeh; cart.).

2840    Prose.   P. Hibeh 2.225 (Brit. Mus.) (ca. 270-230 B.C., Hibeh; cart.).

2841    Prose.   P. Hibeh 2.226 (Brit. Mus.) (ca. 280-230 B.C., Hibeh; cart.).

2842    Prose (speech, dialogue, or treatise on education and poetry?).   P. Hibeh 2.227 (Brit. Mus.) (ca. 280-240 B.C., Hibeh; different literary texts on recto and verso?).

2843    Prose (oratory or philosophy?).   P. Hibeh 2.229 (Brit. Mus.) (ca. 280-240 B.C., Hibeh; cart.).

2844    Prose: Fragment quoting a riddle.   P. Hibeh 2.230 (Brit. Mus.) (ca. 280-250 B.C., Hibeh; cart.). Cf. Petronius 59.

2845    Prose (Christian or secular?).   P. Hibeh 2.232 (Brit. Mus.) (III, Hibeh; on the verso of an official letter or document).

2846    Prose (medicine?).   P. Iand. 1.4 (inv. 45) (IV; Hermupolis Magna?; pap. cod.). Gundel 28.

2847    Prose.   P. Lond. 2.484 c (II). Evidently not in P. Lit. Lond.

2848    Prose.   P. Lit. Lond. 197 (Brit. Mus. inv. 1862 D) (II). Archiv 10.235-36.

2849    Prose (literary?).   P. Lit. Lond. 256 (Brit. Mus. inv. 1862 G) (II).

2850    Prose (or verse?).   A. Traversa, Aeg. 33 (1953) 62-64 (P. Med. inv. 101). (II-III).

2851    Prose (rhetoric or philosophy?).   P. Oslo 3.166 (II-III; on the verso).

2852    Prose.   P. Oslo 3.168 (I-II).

2853    Prose (anthology or doxography?).   P. Oslo 3.169 (II).

2854    Prose (?).   P. Oslo 3.171 (III).

2855    Prose.   P. Oslo 3.172 (II B.C.).

2856    Prose.   P. Oslo 3.174 (II).

2857    Prose.   P. Oslo 3.177 (III-IV).

2858    Prose.   P. Oxy. 3.440 b (Manchester Mus.) (III, Oxy.).

2859    Prose.   P. Oxy. 4.683 (Manchester Mus.) (II, Oxy.). Archiv 3.500.

2860    Scholia on a comedy (?).   P. Oxy. 17.2086, recto (II, Oxy.; text on recto, No. 2300 on verso). Archiv 10.226-28.

2861    Commentary on a poetic text (Lycophron?) or mythography (?).   P. Oxy. 27.2463 (II-III, Oxy.; on the verso of a tax register).   On the story of Poemandrus.   Refers to Rhianus of Bene, Heraclea; and Aristophanes of Thebes, Boeotica.   The editor conjectures that this may be a commentary on Lycophron, Alexandra 326 ff. (e.g., the one by Theon of Alexandria).

2862    Prose (philosophy? Theophrastus?).   P. Petrie 2.49 (e), verso; P. Lit. Lond. 159 b (Brit. Mus. inv. 591 B) (III B.C., Gurob; cart.; on the verso of No. 2593). Archiv 10.236. C. Gorteman, Chr. Ég. 33 (1958) 99-100, believes that this may belong to the same text as the recto.

2863    Prose.   P. Rain. 3.27 (inv. 29248 a) (I, Soknopaiou Nesos; sch. ex.).

2864    Prose (commentary on an unknown author?).   P. Rain. 1.33 (inv. 20275) (V, Fayum; pap. cod.).

2865    Prose (commentary on an unknown text?).   P. Rain. 1.34 (inv. 29780) (V; pap. cod.). Mentions Sophocles.   Archiv 11.278.

2866    Prose (scholia on an oration?).   P. Rain. 3.37 (inv. 26217) (VI, Fayum; pap. cod.). Archiv 14.141-42.

2867    Scholia on an unidentified text.   P. Rain. 3.39 (inv. 17971) (V; Hermupolis Magna; pap. cod.).

2868    Prose (hypothesis of a tragedy? mythology? prose paraphrase of Pindar?).   P. Rain. 3.45 (inv. 29388) (VI-VII, Fayum; pap. cod.). Galiano, Pind., No. 55. Archiv 14.140-41.

2869    Prose (Christian martyrology? romance?).   P. Rain. 3.46 (inv. 19925) (V, Fayum; pap. cod.).

2870    Prose (history? oratory?).   P. Rain. 3.47 (inv. 29833 a) (IV-V; pap. cod.).

2871    Prose (?).   P. Rain. 3.48 (inv. 29366) (II).

2872    Prose (history? oratory?).   P. Rain. 3.49 (inv. 810) (III). Archiv 14.134.

2873    Prose (?).   P. Rain. 3.50 (inv. 29350) (IV?; pap. cod.).

2874    Prose (oratory?).   P. Rain. 3.51 (inv. 26204) (V-VI, Fayum; pap. cod.). Archiv 14.136.

2875    Prose (?).   P. Rain. 3.52 (inv. 29382 + 29791) (II).

2876 Prose (?). P. Rain. 3.54 (inv. 29303) (III-IV, Fayum; on the verso of a document).

2877 Prose (medicine?). P. Rain. 3.59 (inv. 29290) (VI?, Fayum; pap. cod.). Archiv 14.145-46.

2878 Prose (medicine?). P. Rain. 3.61 (inv. 29393) (V-VI; pap. cod.?). Archiv 14.147-48.

2879 Prose. P. Rein. 1.4 (P. Sorbonne inv. 2013) (II B.C.). Archiv 3.500.

2880 Prose (literary?). P. Ryl. 1.33 (II B.C.). Archiv 6.267.

2881 Prose (?). P. Ryl. 1.36 (III). Archiv 6.267.

2882 Prose. P. Ryl. 1.37 (II-III). Archiv 6.267.

2883 Prose. P. Ryl. 1.38 (III; pap. cod.). Archiv 6.267.

2884 Prose. P. Ryl. 2.246 (II B.C.; two texts in different hands, on recto and verso).

2885 Prose. P. Ryl. 3.502 (II B.C.; cart.).

2886 Prose. P. Ryl. 3.503 (II B.C.; cart.).

2887 Prose (Christian apologetics?). P. Ryl. 3.507 (IV; pap. cod.). Archiv 14.148.

2888 Prose. P. Ryl. 3.508 (V; pap. cod.).

2889 Prose. P. Ryl. 3.513 (I-II).

2890 Prose. P. Ryl. 3.514 (II).

2891 Prose. P. Ryl. 3.516 (III B.C., Hibeh?).

2892 Prose. P. Ryl. 3.517 (II; fr. of an opisthograph roll).

2893 Prose. P. Ryl. 3.518 (II).

2894 Prose. P. Ryl. 3.519 (II).

2895 Prose. P. Ryl. 3.520 (V-VI; pap. cod.).

2896 Prose. P. Ryl. 3.521 (II).

2897 Prose (oratory?): On the martial spirit. P. Schubart 36 (III, Fayum; on the verso of documents). Archiv 16.126.

2898 Prose. P. Schubart 41 (II). "Es könnte sich um Briefe des Epicharmus handeln."

2899 Prose (theological?). PSI 2.155 (IV-V, Oxy.).

2900 Prose. PSI 7.853 (I-II). Archiv 8.272.

2901 Prose (?). PSI 13.1368 (II, Oxy.). Five lines, almost illegible, in an illustrated papyrus representing Hermes Psychopompos (?). Ed. pr.: A. Minto and G. Piccardi, Aeg. 32 (1952) 324-32. Weitzmann, Anc. Bk. Ill., pp. 132-33 and fig. 136. M. Hombert, Chr. Ég. 29 (1954) 151-52.

2902 Prose (commentary on a poem or romantic ecphrasis?). N. Terzaghi, PP 11 (1956) 378-86 (PSI inv. 516) (II-III, Oxy.). I. Cazzaniga, Acme 9 (1956) 53-56, revises the text, regarding it as a romantic ecphrasis.

2903 Prose. P. Tebt. 2.680 (II, Tebtunis; on the verso of an account).

2904 Prose. P. Tebt. 2.681 (II, Tebtunis).

2905 Prose. P. Tebt. 2.682 (III, Tebtunis).

2906 Prose. P. Tebt. 2.684 (II-III, Tebtunis).

2907 Prose (science?). P. Tebt. 3.897 (III B.C.?, Tebtunis; cart.).

2908 Prose (literary?). P. Varsov. 1.8 (II, Fayum?; sch. ex.). Eos 34 (1932-33) 200.

2909 Prose (or New Comedy?). A. Bataille, JJP 6 (1952) 185-86 ("P. Clermont-Ganneau" inv. 3, deposited with the Institut de Papyrologie à la Sorbonne, Paris) (II). S. Srebrny, Symbolae R. Taubenschlag Dedicatae 2 (= Eos 48, fasc. 2, 1956) 51-65, regards the text as a fragment of the New Comedy.

2910 Prose (?). C. C. Edgar, Ann. Serv. 26 (1926) 209 (P. Cairo inv. 45623) (?, Oxy.; text on recto, No. 1330 on verso).

2911 Prose (mythology? theology?). E. Egger, CRAI, 1871, 247 (?, Memphis; on the verso of No. 2579).

2912 Prose. J. G. Milne, Archiv 5 (1913) 379-80 (II, Hawara).

2913 Prose. J. G. Milne, Archiv 5 (1913) 380 (I, Hawara).

2914 Prose. J. G. Milne, Archiv 5 (1913) 380 (I, Hawara).

2915 Prose (?). Mentioned by Gerhard, Phoinix, p. 1, note 2 (II B.C.; on the verso of P. Heid., inv. 310, a, c, i, m: see No. 1605).

2916 Prose (?). S. J. Gasiorowski, JEA 17 (1931) 1-9 ("P. Johnson," Oxford) (ca. A.D. 500, Antinoë; pap. cod.?). Scanty traces of three lines of text, in an illustrated papyrus showing a group of charioteers. Weitzmann, Anc. Bk. Ill., p. 132 and fig. 135; idem, Ill. RC, pp. 53-54 and pl. 41, attributes the fragment to a roll of saec. IV-V.

Prose, Unidentified: see also Nos. 339 (ad fin.), 1359, 1590, 1606, 1827, 2153, 3016.

## A. TEXTS IDENTIFIED BY AUTHORS
### (EXCEPT FOR LAW)

2917 AESOP: The fable of the swallow and the other birds (in Latin and Greek). *P. Mich. 7. 457 (inv. 5604 b, verso) (III; on the verso of a Latin legal text). First published as a "bilingual document," identified as Aesopic by C. H. Roberts, JRS 47 (1957) 124-25. B. E. Perry, TAPA 93 (1962) 316.

Aesop: Latin translation of a Greek fable: see No. 52.

Babrius: Latin translation of Fables 11, 16-17: see No. 172.
Cato: see No. 2999.

2918 CICERO: De Imperio Cn. Pompei 60-65, 70-71; In Verrem ii. 1. 1-4, 2, 3, 12; Pro Caelio 26-55. P. Oxy. 8. 1097, 10. 1251; P. Lit. Lond. 143 (Brit. Mus. inv. 2057) (V?, Oxy.; pap. cod.). Lowe, CLA 2. 210; Mallon, PR, pl. XXII. 1. Collart, PLL 10, 11. Cavenaile, CPL 24-25. JAW 167. 283-84, 183. 74. A. Klotz, Berl. Phil. Woch. 34 (1914) 955-60, on the relation to the text tradition.

2919 --- Divinatio in Q. Caecilium 33-37, 44-46, with Greek and Latin scholia. P. Ryl. 3. 477 (V; pap. cod.). The scholium on line 53 recalls Servius on Aeneid ix. 437. Lowe, CLA 2. 226. Collart, PLL 7. Calderini, PL 2; Cavenaile, CPL 23. Archiv 14. 148.

2920 --- In Verrem ii. 2. 3-4. P. Iand. 5. 90 (inv. 210) (I B. C. -I, Medinet-el-Fayum?). Kirchner, Scr. LL, tab. 3b; Lowe, CLA 8. 1201 (bibl.: ibid., p. 68); Mallon, PR, pl. IV. 1. Collart, PLL 8; Gundel 50 ("älteste vorhandene Cicero-Handschrift"); Marichal 18. Calderini, PL 3; Cavenaile, CPL 20.

2921 --- In Verrem ii. 23. 60-61, 24. 62-63. PSI 1. 20 (V-VI, Oxy.; pap. cod.). Lowe, CLA 3. 286; Mallon, PR, pl. XXIV. 2. Collart, PLL 9. Cavenaile, CPL 27. JAW 167. 284.

2922 --- In Catilinam i. 6. 15-16, 7. 17-18, 8. 19-20, with a literal Greek translation. H. Gerstinger, WS 55 (1937) 95-106 (P. Vindob. inv. G. 30885 a + e) (IV-V; pap. cod.; cart.). Lowe, CLA 10. 1519 (bibl.: ibid., p. 50). Collart, PLL 13. Cavenaile, CPL 21. Archiv 13. 131. Y. Geerts, Chr. Ég. 14 (1939) 181-82.

2923 --- In Catilinam ii. 14-15, with a literal Greek translation. P. Ryl. 1. 61 (V; pap. cod.). Lowe, CLA 2. 224; Mallon, PR, pl. XVIII. 2; New Pal. Soc., Ser. 2, vol. 1, pl. 55. Collart, PLL 14. Calderini, PL 4; Cavenaile, CPL 22. JAW 167. 283. C. H. Moore, CP 19 (1924) 321-22.

2924 --- Pro Plancio 11. 27-28, 19. 46-47. S. de Ricci, Mél. Chatelain 442-47 (P. Berol. inv. 13229 A-B) (V, Hermupolis Magna; parch. cod.). Lowe, CLA 8. 1043. Collart, PLL 12. Cavenaile, CPL 26. JAW 167. 282-83.

Ennius: see No. 3000.

Fenestella: see No. 2999.
Isidorianus: Greek translation of a Latin text: see No. 2512.

2925 JUVENAL: Saturae vii. 149-98, with bilingual scholia and glosses. C. H. Roberts, JEA 21 (1935) 199-209 (Egypt Exploration Society, London) (ca. A. D. 500, Antinoë; parch. cod.). Collart, PLL 58. Cavenaile, CPL 37. Aeg. 15. 297-302, 16. 313; Chr. Eg. 11 (1936) 172-73; JAW 260. 103. U. Knoche, Philol., Suppl. 33, Heft 1 (1940) 2.

2926 LIVY i. 5. 6--6. 1. P. Oxy. 11. 1379 (Bodleian Libr., Lat. class. f. 5 (P)) (III-IV, Oxy.). Lowe, CLA 2. 247. Collart, PLL 73. Cavenaile, CPL 35. JAW 188. 25.

2927 --- An epitome of Books xxxvii-xl, xlvii-lv. P. Oxy. 4. 668; P. Lit. Lond. 120 (Brit. Mus. inv. 1532); PSI 12. 1291, from the same pap. (III-IV, Oxy.; on the verso are P. Oxy. 4. 657 and PSI 12. 1292: Paul, Epist. ad Hebraeos). Bassi, MIG, No. 152, tav. LV; Kirchner, Scr. LL, tab. 4c; Lowe, CLA, 2. 208; Mallon, EL, pl. 46; idem, PR, pl. XVII. 3; E. G. Turner, GR 21 (1952), pl. CXXIII. Calderini, PL 5; Cavenaile, CPL 33-34 (bibl.); O. Rossbach, T. Livi Periochae Omnium Librorum, Fragmenta Oxyrhynchi Reperta ... (Lipsiae 1910) 122-48; A. C. Schlesinger, Livy, vol. 14 (Loeb ed., 1959), passim (after the traditional periochae of the same Books). Collart, PLL 74. Archiv 3. 501, 16. 129; JAW 142. 199-200. E. Kornemann, Klio, Beih. 2 (1904), reedits the text; C. H. Moore, AJP 25 (1904) 241-55, on the relation to Julius Obsequens and Cassiodorus; J. S. Reid, CR 18 (1904) 290-300; F. Muenzer, Klio 24 (1931) 333-38, on the evidence for the consuls of 139 B. C.; M. Stuart, CP 39 (1944) 40-44, restores lines 188-90; R. Marichal, Pauli Sent. Fr. Leid., p. 34, on the dating of the papyrus (saec. III).

2928 LUCAN: Bellum Civile ii. 247-48, 265-66. P. Lit. Lond. 42 (Brit. Mus., Add. MS. 34473, art. 6) (V-VI, Fayum?; a small strip of vellum from the binding of a MS.). Lowe, CLA 2. 175. Collart, PLL 59. Cavenaile, CPL 36.

Palaemon, Q. Remmius: see No. 2996.
Pliny the Elder: see No. 2996.

2929 SALLUST: Bellum Iugurthinum 31. 7. P. Ryl. 1. 42 (IV). Identified by Lowe, CLA 2. 223. Bassi, MIG, No. 114, tav. XLI. Collart, PLL 68; Marichal 305. Cavenaile, CPL 30. Archiv 6. 268.

2930 --- 43. 3-4, 44. 3-4, 49. 5-6, 50. 3-4. P. Lehmann, Sitzb. Berl. Akad., 1934, Abh. 4, 19-24 (Staatsbibliothek, Berlin, MS. lat. qu. 914) (IV, Oxy. ?; parch. cod.). Lowe, CLA 8. 1054. Collart, PLL 69; Marichal 304. Cavenaile, CPL 31. W. Kroll, Gnomon 11 (1935) 334.

2931 --- Bellum Catilinae 6. 2, 6-7. P. Oxy. 6. 884 (Bodleian Libr., Lat. class. e. 20 (P)) (V, Oxy.; pap. cod.; sch. ex. ?). Lowe, CLA 2. 246. Collart, PLL 66. Calderini, PL 6; Cavenaile, CPL 32. A. W. Ahlberg, Eranos 9 (1909) 13-29; G. Perl, FF 33 (1959) 57-59.

2932    --- 10.4-5, 11.6-7, with a few Greek glosses.  PSI
        1.110 (IV, Oxy.; pap. cod.).  Lowe, CLA 3.288;
        Mallon, PR, pl. XXIV.4; Van Hoesen 71 (p. 132).
        Collart, PLL 67; Marichal 161.  Calderini, PL 7;
        Cavenaile, CPL 29.

2933    --- Historiae, Bk. ii (?).    P. Ryl. 3.473, and P.
        Oxy. sine numero (II-III, Oxy.; text on recto, No.
        2050 on verso).  Kirchner, Scr. LL, tab. 3a. Col-
        lart, PLL 70; Marichal 294.  Calderini, PL 8;
        Cavenaile, CPL 28.    Archiv 14.148-49.  B. Snell,
        Gnomon 15 (1939) 537; W. Morel, CR 55 (1941) 74-
        75; E. Lepore, Athen. 38 (1950) 280-91.

        Sallust: see also No. 3002.

        Seneca: see No. 3002.

2934    TERENCE: Andria 602-68, 924-50, 957-79, with a
        few Greek glosses.  P. Oxy. 24.2401 (IV?, Oxy.;
        pap. cod.).

        Trogus, Pompeius: see No. 3000.
        Tubero, L. Aelius: see No. 2999.

2935    VERGIL: Eclogae v.17-31.  Lowe, CLA 6.833 (P.
        Strasb., P. lat. 2, inedita) (III-IV?; parch. roll).
        Marichal 306.  R. Marichal, Script. 9 (1955) 133-
        34, dates the text to saec. III or earlier.

2936    --- Georgica i.229-37, with a literal Greek trans-
        lation.  E. M. Husselman, Studi Calderini-
        Paribeni 2.453-59 (collection of Robert S. Allen,
        Oakland, California) (V, Egypt; parch. cod.;
        palimpsest: a Coptic text, Sapientia Salomonis
        ll.4-15, covers the Latin and Greek).

2937    --- Georgica ii.527-42, iii.1-25, with an argument
        (?) to Bk. iii, and a few marginalia.  P. Antin.
        1.29 (IV, Antinoöpolis; pap. cod.).  Cavenaile,
        CPL 17.

2938    --- Georgica iv.1-2, written six times, plus a writ-
        ing exercise in unidentified prose.  P. Tebt. 2.
        686 (II-III, Tebtunis; on the verso are Nos. 2998,
        3015).  Collart, PLL 90; Marichal 82.  Cavenaile,
        CLP 18.

2939    --- Latin-Greek glossary on Aeneid i, ii, iv, with
        a Greek translation of i - ii (lacunae).  P. Colt
        1 (VI, Nessana, Palestine; pap. cod.).  Collart,
        PLL 80.  Cavenaile, CPL 8.  H. D. Colt, Pales-
        tine Exploration Fund Quarterly Statement 68 (1936)
        220 (first mention).  JEA 23 (1937) 105.  C. J.
        Kraemer, Jr., Actes Pap. V, 239-40; R. Mari-
        chal, Rev. Ét. Lat. 35 (1957) 83.

2940    --- Aeneid i.235-43, 247-61, 270-74, 406-14, 418-26,
        633-40, 645-51, 702-7, 711-19, with a literal Greek
        translation.  P. Ryl. 3.478; P. Med. 1.1;  R.
        Rémondon, JJP 4 (1950) 239-51 (P. Cairo inv. 85644
        A-B) (III-V; pap. cod.).  Bassi, MIG, No. 153,
        tav. LV; Lowe, CLA 2.227, 3.367, 10.227 (bibl.:
        ibid., p. 52); Mallon, PR, pl. XIX.1 (P. Ryl.).
        Collart, PLL 78, 79.  Calderini, PL 9; Cavenaile,
        CPL 1-3.  Archiv 14.149.  B. Snell, Gnomon 15
        (1939) 537-38; M. Hombert, Chr. Ég. 26 (1951)
        416-17;  R. Marichal, Pauli Sent. Fr. Leid., pp.
        29, 34-36, on the date (saec. III-IV).

2941    --- Aeneid i.457-67, 495-507.    P. Oxy. 1.31 (Cam-
        bridge Univ. Libr., add. 4031) (V, Oxy.; pap. cod.).
        Lowe, CLA 2.134; Wessely, SALP, Taf. 49. Col-
        lart, PLL 85.  Cavenaile, CPL 10.

2942    --- Aeneid i.477-93, revised.    PSI 2.142 (III-IV; a
        leaf of pap.).  Lowe, CLA 3.289; Mallon, EL, pl.
        51. Collart, PLL 89.  Calderini, PL 10; Cavenaile,
        CPL 19.  Archiv 7.254-55.  R. Cavenaile, Ét. Cl.
        18 (1950) 285-88;  R. Marichal, Pauli Sent. Fr.
        Leid., p. 29, prefers saec. IV (Lowe, saec. V).

2943    --- Aeneid i.588-748 (lacunae), with a Greek trans-
        lation.  J. Galbiati, Aevum 1 (1927) 49-70 (Biblio-
        teca Ambrosiana, Milano) (IV-V, Egypt or Syria;
        140 leaves from a parch. cod.; palimpsest: an
        Arabic text covers the Greek and Latin).  Collart,
        PLL 82.  Cavenaile, CPL 7.  Identified by E. A.
        Lowe, CR 36 (1922) 154-55.  JEA 9.97.

2944    --- Aeneid ii.16-23, 39-46.  P. Oxy. 8.1098 (P.
        Cairo) (IV, Oxy.; parch. cod.).  Bassi, MIG, No.
        139, tav. LII; Lowe, CLA 10.1569 (and p. 52).
        Collart, PLL 86; Marichal 309.  Cavenaile, CPL
        9.

2945    --- Aeneid ii.296-338, iii.559-666, iv.450-686,
        v.8-681, vi.425-880 (lacunae).  P. Colt 2 (VI, Nes-
        sana, Palestine; pap. cod.).

2946    --- Aeneid ii.443-537, with a literal Greek transla-
        tion.  PSI 7.756 (IV-V?, Oxy.; pap. cod.).  Lowe,
        CLA 3.290.  Collart, PLL 81.  Cavenaile, CPL 4.

2947    --- Aeneid ii.601 (written seven times), iv.174 (?),
        198 (?).  P. Hawara 24 (University Coll., London)
        (I, Hawara; writing ex.).  Marichal 19.  Cavenaile,
        CPL 14; Ziebarth, No. 12; Ziebarth 2, No. 34.
        J. G. Milne, JHS 28 (1908) 125.  E. G. Turner,
        Studi Calderini-Paribeni 2.157-61, sees an uniden-
        tified iambic verse in place of iv.174, and observes
        that this is evidently the oldest surviving MS. of
        Vergil, perhaps the work of an apprentice calli-
        grapher; K. Preisendanz, DLZ, 1959, 309, recog-
        nizes the "decorative doodling" as Aeneid iv.198.

2948    --- Aeneid iii.444-68, with a Greek translation.   P.
        Fuad 1.5 (IV-V; pap. cod.; from a teacher's pri-
        vate copy?).  Lowe, CLA 10.1570.  Collart, PLL
        83; Marichal 164.  Cavenaile, CPL 6.

2949    --- Aeneid iv.66-68, 99-102.  PSI 1.21 (V, Oxy.;
        pap. cod.).  Lowe, CLA 3.287; Mallon, EL, pl.
        49. Collart, PLL 87.  Cavenaile, CPL 11.  M.
        Lenchantin de Gubernatis, Riv. Fil. 43 (1915) 448-
        53, on the marked accents; C. H. Moore, CP 19
        (1924) 322-23.

2950    --- Greek paraphrase of Aeneid iv.661-705, v.1-6.
        P. Oxy. 8.1099 (Cambridge Univ. Libr., add. 5896)
        (V-VI, Oxy.; parch. cod.).  Lowe, CLA 2.137.
        Collart, PLL 84.  Calderini, PL 11; Cavenaile,
        CPL 5.  M. Lenchantin de Gubernatis, Riv. Fil.
        43 (1915) 448-53, suggests a school exercise, com-
        menting on the marks of punctuation; C. H. Moore,
        CP 19 (1924) 319-21.

2951 --- Aeneid v. 673-74, 683-84, with a Greek translation. E. A. Lowe, CR 36 (1922) 154-55 (P. Vindob.
inv. Lat. 24) (V, Fayum?; parch. cod.; from a
schoolbook). Lowe, CLA 10.1522 (and p. 50). Collart, PLL 88. Cavenaile, CPL 13. JEA 9.97.

--- Aeneid vi. 698-700, 711, 713: see No. 3018.

--- Aeneid ix. 26: see No. 2996.

2952 --- Aeneid xii. 762-65, 786-90. P. Antin. 1.30 (IV,
Antinoöpolis; parch. cod.). Cavenaile, CPL 15.

## B. LAW

### 1. Texts Identified by Authors

Law: Authors. Anatolius: see No. 2277.

2953 GAIUS: Institutiones iii. 153-54, 167-74, iv. 16-18, with
Greek glosses. PSI 11.1182 (IV-VI, Antinoë?; parch.
cod.). Refers to Paulus, Sententiae ii. 29.14 Bassi,
MIG, No. 172, tav. LXIII; Lowe, CLA 3.292 (saec.
V-VI). Collart, PLL 46. Baviera 195-200 (bibl.);
Calderini, PL 16; Cavenaile, CPL 78 (bibl.); David,
Gaius, pp. 103, 105-7, 120-22; Girard, p. 224;
Wieacker, Textstufen 163-64, 202. Archiv 13.131-
32. E. Albertario, Gnomon 9 (1933) 326-28; P.
Collinet, Rev. Dr. Fr., Sér. 4.13 (1934) 96-113; E.
Levy, Sav. Zeitschr. 54 (1934) 258-311; F. de Zu-
lueta, JRS 24 (1934) 168-86 (bibl.), ibid. 25 (1935)
19-32; C. W. Westrup, Det Kgl. Danske Viden-
skabernes Selskab, Hist.-Fil. Meddelelser 31 (1947),
Nr. 2; L. Wenger, Scritti in onore di C. Ferrini
(Pubblicazioni dell' Univ. Cattolica del Sacro Cuore,
NS 28, Milano 1949) 268-83; E. Kiessling, JJP 4
(1950) 317-25; F. Wieacker, Sav. Zeitschr. 67
(1950) 393; E. Weiss, Festschr. F. Schulz 2 (Weimar 1951) 79-100.

2954 --- Institutiones iv. 57, 68-72. P. Oxy. 17. 2103 (III,
Oxy.). Kirchner, Scr. LL, tab. 3c; Mallon, PR,
pl. XVI.1. Collart, PLL 47; Marichal 130. Ba-
viera 201-4 (bibl.); Cavenaile, CPL 77 (bibl.);
David, Gaius 134-36; Girard 223-24; Wieacker,
Textstufen 197-98. JEA 14.149-50. E. Levy, Studi
Bonfante 2.275-87; F. Wieacker, Sav. Zeitschr.
67 (1950) 381, 388.

Gaius: see also Nos. 2283, 2958.

Javolenus Priscus: see No. 2982.
Julianus: see No. 2960.
Labeo, Antistius: see No. 2972.
Modestinus: see No. 2982.

2955 PAPINIAN: De Bonorum Possessione; Responsa v, ix.
P. Krueger, Monatsberichte Berl. Akad., 1879,
509-18 (P. Berol. inv. 6762 + 6763; P. Louvre inv.
E. 7153) (IV-VI; parch. cod.). According to R.
Marichal, Pauli Sent. Fr. Leid., p. 30, the frag-
ment in the Louvre has now disappeared. Lowe,
CLA 8.1037 (bibl.: ibid., p. 60). Collart, PLL
62, 63. Baviera 435-45; Cavenaile, CPL 93-94
(bibl.); Girard 371-75 (bibl.). R. Dareste, Rev.
Dr. Fr., 1883, 361-85.

Papinian: see also Nos. 2982, 2991.

2956 PAULUS: Sententiae v. 28-29, and some eight new
sententiae. Pauli Sent. Fr. Leid. (Cod. Leiden-
sis B. P. L. 2589) (III-IV, Egypt; parch. cod.). In
the basic publication, David and Nelson present the
text with a philological commentary, Marichal discusses the script and its dating, Levy treats the
source problems, and Archi studies the new material in relation to Roman criminal law. Ed. pr.:
M. David and H. L. W. Nelson, Tijdschr. v. Rechtsg.
23 (1955) 75-82, 286. Lowe, CLA 10.1577 (and p.
53). Cavenaile, CPL 74. A. d'Ors, Est. Clás. 3
(1955) 121-25; F. Serrao, Il frammento Leidense
di Paolo ..., Univ. di Roma, Pubbl. dell' Istituto
di Diritto Romano ... 33 (Milano 1956); M. David
and H. L. W. Nelson, Tijdschr. v. Rechtsg. 25
(1957) 302-8; H. J. Scheltema, ibid. 308; E. Seidl,
Labeo: Rassegna di Diritto Romano 3 (Napoli 1957)
257-59.

2957 --- De Formula Fabiana; Ad Plautium viii (fragments).
Raineri M. 4.1-50 (P. Vindob. inv. Lat. 90); P.
M. Meyer, Sav. Zeitschr. 42 (1921) 42-57 (P. Berol.
inv. 11753) (IV, Hermupolis; parch. cod.). Lowe,
CLA 8.1042 (bibl.: ibid., pp. 60-61), 10.1042 (bibl.:
ibid., p. 50); Mallon, EL, pl. 48; Wessely, SALP,
Taf. 42. Baviera 427-32; Cavenaile, CPL 84, 85
(bibl.); Girard 454-59. Aeg. 3 (1922) 212-14; JEA
8.88; H. Klos, Chr. Eg. 28 (1953) 374-75 (bibl.).

Paulus: see also Nos. 2277-78, 2281, 2953,2958,
2966, 2972, 2982.

2958 Greek commentary on Paulus, Ulpian, and Gaius (?).
R. Dareste, BCH 4 (1880) 449-60 (438-529, Mt.
Sinai; pieces of pap. used as a cover for a codex).
Contains references to the Codex Theodosianus,
Codex Gregorianus, Gaius (?), Paulus, Sabinus,
and Ulpian. Baviera 637-52 (bibl.): "Scholia Sina-
itica ad Ulpiani Libros ad Sabinum." E. O. Winstedt,
CP 2 (1907) 201-7.

Pomponius: see Nos. 2972, 2979.
Sabatius: see No. 2280.
Sabinus: see Nos. 2277, 2958.
Stephanus: see No. 2971.

2959 ULPIAN: Institutiones, Bk. ii (fragments). Girard
492-93 (?; strips of pap. used in binding a codex).
Collart, PLL 76.

2960 --- Ad Edictum, Bk. xxxii, with Greek scholia. PSI
14.1449 (IV?; parch.). Mentions the jurist Julianus.
Wieacker, Textstufen 255-62, 432. V. Arangio-
Ruiz, Archivio Giuridico (Modena 1957) 140-58; H.
J. Wolff, Iura 10, Parte 1 (1959) 1-12; V. Arangio-
Ruiz, BIDR 63 (1960) 281-93.

2961 --- Ad Edictum, Bk. xlv (fragments). P. Fay. 10
(Bodleian Libr., Lat. class. g. 5 (P)); Lowe, CLA
8, p. 6 (P. Berol. inv. 11533, inedita?) (II-III, Thea-
delphia). P. Fay. 10 identified by O. Plasberg,
Woch. Phil. 18 (1901) 141-42. Lowe, CLA 2.249;
Mallon, PR, pl. XVI.2; Van Hoesen, No. 31 (pp.
88-89). Collart, PLL 75; Marichal 53. Cavenaile,
CPL 71; Girard 497; Wieacker, Textstufen 263.

2962    --- Disputationes, Bks. ii-iii (fragments).  O. Lenel,
        Sitzb. Berl. Akad., 1903, 922-36, 1034-35, ibid.,
        1904, 1156-72 (P. Strassb. inv. Lat. 3 + 6 B) (V-VI;
        parch.).  Lowe, CLA 6.834.  Collart, PLL 77.
        Baviera 308-12; Cavenaile,. CPL 76; Girard 494-96.
        JAW 134.67-70.  O. Lenel, Sav. Zeitschr. 23 (1903)
        416-19, ibid. 25 (1904) 368-74.

        Ulpian: see also Nos. 2958, 2974, 2979, 2982, 2985,
        2991.

        Vivianus: see No. 2280.

2963    CODEX THEODOSIANUS vii. 8. 9-14.  P. Oxy. 15.1813;
        P. Lit. Lond. 189 (Brit. Mus. inv. 2485) (VI, Oxy.;
        parch. cod.).  Lowe, CLA 2.211.  Collart, PLL 72.
        Cavenaile, CPL 98.  P. Krueger, Sav. Zeitschr.
        43 (1922) 560-61.

2964    --- Fragment of the Codex Theodosianus (?).  E. W.
        B. Nicholson ap. F. Madan and H. H. E. Craster,
        Summary Catalogue of Western Manuscripts in the
        Bodleian Library ... 6 (1924) 12 (No. 31074) (Bod-
        leian Libr., Gr. bibl. d. 2 (P)) (V-VI, Egypt; parch.
        palimpsest).  Marichal 312.

        Codex Theodosianus: see also No. 2958.

2965    DIGESTA:  Greek index to Digesta ii. 14. 4-7.  PSI 1.
        55 (VI, Oxy.; pap. cod.).  Collart, PLL 17; Mari-
        chal 319.  Cavenaile, CPL, p. 199 (bibl.).

2966    --- Greek scholia on Digesta v. 2.16-19.  O. Graden-
        witz, Sav. Zeitschr. 23 (1902) 458-59 (P. Heid. inv.
        1272) (VI-VII; pap. cod.).  Lowe, CLA 8.1221.
        Marichal 317.  Cavenaile, CPL 87 (bibl.).  Archiv
        3.299.  G. A. Gerhard and O. Gradenwitz, Philol.
        62 (1903) 95-124; Gerhard, ibid. 66 (1907) 477-80;
        A. J. Boyé, Tijdschr. v. Rechtsg. 5 (1924) 464-88,
        prefers to think of scholia on Paulus, Quaestiones;
        L. Wenger, Aus Antike u. Orient: Festschr. ... W.
        Schubart (Leipzig 1950) 137-43.

2967    --- Digesta xxx. 11-13, 22-26, and three unidentified
        fragments.  P. Ryl. 3.479 (VI, Thebaïd?; pap.
        cod.).  Mallon, PR, pl. XXXII. 1.  Collart, PLL
        16.  Cavenaile, CPL 89.  Archiv 14.150.  F. Schulz,
        Tijdschr. v. Rechtsg. 17 (1940) 19-27, prefers to
        think of a pre-Justinianic collection used by the
        compiler of the Digesta; R. Duell and E. Seidl,
        Sav. Zeitschr. 61 (1941) 406-19; L. Wenger, Aus
        Antike u. Orient: Festschr. ... W. Schubart (Leip-
        zig 1950) 143.

2968    --- Digesta xlix. 1. 25, in Greek.  P. Oxy. 17.2104
        (A. D. 241?, Oxy.).  Identified independently by
        P. M. Meyer, Studi Bonfante 2.341-44, and U.
        Wilcken, Archiv 9 (1930) 90.

2969    CODEX IUSTINIANUS:  Index to the Codex Iustinianus.
        P. Oxy. 15.1814 (A. D. 529-535?, Oxy.; pap. cod.).
        Collart, PLL 57.  Cavenaile, CPL 101 (bibl.).  P.
        Bonfante, BIDR 32 (1922) 277-82; P. de Francisci,
        Aeg. 3 (1922) 68-79; P. Krueger, Sav. Zeitschr.
        43 (1922) 561-63.

2970    --- Codex Iustinianus vii. 16. 41-42, 17.1.  PSI 13.
        1347 (VI; pap. cod.).  Ed. pr.: A. Segrè, Studi
        Bonfante 3.429-30.  Lowe, CLA 3.293.  Cavenaile,
        CPL 99 (bibl.).  F. Schulz, Sav. Zeitschr. 51 (1931)
        417-21.

2971    --- Codex Iustinianus xii. 59. 10, 60. 6, 62. 3; Digesta
        xix. 2.54, with Greek glosses.  S. de Ricci, Études
        d'histoire juridique offertes à P. F. Girard 1 (1912)
        273-82 (P. Rein. inv. 2219 + 2173) (VI; pap. cod.).
        Lowe, CLA 5.700.  Marichal 314.  Cavenaile, CPL
        100.  J. C. Naber, Studi in memoria di A. Alber-
        toni 1 (Padova 1935) 21-23, thinks of the first edition
        of the Codex, A. D. 529; H. J. Scheltema, Tijdschr.
        v. Rechtsg. 26 (1958) 5-14, attributes the Greek
        glosses to Stephanus, a commentator on the Diges-
        ta.

## 2.  Adespota

2972    Juridical fragment: On Societas (Sextus Pomponius or
        Julius Paulus?).  P. Grenf. 2.107 (Bodleian Libr.,
        Lat. class. g.1 (P)) (IV-V; parch. cod.).  Refers
        twice to the jurist Labeo.  Lowe, CLA 2.248.  Col-
        lart, PLL 30.  Baviera 423-24; Cavenaile, CPL
        86 (bibl.); Girard 460 (bibl.); Wieacker, Text-
        stufen 271-72.  JAW 109.46-48.

2973    Juridical fragment.  G. A. Gerhard and O. Graden-
        witz, Neue Heidelb. Jahrb. 12 (1903) 141-83 (P. Heid.
        inv. 1000) (III-IV).  Lowe, CLA 8.1219.  Collart,
        PLL 31; Marichal 300.  Cavenaile, CPL 82.  Ar-
        chiv 3.299.

2974    Juridical fragment.  P. Ryl. 3.474 (IV, Thebaid?;
        pap. cod.).  A collection of excerpts from Ulpian
        and other jurists, or a copy of Ulpian's commentary
        on the Edict; includes Digesta xii. 1. 1. 1, De Rebus
        Credendis (Ulpian, Ad Edictum 26).  Collart, PLL
        32.  Baviera 313-14; Cavenaile, CPL 88 (bibl.);
        Wieacker, Textstufen 250-53, queries Schulz' sug-
        gestion (see below), prefers a codex of Ulpian.
        Archiv 14.150.  F. de Zulueta, Actes Pap. v, 609-14,
        BIDR 45 (1938) 380-86, and Studi ... in onore di
        Enrico Besta 1 (Milano 1939) 139-47; L. Wenger,
        Aus Antike u. Orient: Festschr. ... W. Schubart
        (Leipzig 1950) 143-44; F. Wieacker, Sav. Zeitschr.
        67 (1950) 375-78; F. Schulz, ibid. 68 (1951) 1-29,
        thinks of an anthology of the classical jurists (de-
        tailed study, with bibl.).

2975    Juridical fragment.  P. Oxy. 17.2089 (IV-V, Oxy.;
        parch.).  Relates to the laws of inheritance.  Col-
        lart, PLL 34.  Baviera 315-16; Cavenaile, CPL
        92 (bibl.); Girard 509-10; Wieacker, Textstufen
        146.  Archiv 10.236.  R. Marichal, Pauli Sent. Fr.
        Leid. 36, on the dating (saec. IV-V).

2976    Juridical fragment.  F. Bilabel, Actes Pap. V, 81-82
        (P. Heid. inv. 317) (III-IV?; pap. cod.).  Lowe,
        CLA 8.1218 (as of saec. VI).  Collart, PLL 36.
        Cavenaile, CPL 83.

2977    Juridical fragment (part of a literary work?).  P.
        Amh. 2.27 (V-VI).  Collart, PLL 29.

2978   Juridical fragment.   P. Amh. 2.28 (IV-V; pap. cod.). Marichal 315. Cavenaile, CPL 90. A. Schneider, Sav. Zeitschr. 24 (1903) 414-16.

2979   Juridical fragments.   P. Antin. 1.22 (IV, Antinoöpolis; parch. cod.). Text on recto, Ulpian, Ad Edictum xii (?); text on verso unidentified. Refers to Pomponius. Cavenaile, CPL 72; Wieacker, Textstufen 232.

2980   Juridical fragment (?).   P. Ryl. 3.480 (V; recto blank, text on verso). Collart, PLL 35. Cavenaile, CPL 96.

2981   Juridical fragment (?).   P. Ryl. 3.481 (V; small opisthograph fr.). Collart, PLL 35. Cavenaile, CPL 97.

2982   Legal definitions and maxims, in Greek and Latin. PSI 13.1348 (IV-V, Oxy.?; pap. cod.). Cites Javolenus; Modestinus; Papinian, Quaestiones viii and Responsa; Paulus, Quaestiones i and Libri Brevium ii; Ulpian, De Appellationibus i and Libri ad Sabinum xliv. Ed. pr.: A. Segrè, Studi Bonfante 3. 421-28. Collart, PLL 39; Marichal 313. Wieacker, Textstufen 47, 109, 162, 262. F. Schulz, JRS 31 (1941) 63-69.

2983   Legal (?) fragment.   P. Aberdeen 130 (III?, Fayum?). Ed. pr.: E. O. Winstedt, CQ 1 (1907) 266. Lowe, CLA 2.120; Mallon, EL, pl. 53. Collart, PLL 25; Marichal 298.

2984   Rubrics of a work on criminal law. Wessely, SALP, Taf. 24 (P. Vindob. inv. Lat. 110) (VI, Fayum?; pap. cod.). Lowe, CLA 10.1538 (bibl.: ibid., p. 50). Collart, PLL 38.

2985   Juridical fragment.   T. Mommsen, Monatsberichte Berl. Akad., 1879, 502-8 (P. Berol. inv. 6757) (III-V?; parch. cod.). Perhaps from Ulpian, Ad Edictum xvi. Bassi, MIG, No. 157, tav. LVII; Lowe, CLA 8.1033 (bibl.: ibid., p. 60); Mallon, EL, pl. 47; idem, PR, pl. XIX.2; Wessely, SALP, Taf. 43. Collart, PLL 41. Baviera 625-26 (bibl.); Cavenaile, CPL 75 (bibl.).

2986   Juridical fragment.   P. Mich. 7.431 (inv. 513) (I). Marichal 288. Cavenaile, CPL 70.

2987   Juridical fragment (?).   P. Mich. 7.456, recto (inv. 5604 b, recto) (I-II). Identified by A. D'Ors, Emerita 19 (1951) 1-14, as a fragment of an early writer on jurisprudence (Actio ex stipulatu) rather than a "record of court proceedings," as designated by the editor.

2988   Juridical fragment (?).   PSI 13.1346 (IV?, Antinoë; pap. cod.).

2989   Juridical fragment.   Mentioned by R. Marichal, Pauli Sent. Fr. Leid. 27 (P. Berol. inv. 11323) (IV-V, Hermupolis Magna; parch. cod.). Lowe, CLA 8. 1039.

2990   Juridical fragment.   Mentioned by R. Marichal, Pauli Sent. Fr. Leid. 26 (P. Berol. inv. 11324) (IV-V, Hermupolis Magna?; parch. cod.).

2991   Fragment on jurisprudence (Ulpian?).   V. Arangio-Ruiz, Festschr. Fritz Schulz 2 (Weimar 1951) 3-8 (in the editor's collection) (IV; pap. cod.). Cites Papinian. Cavenaile, CPL 73. M. T. Lenger, Chr. Ég. 27 (1952) 291.

2992   Juridical fragment.   Lowe CLA 8.1034 (P. Berol. inv. 6758) (VI; parch.).

2993   Juridical fragment (?).   Lowe, CLA 8.1035 (P. Berol. inv. 6759 + 6761) (VI; parch.).

Law: for legal texts in Greek, see Nos. 2277-86.

## C. ADESPOTA (except for Law)

2994   Catalogue of works of art.   J. Nicole, Un catalogue d'oeuvres d'art conservées à Rome ... (Genève 1906) (P. Genève inv. Lat. VII) (II-III; on the verso of a Greek document). ChLA 1, No. 11 (bibl.); Lowe, CLA 7.885; Van Hoesen, No. 41 (pp. 103-4). Collart, PLL 5; Marichal 77. Cavenaile, CPL 64. R. Cagnat, Journ. Sav., 1906, 609; G. Nicole, Mél. Holleaux (Paris 1913) 145, note 2 (bibl.); R. Marichal, Chr. Ég. 30 (1955) 346-60, reedits both this and No. 2995.

2995   Catalogue of works of art.   G. Nicole, Mél. Holleaux (Paris 1913) 145-52 (P. Genève inv. Lat. V) (post A.D. 211; on the verso of P. Geneve inv. Gr. 65, a philosophical commentary, evidently unedited). ChLA 1, No. 10; Lowe, CLA 7.885. Marichal 77. Cavenaile, CPL 63. R. Cagnat, Journ. Sav., NS 12 (1914) 371-72, reprints the text; R. Marichal, Chr. Ég. 30 (1955) 346-60, reedits both this and No. 2994.

2996   Grammatical treatise (Q. Remmius Palaemon? Pliny the Elder?).   P. Lit. Lond. 184 (Brit. Mus. inv. 2723); J. E. Dunlap, AJP 61 (1940) 330-44, publishes an additional fr. (P. Mich. inv. 4649), rejecting the attribution to Palaemon; P. Mich. 7. 429 (combines both frr.) (II-III, Karanis; on the verso of a military register). Line 18 quotes Vergil, Aeneid ix.26. Bassi, MIG, No. 115, tav. XLI; Lowe, CLA 2.212. Collart, PLL 61; Marichal 292. Cavenaile, CPL 56-57. A. Koerte, Archiv 10.237, regards the attribution to Palaemon as "very probable"; J. Collart, Rev. Phil. 12 (1938) 228-38, accepts it; E. G. Turner, CR 62 (1948) 146, rejects it; R. Merkelbach, Archiv 16..129; G. Pennisi, Hlk. 1 (1961) 503-11, reedits the text and attributes it to Pliny, Dubius Sermo.

2997   Latin-Greek grammar: A text for Greek-speaking pupils.   K. Wessely, WS 8 (1886) 218-21 (Musée du Louvre, Paris, P. Ég. 7332) (V-VI; parts of two parch. leaves). Nine Greek nouns and their Latin equivalents, with declensions of the latter. Lowe, CLA 5.697. Marichal 318.

2998   On the Labors of Hercules.   P. Tebt. 2.686 a, verso (II-III, Tebtunis; on the verso of No. 2938). Collart, PLL 44; Marichal 82.

2999    On Servius Tullius and his constitution. P. Oxy. 17.
2088 (II, Oxy.). Mallon, PR, pl. X.1. Collart,
PLL 71; Marichal 64. Calderini, PL 12; Cavenaile,
CPL 41. Archiv 10.236. M. A. Levi, Riv. Fil. 56
(1928) 511-15, favors the attribution to Fenestella
suggested by the editors; L. Castiglioni, BFC 35
(1929) 212-13, rejects Fenestella; A. Piganiol, Scritti Nogara 373-80, suggests L. Aelius Tubero; F.
M. Heichelheim, Aeg. 37 (1957) 250-58, favors
Cato, Origines.

3000    On Rome's Macedonian Wars. P. Oxy. 1.30; P. Lit.
Lond. 121 (Brit. Mus. inv. 745) (ca. A.D. 100, Oxy.;
parch. cod.). Bassi, MIG, No. 151, tav. LV; Kirchner, Scr. LL, tab. 4a; Lowe, CLA 2.207; Mallon,
EL, pl. 54; idem, PR, pl. X.2; Wessely, SALP,
Taf. 48. Collart, PLL 21; Marichal 302. Archiv
1.119-20. H. Diels, Sitzb. Berl. Akad., 1898, 497-
98, rejects Pompeius Trogus as the author, sees
hexameters, and suggests Ennius, Annales; J. Mallon, Emérita 17 (1949) 1-8, redates the text from
saec. III to ca. A.D. 100, observing that it is the
earliest known Latin manuscript in codex form.

3001    Fragments of triumphal (?) Fasti. BGU 7.1689 (P.
Berol. inv. 11596) (II-III, Philadelphia; opisthograph fr.). Collart, PLL 22; Marichal 295. Calderini, PL 13; Cavenaile, CPL 42.

3002    Unidentified prose (Seneca? Sallust?). A. Mariotti,
Athen. 35 (1947) 166-70 (Castello Sforzesco, Milano)
(II?, Fayum?). Marichal 293. Cavenaile, CPL 46.

3003    Latin-Greek glossary (in Latin characters). Wessely,
SALP, Taf. 20; P. Par. 4 bis (Musée du Louvre,
P. Eg. 2329) (IV-VI?; a separate leaf of papyrus).
Lowe, CLA 5.696 (bibl.: ibid., p. 63); Van Hoesen,
No. 81 (pp. 150-51). Collart, PLL 52; Marichal
181. Cavenaile, CPL 277.

3004    Latin-Greek glossary (in Greek characters): Names
of animals. A. Wifstrand, Årsb., Lund, 1934-35,
59-60 (P. Lund inv. 5) (II). Collart, PLL 50. Cavenaile, CPL 275. Archiv 13.130.

3005    Latin-Greek glossary (in Greek characters). P. Lond.
2.481; P. Lit. Lond. 187 (Brit. Mus. inv. 481) (IV;
opisthograph fr.). Perhaps "a vocabulary to some
particular literary work." Collart, PLL 53. Calderini, PL 15; Cavenaile, CPL 278. C. Haeberlin,
Berl. Phil. Woch. 19 (1899) 474-75.

3006    Latin-Greek glossary: Words in S-V. P. Collart,
Mél. Ernout 61-74 (P. Sorbonne inv. 2069) (III; on
the verso of accounts in Greek). Lowe, CLA 5.
698; Mallon, PR, pl. XVI.3. Collart, PLL 51;
Marichal 112. Cavenaile, CPL 276. Chr. Eg. 18
(1943) 161-62; L. Robert, Hellenica: Recueil d'
épigraphie ... 11-12 (1960) 5-15.

3007    Latin-Greek lexicon. M. Manfredi, SIFC, NS 27-28
(1956) 52-54 (PSI) (IV; pap. cod.?).

3008    Latin-Greek glossary. Lowe, CLA 5.699 (P. Sorbonne, inv. 2140) (V; pap. cod.). Cavenaile, CPL,
p. 439.

3009    Latin-Greek-Coptic manual of conversation. W.
Schubart, Klio 13 (1913) 27-38 (P. Berol. inv. 10582)
(VI; pap. cod.). Collart, PLL 60; Coptic Bibl.,
Nos. 1838-39. Cavenaile, CPL 281. G. Esau, Philol.
73 (1914) 157-58.

3010    Fable of the dog deceived by his reflection. P. Oxy.
11.1404 (Wellesley Coll.) (III, Oxy.; text incomplete; sch. ex.). A paraphrase of the same fable
as in Aesop 339, Phaedrus i.4, and Babrius 79.
Collart, PLL 18; Marichal 129. Cavenaile, CPL
38. Archiv 7.255.

3011    A declamation (?) in dialogue form. P. Hamb. 167
(inv. 80) (II-III). Lowe, CLA 8.1214. Cavenaile,
CPL 65. Archiv 16.129.

3012    Two Latin alphabets. Milne, Gr. Shorthand Man.
70 (P. Antin. inv. 1, fr. 1, verso) (IV-V, Antinoë).
Minuscules and rustic capitals. Mallon, PR, pl.
XXVIII.1. Collart, PLL 2; Marichal 307. Cavenaile, CPL 58. B. L. Ullman, AJP 56 (1935) 147-
48.

3013    Latin alphabet, with some Greek equivalents. P.
Oxy. 10.1315 (Cambridge Univ. Libr., add. 5902)
(V-VI, Oxy.). Van Hoesen, No. 83a (p. 156). Collart, PLL 3; Marichal 184, 311. Cavenaile, CPL
59.

3014    Writing exercise (?). P. Oxy. 10.1314 (Liverpool
Univ. Libr., Class. Gr. Libr. 428) (IV-V?, Oxy.;
sch. ex.?). Van Hoesen, No. 81b (p. 152). Collart, PLL 45; Marichal 166. Cavenaile, CPL 62.

3015    Writing exercise. P. Tebt. 2.686 b, verso (II-III,
Tebtunis; on the verso of No. 2938). Collart, PLL
44; Marichal 82.

3016    Writing exercise (?) and unidentified Greek literary
(?) text. PSI 13.1309 (V-VI, Oxy.; on the verso
of a document). Ed. pr.: M. Norsa, Papiri greci
delle collezioni Italiane 3 (Roma 1946) 41-42 and
tav. XXVI. Marichal 320. (Norsa and Marichal
seemingly err in giving PSI "1310.")

3017    Philosophy (?). P. Oxy. 6.871 (Princeton Univ. Libr.
CC.0174.6.871) (IV-V, Oxy.). Collart, PLL 43;
Marichal 308. Cavenaile, CPL 47. Archiv 6.268.

3018    Latin verse (?). P. Oxy. 6.872 (Muhlenberg Coll.)
(VI, Oxy.; parch. cod.). Collart, PLL 23. Cavenaile, CPL 12. A. Koerte, Archiv 6,267, notes
the possibility of Vergil, Aeneid vi.698-700, 711,
713, in the meager fragments on the verso.

3019    Unidentified. P. Aberdeen 129 (III, Fayum?). Ed.
pr.: E. O. Winstedt, CQ 1 (1907) 266. Lowe, CLA
2.119. Collart, PLL 24; Marichal 297. Cavenaile,
CPL 67.

3020    Unidentified. P. Aberdeen 131 (I, Fayum?). Ed. pr.:
E. O. Winstedt, CQ 1 (1907) 267. Collart, PLL 26;
Marichal 4. Cavenaile, CPL 66.

3021    Unidentified. P. Aberdeen 132 (III?, Fayum?). Ed.
pr.: E. O. Winstedt, CQ 1 (1907) 267. Collart, PLL
27; Marichal 299. Cavenaile, CPL 68.

3022    Unidentified.   P. Hawara, p. 36 (No. 19) (University
        Coll., London?) (I-II).  Marichal 290.

3023    Unidentified.    P. Mich. 7.430 (inv. 4385 + 4390) (ante
        A.D. 115, Karanis).  Marichal 28.  Cavenaile, CPL
        45.  Archiv 16.129.  J. F. Gilliam, AJP 71 (1950)
        432, suggests a collection of maxims; A. Vogliano,
        Prolegom. 1 (1952) 140-42.

3024    Unidentified (history?).    P. Ryl. 4.553 (III).  Cave-
        naile, CPL 44.

3025    Unidentified.   Mentioned by R. Marichal, Pauli Sent.
        Fr. Leid. 27 (P. Berol. inv. 11325) (V-VI?, Her-
        mupolis Magna; parch. cod.).  Lowe, CLA 8.1041
        (as of saec. IV).  Only a few letters.

3026    Unidentified.    Lowe, CLA 9.1342 (P. Monac. inv. Lat.
        1) (III, Abd-el-Nahab, Fayum).

Ausenda, G., "Contributo allo studio dell' omiletica cristiana nei papiri greci dell' Egitto, " Aegyptus 20 (1940) 43-47.

BKT 6 = C. Schmidt und W. Schubart, Berliner Klassikertexte, Heft 6: Altchristliche Texte. Berlin 1910.

Doutreleau, L., et J. Aucagne, "Que savons-nous aujourd'hui des papyrus de Toura?, " Recherches de science religieuse 43 (1955) 161-93 (inaccessible).

Guéraud, O., "Note préliminaire sur les papyrus d' Origène découverts à Toura, " Revue de l' histoire des religions 131 (1946) 85-108.

Harv. Theol. Rev. = Harvard Theological Review. Cambridge, Mass., 1908-.

Joly, R., Hermas: Le Pasteur. Paris 1958. (Sources chrétiennes 53; pp. 58-62: a list of the papyri).

Modena, L. G., "Il cristianesimo ad Ossirinco, " BSAA, NS 10, No. 33 (1939) 293-310 (pp. 307-10: "Elenco dei papiri letterari cristiani").

P. Rain. 4 = H. Gerstinger, Mitteilungen aus der Papyrussammlung der Nationalbibliothek in Wien: Papyrus Erzherzog Rainer, Neue Serie, Vierte Folge: Griechische literarische Papyri christlichen Inhaltes I. Baden bei Wien 1946.

Puech, H. -C., "Les nouveaux écrits d' Origène et de Didyme découverts à Toura, " Revue d' histoire et de philosophie religieuses 31 (1951) 293-329.

Vig. Chr. = Vigiliae Christianae: A Review of Early Christian Life and Language. Amsterdam 1947-.

Wessely, Patr. Or. = C. Wessely, "Les plus anciens monuments du christianisme écrits sur papyrus, " Patrologia Orientalis 4 (1908) 99-210, ibid. 18 (1924) 345-511. (Cited by volume and page.)

Whittaker, M., Der Hirt des Hermas. Berlin 1956. (Die griechischen christlichen Schriftsteller der ersten Jahrhunderte, Band 48; pp. XII-XVI: a list of the papyri).

1    ALEXANDER, Patriarch of Alexandria: A Paschal Epistle. BKT 6.55-109 (inv. 10677) (VIII, Sohag.

2    ARISTIDES: Apologia 5-6. P. Oxy. 15.1778 (IV, Oxy.; pap. cod.). Wessely, Patr. Or. 18.500-2.

3    --- Apologia 15.6 - 16.1. H. J. M. Milne, Journal of Theological Studies 25 (1923) 73-77; P. Lit. Lond. 223 (Brit. Mus. inv. 2486) (IV; from a pap. cod. containing also the Song of Solomon, P. Lit. Lond. 209). JEA 10.155, 11.90. G. Krüger, Theologische Literaturzeitung 49 (1924) 47-48, reprints the text.

4    St. ATHANASIUS: Epistula ad monachos. Mon. Epiphan. 2.585 (VI-VII?, Thebes; graffito).

5    St. BASIL of Caesarea: An anthology comprising Epistulae 5.77 E, 6.79 B, 243.432 B, 150.239 C, 2.72 A (Migne, Patrologia Graeca 32) BKT 6. 21-37 (inv. 6795) (V, Fayum; pap. cod.). H. Landwehr, Philol. 43 (1884) 110-36, ibid. 44 (1885) 19-21 (ed. pr.); F. Blass, Zeitschr. für ägyptische Sprache 18 (1880) 35; C. Haeberlin, Zentralblatt für Bibliothekswesen 14 (1897) 473-74.

6    --- Hexahemeron, Hom. ii.1 (Migne, PG 29.28-29). P. Rein. 2.62 (inv. 2131) (V; pap. cod.).

7    BASILIUS, Bishop of Seleucia: Hom. xxii (a fragment: Migne, PG 85.268). M. Naldini, Aeg. 38 (1958) 139-44 (PSI) (V-VI, Oxy.; on the verso of a blank sheet of pap.).

8    St. John CHRYSOSTOM: Homily on John xxix.2 (Migne, PG 59.169). P. Rain. 4.54 (inv. 26132 B) (VI, Fayum; opisthograph leaf of pap.).

9    --- Ps.-Chrysostom: In decollationem Praecursoris (Migne, PG 59.487 ff.). P. Oxy. 13.1603 (John Rylands Libr., R. 55247) (V-VI, Oxy.). Originally edited as a "Homily Concerning Women"; identified by A. Castiglioni, Rend. Ist. Lomb. 52 (1919) 292-96, and R. Harris, Bull. Ryl. Libr. 5 (1919) 386-87 (giving a revised text by B. P. Grenfell). JAW 230.246; JEA 8.90. S. Mercati, Biblica 2 (1921) 229-39, also revises the text.

10    CLEMENT of Alexandria (?): Praedicatio prophetica (?). H. A. Sanders and C. Schmidt, The Minor Prophets in the Freer Collection and the Berlin Fragment of Genesis (Ann Arbor 1927; University of Michigan, Humanistic Series 21) 228-29 ("Washington MS. V, " Freer Collection, Smithsonian Institution) (III; pap. cod.). H. S. J. Thackeray, Journ. of Theol. Studies 30 (1929) 179-90, proposes the attribution.

11    St. CLEMENT of Rome (?): A patristic (?) fragment. M. Naldini, SIFC, NS 33 (1961) 212 (PSI) (IV). A fragment quoting Ezechiel xxxiii.11, xviii.23.

12    CONSTITUTIONES APOSTOLICAE viii.12.6-7. Wessely, Patr. Or. 18.434-35 (P. Rain. inv. 19937) (VI; six small frr.). G. Mercati, Aeg. 8 (1927) 40-42, identifies the three contiguous fragments and attributes the passage to the liturgy of Clement of Rome.

13    CYRIL of Alexandria: De adoratione et cultu in spiritu et veritate, Bks. vii-ix (Migne, PG 68.520 B — 597 B). J. H. Bernard, Transactions of the Royal Irish Academy 29 (1892) 653-72; D. Serruys, Rev. Phil. 34 (1910) 101-17 (Musée du Louvre, inv. E. 10295); P. Rain. 4.53 (inv. 19899-19908) (VI-VII, Fayum; pap. cod.: 10 leaves in Dublin, 38 in Paris, 5 in Vienna). C. Haeberlin, Zentralbl. Bibliotheksw. 14 (1897) 476-77.

14    --- Duodecim anathemata 1-3, 6-8. Mon. Epiphan. 2.586 (VI-VII?, Thebes; graffito).

15    --- An unallocated fragment. Mentioned by D. Serruys, Rev. Phil. 34 (1910) 102, and H. Gerstinger, P. Rain. 4, p. 111 (P. Rain. inv. 19913) (VI; parch. cod.).

16    --- Cyril (?): An apologetic fragment. J. W. B. Barns, CQ 43 (1949) 5-8 ("P. Johnson, " Egypt Exploration Soc.) (VIII, Arsinoïte nome; parch. cod.).

17 Johannes DAMASCENUS: Easter Canon, in verse
(Migne, PG 96.840). BKT 6.119-20 (inv. 9051)
(X; double leaf from a paper cod.).

18 DIDACHE (The Teachings of the Apostles) 1.3b-4a,
2.7b — 3.2a. P. Oxy. 15.1782 (IV, Oxy.; parch.
cod.). J.-P. Audet, La Didachè: Instructions des
Apôtres (Paris 1958) 26-28, describes and reprints
the text.

19 DIDYMUS the Blind: Commentary on the Psalms.
Mentioned by L. Koenen, Archiv 17 (1960) 61, note
1 (Brit. Mus. inv. 2921 A-C) (V-VI, Tura; 10 leaves
from the pap. cod. containing the Commentary on
Zachariah: see No. 20).

20 --- Commentary on Zachariah. L. Doutreleau,
Didyme l' Aveugle: Sur Zacharie, Tomes 1-3 (Paris
1962), especially 1, pp. 139-65 (VI-VII, Tura; 204
written pages from a pap. cod. in the Cairo Mus.).
According to the editor, 202 pages of the same codex
are in other collections (cf. Nos. 19, 21).

21 --- Commentary on Zachariah ix.11, 16. L. Koenen,
Archiv 17 (1960) 61-105 (Univ.-Bibl., Köln) (V-VI,
Tura; a double leaf from the pap. cod. in the Cairo
Mus.: cf. No. 20).

22 --- Didymus (or Origen?): A Christological fragment.
P. Iand. 5.69 (inv. 272) (IV; pap. cod.).

23 St. EPHRAEM: Lives of Saints Abraham and Theodora.
K. Wessely, WS 11 (1889) 177-91 (Musée du Louvre,
inv. 7404-5, 7408) (VI, Fayum; pap. cod.). C.
Haeberlin, Zentralbl. Bibliotheksw. 14 (1897) 475.

24 --- In pulcherrimum Joseph (in verse). B. de Mont-
faucon, Palaeographica Graeca, p. 214 (facsimile)
(VI-VII?; 5 frr., from a pap. cod., once attached
to the spine of a Ms. of Commentarii in Iob). JEA
8.90. Identified by S. G. Mercati, Biblica 1 (1920)
371-75; idem, Chr. Ég. 7 (1932) 190-91.

25 EUSEBIUS: Epistula ad Carpianum; Canones Evangelici.
Mon. Epiphan. 2.584 (VI-VII?, Thebes; pap. cod.).

26 GREGORY of Nazianzus: De moderatione in disputando,
Or. xxxii.29, 33 (Migne, PG 36.208 B, 212 B).
PSI 5.550 (IX-X; parch. cod., with a Coptic text
written across the Greek on the verso).

27 --- Epistulae 80 (84), 90 (41) (Migne, PG 37.153, 164).
H. Gerstinger, Sitzb. Wien. Akad., 1928, Abh. 3,
pp. 87-91 (P. Rain. inv. 29788 A-C) (V-VI; from
the pap. cod. of Pamprepius: see No. 1334 above).
JEA 16.125.

28 GREGORY of Nyssa: Anthology from the Vita Mosis,
i.344 C ff. (Migne, PG 44). BKT 6.38-54 (inv.
5863) (V, Fayum; pap. cod.). H. Landwehr,
Philol. 44 (1885) 1-19 (ed. pr.); C. Haeberlin,
Zentralbl. Bibliotheksw. 14 (1897) 474-75; J. Dani-
élou, Grégoire de Nysse: La vie de Moïse (Paris
1955), p. XXXII.

Heracleon: see No. 60.

29 HERMAE PASTOR: Fragments of Visions i, iii,
Mandates xii, Similitudes ix. P. Amh. 2.190 (VI;
pap. cod.). Wessely, Patr. Or. 18.472-77.

30 --- Visions v.5.7. P. Harris 128 (V; pap. cod.).

31 --- Mandates ii.6 - iii.1. C. Bonner, A Papyrus
Codex of the Shepherd of Hermas (Ann Arbor 1934)
129-36 (P. Mich. inv. 44-H) (II, Fayum; on the
verso of a document). C. Bonner, Harv. Theol.
Rev. 20 (1927) 105-16 (ed. pr.).

32 --- Mandates ix.2-4. P. Oxy. 15.1783 (Glasgow
Univ. Libr.) (IV, Oxy.; parch. leaf, palimpsest).
Wessely, Patr. Or. 18.503-4.

33 --- Mandates xi.9-10. P. Oxy. 1.5 (Bodleian Libr.,
Gr. theol. f.9 (P)) (III-IV, Oxy.; pap. cod.).
Headed in P. Oxy., "Early Christian Fragment."

34 --- Fragments of Similitudes ii-ix. C. Bonner, A
Papyrus Codex of the Shepherd of Hermas (Ann
Arbor 1934) (P. Mich. inv. 917) (III, Theadelphia?;
pap. cod.). C. Bonner, Harv. Theol. Rev. 18
(1925) 115-27 (preliminary notice). JEA 22.66. M.
Whittaker, Der Hirt des Hermas (Berlin 1956), pp.
XII-XIV, describes the codex; R. Joly, Hermas:
Le Pasteur (Paris 1958) 59-62 (ditto).

35 --- Similitudes ii.4-10. P. Oxy. 9.1172; P. Lit.
Lond. 224 (Brit. Mus. inv. 2067) (IV, Oxy.; pap.
cod.). Wessely, Patr. Or. 18.477-79.

36 --- Similitudes ii.7-10, iv.2-5, viii.1-12. BKT 6.
13-17 (inv. 5513) (III). Edd. pr.: H. Diels and A.
Harnack, Sitzb. Berl. Akad., 1891, 427-31; A.
Ehrhard, Tüb. Theol. Quartalschr. 74 (1892) 294-
303. C. Haeberlin, Zentralbl. Bibliotheksw. 14
(1897) 411-12; Wessely, Patr. Or. 18.468-71.
Wilcken, TAGP, Taf. 3 (merely as a Christian
text).

37 --- Similitudes iv.6-7, v.1.1-5. K. Schmidt and
W. Schubart, Sitzb. Berl. Akad. 42 (1909) 1077-81
(P. Hamb. inv. 24) (IV-V; parch. cod.). Wessely,
Patr. Or. 18.479-81.

38 --- Similitudes v.1.5-2.2, 2.4-6. O. Stegmüller,
Aeg. 17 (1937) 456-59 (P. Berol. inv. 13272) (IV,
Hermupolis Magna; parch. leaf).

39 --- Similitudes vi.5.3, 5. P. Oxy. 15.1828 (III, Oxy.;
parch. leaf). First published as an "ethical" fragment, identified by S. Mercati, Biblica 6 (1925)
336-38. Archiv 7.156.

40 --- Similitudes viii.1.1-12. BKT 6.17-20 (inv. 6789)
(VI; pap. cod.). Wessely, Patr. Or. 18.471-72.

41 --- Similitudes viii.6.4 - 8.3. P. Oxy. 13.1599;
P. Lit. Lond. 225 (Brit. Mus. inv. 2467) (IV, Oxy.;
pap. cod.). Wessely, Patr. Or. 18.504-6.

42 --- Similitudes x.3.3 - 4.3. P. Oxy. 3.404 (Bodleian Libr., Gr. theol. f.10 (P)) (III-IV, Oxy.;
pap. cod.). Wessely, Patr. Or. 4.195-98, 18.468.

43    IGNATIUS of Antioch: Epistula ad Smyrnaeos 3 - 12. BKT 6.1-12 (inv. 10581) (V; pap. cod.).

44    IRENAEUS: Contra Haereses iii. 9.   P. Oxy. 3.405 (Cambridge Univ. Libr., Add. 4413) (cf. P. Oxy. 4, pp. 264-65) (II-III, Oxy.). Identified by J. A. Robinson. Wessely, Patr. Or. 4.200-1.

45    --- Ibid. v. 3.2 - 13.1.   H. Lietzmann, Gött. Nachr., 1912, 291-320 (Philologisches Seminar der Univ. Jena) (IV). JEA 1.54.

       Julius Africanus: see No. 53 above, though it is hardly patristic.

46    MELITO, Bishop of Sardis: Homily on the Passion. F. G. Kenyon, The Chester Beatty Biblical Papyri, fasc. 1 (London 1933), p. 9 (described as a "Christian homily"), ibid., fasc. 8 (1941; facsimiles) (P. Chester Beatty XII); C. Bonner, The Homily on the Passion, by Melito, Bishop of Sardis ... (Studies and Documents edited by Kirsopp and Silva Lake, 12, London and Philadelphia 1940) (P. Mich. inv. 5553) (IV, Fayum; pap. cod.). C. Bonner, Mél. Franz Cumont (Bruxelles 1936) 107-19, and Actes Pap. V, 94-97, writes prolegomena to his edition; idem, Harv. Theol. Rev. 31 (1938) 175-90; M. Rist, ibid. 249-50; G. Zuntz, ibid. 36 (1943) 299-315; C. Bonner, ibid. 317-19; A. Wifstrand, Vig. Chr. 2 (1948) 219-23, and C. Bonner, ibid. 3 (1949) 184-85, on textual points; B. Lohse, Die Passa-Homilie des Bischofs Melito von Sardes (Leiden 1958; bibl., p. 8); idem, Meliton von Sardes, Vom Passa: Die älteste christliche Osterpredigt (Freiburg im Breisgau 1963; translation, introduction, and commentary).

47    --- Ibid. 57-63.   P. Oxy. 13.1600 (Bodleian Libr., Gr. theol. d. 4 (P)) (V, Oxy.; pap. cod.). Identified by C. Bonner, Actes Pap. V, 94-97 (formerly attributed to Hippolytus).

48    --- Ibid. 6 - end, with a colophon. M. Testuz, Papyrus Bodmer XIII: Méliton de Sardes, Homélie sur la Pâque (Cologny-Gèneve 1960) (III-IV; from a pap. cod. of miscellaneous contents, including Phileas, Apologia: see Testuz, Papyrus Bodmer VII-IX, 1959, p. 8).

49    --- De veritate (?).   P. Oxy. 2074 (V, Oxy.; pap. cod.). Edited as an "Apostrophe to Wisdom (?)"; attributed to Melito by C. Bonner, Studies and Documents edited by Kirsopp and Silva Lake, 12 (1940) 50-55.

50    From a Life of St. NEPHON. A. Deissmann und P. Maas, Aeg. 13 (1933) 11-20 (XI-XII; pap. cod.). Identified by S. G. Mercati, Aeg. 21 (1941) 55-92, as the papyrus formerly belonging to L. Lambruschini of Florence (now "P. Fitzroy Fenwick," Cheltenham) and as a part of the as yet unedited Life of St. Nephon.

51    ORIGEN: Commentary on Genesis i. 28. P. Giss. 2.17 (inv. 30) (ca. A.D. 300, Hermupolis Magna; pap. cod.). Gundel 34. A. Puech, BAGB 22 (Jan. 1929) 24-29.

52    --- Commentary on Genesis iii. 11-15. P. Rain. 4. 51 (inv. 29829 + 29883) (IV-V; from the same pap. cod. as P. Rain. 4.52: see No. 59 below).

53    --- Commentary on Exodus xii. 1-11. Described by O. Guéraud, Rev. de l'hist. des religions 131 (1946) 93-94 (VII, Tura; pap. cod.). H.-C. Puech, Rev. d'hist. et de philos. rel. 31 (1951) 307-8 (description); O. Guéraud, JEA 40 (1954) 63-67, gives a preliminary notice, and studies borrowings made by Procopius of Gaza.

54    --- Homily on I Kings (Samuel). O. Guéraud, Rev. de l'hist. des religions 131 (1946) 98-108, gives the ed. pr. (VI-VII, Tura; pap. cod.). H.-C. Puech, Rev. d'hist. et de philos. rel. 31 (1951) 311.

55    --- Fragments of Homilies on Luke (Homil. xxxv) and Matthew (Homil. xxv?). P. Bon. 1.1 (inv. 12) (III; pap. cod.). Edd. pr.: A. Vogliano, Byz. neugr. Jahrb. 15 (1939) 130-36; idem, Acme 1 (1948) 217-25; G. B. Pighi, Vig. Chr. 2 (1948) 109-12. R. M. Grant, Vig. Chr. 2 (1948) 161-62, identifies the text as by Origen.

56    --- Commentary on Ep. ad Romanos iii. 5 - v. 7. J. Scherer, Le commentaire d'Origène sur Rom. III, 5 — V, 7... (Le Caire 1957; Inst. Fr. d'Arch. Or., Bibliothèque d'étude 27) (Cairo Mus., inv. 88748) (VII, Tura; from the same pap. cod. as Nos. 54, 57). O. Guéraud, Rev. de l'hist. des religions 131 (1946) 95-96 (description); H.-C. Puech, Rev. d'hist. et de philos. rel. 31 (1951) 308-10 (ditto); H. Chadwick, Journ. of Theological Studies 10 (1959) 10-42.

57    --- Contra Celsum, Bks. i-ii (extracts). J. Scherer, Extraits des Livres I et II du Contre Celse d'Origène ... (Le Caire 1956; Inst. Fr. d'Arch. Or., Bibliothèque d'étude 28) (Cairo Mus., inv. 88747) (VII, Tura; from the same pap. cod. as Nos. 54, 56). H.-C. Puech, Rev. d'hist. et de philos. rel. 31 (1951) 310-11 (description); H. Chadwick, Origen: Contra Celsum (Cambridge 1953), p. XXX (brief mention); C. Préaux, Chr. Ég. 32 (1957) 352-54.

58    --- Dialogus ad Heraclidem. J. Scherer, Entretien d'Origène avec Héraclide ..., Publications de la Société Fouad I de Papyrologie, Textes et documents 9 (Le Caire 1949) (Cairo Mus., inv. 88745) (VI-VII, Tura; pap. cod.). O. Guéraud, Rev. de l'hist. des religions 131 (1946) 92-93 (description); H.-C. Puech, Rev. d'hist. et de philos. rel. 31 (1951) 300-7 (ditto); L. Fruechtel, Theologische Literaturzeitung 75 (1950) 504-6; H.-C. Puech and P. Hadot, Vig. Chr. 13 (1959) 204-34; J. Scherer, Entretien d'Origène avec Héraclide (Paris 1960; Sources Chrétiennes 67; bibl.).

59    --- Fragments of a homily or an epistle. P. Rain. 4.52 (inv. 29832) (IV-V; from the same pap. cod. as P. Rain. 4.51: see No. 52 above). Addressed to women: perhaps the Exhortatoria ad Pioniam.

60    --- Origen (or Heracleon?): Fragments of a commentary. H. I. Bell and T. C. Skeat, Fragments of an Unknown Gospel (London 1935) 42-51 ("P. Egerton 3," Brit. Mus.) (III; pap. cod.). First

published as "Fragments of a Gospel Commentary (?)"; R. M. Grant, Vig. Chr. 2 (1948) 243-47, proposes Origen as the author; R. Leaney, ibid. 9 (1955) 212-17, and H. Chadwick, Harv. Theol. Rev. 49 (1956) 145-51, support this attribution.

61 --- Origen (?): Fragment of a homily. P. Bouriant 3 (inv. 38) (V, Alexandria?). Attributed to Origen by G. Ausenda, Aeg. 20 (1940) 44.

Origen: see also No. 22.

62 St. ROMANUS: De tribus SS. pueris in fornace (in verse). P. Rain. 3.41 (inv. 29430) (cf. ibid. 4, p. 137) (V; pap. cod.). Identified by P. Maas, Byz. 14 (1939) 381.

63 TATIAN: Diatessaron (a fragment). P. Dura 10 (inv. 24) (III, Dura, Mesopotamia; parch. roll). Ed. pr.: C. H. Kraeling, A Greek Fragment of Tatian's Diatessaron from Dura (Studies and Documents edited by Kirsopp and Silva Lake, 3; London 1935). Roberts, GLH, pl. 21b. M. J. Lagrange, Rev. Biblique 44 (1935) 321-27; H. Lietzmann, Zeitschr. fur die Neutestamentl. Wiss. 34 (1935) 291-93; A. Baumstark, Oriens Christianus, Ser. 3.10 (1935) 244-52, gives the text; A. Merk, Biblica 17 (1936) 234-41.

64 --- Fragment of the Diatessaron (or of a "wild" text of Matthew?). O. Stegmüller, Zeitschr. für die Neutestamentl. Wiss. 37 (1938) 223-29 (P. Berol. inv. 16388) (V-VI; pap. cod.). A. Baumstark, Oriens Christianus, Ser. 3.14 (1939) 111-15; C. Peters, Biblica 21 (1940) 51-55, prefers to think of a text of Matthew influenced by Tatian (cf. ibid. 23, 1942, 68-77).

UNIDENTIFIED and apparently unattributed fragments of homilies or other possibly patristic texts include:
P. Oxy. 3.406, 13.1601, 15.1785, 17.2072-73;
P. Rain. 4.55-60;
P. Rein. 2.64;
H. A. Musurillo, Aeg. 33 (1953) 179-80 (Bodleian Libr., Gr. theol. e.2 (P)
M. Naldini, Aeg. 38 (1958) 144-46 (PSI);
C. H. Roberts, Zeitschr. für die Neutestamentl. Wiss. 37 (1938) 184-85 (Ashmolean Mus. inv. 2).
Nos. 10, 11, 15, 16, 22, 49, 60, 61 in the list above appear to be attributed but not definitely identified.

## NOTE

The following references were collected too late to be included in the List.

An entry number, if not followed by a letter, corresponds to the same number in the List and introduces an addendum to the original entry under that number.

An entry number followed by a letter records a new text, not included in the List, and serves to indicate the point at which that text might have been inserted.

## BIBLIOGRAPHY

Dain, A., "La survie de Ménandre," Maia, NS 15 (1963) 278-309.

Jory, E. J., "'Algebraic' Notation in Dramatic Texts," BICSL 10 (1963) 65-78 (especially 65-67, on papyrus texts).

Lesky, A., Geschichte der griechischen Literatur. Zweite, neu bearbeitete und erweiterte Auflage, Bern u. München 1963. (This revised edition, though not cited here, contains new and valuable bibliographical data.)

Masson = O. Masson, Les Fragments du poète Hipponax. Paris 1962. (Etudes et commentaires 43).

## GREEK

24    Aeschylus. M. L. Cunningham, Rh. Mus. 105 (1962) 189-90, defends the attribution to the Aegyptioi.

50    Aesop. B. E. Perry, TAPA 93 (1962) 315.

82    Alcman. M. L. West, CQ, NS 13 (1963) 154-56.

86    Anacreon. B. Gentili, Maia, NS 15 (1963) 317-21, on the meter.

87    --- J. A. S. Evans, SO 38 (1963) 22-24.

149    Aristophanes. Pasquali, Stor. Testo 198.

186    Callimachus. A. Barigazzi, Rh. Mus. 106 (1963) 214-29, reedits the poem on astronomy quoted in the text.

200    --- L. Pearson, The Local Historians of Attica (Philadelphia 1942) 60, 65, on the citation of Clidemus.

215    --- B. E. Perry, TAPA 93 (1962) 312-13, on the Aesopic fable in Iambus 2, possibly from the collection made by Demetrius of Phalerum.

308    Demosthenes. M. Naoumides, TAPA 93 (1962) 240-43.

391    Euripides. K. Alt, Philol. 107 (1963) 179-81.

432    --- D. Lanza, SIFC, NS 34 (1963) 230-45, on the double chorus.

434    --- P. Hamb. 118 a is from the Archelaüs. H. Lloyd-Jones ap. G. W. Bond, Euripides: Hypsipyle (Oxford 1963) 157-60, attributes 118 b to the prologue to the Hypsipyle and conjectures that the text is a Euripidean anthology (cf. No. 426). W. S. Barrett, ibid. 160, notes that the meager remains of 118 b, col. i, may coincide with Hecuba 28-44.

436    --- H. Lloyd-Jones, Gnomon 35 (1963) 444-46; E. G. Turner, Ant. Class. 32 (1963) 122-27.

438    --- G. W. Bond, Euripides: Hypsipyle (Oxford 1963: text, facsimile, commentary, bibl.).

439    --- G. W. Bond, op. cit. (see No. 438) 40.

440    --- G. W. Bond, op. cit. (see No. 438) 140, reports that this is in Trinity College, Dublin (inv. 193) rather than the British Museum, and that it does not belong to the same papyrus as P. Petrie 2.49 (c) (see No. 439).

443    --- H. Lloyd-Jones, Gnomon 35 (1963) 446-47.

446    --- H. J. Mette, Mus. Helv. 21 (1964) 71-72, restores the text.

451    --- H. Lloyd-Jones, Gnomon 35 (1963) 447-49.

453    --- G. W. Bond, op. cit. (see No. 438) 21-22, reedits the hypothesis to the Hypsipyla; H. Lloyd-Jones, Gnomon 35 (1963) 439-43; B. Snell, Hermes 91 (1963) 495, on the restoration in fr. 19 of a line from the satyr play Busiris.

454    --- H. Lloyd-Jones, Gnomon 35 (1963) 443-44.

459    Hellanicus. L. Pearson, Early Ionian Historians (Oxford 1939) 177-78, queries the attribution.

485    Herondas. A. P. Smotrytsch, Philol. 107 (1963) 315-16, on Mime iii. 50-52.

510    Hesiod. Nos. 510 and 511 are evidently from the same papyrus: see P. Oxy. 28, p. 60.

510a    Hesiod: Catalogus (Mestra, etc.); Ceÿcis Nuptiae; and other pieces (?). P. Oxy. 28.2495 (cf. ibid., p. 44) (II, Oxy.). M. West, Gnomon 35 (1963) 754-57.

514    --- P. Oxy. 28, p. 82 (an addendum on Nos. 514-15).

516     --- P. Oxy. 28, p. 7 (an addendum).

516a     --- Catalogus (Nestor and his sons; The descendants of Leda, Althaea, Hypermestra, and Stratonice). P. Oxy. 28.2481 (cf. ibid., p. 26) (II, Oxy.). By the same copyist as PSI 1301 (see No. 513). M. West, Gnomon 35 (1963) 755.

516b     --- Ibid. P. Oxy. 28.2482 (II, Oxy.). Parts of six lines overlapping No. 516a.

516c     --- Ibid. (Heracles). P. Oxy. 28.2493 (III, Oxy.). M. West, Gnomon 35 (1963) 756.

519a     --- Ibid. (The suitors of Helen). P. Oxy. 28.2491 (II, Oxy.). Overlaps Merkelbach, fr. G 3. M. West, Gnomon 35 (1963) 756.

519b     --- Ibid. (The suitors of Helen). P. Oxy. 28.2492 (III, Oxy.). Overlaps Merkelbach, fr. G 5.

520     --- Ibid. K. Stiewe, Philol. 107 (1963) 1-20.

525     --- Ibid. E. Schwentner, Zeitschr. Vergl. Spr. 77 (1961) 111.

528a     --- Ibid. (The daughters of Proetus; Atalanta). P. Oxy. 28.2488 A-B (II-III, Oxy.; on the verso of an unidentifiable text). 2488 B overlaps Merkelbach, fr. Q (see No. 529).

528b     --- Ibid. (Descendants of Danaüs, including Perseus and the daughters of Proetus). P. Oxy. 28.2487 (III, Oxy.). M. West, Gnomon 35 (1963) 756.

533a     --- Ibid. (Ceÿx and Alcyone; Coronis). P. Oxy. 28.2483 and 2490 (= fr. 3 of the same pap.) (II, Oxy.). M. West, Gnomon 35 (1963) 755-56.

533b     --- Ibid. (two small frr.). P. Oxy. 28.2484 (II, Oxy.).

533c     --- Ibid. (Salmoneus and Tyro; Neleus and his descendants; Periclymenus and Heracles). P. Oxy. 28.2485 (III, Oxy.; 3-4 frr. from at least two different rolls). M. West, Gnomon 35 (1963) 756.

533d     --- Ibid. P. Oxy. 28.2486 (II, Oxy.). Parts of the same verses as in P. Oxy. 2485, fr. 2 (see No. 533c).

533e     --- Ibid. (Cyrene, etc.). P. Oxy. 28.2489 (II, Oxy.).

533f     --- Ibid. (Aerope, etc.); Scutum 1-18. P. Oxy. 28.2494 A-B (II, Oxy.). M. West, Gnomon 35 (1963) 756.

533g     --- Ibid. ? (Iasion). P. Oxy. 28.2496 (I, Oxy.). Meager frr. of the same lines as in No. 533h.

533h     --- Ibid.? (Iasion). P. Oxy. 28.2497 (II, Oxy.). Parts of the same text as in No. 533g. M. West, Gnomon 35 (1963) 757.

533i     --- Ibid. (Melampodia?). P. Oxy. 28.2500 (III, Oxy.). M. West, Gnomon 35 (1963) 757.

533j     --- Ibid. (Descendants of Melampus). P. Oxy. 28.2501 (III, Oxy.; on the verso of a document). The editor (p. 75) conjectures that this may belong to the same papyrus as Merkelbach, fr. I (see No. 521). M. West, Gnomon 35 (1963) 757.

533k     --- Hesiod (?): Catalogus (?). P. Oxy. 28.2502 (I, Oxy.). M. West, Gnomon 35 (1963) 757.

533 l     --- Hesiod (?): Catalogus (?). P. Oxy. 28.2503 (II?, Oxy.). M. West, Gnomon 35 (1963) 758.

533m     --- Catalogus. P. Oxy. 28.2504 (II, Oxy.). The same lines as Merkelbach, fr. H, 90-93.

533n     --- Hesiod (?): Catalogus (?). P. Oxy. 28.2505 (III-IV, Oxy.). Parts of six lines.

535a     --- Megalai Eoiai (Polycreion and Euaechme). P. Oxy. 28.2498 (II, Oxy.). M. West, Gnomon 35 (1963) 757.

535b     --- Hesiod (?): Megalai Eoiai (?). P. Oxy. 28.2499 (II, Oxy.). Parts of 8 lines.

547     Hipponax. Masson, frr. 70-101.

548     --- Masson, frr. 102-14.

549     --- Masson, fr. 92.

550     --- Masson, fr. 95.

551     --- Masson, fr. 118.

636a     Homer: Iliad ii.137-44. H. Hunger, WS 76 (1963) 159-60 (P. Vindob. inv. Gr. 39839) (I).

705a     --- iv.1-6. S. Daris, Aeg. 42 (1962) 115-19 (the editor's collection, Milano, inv. 19) (I).

769a     --- v.891-96. H. Hunger, WS 76 (1963) 160 (P. Vindob. inv. Gr. 39833) (II).

827a     --- viii. 262, 266-68, 292-314. S. Daris, Aeg. 42 (1962) 119-22 (the editor's collection, Milano, inv. 8) (III).

849a     --- ix.486-99. H. Hunger, WS 76 (1963) 160 (P. Vindob. inv. Gr. 39835) (II).

943     --- Arch. Bibliogr., loc. cit., gives 26725 as the inv. number, while P. Rain. 3.2 has 26742. Is this a slip or are there two distinct papyri in question?

970a     --- xx.86-100. H. Hunger, WS 76 (1963) 161 (P. Vindob. inv. Gr. 39701) (ca. A.D. 100).

987a     --- xxii.27-38. H. Hunger, WS 76 (1963) 161-62 (P. Vindob. inv. Gr. 31936) (III; on the verso of a pap. with blank recto).

1217     --- Homerica. M. Naoumides, TAPA 93 (1962) 243-47, restores the names of the grammarians Comanus (line 8) and Crates (line 18).

1295a     Manetho: Apotelesmata. Mentioned by Neugebauer-
          Van Hoesen, Astrol. Pap. Ostr., No. 125 (II, Oxy.;
          on the verso is an astrological treatise, saec. III-
          IV). To appear in P. Oxy.

1298      Menander: Dyscolus. W. Peek, Wissenschaftliche
          Zeitschr. der Martin Luther Univ., Halle-
          Wittenberg, Gesellschafts- u. sprachwissenschaft-
          liche Reihe 8 (1958-59) 1201-17; J. H. Quincey, W.
          Ritchie, G. P. Shipp, and A. P. Treweek, Aus-
          tralian Humanities Research Council, Occasional
          Paper No. 2 (Adelaide 1959); S. Eitrem, SO 38
          (1963) 120-21. On the fragments of the Samia and
          the Aspis from the same papyrus, see A. Dain,
          Maia, NS 15 (1963) 287-89; V. Martin, Script. 14
          (1960) 3, note 2, evidently refers to the fr. of the
          Aspis on the verso of the last leaf.

1300      --- A. Dain, Maia, NS 15 (1963) 290.

1301      --- A. Dain, Maia, NS 15 (1963) 294, 308.

1303      --- A. Dain, Maia, NS 15 (1963) 289.

1318      --- A. Dain, Maia, NS 15 (1963) 293-94, reports that
          this has been identified as from the Aspis.

1320      --- A. Dain, Maia, NS 15 (1963) 280.

1320a     --- Thressa. P. Oxy. inedita (?). Mentioned by
          A. Dain, Maia, NS 15 (1963) 290; to be published
          by E. G. Turner.

1321      --- A. Dain, Maia, NS 15 (1963) 283.

1339      Pherecydes. M. L. West, CQ, NS 13 (1963) 157-72.

1369      Pindar. M. Treu, Rh. Mus. 106 (1963) 200-11.

1457      Satyrus. H. Lloyd-Jones, Gnomon 35 (1963) 453-54.

1479      Sophocles. H. Lloyd-Jones, Gnomon 35 (1963) 434-36,
          queries the attribution.

1486      Stesichorus. R. Merkelbach, Maia, NS 15 (1963)
          165-66, on the meter.

1647      Comedy. A. Dain, Maia, NS 15 (1963) 279, reports
          that this has recently been identified as from
          Menander, Sicyonii.

1656      Comedy. New fragments of this papyrus, to be pub-
          lished in Recherches Pap. 3, show that it belongs
          to Menander, Sicyonii; see A. Dain, Maia, NS 15
          (1963) 279-80. Over 400 lines of the play now sur-
          vive; described in "Life" (a popular American
          periodical), November 15, 1963, pp. 65-68.

1657      Comedy. A. Dain, Maia, NS 15 (1963) 280.

1659      Comedy. A. Dain, Maia, NS 15 (1963) 293.

1711      Tragedy. H. Lloyd-Jones, Gnomon 35 (1963) 438-39.

1739      Satyr play. H. Lloyd-Jones, Gnomon 35 (1963) 436-
          38, on P. Oxy. 2453.

1840      Epic. The citation of Hipponax: Masson, fr. 148 b.

1875a     Didactic poetry. An astrological poem (?). P.
          Schubart, p. 37 (with P. Schubart 16: see No.
          1768) (VI). Neugebauer-Van Hoesen, Astrol. Pap.
          Ostr., No. 107 ("could not be found in the Berlin
          collection.").

1887a     Gnomic verses. M. Papathomopoulos, Recherches
          Pap. 2 (1962) 113-16 (PIFAO inv. 172) (IV; a se-
          parate leaf of pap.). Lines 4-7 resemble Euri-
          pides, Medea 14-15.

1895      Lyric ("Strassburg Epodes"). Masson, frr. 115-17.

2066a     Astrology: A "horoscopic gnomon." Mentioned by
          Neugebauer-Van Hoesen, Astrol. Pap. Ostr., No.
          102 (III, Antinoöpolis). To appear in P. Antin. 3.

2066b     Astrology: Excerpts concerning aspects; character
          of zodiacal signs. Mentioned by Neugebauer-
          Van Hoesen, Astrol. Pap. Ostr., No. 103 (IV,
          Antinoöpolis; on the verso of an account). To
          appear in P. Antin. 3.

2066c     Astrology: A treatise. Mentioned by Neugebauer-
          Van Hoesen, Astrol. Pap. Ostr., No. 139 (I-II).
          To appear as PSI 15.1494.

2066d     Astrology: A fragment. Mentioned by Neugebauer-
          Van Hoesen, Astrol. Pap. Ostr., No. 140 (III).
          To appear as PSI 15.1495.

2103      Dialogue. W. Morel, Gymnas. 70 (1963) 545-47.

2131      Glossary. The quotation from Hipponax: Masson,
          fr. 49.

2309      Mathematics. F. E. Robbins, Isis 22 (1934-35) 95-
          103 (first description).

2322      Mathematics. H. Gerstinger, FF 9 (1933) 142-43.

2440      Music. E. K. Borthwick, AJP 84 (1963) 225-43, dis-
          cusses a possible allusion to a fertility super-
          stition.

2465a     Religion: Commentary on the Orphic Theogony.
          S. G. Kapsomenos, Gnomon 35 (1963) 222-23,
          gives a preliminary notice (ca. 350 B.C., Derveni,
          near Thessalonica!). To be published in full by
          Kapsomenos and K. Tsantsanoglu.

2499      Oratory. H. Lloyd-Jones, Gnomon 35 (1963) 450-53.

2576      Philosophy. W. Schmid, Rh. Mus. 105 (1962) 368-76.

2659a     Writing exercise (or account?). P. Mur. 122 and pl.
          XCIII (?, Murabba'at, Judaea; pap.).

2759      Shorthand. A. Dain, Maia, NS 15 (1963) 286, on the
          list of Menander's plays.

2779a     Shorthand: A document written in Greek shorthand.
          P. Mur. 164 and pll. CIII-CV (II, Murabba'at,
          Judaea; two pieces of leather joined to form a
          sack).

2850a     Unidentified prose (history? philosophy?). P. Mur.
          109 and pl. LXXXII (I-II, Murabba'at, Judaea;
          pap.; No. 2850b is on the verso).

2850b   Unidentified prose (literary?).   P. Mur. 110 (I-II?,
        Murabba'at, Judaea; pap.; on the verso of No.
        2850a).

2850c   Unidentified prose (?).   P. Mur. 111 and pl. LXXXII
        (I-II, Murabba'at, Judaea; pap.).

2850d   Unidentified prose (natural science? medicine?).
        P. Mur. 112 and pl. LXXXIII (II, Murabba'at,
        Judaea; opisthograph pap., seven small frr.).

2861    Unidentified prose.  H. Lloyd-Jones, Gnomon 35
        (1963) 449-50.

## LATIN

2933a   Terence: Andria 489-99, 514-21, 539-54, 575-82.
        Lowe, CLA 10.1537 (P. Vindob. inv. L 103) (IV-
        V, Fayum?; pap. cod.).

2964a   Codex Theodosianus (?).   Lowe, CLA 10.1529 (P.
        Vindob. inv. L 81) (V, Fayum?; a small scrap of
        pap., written on the recto only).

2993a   Juridical fragment.   Lowe, CLA 10.1524 (P. Vindob.
        inv. L 26) (V, Fayum?; a strip of parch.).

2993b   Legal fragment.   Lowe, CLA 10.1527 (P. Vindob.
        inv. L 59 + 92) (IV-V, Fayum?; pap. cod.).

2993c   Legal fragment.   Lowe, CLA 10.1534 (P. Vindob.
        inv. L 94) (V, Fayum?; a strip of parch.).

2993d   Legal fragment.   Lowe, CLA 10.1535 (P. Vindob.
        inv. L 95) (VI, Fayum?; parch. cod.).

2993e   Legal fragments, with commentary in Greek.   Lowe,
        CLA 10.1536 (P. Vindob. inv. L 101 + 102 + 107)
        (V-VI; pap. cod.).

3000a   Historical (?) fragment.   Lowe, CLA 10.1539 (P.
        Vindob. inv. L 117) (IV-V, Fayum?; parch. cod.).

3008a   Fragment of a Latin-Greek glossary.  Lowe, CLA
        10.1525 (P. Vindob. inv. L 27) (V, Fayum?; parch.).

3026a   Unidentified (literary?).   Lowe, CLA 10.1520 (P.
        Vindob. inv. L 16) (III, Fayum?; on the verso is
        a Greek cursive text).

3026b   Unidentified (literary?).   Lowe, CLA 10.1521 (P.
        Vindob. inv. L 17) (V, Fayum?).

3026c   Unidentified.   Lowe, CLA 10.1523 (P. Vindob. inv.
        L 25) (V, Fayum?; parch.).

3026d   Unidentified (mythography?).   Lowe, CLA 10.1526
        (P. Vindob. inv. L 44) (V, Fayum?; pap. cod.).

3026e   Unidentified Latin text with a Greek translation.
        Lowe, CLA 10.1528 (P. Vindob. inv. L 62) (V-VI,
        Fayum?; pap. cod.).

3026f   Unidentified (literary?).   Lowe, CLA 10.1530 (P.
        Vindob. inv. L 87) (IV-V, Fayum?; parch. cod.).

3026g   Unidentified.   Lowe, CLA 10.1531 (P. Vindob. inv.
        L 88) (V, Fayum?; parch. cod.).

3026h   Unidentified.   Lowe, CLA 10.1532 (P. Vindob. inv.
        L 89) (IV-V, Fayum?; parch. cod.).

## CORRIGENDA

1751    Bartoletti's article has eluded search owing to the
        accidental disappearance of the fascicle in which
        it appeared.  According to Peek, loc. cit., Bar-
        toletti has perceived that a fragment (PSI) pub-
        lished by N. Terzaghi belongs to the same poem
        as this.

2003    This should now be ranged under Astrology.  (Neu-
        gebauer-Van Hoesen, Astrol. Pap. Ostr. came to
        hand only after the renumbering.)

2063    This no longer falls within the defined scope of the
        repertory.

## CONSPECTUS OF TEXTS IDENTIFIED OR REATTRIBUTED

Note. This comprises those texts which have been identified by author since their first publication and those which have been attributed to other authors or genres, as far as the new attributions have determined their classification in the List and the Appendix.

Abh. Berl. Akad., 1865, 140: see No. 1883.
Aeg. 1 (1920) 154-58: No. 2518. Ibid. 13 (1933) 11-20: see Appendix, No. 50. Ibid. 15 (1935) 282-96: No. 1365.
Bell and Skeat, Fragments of an Unknown Gospel 42-51: Appendix, No. 60.
BKT 5.2.64-72: No. 449.
Bowra, Pindar, No. 341: No. 1907. Ibid., No. 342: No. 1906.
BSAA 14 (1912) 192: No. 29. Ibid., NS 6 (1928) 294-95: No. 533.
CRAI, 1877, 92-95: No. 1378.
Crum, Short Texts from Coptic Ostraca ..., No. 403: No. 1322.
Hermathena 5 (1885) 237-57: No. 1844.
JHS 25 (1905) 118: No. 1982.
Keil, Anonymus Argentinensis: No. 310.
Kenyon, Album Gratulatorium ... Van Herwerden 137-42: No. 343. Idem, The Chester Beatty Biblical Papyri, fasc. 1, p. 9: Appendix, No. 46.
Lefebvre, Papyrus de Ménandre, pp. xxi-xxiii: No. 375.
Mél. Nicole 220-22: No. 1299.
Nicole, Procès de Phidias ... : No. 2532.
O. Berol. inv. 12605: No. 2131.
P. Aberdeen 17, 133, 188: see note following the Concordance. 136: No. 2236.
P. Amh. 10: No. 169.
P. Bad. 6.179: No. 2752.
P. Berol. inv. 9908: No. 449. 13411: No. 1365. 16139: No. 1906. 16140: No. 1907.
P. Bon. 1.1: Appendix, No. 55.
P. Bouriant 3: Appendix, No. 61.
P. Cairo G.H. 10244: No. 545.
P. Colt 8: No. 2119.
P. Didot 2-15: No 1319. 25-28: No. 1320.
P. Erl. 8: No. 1257. 11: No. 9.
P. Fay. 10: No. 2961. 204: No. 545. 217: No. 2234.
P. Fuad 8: No. 2223.
P. Genève inv. 97: No. 1338. 263 + 264: No. 2532.
P. Grenf. 1.52: No. 2396. 2.6 (a): No. 1477. 2.7 (b): No. 342. 2.8 (a): No. 1538. 2.12: No. 1625. 2.13: No. 1558.
P. Harris 1: No. 1325. 21: No. 1376. 31: identified as Psalm 43.20-23, and now omitted. 56: No. 1602.

P. Heid. Siegmann 190: No. 2752.
P. Iand. 5.84: No. 2012.
P. Lit. Lond. 40: No. 343. 49: No. 1538. 53: No. 1581. 55: No. 131. 60: No. 1593. 77: No. 1709. 142: No. 1188. 184: No. 2996. 253: No. 2713.
P. Lond. 2.184: No. 1565. 2.186: No. 2402. 2.273: No. 343. 2.274: No. 2618. 3.1109 (a): No. 476. 5.1812: No. 1581. 5.1816 (c): No. 1188.
P. Maspero 2.67176, 67275, 67351: No. 355.
P. Mich. 139: No. 1458. 456: No. 2987. 457: No. 2917.
P. Mur. 108 b: No. 1983.
P. Oxy. 5: Appendix, No. 33. 33: No. 2232. 303: No. 2022. 405: Appendix, No. 44. 414: No. 94. 416: No. 168. 417: No. 2474. 426: No. 178. 440 (a): No. 8. 470: No. 2044. 471: No. 2225. 680: No. 2178. 865: No. 2455. 870: No. 546. 887: see the note following the Concordance. 1401: No. 1578. 1600: Appendix, No. 47. 1603: Appendix, No. 9. 1828: Appendix, No. 39. 2074: Appendix, No. 49. 2078: No. 254. 2104: No. 2968. 2317: No. 134. 2318: No. 127. 2319: No. 124. 2320: No. 135. 2326: No. 486. 2460: No. 448. 2461: No. 451.
P. Par. 2: No. 246.
P. Petrie 1.3 (3): No. 529. 1.4 (2): No. 131. 2.45: No. 2206. 2.49 (a): No. 1593. 2.49 (c): No. 439. 2.49 (d): No. 440.
P. Rain. 1.7: No. 2201. 3.38: No. 2286. 3.41: Appendix, No. 62. 3.42: No. 1275.
P. Rein. 1.5: No. 2444.
PRIMI 1.21: No. 2199.
P. Ryl. 14: No. 1375. 39: No. 342. 42: No. 2929. 437: No. 2239. 482: No. 450. 524: No. 2063. 526: No. 2314.
P. Schubart 15: No. 96. 21: No. 1203.
PSI 724: No. 1287. 743: No. 2100. 762: No. 1265. 844: No. 1862. 1162: No. 2472. 1368: No. 2901. 1399: No. 2518.
P. Strassb. inv. 84: No. 310.
P. Tebt. 271: No. 512.
Rev. Ét. Gr. 17 (1904) 215-29: No. 1338.
Rev. Phil. 21 (1897) 1-4: No. 358.
Sanders and Schmidt, The Minor Prophets in the Freer Collection ... 228-29: Appendix, No. 10.
SIFC, NS 12 (1935) 87-91: No. 513.
Sitzb. Berl. Akad., 1887, 819-20: No. 1599. Ibid., 1918, 739-42: No. 2131. Ibid., 1923, 160-83: No. 2099.
TAPA 53 (1922) 133-36: No. 1458.

# CONCORDANCE: PACK AND PACK 2

| P=P 2 | P=P 2 | P=P 2 | P=P 2 | P=P 2 | P=P 2 | P=P 2 | P=P 2 | P=P 2 | P=P 2 |
|---|---|---|---|---|---|---|---|---|---|
| 1=2 | 61=108 | 122=208 | 178=268 | 238=335 | 296a=406 | 355=481 | 415=555 | 476=623 | 537=700 |
| 1a=1 | 62=109 | 123=209 | 179=271 | 239=337 | 297=407 | 356=482 | 416=556 | 477=624 | 538=701 |
| 2=3 | 63=110 | 124=210 | 180=272 | 240=338 | 298=409 | 357=483 | 417=557 | 478=626 | 539=703 |
| 3=5 | 64=111 | 125=211 | 181=273 | 241=339 | 299=410 | 358=484 | 418=558 | 479=628 | 540=705 |
| 4=6 | 65=112 | 126=212 | 182=274 | 242=341 | 300=411 | 359=485 | 419=559 | 480=629 | 541=706 |
| 5=7 | 66=113 | 126a=186 | 183=275 | 243=342 | 301=412 | 360=487 | 420=561 | 481=630 | 542=707 |
| 6=8 | 67=114 | 127=213 | 184=276 | 244=343 | 302=413 | 361=488 | 421=563 | 482=631 | 543=708 |
| 7=10 | 68=115 | 128=214 | 185=277 | 245=344 | 303=414 | 362=489 | 422=565 | 483=632 | 544=709 |
| 8=12 | 69=116 | 129=215 | 186=279 | 246=345 | 304=416 | 363=490 | 423=566 | 484=634 | 545=710 |
| 9=14 | 70=117 | 130=207 | 186a=280 | 247=346 | 305=417 | 364=491 | 424=567 | 485=635 | 546=712 |
| 10=15 | 71=118 | 131=216 | 187=281 | 248=347 | 306=418 | 365=492 | 425=568 | 486=636 | 547=713 |
| 11=16 | 72=119 | 132=217 | 188=282 | 249+ | 307=419 | 366=493 | 426=569 | 487=637 | 548=714 |
| 12=17 | 73=122 | 133=218 | 189=283 | 250=348 | 308=420 | 367=494 | 427=570 | 488=638 | 549=715 |
| 13=19 | 74=130 | 134=219 | 190=284 | 251=349 | 309=421 | 368=495 | 428=571 | 489=639 | 550=716 |
| 14=20 | 75=131 | 135=220 | 191+ | 252=350 | 310=423 | 369=497 | 429=572 | 490=640 | 551=717 |
| 15=21 | 76=138 | 136=221 | 192=285 | 253+ | 311=424 | 370=499 | 430=573 | 491=641 | 552=718 |
| 16=31 | 77=139 | 137=222 | 193=286 | 257=351 | 312=425 | 371=500 | 431=574 | 492=642 | 553=721 |
| 17=26 | 78=140 | 137a=225 | 194=287 | 254=354 | 313=426 | 372=502 | 432=575 | 493=643 | 554=722 |
| 18=27 | 79=141 | 138=223 | 195=288 | 255=352 | 314=415 | 373=503 | 433=576 | 494=644 | 555=723 |
| 19=28 | 80=142 | 139=224 | 196=289 | 256=353 | 315=427 | 374=504 | 434=577 | 495=645 | 556=724 |
| 20=32 | 81=144 | 140=226 | 197=290 | 257+ | 316=428 | 375=505 | 435=578 | 496=646 | 557=725 |
| 21=33 | 82=145 | 141=227 | 198=291 | 253=351 | 317=430 | 376=506 | 436=579 | 497=648 | 558=727 |
| 22=34 | 83=146 | 142=228 | 199=292 | 258=357 | 317a=431 | 377=507 | 437=580 | 498=650 | 559=728 |
| 23=35 | 84=147 | 143=233 | 200=293 | 259=358 | 318=432 | 378=530 | 438=582 | 499=651 | 560=729 |
| 24=36 | 85=148 | 144=234 | 201=294 | 260=361 | 319=433 | 379=529 | 439=583 | 500=652 | 561=731 |
| 25=37 | 86=149 | 144a=187 | 202=295 | 261=363 | 320=435 | 380=519 | 440=584 | 501=653 | 562=732 |
| 26=42 | 87=150 | 144b=188 | 203=296 | 262=364 | 321=437 | 381=520 | 441=585 | 502=654 | 563=733 |
| 27=44 | 88=151 | 145=189 | 204=297 | 263=365 | 322=438 | 382=527 | 442=586 | 503=658 | 564=734 |
| 28=50 | 89=152 | 146=190 | 205=298 | 264=366 | 323=439 | 383=509 | 443=587 | 504=659 | 565=735 |
| 29=51 | 90=153 | 147=191 | 206=299 | 265=367 | 324=440 | 384=511 | 444=588 | 505=661 | 566=737 |
| 30=52 | 91=154 | 148=193 | 207=300 | 266=368 | 325=441 | 385=531 | 445=589 | 506=662 | 567=738 |
| 31=53 | 92=155 | 149=194 | 208=301 | 267=369 | 326=442 | 386=512 | 446=590 | 507=663 | 568=739 |
| 32=55 | 93=156 | 150=1338 | 209=302 | 268=370 | 327=444 | 387=522 | 447=592 | 508=664 | 569=740 |
| 33=56 | 94=157 | 151=2201 | 210=303 | 269=371 | 328=446 | 388=523 | 448=593 | 509=665 | 570=741 |
| 34=58 | 95=158 | 152=237 | 211=305 | 270=372 | 328a=1203 | 389=517 | 449=594 | 510=666 | 571=742 |
| 35=59 | 96=161 | 153=238 | 212=306 | 271=373 | 329=447 | 390=516 | 450=595 | 511=667 | 572=744 |
| 36=60 | 97=162 | 154=239 | 213=307 | 272=374 | 330=455 | 391=533 | 451=596 | 512=668 | 573=746 |
| 37=61 | 98=163 | 155=240 | 214=308 | 273=375 | 331=456 | 392=1458 | 452=597 | 513=669 | 574=748 |
| 38=62 | 99=164 | 156=241 | 215=309 | 274=376 | 332=457 | 393=534 | 453=598 | 514=670 | 575=750 |
| 39=57 | 100=165 | 156a=242 | 216=310 | 275=377 | 333=458 | 394=535 | 454=599 | 515=672 | 576=751 |
| 40=76 | 101=166 | 157=243 | 217=312 | 276=378 | 334=459 | 395=526 | 455=600 | 516=673 | 577=753 |
| 41=77 | 102=167 | 158=244 | 218=313 | 277=379 | 335=460 | 396=525 | 456=602 | 517=674 | 578=754 |
| 42=78 | 103=168 | 159=245 | 219=314 | 278=380 | 336=461 | 397=524 | 457=603 | 518=675 | 579=755 |
| 43=88 | 104=169 | 160=246 | 220=315 | 279=382 | 337=462 | 398=513 | 458=604 | 519=676 | 580=756 |
| 44=89 | 105=170 | 161=250 | 221=316 | 280=383 | 338=463 | 399=521 | 459=605 | 520=677 | 581=757 |
| 45=90 | 106=172 | 162=251 | 222=317 | 281=384 | 339=464 | 400=536 | 460=606 | 521=678 | 582=758 |
| 46=91 | 107=173 | 163=252 | 223=318 | 282=385 | 340=465 | 401=538 | 461=607 | 522=679 | 583=759 |
| 47=92 | 108=174 | 164=253 | 224=319 | 283=386 | 341=466 | 402=539 | 462=608 | 523=680 | 584=760 |
| 48=93 | 109=175 | 165=254 | 225=320 | 284=388 | 342=467 | 403=540 | 463=609 | 524=682 | 585=761 |
| 49=94 | 109a=176 | 166=256 | 226=322 | 285=389 | 343=468 | 404=541 | 464=610 | 525=683 | 586=762 |
| 50=95 | 110=177 | 167=257 | 227=323 | 286=390 | 344=469 | 405=542 | 465=611 | 526=684 | 587=763 |
| 51=97 | 111=178 | 168=258 | 228=324 | 287=394 | 345=470 | 405a=543 | 466=612 | 527=687 | 588=765 |
| 52=98 | 112=179 | 169=259 | 229=325 | 288=395 | 346=472 | 406=545 | 467=613 | 528=689 | 589=766 |
| 53=99 | 113=195 | 170=260 | 230=326 | 289=396 | 347=473 | 407=546 | 468=614 | 529=690 | 590=769 |
| 54=100 | 114=196 | 171=261 | 231=327 | 290=397 | 348=474 | 408=547 | 469=615 | 530=691 | 591=770 |
| 55=101 | 115=197 | 172=262 | 232=328 | 291=400 | 349=475 | 409=548 | 470=616 | 531=692 | 592=772 |
| 56=102 | 116=198 | 173=263 | 233=329 | 292=401 | 350=476 | 410=549 | 471=618 | 532=694 | 593=773 |
| 57=104 | 117=200 | 174=264 | 234=330 | 293=402 | 351=477 | 411=551 | 472=619 | 533=695 | 594=776 |
| 58=105 | 118=201 | 175=265 | 235=331 | 294=403 | 352=478 | 412=552 | 473=620 | 534=697 | 595=777 |
| 59=106 | 119=202 | 176=266 | 236=332 | 295=404 | 353=479 | 413=553 | 474=621 | 535=698 | 596=778 |
| 60=107 | 120=203 | 177=267 | 237=334 | 296=405 | 354=480 | 414=554 | 475=622 | 536=699 | 597=779 |
| | 121=206 | | | | | | | | |

| P=P 2 | P=P 2 | P=P 2 | P=P 2 | P=P 2 | P=P 2 | P=P2 | P=P 2 | P=P 2 | P=P 2 |
|---|---|---|---|---|---|---|---|---|---|
| 598=780 | 664=862 | 722=929 | 788=1015 | 854=1093 | 913=1172 | 975=1246 | 1040=1322 | 1105=1404 | 1168b=1494 |
| 599=781 | 665=864 | 723=931 | 789=1016 | 854a=1094 | 914=1173 | 976=1248 | 1041=1325 | 1106=1405 | 1169=1495 |
| 600=782 | 666=865 | 724=932 | 790=1017 | 855=1095 | 915=1174 | 977=1249 | 1042=1327 | 1107=1406 | 1170=1496 |
| 601=783 | 667=866 | 725=933 | 791=1008 | 856=1096 | 916=1175 | 978=1250 | 1043=1329 | 1108=1418 | 1171=1498 |
| 602=784 | 668=867 | 726=934 | 792=1018 | 857=1098 | 917=1177 | 979=1251 | 1044=1330 | 1109=1419 | 1172=1499 |
| 603=785 | 669=868 | 727=935 | 793=1019 | 858=1099 | 918=1178 | 980=1252 | 1045=1331 | 1110=1420 | 1173=1500 |
| 604=787 | 670=869 | 728=937 | 794=1020 | 859=1100 | 919=1179 | 981=1253 | 1046=1332 | 1111=1432 | 1174=1501 |
| 605=719 | 671=870 | 729=938 | 795=1022 | 860=1101 | 920=1180 | 982=1254 | 1047=1333 | 1112=1422 | 1175=1503 |
| 606=788 | 672=872 | 730=940 | 796=1023 | 861=1102 | 921=1181 | 983=1255 | 1048=1334 | 1113=1423 | 1176=1505 |
| 607=790 | 673=873 | 731=941 | 797=1024 | 862=1104 | 922=1182 | 984=1256 | 1049=1335 | 1114=1424 | 1177=1506 |
| 608=791 | 674=874 | 732=942 | 798=1025 | 863=1105 | 923=1183 | 985=1258 | 1050=1336 | 1115=1425 | 1178=1507 |
| 609=792 | 675=876 | 733=943 | 799=1026 | 864=1106 | 924=1184 | 986=1259 | 1051=1337 | 1116=1426 | 1179=1508 |
| 610=793 | 676=877 | 734=944 | 800=1027 | 865=1107 | 925=1185 | 987=1260 | 1052=1339 | 1117=1428 | 1180=1509 |
| 611=795 | 677=878 | 735=945 | 801=1028 | 866=1108 | 926=1186 | 988=1261 | 1053=1340 | 1118=1430 | 1181=1510 |
| 612=796 | 678=879 | 736=946 | 802=1029 | 867=1109 | 927+ | 989=1262 | 1054=1341 | 1119=1433 | 1182=1511 |
| 613=797 | 679=880 | 737=947 | 803=1030 | 868=1110 | 1973=1188 | 990=1263 | 1055=1342 | 1120=1435 | 1183=1512 |
| 614=799 | 680=881 | 738=948 | 804=1031 | 869=1111 | 928=1189 | 991=1264 | 1056=1343 | 1121=1593 | 1184=1513 |
| 615=801 | 681=882 | 739=949 | 805=1032 | 870=1112 | 929=1190 | 992=1265 | 1057=1344 | 1122=1436 | 1185=1514 |
| 616=802 | 682=883 | 740=950 | 806=1034 | 871=1113 | 930=1191 | 993=1267 | 1058=1345 | 1123=1437 | 1186=1515 |
| 617=803 | *683=884 | 741=952 | 807=1036 | 872=1114 | 931=1192 | 994=1268 | 1059=1346 | 1124=1441 | 1187=1516 |
| 618=805 | 685=888 | 742=953 | 808=1037 | 872a+ | 932=1193 | 995=1269 | 1060=1347 | 1125=1442 | 1188=1517 |
| 619=806 | 686=889 | 743=954 | 809=1038 | 874=1115 | 933=1194 | 996=1270 | 1061=1348 | 1126=1440 | 1189=1519 |
| 620=807 | 687=890 | 744=957 | 810=1039 | 873=1116 | 934=1195 | 997=1271 | 1062=1349 | 1127=1444 | 1190=1520 |
| 621=808 | 688=892 | 745=958 | 811=1041 | 874+ | 935=1196 | 998=1272 | 1063=1350 | 1128=1445 | 1191=1521 |
| 622=810 | 689=894 | 746=959 | 812=1042 | 872a=1115 | 936=1197 | 999=1274 | 1064=1352 | 1129=1447 | 1192=1522 |
| 623=811 | 690+ | 747=960 | 813=1043 | 875=1118 | 937=1198 | 1000=1275 | 1065=1353 | 1130=1448 | 1193=1523 |
| 624=812 | 695=894 | 748=961 | 814=1044 | 876=1120 | 938=1199 | 1001=1278 | 1066=1355 | 1131=1449 | 1194=1524 |
| 625=813 | 691=895 | 749=962 | 815=1045 | 877=1121 | 939=1200 | 1002=1279 | 1067=1356 | 1132=1451 | 1195=1525 |
| 626=816 | 692=896 | 750=963 | 816=1046 | 878=1123 | 940=1202 | 1003=1280 | 1068=1357 | 1133=1452 | 1196=1526 |
| 627=817 | 693=897 | 751=964 | 817=1047 | 879=1125 | 941=1204 | 1004=1281 | 1069=1361 | 1134=1439 | 1197=1527 |
| 628=818 | 694=898 | 752=965 | 818=1048 | 880=1126 | 942=1205 | 1005=1282 | 1070=1362 | 1135=1456 | 1198=1528 |
| 629=819 | 695+ | 753=966 | 819=1050 | 881=1127 | 943=1207 | 1006=1283 | 1071=1363 | 1136+ | 1199=1530 |
| 630=820 | 690=894 | 754=969 | 820=1051 | 882=1128 | 944=1208 | 1007=1285 | 1072=1364 | 1357=1581 | 1200=1531 |
| 631=821 | 696+ | 755=970 | 821=1052 | 883=1130 | 945=1209 | 1008=1286 | 1073=1365 | 1137=1459 | 1201=1529 |
| 632=822 | 698+ | 756=971 | 822=1053 | 884=1131 | 946=1211 | 1009=1287 | 1074=1367 | 1138=1908 | 1202=1532 |
| 633=823 | 701=900 | 757=972 | 823=1054 | 885=1132 | 947=1212 | 1010=1288 | 1075=1371 | 1139=1909 | 1202a=1533 |
| 634=824 | 697=899 | 758=974 | 824=1055 | 886=1133 | 948=1213 | 1011=1289 | 1076=1379 | 1140=1461 | 1203=1534 |
| 635=825 | 698+ | 759=975 | 825=1056 | 887=1134 | 949=2131 | 1012=1290 | 1077=1373 | 1141=1462 | 1204=1535 |
| 636=827 | 696+ | 760=976 | 826=1057 | 888=1135 | 950=1214 | 1013=1291 | 1078=1380 | 1142=1463 | 1205=1536 |
| 637=829 | 701=900 | 761=978 | 827=1058 | 889=1138 | 951=1215 | 1014=1292 | 1079=1378 | 1143=1465 | 1206=1537 |
| 638=830 | 699=901 | 762=979 | 828=1059 | 890=1139 | 951a=1229 | 1015=1293 | 1080=1381 | 1144=1466 | 1207=1538 |
| 639=831 | 700=902 | 763=981 | 829=1060 | 891=1140 | 952=1216 | 1016=1294 | 1081=1382 | 1145=1467 | 1208=1539 |
| 640=832 | 701+ | 764=982 | 830=1061 | 892=1142 | 953=1217 | 1017=1295 | 1082+ | 1146=1468 | 1209=1541 |
| 641=833 | 696+ | 765=983 | 831=1062 | 893=1143 | 954+ | 1018=1296 | 1082a=1387 | 1147=1469 | 1210=1542 |
| 642=834 | 698=900 | 766=984 | 832=1063 | 894=1147 | 1668=1218 | 1019=1301 | 1083=1388 | 1148=1470 | 1211=1543 |
| 643=836 | 702=903 | 767=985 | 833=1064 | 895=1148 | 955=1219 | 1020=1302 | 1084=1389 | 1149=1471 | 1212=1544 |
| 644=837 | 702a=904 | 768=986 | 834=1066 | 896=1149 | 956=1220 | 1021=1303 | 1085=1391 | 1150=449 | 1213=1545 |
| 645=838 | 703=905 | 769=987 | 835=1067 | 897=1151 | 957=1223 | 1022=1304 | 1086=1392 | 1151=450 | 1214=1548 |
| 646=839 | 704=906 | 770=988 | 836=1068 | 898=1152 | 958=1224 | 1023=1305 | 1087=1393 | 1152=1472 | 1215=1546 |
| 647=840 | 705=907 | 771=989 | 837=1070 | 899=1153 | 959+ | 1024=1306 | 1088=1412 | 1153=1473 | 1216=1547 |
| 648=841 | 706=908 | 772=993 | 838=1071 | 900=1155 | 959a=1225 | 1025=1307 | 1089=1413 | 1154=1475 | 1217=1549 |
| 649=842 | 707=909 | 773=994 | 839=1072 | 901=1156 | 960=1226 | 1026=1308 | 1090=1414 | 1155=1476 | 1218=1550 |
| 650=843 | 708=911 | 774=995 | 840=1073 | 902=1157 | 961=1227 | 1027=1309 | 1091=1415 | 1156=1477 | 1219=1551 |
| 651=844 | 709=912 | 775=996 | 841=1074 | 903+ | 962=1228 | 1028=1310 | 1092=1416 | 1157=1478 | 1220=1552 |
| 652=845 | 710=914 | 776=998 | 842=1076 | 906=1158 | 963=1233 | 1029=1311 | 1093=1417 | 1158=1480 | 1221=1553 |
| 653=846 | 711=915 | 777=999 | 843=1077 | 904=1159 | 964=1234 | 1030=1312 | 1094=1407 | 1159=1481 | 1222=1554 |
| 654=847 | 712=916 | 778=1000 | 844=1078 | 905=1160 | 965=1235 | 1031=1313 | 1095=1408 | 1160=1482 | 1223=1555 |
| 655=848 | 713=917 | 779=1001 | 845=1080 | 906+ | 966=1236 | 1032=1314 | 1096=1409 | 1161=1483 | 1224=1556 |
| 656=849 | 714=918 | 780=1003 | 846=1081 | 903=1158 | 967=1237 | 1033=1315 | 1097=1410 | 1162=1484 | 1225=1558 |
| 657=850 | 715=920 | 781=1006 | 847=1082 | 907=1163 | 968=1238 | 1034=1316 | 1098=1411 | 1163=1487 | 1226=1559 |
| 658=852 | 716=921 | 782=1007 | 848=1083 | 908=1164 | 969=1239 | 1035=1317 | 1099=1397 | 1164=1488 | 1227=1560 |
| 659=853 | 717=922 | 783=1009 | 849=1084 | 908a=1165 | 970=1241 | 1036+ | 1100=1398 | 1165=1489 | 1228=1561 |
| 660=854 | 718=924 | 784=1010 | 850=1085 | 909=1166 | 971=1242 | 1036a=1318 | 1101=1399 | 1166=1490 | 1229=1562 |
| 661=991 | 719=925 | 785=1012 | 851=1089 | 910=1163 | 972=1243 | 1037=1319 | 1102=1400 | 1167=1491 | 1230=1563 |
| 662=858 | 720=926 | 786=1013 | 852=1090 | 911=1170 | 973=1244 | 1038=1320 | 1103=1401 | 1168=1492 | 1230a+ |
| 663=861 | 721=927 | 787=1014 | 853=1092 | 912=1171 | 974=1245 | 1039=1321 | 1104=1402 | 1168a=1493 | 1232=1564 |
| | *684=886 | | | | | | | | |

| P=P 2 | P=P 2 | P=P 2 | P=P 2 | P=P 2 | P=P 2 | P=P 2 | P=P 2 | P=P 2 | P=P 2 |
|---|---|---|---|---|---|---|---|---|---|
| 1231=1565 | 1285=1630 | 1345=1702 | 1402=1771 | 1460=1833 | 1524=1935 | 1581=2018 | 1642=2102 | 1703=2180 | 1763=2262 |
| 1232+ | 1286=1631 | 1346=1703 | 1403=1772 | 1461=1834 | 1525+ | 1582=2019 | 1643=2103 | 1704=2181 | 1764=2263 |
| 1230a=1564 | 1287=1632 | 1347=1705 | 1403a=532 | 1462=1862 | 1373=1936 | 1583=2028 | 1644=2104 | 1705=2182 | 1765=2264 |
| 1233=1566 | 1288=1633 | 1348=1708 | 1404=1773 | 1463=1835 | 1526=1937 | 1584=2051 | 1645=2105 | 1706=2183 | 1766=2265 |
| 1234=1567 | 1289=1634 | 1349=1709 | 1405=1774 | 1464=1841 | 1527=1938 | 1585=2015 | 1646=2106 | 1707=2184 | 1767=2266 |
| 1235=1568 | 1290=1635 | 1349a=1713 | 1406=1775 | 1465=1842 | 1528=1939 | 1586=2016 | 1647=2107 | 1708=2185 | 1768=2267 |
| 1236=1569 | 1291=1639 | 1350=1710 | 1407=1776 | 1466=1843 | 1529=1940 | 1587=2011 | 1648=2108 | 1709=2186 | 1769=2268 |
| 1237=1571 | 1292=1640 | 1351=1712 | 1408=1781 | 1467=1844 | 1530 omitted | | 1649=2109 | 1709a=2187 | 1770=2273 |
| 1238=1572 | 1293=1641 | 1352=1714 | 1409=1782 | 1468=1845 | 1531 omitted | | 1650=2110 | 1710=2188 | 1771=2274 |
| 1239=1573 | 1294=1644 | 1352a=1715 | 1410=1858 | 1469=1846 | 1532=1941 | 1588=2034 | 1651=2111 | 1711=2189 | 1772=2275 |
| 1240=1575 | 1295=1646 | 1353=1716 | 1411=1783 | 1470=1847 | 1533=1942 | 1589=2035 | 1652=2112 | 1712=2190 | 1773=2276 |
| 1241=1576 | 1296=1647 | 1354=1717 | 1412=1787 | 1471=1848 | 1534=1943 | 1589a=2029 | 1653=2113 | 1713=2191 | 1774=2277 |
| 1242=1577 | 1297=1648 | 1355=1718 | 1413=1788 | 1472=1849 | 1534a=1921 | 1590=2039 | 1654=2114 | 1714=2192 | 1775=2280 |
| 1243=1580 | 1298=1649 | 1356=1719 | 1414=1789 | 1473=1850 | 1535=1944 | 1591=2040 | 1655=2115 | 1715=2193 | 1775a=2281 |
| 1243a=1579 | 1299=1651 | 1357+ | 1415=1790 | 1474=1851 | 1536=1945 | 1592=2041 | 1656=2116 | 1716=2195 | 1776=2282 |
| 1244=1582 | 1300=1652 | 1136=1581 | 1416=1791 | 1475=1852 | 1536a=1947 | 1593=2045 | 1657=2117 | 1717=2197 | 1776a=2283 |
| 1245=1584 | 1301=1653 | 1358+ | 1417=1792 | 1476=1853 | 1537=1948 | 1594=2046 | 1657a=2118 | 1718=2198 | 1776b=2284 |
| 1246=1585 | 1302=1654 | 1359=1721 | 1417a=1784 | 1477=1854 | 1538=1953 | 1595=2048 | 1658=2120 | 1719=2726 | 1776c=2285 |
| 1247=1586 | 1303=1655 | 1360=1722 | 1417b=1777 | 1478=1863 | 1539=1954 | 1596=2049 | 1659=2121 | 1720+ | 1777=2287 |
| 1248=1587 | 1304=1656 | 1361=1723 | 1417c=1785 | 1479=1864 | 1540=1955 | 1597=2050 | 1660=2127 | 1721=2203 | 1778=2288 |
| 1249+ | 1305=1657 | 1362=1578 | 1417d=1838 | 1480=1865 | 1541=1956 | 1598=2052 | 1661=2126 | 1722=2204 | 1779=2289 |
| 1250b=1588 | 1306=1299 | 1363=1724 | 1417e=1839 | 1481=1866 | 1542=1960 | 1599=2054 | 1662=2125 | 1723=2205 | 1780=2290 |
| 1250=1589 | 1307=1658 | 1364=1725 | 1417f=1840 | 1482=1867 | 1543=1967 | 1600=2055 | 1663=2128 | 1724=2206 | 1781=2291 |
| 1250a=1570 | 1308=1660 | 1365=1726 | 1418=1793 | 1483=1868 | 1544=1968 | 1601=2056 | 1663a=2119 | 1725=2207 | 1782=2292 |
| 1250b+ | 1309=1661 | 1366=1727 | 1418a=1786 | 1484=1870 | 1545=1969 | 1602=2010 | 1664=2134 | 1726=2208 | 1783=2293 |
| 1249=1588 | 1310=1662 | 1367=1728 | 1419=1794 | 1484a=2482 | 1546=1970 | 1603=2057 | 1665=2132 | 1727=2209 | 1784=2294 |
| 1251=1590 | 1311=1663 | 1368=1729 | 1420=1795 | 1485=1871 | 1547=1971 | 1604=2027 | 1665a=2133 | 1728=2210 | 1785=2295 |
| 1252+ | 1312=1664 | 1369=1730 | 1421=1796 | 1486=1873 | 1548=1972 | 1605=2058 | 1666=2136 | 1728a=2211 | 1786=2297 |
| 2129=2713 | 1313=1665 | 1370=1731 | 1422=1797 | 1487=1874 | 1549=1973 | 1606=2059 | 1667=2137 | 1729=2212 | 1787=2298 |
| 1253=1591 | 1314=1666 | 1371=1732 | 1423=1798 | 1488=1876 | 1550=1974 | 1607=2060 | 1668+ | 1730=2213 | 1788=2299 |
| 1254+ | 1315=1667 | 1372=1733 | 1424=1799 | 1489=1877 | 1551=1975 | 1608=2061 | 954=1218 | 1731=2214 | 1789=2300 |
| 2137=2721 | 1316=1668 | 1373+ | 1425=1800 | 1490=1878 | 1552=1976 | 1609=2062 | 1669=2138 | 1732=2218 | 1790=2303 |
| 1255=1592 | 1317=1669 | 1525=1936 | 1426=1801 | 1491=1879 | 1552a=1982 | 1610=2068 | 1670=2139 | 1733=2219 | 1791=2304 |
| 1256=1594 | 1318=1670 | 1374=1734 | 1427=1802 | 1492=1880 | 1553=1984 | 1611=2069 | 1671=2141 | 1734=2220 | 1792=2305 |
| 1257=1595 | 1318a=1659 | 1374a=1691 | 1428=1803 | 1493=1881 | 1553a=1978 | 1612=2070 | 1672=2142 | 1735=2221 | 1793=2306 |
| 1258+ | 1319=1671 | 1375=1735 | 1429=1804 | 1494=1882 | 1553b=1979 | 1613=2071 | 1673=2143 | 1736=2217 | 1794=2307 |
| 1393=1596 | 1319a=1672 | 1376=1738 | 1430=1805 | 1495+ | 1553c=1980 | 1614=2072 | 1674=2144 | 1736a=2224 | 1795=2309 |
| 1259=1597 | 1320=1673 | 1377=1739 | 1431=1807 | 2079a=1883 | 1554=1987 | 1615=2075 | 1675=2145 | 1737=2227 | 1796=2310 |
| 1260=1598 | 1321=1674 | 1378=1741 | 1432=1808 | 1496=1884 | 1555=1988 | 1616=2073 | 1676=2147 | 1738=2228 | 1797=2311 |
| 1261=1599 | 1322=1675 | 1379=1743 | 1433=1809 | 1497=1885 | 1556=1989 | 1617=2074 | 1677=2148 | 1739=2229 | 1798=2314 |
| 1262=1600 | 1323=1676 | 1380=1744 | 1434=1859 | 1498=1886 | 1557=1990 | 1618=2076 | 1678=2149 | 1740=2231 | 1799=2315 |
| 1263=1601 | 1324=1677 | 1381=1745 | 1435=1810 | 1499=1887 | 1557a=1991 | 1619=2077 | 1679=2150 | 1740a=2226 | 1800=2316 |
| 1263a=1602 | 1325=1678 | 1382=1746 | 1436=1811 | 1500=1888 | 1558=1992 | 1620=2099 | 1680=2151 | 1741=2232 | 1801=2318 |
| 1263b=1603 | 1326=1679 | 1383=1747 | 1437=1812 | 1501=1889 | 1559=1993 | 1621=2100 | 1681=2154 | 1742=2238 | 1802=2319 |
| 1263c=1574 | 1327=1680 | 1384=1748 | 1438+ | 1502=1895 | 1560=1994 | 1622=2078 | 1682=2155 | 1743=2233 | 1803=2320 |
| 1264=1604 | 1328=1681 | 1385=1749 | 1439=1813 | 1503=1898 | 1561=1995 | 1623=2079 | 1683=2156 | 1744=2234 | 1804=2321 |
| 1265=1605 | 1329=1682 | 1386=1751 | 1440=1814 | 1504=1899 | 1562=1996 | 1624=2080 | 1684=2157 | 1745=2230 | 1805=2322 |
| 1266=1606 | 1330=1683 | 1387=1754 | 1441=1815 | 1505=1904 | 1563=1997 | 1625=2081 | 1685=2159 | 1746=2243 | 1806=2012 |
| 1267=1607 | 1331=1684 | 1387a=1753 | 1442=1816 | 1506=1376 | 1564=1998 | 1626=2083 | 1686=2161 | 1747=2244 | 1807=2044 |
| 1268=1608 | 1332=1685 | 1388=1755 | 1443=1818 | 1507=1905 | 1565=1999 | 1627=2085 | 1687=2162 | 1748=2246 | 1808=2324 |
| 1269=1609 | 1333=1686 | 1389=1757 | 1444=1819 | 1508=1375 | 1566=2000 | 1628=2086 | 1688=2164 | 1749=2237 | 1809=2325 |
| 1270=1610 | 1334=1687 | 1390=1758 | 1445=1820 | 1509=1906 | 1567=2001 | 1629=2087 | 1689=2166 | 1750=2247 | 1810=2326 |
| 1271=2752 | 1335=1688 | 1391=1759 | 1446=1821 | 1510=1907 | 1568=2002 | 1630=2088 | 1690=355 | 1751=2248 | 1811=2327 |
| 1272=1611 | 1336=1689 | 1392=1760 | 1447=1860 | 1511=1915 | 1569=2003 | 1631=2089 | 1691=2167 | 1752=2249 | 1812=2328 |
| 1273=1614 | 1337=1690 | 1393+ | 1448=1822 | 1512=1916 | 1570=2017 | 1632=2090 | 1692=2168 | 1753=2250 | 1813=2329 |
| 1274=1615 | 1338=1695 | 1258=1596 | 1449=1823 | 1513=1922 | 1571=2026 | 1633=2091 | 1693=2170 | 1754=2251 | 1814=2330 |
| 1275=1616 | 1338a=1692 | 1394=1761 | 1450=1824 | 1514=1923 | 1572=2063 | 1634=2092 | 1694=2171 | 1755=2253 | 1815=2331 |
| 1276=1617 | 1338b=1693 | 1395=1762 | 1451=1825 | 1515=1924 | 1573 omitted* | 1635=2093 | 1695=2172 | 1756=2254 | 1816=2333 |
| 1277=1618 | 1338c=1694 | 1396=1763 | 1452=1826 | 1516=1925 | 1574=2036 | 1636=2094 | 1696=2173 | 1757=2255 | 1817=2334 |
| 1278=1619 | 1339=1696 | 1397=1764 | 1453=1827 | 1517=1926 | 1575=2020 | 1637=2095 | 1697=2174 | 1758=2256 | 1818=2336 |
| 1279=1620 | 1340=1697 | 1398=1765 | 1454=1828 | 1518=1927 | 1576=2021 | 1638=2096 | 1698=2175 | 1759=2257 | 1819=2338 |
| 1280=1625 | 1341=1698 | 1399=1766 | 1455=1861 | 1519=1928 | 1577=2023 | 1639=2097 | 1699=2176 | 1760=2258 | 1820=2339 |
| 1281=1626 | 1342=29 | 1400=1767 | 1456=1829 | 1520=1929 | 1578=2047 | 1640=2098 | 1700=2177 | 1761=2260 | 1821=2340 |
| 1282=1627 | 1343=1700 | 1400a=96 | 1457=1830 | 1521=1930 | 1579=2004 | 1641=2101 | 1701=2178 | 1762=2261 | 1822=2341 |
| 1283=1628 | 1344=1701 | 1400b=1768 | 1458=1831 | 1522=1932 | 1580=2009 | | 1702=2179 | | 1823=2342 |
| 1284=1629 | 1344a=1707 | 1401=1769 | 1459=1832 | 1523=1933 | | | | | |

* See Neugebauer, Astron. Pap. Ostr., p. 389.

| P=P 2 | P=P 2 | P=P 2 | P=P 2 | P=P 2 |
|---|---|---|---|---|
| 1824=2343 | 1890=2423 | 1952=2515 | 2009=2578 | 2069=2643 |
| 1825=2344 | 1891=2402 | 1953=2516 | 2010=2579 | 2070=2644 |
| 1826=2345 | 1892=2434 | 1954=2517 | 2011=2581 | 2071=2646 |
| 1827=2346 | 1893=2435 | 1955=2519 | 2012=2582 | 2072=2647 |
| 1828=2347 | 1894=2436 | 1956=2521 | 2013=2583 | 2073=2648 |
| 1829=2349 | 1895=2437 | 1957=2225 | 2014=2584 | 2074=2649 |
| 1830=2350 | 1896=2438 | 1958=2522 | 2015=2585 | 2075=2650 |
| 1831=2351 | 1897=2439 | 1959=2523 | 2016=2588 | 2076=2652 |
| 1832=2352 | 1898=2443 | 1960=2524 | 2017=2589 | 2077=2653 |
| 1833=2353 | 1899=2444 | 1961=2526 | 2018=2590 | 2078=2654 |
| 1834=2354 | 1900=2446 | 1962=2527 | 2019=2591 | 2079=2655 |
| 1835=2355 | 1901=2447 | 1963=2528 | 2020=2592 | 2079a+ |
| 1836=2356 | 1902=2448 | 1964=2530 | 2021=2593 | 1495=1883 |
| 1837=2358 | 1903=2450 | 1965=2531 | 2022=2598 | 2080=2656 |
| 1838=2359 | 1904=2453 | 1966=2532 | 2023=2599 | 2081=2657 |
| 1839=2360 | 1905=2454 | 1967=2533 | 2024=2600 | 2082=2658 |
| 1840=2361 | 1906=2455 | 1968=2534 | 2025=2601 | 2083=2659 |
| 1841=2362 | 1907=2456 | 1969=2535 | 2026=2602 | 2084=2660 |
| 1842=2363 | 1908=2457 | 1970=2536 | 2027=2603 | 2085=2661 |
| 1843=2364 | 1909=2458 | 1971=2540 | 2028=2604 | 2086=2662 |
| 1844=2365 | 1910=2459 | 1972+ | 2029=1257 | 2087=2663 |
| 1845=2366 | 1911=2460 | 1720=2200 | 2030=2605 | 2088=2664 |
| 1846=2367 | 1912=2461 | 1973+ | 2031=2606 | 2089=2665 |
| 1847=2368 | 1913=2462 | 927=1188 | 2032=2607 | 2090=2666 |
| 1848=2369 | 1914=2463 | 1974+ | 2033=2608 | 2091=2667 |
| 1849=2370 | 1915=2464 | 2218=2541 | 2034=2609 | 2092=2668 |
| 1850=2371 | 1916=2465 | 1975=2542 | 2035=2610 | 2093=2669 |
| 1851=2372 | 1917=2468 | 1976=2543 | 2036=2611 | 2094=2670 |
| 1852=2373 | 1917a=2469 | 1977=2544 | 2037=2612 | 2095=2671 |
| 1853=2374 | 1918=2470 | 1978=2545 | 2038=2613 | 2096=2672 |
| 1854=2375 | 1919 omitted* | | 2039=2614 | 2097=2680 |
| 1855=2376 | 1919a=2466 | 1979=2546 | 2039a=2594 | 2098=2681 |
| 1856=2377 | 1920=2472 | 1980=2547 | 2039b=2595 | 2099=2682 |
| 1857=2378 | 1921=2473 | 1981=2548 | 2039c=2596 | 2100=2683 |
| 1858=2379 | 1922=2474 | 1982=2549 | 2039d=2597 | 2101=2685 |
| 1859=2380 | 1923=2475 | 1983=2550 | 2040=2615 | 2102=2686 |
| 1860=2381 | 1924=2476 | 1984=2551 | 2041=2616 | 2103=2687 |
| 1861=2382 | 1925=2477 | 1985=2552 | 2042=2617 | 2104=2688 |
| 1862=2384 | 1926=2479 | 1986=2553 | 2043=2618 | 2105=2689 |
| 1863=2385 | 1927=2480 | 1987=2555 | 2044=2619 | 2106=2690 |
| 1864=2386 | 1928=2482 | 1988=2556 | 2045=2620 | 2107=2691 |
| 1865=2387 | 1929=2483 | 1989=2557 | 2046=2621 | 2108=2692 |
| 1866=2388 | 1930=2485 | 1990=2558 | 2047=2622 | 2109=2693 |
| 1867=2389 | 1931=2199 | 1991=2559 | 2048=2623 | 2110=2694 |
| 1868=2414 | 1932=2486 | 1991a=2507 | 2049=2518 | 2111=2695 |
| 1869=2392 | 1933=2491 | 1991b=2514 | 2050=2624 | 2112=2696 |
| 1870=2393 | 1934=2492 | 1991c=2897 | 2051=2625 | 2113=2697 |
| 1871=2394 | 1935=2493 | 1992=2560 | 2052=2626 | 2114=2698 |
| 1872=2395 | 1936=2494 | 1993=2561 | 2053=2627 | 2115=2699 |
| 1873=2397 | 1937=2495 | 1994=2562 | 2054=2628 | 2116=2700 |
| 1874=2398 | 1938=2496 | 1995=2563 | 2055=2629 | 2117=2701 |
| 1875=2400 | 1939=2497 | 1996=2564 | 2056=2630 | 2118=2702 |
| 1876=2402 | 1940=2498 | 1997=2565 | 2057=2631 | 2119=2703 |
| 1877=2403 | 1941=2500 | 1998=2566 | 2058=2632 | 2120=2704 |
| 1878=2404 | 1942=2501 | 1999=2567 | 2059=2633 | 2121=2705 |
| 1879=2405 | 1943=2502 | 2000=2569 | 2060=2634 | 2122=2706 |
| 1880=2409 | 1944=2504 | 2001=2570 | 2061=2635 | 2123=2707 |
| 1881=2410 | 1945=2505 | 2002=2571 | 2062=2636 | 2124=2708 |
| 1882=2411 | 1946=2506 | 2003=2572 | 2063=2637 | 2125=2709 |
| 1883=2412 | 1947=2508 | 2004=2573 | 2064=2638 | 2126=2710 |
| 1884=2415 | 1948=2509 | 2005=2574 | 2065=2639 | 2127=2711 |
| 1885=2416 | 1949=2510 | 2006=2575 | 2066=2640 | 2128=2712 |
| 1886=2417 | 1950=2511 | 2007=2576 | 2067=2641 | 2129+ |
| 1887=2418 | 1951=2512 | 2008=2577 | 2068=2642 | 1252=2713 |
| 1888=2421 | | | | |
| 1889=2422 | | | | |

*This is actually a private letter; see V. Martin, Studies Presented to F. LL. Griffith (London 1932) 245-47.

| P=P 2 | P=P 2 | P=P 2 | P=P 2 |
|---|---|---|---|
| 2130=2714 | 2192=2795 | 2255=2884 | 2312a=2952 |
| 2131=2715 | 2193=2796 | 2256=2885 | 2313=2954 |
| 2132=2716 | 2194=2797 | 2257=2886 | 2314=2953 |
| 2133=2717 | 2195=2798 | 2258=2887 | 2315=2955 |
| 2134=2718 | 2196=2799 | 2259=2888 | 2316=2957 |
| 2135=2719 | 2197=2806 | 2260=2889 | 2317=2958 |
| 2136=2720 | 2198=2807 | 2261=2890 | 2318=2959 |
| 2137+ | 2199=9 | 2262=2891 | 2319=2961 |
| 1254=2721 | 2200=2808 | 2263=2892 | 2320=2962 |
| 2138=2722 | 2201=2809 | 2264=2893 | 2321=2963 |
| 2139=2723 | 2202=2810 | 2265=2894 | 2322=2965 |
| 2140=2725 | 2203=2826 | 2266=2895 | 2323=2966 |
| 2141=2727 | 2204=2827 | 2267=2896 | 2324=2967 |
| 2142=2728 | 2205=2828 | 2268=2899 | 2325 omitted |
| 2143=2729 | 2206=2829 | 2269=2900 | (see note |
| 2144=2730 | 2207=2830 | 2270=2903 | at end) |
| 2145=2731 | 2208=2831 | 2271=2904 | 2326=2968 |
| 2146=2732 | 2209=2832 | 2272=2905 | 2327=2969 |
| 2147=2733 | 2210=2833 | 2273=2906 | 2328=2970 |
| 2148=2734 | 2211=2834 | 2274=2907 | 2329=2972 |
| 2149=2735 | 2212 omitted* | | 2330=2973 |
| 2150=2736 | 2213=2835 | 2275=2908 | 2331=2974 |
| 2151=2737 | 2214=2836 | 2276=2910 | 2332=2975 |
| 2152=2738 | 2215=2837 | 2277=2911 | 2333=2976 |
| 2153=2739 | 2216=2846 | 2278=2912 | 2334=2977 |
| 2154=2740 | 2217=2847 | 2279=2913 | 2335=2978 |
| 2155=2741 | 2218+ | 2280=2914 | 2335a=2979 |
| 2156=2742 | 1974=2541 | 2281=2915 | 2336=2980 |
| 2157=2743 | 2219=2848 | 2281a=2898 | 2337=2981 |
| 2158=2753 | 2220=2849 | 2282=2783 | 2338=2982 |
| 2159=2754 | 2221=2851 | 2283=2918 | 2339=2983 |
| 2160=2755 | 2222=2852 | 2284=2919 | 2340=2984 |
| 2161=2756 | 2223=2853 | 2285=2920 | 2341=2985 |
| 2162=2757 | 2224=2854 | 2286=2921 | 2342=2986 |
| 2163=2758 | 2225=2855 | 2287=2922 | 2343=2994 |
| 2164=2759 | 2226=2856 | 2288=2923 | 2344=2995 |
| 2165=2760 | 2227=2857 | 2289=2924 | 2345=2996 |
| 2166=2761 | 2228=2022 | 2290 omitted | |
| 2167=2762 | 2229=2858 | (see note | 2346=2998 |
| 2168=2763 | 2230=2859 | at end) | 2347=2999 |
| 2169=2764 | 2231=2860 | 2291=2925 | 2348=3000 |
| 2170=2771 | 2232=2862 | 2292=2926 | 2349=3001 |
| 2171=2769 | 2233=2863 | 2293=2927 | 2350=3002 |
| 2172=2770 | 2234=2864 | 2294=2928 | 2351=3003 |
| 2173=2773 | 2235=2865 | 2295=2929 | 2352+ |
| 2174=2774 | 2236=2866 | 2296=2930 | 2354 omitted |
| 2175=2775 | 2237=2286 | 2297=2931 | (see note |
| 2175a=2777 | 2238=2867 | 2298=2932 | at end) |
| 2176=2778 | 2239=2868 | 2299=2933 | 2353=3004 |
| 2177=2779 | 2240=2869 | 2300=2938 | 2354+ |
| 2177a | 2241=2870 | 2300a=2937 | 2352 omitted |
| follows 2779 | | 2301=2939 | 2355=3005 |
| 2178=2780 | 2242=2871 | 2302+ | 2356=3006 |
| 2179=2781 | 2243=2872 | 2302a=2940 | 2357=3009 |
| 2180=2784 | 2244=2873 | 2303=2941 | 2358=3010 |
| 2181=2785 | 2245=2874 | 2304=2942 | 2359=3012 |
| 2182=2786 | 2246=2875 | 2305=2943 | 2360=3013 |
| 2183=2787 | 2247=2876 | 2306=2944 | 2361=3014 |
| 2184=2788 | 2248=2877 | 2306a=2945 | 2362=3015 |
| 2185=2236 | 2249=2878 | 2307=2946 | 2363=3017 |
| 2186=2789 | 2250=2879 | 2308=2947 | 2364=3018 |
| 2187=2790 | 2251=2880 | 2309=2948 | 2365=3019 |
| 2188=2791 | 2252=2881 | 2310=2949 | 2366=3020 |
| 2189=2792 | 2253=2882 | 2311=2950 | 2367=3021 |
| 2190=2793 | 2254=2883 | 2312=2951 | 2368=3023 |
| 2191=2794 | | | |

*Identified as Psalm 43. 20-23.

Pack 2290, 2325, 2352 (=2354): these medieval papyrus codices, not of Egyptian provenience, are now omitted at the instance of J.-O. Tjäder, Die nicht-literarischen lateinischen Papyri Italiens aus der Zeit 445 - 700 (Skrifter utgivna av Svenska Institutet i Rom 4.19, 1954-55) 17, 37-38, 40.

See Pack, pp. 79, 105, for the omission of P. Oxy. 6. 887 and P. Aberdeen 17 and 188. P. Oxy. 15.1828 (Hermas; cf. Pack, p. 105) now appears in the Appendix.

P. Aberdeen 133 (E. O. Winstedt, CQ 1, 1907, 267, ed. pr.; Collart, PLL 28), at first regarded as literary, was omitted from Pack because it had been identified by E. G. Turner, JEA 33 (1947) 92, as a fragment of P. Berol. inv. 6866, a military document (see Cavenaile, CPL 122-23).

## ADDENDA

The materials which precede were assembled before April 1, 1964. Conscious that his task is never finished, the compiler notes here a few of the more important publications that he has seen since that date.

H. Cadell, Rech. Pap. 2 (1962) 25-36 (No. 393 above). Add: III-II B.C., Ghoran; cart.

C. Corbato, "Il 'Dyskolos' di Menandro: Un saggio e una bibliografia," Dion. 37 (1963) 5-69.

B. M. Metzger, "Check-list of the Greek Papyri of the New Testament," The Text of the New Testament (Oxford 1964) 247-56.

O. Neugebauer and H. B. Van Hoesen. Astrol. Pap. Ostr. (cited above by serial number) has now appeared in Proc. Amer. Philos. Soc. 108 (1964) 57-72.

D. L. Page, Oxyrhynchus Papyri, Part 29 (P. Oxy. 29.2506: A commentary on lyric poems, with quotations from Alcaeus, Alcman, Sappho, and Stesichorus; II, Oxy.).

M. Papathomopoulos, Rech. Pap. 2 (1962) 99-111 (No. 1756 above). Add: II B.C.; cart.

M. Papathomopoulos, Rech. Pap. 2 (1962) 113-16 (Gnomic verses, including Euripides, Medea 14-15; PIFAO, inv. PSP 172; IV; a separate sheet of papyrus).

A. Rostagni: Miscellanea di studi alessandrini in memoria di Augusto Rostagni. Torino 1963.

P. J. Sijpesteijn, "Les parchemins et les papyrus de Démosthène trouvés en Égypte," Chr. Ég. 38 (1963) 297-305.

B. Snell: A. Nauck, Tragicorum Graecorum Fragmenta: Supplementum Continens Nova Fragmenta Euripidea et Adespota . . . adiecit Bruno Snell. Hildesheim 1964.